AN INTRODUCTION TO POETRY

LOUIS SIMPSON

*State University of New York,
Stony Brook*

An Introduction to Poetry

THIRD EDITION

ST. MARTIN'S PRESS   NEW YORK

ACKNOWLEDGMENTS

ROBERT BLY: "Late at Night During a Visit of Friends" by Robert Bly. Reprinted from *Silence in the Snowy Fields*, published by Wesleyan University Press, 1962. Copyright © 1961 by Robert Bly. Reprinted by permission of the author.

"Morning Bird Songs" by Tomas Tranströmer. Reprinted from *Twenty Poems of Tomas Tranströmer*, translated by Robert Bly, published by Seventies Press. Copyright © 1971 by Robert Bly. Reprinted with permission of Robert Bly.

BOA EDITIONS, LTD: "The Battle," Copyright © 1983 by Louis Simpson. Reprinted from *People Live Here: Selected Poems 1949–1983* with the permission of BOA Editions, Ltd.

GEORGES BORCHARDT, INC.: "The Instruction Manual" by John Ashbery. Reprinted from *Some Trees*, published by The Ecco Press, 1956. Reprinted by permission of Georges Borchardt, Inc. and the author. Copyright © 1956 by John Ashbery.

GEORGE BRAZILLER, INC.: "Stone" from *Dismantling the Silence* by Charles Simic. Reprinted by permission of George Braziller Inc., Publishers.

JONATHAN CAPE LTD.: "Naming of Parts" from A *Map of Verona and Other Poems* by Henry Reed. London: Jonathan Cape, Ltd. Reprinted by permission of the author.

TOI DERRICOTTE: "Fears of the Eighth Grade," "Hamtramck: The Polish Women," "The Good Old Dog," and "Stopping Late in the Afternoon for Steamed Dumplings" by Toi Derricotte. Reprinted by permission of the author.

DEVIN-ADAIR PUBLISHERS: "Gold Watch," "Tinker's Wife," "Memory of My Father," "If Ever You Go to Dublin Town," and "Lines Written on a Seat on the Grand Canal, Dublin" from *Collected Poems* by Patrick Kavanagh. Permission to reprint is granted by the Devin-Adair Publishers. Copyright © 1964 by Patrick Kavanagh.

DOUBLEDAY: "For My Son Noah, Ten Years Old," copyright © 1979 by Holy Cow! Press, and "My Father's Wedding 1924," copyright © 1981 by Robert Bly. From the book *The Man in the Black Coat Turns* by Robert Bly. Reprinted by permission of Doubleday & Co., Inc.

"Danny Deever" from *Rudyard Kipling's Verse: Definitive Edition*, by Rudyard Kipling. Reprinted by permission of Doubleday & Co., Inc.

"My Papa's Waltz," "The Waking," "Praise to the End," and "Elegy for Jane" by Theodore Roethke. Copyright 1942 by Hearst Magazine Inc., 1953 by Theodore Roethke, 1950 by Theodore Roethke. From *The Collected Poems of Theodore Roethke*. Reprinted by permission of Doubleday & Co., Inc.

"In Uganda an Early King" by Alice Walker. From the book *Good Night Willie Lee, I'll See You in the Morning*. Copyright © 1979 by Alice Walker. Reprinted by permission of Doubleday & Co., Inc.

NORMA MILLAY ELLIS: "Love is not all; it is not meat nor drink," from *Collected Poems*, Harper & Row. Copyright 1923, 1931, 1951, 1958 by Edna St. Vincent Millay and Norma Millay Ellis. Reprinted by permission of Norma Millay Ellis.

FABER & FABER PUBLISHERS: "At Last the Secret is Out," "On This Island," and "Musée des Beaux Arts" from *Collected Short Poems* by W. H. Auden. "Get There If You Can and See the Land" from *The English Auden: Poems, Essays and Dramatic Writings 1927–1939*, by W. H. Auden. Reprinted by permission of Faber & Faber Publishers Ltd.

Acknowledgments and copyrights continue at the back of the book beginning on page 636, which constitutes an extension of the copyright page.

PREFACE

In this new edition of *An Introduction to Poetry*, as in previous editions, the emphasis is on reading for enjoyment and understanding. There is no understanding of poetry if we do not, first, enjoy it. And as the pleasure of reading is in noticing things for ourselves and proving an idea, as Keats said, "upon our pulses," I have given neither directions for reading individual poems nor lists of questions to be answered. Directions of this kind interrupt the immediate experience of a work and can turn reading poetry into an exercise devoid of intellectual or emotional engagement.

On the other hand, the book does offer considerable assistance toward achieving its main intention—not to tell readers what to think, but to enable them to understand and enjoy poetry for themselves. Without usurping the function of the reader or the teacher, I have undertaken to explain the elements of poetry in three introductory sections on "The Art of Poetry," "Reading the Poem," and "Meter, Rhyme, Stanza, and Sound." In addition, an extensive Glossary provides detailed definitions of poetic concepts and terms, including numerous examples from and cross-references to specific poems. Separating these discussions from the anthology proper allows readers to study any poem in the text without feeling constrained by a single approach.

In putting together the third edition I have been guided by the advice of others as well as my own experience in the classroom. "The Art of Poetry"—particularly in its opening pages—has been revised for clarity and with the needs of novice readers of poetry in mind. The latter half of "Reading the Poem" has been thoroughly rewritten and now traces a line of poetic development from the 1890s to the present. Only the section "Meter, Rhyme, Stanza, and Sound" has not undergone significant alteration—readers have found it useful and comprehensive as it stands.

The "Anthology of Poems," which constitutes the main body of the text, has been revised and greatly expanded. A glance at the Table of Contents will show larger selections of poems by Wyatt, Spenser, Sidney, Shakespeare, Donne, Jonson, Herrick, and Herbert. The reader will now find Henry King's "The Exequy," Milton's "L'Allegro" and "Il Penseroso," and Marvell's "A Dialogue between the Soul and Body." This broadening holds true of later periods as well: there are more representative selections of Wordsworth, Shelley, Keats, Tennyson, Browning, Whitman, Hardy, and Yeats. A group of poems by Christina Rossetti stands next to the poems of Emily Dickinson.

I have given particular attention to the selection of modern and contemporary poets. The anthology was always considered strong, even innovative, in this department—and it has, I hope, been made stronger with new selections of Frost, Stevens, Williams, Pound, Hilda Doolittle, Marianne Moore, Eliot, Hart Crane, and Auden. I have included important poets of the first half of this century who deserve to be better known—Hugh MacDiarmid and Patrick Kavanagh. Coming down to recent times, there are poems by Elizabeth Bishop, Ruth Stone, Robert Hayden, Denise Levertov, Frank O'Hara, Robert Bly, Allen Ginsberg, Galway Kinnell, Adrienne Rich, and other contemporaries who are already part of the tradition of verse in English. There are large selections of poems by Seamus Heaney and Alice Walker. I could not include all the good poets who have written in this century—still, I have been reasonably eclectic. Charles Olson's "The Kingfishers" is included, but so is a sonnet by Edna St. Vincent Millay. There are poems by Philip Larkin as well as by John Ashbery. I have also provided a sampling of the important work now being done by young poets from diverse backgrounds, like Jimmy Santiago Baca and Garrett Kaoru Hongo. I have asked of each poem: Is it well written? Is it interesting and rewarding to study? I have not included any poem that I do not consider excellent of its kind.

As stated earlier, I have not undertaken to interpret the meaning of particular lines or tell the reader how to read any poem. The footnotes I have provided are purely informative. They explain references to names and places, to myths, fables, and historical events. They elucidate obscure words and phrases, and explain technical terms. On a few occasions, however, I could not resist making a suggestion: to compare Lewis Carroll's "The White Knight's Song" with the poem by Wordsworth it parodies; Ogden Nash's observations on metaphor in "Very Like a Whale" with the poem by Byron it pokes fun at; Hardy's description of the eve of the battle of Waterloo with Byron's.

The poems are arranged chronologically but may be read in any order you please. One could begin a study of the ballad with Elizabeth Bishop's about Micuçú the Burglar of Babylon. Set in Rio de Janeiro, its contemporaneity should be appealing. One could then move back in time to Keats's "La Belle Dame Sans Merci," Coleridge's "The Rime of the Ancient Mariner," and the Scottish border ballads, "Sir Patrick Spens" and "Thomas the Rhymer."

One could make a study of sonnets, beginning with the selections of Surrey and Wyatt, of Spenser's *Amoretti* and Sidney's *Astrophel and Stella*, of Shakespeare. One could study the elegy in various forms by Tichborne, Donne, Ben Jonson, Milton, Dryden, Samuel Johnson, Gray, Whitman, Williams, Roethke, and Robert Lowell. There is a wonderful elegy for himself written by Patrick Kavanagh.

One could group poems by theme, being careful, however, not to think of the poem merely in terms of what it "says." There is the poetry of love, by poets in every age; the poetry of war in Byron, Whitman, Hardy, Wilfred Owen, E. E. Cummings, Keith Douglas, and Denise Levertov. In making this collection I noticed for the first time how many poems there are comparing youth and age. And, of course, poets have often gone to nature for a theme.

In line with other revisions, the Glossary has been expanded and brought up to date. When I made a Glossary for the first edition of *An Introduction to Poetry*, other textbooks on poetry did not include one. It has proved a most useful feature, however, and this revised version, with its broad range and numerous examples, may be read for pleasure as well as instruction. It would be possible, of course, to make a Glossary three times the size if all the terms invented by critics were admitted, but I have admitted only those that seem useful.

A final note about the texts themselves. I have used the best texts of poems I could find, revising some of the older ones slightly to make them readable. Anyone who is familiar with the poetry of the sixteenth and seventeenth centuries knows what a muddle of erratic spelling and punctuation it can be. I have tried to avoid making changes that would alter the meter, sound, or meaning of a line. Here and there a scholar will take exception, but where so many disagree I hope I may be allowed to use my own best judgment.

Louis Simpson

CONTENTS

An Introduction
to Poetry

An Anthology
of Poems

xii

AN INTRODUCTION TO POETRY

A poem has an organic unity. Each part—imagery, rhythm, structure, the choice and arrangement of language—contributes to the effect of the whole. This chapter is a general introduction to the subject. There follows a discussion of how the elements work together in several poems from different periods and in different modes ("Reading the Poem"), and finally a description of the technique of verse ("Meter, Rhyme, Stanza, and Sound").

Images and Metaphors

Poets embody their thought in images, words that appeal to the senses, for, as John Locke said, "There is nothing in the mind that was not first in the senses." The first task of the poet is to make the reader "feel" the thought.

While visual imagery is frequent, poetry may also lead us to imagine that we can touch, smell, or taste a thing. And often how the words of a poem sound is as important as what they say. The following lines from Keats's ode "To Autumn," for example, appeal to the auditory as well as the visual imagination:

> Where are the songs of Spring? Ay, where are they?
> Think not of them, thou hast thy music too,—
> While barred clouds bloom the soft-dying day,
> And touch the stubble-plains with rosy hue;
> Then in a wailful choir the small gnats mourn
> Among the river sallows, borne aloft
> Or sinking as the light wind lives or dies . . .

To evoke the music of Autumn the poet uses consonants and vowels harmoniously—note the recurrence of *s, a, o,* and *m* throughout. In this passage the sound of the words is as important to the overall effect as the visual image of clouds reflecting a rosy light onto the plain.

The poet may use a simile or metaphor to give a clear mental image. Simile, usually introduced by the preposition *like* or *as*, compares one thing with another to show a likeness between them. The poet Burns writes: "My luve is like a red, red rose," comparing the woman he loves to a rose, an object we can imagine as colorful and perfectly formed. The woman is then invested with the beauty of the rose.

1

Metaphor omits *like* and *as*, speaking of one thing as though it were another:

> The swell foams where they float and crawl,
> A catherine wheel of arm and hand . . .
>> Seamus Heaney, "Girls Bathing, Galway 1965"

A girl's arm revolving in the water becomes a catherine wheel, the fireworks device named after the saint, martyred on a wheel, who is the patron saint of young women.

Metaphor is translation and, in fact, used to be called *translatio*. An object or action, A, is presented in terms of another object or action, B, that has vivid associations. In this way our sense of A is enlarged and enhanced. This is particularly useful when we are trying to explain ideas. "An idea," said Remy de Gourmont, "is an image that has faded." But we may reverse the process and give new life to an idea by turning it into an image. Consider Hamlet's soliloquy:

> To be, or not to be: that is the question.
> Whether 'tis nobler in the mind to suffer
> The slings and arrows of outrageous fortune,
> Or to take arms against a sea of troubles,
> And by opposing end them.

Mental suffering is translated into the image of a man being shot at with stones and arrows. The second metaphor translates suffering into the image of a man fighting with the sea. Ideas have been translated into scene and drama. Now suppose Hamlet said:

> To be, or not to be, that is the question.
> Whether 'tis nobler in the mind to suffer
> The insults and misfortunes of our life,
> Or make a strenuous effort to resist,
> And by opposing end them.

How dull this is! All the life has gone out of it. We do not see the man being shot at and fighting the sea, and we do not feel what it would be like to be in his situation.

Besides presenting ideas in terms that may be perceived through the senses, metaphors unify our perceptions. The critic Owen Barfield has written that primitive people continually saw relations between objects and reported them in metaphors. But as we have grown sophisticated and distanced ourselves from nature we have lost the ability to see connections. "To primitive men and children, everything is infused with the same life. But we have lost the ability to perceive the unity of things." And now "it is the language of poets, in so far as they create true metaphors, which must restore this unity conceptually, after it has been lost from perception" (*Poetic Diction*, 1928).

"The greatest thing for a poet," Aristotle said, "is to be a master of metaphor. It is the one thing that cannot be learned from others; and it is also a sign of genius, since a good metaphor implies an intuitive perception of the similarity in dissimilars."[1]

Rhythm[2]

Rhythm, repeated stress, is essential in poetry. We expect the stress to come again, and so we keep listening.

It is easy to see the pattern of rhythm when poetry is in meter, a regular pattern of stressed and unstressed syllables. The following lines are in meter:

> Since brass, nor stone, nor earth, nor boundless sea,
> But sad mortality o'er-sways their power,
> How with this rage shall beauty hold a plea,
> Whose action is no stronger than a flower?
>
> William Shakespeare, Sonnet 65

To see the pattern of meter, lines are divided into feet. A foot is a unit of stressed (´) and unstressed (˘) syllables. The foot being used here is the iamb—an unstressed syllable followed by a stressed (˘´). The first line therefore may be scanned as follows:

$$\text{S\u{i}nce br\'ass,} \mid \text{n\u{o}r st\'one,} \mid \text{n\u{o}r e\'arth,} \mid \text{n\u{o}r b\'ound} \mid \text{l\u{e}ss s\'ea} \mid$$

The second line also is regular. In the third line, however, there is a substitution: at the start of the line a trochee is substituted for the iamb:

H\'ow w\u{i}th

In any use of meter there will occasionally be substitutions where the need to accent syllables for meaning (the rhetorical accent) comes in conflict with the stress of the prevailing meter.

1 In contradiction to Aristotle some poets have attempted to eliminate similes and metaphors from their writing. It can be argued that the habit of comparing one thing with another prevents one from seeing what is actually there. As for unifying our perceptions, the very idea of unifying them ensures that they are conceived as separate and distinct. William Carlos Williams and the Objectivist poets who followed in his steps used few if any similes or metaphors as the basis of their imagery. See the poems by Williams and the discussion of Williams's "Nantucket" on pages 25–26.
2 See the Glossary for fuller explanations of technical terms, and also the section titled "Meter, Rhyme, Stanza, and Sound."

In this sonnet by Shakespeare, the iambic feet are moving like the thought, at a steady pace from one thing to another: "brass . . . earth . . . mortality . . . rage . . . beauty . . . flower." The meter is well-suited to the thought, which is meditative. Indeed, to some extent the meter *is* the thought, for a different meter would make for a different mood. Rhythm is not everything; there are other elements in poetry; but rhythm is essential.

In free verse, on the other hand, it is not easy to see the pattern of the rhythm, for it is irregular:

> Among the rain
> and lights
> I saw the figure 5
> in gold
> on a red
> firetruck
> moving
> tense
> unheeded
> to gong clangs
> siren howls
> and wheels rumbling
> through the dark city.

William Carlos Williams, "The Great Figure"

This poem does not have a regular pattern of stressed and unstressed syllables. Yet there is a rhythm—of cadences, an irregular pattern of stressed and unstressed syllables. The measurable unit is not the foot but the phrase. In "The Great Figure" the phrase may have as many as six syllables or only one or two.

> Among the rain   1st phrase
> and lights   2nd   "
> I saw the figure 5 3rd   "
> in gold   4th   "

In this poem each phrase is written as a separate line; this enables us to see the phrase. But in free verse there may be several phrases to the line, as in this line by Whitman:

>   1   2   3   4
> Dumb swimmers there | among the rocks— | coral, | gluten, |
>   5   6   7   8
> grass, | rushes— | and the aliment | of the swimmers |

Whitman's phrases could be written as separate lines, as Williams writes his; or Williams's poem could be written as one long line.

4

In some of his later poems Williams would arrange phrases in three steps across the page. The phrase, he said, was a "variable foot"; it was to be counted as a single stress. The three steps formed a kind of trimeter. If "The Great Figure" had been written later, it might have looked like this:

Among the rain
                    and lights
                              I saw the figure 5
        in gold
              on a red
                    firetruck . . .

Free verse, as I have said, is written in cadences. To follow the cadences, we must follow the movement of the thought, we must understand what the poet intends at every moment. Only in this way can we tell where the stress falls and where the phrase ends. Reading in a sing-song won't do. In reading "The Great Figure" we have to pay attention to exactly what is said, and seen, and heard: "the figure 5," the clanging gong, the rumbling wheels. We have to concentrate on these things as the speaker in the poem is concentrating.

Indeed, the objects in the poem seem to be compelling the observer to pay attention to them. They seem to be determining the language, the phrases, the rhythm. The rhythm of the poem depends upon what the poem is about—far more, it might be argued, than if the poem were in meter.

There are readers of poetry who find it difficult to read free verse. They want a poem to be written in meter—regular feet, and so many feet to the line. Also, they would like a regular pattern of rhymes. Free verse strikes them as unpoetic. What, they ask, makes it different from prose? One possible answer is that the difference is a matter of degree: in free verse there is a greater concentration of thought, selectivity in the use of words, intensity through the use of images. But though these are certainly qualities of free verse, they can also be found in prose. Then, perhaps, the difference is in rhythm. Perhaps rhythm plays a greater part in free verse than it does in prose.

So important is rhythm in poetry that in the first edition of this book I said that poetry was "thought expressed in rhythm," and that in poetry rhythm was essential to the meaning, while in prose it was not. Some readers objected, saying that there are passages of prose—"John Donne's Meditation XVII, for example"—in which rhythm is essential. They may have been right. In any case, as a poem consists of several elements, it is not possible to isolate one element and show that this is what poetry consists of; and we cannot say exactly what the difference is between poetry and prose, for they have several elements in common. Many people have tried to define poetry—there are eleven instances in the Glossary—but no definition seems conclusive. The reason for life in the poem, as in the human being, eludes analysis. This should not prevent us, however, from understanding how the parts work, separately and together.

Structure

Just as there is rhythm in the lines of a poem, there is a rhythm of the poem as a whole. This is evident where the poem is written in stanzas, groups of lines recurring in the same pattern:

> It is an ancient Mariner,
> And he stoppeth one of three.
> "By thy long gray beard and glittering eye,
> Now wherefore stopp'st thou me?
>
> The Bridegroom's doors are opened wide,
> And I am next of kin,
> The guests are met, the feast is set:
> May'st hear the merry din."

The pattern here is of ballad stanzas, tetrameters and trimeters rhyming *a b c b*. (These terms are explained in the Glossary.)

Structure does not consist only of rhythmic patterns such as stanzas; there may be a pattern of symbols, or a structure of language. And there may be two or more structures in combination; indeed, as there are so many patterns in the use of words, syntax, plot, and symbolism, it would be hard to imagine a poem that had only a single, discernible structure.

Some twentieth-century poets have said that they are writing poetry without a structure, imitating a flow of experience, with no beginning, middle, or end. When we read some of these poems we really do have the impression of a mind moving freely:

> Three gas lamps lighted
> The boss has T.B.
> When you've finished we'll play backgammon
> A conductor who has a sore throat . . .
>
> Guillaume Apollinaire, "Lundi Rue Christine"

But there is a structure in this poetry, though it is hidden. Everything that comes into the mind takes on a kind of structure; and though poets may not be aware of it, everything they write gives back a pattern of the mind.

The poem by William Carlos Williams that we have seen, "The Great Figure," has the structure of a narrative: "I saw this, I heard that." Narrative poems and songs go back to the beginnings of history; it seems that people always wanted to sing a song or tell a story, and patterns of song and story were given to poetry from the start. But I shall not try to describe all the patterns that can be found in poems. This would be tedious and not in keeping with the purpose of this book. There is more to be learned from reading poems and discovering what is in the individual poem than from any amount of generalization. As an example, however, let us consider one passage of poetry in order to see the struc-

6

ture, and also the use of rhythm and images, the elements of poetry touched on so far.

The passage is taken from *The Prelude*, Wordsworth's autobiographical poem:

> So feeling comes in aid
> Of feeling, and diversity of strength
> Attends us, if but once we have been strong.
> Oh! mystery of man, from what a depth
> Proceed thy honours. I am lost, but see
> In simple childhood something of the base
> On which thy greatness stands; but this I feel,
> That from thyself it comes, that thou must give,
> Else never canst receive. The days gone by
> Return upon me almost from the dawn
> Of life: the hiding-places of man's power
> Open; I would approach them, but they close.
> I see by glimpses now; when age comes on,
> May scarcely see at all; and I would give,
> While yet we may, as far as words can give,
> Substance and life to what I feel, enshrining,
> Such is my hope, the spirit of the Past
> For future restoration.

In *The Prelude*, Wordsworth undertakes to trace "the growth of a poet's mind." The poem ranges from scene and incident to passages in which he attempts to describe the workings of his mind at certain times and explain how this contributed to his development as a poet. It is admirable to see how he manages to give passages of explanation a forward movement. When poets undertake to argue and explain they often fall into prose, but these lines have a deepening excitement.

How does Wordsworth accomplish this? Not by the weight of his ideas, though they are profound. The poetry comes of his skill in writing verse and of what Aristotle called mastery of metaphor. For at the center of this passage of explanation there is a powerful and original metaphor, the vision of the "hiding-places of man's power" opening and closing. This lifts the passage above the level of rational argument, toward a place where truths are seen in a flash. The image is vague, but so is a mystery; the poet is describing mysterious and awe-inspiring things, glimpsed only to be hidden again.

A vision can hardly be analyzed. The technique of verse is more understandable. When we scan the passage, we find that Wordsworth has broken the lines, unrhymed iambic pentameters (blank verse), into shorter units. Several of the lines are divided with a pause (caesura), and phrases run from the middle of a line to the middle of the next, running past the end of the pentameter as though there were an urgency, a thought too pressing to be contained within the five-foot measure:

Oh! mystery of man, | | from what a depth
Proceed thy honours. | | I am lost, but see
In simple childhood | | something of the base
On which thy greatness stands; | | but this I feel,
That from thyself it comes, | | that thou must give,
Else never canst receive. | | The days gone by . . .

This overriding of the line by the sentence makes the idea in the sentence seem irresistible. So the argument moves forward and carries us with it.

Toward the end Wordsworth makes parenthetical remarks. This is what he has to say: "I would give substance and life to what I feel, enshrining the spirit of the Past for future restoration." In the course of saying it, however, he makes these digressions: "While yet we may, as far as words can give . . . Such is my hope." These interruptions make us impatient to see to the end of the thought; we are not just drawn forward, we push forward to the end ourselves. The purpose of this delaying, keeping us in suspense, is to involve us more. Of course, a writer cannot digress too much, otherwise the reader may be confused or lose interest. Wordsworth has a lively sense of the drama of a sentence, what must be said right away and what may be delayed.

Moreover, there is an ingenious structure in the passage that we have not yet seen. By repeating a word, or by following a word with another that the first word has led us to expect, Wordsworth sets up a pattern of anticipation and reward. Then, suddenly, at the image of the "hiding-places," anticipation is disappointed: the "hiding-places" suddenly "close" rather than remain "open." This is a stroke of genius in sentence structure. Just as rhythm may contribute essentially to the effect of a poem, so may sentence structure. The syntax corresponds to, indeed helps to create, the idea:

feeling . . . feeling
strength . . . strong
give . . . receive
[but the hiding-places] open . . . close
see by glimpses . . . scarcely see
[then, resoundingly, like the resolution of a Beethoven symphony]
give . . . give

When we consider the content of the passage, it is remarkable how many ideas have been put in a few lines. Much of Wordsworth's thinking is touched upon in this brief space. He states his belief that feeling is primary and that we develop by feeling, one feeling and thought leading to another. He affirms his faith in human dignity and asks the question he is frequently pondering: Where do we obtain the power to feel and think? He answers his own question, saying that we obtain the power from ourselves, by giving, whereupon something is given to us. He hints at mysteries we apprehend at certain moments from a contact with nature, and he describes the poet's task: by a process of recollection to recreate those moments in poems that will serve as a restorative.

These ideas, however, would not be as persuasive had Wordsworth not used rhythm, sentence structure, and words in ways that support the argument. And it needed more than philosophy, it required poetic genius, to see the hiding-places opening and closing. What were they? But we are left to wonder.

Language and Style

The following little poem has been remembered for hundreds of years:

> Western wind, when will thou blow
> The small rain down can rain?
> Christ, if my love were in my arms,
> And I in my bed again.

This is as simple and direct as the language a man might use in conversation. And if we look again at the passage from *The Prelude*, we see that though Wordsworth is philosophizing and speaking of difficult matters, he is for the most part using ordinary words. Poetry is the most expressive way of saying a thing, and sometimes plain words are best.

The language of some poetry, however, is difficult, for the poet is trying to convey a subtle or difficult idea. But still he or she is choosing the best words and putting them in the best order. (Bad poets use vague words and difficult constructions when they don't have to; when they say something we feel that it could have been said better.)

Milton has sometimes been accused of using pompous words and writing Latin rather than English sentences. If this were all there was to Milton's style, then we would not be able to read him with pleasure. But when we examine a passage of his writing we are likely to find that the construction of a sentence, if it is peculiar, has a definite purpose. Putting the subject after the predicate, for example, may be an attempt to represent the order in which things are actually happening. Milton wants to make us see and feel, and therefore he changes the usual sentence order in which, all too often, words are used in a nonspecific way and have lost their connection to the senses.

For the same reason Milton uses unusual words. In the following passage from *Paradise Lost*, Moloch, an angel who has been driven out of Heaven, is describing the battle in which the angels fell. He is arguing that as there is a kind of gravity that draws spirits upward, it will not be too hard for the fallen angels to fly up again:

> Who but felt of late
> When the fierce foe hung on our broken rear
> Insulting, and pursued us through the deep,
> With what compulsion and laborious flight
> We sunk thus low?

Consider the words Milton is using, particularly "compulsion" and "laborious." The sound of these words is like the action they describe. In *compulsion* and *laborious*, the plosives *p* and *b*, the following vowel sounds, and the ponderous length of the words give a sense of wings pushing back against a pressure that is forcing them downward, a pressure greater than the strength of wings but not irresistible.

Every poet has a style, a certain way of using language, figurative and rhetorical devices, tones, and patterns of sound. Just as we can tell from a few bars of music that they were composed by Mozart, from a few lines of verse we can tell that they are by Emily Dickinson or by Gerard Manley Hopkins.

But as people live in communities they think and speak alike, and though poets may have a distinctive style they owe something to the style of their time and place. Therefore we speak of the style of a period: Elizabethan, Augustan, Romantic, Victorian. In the early eighteenth century, Pope and Swift moved in elegant society. Though they were very different men, they both wrote wittily, with turns of speech that were fashionable in drawing rooms. A hundred years later, after the French Revolution and the industrial revolution, poets were not so often in society and were given to taking long walks in the country and writing about nature. Wordsworth and Keats, who lived in this period, are closer to each other in their styles than they are to Pope and Swift.

At the beginning of the Romantic period, Wordsworth argued against the farfetched words and euphemisms of verse in the late eighteenth century. He cited a passage from the Bible:

> Go to the Ant, thou sluggard, consider her ways, and be wise: which having no guide, overseer, or ruler, provideth her meat in the summer, and gathereth her food in the harvest.

Then he quoted Samuel Johnson's version of the passage:

> Turn on the prudent Ant thy heedless eyes,
> Observe her labors, Sluggard, and be wise;
> No stern command, no monitory voice,
> Prescribes her duties, or directs her choice.

This, Wordsworth said, was a hubbub of words, and indeed it does seem that the busy housekeeping little ant has been crushed under the weight of Doctor Johnson's attention.

In literary generations, writing swings like a pendulum from one style to another. Wordsworth's liking for simplicity enabled him to write lines of his own that have a Biblical grandeur:

> The silence that is in the starry sky,
> The sleep that is among the lonely hills . . .

However, later in the century Browning is anything but simple:

> While Paul looked archly on, pricked brow at whiles
> With the pen-point as to punish triumph there,
> And said "Count Guido, take your lawful wife
> Until death part you!"

The eccentricities of Gerard Manley Hopkins would have puzzled Wordsworth:

> In a flash, at a trumpet crash,
> I am all at once what Christ is, since he was what I am, and
> This Jack, joke, poor potsherd, patch, matchwood, immortal
> diamond,
>   Is immortal diamond.

At the beginning of the present century, poets seemed again to be out of touch with common speech. The language of poems was vaguely romantic, but without the Romantics' power of thought. In reaction against this there was a swing toward a kind of "hardness," and about 1910 a group of poets who called themselves Imagists began to write a new kind of poetry with short, simple phrases, as in these lines by Hilda Doolittle:

> O wind, rend open the heat,
> cut apart the heat,
> rend it to tatters.

Thirty years later, in the writing of Dylan Thomas the pendulum will have swung the other way—sound is more impressive than sense:

> Who blows death's feather? What glory is color?
> I blow the stammel feather in the vein.

In modern writing there have been attempts to separate style from content, attributable, I think, to the separation of the writer from the community. Chaucer who was a civil servant, Shakespeare who wrote for the theater, and Milton who was Latin Secretary to the Council of State, did not feel that they were different from the people around them. But as the old communities disappeared the artist felt increasingly isolated. At the end of the eighteenth century Rousseau made a virtue out of seeming different; in the *Confessions* he claimed proudly, "I am made unlike anyone I have ever met," and other writers would make a similar claim.

Their individuality was expressed through style. The novelist Flaubert spoke of style as "absolute"—he said that he would like to write "a book about nothing, a book dependent on nothing external, which would be held together by the strength of its style." But even Flaubert was not able to do this—*Madame*

Bovary has a subject, the life of an unhappy woman in a French provincial town.

Mallarmé, leader of the Symbolists, declared that poetry should not be explicit. It was only to suggest—"suggestion makes the dream." Yet even the most "suggestive" of his poems contain a grain of matter, like the grain of sand that irritates the oyster into producing a pearl.

It seems that we cannot think without thinking about something.

READING THE POEM

In discussing the following poems I have used technical terms and references that may be unfamiliar to the reader. These words are explained in the Glossary.

When Icicles Hang by the Wall

> When icicles hang by the wall,
>   And Dick the shepherd blows his nail,
> And Tom bears logs into the hall,
>   And milk comes frozen home in pail,
> When blood is nipped, and ways be foul,
> Then nightly sings the staring owl,
>   To-whit!
> To-who!—a merry note,
> While greasy Joan doth keel the pot.
>
> When all aloud the wind doth blow,
>   And coughing drowns the parson's saw,
> And birds sit brooding in the snow,
>   And Marian's nose looks red and raw,
> When roasted crabs hiss in the bowl,
> Then nightly sings the staring owl,
>   To-whit!
> To-who!—a merry note,
> While greasy Joan doth keel the pot.
>   William Shakespeare, *Love's Labour's Lost*, 1593–97

The origins of poetry are unknown, but I think there must always have been songs, and some songs are poetry. The words of this song by Shakespeare evoke a situation and mood, describing an English country scene in the winter. There is an intense selectivity of detail, a pleasure in everything, rising from the delight in his mind.

To a country-dweller today the scene would be almost as familiar as it was hundreds of years ago when Shakespeare was alive. The kitchen may be different, and milk may be delivered in bottles, but people still get red noses. A cold day can be exhilarating, and it is good to be warm inside when it is freezing out. It would be the same in China; a good poem can be understood by strangers and it may last for centuries.

There are, however, two or three places in the poem where the reader may have difficulty in understanding, due to changes in the use of words between Shakespeare's time and our own. Some difficulties will disappear when we look at the words carefully and think of all the possible meanings. The phrase "blows his nail," for instance, makes sense if we just think about it. The mind moves to "blows on his nail," and then to "blows on his fingernail," whereupon the difficulty vanishes. Dick is blowing on the ends of his fingers to warm them. "Parson's saw" is a little more difficult. But what is it that parsons do in church? They make sermons. So *saw* probably means sermon. We cannot be certain of this, however, so we had better look in a dictionary. There we find that we are right: "A saying; discourse; speech. *Obs.*" Also, when we look up *crabs* we find that one of the meanings is: "*Brit.*—the wild form of the common apple." In the context, a description of an English countryside, "wild apples" is clearly the right meaning. These crabs are not crustaceans.

"Keel the pot" presents a serious obstacle. If I were to rely on my own ideas, my thinking would go like this: the bottom of a boat is called the keel, and Joan is described as greasy, so keeling the pot probably means greasing the bottom of the pot. A strange thing for her to do, but there it is. So I would settle the meaning of the line to my own satisfaction—and I would be mistaken. If, on the other hand, I went to a dictionary, I would find that one of the meanings given for *keel* is: "*Obs.* To cool (a hot or boiling liquid) by stirring, skimming, or pouring in something cold, in order to prevent it from boiling over; hence freq. in phr. to *keel the pot*." A little further on I would find: "Shaks. L L L 5.2.930 While greasie Ione doth keele the pot."

The way to read, then, seems to be: use imagination and a dictionary.

"Greasy Joan" is unforgettable. Details such as this remind us, if ever we are inclined to doubt it, what a writer Shakespeare is. Many people think that poetry consists of high-flown, fanciful, euphemistic language. On the contrary, poets want to make their readers see and feel; therefore they say what they mean as exactly and vividly as possible. It is "officialese," the language bureaucrats speak, or the language used in politics or advertising, that is euphemistic. We know all too well the politician's speech that conceals a meaning in circumlocutions. Every day we are bombarded with language that tries to sell us something by calling it something else, or language which, out of a false sense of delicacy, tries to disguise plain functions.

But Shakespeare was happy with the word *greasy* because he liked Joan, greasy or not; he did not have to think of people as disinfected before he could put up with them. Having found this phrase he liked it so well that he used it twice, and it is the climax of his series of winter images—icicles, frozen milk, muddy footpaths, Marian's nose, roast apples, the owl. The image of greasy Joan keeling the pot, right at the end, makes the whole poem stick in the mind.

The Sun Rising

> Busy old fool, unruly sun,
> Why dost thou thus

Through windows and through curtains call on us?
Must to thy motions lovers' seasons run?
    Saucy, pedantic wretch, go chide
    Late schoolboys and sour 'prentices,
   Go tell court huntsmen that the king will ride,
   Call country ants to harvest offices.
Love, all alike, no season knows nor clime,
Nor hours, days, months, which are the rags of time.

    Thy beams, so reverend and strong
      Why shouldst thou think?
I could eclipse and cloud them with a wink,
But that I would not lose her sight so long.
    If her eyes have not blinded thine,
    Look, and tomorrow late tell me
   Whether both th' Indias of spice and mine
   Be where thou left'st them, or lie here with me;
Ask for those kings whom thou saw'st yesterday,
And thou shalt hear: All here in one bed lay.

    She's all states, and all princes I;
      Nothing else is.
Princes do but play us; compared to this,
All honor's mimic, all wealth alchemy.
    Thou, sun, art half as happy's we,
    In that the world's contracted thus;
   Thine age asks ease, and since thy duties be
   To warm the world, that's done in warming us.
Shine here to us, and thou art everywhere;
This bed thy center is, these walls thy sphere.

                         John Donne, 1633

In the twentieth century much has been written about Donne and the metaphysical poets. T. S. Eliot discovered in Donne's verse the "unified sensibility" that he was aiming at in his own lines. Donne was able to make sense of a variety of experiences at the same time; sense perception and reflection took place at once. Eliot, himself working out images that could render simultaneously thought, the smell of cabbage, and the clatter of typewriting, found Donne usable in a way that Milton and Dryden were not. Between their thoughts and feelings there were gaps.

Several critics—including, it seems, the later Eliot—have found fault with his first enthusiastic validation of Donne. In *The Monarch of Wit*, J. B. Leishman argues that Donne's main quality is not metaphysical thinking, nor does he have "unified sensibility." To the contrary, he is, like Hamlet, subject to fits and starts. He wants to be witty at any price, and is never happier than when developing an outrageous paradox. Donne's most striking characteristics, says Leishman, are wit, self-dramatization, and the use of the colloquial.

Certainly, the actor in Donne strikes us forcibly. He is always throwing himself into one role or another. He is John Donne pretending to be a cynic, or a Platonic lover, or a man terrified at the thought of death. He thinks best in dialogue. Even when he is not addressing another person or God, he carries on a dialogue with himself. The poems are a little theater, with curtain raisers:

Busy old fool, unruly sun . . .

For Godsake hold your tongue, and let me love . . .

Batter my heart, three-personed God . . .

The poems have the scenery and furniture of stage sets: a bedroom into which the sun is shining, a sick room, an open grave, a panorama of the Last Judgment. A poem to his mistress suddenly lets in a view of Alps where a traveler, attacked by brigands, is stabbed and falling. This is the Donne of whom Sir Richard Baker said that after leaving Oxford he "lived at the *Inns of Court*, not dissolute, but very neat, a great visiter of ladies, a great frequenter of Plays, a great writer of conceited verses," and of whom it is reported that when he was dying he had his portrait painted in grave clothes and kept it beside his bed. This also is the man who ruined his chances of preferment by running off with Sir George More's daughter: "John Donne, Anne Donne, Un-done."

How serious is the drama? Donne seems in dead earnest, and then he is off on the scent of a pun or some wild comparison. In this he appears to deserve the criticism Johnson makes of Shakespeare—he would throw away everything for a quibble. Does this mean Donne was not serious? I do not think so. Men of the Elizabethan age were serious in humorous ways. Hamlet was in earnest when he ran his sword through the arras and Polonius fell out, but at the same time Hamlet jested. This was barbarous to the age of Johnson, and must have seemed sheer fantasy to the Victorians. But in our century, which has seen violent extremes, peace and war, juxtaposed, and like the age of Donne sees new gulfs of science opening, Donne's taste for shock does not invalidate his seriousness.

To emphasize Donne's playfulness, J. B. Leishman says that he did not care what happened to his poems, once he wrote them. However, though Donne may have given the impression of tossing off his poems—a manner of acting that can be observed at any gathering of poets today—they are too well written to be jokes, and besides he knew there were copies in circulation and people were keeping them.

The sign of metaphysical poetry, as Johnson said, is a use of wild conceits, ransacking all fields of knowledge for comparisons. The technique has often been described: images are taken from science as well as nature, and the poet goes ranging over heaven and earth. But I do not think the purpose of the technique has been sufficiently underscored, and it is serious. The aim is not merely to astonish by showing how seemingly contradictory things can be yoked together. True, when Donne compares a flea to a marriage bed, something odd is happening for the sake of oddness. But when, as in "The Sun Rising," he brings into the bedroom of two lovers a vision of "Both th' Indias of spice and mine," the leap does more than astonish, it joins two disparate areas of experience.

This is the real function of the metaphysical conceit: to join again the parts of a fractured world. In Donne's time, because of the new discoveries in astronomy, the earth is no longer at the center of the universe, no longer at the center of God's attention. Humankind is suddenly diminished. As Donne says, this new philosophy "calls all in doubt." On the earth itself, things are sliding off, east and west, as the explorers circumnavigate the globe. But the metaphysical conceit pulls the fractions together again; it draws the disordered parts back into order, the order of the poem and the mind. The one who controls the poem controls the world. Then, if the poet is religious, God still orders the universe.

"The Sun Rising" is one of Donne's complimentary love poems. Here he is not proving that women are all untrue, nor is he engaged in a Platonic disquisition. The subject is clear: the centering, controlling power of love. A man and woman are in bed, and the sun looks in. The poet tells the sun to go about his business. There is a man-about-town's contemptuous reference to "country ants," a topical reference to King James' passion for hunting, and a picture of "Late schoolboys and sour 'prentices" which shows that morning scenes have not changed from that time to this. Then the theme of the poem is stated:

> Love, all alike, no season knows nor clime,
> Nor hours, days, months, which are the rags of time.

There follows a solipsism that has occurred to everyone, at one time or another: if you simply shut your eyes, reality goes away. Is reality in the perceiver or in the world perceived? This question, which has occupied some poets greatly—Wordsworth answered "half-and-half"—Donne solves, or rather evades, by tossing off a pretty compliment to the woman. He does not want to stop looking at her for as long as the wink of an eye. Then comes the advice to the sun which brings the Indies into the poem with a glimpse of potentates on their thrones. If the sun comes back tomorrow, it will have to confess that the woman is more beautiful than anything else in the world.

"She is all states." And by possessing her, the persona—Donne in one of his speaking roles—is "all princes." Everything but love is play-acting; honor and riches are poor imitations of the reality, love. Then, to polish off the poem, Donne has a happy conceit. The sun should be pleased to have them stay in bed, for the sun is old and tired, and here it can do its job all at once—warm the world by warming them. In the lovers' astronomy:

> This bed thy center is, these walls thy sphere.

(Donne is perfectly aware of the theory that the sun does not go round the world, but it appears to do so, and that is enough for a poem.)

Donne wrote "strong lines." Leishman speaks of the "colloquial vigor of the language, together with the absence of classical allusions, traditional ornaments, and, generally speaking, of anything obviously 'poetical.'" However, I do not agree with his opinion that Donne was the first to introduce into lyrical verse "those natural speech-rhythms . . . that colloquial diction" which Shakespeare and his fellows introduced into dramatic verse. Wyatt had already done this, when he tuned his speech to the lute.

If we take Spenser as one extreme, with smoothness and softness:

> Sweete *Themmes* run softlie, till I end my Song

then Donne is the other. Spenser is all for smoothness and purity of effect; he uses classical allusions, ornaments, and Petrarchan conceits; he attaches his feelings to ideal things and so climbs the Platonic ladder. Donne's thoughts, on the other hand, are attracted to whatever he sees; he is fascinated with strange sights and ideas; his manner of speaking is informal, seeming at times abrupt. It is tempting to divide the poets of the early seventeenth century into two camps, those who followed Spenser and those who followed Donne. But this is too simple; poets do not fit neatly into categories. Also, among the poets—Donne, Vaughan, Crashaw, Herbert, and others—who are grouped together as metaphysicals, there is so much temperamental variety that perhaps their only resemblance is in the use of metaphysical conceits.

from *Absalom and Achitophel*

> Of these the false Achitophel was first;
> A name to all succeeding ages curst:
> For close designs and crooked counsels fit;
> Sagacious, bold, and turbulent of wit;
> Restless, unfixed in principles and place;
> In power unpleased, impatient of disgrace:
> A fiery soul, which, working out its way,
> Fretted the pigmy body to decay,
> And o'er-informed the tenement of clay.
> A daring pilot in extremity;
> Pleased with the danger, when the waves went high,
> He sought the storms; but, for a calm unfit,
> Would steer too nigh the sands, to boast his wit.
> Great wits are sure to madness near allied,
> And thin partitions do their bounds divide;
> Else why should he, with wealth and honor blest,
> Refuse his age the needful hours of rest?
> Punish a body which he could not please;
> Bankrupt of life, yet prodigal of ease?
> And all to leave what with his toil he won,
> To that unfeathered two-legged thing, a son;
> Got, while his soul did huddled notions try,
> And born a shapeless lump, like anarchy.
> In friendship false, implacable in hate;
> Resolved to ruin or to rule the State.

To compass this the triple bond he broke,
The pillars of the public safety shook;
And fitted Israel for a foreign yoke;
Then seized with fear, yet still affecting fame,
Usurped a patriot's all-atoning name.
So easy still it proves in factious times,
With public zeal to cancel private crimes.

John Dryden, 1681

Absalom and Achitophel is political satire in the form of an allegory. The satire is strong and biting. Dryden exhibits the despicable traits of his characters and holds them up to ridicule.

The poet pretends to be retelling the Biblical story of the revolt of Absalom and Achitophel against King David (2 Samuel, 14–18), but actually it is the story of the treason of the Duke of Monmouth and the Earl of Shaftesbury against King Charles II. They had plotted to secure the succession for Monmouth, Charles' illegitimate son, though rightfully it belonged to the Duke of York, the king's brother.

In Dryden's allegory Israel represents England; David is King Charles; Absalom is his son Monmouth; Achitophel is Shaftesbury. In the Bible story the illegitimate Absalom was the apple of his father's eye, and Charles dotes on Monmouth. Prudently Dryden avoids harsh criticism of Monmouth and throws all the blame on Shaftesbury, Lord Chancellor and leader of the Whig faction that plotted to cut out the Catholic Duke of York.

The poem is written in heroic couplets—that is, couplets of iambic pentameter, the lines end-stopped, the statement completed at the end of the second line. (Occasionally there is a third rhyming line, for variety.) The meter is fairly regular, except for an occasional trochaic opening to a line. The thought is organized by the regular meter and by rhyme, but it is especially the syntax that creates the special sense of the line.

In the portrait of Achitophel, the first two lines are very even iambic, with no caesuras. Moving relentlessly, they declare Dryden's point of view. In line 3 the cramped parallel structure of "close designs" and "crooked counsels" emphasizes Achitophel's secretive character; the inversion of the syntactical order suggests his crooked and inverted ways. The repetition of p in lines 5 and 6 ("*p*ower un*p*leased, im*p*atient of disgrace"), with its explosive quality, creates a tone of contempt. The zeugma in line 5, "principles" and "place" both depending on the word "unfixed," produces an ironic effect—Achitophel is as unsure of his footing as he is confused in his mind. The chiasmus in line 6 makes a cross structure:

As these nouns and adjectives cross over, so does Achitophel; perversely he hastens from honor to dishonor.

The lines linked by the triple rhyme "way," "decay," "clay" may be read in different ways. Achitophel's body was puny; his soul "fretted" it like the teeth of an animal; his soul "o'er-informed," over-filled his little body. Or Dryden may be using "fret" not in the sense of "gnaw," but to mean "fermentation" or "working" (heating and agitating), for it is a "fiery" soul that is "working out its way." In "o'er-informed" Dryden is playing on the scholastic notion of the soul as the "form" of the body. All these meanings are valid; they do not exclude each other; to the contrary, from different directions they reinforce the central argument.

Another image dominates the following lines. Achitophel is a pilot steering a ship, an eccentric pilot who welcomes storms but is incompetent in calm seas. In the line "Would steer too nigh the sands, to boast his wit," the syntactical inversion creates an anticlimax—just as Achitophel's grandiose, dangerous actions reveal small motives.

For Dryden, Achitophel's wit is close to madness; otherwise why should he "Refuse his age the needful hours of rest"? The word *age* has a double meaning. It means not only his "many years" but also his "times." The present age would like Achitophel to retire so that the body politic may rest. Instead, he is working himself to death, punishing both himself and the state, so that his son may inherit the fruits of his toil.

The son is an "unfeathered two-legged thing," an allusion to Plato's definition of humanity. The comparison becomes more ludicrous when we recall that Diogenes plucked the feathers of a cock and presented it as Plato's human being. The heavy stress on the monosyllable "Got" and the caesura after the first syllable of the line, an unusual position, ironically emphasizes the word. It means not only "begot" but also "acquired," and his son is reduced to a thing acquired, like his other possessions, by hard work. The son is born a "shapeless lump," an image of formlessness and insignificance. He is further compared, in a simile, to anarchy, an abstract term. He is thus reduced from a thing to an abstraction, to nothingness.

Anticipating Dr. Johnson's remark that patriotism is the last refuge of scoundrels, Dryden goes on to knock this prop from under the figure he is demolishing. And this is not all, but perhaps it is enough to show what could be done by Dryden, and by Pope some years later, in the heroic couplet as a vehicle for satire. The couplet bites off a statement neatly in two lines; it has a logical movement, and with syntactical devices such as I have shown, lends itself to strokes of wit.

About forty years ago, Dryden was "rediscovered" by critics. T. S. Eliot said, "The effect of the portraits of Dryden is to transform the object into something greater." Quoting the lines

> A fiery soul, which, working out its way,
> Fretted the pigmy body to decay,
> And o'er-informed the tenement of clay

he commented: "These lines are not merely a magnificent tribute. They create the object which they contemplate." Dryden, he said, had great comic talent.

I think this is true. Dryden's portrait of Achitophel is entertaining; I am not sure that it improved anyone's morals. Writers of satire such as Dryden, Swift, and Pope claimed that their purpose in writing was to improve morals and make the world a better place to live in. However, the world goes on much as it has, and satirists are remembered only because they are amusing.

Ode on Melancholy

No, no, go not to Lethe, neither twist
    Wolf's-bane, tight-rooted, for its poisonous wine;
Nor suffer thy pale forehead to be kiss'd
    By nightshade, ruby grape of Proserpine;
Make not your rosary of yew-berries,
    Nor let the beetle, nor the death-moth be
        Your mournful Psyche, nor the downy owl
A partner in your sorrow's mysteries;
    For shade to shade will come too drowsily,
        And drown the wakeful anguish of the soul.

But when the melancholy fit shall fall
    Sudden from heaven like a weeping cloud,
That fosters the droop-headed flowers all,
    And hides the green hill in an April shroud;
Then glut thy sorrow on a morning rose,
    Or on the rainbow of the salt sand-wave,
    Or on the wealth of globed peonies;
Or if thy mistress some rich anger shows,
    Emprison her soft hand, and let her rave,
        And feed deep, deep upon her peerless eyes.

She dwells with Beauty—Beauty that must die;
    And Joy, whose hand is ever at his lips
Bidding adieu; and aching Pleasure nigh,
    Turning to poison while the bee-mouth sips:
Ay, in the very temple of Delight
    Veil'd Melancholy has her sovran shrine,
        Though seen of none save him whose strenuous tongue
    Can burst Joy's grape against his palate fine;
His soul shall taste the sadness of her might,
        And be among her cloudy trophies hung.

John Keats, 1819

Keats said that if English had to be "chained" in rhymes, he wished to discover complex, satisfying patterns of rhyme and sound. Also he wished to "load every rift with ore," by which he meant that poetry should be full of images and as sensuous as possible.

The first stanza is filled with images evoking death: Lethe, the river of forgetfulness that spirits cross on their way to the Underworld; wolf's-bane and nightshade, which are poisonous; Proserpine, queen of the Underworld; yew-berries, from the tree that grows in graveyards; the beetle, the death-moth, the owl, and shadows. Also there are sounds like a dirge accompanying a funeral: the *o* sounds with which the ode begins: "No, no, go not," "wolf's," "rooted," "poisonous"—and continues: "Proserpine," "rosary," "moth," "mournful," "downy owl," "your sorrow's," "come too drowsily," "drown," "soul."

In the second stanza, strong, fresh images of nature—rain, flowers, a green hill, a morning rose—oppose the dying mood. These are not merely pictures, they are images of taste and touch. The sand-wave is salt, the peonies are globed. The word *globed* fits the hand; we think that we are holding a flower, a round, globed peony, in the cup of the hand. A woman appears immediately after the peony, so that she is globed and we seem to touch her. She is in an angry mood, with streaks of rich color. As we are still thinking of weeping clouds, hills after showers, waves and peonies, the woman's anger seems a natural phenomenon and she herself is like nature.

"She dwells with Beauty." Some confusion may set in here. Does "She" refer to the mistress or to Melancholy? The difficulty exists only if we try to choose. "She" refers to both the woman and the mood, for in the keenest of pleasures, sexual intercourse, there is melancholy:

> in the very temple of Delight
> Veil'd Melancholy has her sovran shrine

And "Pleasure," a word that for Keats and his contemporaries in this context would have meant sexual intercourse, is "Turning to poison while the bee-mouth sips."

But who, for thinking of that, would refrain? If the lover is sad it is because he has been happy—he has "burst Joy's grape against his palate fine." (In Keats, sexual intercourse is sometimes represented by images such as this, substituting food for sex. In "The Eve of St. Agnes," Porphyro heaps the table with "candied apple, quince, and plum, and gourd" and other delicacies, before waking Madeline.)

The argument of the ode runs as follows. "Do not try to escape from melancholy, for sadness and joy are two sides of the same coin. Instead, 'glut' your sorrow and study the results. The study of melancholy is a kind of pleasure." Keats is recommending a poet's receptivity to all kinds of experience, in the spirit of the letter to Woodhouse (see under Poetry in the Glossary) where he speaks of enjoying light and shade, foul or fair. The ode concludes with the idea that to be melancholy is a privilege. Some men seem possessed by melancholy; they have "cloudy" fates. These are men who have a heightened awareness of joy; they are the lovers of beauty.

This thought should be consoling, and to some extent it is, but the final image has a contrary effect.

His soul shall taste the sadness of her might,
And be among her cloudy trophies hung.

This is disturbing; it calls up the image of a hanged man. A frightening idea of sexual intercourse is surfacing here. Whether or not Keats consciously intended this effect, the image suggests that the lover is executed by the mistress he seeks. And the poet is consumed by beauty, converted into one of her trophies. This is a sad distinction. Though Keats has resolved to be strong, he holds some resentment against fate and the nature he professes to love.

from *Meditations in Time of Civil War*
    VI   *The Stare's Nest by My Window*

> The bees build in the crevices
> Of loosening masonry, and there
> The mother bird brings grubs and flies.
> My wall is loosening; honey-bees,
> Come build in the empty house of the stare.
>
> We are closed in, and the key is turned
> On our uncertainty; somewhere
> A man is killed, or a house burned,
> Yet no clear fact to be discerned:
> Come build in the empty house of the stare.
>
> A barricade of stone or of wood;
> Some fourteen days of civil war;
> Last night they trundled down the road
> That dead young soldier in his blood:
> Come build in the empty house of the stare.
>
> We had fed the heart on fantasies,
> The heart's grown brutal from the fare;
> More substance in our enmities
> Than in our love; O honey-bees,
> Come build in the empty house of the stare.

W. B. Yeats, 1923

When Yeats was a young man, he attended meetings of the Theosophical Society at which the members discussed correspondences between nature and the spiritual world; he belonged to the Society of the Golden Dawn whose members believed that symbols evoked certain dreams or visions; and he edited William Blake's poems and became familiar with Blake's use of symbols. Symbolism was in the air; in Paris there was a Symbolist school of poets, headed by Stéphane Mallarmé. Evocation, allusion, and suggestion, said Mallarmé, are the essence of poetry. The Symbolist "shuns the materials in nature, avoids any thought that might tend to arrange them too directly or precisely, and retains only the suggestiveness of things." Mallarmé had a theory of the image: the

Symbolist "must establish a careful relationship between two images, from which a third element, clear and fusible, will be distilled and caught by our imagination." The main Symbolist idea, however, had been stated by Baudelaire before the Symbolists appeared: all things are part of a larger synthesis.

> Like long echoes that mingle in the distance
> In a somber and profound unity,
> Vast as night and as daylight,
> Perfumes, colors and sounds respond to one another.
>
> "Correspondences"

From his studies of the occult, Yeats developed his own system of correspondences. In the poems he wrote in the 1890's there are correspondences among the four elements, seasons, times of day, stages of human life, points of the compass, and certain magical objects—sword, stone, spear, and cauldron. For example, the word *wave* or *dew* evokes the element of water. This is connected with autumn, evening, adult life, and the west.

In "Who Goes with Fergus?" Yeats writes:

> Fergus rules the brazen cars,
> And rules the shadows of the wood,
> And the white breast of the dim sea
> And all dishevelled wandering stars.

I interpret "the brazen cars" to stand for the business of life, "the shadows of the wood" for death (trees are an extension of the earth), and "the dim sea" and "wandering stars" for the passions. Throughout his life Yeats would use such symbols in his writing—words such as sun, moon, tower, mask, and gyre have hidden meanings.

The concealment is not out of a perverse unwillingness to be understood. The poet wishes to restore the mystery that is vanishing from the world, and to do so he must make things new, investing them with his own thought and feeling. But what they mean to him may not be apparent to others—hence the so-called obscurity of much modern writing.

In "The Stare's Nest by My Window," Yeats speaks of the civil war that followed the founding of the Irish Free State in 1922. According to the treaty with England, there was to be a Free State in the south while six counties in the north would remain in the United Kingdom. Not all of the Irish accepted the treaty—some rejected it vehemently, and there was civil war. Yeats deplores political fanaticism and the bloodshed it has caused:

> We had fed the heart on fantasies,
> The heart's grown brutal from the fare . . .

There are a number of objects in the poem that seem to have a meaning beyond the literal, surface meaning. Yeats speaks of the wall of his house, but "wall" appears to stand for something more. The bees and the mother bird may have a meaning beyond the literal. And what is meant by "the empty house of the stare"?

The crumbling wall is the new republic imperiled by civil war—Yeats's sympathies are with the republic. The "house of the stare" is literally the nest of a starling, but it is also the countryside that has been emptied by war. And to stare is to gaze—I see a man sitting and gazing, the poet himself, contemplating what is passing and allowing poetry to gather like honey, cell by cell. The poem is about being a poet—a subject never far from Yeats's thoughts. It is a defense of poetry and the idleness of being a poet in a time of civil war.

In another poem, "Adam's Curse," Yeats says that writing poetry is harder work than scrubbing pavements or breaking stones, and yet to be a poet is to be thought an idler "by the noisy set/ Of bankers, schoolmasters, and clergymen/ The martyrs call the world." He is thinking so now as he envisions the barricades and the dead soldier being "trundled down the road." The justification for his idle staring is the honey-bees that come bearing words for poems. The world passes but poetry is being secreted, like honey in the cracks.

O yes, the mother bird . . . Mother Ireland perhaps?

Separation on the River Kiang

> Ko-Jin goes west from Ko-kaku-ro,
> The smoke-flowers are blurred over the river.
> His lone sail blots the far sky.
> And now I see only the river,
> > The long Kiang, reaching heaven.

Ezra Pound, 1915

In 1907 Ezra Pound left the United States and traveled to Venice, then to London because Yeats was there. Within a few years Pound had become the leader of a group of poets called Imagists—he said that he invented the name in order to launch the poems of H. D. (Hilda Doolittle). As dictated by Pound to F. S. Flint, the principles of Imagist writing were:

1. Direct treatment of the "thing" whether subjective or objective.

2. To use absolutely no word that does not contribute to the presentation.

3. As regarding rhythm: to compose in the sequence of the musical phrase, not in sequence of a metronome.

The centrality of the image was the idea of T. E. Hulme, who derived it from Henri Bergson's theory of intuition. According to Hulme, poetry should be "a compromise for a language of intuition that would hand over sensations bodily. It always endeavors to arrest you and to make you continuously see a physical thing, to prevent you gliding through an abstract process."

25

Pound explains that an image is "that which presents an intellectual and emotional complex in an instant of time." So imagism is not just a matter of making you see a physical thing—there must also be an intuition. In an imagist poem "one is trying to record the precise instant when a thing outward and objective transforms itself, or darts into a thing inward and subjective." This can be seen in "Separation on the River Kiang," Pound's translation of a poem by Li Po. The image of "The long Kiang, reaching heaven" evokes the sadness of the observer at parting from his friend. His loneliness seems as large as the universe.

The Imagists insisted on using the language of "common speech" and employing the exact word, and they wrote by preference in simple, declarative sentences, as Pound does in his translation.

Nantucket

> Flowers through the window
> lavender and yellow
>
> changed by white curtains—
> Smell of cleanliness—
>
> Sunshine of late afternoon—
> On the glass tray
>
> a glass pitcher, the tumbler
> turned down, by which
>
> a key is lying—And the
> immaculate white bed

William Carlos Williams, 1934

William Carlos Williams was the most faithful of the Imagists—he held to the principles long after Pound, H. D., and Eliot had moved on to other ways of writing. The strictly Imagist poem tended to be a fragment, a small, precise observation. It would be difficult, if not impossible, to write narrative or discursive poetry according to Imagist principles: at some point one would want to use abstract language or write an involved sentence. Pound in his *Cantos*, H. D. in *Trilogy*, and Eliot in *Four Quartets* wrote extended discursive poems that used images but also made statements, and frequently they wrote in a heightened language that was not "common speech." But Williams adhered to the main Imagist principle and expressed it in a formula of his own: "No ideas but in things."

The Imagist poet avoids using metaphors and similes—identifying one thing with another would abstract from experience of the thing itself. But poems such as "Nantucket," are not a meaningless clutter of objects. "No ideas but in things," does not mean "no ideas"—it means that ideas in a poem must seem to rise out of the situation rather than the other way round, being imposed by the author. The flowers, curtains, glass tray, pitcher, tumbler, key, and bed stand in a relationship to the observer. How is this effect brought about? By the rhythm of the lines. There will be a pause at the end of the line, and sometimes also within the line. The pause is indicated by the structure of the sentence.

On the glass tray

a glass pitcher, the tumbler
turned down . . .

In this way movement is suspended and we feel the serene, unhurried mood, the attentiveness of the observer. Though the objects are ordinary the poem takes us out of life as though we were gazing at a picture.

*

Before the Great War of 1914–18 there were successive movements in art and literature. One of these, Futurism, produced something like a revolution in poetry. Whereas the Symbolists had exalted the dream, the Futurists exalted action—and machinery. They enthused over the automobile, airplane, cinema, cannon, and battleship. The leader of the Futurists, F. T. Marinetti, gave public recitals of his "Battle of Adrianople" with cannon and machine-gun noises, whinnies and yells, to the beating of a bass drum. The Futurists invented words at liberty, *parole in libertà*. Arithmetic and geometric formulas, colors, the cries of wild beasts, and motor noises, went into the making of words at liberty.

Futurism prepared the way for Dada and Surrealism. Dada began among some artists and writers who were sitting out the war in Zurich. They did not share the Futurists's enthusiasm for big guns—they detested militarism and all rhetorical gestures, and poked fun at everything, including themselves. A Dada performance might include poems, manifestoes, skits, and insults to the audience. This is a Dada poem:

Their rubber hammer strikes the sea
Down the black general so brave.
With silken braid they deck him out
A fifth wheel on the common grave.

All striped in yellow with the tides
They decorate his firmament.
The epaulettes they then construct
Of June July and wet cement . . .

Hans Arp, "The Guest Expulsed"[1]

The poem is a joke, as you see, holding military pomp up to ridicule.

1 Translated by Hans Richter. In Hans Richter, *Dada: Art and Anti-Art*, London, Thames and Hudson, 1970. 52.

The Dadaists claimed to have invented "static, simultaneous and phonetic poetry." There is a poem by Tristan Tzara in which he gives instructions for making an "accidental poem": cut words out of a newspaper, put them in a bag, and take them out at random.

During the war André Breton, an intern in a psychiatric ward that received cases from the front, became interested in Sigmund Freud's treatment of neurosis by free association. By having the patient utter his thoughts just as they came, the "unconscious" and the cause of neurosis might be uncovered. After the war Breton was active in Dada and carried out experiments in automatic writing. Then he quarreled with Tzara—Breton wanted to study the unconscious systematically, Tzara wanted only to make jokes. Breton broke with Dada and, taking a word from Apollinaire, organized his own movement, Surrealism, which he defined as "psychic automatism in its pure state, by which one proposes to express—verbally, by means of the written word, or in any other manner—the actual functioning of thought. Dictated by thought, in the absence of any control exercised by reason, exempt from any aesthetic or moral control."[2]

Breton said that there was a "secret" of Surrealism: something was hidden behind visible objects. He spoke of "facts which . . . present all the appearance of a signal."[3] This sounds like Symbolist theory. There is a difference, however. The symbol was a thing one might actually experience . . . a swan or a rose. The Surrealist image was "a pure creation of the mind. It cannot," said Pierre Reverdy, "be born from a comparison but from a juxtaposition of two more or less distant realities. The more the relationship between the two juxtaposed realities is distant and true, the stronger the image will be—the greater its emotional power and poetic reality . . ."[4]

The Surrealist image, then, was made by juxtaposing apparently unrelated objects:

> An old suitcase a sock and an endive
> have arranged for a rendezvous between two blades of grass . . .
> Benjamin Péret, "It Keeps Going On"[5]

The image might be suggested merely by a similarity of sounds between words: "the vertical desert"—*le desert vertical*; "the sexual eagle"—*l'aigle sexuel*.

Breton made a classification of seven kinds of Surrealist images, including "contradictions," for example, simultaneous use of past, present, and future tenses: "The curtains that have never been raised/ Are floating at the windows of houses that will be built"; images that imply negation of some elementary

2 André Breton, *Manifestoes of Surrealism*, trans. Richard Seaver and Helen R. Lane. Ann Arbor, University of Michigan Press, 1969. 26.
3 *Nadja*, New York, Grove Press, 1960. 19.
4 Cited by Breton in *Manifestoes of Surrealism*. 20.
5 Translated by Michael Benedikt. In Michael Benedikt, *The Poetry of Surrealism: An Anthology*. Boston, Little, Brown and Company, 1974. 225.

physical property, as when Eluard writes, "The earth is blue like an orange"; and, simply, images that provoke laughter, as in this by Benjamin Péret: "Stupid, like sausages whose sauerkraut has already been eaten away."

Fifty years before Surrealism, Arthur Rimbaud had called for the poet to make himself a "seer" through a "long, immense and reasoned derangement of all the senses." The Surrealists were realizing this idea. To what purpose? To show the absolute power of mind. "If Surrealism wished to bring together in its images the most distant realities, is it not because of its unlimited confidence in the powers of the spirit?" Surrealism demonstrates that "man is the creator of values, which have their sense only from him and relative to him."[6]

Directed by Breton, who expelled from the group anyone who disagreed with his theories, Surrealism became a successful movement in literature and art, spreading to other countries. Its effect in England and the United States, however, was tangential—Surrealism in English was a tributary, not a main stream. In the 1930s the English poet David Gascoyne imitated French Surrealism. In the United States Charles Henri Ford and Kenneth Patchen wrote in a Surrealistic manner, and there are patches of Surrealism in the novels of Henry Miller.

During the Second World War a number of French Surrealists fled from Europe to the United States. Breton, Dali, Max Ernst, Tanguy, Duchamp, and Seligmann took up residence in the States. The ascendancy of American "nonrepresentational" painting dates from these years. The influence of French Surrealism on American poetry can be seen plainly in the writings of Frank O'Hara and the "New York Poets," one of whom, John Ashbery, is also a critic of art.

Allen Ginsberg, whose "Howl" made a sensation in the late 1950s, had read the French Surrealists but owed as much to the eighteenth-century poet Christopher Smart, and Blake and Whitman. In the 1960s Robert Bly and James Wright made translations from Surrealist poets writing in other languages than French: from the German of Georg Trakl, the Spanish of Pablo Neruda and César Vallejo, and the Swedish of Tomas Tranströmer.

Surrealism according to the rules laid down by André Breton made for monotony. To exclude reason is to censor part of the mind—could anything be more inhibiting? The flaw in Breton's theory was to assume that there is something more "real" about the unconscious functioning of thought than its rational functioning.

Poets such as Tranströmer, whose "Morning Bird Songs" appears below, express the observed, exterior world as well as their own thoughts. There is a side of mind that is turned away from the light of day—in great poetry we feel that the shadow side has been allowed to express itself. But reason has not been excluded—"it is only by its contact with the verities of reason . . . that the dream seems marvelous."[7]

6 Ferdinand Alquié, *The Philosophy of Surrealism*. Ann Arbor, University of Michigan Press, 1969. 101–102.
7 Alquié, 140.

Morning Bird Songs

I wake up my car;
pollen covers the windshield.
I put my dark glasses on.
The bird songs all turn dark.

Meanwhile someone is buying a paper
at the railroad station
not far from a big freight car
reddened all over with rust.
It shimmers in the sun.

The whole universe is full.

A cool corridor cuts through the spring warmth;
a man comes hurrying past
describing how someone right up in the main office
has been telling lies about him.

Through a backdoor in the landscape
the magpie arrives,
black and white, bird of the death-goddess.
A blackbird flies back and forth
until the whole scene becomes a charcoal drawing,
except for the white clothes on the line:
a palestrina choir.

The whole universe is full!

Fantastic to feel how my poem is growing
while I myself am shrinking.
It's getting bigger, it's taking my place,
it's pressing against me.
It has shoved me out of the nest.
The poem is finished.

Tomas Tranströmer, translated by Robert Bly, 1970

Boswell: Then, Sir, what is poetry?
Johnson: Why, Sir, it is much easier to say what it is not. We all *know*
what light is; but it is not easy to *tell* what it is.

It is no easier to define poetry now than it was two hundred years ago when Samuel Johnson gave his opinion. But the behavior of light may be described and so may the sound and movement of a poem. Here are terms generally used in describing lines of verse, how they are formed, and move, and sound.

Meter

In English, meter is the pattern of stressed and unstressed syllables—also commonly called accented and unaccented syllables.

Prosodists sometimes attempt to distinguish between heavily stressed and lightly stressed syllables, but prosody, the "science" of poetical forms, is not an exact science, and if we attempt to make it so, it disappears. If we mark half-stresses there is no reason that we should not mark quarter-stresses, and so on. But when we think we hear half- and quarter-stresses we can be sure that others do not hear them. At that point, either we must impose our own way of hearing upon others, which is impossible, or agree that it is up to the individual to say exactly how he or she hears the beat of verse. The only system we can agree upon is the division of meter into stressed and unstressed syllables.

As we read lines of verse, each stressed sound combines with one or two unstressed sounds. This combination is called a foot. In the following line I have separated the feet by putting a vertical bar (|) between them. I have marked each stressed syllable: ′. Unstressed syllables are marked: ˘.

Ro˘mán | tĭc Íre | lănd's déad | ănd góne.

Here each foot consists of an unstressed syllable followed by a stressed. A foot of this kind is called an iamb, and verse in which such feet predominate is iambic. In the line above there are four feet. A line with four feet is called a tetrameter. Therefore, the complete description of the meter of the line above is iambic tetrameter.

Besides the stresses, or accents, of meter, there are rhetorical accents. Rhetorical accent is the emphasis given to a word because of its importance in the sentence. The meter of verse, the regular pattern of stressed and unstressed sounds, is sometimes wrenched by a rhetorical accent. It would be a rare poem that followed its meter exactly, without variation, and a poem like that would sound mechanical.

Though the poem by Yeats from which I have taken the line above is in iambic tetrameter—that is, most of the lines are in iambic tetrameter—there are places where the rhetorical accent wrenches the meter, substituting irregular feet and giving the line a more passionate, natural sound, as though a person were thinking and feeling:

> Wás ĭt | fŏr thís | thĕ wíld | gĕése spréad
>
> Thĕ gráy | wĭng úp | ŏn év | ĕry tíde;
>
> Fŏr thís | thăt áll | thăt blóod | wăs shéd,
>
> Fŏr thís | Édwărd | Fítzgĕr | ăld díed,
>
> Ănd Rób | ĕrt Émm | ĕt ănd | Wólfe Tóne;
>
> Áll thăt | dĕlír | ĭum ŏf | thĕ bráve?

I am not sure that Yeats would have stressed the sounds as I have done, for everyone reads in a different way, but I think he would have played as many variations, of one kind or another, upon the basic meter.

Meter is like waves of the sea, and rhetorical accents are like crosscurrents. The waves come on at a regular pace. They are crossed by the currents, and writhe, and seem to break. Then they resume their pace.

In English the basic feet are:

> the iamb (adjective, iambic) ˘´
> trochee (trochaic) ´˘
> anapest (anapestic) ˘˘´
> dactyl (dactylic) ´˘˘

Less common are:

> the spondee (spondaic) ´´
> pyrrhus (pyrrhic) ˘˘
> amphibrach (amphibrachic) ˘´˘
> amphimacer (cretic) ´˘´

And there are other feet so rarely used that we do not need to know them. Lines of verse are named for the number of feet they contain.

A line of one foot is a monometer

two feet	dimeter
three feet	trimeter
four feet	tetrameter
five feet	pentameter
six feet	hexameter
seven feet	heptameter

and so on.

Or else the line may be named for the number of syllables in it. A line of eight syllables is called octosyllabic; a line of ten syllables, decasyllabic.

Unrhymed iambic pentameter, the line in which Marlowe and Shakespeare wrote plays, is often called blank verse (not to be confused with free verse). The iambic hexameter is sometimes called an Alexandrine. In the following couplet, Pope shows the difference between a line of iambic pentameter and an Alexandrine:

Ă néed | lĕss Ăl | ĕxánd | rĭne énds, | hĭs sóng,   (*iambic pentameter*)

Whĭch, | lĭke ă wóund | ĕd snáke, | | drăws ĭts | slŏw léngth |

ălóng.   (*iambic hexameter* or *Alexandrine*)

In this Alexandrine I have marked the caesura—that is, a "cutting" or pause in the line—with a double bar. Here the caesura is in the middle of the line, dividing it into two equal parts, each of which contains three feet. But a pause may occur anywhere in a line.

Here are other lines and meters. The first two examples are not very good poetry, but they are good enough for our purpose:

Whĕn thréads | căn máke   *iambic dimeter*
A heartstring shake,
Philosophy
Can scarce deny

Thĕ sóul | cŏnsísts | ŏf hárm | ŏnÿ.   *iambic tetrameter*

Nŏ, thĕ héart | thăt hăs trú | lÿ lŏved név | ĕr fŏrgéts,
                                              anapestic tetrameter

Bŭt ăs trú | lÿ lóves ón | tŏ thĕ clóse,   *anapestic trimeter*
As the sunflower turns on her god when he sets,
    The same look which she turned when he rose.

Lóng-ĕx | pécted | óne ănd | twénty,   *trochaic tetrameter*
Ling'ring year, at last is flown;
Pomp and pleasure, pride and plenty,
Great Sir John, are all your own.

Mídnight hăs | cóme, ănd thĕ | gréat Chrĭst Chŭrch | Béll

dactylic tetrameter

Ănd mánў ā | léssĕr bĕll | sóund thrŏugh thĕ | róom.

Though meter may reinforce the meaning of poetry, it cannot *be* the meaning. Reading these lines by Tennyson, we may think we feel the gallop of horses:

> Half a league, half a league,
>   Half a league, onward,
> All in the valley of Death
>   Rode the six hundred.
> "Forward the Light Brigade!
> Charge for the guns!" he said.
> Into the valley of Death
>   Rode the six hundred.

But if we think we feel the pace of a cavalry charge, it is because the words tell us it is a cavalry charge. The meter alone does not call up the scene. A poet could write lines with the same meter but with different words that would make us think of something entirely different. Once we have a meaning, meter can support it; but without meaning, meter drifts in a void.

In his *Life of Pope*, Samuel Johnson argues against the fallacy of thinking that meter alone can represent meaning. Johnson says that through meter:

> Motion . . . may be in some sort exemplified; and yet it may be suspected that in such resemblances the mind often governs the ear, and the sounds are estimated by their meaning.

He shows that Pope uses the same meter when describing a running girl, and, in another place, a slow march. Pope himself says, "The sound must seem an echo to the sense." But this is a far cry from saying that sound is sense. Poetry has both meaning and meter, and in a good poem they are so closely related that they seem one thing.

Though meter and sound cannot by themselves represent the subject, frequently they represent the author's feelings about it—in Pope's phrase, the sound echoes the sense. If the poet wishes to express a heroic mood, he or she may choose a long, slowly moving line. To express lyrical feeling, the poet may write in short lines with tripping meters. But there are no standard correlations between lines and feelings. A long, slow line may be humorous, and a tripping line satirical.

There is no end to descriptions of meter. *Secondary stress* and *hovering accent*, and other kinds of rhythmic organization—*cadence* and *syllabic verse*—are described in the Glossary. We could go on talking about prosody, but it makes more sense, and it is certainly more enjoyable, to read poems than to try to think of all the kinds of poems there might possibly be.

Rhyme, Stanza, and Sound

Poems used to be called rhymes, and some people think that anything that rhymes is a poem. But, as Ben Jonson said, "A rhymer, and a poet, are two things." Poems are made with words that express thought and feeling; merely repeating sounds is not enough. Of course, many poets have written in rhyme— great poets use it, little poets depend on it. There may be a pleasure in the sound of rhyme even where sense is lacking:

> Lives of great men all remind us
>   We can make our lives sublime,
> And, departing, leave behind us
>   Footprints on the sands of time.
>
> Longfellow, "A Psalm of Life"

Rhymes are memorable. And writers of light verse entertain us with their ingenuity in making rhymes:

> I'm very well acquainted too with matters mathematical,
> I understand equations, both the simple and quadratical,
> About binomial theorem I'm teeming with a lot of news,
> With many cheerful facts about the square of the hypotenuse.
>
> W. S. Gilbert, "Major General's Song"

In the twentieth century, however, many poets have dispensed with rhyme in order to make new forms of verse.

Rhyme does not have a very long history. The ancient Greek, Hebrew, and Roman poets did not use rhyme. It was invented by monks in the Middle Ages as a memory aid; they found it easier to memorize chants if the ends of lines had the same sound. Then rhyme was taken up by Italian poets and their imitators, and by the time of Chaucer (c. 1340-1400) we find it ensconced in English.

In the history of verse, there has been a running quarrel between poets such as Samuel Daniel (1562-1619), who *would* rhyme, and poets such as Thomas Campion (c. 1567-1620), who *wouldn't*. Daniel defended rhyming on the ground that it was customary (though it was not customary with the ancients); Campion called rhyme, together with the English system of meter, a "vulgar and easie kind of Poesie." Milton, who had written several poems in rhyme, broke with it scornfully:

> rhyme being no necessary adjunct or true ornament of poem or good verse, in longer works especially, but the invention of a barbarous age, to set off wretched matter and lame meter.

The defenders of rhyme say that the sound is pleasing. Moreover, searching for rhymes makes the poet have thoughts he or she would not otherwise have had. Those who attack rhyme say that in searching for a rhyme the poet loses the thought he or she had to start with. As for sound, there are other, more subtle devices than the correspondence of terminal sounds. And besides, writing without rhyme is more *natural*. To this the defenders of rhyme reply that all art is artificial, and poets are free to do as they like.

In comparison with other languages, English does not have a large variety of rhyming words. This is evident if we read the poems of an English rhymer such as Pope, who is frequently compelled to use the same terminal words. Rhyme schemes that in other languages are easy—*terza rima*, for example—are hard to find rhymes for in English.

In scansion, rhymes are marked by placing the same letter of the alphabet after words that rhyme with each other. I have marked the following couplets from Pope's *The Rape of the Lock* in this manner:

The hungry Judges soon the Sentence sign,	*a*
And wretches hang that Jurymen may dine;	*a*
The Merchant from th'*Exchange* returns in Peace,	*b*
And the long Labors of the *Toilet* cease.	*b*

Actually, in this instance, the letters *a a b b* are not needed to describe the lines, for the word *couplet* means two consecutive lines that rhyme with each other. But if we wish to describe other rhyme schemes, letters are useful. Here is a ballad stanza:

It is an ancient Mariner,	*a*
And he stoppeth one of three.	*b*
"By thy long gray beard and glittering eye,	*c*
Now wherefore stopp'st thou me?	*b*

We could describe this rhyme scheme simply by saying "a ballad stanza rhyming *a b c b*." This would differentiate the stanza from others—for example, stanzas rhyming *a b a b*.

At the same time we could describe the meter by placing numbers after the letters to show the number of feet in each line: $a^4 b^3 c^4 b^3$.

A stanza is a group of lines forming a unit of a poem. It is recurrent, with a regular pattern of lines, meter, and rhyme—though the pattern may vary. Some of the stanza forms—quatrain, *rime royal*, *ottava rima*, Spenserian stanza, and so on—are described in the Glossary.

Before rhyme came into English, there was an entirely different system of sound-correspondence: by alliteration, the repetition of initial consonants or vowels in words placed close together. William Langland, a contemporary of Chaucer, wrote in this manner:

In a somer seson whan soft was the sonne,
I shope me in shroudes as I a shepe were,

In habite as an heremite unholy of workes,
Went wyde in this world wondres to here.

Piers Plowman

Though alliteration is no longer used as a system, in most poetry there is some alliteration:

Now the old come out to look,
    Winter past and winter's pains,
How the sky in pool and brook
    Glitters on the grassy plains.

A. E. Housman, "Spring Morning"

In this quatrain the initial consonant *p* occurs four times, and the *g* twice. (The initial consonant *w* occurs twice, in "Winter" and "winter's," but as it is the same word this is not alliteration but just repetition.)

Besides alliteration, in this quatrain there is another sound device: assonance, the repetition of vowel sounds within different words placed close together. "Past" and "pains" are assonant; so are "pool" and "brook."

On the other hand, if the main vowel sounds change but consonantal sounds recur, this is consonance. The word *consonance* may be used also to mean line endings where the final consonants agree but the vowels that precede them differ.

But cursed are dullards whom no cannon stu*ns*,
That they should be as sto*nes*.

Wilfred Owen, "Insensibility"

And there is cacophony, a combination of discordant sounds:

The ice was here, the ice was there,
The ice was all around:
It *cracked* and *growled*, and roared and howled,
Like noises in a swound!

Coleridge, "The Rime of the Ancient Mariner"

I have said that meter alone cannot convey meaning. Nor can onomatopoeia, the forming of words in imitation of sounds. In the following lines from Tennyson's *The Princess*, we may think that we hear, in the alliterative and consonant *m* sounds, and the assonant *o* and *u* sounds, the moaning of doves and humming of bees:

The moan of doves in immemorial elms,
And murmuring of innumerable bees

But without the nouns *doves* and *bees*, these sounds would not conjure up doves and bees. We might be thinking of the ocean, or wind in the grass. In the "cracked" and "growled" of Coleridge's description we may think that we hear ice grinding and splitting, but without the word *ice* it might as well be breaking timber. Like meter, sound can reinforce meaning, but sounds alone are . . . Sound Poetry. See the entry in the Glossary.

Free Verse

Free verse—verse with an irregular metrical pattern—is an old form. The Hebrew psalms were written in lines that are more or less free; in the last century Whitman wrote free verse, so did some of the Symbolists, and nowadays many poets write in this form. Free verse is not just prose broken into irregular lines. As Eliot said, no verse is free for the poet who wants to do a good job—and free verse, to be written well, requires as much art as writing in regular meters. However, this has not been apparent to some people. Robert Frost said he would as soon play tennis without a net as try to write free verse. Even if we think that poetry is a game, there are games—jai alai, for example—that do not use a net.

Free verse is discussed on pp. 4–5, in the reading of a poem by Williams and a line by Whitman. Also see Free Verse in the Glossary.

AN ANTHOLOGY OF POEMS

GEOFFREY CHAUCER [1340?–1400]

from *The Canterbury Tales*

Whan that Aprill with his shoures° soote°	*showers / sweet*
The droghte of March hath perced to the roote,	
And bathed every veyne in swich licour°	*such liquid*
Of which vertu° engendred is the flour;	*by power of which*
Whan Zephirus eek° with his sweete breeth	*also*
Inspired hath in every holt° and heeth	*wood*
The tendre croppes, and the yonge sonne	
Hath in the Ram his halve cours yronne,°	*run*
And smale foweles° maken melodye,	*birds*
That slepen al the nyght with open ye°	*eye*
(So priketh hem° nature in hir	*inspires them*
corages°),	*their hearts*
Thanne longen° folk to goon on pilgrimages,	*long*
And palmeres° for to seken straunge strondes,°	*pilgrims / shores*
To ferne halwes,° kowthe° in sondry londes;	*distant shrines / known*
And specially from every shires ende	
Of Engelond to Caunterbury they wende,	
The hooly blisful martir[1] for to seke,	
That hem hath holpen° whan that they were seeke.°	*helped / sick*
Bifil° that in that seson on a day,	*It befell*
In Southwerk at the Tabard as I lay	
Redy to wenden° on my pilgrymage	*go*
To Caunterbury with ful devout corage,°	*heart*
At nyght was come into that hostelrye°	*inn*
Wel nyne and twenty in a compaigyne,	
On sondry folk, by aventure yfalle°	*by chance fallen*
In felaweshipe, and pilgrimes were they alle,	
That toward Caunterbury wolden° ryde.	*wanted to*
The chambres and the stables weren wyde,	
And wel we weren esed° atte beste.	*entertained*
And shortly, whan the sonne was to reste,	
So hadde I spoken with hem everichon°	*every one*
That I was of hir felaweshipe anon,	
And made forward° erly for to ryse,	*agreement*
To take oure wey ther as I yow devyse.°	*impart*

♦

A Knyght ther was, and that a worthy man,	
That fro the tyme that he first bigan	
To riden out,° he loved chivalrie,	*go on expeditions*
Trouthe and honour, fredom and curteisie.	

---

1 Thomas à Beckett, Archbishop of Canterbury, murdered in 1170.

Ful worthy was he in his lordes werre,°   *war*
And therto hadde he riden, no man ferre,°   *farther*
As wel in cristendom as in hethenesse,°   *heathen lands*
And evere honoured for his worthynesse.
At Alisaundre° he was whan it was wonne.   *Alexandria*
Ful ofte tyme he hadde the bord bigonne°   *headed the table*
Aboven alle nacions in Pruce;°   *Prussia*
In Lettow° hadde he reysed° and in   *Lithuania / made a raid*
    Ruce,°   *Russia*
No Cristen man so ofte of his degree.°   *rank*
In Gernade° at the seege eek hadde he be   *Granada*
Of Algezir,° and riden in Belmarye.°   *Algeciras / Benmarin*
At Lyeys° was he and at Satalye,°   *Ayas / Attalia*
Whan they were wonne; and in the Grete See°   *Mediterranean Sea*
At many a noble armee° hadde he be.   *armed expedition*
At mortal batailles° hadde he been
    fiftene,   *tournaments fought to the death*
And foughten for oure feith at Tramyssene°   *Tlemcen*
In lystes° thries, and ay slayn his foo.   *tournaments*
This ilke° worthy knyght hadde been also   *same*
Somtyme with the lord of Palatye°   *Palathia*
Agayn another hethen in Turkye.
And everemoore he hadde a sovereyn prys;°   *supreme reputation*
And though that he were worthy, he was wys,
And of his port° as meeke as is a mayde.   *demeanor*
He nevere yet no vileynye° ne sayde   *insult*
In al his lyf unto no maner wight.°   *person*
He was a verray, parfit gentil° knyght.   *true / perfect / noble*
But, for to tellen yow of his array,
His hors were goode, but he was nat gay.
Of fustian° he wered a gypon°   *thick cotton / tunic*
Al bismotered with his
    habergeon,°   *marked with rust from his coat of mail*
For he was late ycome from his viage,°   *expedition*
And wente for to doon his pilgrymage.

◆

A Clerk° ther was of   *ecclesiastical student*
    Oxenford° also,   *Oxford*
That unto logyk hadde longe ygo.
As leene was his hors as is a rake,
And he nas nat right fat, I undertake,
But looked holwe, and therto sobrely.
Ful thredbare was his overeste courtepy;°   *outer cloak*
For he hadde geten hym yet no benefice,
Ne was so worldy for to have office.°   *secular employment*
For hym was levere° have at his beddes heed   *would rather*
Twenty bookes, clad in blak or reed,

Of Aristotle[2] and his philosophie,
Than robes riche, or fithele,° or gay sautrie.°   *fiddle / psaltery*
But al be that he was a philosophre,
Yet hadde he but litel gold in cofre;[3]
But al that he myghte of his freendes hente,°   *obtain*
On bookes and on lernynge he it spente,
And bisily gan for the soules preye
Of hem that yaf hym wherwith to scoleye.°   *study*
Of studie took he moost cure° and moost heede.   *care*
Noght o word spak he moore than was neede,
And that was seyd in forme° and reverence,   *with decorum*
And short and quyk and ful of hy sentence;°   *thought*
Sownynge in° moral vertu was his speche,   *tending towards*
And gladly wolde he lerne and gladly teche.

◆

A good Wif was ther of biside° Bathe,   *near*
But she was somdel° deef, and that was scathe.°   *somewhat / a pity*
Of clooth-makyng she hadde swich an haunt,°   *skill*
She passed° hem of Ypres and of Gaunt.[4]   *surpassed*
In al the parisshe wif ne was ther noon
That to the offrynge° bifore hire sholde goon;   *offering of alms*
And if ther° dide, certeyn so wrooth was she,   *they*
That she was out of alle charitee.
Hir coverchiefs° ful fyne weren of ground;°   *kerchiefs / texture*
I dorste° swere they weyeden° ten pound   *dare / weighed*
That on a Sonday weren upon hir heed.
Hir hosen weren of fyn scarlet reed,
Ful streite yteyd,° and shoes ful moyste and newe.   *tied*
Boold was hir face, and fair, and reed of hewe.
She was a worthy womman al hir lyve:
Housbondes at chirche dore she hadde fyve,
Withouten° oother compaignye in youthe,—   *apart from*
But therof nedeth° nat to speke as nowthe.°   *need / now*
And thries hadde she been at Jerusalem;
She hadde passed many a straunge strem;
At Rome she hadde been, and at Boloigne,
In Galice at Seint-Jame, and at Coloigne.
She koude° muchel of wandrynge by the weye.   *knew*
Gat-tothed° was she, soothly for to seye.   *teeth wide apart*
Upon an amblere° esily she sat,   *slow horse*
Ywympled° wel, and on hir heed an hat   *veiled*
As brood as is a bokeler° or a targe;°   *buckler / shield*

---

2 famous Greek philosopher whose writings were particularly influential in the
Middle Ages.
3 a punning reference to the "philosopher's stone," which alchemists believed would
change base metals into gold.
4 Flemish towns famous for cloth-making.

A foot-mantel° aboute hir hipes large,	*skirt*
And on hir feet a paire of spores° sharpe.	*spurs*
In felaweshipe wel koude she laughe and carpe.°	*talk*
Of remedies of love she knew per chaunce,	
For she koude° of that art the olde daunce.°	*knew / dance*

ANONYMOUS

I Sing of a Maiden

I sing of a maiden	
That is makeles;°	*matchless, without a mate*
King of all kings	
To° her son she ches.°	*for / chose*

He came al so still
    There his mother was,
As dew in April
    That falleth on the grass.

He came al so still
    To his mother's bour,
As dew in April
    That falleth on the flour.

He came al so still
    There his mother lay,
As dew in April
    That falleth on the spray.

Mother and maiden
    Was never none but she;
Well may such a lady
    Goddes mother be.

Adam Lay I-bowndyn

Adam lay I-bowndyn,° bowndyn in a bond,	*bound*
Forwe° thowsand wynter thowt he not to long;[1]	*four*
And al was for an appil, an appil that he tok,	
As clerkis° fyndyn wretyn in here° book.	*clergy / their*

1 The Creation was thought to have taken place in 4004 B.C. From this to the birth of Christ was four thousand years.

Ne hadde the appil take ben, the appil taken ben,
Ne hadde neuer our lady a ben heuene qwen;[2]
Blyssid be the tyme that appil take was,
Ther-fore we mown° syngyn, "deo gracias!"[3]   *may*

2   Our Lady would never have been Queen of Heaven.
3   "thanks be to God."

Who Wot Nowe
That Ys Here

Who wot° nowe that ys here,   *knows*
   Where he schall be anoder yere?
Anoder yere hit may betyde
This compeny to be full wyde,°   *far off*
And neuer on-odyr to abyde;
   Criste may send now sych a yere.

Another yere hit may befall
The lest° that is withyn this hall   *lowest*
To be more mastur then we all;
   Cryste may send now sych a yere.

This lordis that ben wonder grete,
They threton powre men for to bete;
Hyt lendith° lytull in hur° threte;   *there is / their*
   Cryste may send sich a yere.

Sumer Is
Icumen In

Sumer is icumen in,
   Lhudé° sing cuccu;   *loud*
Groweth sed and bloweth° med°   *blossoms / meadow*
   And springth the wudé nu.°   *wood now*
      Sing cuccu!
Awé° bleteth after lomb,   *ewe*
   Lhouth° after calvé cu;°   *lows / cow*
Bulluc sterteth, bucké verteth;°   *breaks wind*
   Murie sing cuccu.
      Cuccu, cuccu,
   Wel singés thu, cuccu,
      Ne swik° thu naver nu.°   *stop / now*
Sing cuccu nu! Sing cuccu!
Sing cuccu! Sing cuccu nu!

I Haue
a Yong Suster

I haue a yong suster
   ffer be-yondyn the se,
many be the drowryis°   *love-tokens*
   that che sente me.

che sente me the cherye
   with-outyn ony ston,
& so che ded the dowe°   *dove*
   with-outyn ony bon.

sche sente me the brer°   *briar*
   with-outyn ony rinde,°   *branch*
sche bad me loue my lemman°   *sweetheart*
   with-oute longgyng.

how shuld ony cherye
   be with-oute ston?
& how shuld ony dowe
   ben with-oute bon?

how shuld ony brer
   ben with-oute rynde?
how shuld y loue myn lemman
   with-out longyng?

Quan° the cherye was a flour,   *when*
   than hadde it non ston.
quan the dowe was an ey,°   *egg*
   than hadde it non bon.

Quan the brer was on-bred,°   *unborn*
   than hadde it non rynd.
quan the maydyn hast that che louit,
   che is with-out longing.

Westron Winde, When
Will Thou Blow

Westron winde, when will thou blow,
The smalle raine downe can raine?
Crist, if my love wer in my armis,
And I in my bed againe.

Sir Patrick Spens

The king sits in Dumferling toune,
    Drinking the blude-reid wine;
"O whar will I get guid sailor,
    To sail this schip of mine?"

Up and spak an eldern knicht,
    Sat at the kings richt kne:
"Sir Patrick Spens is the best sailor
    That sails upon the se."

The king has written a braid° letter,   *broad*
    And signd it wi his hand,   10
And sent it to Sir Patrick Spens,
    Was walking on the sand.

The first line that Sir Patrick red,
    A loud lauch lauched he;
The next line that Sir Patrick red,
    The teir blinded his ee.°   *eye*

"O wha° is this has don this deid,   *who*
    This ill deid don to me,
To send me out this time o' the yeir,
    To sail upon the se!   20

"Mak haste, mak haste, my mirry men all,
    Our guid° schip sails the morne."   *good*
"O say na sae,° my master deir,   *so*
    For I feir a deadlie storme.

"Late late yestreen I saw the new moone,
    Wi the auld moone in hir arme,
And I feir, I feir, my deir master,
    That we will cum to harme."

O our Scots nobles wer richt laith°   *loath*
    To weet their cork-heild schoone;°   *cork-heeled shoes*
Bot lang owre° a' the play wer playd,   *before*
    Thair hats they swam aboone.°   *above*

O lang, lang may their ladies sit,
    Wi thair fans into their hand,
Or eir° they se Sir Patrick Spens   *before*
    Cum sailing to the land.

O lang, lang may the ladies stand
    Wi thair gold kems° in their hair,   *combs*

Waiting for thair ain deir lords,
   For they'll se thame na mair.   40

Haf owre,° haf owre to Abedour,   *half over*
   It's fiftie fadom deip,
And thair lies guid Sir Patrick Spens,
   Wi the Scots lords at his feit.

Thomas the Rhymer

True Thomas lay on Huntlie bank;
   A ferlie° he spied wi' his e'e;   *marvel*
And there he saw a ladye bright
   Come riding doun by Eildon Tree.

Her skirt was o' the grass-green silk,
   Her mantle o' the velvet fyne;
At ilka° tett° o' her horse's mane   *each / lock*
   Hung fifty siller bells and nine.

True Thomas he pu'd aff his cap,
   And louted° low doun on his knee: *bowed*
"Hail to thee, Mary, Queen of Heaven!   11
   For thy peer on earth could never be."

"O no, O no, Thomas," she said,
   "That name does not belang to me;
I'm but the Queen o' fair Elfland,
   That am hither come to visit thee."

"Harp and carp,° Thomas," she said;   *sing*
   "Harp and carp along wi' me;
And if ye dare to kiss my lips,
   Sure of your bodie I will be."   20

"Betide me weal, betide me woe,
   That weird° shall never daunten me."   *fate*
Syne° he has kissed her rosy lips,   *soon*
   All underneath the Eildon Tree.

"Now ye maun° go wi' me," she said,   *must*
   "True Thomas, ye maun go wi' me;
And ye maun serve me seven years,
   Thro' weal or woe as may chance to be."

She's mounted on her milk-white steed;
   She's ta'en true Thomas up behind;   30

And aye, whene'er her bridle rang.
　　The steed gaed° swifter than the wind.　　　　　　　　　　　　*went*

O they rade on, and farther on,
　　The steed gaed swifter than the wind;
Until they reached a desert wide,
　　And living land was left behind.

"Light down, light down now, true Thomas,
　　And lean your head upon my knee;
Abide ye here a little space,
　　And I will show you ferlies three.　　　　　　　　　　　　　　40

"O see ye not yon narrow road,
　　So thick beset wi' thorns and briars?
That is the Path of Righteousness,
　　Though after it but few inquires.

"And see ye not yon braid,° braid road,　　　　　　　　　　　*broad*
　　That lies across the lily leven?°　　　　　　　　　　　*white light*
That is the Path of Wickedness,
　　Though some call it the Road to Heaven.

"And see ye not yon bonny road
　　That winds about the fernie brae?°　　　　　　　　　　　　*hill*
That is the road to fair Elfland,　　　　　　　　　　　　　　51
　　Where thou and I this night maun gae.

"But, Thomas, ye sall haud° your tongue,　　　　　　　　　　*hold*
　　Whatever ye may hear or see;
For speak ye word in Elfyn-land,
　　Ye'll ne'er win back to your ain countrie."

O they rade on, and farther on,
　　And they waded rivers abune° the knee;　　　　　　　　　*above*
And they saw neither sun nor moon,
　　But they heard the roaring of the sea.　　　　　　　　　　60

It was mirk,° mirk night, there was nae starlight,　　　　　　*dark*
　　They waded thro' red blude to the knee;
For a' the blude that's shed on the earth
　　Rins° through the springs o' that countrie.　　　　　　　　*runs*

Syne they came to a garden green,
　　And she pu'd an apple frae a tree:
"Take this for thy wages, true Thomas;
　　It will give thee the tongue that can never lee.°"　　　　　*lie*

"My tongue is my ain,°" true Thomas he said;　　　　　　　　*own*
　　"A gudely gift ye wad gie° to me!　　　　　　　　　　　*would give*

I neither dought° to buy or sell   *am able*
    At fair or tryst° where I might be.   *appointed place*

"I dought neither speak to prince or peer,
    Nor ask of grace from fair ladye!"
"Now haud° thy peace, Thomas," she said,   *hold*
    "For as I say, so must it be."

He has gotten a coat of the even cloth,
    And a pair o' shoon° of the velvet green;   *shoes*
And till seven years were gane and past,
    True Thomas on earth was never seen.   80

Edward, Edward

"Why does your brand° sae drop wi' blude,   *sword*
    Edward, Edward?
Why does your brand sae drop wi' blude,
    And why sae sad gang ye, O?"—
"O I hae kill'd my hawk sae gude,
    Mither, mither;
O I hae kill'd my hawk sae gude,
    And I had nae mair but he, O."

"Your hawk's blude was never sae red,
    Edward, Edward;   10
Your hawk's blude was never sae red,
    My dear son, I tell thee, O."—
"O I hae kill'd my red-roan° steed,   *reddish-brown*
    Mither, mither;
O I hae kill'd my red-roan steed,
    That earst° was sae fair and free, O."   *previously*

"Your steed was auld, and ye hae got mair,°   *more*
    Edward, Edward;
Your steed was auld, and ye hae got mair;
    Some other dule° ye dree,° O."   *grief / suffer*
"O I hae kill'd my father dear,   21
    Mither, mither;
O I hae kill'd my father dear,
    Alas, and wae is me, O!"

"And whatten penance will ye dree° for that,   *undergo*
    Edward, Edward?
Whatten penance will ye dree for that?
    My dear son, now tell me, O."—
"I'll set my feet in yonder boat,

30

Mither, mither;
I'll set my feet in yonder boat,
    And I'll fare over the sea, O."

"And what will ye do wi' your tow'rs and your ha',°   *hall*
    Edward, Edward?
And what will ye do wi' your tow'rs and your ha',
    That were sae fair to see, O?"
"I'll let them stand till they doun fa',°   *fall*
    Mither, mither;
I'll let them stand till they doun fa',
    For here never mair maun° I be, O."   *must*

"And what will ye leave to your bairns° and your wife,   *children*
    Edward, Edward?
And what will ye leave to your bairns and your wife,
    When ye gang owre the sea, O?"—
"The warld's room: let them beg through life,
    Mither, mither;
The warld's room: let them beg through life;
    For them never mair will I see, O."

"And what will ye leave to your ain mither dear,
    Edward, Edward?   50
And what will ye leave to your ain mither dear,
    My dear son, now tell me, O?"—
"The curse of hell frae me sall ye bear,
    Mither, mither;
The curse of hell frae me sall ye bear:
    Sic° counsels ye gave to me, O!"   *such*

JOHN SKELTON [1460?–1529]

from *The Garlande of Laurell*

11   *To maystres Isabell Pennell*[1]

By saynt Mary, my lady,
Your mammy and your dady
Brought forth a godely babi!
    My mayden Isabell,

---

1   *maystres*: mistress. Isabell Pennell was the daughter of John Paynell and related on her mother's side to the Countess of Surrey.

Reflaring rosabell,°   *redolent rose*
The flagrant camamell;
        The ruddy rosary,°   *rose bush*
The soverayne rosemary,
The praty° strawbery;   *pretty*
        The columbyne, the nepte,°   *catnip*
The jeloffer° well set,   *gillyflower*
The propre° vyolet;   *excellent*
        Enuwyd° your colowre   *tinted*
Is lyke the dasy flowre
After the Aprill showre;
        Sterre° of the morow° gray,   *star / morning*
The blossom on the spray,
The fresshest flowre of May;
        Maydenly demure,
Of womanhode the lure;   20
Wherefore I make you sure,
        It were an hevenly helth,
It were an endeles welth,
A lyfe for God hymselfe,
        To here this nightingale,
Amonge the byrdes smale,
Warbelynge in the vale,
Dug, dug,
Jug, jug,
Good yere and good luk,   30
With chuk, chuk, chuk, chuk!

12   To maystres Margaret Hussey[1]

Mirry Margaret,
As mydsomer flowre,
Jentill as fawcoun°   *falcon*
Or hawke of the towre;
        With solace and gladnes,
Moche mirthe and no madnes,   *much*
All good and no badnes,
So joyously,
So maydenly,
So womanly   10
Her demenyng°   *demeanor*
In every thynge,
Far, far passynge
That I can endyght,°   *write, proclaim*

1 Margaret Hussey has not been identified.

Or suffyce to wryght
Of mirry Margarete,
As mydsomer flowre,
Jentyll as fawcoun
Or hawke of the towre;
As pacient and as styll,   20
And as full of good wyll,
As fayre Isaphill;[2]
Colyaunder,°   *coriander*
Swete pomaunder,°   *pomander*
Good cassaunder;[3]
Stedfast of thought,
Wele made, wele wrought;
Far may be sought
Erst° that ye can fynde   *before*
So corteise, so kynde   *courteous*
As mirry Margarete,   31
This midsomer flowre,
Jentyll as fawcoun
Or hawke of the towre.

2   Hypsipyle, a princess of Lemnos, daughter of King Thoas. She saved her father's life
when the women killed the men on the island.
3   Cassandra, a princess of Troy, daughter of Priam and Hecuba. She had the gift of
prophecy but no one would believe her.

SIR THOMAS WYATT   [1503?–1542]

The Long Love[1]

The long love that in my thought doth harbor,
And in my heart doth keep his residence,
Into my face presseth with bold pretense
And therein campeth, spreading his banner.
She that me learneth to love and suffer
And wills that my trust and lust's negligence
Be reined by reason, shame and reverence,
With his hardiness taketh displeasure.
Wherewithal, unto the heart's forest he fleeth,
Leaving his enterprise with pain and cry,
And there him hideth, and not appeareth.
What may I do, when my master feareth,
But in the field with him to live and die?
For good is the life ending faithfully.

1   Translated from Petrarch, *Sonnetto in Vita* 91.

My Galley[1]

My galley charged with forgetfulness
Thorough sharp seas in winter nights doth pass
'Tween rock and rock; and eke[2] mine enemy, alas,
That is my lord, steereth with cruelness;
And every oar a thought in readiness,
As though that death were light in such a case.
An endless wind doth tear the sail apace
Of forced sighs and trusty fearfulness.
A rain of tears, a cloud of dark disdain,
Hath done the wearied cords great hinderance,
Wreathed with error and eke with ignorance.
The stars be hid that led me to this pain,
Drowned is reason that should me comfort,
And I remain despairing of the port.

1 Translated from Petrarch, *Sonnetto in Vita* 137.
2 also.

The Lover Showeth
How He Is Forsaken
of Such as He Sometime Enjoyed

They flee from me that sometime did me seek,
    With naked foot stalking in my chamber.
I have seen them gentle, tame and meek,
    That now are wild and do not remember
    That sometime they put themselves in danger
        To take bread at my hand; and now they range
        Busily seeking with a continual change.

Thanked be fortune, it hath been otherwise
    Twenty times better; but once, in special,
In thin array, after a pleasant guise,
    When her loose gown from her shoulders did fall,
    And she me caught in her arms long and small,
        Therewith all sweetly did me kiss,
        And softly said: "Dear heart, how like you this?"

It was no dream; I lay broad waking:
    But all is turned thorough my gentleness
Into a strange fashion of forsaking;
    And I have leave to go of her goodness;
    And she also to use new-fangleness.
        But since that I so kindely[1] am served,
        I fain would know what she hath deserved.

1 naturally.

56

My Lute, Awake!

My lute, awake! Perform the last
Labor that thou and I shall waste,
   And end that I have now begun;
For when this song is sung and past,
   My lute, be still, for I have done.

As to be heard where ear is none,
As lead to grave in marble stone,
   My song may pierce her heart as soon.[1]
Should we then sigh or sing or moan?
   No, no, my lute, for I have done.   10

The rocks do not so cruelly
Repulse the waves continually
   As she my suit and affection,
So that I am past remedy,
   Whereby my lute and I have done.

Proud of the spoil that thou hast got
Of simple hearts, thorough love's shot;
   By whom, unkind, thou hast them won,
Think not he hath his bow forgot,
   Although my lute and I have done.   20

Vengeance shall fall on thy disdain
That makest but game on earnest pain.
   Think not alone under the sun
Unquit to cause thy lover's plain,
   Although my lute and I have done.

Perchance thee lie withered and old
The winter nights that are so cold,
   Plaining in vain unto the moon.
Thy wishes then dare not be told.
   Care then who list, for I have done.   30

And then may chance thee to repent
The time that thou hast lost and spent
   To cause thy lovers sigh and swoon.
Then shalt thou know beauty but lent,
   And wish and want as I have done.

Now cease, my lute. This is the last
Labor that thou and I shall waste,
   And ended is that we begun.

---

1   My song may pierce her heart as soon as sound may be heard without ears or marble
be engraved by lead.

Now is this song both sung and past;
  My lute, be still, for I have done.   40

HENRY HOWARD, EARL OF SURREY [1517?–1547]

The Soote Season[1]

The soote[2] season, that bud and bloom forth brings,
With green hath clad the hill and eke[3] the vale;
The nightingale with feathers new she sings;
The turtle to her make[4] hath told her tale.
Summer is come, for every spray now springs;
The hart hath hung his old head on the pale;
The buck in brake his winter coat he flings,
The fishes float with new repaired scale;
The adder all her slough away she slings,
The swift swallow pursueth the flies small;
The busy bee her honey now she mings.[5]
Winter is worn, that was the flowers' bale.
And thus I see among these pleasant things,
Each care decays, and yet my sorrow springs.

1 Adapted from Petrarch, *Sonnetto in Morte* 42.
2 sweet.
3 also.
4 *turtle*: turtle dove; *make*: mate.
5 remembers.

BARNABE GOOGE [1540–1594]

Out of Sight,
Out of Mind

The oftener seen, the most I lust,
  The more I lust, the more I smart,
The more I smart, the more I trust,
  The more I trust, the heavier heart;
The heavy heart breeds mine unrest,
Thy absence, therefore, like I best.

The rarer seen, the less in mind,
  The less in mind, the lesser pain,
The lesser pain, less grief I find,
  The lesser grief, the greater gain,
The greater gain, the merrier I,
Therefore I wish thy sight to fly.

The further off, the more I joy,
    The more I joy, the happier life,
The happier life, less hurts annoy,
    The lesser hurts, pleasure most rife:
Such pleasures rife shall I obtain
When distance doth depart us twain.

SIR WALTER RALEGH [1552?–1618]

The Nymph's Reply
to the Shepherd

If all the world and love were young,
And truth in every shepherd's tongue,
These pretty pleasures might me move,
To live with thee, and be thy love.

Time drives the flocks from field to fold
When rivers rage, and rocks grow cold,
And Philomel[1] becometh dumb;
The rest complains of cares to come.

The flowers do fade, and wanton fields
To wayward winter reckoning yields;
A honey tongue, a heart of gall,
Is fancy's spring, but sorrow's fall.

Thy gowns, thy shoes, thy bed of roses,
Thy cap, thy kirtle,[2] and thy posies
Soon break, soon wither, soon forgotten:
In folly ripe, in reason rotten.

Thy belt of straw and ivy buds,
Thy coral clasps and amber studs,
All these in me no means can move,
To come to thee, and be thy love.

But could youth last, and love still[3] breed,
Had joys no date, nor age no need,
Then these delights my mind might move,
To live with thee, and be thy love.

1 the nightingale.
2 skirt.
3 always.

As You Came
from the Holy Land[1]

As you came from the holy land
   · Of Walsingham,
Met you with my true love
   By the way as you came?

How shall I know your true love
   That have met many one,
As I went to the holy land
   That have come, that have gone?

She is neither white nor brown
   But as the heavens fair,   10
There is none hath a form so divine
   In the earth or the air.

Such an one did I meet, good sir,
   Such an angel-like face,
Who like a queen, like a nymph, did appear
   By her gate, by her grace.

She hath left me here all alone,
   All alone as unknown,
Who sometimes[2] did me lead with herself,
   And me loved as her own.   20

What's the cause that she leaves you alone
   And a new way doth take,
Who loved you once as her own
   And her joy did you make?

I have loved her all my youth,
   But now old, as you see;
Love likes not the falling fruit
   From the withered tree.

Know that love is a careless child
   And forgets promise past;   30
He is blind, he is deaf when he list[3]
   And in faith never fast.

1   based on a popular song. Walsingham is in Norfolk, east central England. It is the site of Walsingham Abbey, one of the shrines of medieval England.
2   once.
3   wishes.

His desire is a dureless[4] content
    And a trustless joy;
He is won with a world of despair
    And is lost with a toy.

Of womankind such indeed is the love,
    Or the word love abused,
Under which many childish desires
    And conceits[5] are excused.   40

But true love is a durable fire
    In the mind ever burning;
Never sick, never old, never dead,
    From itself never turning.

4   not enduring.
5   fanciful ideas.

To His Son

Three things there be that prosper all apace
And flourish, while they are asunder far;
But on a day they meet all in a place,
And when they meet, they one another mar.
And they be these: the wood, the weed, the wag.
The wood is that that makes the gallows tree;
The weed is that that strings the hangman's bag;
The wag, my pretty knave, betokens thee.
Now mark, dear boy: while these assemble not,
Green springs the tree, hemp grows, the wag is wild;
But when they meet, it makes the timber rot,
It frets the halter, and it chokes the child.
     God bless the child!

EDMUND SPENSER   [1552?–1599]

from *Amoretti*

68

Most glorious Lord of lyfe, that on this day
Didst make thy triumph over death and sin,
And having harrowd hell, didst bring away
Captivity thence captive, us to win:

This joyous day, deare Lord, with joy begin,
And grant that we, for whom thou diddest dye,
Being with thy deare blood clene washt from sin,
May live for ever in felicity:
And that thy love we weighing worthily,
May likewise love thee for the same againe:
And for thy sake, that all lyke deare didst buy,
With love may with one another entertayne.
So let us love, deare love, lyke as we ought:
Love is the lesson which the Lord us taught.

70

Fresh Spring the herald of loves mighty king,
In whose cote armour[1] richly are displayd
All sorts of flowers the which on earth do spring,
In goodly colours gloriously arrayd,
Goe to my love, where she is carelesse layd,
Yet in her winters bowre, not well awake:
Tell her the joyous time will not be staid
Unlesse she doe him by the forelock take.
Bid her therefore her selfe soone ready make
To wayt on love amongst his lovely crew,
Where every one that misseth then her make
Shall be by him amearst[2] with penance dew.
Make haste therefore, sweet love, whilest it is prime;
For none can call againe the passed time.

1 *cote armour*: a herald's official garment.
2 punished.

75

One day I wrote her name upon the strand,
But came the waves and washed it away:
Agayne I wrote it with a second hand,
But came the tyde, and made my paynes his pray.
Vayne man, sayde she, that doest in vaine assay
A mortal thing so to immortalize,
For I my selve shall lyke to this decay,
And eek[1] my name bee wyped out lykewize.
Not so, (quod I) let baser things devize[2]
To dy in dust, but you shall live by fame:
My verse your vertues rare shall eternize,
And in the hevens wryte your glorious name.
Where whenas death shall al the world subdew,
Our love shall live, and later life renew.

1 also.
2 contrive.

Epithalamion[1]

Ye learned sisters[2] which have oftentimes
Beene to me ayding, others to adorne:
Whom ye thought worthy of your gracefull rymes,
That even the greatest did not greatly scorne
To heare theyr names sung in your simple layes,
But joyéd in theyr prayse.
And when ye list your owne mishaps to mourne,
Which death, or love, or fortunes wreck did rayse,
Your string could soone to sadder tenor turne,
And teach the woods and waters to lament   10
Your dolefull dreriment.
Now lay those sorrowfull complaints aside,
And having all your heads with girland crownd,
Helpe me mine owne loves prayses to resound,
Ne let the same of any be envide:
So Orpheus did for his owne bride,[3]
So I unto my selfe alone will sing,
The woods shall to me answer and my Eccho ring.

Early before the worlds light giving lampe,
His golden beame upon the hils doth spred,   20
Having disperst the nights unchearefull dampe,
Doe ye awake, and with fresh lusty hed
Go to the bowre of my belovéd love,
My truest turtle dove,
Bid her awake; for Hymen[4] is awake,
And long since ready forth his maske to move,
With his bright Tead[5] that flames with many a flake,
And many a bachelor to waite on him,
In theyr fresh garments trim.
Bid her awake therefore and soone her dight,[6]   30
For lo the wishéd day is come at last,
That shall for al the paynes and sorrowes past,
Pay to her usury of long delight:
And whylest she doth her dight,
Doe ye to her of joy and solace sing,
That all the woods may answer and your eccho ring.

Bring with you all the Nymphes that you can heare
Both of the rivers and the forrests greene:
And of the sea that neighbours to her neare,

1 a wedding song, celebrating Spenser's marriage to Elizabeth Boyle in 1594.
2 the Muses.
3 Orpheus, on the death of his wife, Eurydice, descended to Hades and charmed the
god of the underworld with his song so that she was released.
4 god of marriage.
5 a torch used in Roman wedding ceremonies.
6 dress.

Al with gay girlands goodly wel beseene.   40
And let them also with them bring in hand,
Another gay girland
For my fayre love of lillyes and of roses,
Bound truelove wize with a blew silke riband.
And let them make great store of bridale poses,
And let them eeke bring store of other flowers
To deck the bridale bowers.
And let the ground whereas her foot shall tread,
For feare the stones her tender foot should wrong
Be strewed with fragnant flowers all along,   50
And diapred lyke the discolored mead.[7]
Which done, doe at her chamber dore awayt,
For she will waken strayt,
The whiles doe ye this song unto her sing,
The woods shall to you answer and your Eccho ring.

Ye Nymphes of Mulla[8] which with carefull heed,
The silver scaly trouts doe tend full well,
And greedy pikes which use therein to feed,
(Those trouts and pikes all others doo excell)
And ye likewise which keepe the rushy lake,   60
Where none doo fishes take,
Bynd up the locks the which hang scatterd light,
And in his waters which your mirror make,
Behold your faces as the christall bright,
That when you come whereas my love doth lie,
No blemish she may spie.
And eke ye lightfoot mayds which keepe the deere,
That on the hoary mountayne use to towre,
And the wylde wolves which seeke them to devoure,
With your steele darts doo chace from comming neer   70
Be also present heere,
To helpe to decke her and to help to sing,
That all the woods may answer and your eccho ring.

Wake, now my love, awake; for it is time,
The Rosy Morne long since left Tithones bed,[9]
All ready to her silver coche to clyme,
And Phoebus[10] gins to shew his glorious hed.
Hark how the cheerefull birds do chaunt theyr laies
And carroll of loves praise.
The merry Larke hir mattins sings aloft,   80
The thrush replyes, the Mavis descant playes,

7   diversified like the many-colored meadow.
8   a river near Spenser's home in Ireland.
9   Tithonus' wife, the dawn goddess Aurora ("Rosy Morne"), obtained immortality for
him but not eternal youth.
10   Apollo, the sun god, also god of music and the arts.

The Ouzell shrills, the Ruddock warbles soft,[11]
So goodly all agree with sweet consent,
To this dayes merriment.
Ah my deere love why doe ye sleepe thus long,
When meeter were that ye should now awake,
T' awayt the comming of your joyous make,[12]
And hearken to the birds lovelearnéd song,
The deawy leaves among.
For they of joy and pleasance to you sing,   90
That all the woods them answer and theyr eccho ring.

My love is now awake out of her dreame,
And her fayre eyes like stars that dimméd were
With darksome cloud, now shew theyr goodly beams
More bright then Hesperus[13] his head doth rere.
Come now ye damzels, daughters of delight,
Helpe quickly her to dight,
But first come ye fayre houres which were begot
In Joves sweet paradice, of Day and Night,
Which doe the seasons of the yeare allot,   100
And al that ever in this world is fayre
Doe make and still repayre.
And ye three handmayds of the Cyprian Queene,[14]
The which doe still adorne her beauties pride,
Helpe to addorne my beautifullest bride:
And as ye her array, still throw betweene
Some graces to be seene,
And as ye use to Venus, to her sing,
The whiles the woods shal answer and your eccho ring.

Now is my love all ready forth to come,   110
Let all the virgins therefore well awayt,
And ye fresh boyes that tend upon her groome
Prepare your selves; for he is comming strayt.
Set all your things in seemely good aray
Fit for so joyfull day,
The joyfulst day that ever sunne did see.
Faire Sun, shew forth thy favourable ray,
And let thy lifull[15] heat not fervent be
For feare of burning her sunshyny face,
Her beauty to disgrace.   120
O fayrest Phoebus, father of the Muse,
If ever I did honour thee aright,
Or sing the thing, that mote thy mind delight,

11   Mavis, Ouzell, and Ruddock are birds.
12   mate.
13   evening star.
14   Venus, to whom a temple on Cyprus was dedicated.
15   vital.

Doe not thy servants simple boone refuse,
But let this day let this one day be myne,
Let all the rest be thine.
Then I thy soverayne prayses loud wil sing,
That all the woods shal answer and theyr eccho ring.

Harke how the Minstrels gin to shrill aloud
Their merry Musick that resounds from far,   130
The pipe, the tabor, and the trembling Croud,[16]
That well agree withouten breach or jar.
But most of all the Damzels doe delite,
When they their tymbrels smyte,
And thereunto doe daunce and carrol sweet,
That all the sences they doe ravish quite,
The whyles the boyes run up and down the street,
Crying aloud with strong confuséd noyce,
As if it were one voyce.
Hymen iô Hymen, Hymen they do shout,   140
That even to the heavens theyr shouting shrill
Doth reach, and all the firmanent doth fill,
To which the people standing all about,
As in approvance doe thereto applaud
And loud advaunce her laud,
And evermore they *Hymen Hymen* sing,
That al the woods them answer and theyr eccho ring.

Loe where she comes along with portly pace
Lyke Phoebe[17] from her chamber of the East,
Arysing forth to run her mighty race,   150
Clad all in white, that seemes a virgin best.
So well it her beseemes that ye would weene
Some angell she had beene.
Her long loose yellow locks lyke golden wyre,
Sprinckled with perle, and perling flowres a tweene,
Doe lyke a golden mantle her attyre,
And being crownéd with a girland greene,
Seeme lyke some mayden Queene.
Her modest eyes abashéd to behold
So many gazers, as on her do stare,   160
Upon the lowly ground affixéd are.
Ne dare lift up her countenance too bold,
But blush to heare her prayses sung so loud,
So farre from being proud.
Nathlesse doe ye still loud her prayses sing,
That all the woods may answer and your eccho ring.

Tell me ye merchants daughters did ye see
So fayre a creature in your towne before,

16   violin.
17   Diana, goddess of the moon; also called Cinthia (*l.* 374).

So sweet, so lovely, and so mild as she,
Adornd with beautyes grace and vertues store,   170
Her goodly eyes lyke Saphyres shining bright,
Her forehead yvory white,
Her cheekes lyke apples which the sun hath rudded,
Her lips lyke cherryes charming men to byte,
Her brest lyke to a bowle of creame uncrudded,
Her paps lyke lyllies budded,
Her snowie necke lyke to a marble towre,
And all her body like a pallace fayre,
Ascending uppe with many a stately stayre,
To honors seat and chastities sweet bowre.   180
Why stand ye still ye virgins in amaze,
Upon her so to gaze,
Whiles ye forget your former lay to sing,
To which the woods did answer and your eccho ring.

But if ye saw that which no eyes can see,
The inward beauty of her lively spright,[18]
Garnisht with heavenly guifts of high degree,
Much more then would ye wonder at that sight,
And stand astonisht lyke to those which red
Medusaes mazeful hed.[19]   190
There dwels sweet love and constant chastity,
Unspotted fayth and comely womanhood,
Regard of honour and mild modesty,
There vertue raynes as Queene in royal throne,
And giveth lawes alone.
The which the base affections doe obay,
And yeeld theyr services unto her will,
Ne thought of thing uncomely ever may
Thereto approch to tempt her mind to ill.
Had ye once seene these her celestial threasures,   200
And unrevealéd pleasures,
Then would ye wonder and her prayses sing,
That al the woods should answer and your eccho ring.

Open the temple gates unto my love,
Open them wide that she may enter in,
And all the postes adorne as doth behove,
And all the pillours deck with girlands trim,
For to recyve this Saynt with honour dew,
That commeth in to you.
With trembling steps and humble reverence,
She commeth in, before th' almighties vew,   210
Of her ye virgins learne obedience,
When so ye come into those holy places,

18   soul.
19   Medusa had serpents instead of hair, and those who saw ("red") her were turned to
stone.

To humble your proud faces:
Bring her up to th' high altar, that she may
The sacred ceremonies there partake,
The which do endlesse matrimony make,
And let the roring Organs loudly play
The praises of the Lord in lively notes,
The whiles with hollow throates,   220
The Choristers the joyous Antheme sing,
That al the woods may answere and their eccho ring.

Behold whiles she before the altar stands
Hearing the holy priest that to her speakes
And blesseth her with his two happy hands,
How the red roses flush up in her cheekes,
And the pure snow with goodly vermill stayne,
Like crimsin dyde in grayne,
That even th' Angels which continually,
About the sacred Altare doe remaine,   230
Forget their service and about her fly,
Ofte peeping in her face that seemes more fayre,
The more they on it stare.
But her sad eyes still fastened on the ground,
Are governéd with goodly modesty,
That suffers not one looke to glaunce awry,
Which may let in a little thought unsownd.
Why blush ye love to give to me your hand,
The pledge of all our band?
Sing ye sweet Angels, Alleluya sing,   240
That all the woods may answere and your eccho ring.

Now al is done; bring home the bride againe,
Bring home the triumph of our victory,
Bring home with you the glory of her gaine,
With joyance bring her and with jollity.
Never had man more joyfull day then this,
Whom heaven would heape with blis.
Make feast therefore now all this live long day,
This day for ever to me holy is,
Poure out the wine without restraint or stay,   250
Poure not by cups, but by the belly full,
Poure out to all that wull,
And sprinkle all the postes and wals with wine,
That they may sweat, and drunken be withall.
Crowne ye God Bacchus[20] with a coronall,
And Hymen also crowne with wreathes of vine,
And let the Graces daunce unto the rest;
For they can doo it best:

20   god of wine and festivity.

The whiles the maydens doe theyr carroll sing,
To which the woods shal answer and theyr eccho ring.   260

Ring ye the bels, ye yong men of the towne,
And leave your wonted labors for this day:
This day is holy; doe ye write it downe,
That ye for ever it remember may.
This day the sunne is in his chiefest hight,
With Barnaby[21] the bright,
From whence declining daily by degrees,
He somewhat loseth of his heat and light,
When once the Crab[22] behind his back he sees.
But for this time it ill ordainéd was,   270
To chose the longest day in all the yeare,
And shortest night, when longest fitter weare:
Yet never day so long, but late would passe.
Ring ye the bels, to make it weare away,
And bonefiers make all day,
And daunce about them, and about them sing:
That all the woods may answer, and your eccho ring.

Ah when will this long weary day have end,
And lende me leave to come unto my love?
How slowly do the houres theyr numbers spend?   280
How slowly does sad Time his feathers move?
Hast thee O fayrest Planet to thy home
Within the Westerne fome:
Thy tyred steedes long since have need of rest.
Long though it be, at last I see it gloome,
And the bright evening star with golden creast
Appeare out of the East.
Fayre childe of beauty, glorious lampe of love
That all the host of heaven in rankes doost lead,
And guydest lovers through the nightés dread,   290
How chearefully thou lookest from above,
And seemst to laugh atweene thy twinkling light
As joying in the sight
Of these glad many which for joy doe sing,
That all the woods them answer and their eccho ring.

Now ceasse ye damsels your delights forepast;
Enough is it, that all the day was youres:
Now day is doen, and night is nighing fast:
Now bring the Bryde into the brydall boures.
Now night is come, now soone her disaray,   300
And in her bed her lay;
Lay her in lillies and in violets,

21   the wedding took place on June 11, St. Barnabas' day.
22   a sign of the zodiac, which the sun enters in June.

And silken courteins over her display,
And odourd sheetes, and Arras coverlets.
Behold how goodly my faire love does ly
In proud humility;
Like unto Maia;[23] when as Jove her tooke,
In Tempe, lying on the flowry gras,
Twixt sleepe and wake, after she weary was,
With bathing in the Acidalian brooke.   310
Now it is night, ye damsels may be gon,
And leave my love alone,
And leave likewise your former lay to sing:
The woods no more shal answere, nor your eccho ring.

Now welcome night, thou night so long expected,
That long daies labour doest at last defray,
And all my cares, which cruell love collected,
Hast sumd in one, and cancelléd for aye:
Spread thy broad wing over my love and me,
That no man may us see,   320
And in thy sable mantle us enwrap,
From feare of perrill and foule horror free.
Let no false treason seeke us to entrap,
Nor any dread disquiet once annoy
The safety of our joy:
But let the night be calme and quietsome,
Without tempestuous storms or sad afray:
Lyke as when Jove with fayre Alcmena[24] lay,
When he begot the great Tirynthian groome:
Or lyke as when he with thy selfe did lie,   330
And begot Majesty.
And let the mayds and yongmen cease to sing:
Ne let the woods them answer, nor theyr eccho ring.

Let no lamenting cryes, nor dolefull teares,
Be heard all night within nor yet without:
Ne let false whispers, breeding hidden feares,
Breake gentle sleepe with misconceivéd dout.
Let no deluding dreames, nor dreadful sights
Make sudden sad affrights;
Ne let housefyres, nor lightnings helpelesse harmes,   340
Ne let the Pouke, nor other evill sprights,
Ne let mischivous witches with theyr charmes,
Ne let hob Goblins, names whose sence we see not,
Fray us with things that be not.
Let not the shriech Oule, nor the Storke be heard:
Nor the night Raven that still deadly yels,

23 mother of Mercury by Jove.
24 mother, by Jove, of Hercules (the "great Tirynthian groome").

Nor damnéd ghosts cald up with might spels,
Nor griesly vultures make us once affeard:
Ne let th' unpleasant Quyre of Frogs still croking
Make us to wish theyr choking.   350
Let none of these theyr drery accents sing;
Ne let the woods them answer, nor theyr eccho ring.

But let stil Silence trew night watches keepe,
That sacred peace may in assurance rayne,
And tymely sleep, when it is tyme to sleepe,
May poure his limbs forth on your pleasant playne,
The whiles an hundred little wingéd loves,
Like divers fethered doves,
Shall fly and flutter round about your bed,
And in the secret darke, that none reproves,   360
Their prety stealthes shal worke, and snares shal spread
To filch away sweet snatches of delight,
Conceald through covert night.
Ye sonnes of Venus, play your sports at will,
For greedy pleasure, carelesse of your toyes,
Thinks more upon her paradise of joyes,
Then what ye do, albe it good or ill.
All night therefore attend your merry play,
For it will soone be day:
Now none doth hinder you, that say or sing,   370
Ne will the woods now answer, nor your Eccho ring.

Who is the same, which at my window peepes?
Or whose is that faire face, that shines so bright,
Is it not Cinthia, she that never sleepes,
But walkes about high heaven al the night?
O fayrest goddesse, do thou not envy
My love with me to spy:
For thou likewise didst love, though now unthought.
And for a fleece of woll, which privily,
The Latmian shephard[25] once unto thee brought,   380
His pleasures with thee wrought.
Therefore to us be favorable now;
And sith of wemens labours thou hast charge,
And generation goodly dost enlarge,
Encline thy will t' effect our wishfull vow,
And the chast wombe informe with timely seed,
That may our comfort breed:
Till which we cease our hopefull hap to sing,
Ne let the woods us answere, nor our Eccho ring.

25   The goddess of the moon fell in love with the shepherd Endymion while he was
sleeping on Mt. Latmus.

And thou great Juno, which with awful might   390
The lawes of wedlock still dost patronize,
And the religion of the faith first plight
With sacred rites hast taught to solemnize:
And eeke for comfort often calléd art
Of women in their smart,
Eternally bind thou this lovely band,
And all thy blessings unto us impart.
And thou glad Genius,[26] in whose gentle hand,
The bridale bowre and geniall bed remaine,
Without blemish or staine,   400
And the sweet pleasures of theyr loves delight
With secret ayde doest succour and supply,
Till they bring forth the fruitfull progeny,
Send us the timely fruit of this same night.
And thou fayre Hebe,[27] and thou Hymen free,
Grant that it may so be.
Til which we cease your further prayse to sing,
Ne any woods shal answer, nor your Eccho ring.

And ye high heavens, the temple of the gods,
In which a thousand torches flaming bright   410
Doe burne, that to us wretched earthly clods,
In dreadful darknesse lend desired light;
And all ye powers which in the same remayne,
More then we men can fayne,
Poure out your blessing on us plentiously,
And happy influence upon us raine,
That we may raise a large posterity,
Which from the earth, which they may long possesse,
With lasting happinesse,
Up to your haughty pallaces may mount,   420
And for the guerdon of theyr glorious merit
May heavenly tabernacles there inherit,
Of blessed Saints for to increase the count.
So let us rest, sweet love, in hope of this,
And cease till then our tymely joyes to sing,
The woods no more us answer, nor our eccho ring.

Song made in lieu of many ornaments,
With which my love should duly have bene dect,
Which cutting off through hasty accidents,
Ye would not stay your dew time to expect,   430
But promist both to recompens,
Be unto her a goodly ornament,
And for short time an endlesse moniment.

---

26 god of reproduction.
27 the goddess of youth and cupbearer to Jove. She became the wife of Hercules after
he was deified.

SIR PHILIP SIDNEY [1554–1586]

from *Astrophel and Stella*

1

Loving in truth, and fain in verse my love to show,
That she, dear she, might take some pleasure of my pain,
Pleasure might cause her read, reading might make her know,
Knowledge might pity win, and pity grace obtain,
I sought fit words to paint the blackest face of woe:
Studying inventions fine, her wits to entertain,
Oft turning others' leaves, to see if thence would flow
Some fresh and fruitful showers upon my sunburn'd brain.
But words came halting forth, wanting Invention's stay;
Invention, Nature's child, fled stepdame Study's blows;
And others' feet still seemed but strangers in my way.
Thus, great with child to speak, and helpless in my throes,
Biting my truant pen, beating myself for spite:
"Fool," said my Muse to me, "look in thy heart and write!"

31

With how sad steps, O Moon, thou climb'st the skies,
How silently, and with how wan a face!
What, may it be that even in heav'nly place
That busy archer his sharp arrows tries?
Sure, if that long with love acquainted eyes
Can judge of love, thou feel'st a lover's case;
I read it in thy looks, thy languisht grace
To me that feel the like, thy state descries.
Then, ev'n of fellowship, O Moon, tell me,
Is constant love deem'd there but want of wit?
Are beauties there as proud as here they be?
Do they above love to be lov'd, and yet
Those lovers scorn whom that love doth possess?
Do they call Virtue there ungratefulness?

45

Stella oft sees the very face of woe
Painted in my beclouded stormy face,
But cannot skill to pity my disgrace,
Not though thereof the cause herself she know.
Yet hearing late a fable which did show
Of lovers never known a grievous case,
Pity thereof gat in her breast such place
That, from that sea derived, tears' spring did flow.
Alas, if fancy, drawn by imaged things
Though false, yet with free scope more grace doth breed
Than servant's wreck, where new doubts honor brings;
Then think, my dear, that you in me do read

Of lovers' ruin some sad tragedy.
I am not I; pity the tale of me.

54

Because I breathe not love to everyone,
Nor do not use set colors for to wear,
Nor nourish special locks of vowed hair,[1]
Nor give each speech a full point[2] of a groan,
The courtly nymphs, acquainted with the moan
Of them who in their lips Love's standard bear,
"What, he!" say they of me, "now I dare swear
He cannot love; no, no, let him alone."
And think so still, so Stella know my mind;
Profess indeed I do not Cupid's art;
But you, fair maids, at length this true shall find,
That his right badge is but worn in the heart.
Dumb swans, not chattering pies,[3] do lovers prove;
They love indeed who quake to say they love.

1 locks of hair given as a pledge.
2 period.
3 Swans were said to sing once, before dying; *pies*: magpies.

71

Who will in fairest book of Nature know
How virtue may best lodged in beauty be,
Let him but learn of love to read in thee,
Stella, those fair lines which true goodness show.
There shall he find all vices' overthrow,
Not by rude force, but sweetest sovereignty
Of reason, from whose light those night birds fly,
That inward sun in thine eyes shineth so.
And, not content to be perfection's heir
Thyself, dost strive all minds that way to move,
Who mark in thee what is in thee most fair.
So while thy beauty draws the heart to love,
As fast thy virtue bends that love to good.
But, ah, Desire still cries, "Give me some food."

CHIDIOCK TICHBORNE [1558–1586]

Tichborne's Elegy
Written with His Own Hand in the Tower Before His Execution

My prime of youth is but a frost of cares,
My feast of joy is but a dish of pain,
My crop of corn is but a field of tares,

And all my good is but vain hope of gain;
The day is past, and yet I saw no sun,
And now I live, and now my life is done.

My tale was heard and yet it was not told,
My fruit is fallen and yet my leaves are green,
My youth is spent and yet I am not old,
I saw the world and yet I was not seen;
My thread is cut and yet it is not spun,
And now I live, and now my life is done.

I sought my death and found it in my womb,
I looked for life and saw it was a shade,
I trod the earth and knew it was my tomb,
And now I die, and now I was but made;
My glass is full, and now my glass is run,
And now I live, and now my life is done.

GEORGE PEELE [1559–1596]

Gently Dip

Gently dip, but not too deep,
For fear you make the golden beard to weep.
Fair maiden white and red,
Comb me smooth, and stroke my head,
And thou shalt have some cockle bread.
Gently dip, but not too deep,
For fear thou make the golden beard to weep.
Fair maiden white and red,
Comb me smooth, and stroke my head,
And every hair a sheaf shall be,
And every sheaf a golden tree.

A Sonnet

His golden locks time hath to silver turned;
O time too swift, O swiftness never ceasing!
His youth gainst time and age hath ever spurned,
But spurned in vain; youth waneth by increasing.
    Beauty, strength, youth, are flowers but fading seen,
    Duty, faith, love are roots and ever green.

His helmet now shall make a hive for bees,
And, lovers' sonnets turned to holy psalms,

A man at arms must now serve on his knees,
And feed on prayers, which are age his alms.
    But though from court to cottage he depart,
    His saint is sure of his unspotted heart.

And when he saddest sits in homely cell,
He'll teach his swains this carol for a song,
Blessed be the hearts that wish my sovereign well,
Cursed be the souls that think her any wrong.
    Goddess, allow this agéd man his right,
    To be your bedesman now, that was your knight.

ROBERT SOUTHWELL   [1561–1595]

The Burning Babe

As I in hoary winter's night stood shivering in the snow,
Surprised I was with sudden heat, which made my heart to glow;
And lifting up a fearful eye to view what fire was near,
A pretty babe all burning bright, did in the air appear,
Who scorched with excessive heat, such floods of tears did shed,
As though his floods should quench his flames which with his tears
      were fed;
"Alas!" quoth he, "but newly born, in fiery heats I fry,
Yet none approach to warm their hearts or feel my fire but I!
My faultless breast the furnace is, the fuel wounding thorns,
Love is the fire, and sighs the smoke, the ashes shame and scorns;
The fuel justice layeth on, and mercy blows the coals,
The metal in this furnace wrought are men's defiled souls,
For which, as now on fire I am to work them to their good,
So will I melt into a bath to wash them in my blood."
With this he vanished out of sight, and swiftly shrank away,
And straight I called unto mind that it was Christmas day.

SAMUEL DANIEL   [1562–1619]

45   Care-Charmer Sleep[1]

Care-charmer sleep, son of the sable night,
Brother to death, in silent darkness born,
Relieve my languish and restore the light;
With dark forgetting of my cares, return.
And let the day be time enough to mourn
The shipwreck of my ill-adventured youth;

1   from *Delia*.

Let waking eyes suffice to wail their scorn
Without the torment of the night's untruth.
Cease, dreams, th' imagery of our day desires,
To model forth the passions of the morrow;
Never let rising sun approve you liars,
To add more grief to aggravate my sorrow.
Still let me sleep, embracing clouds in vain,
And never wake to feel the day's disdain.

MICHAEL DRAYTON [1563–1631]

61 Since There's No Help[1]

Since there's no help, come let us kiss and part;
Nay, I have done, you get no more of me;
And I am glad, yea, glad with all my heart,
That thus so cleanly I myself can free.
Shake hands for ever, cancel all our vows,
And when we meet at any time again,
Be it not seen in either of our brows
That we one jot of former love retain.
Now at the last gasp of love's latest breath,
When, his pulse failing, passion speechless lies,
When faith is kneeling by his bed of death,
And innocence is closing up his eyes,
Now if thou wouldst, when all have given him over,
From death to life thou might'st him yet recover.

1 from *Idea*.

CHRISTOPHER MARLOWE [1564–1593]

The Passionate Shepherd to His Love

Come live with me, and be my love,
And we will all the pleasures prove,
That valleys, groves, hills and fields,
Woods, or steepy mountains yields.

And we will sit upon the rocks,
Seeing the shepherds feed their flocks,
By shallow rivers, to whose falls
Melodious birds sing madrigals.

And I will make thee beds of roses,
And a thousand fragrant posies,
A cap of flowers, and a kirtle[1]
Embroidered all with leaves of myrtle;

A gown made of the finest wool,
Which from our pretty lambs we pull,
Fair-linéd slippers for the cold,
With buckles of the purest gold;

A belt of straw and ivy buds
With coral clasps and amber studs:
And if these pleasures may thee move,
Come live with me, and be my love.

The shepherd swains shall dance and sing,
For thy delight each May morning:
If these delights thy mind may move,
Then live with me, and be my love.

1   skirt.

ANONYMOUS

Crabbed Age and Youth

Crabbed age and youth cannot live together:
Youth is full of pleasance, age is full of care;
Youth like summer morn, age like winter weather;
Youth like summer brave, age like winter bare.
Youth is full of sport, age's breath is short;
Youth is nimble, age is lame;
Youth is hot and bold, age is weak and cold;
Youth is wild, and age is tame.
Age, I do abhor thee, youth, I do adore thee;
Oh! my love, my love is young:
Age, I do defy thee: Oh! sweet shepherd, hie thee,
For methinks thou stay'st too long.

WILLIAM SHAKESPEARE   [1564–1616]

Under the Greenwood Tree

Under the greenwood tree
Who loves to lie with me,

And turn his merry note
Unto the sweet bird's throat,
Come hither, come hither, come hither:
Here shall he see
No enemy
But winter and rough weather.

Who doth ambition shun
And loves to lie i' the sun,
Seeking the food he eats
And pleased with what he gets,
Come hither, come hither, come hither:
Here shall he see
No enemy
But winter and rough weather.

(As You Like It)

Blow, Blow, Thou Winter Wind!

Blow, blow, thou winter wind!
Thou art not so unkind
As man's ingratitude;
Thy tooth is not so keen
Because thou art not seen,
Although thy breath be rude.
Heigh ho! sing heigh ho! unto the green holly:
Most friendship is feigning, most loving mere folly:
Then, heigh ho! the holly!
This life is most jolly.

Freeze, freeze, thou bitter sky,
Thou dost not bite so nigh
As benefits forgot:
Though thou the waters warp,
Thy sting is not so sharp
As friend remembered not.
Heigh ho! sing heigh ho! unto the green holly:
Most friendship is feigning, most loving mere folly:
Then, heigh ho! the holly!
This life is most jolly.

(As You Like It)

It Was a Lover

It was a lover and his lass,
With a hey, and a ho, and a hey nonino!

That o'er the green corn-field did pass,
    In spring time, the only pretty ring time,
When birds do sing, hey ding a ding, ding;
    Sweet lovers love the spring.

Between the acres of the rye,
    With a hey, and a ho, and a hey nonino!
Those pretty country folks would lie,
    In spring time, the only pretty ring time,
When birds do sing, hey ding a ding, ding;
    Sweet lovers love the spring.

This carol they began that hour,
    With a hey, and a ho, and a hey nonino!
How that a life was but a flower
    In spring time, the only pretty ring time,
When birds do sing, hey ding a ding, ding;
    Sweet lovers love the spring.

And therefore take the present time,
    With a hey, and a ho, and a hey nonino!
For love is crownéd with the prime
    In spring time, the only pretty ring time,
When birds do sing, hey ding a ding, ding;
    Sweet lovers love the spring.
                          (As You Like It)

O Mistress Mine

O mistress mine, where are you roaming?
O stay and hear; your true love's coming,
    That can sing both high and low.
Trip no further, pretty sweeting;
Journeys end in lovers' meeting,
    Every wise man's son doth know.

What is love? 'Tis not hereafter;
Present mirth hath present laughter;
    What's to come is still unsure.
In delay there lies no plenty;
Then come kiss me, sweet and twenty;
    Youth's a stuff will not endure.
                          (Twelfth Night)

Take, O! Take

Take, O! take those lips away,
    That so sweetly were forsworn,
And those eyes, the break of day,
    Lights that do mislead the morn;
But my kisses bring again, bring again,
Seals of love, but sealed in vain, sealed in vain.
                    (Measure for Measure)

Fear No More

Fear no more the heat o' the sun
    Nor the furious winter's rages;
Thou thy worldly task hast done,
    Home art gone and ta'en thy wages.
Golden lads and girls all must,
As chimney-sweepers, come to dust.

Fear no more the frown o' the great,
    Thou art past the tyrant's stroke;
Care no more to clothe and eat;
    To thee the reed is as the oak.
The scepter, learning, physic, must
All follow this, and come to dust.

Fear no more the lightning-flash,
    Nor the all-dreaded thunder-stone:
Fear not slander, censure rash;
    Thou hast finished joy and moan.
All lovers young, all lovers must
Consign to thee, and come to dust.
                    (Cymbeline)

Full Fathom Five

Full fathom five thy father lies;
    Of his bones are coral made;
Those are pearls, that were his eyes;
    Nothing of him that doth fade
But doth suffer a sea-change
Into something rich and strange.
Sea-nymphs hourly ring his knell.
    Ding-dong!
Hark, now I hear them
    Ding dong, bell!
                    (The Tempest)

from *Sonnets*

When I do count the clock that tells the time,
And see the brave day sunk in hideous night,
When I behold the violet past prime,
And sable curls all silvered o'er with white:
When lofty trees I see barren of leaves,
Which erst[1] from heat did canopy the herd
And summer's green all girded up in sheaves
Borne on the bier with white and bristly beard:
Then of thy beauty do I question make
That thou among the wastes of time must go,
Since sweets and beauties do themselves forsake,
And die as fast as they see others grow,
    And nothing 'gainst Time's scythe can make defence
    Save breed[2] to brave him, when he takes thee hence.

1 formerly.
2 offspring.

18

Shall I compare thee to a summer's day?
Thou art more lovely and more temperate.
Rough winds do shake the darling buds of May,
And summer's lease hath all too short a date.
Sometime too hot the eye of heaven shines,
And often is his gold complexion dimmed;
And every fair from fair sometime declines,
By chance, or nature's changing course, untrimmed;
But thy eternal summer shall not fade
Nor lose possession of that fair thou ow'st,[1]
Nor shall Death brag thou wand'rest in his shade
When in eternal lines to time thou grow'st.
    So long as men can breathe or eyes can see,
    So long lives this, and this gives life to thee.

1 beauty you possess.

29

When, in disgrace with Fortune and men's eyes,
I all alone beweep my outcast state,
And trouble deaf heaven with my bootless cries,
And look upon myself and curse my fate,
Wishing me like to one more rich in hope,
Featured like him, like him with friends possessed,
Desiring this man's art, and that man's scope,
With what I most enjoy contented least;
Yet in these thoughts myself almost despising,
Haply I think on thee, and then my state,

Like to the lark at break of day arising
From sullen earth, sings hymns at heaven's gate;
    For thy sweet love rememb'red such wealth brings
    That then I scorn to change my state with kings.

30

When to the sessions[1] of sweet silent thought
I summon up remembrance of things past,
I sigh the lack of many a thing I sought
And with old woes new wail my dear time's waste.
Then can I drown an eye (unused to flow)
For precious friends hid in death's dateless night,
And weep afresh love's long since canceled woe,
And moan th' expense[2] of many a vanished sight.
Then can I grieve at grievances foregone,
And heavily from woe to woe tell o'er
The sad account of fore-bemoanéd moan,
Which I new pay as if not paid before.
    But if the while I think on thee, dear friend,
    All losses are restored and sorrows end.

1   sittings of a court of justice.
2   loss.

65

Since brass, nor stone, nor earth, nor boundless sea,
But sad mortality o'ersways their power,
How with this rage shall beauty hold a plea,
Whose action is no stronger than a flower?
O how shall summer's honey breath hold out
Against the wrackful[1] siege of batt'ring days,
When rocks impregnable are not so stout,
Nor gates of steel so strong but time decays?
O fearful meditation, where alack,
Shall Time's best jewel from Time's chest lie hid?
Or what strong hand can hold his swift foot back,
Or who his spoil of beauty can forbid?
    O none, unless this miracle have might,
    That in black ink my love may still shine bright.

1   destructive.

66

Tired with all these, for restful death I cry:
As, to behold desert[1] a beggar born,
And needy nothing trimmed in jollity,[2]
And purest faith unhappily forsworn,
And gilded honor shamefully misplaced,
And maiden virtue rudely strumpeted,
And right perfection wrongfully disgraced,

And strength by limping sway disabled,
And art made tongue-tied by authority,
And folly (doctor-like) controlling skill,
And simple truth miscalled simplicity,[3]
And captive good attending captain ill.
    Tired with all these, from these would I be gone,
    Save that, to die, I leave my love alone.

1   merit.
2   emptiness clothed in finery.
3   ignorance, silliness.

73

That time of year thou mayst in me behold
When yellow leaves, or none, or few, do hang
Upon those boughs which shake against the cold,
Bare ruined choirs where late the sweet birds sang.
In me thou see'st the twilight of such day
As after sunset fadeth in the West,
Which by-and-by black night doth take away,
Death's second self, that seals up all in rest.
In me thou see'st the glowing of such fire
That on the ashes of his youth doth lie,
As the deathbed whereon it must expire,
Consumed with that which it was nourished by.
    This thou perceiv'st, which makes thy love more strong,
    To love that well which thou must leave ere long.

87

Farewell! thou art too dear[1] for my possessing,
And like enough thou know'st thy estimate.[2]
The charter[3] of thy worth gives thee releasing:
My bonds in thee are all determinate.[4]
For how do I hold thee but by thy granting,
And for that riches where is my deserving?
The cause of this fair gift in me is wanting,
And so my patent[5] back again is swerving.[6]
Thy self thou gav'st, thy own worth then not knowing,
Or me to whom thou gav'st it, else mistaking,
So thy great gift upon misprision[7] growing,
Comes home again, on better judgment making.
    Thus have I had thee as a dream doth flatter,
    In sleep a king, but waking no such matter.

1   precious.
2   value.
3   contract.
4   limited.
5   grant of a monopoly.
6   returning.
7   contempt, undervaluing.

94

They that have power to hurt, and will do none,
That do not do the thing, they most do show,[1]
Who moving others, are themselves as stone,
Unmovéd, cold, and to temptation slow:
They rightly do inherit heaven's graces,
And husband nature's riches from expense;[2]
They are the lords and owners of their faces,
Others, but stewards[3] of their excellence.
The summer's flower is to the summer sweet,
Though to itself it only live and die,
But if that flower with base infection meet,
The basest weed outbraves his dignity:
    For sweetest things turn sourest by their deeds,
    Lilies that fester, smell far worse than weeds.

1   seem capable of doing.
2   expenditure.
3   A steward manages property on behalf of the owner.

116

Let me not to the marriage of true minds
Admit impediments. Love is not love
Which alters when it alteration finds,
Or bends with the remover to remove.[1]
O no, it is an ever-fixéd mark[2]
That looks on tempests and is never shaken;
It is the star[3] to every wand'ring bark,[4]
Whose worth's unknown, although his height be taken.
Love's not Time's fool, though rosy lips and cheeks
Within his bending sickle's compass come;
Love alters not with his brief hours and weeks,
But bears it out[5] even to the edge of doom.
    If this be error and upon me proved,
    I never writ, nor no man ever loved.

1   *Remove* was used both in a transitive and an intransitive sense—to move someone or something, or to go from one place to another.
2   beacon.
3   the North Star, a navigational aid.
4   ship.
5   endures.

129

Th' expense[1] of spirit in a waste of shame
Is lust in action, and till action, lust
Is perjured, murd'rous, bloody, full of blame,
Savage, extreme, rude,[2] cruel, not to trust;
Enjoyed no sooner but despised straight;
Past reason hunted, and no sooner had,
Past reason hated as a swallowed bait

On purpose laid to make the taker mad:
Mad in pursuit and in possession so;
Had, having, and in quest to have, extreme;
A bliss in proof,[3] and proved, a very woe;
Before a joy proposed, behind a dream.
    All this the world well knows, yet none knows well
    To shun the heaven that leads men to this hell.

1   expenditure.
2   brutal.
3   while being experienced.

130

My mistress' eyes are nothing like the sun;
Coral is far more red than her lips' red;
If snow be white, why then her breasts are dun;
If hairs be wires, black wires grow on her head.
I have seen roses damasked,[1] red and white,
But no such roses see I in her cheeks,
And in some perfumes there is more delight
Than in the breath that from my mistress reeks.[2]
I love to hear her speak, yet well I know
That music hath a far more pleasing sound;
I grant I never saw a goddess go:
My mistress when she walks treads on the ground.
    And yet by heaven I think my love as rare
    As any she belied with false compare.

1   arranged in ornamental patterns.
2   is exhaled.

146

Poor soul, the center of my sinful earth,[1]
Fooled by[2] these rebel pow'rs that thee array,
Why dost thou pine within and suffer dearth,
Painting thy outward walls so costly gay?
Why so large cost, having so short a lease,
Dost thou upon thy fading mansion spend?
Shall worms, inheritors of this excess,
Eat up thy charge? Is this thy body's end?
Then, soul, live thou upon thy servant's loss,
And let that pine to aggravate[3] thy store;
Buy terms divine[4] in selling hours of dross;[5]
Within be fed, without be rich no more.
    So shalt thou feed on Death, that feeds on men.
    And Death once dead, there's no more dying then.

1   body.
2   The text here is corrupt, repeating "my sinful earth." Malone conjectures *Fooled by*.
3   increase.
4   immortality in heaven.
5   wasted hours.

THOMAS CAMPION [1567–1620]

My Sweetest Lesbia[1]

My sweetest Lesbia, let us live and love,
And, though the sager sort our deeds reprove,
Let us not weigh them: heaven's great lamps do dive
Into their west, and straight again revive,
But, soon as once set is our little light,
Then must we sleep one ever-during[2] night.

If all would lead their lives in love like me,
Then bloody swords and armor should not be,
No drum nor trumpet peaceful sleeps should move,
Unless alarm came from the camp of love:
But fools do live, and waste their little light,
And seek with pain their ever-during night.

When timely death my life and fortune ends,
Let not my hearse be vexed with mourning friends,
But let all lovers, rich in triumph, come,
And with sweet pastimes grace my happy tomb;
And, Lesbia, close up thou my little light,
And crown with love my ever-during night.

1 based on Catullus, 5, "Vivamus, mea Lesbia, atque amemus."
2 everlasting.

Rose-Cheeked Laura

Rose-cheeked Laura, come,
Sing thou smoothly with thy beauty's
Silent music, either other
    Sweetly gracing.

Lovely forms do flow
From concent divinely framéd;
Heav'n is music, and thy beauty's
    Birth is heavenly.

These dull notes we sing
Discords need for helps to grace them;
Only beauty purely loving
    Knows no discord,

But still moves delight,
Like clear springs renewed by flowing,
Ever perfect, ever in them-
    Selves eternal.

THOMAS DEKKER[1] [1570?–1632?]

Art Thou Poor

Art thou poor, yet hast thou golden slumbers?
    O sweet content!
Art thou rich, yet is thy mind perplexed?
    O punishment!
Dost thou laugh to see how fools are vexed
To add to golden numbers, golden numbers?
O sweet content! O sweet content!
    Work apace, apace, apace, apace;
    Honest labor bears a lovely face;
   Then hey nonny nonny, hey nonny nonny!

Canst drink the waters of the crisped[2] spring?
    O sweet content!
Swim'st thou in wealth, yet sink'st in thine own tears?
    O punishment!
Then he that patiently want's burden bears
No burden bears, but is a king, a king!
O sweet content! O sweet content!
    Work apace, apace, apace, apace;
    Honest labor bears a lovely face:
   Then hey nonny nonny, hey nonny nonny!

1   This poem may have been written by Dekker's coauthor, Henry Chettle.
2   rippling.

JOHN DONNE [1572–1631]

The Good-morrow

I wonder by my troth, what thou and I
Did, till we lov'd? were we not wean'd till then?
But suck'd on country pleasures, childishly?
Or snorted[1] we in the seven sleepers' den?[2]
'Twas so; but[3] this, all pleasures fancies be.
If ever any beauty I did see,
Which I desir'd, and got, 'twas but a dream of thee.

And now good-morrow to our waking souls,
Which watch not one another out of fear;
For love all love of other sights controls,
And makes one little room an everywhere.
Let sea-discoverers to new worlds have gone,
Let maps to other, worlds on worlds have shown,
Let us possess one world, each hath one, and is one.

My face in thine eye, thine in mine appears,
And true plain hearts do in the faces rest;
Where can we find two better hemispheres
Without sharp North, without declining West?[4]
What ever dies, was not mixt equally;[5]
If our two loves be one, or thou and I
Love so alike that none do slacken, none can die.

1   snored.
2   It is said that during the persecution of Decius (250 A.D.), seven Christian soldiers
were walled up in a cave, where they slept for 200 years.
3   except for.
4   A hemisphere is half the globe, containing the points of the compass, e.g., the cold
North, and the West where the sun goes down.
5   This refers to the idea that death or corruption was due to a disproportionate
mixture of opposing elements.

Song:
Go and Catch
a Falling Star

Go and catch a falling star,
    Get with child a mandrake root,
Tell me where all past years are,
    Or who cleft the devil's foot;
Teach me to hear mermaids singing,
Or to keep off envy's stinging,
        And find
        What wind
Serves to advance an honest mind.

If thou be'st born to strange sights,
    Things invisible to see,
Ride ten thousand days and nights
    Till age snow white hairs on thee;
Thou, when thou return'st, wilt tell me
All strange wonders that befell thee,
        And swear
        No where
Lives a woman true, and fair.

If thou find'st one, let me know;
    Such a pilgrimage were sweet.
Yet do not; I would not go,
    Though at next door we might meet.
Though she were true when you met her,
And last, till you write your letter,
        Yet she
        Will be
False, ere I come, to two, or three.

The Bait

Come live with me, and be my love,[1]
And we will some new pleasures prove
Of golden sands, and crystal brooks,
With silken lines, and silver hooks.

There will the river whispering run
Warm'd by thy eyes, more than the Sun.
And there th' enamour'd fish will stay,
Begging themselves they may betray.

When thou wilt swim in that live bath,
Each fish, which every channel hath,
Will amorously to thee swim,
Gladder to catch thee, than thou him.

If thou, to be so seen, be'st loth,
By Sun, or Moon, thou dark'nest both,
And if myself have leave to see,
I need not their light, having thee.

Let others freeze with angling reeds,
And cut their legs, with shells and weeds,
Or treacherously poor fish beset,
With strangling snare, or windowy net:

Let coarse bold hands, from slimy nest
The bedded fish in banks out-wrest,[2]
Or curious[3] traitors, sleeve-silk[4] flies
Bewitch poor fishes' wand'ring eyes.

For thee, thou need'st no such deceit,
For thou thyself art thine own bait;
That fish, that is not catch'd thereby,
Alas, is wiser far than I.

1 Compare Marlowe's "The Passionate Shepherd to His Love" and Ralegh's "The
Nymph's Reply to the Shepherd."
2 drag out.
3 beautifully made.
4 *sleeve-silk*: a kind of silk which can be divided into fine filaments.

The Flea

Mark but this flea, and mark in this,
How little that which thou deny'st me is;
Me it sucked first, and now sucks thee,
And in this flea, our two bloods mingled be;[1]

Confess it, this cannot be said
A sin, or shame, or loss of maidenhead,
   Yet this enjoys before it woo,
     And pampered swells with one blood made of two,
     And this, alas, is more than we would do.

Oh stay, three lives in one flea spare,
Where we almost, nay more than married are.
This flea is you and I, and this
Our marriage bed, and marriage temple is;
Though parents grudge, and you, we'are met,
And cloistered in these living walls of jet.
   Though use make you apt to kill me,
   Let not to this, self murder added be,
   And sacrilege, three sins in killing three.

Cruel and sudden, hast thou since
Purpled thy nail, in blood of innocence?
In what could this flea guilty be,
Except in that drop which it sucked from thee?
Yet thou triumph'st, and say'st that thou
Find'st not thyself, nor me the weaker now;
   'Tis true, then learn how false, fears be;
   Just so much honour, when thou yield'st to me,
   Will waste, as this flea's death took life from thee.

1   It was commonly thought that during sexual intercourse the blood of the lovers mingled—a notion derived from Aristotle.

The Canonization[1]

For God's sake hold your tongue, and let me love,
   Or chide my palsy, or my gout,
My five grey hairs, or ruined fortune flout,
   With wealth your state, your mind with arts improve,
     Take you a course, get you a place,
     Observe his Honour, or his Grace,
Or the King's real, or his stamped face
   Contemplate; what you will, approve,
   So you will let me love.

Alas, alas, who's injured by my love?   10
   What merchant's ships have my sighs drowned?
Who says my tears have overflowed his ground?
   When did my colds a forward spring remove?
     When did the heats which my veins fill

1   the making of saints. Here used to mean the making of saints out of lovers.

Add one more to the plaguy bill?[2]
Soldiers find wars, and lawyers find out still
    Litigious men, which quarrels move,
    Though she and I do love.

Call us what you will, we are made such by love;
    Call her one, me another fly,   20
We are tapers too, and at our own cost die,[3]
    And we in us find the eagle and the dove,
        The phoenix riddle hath more wit
        By us;[4] we two being one, are it.
So to one neutral thing both sexes fit
    We die and rise the same, and prove
    Mysterious by this love.

We can die by it, if not live by love,
    And if unfit for tombs and hearse
Our legend be, it will be fit for verse;   30
    And if no piece of chronicle we prove,
        We'll build in sonnets pretty rooms;
        As well a well wrought urn becomes
The greatest ashes, as half-acre tombs,
    And by these hymns, all shall approve
    Us canonized for love:

And thus invoke us; "You whom reverend love
    Made one another's hermitage;
You, to whom love was peace, that now is rage;
    Who did the whole world's soul contract, and drove   40
        Into the glasses of your eyes
        (So made such mirrors, and such spies,
That they did all to you epitomize,)
    Countries, towns, courts: beg from above
    A pattern of your love!"

2 the list of victims of the plague.
3 *To die* also meant to have an orgasm. It was thought that each orgasm shortened life by a day.
4 The phoenix was a mythical bird. There was only one phoenix; it renewed itself by burning itself on the altar of the temple of the sun at Heliopolis and rising again from the ashes.

Song: Sweetest Love, I Do Not Go

Sweetest love, I do not go,
    For weariness of thee,
Nor in hope the world can show

A fitter love for me;
    But since that I
Must die at last, 'tis best,
To use my self in jest
    Thus by feigned deaths to die.

Yesternight the sun went hence,
    And yet is here today,
He hath no desire nor sense,
    Nor half so short a way:
        Then fear not me,
But believe that I shall make
Speedier journeys, since I take
    More wings and spurs than he.

O how feeble is man's power,
    That if good fortune fall,
Cannot add another hour,
    Nor a lost hour recall!
        But come bad chance,
And we join to it our strength,
And we teach it art and length,
    Itself o'er us to advance.

When thou sigh'st, thou sigh'st not wind,
    But sigh'st my soul away,
When thou weep'st, unkindly kind,
    My life's blood doth decay.
        It cannot be
That thou lov'st me, as thou say'st,
If in thine my life thou waste,
    Thou art the best of me.

Let not thy divining heart
    Forethink me any ill,
Destiny may take thy part,
    And may thy fears fulfil;
        But think that we
Are but turned aside to sleep;
They who one another keep
    Alive, ne'er parted be.

10

20

30

40

A Valediction:
of Weeping

    Let me pour forth
My tears before thy face, whilst I stay here.

For thy face coins them,[1] and thy stamp they bear,
And by this mintage they are something worth,
　　For thus they be
　　Pregnant of thee;
Fruits of much grief they are, emblems of more,
When a tear falls, that thou falst which it bore,
So thou and I are nothing then, when on a divers shore.

　　On a round ball
A workman that hath copies by, can lay
An Europe, Afric, and an Asia,
And quickly make that, which was nothing, all,
　　So doth each tear,
　　Which thee doth wear,
A globe, yea world by that impression grow,
Till thy tears mixed with mine do overflow
This world, by waters sent from thee, my heaven dissolved so.

　　O more than moon,
Draw not up seas to drown me in thy sphere,[2]
Weep me not dead, in thine arms, but forbear
To teach the sea, what it may do too soon;
　　Let not the wind
　　Example find,
To do me more harm, than it purposeth;
Since thou and I sigh one another's breath,
Whoe'er sighs most, is cruellest, and hastes the other's death.

1　Your face causes them, and they bear the image of your face.
2　the sphere of an astral body. The poet is saying that the sphere—the outer limit of
the astral body—might have a greater attraction than the moon, and pull the seas up to
itself.

The Ecstasy[1]

Where, like a pillow on a bed,
　A pregnant bank swell'd up, to rest
The violet's reclining head,
　Sat we two, one another's best.
Our hands were firmly cemented[2]
　With a fast balm,[3] which thence did spring,
Our eye-beams twisted, and did thread
　Our eyes, upon one double string;
So t' intergraft our hands, as yet
　Was all the means to make us one,　　　　　　　　　　10
And pictures in our eyes to get

1　*Ecstasy* is the state in which the soul escapes from the body to achieve a vision of
God, or the Absolute.
2　joined.
3　moisture.

94

Was all our propagation.
As 'twixt two equal Armies, Fate
   Suspends uncertain victory,
Our souls, (which to advance their state,
   Were gone out,) hung 'twixt her, and me.
And whilst our souls negotiate there,
   We like sepulchral statues lay;
All day, the same our postures were,
   And we said nothing, all the day.   20
If any, so by love refin'd,
   That he soul's language understood,
And by good love were grown all mind,
   Within convenient distance stood,
He (though he knew not which soul spake,
   Because both meant, both spake the same)
Might thence a new concoction[4] take,
   And part far purer than he came.
This Ecstasy doth unperplex
   (We said) and tell us what we love,   30
We see by this, it was not sex,
   We see, we saw not what did move:
But as all several souls contain
   Mixture of things, they know not what,
Love these mix'd souls doth mix again,
   And makes both one, each this and that.
A single violet transplant,
   The strength, the colour, and the size,
(All which before was poor, and scant,)
   Redoubles still, and multiples.   40
When love, with one another so
   Interinanimates two souls,
That abler soul, which thence doth flow,
   Defects of loneliness[5] controls.
We then, who are this new soul, know,
   Of what we are compos'd, and made,
For, th' Atomies of which we grow,
   Are souls, whom no change can invade.
But O alas, so long, so far
   Our bodies why do we forbear?[6]   50
They are ours, though they are not we, We are
   The intelligences, they the spheres.[7]
We owe them thanks, because they thus,
   Did us, to us, at first convey,
Yielded their forces, sense, to us,
   Nor are dross to us, but allay.
On man heaven's influence works not so,

4   a process used in refining metals.
5   separateness.
6   avoid.
7   In astronomy the heavenly bodies were thought of as attached to moving spheres.

But that it first imprints the air,
So soul into the soul may flow,
   Though it to body first repair.   60
As our blood labours to beget
   Spirits, as like souls as it can,
Because such fingers need to knit
   That subtle knot, which makes us man:
So must pure lovers' souls descend
   T' affections, and to faculties,
Which sense may reach and apprehend,
   Else a great Prince in prison lies.
To our bodies turn we then, that so
   Weak men on love reveal'd may look;   70
Love's mysteries in souls do grow,
   But yet the body is his book,
And if some lover, such as we,
   Have heard this dialogue of one,
Let me still mark us, he shall see
   Small change, when we're to bodies gone.

Elegy 9
The Autumnal

No spring, nor summer beauty hath such grace,
   As I have seen in one autumnal face.
Young beauties force our love, and that's a rape,
   This doth but counsel, yet you cannot 'scape.
If t'were a shame to love, here t'were no shame,
   Affection here takes reverence's name.
Were her first years the Golden Age; that's true,
   But now she's gold oft tried, and ever new.
That was her torrid and inflaming time,
   This is her tolerable tropic clime.   10
Fair eyes, who asks more heat than comes from hence,
   He in a fever wishes pestilence.
Call not these wrinkles, graves; if graves they were,
   They were love's graves; for else he is no where.
Yet lies not love dead here, but here doth sit
   Vowed to this trench, like an anchorite.
And here, till hers, which must be his death, come,
   He doth not dig a grave, but build a tomb.
Here dwells he, though he sojourn every where,
   In progress,[1] yet his standing house is here.   20
Here, where still evening is; not noon, nor night,
   Where no voluptuousness, yet all delight.

1   state journey of royalty.

In all her words, unto all hearers fit,
    You may at revels, you at counsel, sit.
This is love's timber, youth his under-wood;
    There he, as wine in June, enrages blood,
Which then comes seasonabliest, when our taste
    And appetite to other things, is past.
Xerxes' strange Lydian love, the platan tree,[2]
    Was loved for age, none being so large as she, 30
Or else because, being young, nature did bless
    Her youth with age's glory, barrenness.
If we love things long sought, age is a thing
    Which we are fifty years in compassing.
If transitory things, which soon decay,
    Age must be loveliest at the latest day.
But name not winter faces, whose skin's slack;
    Lank, as an unthrift's purse; but a soul's sack;
Whose eyes seek light within, for all here's shade;
    Whose mouths are holes, rather worn out, than made. 40
Whose every tooth to a several place is gone,
    To vex their souls at resurrection;
Name not these living deaths-heads unto me,
    For these, not ancient, but antique be.
I hate extremes; yet I had rather stay
    With tombs than cradles, to wear out a day.
Since such love's natural lation[3] is, may still
    My love descend, and journey down the hill,
Not panting after growing beauties, so
    I shall ebb out with them, who homeward go. 50

2   Xerxes the Great was smitten by the plane-tree's beauty and had it decorated with gold.
3   motion (astrology).

from *Holy Sonnets*

7

At the round earth's imagin'd corners, blow
Your trumpets, Angels, and arise, arise
From death, you numberless infinities
Of souls, and to your scatter'd bodies go,
All whom the flood did, and fire shall o'erthrow,
All whom war, dearth, age, agues, tyrannies,
Despair, law, chance, hath slain, and you whose eyes,
Shall behold God, and never taste death's woe.
But let them sleep, Lord, and me mourn a space,
For, if above all these, my sins abound,
'Tis late to ask abundance of Thy grace,
When we are there; here on this lowly ground,

Teach me how to repent; for that's as good
As if Thou hadst seal'd my pardon, with Thy blood.

10

Death be not proud, though some have called thee
Mighty and dreadful, for, thou art not so,
For, those, whom thou think'st, thou dost overthrow,
Die not, poor death, nor yet canst thou kill me;
From rest and sleep, which but thy pictures be,
Much pleasure, then from thee, much more must flow,
And soonest our best men with thee do go,
Rest of their bones, and soul's delivery.
Thou art slave to fate, chance, kings, and desperate men,
And dost with poison, war, and sickness dwell,
And poppy, or charms can make us sleep as well,
And better than thy stroke; why swell'st thou then?
One short sleep past, we wake eternally,
And death shall be no more, Death thou shalt die.

14

Batter my heart, three-person'd God; for you
As yet but knock, breathe, shine, and seek to mend;
That I may rise, and stand, o'erthrow me, and bend
Your force, to break, blow, burn, and make me new.
I, like an usurp'd town, to another due,
Labour to admit you, but Oh, to no end,
Reason your viceroy in me, me should defend,
But is captiv'd, and proves weak or untrue.
Yet dearly I love you, and would be loved fain,
But am betroth'd unto your enemy:
Divorce me, untie, or break that knot again,
Take me to you, imprison me, for I
Except you enthral me, never shall be free,
Nor ever chaste, except you ravish me.

A Valediction: Forbidding Mourning

As virtuous men pass mildly away,
    And whisper to their souls to go,
Whilst some of their sad friends do say,
    The breath goes now, and some say, No:

So let us melt, and make no noise,
    No tear-floods, nor sigh-tempests move;
'Twere profanation of our joys
    To tell the laity our love.

Moving of th' earth brings harms and fears,
    Men reckon what it did, and meant;   10
But trepidation of the spheres,[1]
    Though greater far, is innocent.

Dull sublunary[2] lovers' love
    (Whose soul is sense) cannot admit
Absence, because it doth remove
    Those things which elemented it.

But we by a love so much refined
    That ourselves know not what it is,
Inter-assuréd of the mind,
    Care less eyes, lips and hands to miss.   20

Our two souls therefore, which are one,
    Though I must go, endure not yet
A breach, but an expansion,
    Like gold to airy thinness beat.

If they be two, they are two so
    As still twin compasses are two;
Thy soul, the fixed foot, makes no show
    To move, but doth, if th' other do.

And though it in the center sit,
    Yet, when the other far doth roam,   30
It leans, and hearkens after it,
    And grows erect, as that comes home.

Such wilt thou be to me, who must,
    Like th' other foot, obliquely run;
Thy firmness makes my circle just,
    And makes me end where I begun.

1   a reference to the theory that attempted to explain oscillation of heavenly bodies while still maintaining the belief in a stationary earth.
2   under the moon, earthly, and therefore subject to mutability.

Good Friday, 1613.
Riding Westward

Let man's soul be a sphere, and then, in this,
The intelligence that moves, devotion is,[1]

1   If the soul is compared to a sphere, as the sphere is moved by intelligence, the soul is moved by devotion.

And as the other spheres, by being grown
Subject to foreign motions, lose their own,
And being by others hurried every day,
Scarce in a year their natural form obey:
Pleasure or business, so, our souls admit
For their first mover, and are whirled by it.
Hence is't, that I am carried towards the west
This day, when my soul's form bends toward the east.   10
There I should see a sun, by rising set,
And by that setting endless day beget;
But that Christ on this Cross, did rise and fall,
Sin had eternally benighted all.
Yet dare I' almost be glad, I do not see
That spectacle of too much weight for me.
Who sees God's face, that is self life, must die;[2]
What a death were it then to see God die?
It made his own lieutenant Nature shrink,
It made his footstool crack, and the sun wink.[3]   20
Could I behold those hands which span the poles,
And turn[4] all spheres at once, pierced with those holes?
Could I behold that endless height which is
Zenith to us, and to' our antipodes,[5]
Humbled below us? or that blood which is
The seat of all our souls,[6] if not of his,
Made dirt of dust,[7] or that flesh which was worn,
By God, for his apparel, ragged, and torn?
If on these things I durst not look, durst I
Upon his miserable mother cast mine eye,   30
Who was God's partner here, and furnished thus
Half of that sacrifice, which ransomed us?
Though these things, as I ride, be from mine eye,
They are present yet unto my memory,
For that looks towards them; and thou look'st towards me,
O Saviour, as thou hang'st upon the tree;
I turn my back to thee, but to receive
Corrections, till thy mercies bid thee leave.
O think me worth thine anger, punish me,
Burn off my rusts, and my deformity,   40
Restore thine image, so much, by thy grace,
That thou mayst know me, and I'll turn my face.

2   God told Moses that he could not see His face and live (Exodus, 33. 20).
3   Matthew, 17. 51–4 tells of the disturbances in nature when Jesus died.
4   variant reading: *tune*.
5   God is the highest point to us and to the people on the other side of the world.
6   Some people thought that the soul was in the blood.
7   (a) mixed with the dust and so turned into mud; (b) made of less worth than the dust
of which man is created.

Hymn to
God my God,
in my Sickness

Since I am coming to that holy room,
   Where, with thy choir of saints for evermore,
I shall be made thy music; as I come
   I tune the instrument here at the door,
   And what I must do then, think here before.

Whilst my physicians by their love are grown
   Cosmographers[1] and I their map, who lie
Flat on this bed, that by them may be shown
   That this is my south-west discovery
   Per fretum febris,[2] by these straits to die,   10

I joy, that in these straits, I see my west;
   For, though their currents yield return to none,
What shall my west hurt me? As west and east
   In all flat maps (and I am one) are one,
   So death doth touch the resurrection.

Is the Pacific Sea my home? Or are
   The eastern riches? Is Jerusalem?
Anyan,[3] and Magellan, and Gibraltar,
   All straits, and none but straits, are ways to them,
   Whether where Japhet dwelt, or Cham, or Shem.[4]   20

We think that Paradise and Calvary,
   Christ's Cross, and Adam's tree, stood in one place;[5]
Look Lord, and find both Adams met in me;
   As the first Adam's sweat surrounds my face,
   May the last Adam's blood my soul embrace.

So, in his purple wrapped receive me Lord,
   By these his thorns give me his other crown;
And as to others' souls I preached thy word,
   Be this my text, my sermon to mine own,
   Therefore that he may raise the Lord throws down.   30

1   geographers.
2   by the strait of fever.
3   According to old geographers, America and Asia were separated by the "Straits of Anyan." Or the reference may be to the Mozambique Channel where there is an island called Anyouam.
4   the sons of Noah. The world was divided between them: Europe was given to Japhet, Africa to Ham, and Asia to Shem.
5   The Golden Legend says that Christ died in the same place where Adam was buried.

BEN JONSON [1572–1637]

On My
First Daughter

Here lies to each her parents' ruth,
Mary, the daughter of their youth:
Yet, all heaven's gifts, being heaven's due,
It makes the father, less, to rue.
At six months' end, she parted hence
With safety of her innocence;
Whose soul heaven's Queen, (whose name she bears)
In comfort of her mother's tears,
Hath placed amongst her virgin-train:
Where, while that severed doth remain,
This grave partakes the fleshly birth.
Which cover lightly, gentle earth.

On My
First Son

Farewell, thou child of my right hand, and joy;
      My sin was too much hope of thee, loved boy.
Seven years tho'wert lent to me, and I thee pay,
      Exacted by thy fate, on the just day.
O, could I lose all father now. For why
      Will man lament the state he should envy?
To have so soon scaped world's, and flesh's rage,
      And, if no other misery, yet age?
Rest in soft peace, and, asked, say here doth lie
      Ben Jonson his best piece of poetry.
For whose sake, henceforth, all his vows be such,
      As what he loves may never like too much.

Song:
To Celia[1]

Come my Celia, let us prove
While we may, the sports of love;
Time will not be ours, for ever:
He, at length, our goods will sever.
Spend not then his gifts in vain.
Suns, that set, may rise again:

1   from Jonson's *Volpone*, 3. 7.

102

But if once we lose this light,
'Tis with us, perpetual night.
Why should we defer our joys?
Fame and rumor are but toys.
Cannot we delude the eyes
Of a few poor household spies?
Or his[2] easier ears beguile,
So removed by our wile?
'Tis no sin, love's fruit to steal,
But the sweet theft to reveal:
To be taken, to be seen,
These have crimes accounted been.

2   Celia's husband, Corvino.

Her Triumph[1]

See the chariot at hand here of Love
    Wherein my Lady rideth!
Each that draws, is a swan, or a dove
    And well the car Love guideth.
As she goes, all hearts do duty
    Unto her beauty;
And enamour'd, do wish, so they might
    But enjoy such a sight,
    That they still[2] were, to run by her side,
Through swords, through seas, whether[3] she would ride.   10

Do but look on her eyes, they do light
    All that Love's world compriseth!
Do but look on her hair, it is bright
    As Love's star[4] when it riseth!
Do but mark her forehead's smoother
    Than words that soothe her!
And from her arched brows, such a grace
    Sheds itself through the face,
    As alone there triumphs to the life
All the gain, all the good, of the elements' strife.[5]   20

Have you seen but a bright lily grow,
    Before rude hands have touched it?
Ha' you marked but the fall of the snow
    Before the soil hath smutched it?

1   no. 4 in "A Celebration of Charis in Ten Lyrick Peeces."
2   always.
3   wherever.
4   Venus.
5   the elements—earth, air, fire, water—were supposedly always at war.

Ha' you felt the wool of beaver?
        Or swan's down ever?
Or have smelt o' the bud o' the briar?
        Or the nard[6] in the fire?
        Or have tasted the bag of the bee?
O so white! O so soft! O so sweet is she!   30

6   spikenard, a fragrant ointment of the ancients.

Hymn[1]

Queen and Huntress, chaste, and fair,
Now the Sun is laid to sleep,
Seated in thy silver chair,
State in wonted manner keep:
    Hesperus[2] intreats thy light,
    Goddess, excellently bright.

Earth, let not thy envious shade
Dare it self to interpose;
Cynthia's shining orb was made
Heaven to clear, when day did close:
    Bless us then with wished sight,
    Goddess, excellently bright.

Lay thy bow of pearl apart,
And thy crystal-shining quiver;
Give unto the flying hart
Space to breathe, how short soever:
    Thou, that mak'st a day of night,
    Goddess, excellently bright.

1   from *Cynthia's Revels*, 5. 6.
2   the evening star.

Still to be Neat[1]

Still[2] to be neat, still to be drest,
As you were going to a feast;
Still to be powdered, still perfumed:
Lady, it is to be presumed,
Though art's hid causes are not found,
All is not sweet, all is not sound.

1   from *Epicoene or The Silent Woman*, 1.1.
2   always.

Give me a look, give me a face,
That makes simplicity a grace;
Robes loosely flowing, hair as free:
Such sweet neglect more taketh me,
Than all th'adulteries of art.
They strike mine eyes, but not my heart.

Slow, Slow, Fresh Fount[1]

Slow, slow, fresh fount, keep time with my salt tears;
    Yet slower yet, oh faintly gentle springs:
List to the heavy part the music bears,
    "Woe weeps out her division[2] when she sings."
    Droop herbs and flowers;
    Fall grief in showers;
    "Our beauties are not ours":
                Oh, I could still,
Like melting snow upon some craggy hill,
    Drop, drop, drop, drop,
Since nature's pride is, now, a withered daffodil.

1   from *Cynthia's Revels*, 1.2. Sung by Echo. I have followed G. A. Wilkes's edition (Oxford, 1981).
2   descant. A melody or counterpoint sung above the plainsong of the tenor.

ROBERT HERRICK   [1591–1674]

Delight in Disorder

A sweet disorder in the dress
Kindles in clothes a wantonness:
A lawn about the shoulders thrown
Into a fine distraction:
An erring lace, which here and there
Enthrals the crimson stomacher:[1]
A cuff neglectful, and thereby
Ribbands to flow confusedly:
A winning wave (deserving note)
In the tempestuous petticoat:
A careless shoe-string, in whose tie
I see a wild civility:
Do more bewitch me than when art
Is too precise in every part.

1   bodice.

Corinna's Going a-Maying

Get up, get up for shame! The blooming morn
Upon her wings presents the god unshorn.[1]
   See how Aurora[2] throws her fair,
   Fresh-quilted colors through the air.
   Get up, sweet slug-a-bed, and see
   The dew bespangling herb and tree!
Each flower has wept and bowed toward the east
Above an hour since, yet you not drest;
   Nay! not so much as out of bed?
   When all the birds have matins said   10
   And sung their thankful hymns, 'tis sin,
   Nay, profanation, to keep in,
Whenas a thousand virgins on this day
Spring sooner than the lark, to fetch in May.

Rise and put on your foliage, and be seen
To come forth, like the springtime, fresh and green,
   And sweet as Flora.[3] Take no care
   For jewels for your gown or hair.
   Fear not; the leaves will strew
   Gems in abundance upon you.   20
Besides, the childhood of the day has kept
Against you come, some orient pearls unwept.
   Come, and receive them while the light
   Hangs on the dew-locks of the night;
   and Titan[4] on the eastern hill
   Retires himself, or else stands still
Till you come forth! Wash, dress, be brief in praying;
Few beads[5] are best when once we go a-Maying.

Come, my Corinna, come; and coming, mark
How each field turns a street, each street a park,   30
   Made green and trimmed with trees! see how
   Devotion gives each house a bough
   Or branch! each porch, each door, ere this,
   An ark, a tabernacle is,
Made up of white-thorn neatly interwove,
As if here were those cooler shades of love.
   Can such delights be in the street
   And open fields, and we not see't?
   Come, we'll abroad; and let's obey

1   Apollo. As with Samson, Apollo's strength was greatest when his hair was uncut.
2   Roman goddess of dawn.
3   Roman goddess of flowers.
4   the sun god.
5   prayers.

The proclamation made for May,   40
And sin no more, as we have done, by staying;
But, my Corinna, come, let's go a-Maying.

There's not a budding boy or girl this day
But is got up and gone to bring in May.
   A deal of youth ere this is come
   Back, and with white-thorn laden home.
   Some have dispatched their cakes and cream,
   Before that we have left to dream;
And some have wept and wooed, and plighted troth,
And chose their priest, ere we can cast off sloth.   50
   Many a green-gown has been given,
   Many a kiss, both odd and even;
   Many a glance, too, has been sent
   From out the eye, love's firmament;
Many a jest told of the keys betraying
This night, and locks picked; yet we're not a-Maying!

Come, let us go, while we are in our prime,
And take the harmless folly of the time!
   We shall grow old apace, and die
   Before we know our liberty.   60
   Our life is short, and our days run
   As fast away as does the sun.
And, as a vapor or a drop of rain,
Once lost, can ne'er be found again,
   So when or you or I are made
   A fable, song, or fleeting shade,
   All love, all liking, all delight
   Lies drowned with us in endless night.
Then, while time serves and we are but decaying,
Come, my Corinna, come, let's go a-Maying.   70

To the Virgins, to Make Much of Time

Gather ye rosebuds while ye may:
   Old Time is still a-flying,
And this same flower that smiles today
   Tomorrow will be dying.

The glorious lamp of heaven, the sun,
   The higher he's a-getting,
The sooner will his race be run,
   And nearer he's to setting.

That age is best which is the first,
    When youth and blood are warmer;
But, being spent, the worse, and worst
    Times, still succeed the former.

Then be not coy, but use your time,
    And while ye may, go marry:
For having lost but once your prime,
    You may for ever tarry.

To Daffodils

Fair daffodils, we weep to see
    You haste away so soon:
As yet the early rising sun
    Has not attained his noon.
        Stay, stay,
    Until the hasting day
        Has run
    But to the Evensong;
And, having prayed together, we
    Will go with you along.

We have short time to stay, as you,
    We have as short a spring;
As quick a growth to meet decay,
    As you, or any thing.
        We die,
    As your hours do, and dry
        Away,
    Like to the summer's rain;
Or as the pearls of morning's dew
    Ne'er to be found again.

Upon
Julia's Clothes

Whenas in silks my Julia goes,
Then, then, methinks how sweetly flows
The liquefaction of her clothes.

Next, when I cast mine eyes, and see
That brave vibration, each way free,
O, how that glittering taketh me!

Grace
for a Child

Here a little child I stand,
Heaving[1] up my either hand:
Cold as paddocks[2] though they be,
Here I lift them up to Thee,
For a benison to fall
On our meat, and on us all. Amen.

1 raising.
2 toads.

HENRY KING   [1592–1669]

The Exequy[1]

Accept, thou shrine of my dead saint,
Instead of dirges this complaint;
And for sweet flowers to crown thy hearse,
Receive a strew of weeping verse
From thy grieved friend, whom thou might'st see
Quite melted into tears for thee.

    Dear loss! since thy untimely fate
My task hath been to meditate
On thee, on thee: thou art the book,
The library whereon I look   10
Though almost blind. For thee (loved clay)
I languish out, not live the day,
Using no other exercise
But what I practise with mine eyes:
By which wet glasses I find out
How lazily time creeps about
To one that mourns: this, only this
My exercise and business is:
So I compute the weary hours
With sighs dissolved into showers.   20

    Nor wonder if my time go thus
Backward and most preposterous;
Thou hast benighted me, thy set[2]
This eve of blackness did beget,
Who was't my day (though overcast

1 *exequy*: funeral rites. King's wife, Anne, was buried on January 5, 1624. His use of
the word *exequy* has led to its meaning "funeral ode."
2 setting, as of the sun.

Before thou had'st thy noon-tide past)
And I remember must in tears,
Thou scarce had'st seen so many years
As day tells hours.[3] By thy clear sun
My love and fortune first did run;   30
But thou wilt never more appear
Folded within my hemisphere,
Since both thy light and motion
Like a fled star is fall'n and gone,
And twixt me and my soul's dear wish
The earth now interposed is,
Which such a strange eclipse doth make
As ne'er was read in almanake.

    I could allow thee for a time
To darken me and my sad clime;   40
Were it a month, a year, or ten,
I would thy exile live till then,
And all that space my mirth adjourn,
So thou wouldst promise to return,
And putting off thy ashy shroud
At length dispense this sorrow's cloud.

    But woe is me! the longest date
Too narrow is to calculate
These empty hopes: never shall I
Be so much blest as to descry   50
A glimpse of thee, till that day come
Which shall the earth to cinders doom,
And a fierce fever must calcine[4]
The body of this world like thine
(My Little World!) that fit of fire
Once off, our bodies shall aspire
To our souls' bliss: then we shall rise,
And view ourselves with clearer eyes
In that calm region, where no night
Can hide us from each other's sight.   60

    Meantime thou hast her, earth: much good
May my harm do thee. Since it stood
With Heaven's will I might not call
Her longer mine, I give thee all
My short-lived right and interest
In her, whom living I loved best:
With a most free and bounteous grief,
I give thee what I could not keep.
Be kind to her, and prithee[5] look

3 She was only about twenty-four when she died.
4 burn to dust.
5 I pray thee.

110

Thou write into thy Doomsday[6] book   70
Each parcel of this rarity
Which in thy casket shrined doth lie:
See that thou make thy reck'ning straight,
And yield her back again by weight;
For thou must audit on thy trust
Each grain and atom of this dust,
As thou wilt answer Him that lent,
Not gave thee my dear monument.

     So close the ground, and 'bout her shade
Black curtains draw, my bride is laid.   80

     Sleep on, my love, in thy cold bed
Never to be disquieted!
My last goodnight! Thou wilt not wake
Till I thy fate shall overtake:
Till age, or grief, or sickness must
Marry my body to that dust
It so much loves, and fill the room
My heart keeps empty in thy tomb.
Stay for me there; I will not fail
To meet thee in that hollow vale.   90
And think not much of my delay;
I am already on the way,
And follow thee with all the speed
Desire can make, or sorrows breed.
Each minute is a short degree,
And ev'ry hour a step towards thee.
At night when I betake to rest,
Next morn I rise nearer my west
Of life, almost by eight hours' sail,
Than when sleep breathed his drowsy gale.   100

     Thus from the sun my bottom[7] steers,
And my days' compass downward bears:
Nor labor I to stem the tide
Through which to thee I swiftly glide.

     'Tis true, with shame and grief I yield,
Thou like the van[8] first took'st the field,
And gotten hast the victory
In thus adventuring to die
Before me, whose more years might crave
A just precedence in the grave.   110
But hark! My pulse like a soft drum

6 Judgment Day.
7 boat, ship.
8 vanguard, head of an army.

Beats my approach, tells thee I come;
And slow howe'er my marches be,
I shall at last sit down by thee.

    The thought of this bids me go on,
And wait my dissolution
With hope and comfort. Dear (forgive
The crime) I am content to live
Divided, with but half a heart,
Till we shall meet and never part.   120

GEORGE HERBERT [1593–1633]

from *The Temple*

The Altar

A broken ALTAR, Lord, thy servant rears,
Made of a heart, and cemented with tears:
  Whose parts are as thy hand did frame;
  No workman's tool hath touched the same.
        A   HEART   alone
        Is   such   a   stone,
        As   nothing   but
        Thy power doth cut.
        Wherefore each part
        Of my hard heart
        Meets in this frame,
        To praise thy Name:
  That, if I chance to hold my peace,
  These stones to praise thee may not cease.
O let thy blessed SACRIFICE be mine,
And sanctify this ALTAR to be thine.

Redemption

Having been tenant long to a rich Lord,
  Not thriving, I resolved to be bold,
  And make a suit unto him, to afford
A new small-rented lease, and cancel th' old.

In heaven at his manor I him sought:
  They told me there, that he was lately gone
  About some land, which he had dearly bought
Long since on earth, to take possession.

I straight returned, and knowing his great birth,
　　Sought him accordingly in great resorts:
　　In cities, theaters, gardens, parks, and courts:
At length I heard a ragged noise and mirth

　　Of thieves and murderers: there I him espied,
　　Who straight, *Your suit is granted*, said, and died.

Easter Wings

Lord, who createdst man in wealth and store,
　　Though foolishly he lost the same,
　　　　Decaying more and more,
　　　　　　Till he became
　　　　　　　　Most poor;
　　　　　　　　With Thee
　　　　　　O let me rise
　　　　As larks, harmoniously,
　　And sing this day Thy victories:
Then shall the fall further the flight in me.[1]

My tender age in sorrow did begin:
　　And still with sicknesses and shame
　　　　Thou did'st so punish sin,
　　　　　　That I became
　　　　　　　　Most thin.
　　　　　　　　With Thee
　　　　　　Let me combine
　　　　And feel this day Thy victory;
　　For, if I imp[2] my wing on Thine,
Affliction shall advance the flight in me.

1　a reference to the doctrine of "felix culpa," happy fault, in which Adam's fall was thought of as "happy," for had there not been a fall there would not have been the promise of Redemption. See the anonymous song, "Adam Lay I-bowndyn":
　　Ne hadde the appil take ben, the appil taken ben,
　　Ne hadde neuer our lady a ben heuene qwen;
　　Blyssid be the tyme that appil take was . . .
2　engraft feathers on a damaged wing to restore the ability to fly.

Prayer

Prayer the Church's banquet, angels' age,
　　God's breath in man returning to his birth,
　　The soul in paraphrase, heart in pilgrimage,
The Christian plummet sounding heaven and earth;

Engine against th'Almighty, sinners' tower,
　　Reversed thunder, Christ-side-piercing spear,

The six-days world transposing in an hour,
A kind of tune, which all things hear and fear;

Softness, and peace, and joy, and love, and bliss,
    Exalted manna, gladness of the best,
    Heaven in ordinary, man well dressed,
The Milky Way, the bird of paradise,

        Church bells beyond the stars heard, the soul's blood,
        The land of spices; something understood.

Jordan

Who says that fictions only and false hair
Become a verse? Is there in truth no beauty?
Is all good structure in a winding stair?
May no lines pass, except they do their duty
    Not to a true, but painted chair?

Is it no verse, except enchanted groves
And sudden arbours shadow coarse-spun lines?
Must purling streams refresh a lover's loves?
Must all be veiled, while he that reads, divines,[1]
    Catching the sense at two removes?

Shepherds are honest people; let them sing:
Riddle who list,[2] for me, and pull for prime:[3]
I envy no man's nightingale or spring;
Nor let them punish[4] me with loss of rhyme,
    Who plainly say, *My God, My King.*

1   discovers intuitively.
2   wants.
3   Whoever wants may make riddles, for all I care, and we shall see who draws ("pulls") the winning card ("prime").
4   blame.

Virtue

Sweet day, so cool, so calm, so bright,
The bridal[1] of the earth and sky:
The dew shall weep thy fall tonight;
        For thou must die.

Sweet rose, whose hue angry[2] and brave
Bids the rash gazer wipe his eye:
Thy root is ever in its grave,
        And thou must die.

Sweet spring, full of sweet days, and roses,
A box where sweets[3] compacted lie;
My music shows ye have your closes,[4]
      And all must die.

Only a sweet and virtuous soul,
Like seasoned timber, never gives;
But though the whole world turn to coal,[5]
      Then chiefly lives.

1   wedding.
2   red.
3   fragrances.
4   cadences in music. Herbert is making a pun on the word so that it also means "closings" or "endings."
5   cinder.

Artillery

As I one evening sat before my cell,
Me thoughts a star did shoot into my lap.
I rose, and shook my clothes, as knowing well,
That from small fires comes oft no small mishap.
   When suddenly I heard one say,
   Do as thou usest, disobey,
   Expel good motions[1] from thy breast,
Which have the face of fire, but end in rest.

I, who had heard of music in the spheres,
But not of speech in stars, began to muse: 10
But turning to my God, whose ministers
The stars and all things are; If I refuse,
   Dread Lord, said I, so oft my good;
   Then I refuse not ev'n with blood
   To wash away my stubborn thought:
For I will do or suffer what I ought.

But I have also stars and shooters[2] too,
Born where thy servants both artilleries use.
My tears and prayers night and day do woo,
And work up to thee; yet thou dost refuse.   20
   Not but I am (I must say still)
   Much more obliged to do thy will,
   Than thou to grant mine: but because
Thy promise now hath ev'n set thee thy laws.

Then we are shooters both, and thou dost deign
To enter combat with us, and contest

1   impulses.
2   shooting stars.

With thine own clay. But I would parley fain:
Shun not my arrows, and behold my breast.
   Yet if thou shunnest, I am thine:
   I must be so, if I am mine.   30
   There is no articling[3] with thee:
I am but finite, yet thine infinitely.

  3 bargaining.

The Collar

   I struck the board,[1] and cried, No more.
         I will abroad.
  What? shall I ever sigh and pine?
My lines and life are free; free as the road,
   Loose as the wind, as large as store.[2]
        Shall I be still[3] in suit?
  Have I no harvest but a thorn
  To let me blood,[4] and not restore
What I have lost with cordial fruit?
        Sure there was wine   10
       Before my sighs did dry it: there was corn
       Before my tears did drown it.
   Is the year only lost to me?
       Have I no bays to crown it?
No flowers, no garlands gay? all blasted?
       All wasted?
  Not so, my heart: but there is fruit,
       And thou hast hands.
       Recover all thy sigh-blown age
On double pleasures: leave thy cold dispute   20
Of what is fit, and not. Forsake thy cage,
       Thy rope of sands,
Which petty thoughts have made, and made to thee
      Good cable, to enforce and draw,
       And be thy law,
    While thou didst wink and wouldst not see.
       Away; take heed:
       I will abroad.
Call in thy death's head there: tie up thy fears.
       He that forbears   30
     To suit and serve his need,
       Deserves his load.

  1 table.
  2 abundance.
  3 always.
  4 As a cure, physicians would let blood, i.e., make an incision and let some blood
escape from the body.

But as I raved and grew more fierce and wild
        At every word,
Methought I heard one calling, *Child*;
        And I replied, *My Lord*.

The Pulley

        When God at first made man,
Having a glass of blessings standing by,
"Let us," said He, "pour on him all we can:
Let the world's riches, which dispersed lie,
        Contract into a span."[1]

        So Strength first made a way;
Then Beauty flowed, then Wisdom, Honor, Pleasure:
When almost all was out, God made a stay,
Perceiving that alone of all His treasure
        Rest in the bottom lay.

        "For if I should," said He,
"Bestow this jewel also on My creature,
He would adore My gifts instead of Me,
And rest in Nature, not the God of Nature:
        So both should losers be.

        "Yet let him keep the rest,
But keep them with repining restlessness:
Let him be rich and weary, that at least,
If goodness lead him not, yet weariness
        May toss him to My breast."

1   a small space.

Love

Love bade me welcome: yet my soul drew back,
        Guilty of dust and sin.
But quick-eyed Love, observing me grow slack
        From my first entrance in,
Drew nearer to me, sweetly questioning,
        If I lacked anything.

"A guest," I answered, "worthy to be here."
        Love said, "You shall be he."
"I the unkind, ungrateful? Ah my dear,
        I cannot look on thee."

Love took my hand, and smiling did reply,
        "Who made the eyes but I?"

"Truth Lord, but I have marred them: let my shame
        Go where it doth deserve."
"And know you not," says Love, "who bore the blame?"
        "My dear, then I will serve."[1]
"You must sit down," says Love, "and taste my meat":
        So I did sit and eat.

1 Herbert and his contemporaries did not use quotation marks, and there is some
obscurity in the dialogue at this point. I have attributed the line, "My dear, then I will
serve," to the narrator.

THOMAS CAREW [1594?–1640?]

A Song

Ask me no more where Jove bestows,
When June is past, the fading rose;
For in your beauty's orient deep
These flowers, as in their causes, sleep.

Ask me no more whither do stray
The golden atoms of the day;
For, in pure love, heaven did prepare
Those powders to enrich your hair.

Ask me no more whither doth haste
The nightingale, when May is past;
For in your sweet dividing throat
She winters, and keeps warm her note.

Ask me no more where those stars light
That downwards fall in dead of night;
For in your eyes they sit, and there
Fixed become, as in their sphere.

Ask me no more if east or west
The phoenix[1] builds her spicy nest;
For unto you at last she flies,
And in your fragrant bosom dies.

1 a mythical Egyptian bird believed to live for five hundred years, to consume itself in
flames, and to rise from its own ashes.

JOHN MILTON   [1608–1674]

L'Allegro¹

Hence loathed Melancholy
   Of Cerberus² and blackest Midnight born,
In Stygian³ cave forlorn
    'Mongst horrid shapes, and shrieks, and sights unholy,
Find out some uncouth⁴ cell,
   Where brooding Darkness spreads his jealous wings,
And the night-raven sings;
   There under ebon shades and low-browed rocks,
As ragged as thy locks,
   In dark Cimmerian⁵ desert ever dwell.   10
But come thou Goddess fair and free,
In Heaven yclept⁶ Euphrosyne,⁷
And by men, heart-easing Mirth,
Whom lovely Venus at a birth
With two sister Graces more
To ivy-crowned Bacchus⁸ bore;
Or whether (as some sager sing)
The frolic wind that breathes the spring,
Zephyr⁹ with Aurora¹⁰ playing,
As he met her once a-Maying,   20
There on beds of violets blue,
And fresh-blown roses washed in dew,
Filled her with thee, a daughter fair,
So buxom, blithe, and debonair.
    Haste thee Nymph, and bring with thee
Jest and youthful Jollity,
Quips and Cranks, and wanton Wiles,¹¹
Nods, and Becks, and wreathed Smiles,
Such as hang on Hebe's¹² cheek,
And love to live in dimple sleek;   30
Sport that wrinkled Care derides,
And Laughter holding both his sides.
Come, and trip it as ye go
On the light fantastic toe,

1   the lighthearted, joyful man.
2   the three-headed dog that guarded the gate of Hades.
3   belonging to the infernal regions.
4   unknown, savage.
5   *Cimmeria*: a gloomy, misty land described in Homer's *Odyssey*.
6   called.
7   one of the three Graces.
8   god of wine.
9   the west wind.
10 goddess of dawn.
11 *quips*: witty remarks; *cranks*: twists or turns of speech, conceits; *wiles*: tricks.
12 goddess of youth.

And in thy right hand lead with thee,
The mountain nymph, sweet Liberty;
And if I give thee honor due,
Mirth, admit me of thy crew,
To live with her, and live with thee,
In unreproved pleasures free;   40
To hear the lark begin his flight,
And singing startle the dull night,
From his watch-tower in the skies,
Till the dappled dawn doth rise;
Then to come in spite of sorrow,[13]
And at my window bid good-morrow,
Through the sweet-briar, or the vine,
Or the twisted eglantine.
While the cock with lively din,
Scatters the rear of darkness thin,   50
And to the stack or the barn door,
Stoutly struts his dames before;
Oft listening how the hounds and horn
Cheerly rouse the slumbering Morn,
From the side of some hoar hill,
Through the high wood echoing shrill.
Sometime walking not unseen
By hedgerow elms, on hillocks green,
Right against the eastern gate,
Where the great sun begins his state,   60
Robed in flames and amber light,
The clouds in thousand liveries dight;[14]
While the ploughman near at hand,
Whistles o'er the furrowed land,
And the milkmaid singeth blithe,
And the mower whets his scythe,
And every shepherd tells his tale[15]
Under the hawthorn in the dale.
    Straight mine eye hath caught new pleasures
Whilst the landscape round it measures: 70
Russet lawns and fallows gray,
Where the nibbling flocks do stray,
Mountains on whose barren breast
The laboring clouds do often rest,
Meadows trim with daisies pied,[16]
Shallow brooks and rivers wide.
Towers and battlements it sees
Bosomed high in tufted trees,
Where perhaps some beauty lies,

13   to spite sorrow.
14   clothed.
15   counts his sheep, or tells his story.
16   colored.

The cynosure[17] of neighboring eyes.   80
Hard by, a cottage chimney smokes,
From betwixt two aged oaks,
Where Corydon and Thyrsis[18] met,
Are at their savory dinner set
Of herbs and other country messes,[19]
Which the neat-handed Phillis dresses;
And then in haste her bower she leaves,
With Thestylis to bind the sheaves;
Or if the earlier season lead,
To the tanned haycock in the mead.   90
   Sometimes with secure delight
The upland hamlets will invite,
When the merry bells ring round,
And the jocund rebecks[20] sound
To many a youth and many a maid,
Dancing in the chequered shade;
And young and old come forth to play
On a sunshine holiday,
Till the livelong daylight fail;
Then to the spicy nut-brown ale,   100
With stories told of many a feat,
How fairy Mab[21] the junkets eat;
She was pinched and pulled she said,
And he by friar's lantern[22] led
Tells how the drudging goblin[23] sweat,
To earn his cream-bowl duly set,
When in one night, ere glimpse of morn,
His shadowy flail hath threshed the corn
That ten day-laborers could not end;
Then lies him down the lubber fiend,   110
And stretched out all the chimney's length,
Basks at the fire his hairy strength;
And crop-full out of doors he flings,
Ere the first cock his matin rings.
Thus done the tales, to bed they creep,
By whispering winds soon lulled asleep.
   Towered cities please us then,
And the busy hum of men,
Where throngs of knights and barons bold
In weeds[24] of peace high triumphs hold,   120

17   center of attraction.
18   names of characters in pastoral poetry—as are Phillis and Thestylis.
19   dishes.
20   three-stringed musical instruments.
21   queen of the fairies.
22   *friar's lantern*: will-o'-the-wisp.
23   Robin Goodfellow, or Puck, a mischievous fairy. If well treated he would see to it that farm chores ran smoothly. If ignored or mistreated, he would cause all kinds of trouble and discord.
24   garments.

With store of ladies, whose bright eyes
Rain influence, and judge the prize
Of wit or arms, while both contend
To win her grace whom all commend.
There let Hymen[25] oft appear
In saffron robe, with taper clear,
And pomp, and feast, and revelry,
With masque and antique pageantry;
Such sights as youthful poets dream
On summer eves by haunted stream.   130
Then to the well-trod stage anon,
If Jonson's learned sock[26] be on,
Or sweetest Shakespeare, Fancy's child,
Warble his native wood-notes wild;
And ever against eating cares,
Lap me in soft Lydian[27] airs,
Married to immortal verse,
Such as the meeting soul may pierce
In notes with many a winding bout
Of linked sweetness long drawn out,   140
With wanton heed and giddy cunning,
The melting voice through mazes running,
Untwisting all the chains that tie
The hidden soul of harmony;
That Orpheus'[28] self may heave his head
From golden slumber on a bed
Of heaped Elysian[29] flowers, and hear
Such strains as would have won the ear
Of Pluto, to have quite set free
His half-regained Eurydice.   150
    These delights if thou canst give,
Mirth with thee I mean to live.

25   god of marriage.
26   *sock*: the *soccus*, a low-heeled slipper worn by actors in classical comedy, in contrast to the *cothurnus* or buskin worn in tragedy.
27   a mode of Greek music, soft and sweet.
28   In Greek legend, Orpheus was a wonderfully gifted musician. His wife Eurydice died and went down to the underworld. Orpheus charmed Pluto, god of the underworld, with his playing, and won his permission to take Eurydice back to earth. There was one condition: Orpheus must not look back during his passage through the underworld. He looked back to see if Eurydice were following, and she had to return forever to Hades.
29   pertaining to Elysium, abode of the blessed after death.

Il Penseroso[1]

Hence vain deluding Joys,
    The brood of Folly without father bred,

1   the contemplative man.

How little you bested,[2]
   Or fill the fixed mind with all your toys;
Dwell in some idle brain,
   And fancies fond[3] with gaudy shapes possess,
As thick and numberless
   As the gay motes that people the sunbeams,
Or likest hovering dreams,
   The fickle pensioners of Morpheus'[4] train.   10
But hail thou Goddess, sage and holy,
Hail divinest Melancholy,
Whose saintly visage is too bright
To hit the sense of human sight,
And therefore to our weaker view
O'erlaid with black, staid Wisdom's hue;
Black, but such as in esteem
Prince Memnon's sister[5] might beseem,
Or that starred Ethiop queen[6] that strove
To set her beauty's praise above   20
The sea nymphs, and their powers offended;
Yet thou art higher far descended:
Thee bright-haired Vesta long of yore
To solitary Saturn bore;[7]
His daughter she (in Saturn's reign
Such mixture was not held a stain).
Oft in glimmering bowers and glades
He met her, and in secret shades
Of woody Ida's[8] inmost grove,
Whilst yet there was no fear of Jove.[9]   30
   Come pensive Nun, devout and pure,
Sober, stedfast, and demure,
All in a robe of darkest grain,[10]
Flowing with majestic train,
And sable stole of cypress lawn,
Over thy decent shoulders drawn.
Come, but keep thy wonted state,
With even step and musing gait,
And looks commercing with the skies,
Thy rapt soul sitting in thine eyes;   40
There held in holy passion still,
Forget thyself to marble,[11] till

2   benefit.
3   foolish.
4   Greek god of dreams.
5   Memnon was a legendary Ethiopian king, dark of skin and noted for his beauty—a beauty presumably shared by his sister.
6   Cassiopeia. After her death she became one of the constellations.
7   Saturn was ruler of the gods during the Golden Age. His daughter Vesta was goddess of the hearth.
8   Mount Ida in Crete.
9   Jove overthrew his father, Saturn, and seized the throne.
10   color.
11   become as still as a statue.

With a sad leaden downward cast,
Thou fix them on the earth as fast.
And join with thee calm Peace and Quiet,
Spare Fast, that oft with gods doth diet,
And hears the Muses in a ring
Aye round about Jove's altar sing.
And add to these retired Leisure,
That in trim gardens takes his pleasure;   50
But first and chiefest, with thee bring
Him that yon soars on golden wing,
Guiding the fiery-wheeled throne,
The Cherub Contemplation;
And the mute Silence hist[12] along,
'Less Philomel[13] will deign a song,
In her sweetest saddest plight,
Smoothing the rugged brow of Night,
While Cynthia[14] checks her dragon yoke,
Gently o'er the accustomed oak;   60
Sweet bird that shunn'st the noise of folly,
Most musical, most melancholy!
Thee chauntress of the woods among,
I woo to hear thy even-song;
And missing thee, I walk unseen
On the dry smooth-shaven green,
To behold the wandering moon,
Riding near her highest noon,
Like one that had been led astray
Through the Heaven's wide pathless way;   70
And oft, as if her head she bowed,
Stooping through a fleecy cloud.
Oft on a plat of rising ground
I hear the far-off curfew sound,
Over some wide-watered shore,
Swinging slow with sullen roar;
Or if the air will not permit,
Some still removed place will fit,
Where glowing embers through the room
Teach light to counterfeit a gloom,   80
Far from all resort of mirth,
Save the cricket on the hearth,
Or the bellman's drowsy charm,
To bless the doors from nightly harm.
Or let my lamp at midnight hour
Be seen in some high lonely tower,
Where I may oft outwatch the Bear,[15]

12   call quietly.
13   the nightingale.
14   the moon.
15   stay awake all night. The constellation Ursa Major, the Bear, is visible all night in
northern latitudes.

With thrice great Hermes,[16] or unsphere
The spirit of Plato[17] to unfold
What worlds or what vast regions hold   90
The immortal mind that hath forsook
Her mansion in this fleshly nook;
And of those dæmons that are found
In fire, air, flood, or under ground,
Whose power hath a true consent
With planet or with element.
Sometime let gorgeous Tragedy
In sceptred pall[18] come sweeping by,
Presenting Thebes, or Pelops' line,
Or the tale of Troy divine,[19]   100
Or what (though rare) of later age
Ennobled hath the buskined stage.[20]
   But, O sad Virgin, that thy power
Might raise Musæus[21] from his bower,
Or bid the soul of Orpheus sing
Such notes as, warbled to the string,
Drew iron tears down Pluto's cheek,
And made Hell grant what Love did seek;[22]
Or call up him[23] that left half told
The story of Cambuscan bold,
Or Camball, and of Algarsife,   110
And who had Canace to wife,
That owned the virtuous ring and glass,
And of the wondrous horse of brass,
On which theTartar king did ride;
And if aught else great bards beside
In sage and solemn tunes have sung,
Of tourneys and of trophies hung,
Of forests and enchantments drear,
Where more is meant than meets the ear.   120
   Thus Night oft see me in thy pale career,
Till civil-suited[24] Morn appear,
Not tricked and frounced as she was wont
With the Attic boy[25] to hunt,

16   Hermes Trismegistus, author (or authors) of Neo-Platonic writings.
17   call the soul of Plato back from its dwelling in the heavens.
18   cloak.
19   Milton is referring to works by Aeschylus, Sophocles, and Euripides. The Greek
writers of tragedy frequently wrote on themes taken from legends of Thebes and Troy
and the house of Atreus ("Pelops' line").
20   The actors in Greek tragedy wore *buskins*, boots reaching halfway to the knee with
high heels that gave the actor dignity.
21   mythical Greek poet to whom were attributed poems dealing with the mysteries of
Demeter at Eleusis.
22   see "L'Allegro," footnote 28.
23   Chaucer, who left unfinished "The Squire's Tale" of Cambuscan, king of Tartary,
and his children, Camball, Algarsife, and Canace.
24   dressed in ordinary day clothes.
25   Cephalus, grandson of the king of Attica. Cephalus was loved by Eos, goddess of
dawn.

But kerchieft in a comely cloud,
While rocking winds are piping loud,
Or ushered with a shower still,
When the gust hath blown his fill,
Ending on the rustling leaves,
With minute-drops[26] from off the eaves.   130
And when the sun begins to fling
His flaring beams, me Goddess bring
To arched walks of twilight groves,
And shadows brown that Silvan[27] loves,
Of pine or monumental oak,
Where the rude axe with heaved stroke
Was never heard the nymphs to daunt,
Or fright them from their hallowed haunt.
There in close covert by some brook,
Where no profaner eye may look,   140
Hide me from Day's garish eye,
While the bee with honied thigh,
That at her flowery work doth sing,
And the waters murmuring,
With such consort as they keep,
Entice the dewy-feathered Sleep;
And let some strange mysterious dream
Wave at his wings in airy stream
Of lively portraiture displayed,
Softly on my eyelids laid.   150
And as I wake, sweet music breathe
Above, about, or underneath,
Sent by some spirit to mortals good,
Or the unseen Genius of the wood.
    But let my due feet never fail
To walk the studious cloister's pale,
And love the high embowed roof,
With antic pillars massy proof,
And storied windows richly dight,
Casting a dim religious light.   160
There let the pealing organ blow
To the full-voiced choir below,
In service high and anthems clear,
As may with sweetness, through mine ear,
Dissolve me into ecstasies,
And bring all Heaven before mine eyes.
    And may at last my weary age
Find out the peaceful hermitage,
The hairy gown and mossy cell,
Where I may sit and rightly spell
Of every star that Heaven doth shew,   170

26 drops falling one a minute.
27 Silvanus, god of the woods and fields.

And every herb that sips the dew;
Till old experience do attain
To something like prophetic strain.
    These pleasures Melancholy give,
And I with thee will choose to live.

How Soon
Hath Time

How soon hath Time, the subtle thief of youth,
    Stol'n on his wing my three and twentieth year!
    My hasting days fly on with full career,
    But my late spring no bud or blossom shew'th.
Perhaps my semblance might deceive the truth,
    That I to manhood am arrived so near,[1]
    And inward ripeness doth much less appear,
    That some more timely-happy spirits indu'th.
Yet be it less or more, or soon or slow,
    It shall be still in strictest measure ev'n,
    To that same lot, however mean or high,
Towards which Time leads me, and the will of heav'n;
    All is, if I have grace to use it so,
    As ever in my great task Master's eye.

1 a reference to Milton's youthful appearance. He was known at Cambridge as "The Lady of Christ's" (College).

Lycidas

Yet once more, O ye laurels, and once more
Ye myrtles brown, with ivy never sere,
I come to pluck your berries harsh and crude,
And with forced fingers rude,
Shatter your leaves before the mellowing year.
Bitter constraint, and sad occasion dear,
Compels me to disturb your season due;
For Lycidas[1] is dead, dead ere his prime,
Young Lycidas, and hath not left his peer.
Who would not sing for Lycidas? he well knew   10
Himself to sing, and build the lofty rhyme.
He must not float upon his watery bier
Unwept, and welter[2] to the parching wind,

1 a pastoral name for Edward King, a fellow student of Milton at Cambridge, who drowned in the Irish seas in 1637.
2 toss about.

Without the meed[3] of some melodious tear.
   Begin then, Sisters[4] of the sacred well,
That from beneath the seat of Jove doth spring,
Begin, and somewhat loudly sweep the string.
Hence with denial vain, and coy excuse;
So may some gentle muse
With lucky words favor my destined urn,   20
And as he passes turn,
And bid fair peace be to my sable shroud.
For we were nursed upon the self-same hill,
Fed the same flock, by fountain, shade, and rill.
   Together both, ere the high lawns appeared
Under the opening eyelids of the Morn,
We drove a-field, and both together heard
What time the gray-fly winds her sultry horn,
Battening our flocks with the fresh dews of night,
Oft till the star that rose, at evening, bright   30
Toward Heaven's descent had sloped his westering wheel.
Meanwhile the rural ditties were not mute,
Tempered to the oaten flute;
Rough Satyrs danced, and Fauns with cloven heel
From the glad sound would not be absent long,
And old Damœtas[5] loved to hear our song.
   But O the heavy change, now thou art gone,
Now thou art gone, and never must return!
Thee Shepherd, thee the woods and desert caves,
With wild thyme and the gadding vine o'ergrown,   40
And all their echoes mourn.
The willows and the hazel copses green
Shall now no more be seen
Fanning their joyous leaves to thy soft lays.
As killing as the canker to the rose,
Or taint-worn to the weanling herds that graze,
Or frost to flowers that their gay wardrobe wear,
When first the white-thorn blows,
Such, Lycidas, thy loss to shepherd's ear.
   Where were ye Nymphs when the remorseless deep   50
Closed o'er the head of your loved Lycidas?
For neither were ye playing on the steep,
Where your old bards, the famous Druids, lie,
Nor on the shaggy top of Mona high,
Nor yet where Deva[6] spreads her wizard stream.
Ay me, I fondly dream!
Had ye been there—for what could that have done?

3 gift.
4 the Muses.
5 probably a Cambridge tutor.
6 Deva is a river in Wales; Mona, an island off Wales where the Druids, poets and
priests of the ancient Celtic religion, celebrated their rites.

What could the Muse herself that Orpheus bore,[7]
The Muse herself, for her enchanting son
Whom universal Nature did lament,   60
When by the rout that made the hideous roar,
His gory visage down the stream was sent,
Down the swift Hebrus to the Lesbian[8] shore.
   Alas! what boots it with uncessant care
To tend the homely slighted shepherd's trade,
And strictly meditate the thankless Muse?
Were it not better done as others use,
To sport with Amaryllis in the shade,
Or with the tangles of Neæra's[9] hair?
Fame is the spur that the clear spirit doth raise   70
(That last infirmity of noble mind)
To scorn delights, and live laborious days;
But the fair guerdon when we hope to find,
And think to burst out into sudden blaze,
Comes the blind Fury[10] with the abhorred shears,
And slits the thin-spun life. "But not the praise,"
Phœbus[11] replied, and touched my trembling ears;
"Fame is no plant that grows on mortal soil,
Nor in the glistering foil
Set off to the world, nor in broad rumor lies,   80
But lives and spreads aloft by those pure eyes
And perfect witness of all-judging Jove;
As he pronounces lastly on each deed,
Of so much fame in Heaven expect thy meed."
   O fountain Arethuse, and thou honored flood,
Smooth-sliding Mincius,[12] crowned with vocal reeds,
That strain I heard was of a higher mood.
But now my oat proceeds,
And listens to the Herald of the Sea
That came in Neptune's plea.   90
He asked the waves, and asked the felon winds,
What hard mishap hath doomed this gentle swain?
And questioned every gust of rugged wings
That blows from off each beaked promontory;
They knew not of his story,
And sage Hippotades[13] their answer brings,
That not a blast was from his dungeon strayed,
The air was calm, and on the level brine,

7   Orpheus was the son of Calliope, the muse of epic poetry. He was torn to pieces by
the Thracian women.
8   Orpheus's head was thrown into the Hebrus river, and floated to the island of
Lesbos.
9   Amaryllis and Neaera are pastoral maidens.
10   Atropos, one of the three Fates, who cuts the thread of life.
11   Apollo, god of poetry.
12   Arethuse and Mincius are a fountain and river associated with pastoral poetry.
13   Aeolus, god of winds.

Sleek Panope[14] with all her sisters played.
It was that fatal and perfidious bark,   100
Built in the eclipse, and rigged with curses dark,
That sunk so low that sacred head of thine.
    Next Camus,[15] reverend sire, went footing slow,
His mantle hairy, and his bonnet sedge,
Inwrought with figures dim, and on the edge
Like to that sanguine flower[16] inscribed with woe.
"Ah, who hath reft" (quoth he) "my dearest pledge?"
Last came, and last did go,
The Pilot of the Galilean Lake;
Two massy keys[17] he bore of metals twain   110
(The golden opes, the iron shuts amain).
He shook his mitred[18] locks, and stern bespake,
"How well could I have spared for thee, young swain,
Enough of such as for their bellies' sake,
Creep and intrude and climb into the fold!
Of other care they little reckoning make,
Than how to scramble at the shearers' feast,
And shove away the worthy bidden guest;
Blind mouths! that scarce themselves know how to hold
A sheep-hook, or have learnt aught else the least   120
That to the faithful herdsman's art belongs!
What recks it them? What need they? They are sped;
And when they list, their lean and flashy songs
Grate on their scrannel pipes of wretched straw;
The hungry sheep look up, and are not fed,
But swoln with wind and the rank mist they draw,
Rot inwardly, and foul contagion spread;
Besides what the grim wolf with privy paw
Daily devours apace, and nothing said;
But that two-handed engine at the door   130
Stands ready to smite once, and smite no more."
    Return Alpheus,[19] the dread voice is past
That shrunk thy streams; return Sicilian Muse,
And call the vales, and bid them hither cast
Their bells and flowrets of a thousand hues.
Ye valleys low where the mild whispers use
Of shades and wanton winds and gushing brooks,
On whose fresh lap the swart star[20] sparely looks,
Throw hither all your quaint enamelled eyes,

---

14   a sea nymph.
15   personification of the River Cam, Cambridge.
16   the hyacinth, which sprang from the blood of Hyacinthus, a young boy loved and accidentally killed by Apollo.
17   keys of the kingdom of heaven given to St. Peter (the "Pilot") by Christ.
18   *miter*: bishop's headdress.
19   river god in love with Arethusa.
20   Sirius, the Dog Star, whose rising in the late summer brings heat which may burn the landscape.

That on the green turf suck the honied showers,   140
Bring the rathe primrose that forsaken dies,
The tufted crow-toe, and pale jessamine,
The white pink, and the pansy freaked with jet,
The glowing violet,
The musk-rose, and the well-attired woodbine,
With cowslips wan that hang the pensive head,
And every flower that sad embroidery wears.
Bid amaranthus[21] all his beauty shed,
And daffadillies fill their cups with tears,   150
To strew the laureate hearse where Lycid' lies.
For so to interpose a little ease,
Let our frail thoughts dally with false surmise;
Ay me! whilst thee the shores and sounding seas
Wash far away, where'er thy bones are hurled,
Whether beyond the stormy Hebrides,
Where thou perhaps under the whelming tide
Visit'st the bottom of the monstrous world;
Or whether thou to our moist vows denied,
Sleep'st by the fable of Bellerus old,   160
Where the great Vision of the guarded mount[22]
Looks toward Namancos and Bayona's hold;[23]
Look homeward Angel now, and melt with ruth;
And, O ye dolphins, waft the hapless youth.
    Weep no more, woeful shepherds weep no more,
For Lycidas your sorrow is not dead,
Sunk though he be beneath the watery floor,
So sinks the day-star in the ocean bed,
And yet anon repairs his drooping head,
And tricks his beams, and with new-spangled ore,   170
Flames in the forehead of the morning sky:
So Lycidas, sunk low, but mounted high,
Through the dear might of Him that walked the waves,
Where other groves and other streams along,
With nectar pure his oozy locks he laves,
And hears the unexpressive nuptial song,
In the blest kingdoms meek of joy and love.
There entertain him all the saints above,
In solemn troops and sweet societies
That sing, and singing in their glory move,   180
And wipe the tears for ever from his eyes.
Now Lycidas, the shepherds weep no more;
Henceforth thou art the Genius of the shore,
In thy large recompense, and shalt be good

---

21   an imaginary flower that never fades.
22   Bellerus is a legendary hero after whom the Romans named a part of Cornwall,
where there is a mountain guarded by the archangel Michael.
23   a Spanish fortification in Namancos, a mountainous region on the northwest coast
of Spain.

To all that wander in that perilous flood.
   Thus sang the uncouth swain to the oaks and rills,
While the still Morn went out with sandals gray;
He touched the tender stops of various quills,
With eager thought warbling his Doric[24] lay.
And now the sun had stretched out all the hills,   190
And now was dropped into the western bay;
At last he rose, and twitched his mantle blue:
To-morrow to fresh woods, and pastures new.

24   the dialect in which Greek pastorals were written.

When I Consider

When I consider how my light is spent,
      Ere half my days, in this dark world and wide,
      And that one talent[1] which is death to hide
Lodged with me useless, though my soul more bent
To serve therewith my Maker, and present
      My true account, lest He returning chide,
      "Doth God exact day-labor, light denied,"
I fondly[2] ask. But Patience to prevent
That murmur, soon replies, "God doth not need
      Either man's works or his own gifts. Who best
      Bear his mild yoke, they serve him best. His state
Is kingly: thousands at his bidding speed
      And post o'er land and ocean without rest;
      They also serve who only stand and wait."

1   refers to the parable of the servants to whom various talents (weights of gold) were
entrusted. The man who received only one talent neglected it and deserved the reproach
of his master (Matthew, 25. 14–30).
2   foolishly.

SIR JOHN SUCKLING   [1609–1642]

Song

Why so pale and wan, fond lover?
      Prithee why so pale?
Will, when looking well can't move her,
      Looking ill prevail?
      Prithee why so pale?

Why so dull and mute, young sinner?
      Prithee why so mute?
Will, when speaking well can't win her,

Saying nothing do 't?
Prithee why so mute?

Quit, quit, for shame; this will not move,
    This cannot take her;
If of herself she will not love,
    Nothing can make her:
    The devil take her!

RICHARD LOVELACE   [1618–1658]

To Lucasta, Going to the Wars

Tell me not, Sweet, I am unkind
    That from the nunnery
Of thy chaste breast and quiet mind
    To war and arms I fly.

True, a new mistress now I chase,
    The first foe in the field;
And with a stronger faith embrace
    A sword, a horse, a shield.

Yet this inconstancy is such
    As you too shall adore;
I could not love thee, Dear, so much,
    Loved I not Honor more.

To Althea, from Prison[1]

When Love with unconfined wings
    Hovers within my gates,
And my divine Althea brings
    To whisper at the grates;
When I lie tangled in her hair,
    And fetter'd to her eye,
The gods that wanton in the air
    Know no such liberty.

---

1   Lovelace was imprisoned for a while in 1642 for political reasons.

When flowing cups run swiftly round
    With no allaying Thames,   10
Our careless heads with roses bound,
    Our hearts with loyal flames;
When thirsty grief in wine we steep,
    When healths and draughts go free,
Fishes that tipple in the deep
    Know no such liberty.

When, like committed[2] linnets, I
    With shriller throat shall sing
The sweetness, mercy, majesty,
    And glories of my king;   20
When I shall voice aloud how good
    He is, how great should be;
Enlarged winds that curl the flood
    Know no such liberty.

Stone walls do not a prison make,
    Nor iron bars a cage;
Minds innocent and quiet take
    That for an hermitage;
If I have freedom in my love,
    And in my soul am free,   30
Angels alone that soar above
    Enjoy such liberty.

2   imprisoned.

ANDREW MARVELL   [1621–1678]

The Definition of Love

My love is of a birth as rare
As 'tis for object[1] strange and high;
It was begotten by despair
Upon impossibility.

Magnanimous despair alone
Could show me so divine a thing,
Where feeble hope could ne'er have flown,
But vainly flapped its tinsel wing.

And yet I quickly might arrive
Where my extended soul is fixed,   10

1   in the philosophical sense of *objectum*, a thing thrown before the mind.

But fate does iron wedges drive,
And always crowds itself betwixt.

For fate with jealous eye does see
Two perfect loves, nor lets them close;[2]
Their union would her ruin be,
And her tyrannic power depose.

And therefore her decrees of steel
Us as the distant poles have placed,
Though love's whole world on us doth wheel,
Not by themselves to be embraced;   20

Unless the giddy heaven fall,
And earth some new convulsion tear,
And, us to join, the world should all
Be cramped into a planisphere.[3]

As lines, so loves, oblique may well
Themselves in every angle greet;
But ours so truly parallel,
Though infinite, can never meet.

Therefore the love which us doth bind,
But fate so enviously debars,   30
Is the conjunction of the mind,
And opposition[4] of the stars.

2   unite.
3   a sphere represented on a plane.
4   *conjunction*: the astronomical term for the apparent proximity of two planets or
stars; *opposition*: the relative position of two heavenly bodies when exactly opposite each
other as seen from the earth's surface.

To His
Coy Mistress

Had we but world enough, and time,
This coyness, lady, were no crime.
We would sit down, and think which way
To walk, and pass our long love's day.
Thou by the Indian Ganges' side
Should'st rubies find: I by the tide
Of Humber[1] would complain. I would
Love you ten years before the Flood,
And you should, if you please, refuse
Till the conversion of the Jews.   10

1   river flowing by Hull, where Marvell lived.

My vegetable love should grow
Vaster than empires, and more slow.
An hundred years should go to praise
Thine eyes, and on thy forehead gaze:
Two hundred to adore each breast:
But thirty thousand to the rest;
An age at least to every part,
And the last age should show your heart.
For, lady, you deserve this state,
Nor would I love at lower rate.   20
    But at my back I always hear
Time's wingéd chariot hurrying near:
And yonder all before us lie
Deserts of vast eternity.
Thy beauty shall no more be found;
Nor, in thy marble vault, shall sound
My echoing song: then worms shall try
That long-preserved virginity,
And your quaint honor turn to dust,
And into ashes all my lust.   30
The grave's a fine and private place,
But none, I think, do there embrace.
    Now, therefore, while the youthful glew[2]
Sits on thy skin like morning dew,
And while thy willing soul transpires
At every pore with instant fires,
Now let us sport us while we may;
And now, like amorous birds of prey,
Rather at once our Time devour,
Than languish in his slow-chapt[3] power.   40
Let us roll all our strength and all
Our sweetness up into one ball,
And tear our pleasures with rough strife
Thorough the iron gates of life.
Thus, though we cannot make our sun
Stand still, yet we will make him run.

2   glow.
3   slow-devouring.

An Horatian Ode

Upon Cromwell's Return from Ireland[1]

The forward youth that would appear
Must now forsake his Muses dear,

1   Oliver Cromwell (1599–1658) was responsible for the execution of King Charles I and became Lord Protector of England during its only period of republican rule. This poem was written after his suppression of mutiny in Ireland, following the king's execution, and before his march against Scotland where Charles II had been proclaimed king.

Nor in the shadows sing
His numbers languishing.
'Tis time to leave the books in dust,
And oil the unused armor's rust,
    Removing from the wall
    The corslet of the hall.
So restless Cromwell could not cease
In the inglorious arts of peace,   10
    But through adventurous war
    Urged his active star:
And, like the three-fork'd lightning, first
Breaking the clouds where it was nursed,
    Did thorough his own side
    His fiery way divide.
For 'tis all one to courage high,
The emulous, or enemy;
    And with such, to enclose
    Is more than to oppose.   30
Then burning through the air he went,
And palaces and temples rent:
    And Caesar's[2] head at last
    Did through his laurels blast.[3]
'Tis madness to resist or blame
The force of angry Heaven's flame;
    And, if we would speak true,
    Much to the man is due,
Who, from his private gardens, where
He lived reserved and austere,   30
    As if his highest plot
    To plant the bergamot,[4]
Could by industrious valor climb
To ruin the great work of time,
    And cast the Kingdom old
    Into another mould.
Though Justice against Fate complain,
And plead the ancient rights in vain:
    But those do hold or break
    As men are strong or weak: 40
Nature, that hateth emptiness,
Allows of penetration[5] less,
    And therefore must make room
    Where greater spirits come.
What field of all the Civil Wars,
Where his were not the deepest scars?

2   Charles I.
3   Laurels were believed to be lightning-proof. They were traditionally worn by
emperors.
4   a kind of pear.
5   occupation of space by two bodies at the same time.

And Hampton[6] shows what part
    He had of wiser art:
Where, twining subtle fears with hope,
He wove a net of such a scope   50
    That Charles himself might chase
    To Carisbrook's narrow case:
That thence the Royal Actor borne
The tragic scaffold might adorn;
    While round the armed bands
    Did clap their bloody hands.
He nothing common did or mean
Upon that memorable scene,
    But with his keener eye
    The axe's edge did try: 60
Nor called the Gods, with vulgar spite,
To vindicate his helpless Right,[7]
    But bowed his comely head
    Down, as upon a bed.
This was that memorable hour
Which first assured the forced power.
    So when they did design
    The Capitol's first line,
A bleeding Head, where they begun,
Did fright the architects to run;   70
    And yet in that the State
    Foresaw its happy fate.[8]
And now the Irish are ashamed
To see themselves in one year tamed:
    So much can one man do,
    That does both act and know.
They can affirm his praises best,
And have, though overcome, confessed
    How good he is, how just,
    And fit for highest trust;   80
Nor yet grown stiffer with command,
But still in the Republic's hand:
    How fit he is to sway[9]
    That can so well obey.
He to the Commons' feet presents
A Kingdom, for his first year's rents,
    And, what he may, forbears
    His fame, to make it theirs;
And has his sword and spoils ungirt,

6   In 1647, Charles I fled from Hampton Court to Carisbrooke Castle in the Isle of
Wight. It was rumored at the time that Cromwell had engineered this.
7   Divine Right, the doctrine that kings derived their authority directly from God and
were therefore responsible to Him alone.
8   When foundations were dug for the Capitol temple in Rome, a human head was
found intact. This was considered a good omen for the city's future.
9   rule.

To lay them at the public's skirt,   90
   So when the falcon high
   Falls heavy from the sky,
She, having killed, no more does search
But on the next green bow[10] to perch,
   Where, when he first does lure,
   The falconer has her sure.
What may not then our Isle presume
While victory his crest does plume!
   What may not others fear
   If thus he crown each year!   100
A Caesar he, ere long, to Gaul,
To Italy an Hannibal,[11]
   And to all States not free
   Shall climacteric be.[12]
The Pict no shelter now shall find
Within his particolor'd mind,[13]
   But, from this valour, sad
   Shrink underneath the plaid.[14]
Happy if in the tufted brake
The English hunter him mistake,   110
   Nor lay his hounds in near
   The Caledonian[15] deer.
But thou, the War's and Fortune's son,
March indefatigably on:
   And for the last effect
   Still keep thy sword erect:
Besides the force it has to fright
The spirits of the shady night,[16]
   The same arts that did gain
   A power must it maintain.   120

10   bough.
11   Julius Caesar, the Roman dictator, conquered Gaul (France) in his most famous
campaign. Hannibal was a Carthaginian general who occupied Italy for some years.
12   make a climax.
13   a pun on the derivation of the word *Pict*, meaning "painted." The Picts were a
Scottish tribe.
14   a Scottish cloak.
15   Scottish.
16   an allusion to the cross-hilt of the sword, which had the power to avert demons and
witches.

The Garden

How vainly men themselves amaze
To win the palm, the oak, or bays;
And their uncessant labors see
Crowned from some single herb or tree,
Whose short and narrow verged shade

Does prudently their toils upbraid;
While all flow'rs and all trees do close
To weave the garlands of repose.

Fair Quiet, have I found thee here,
And Innocence, thy sister dear?   10
Mistaken long, I sought you then
In busy companies of men.
Your sacred plants, if here below,
Only among the plants will grow.
Society is all but rude
To this delicious solitude.

No white nor red was ever seen
So am'rous as this lovely green.
Fond lovers, cruel as their flame,
Cut in these trees their mistress' name.   20
Little, alas, they know, or heed,
How far these beauties hers exceed!
Fair trees! where s'eer your barks I wound,
No name shall but your own be found.

When we have run our passions' heat,
Love hither makes his best retreat.
The gods, that mortal beauty chase,
Still in a tree did end their race.
Apollo hunted Daphne so,
Only that she might laurel grow.   30
And Pan did after Syrinx speed
Not as a nymph, but for a reed.[1]

What wond'rous life in this I lead!
Ripe apples drop about my head;
The luscious clusters of the vine
Upon my mouth do crush their wine;
The nectarine, and curious[2] peach
Into my hands themselves do reach;
Stumbling on melons, as I pass,
Ensnared with flow'rs, I fall on grass.   40

Meanwhile the mind from pleasure less
Withdraws into its happiness:
The mind, that ocean where each kind
Does straight its own resemblance find;[3]
Yet it creates, transcending these,

1 Daphne was a river-god's daughter. Pursued by Apollo, she changed into a laurel
tree to escape him. Syrinx, in order to escape from Pan, turned into a reed; Pan made his
pipes from the reed.
2 exquisite.
3 an allusion ot the idea that all land animals had a counterpart in the sea.

140

Far other worlds, and other seas;
Annihilating all that's made
To a green thought in a green shade.

Here at the fountain's sliding foot,
Or at some fruit-tree's mossy root,   50
Casting the body's vest aside,
My soul into the boughs does glide;
There, like a bird, it sits and sings,
Then whets,[4] and combs its silver wings,
And, till prepared for longer flight,
Waves in its plumes the various light.

Such was that happy Garden-state[5]
While man there walked without a mate;
After a place so pure, and sweet,
What other help could yet be meet!   60
But 'twas beyond a mortal's share
To wander solitary there:
Two Paradises 'twere in one
To live in Paradise alone.

How well the skilful Gard'ner drew
Of flow'rs and herbs this dial new;[6]
Where, from above, the milder sun
Does from a fragrant Zodiac[7] run;
And, as it works, th' industrious bee
Computes its time as well as we.   70
How could such sweet and wholesome hours
Be reckoned, but with herbs and flow'rs!

4   preens.
5   the Garden of Eden.
6   a flower dial, a bed made up of flowers opening at different times, which formed a
clock.
7   an imaginary belt in the sky which contained the planets.

A Dialogue between
the Soul and Body

Soul

O who shall from this dungeon raise
A soul enslaved so many ways?
With bolts of bones, that fettered stands
In feet, and manacled in hands.
Here blinded with an eye; and there
Deaf with the drumming of an ear.
A soul hung up, as 'twere, in chains

Of nerves, and arteries, and veins.
Tortured, besides each other part,
In a vain head, and double heart.   10

Body

O who shall me deliver whole
From bonds of this tyrannic soul?
Which, stretched upright, impales me so,
That mine own precipice I go;
And warms and moves this needless frame:
(A fever could but do the same.)
And, wanting where its spite to try,
Has made me live to let me die.
A body that could never rest,
Since this ill spirit it possessed.   20

Soul

What magic could me thus confine
Within another's grief to pine?
Where whatsoever it complain,
I feel, that cannot feel, the pain.
And all my care itself employs,
That to preserve, which me destroys:
Constrained not only to endure
Diseases, but, what's worse, the cure:
And ready oft the port to gain,
Am shipwrecked into health again.   30

Body

But physic[1] yet could never reach
The maladies thou me dost teach;
Whom first the cramp of hope does tear;
And then the palsy shakes of fear.
The pestilence of love does heat:
Or hatred's hidden ulcer eat.
Joy's cheerful madness does perplex:
Or sorrow's other madness vex.
Which knowledge forces me to know;
And memory will not forgo.   40
What but a soul could have the wit
To build me up for sin so fit?
So architects do square and hew,
Green trees that in the forest grew.

1 medicine.

HENRY VAUGHAN   [1622–1695]

The Retreat

Happy those early days! when I
Shined in my angel-infancy.
Before I understood this place
Appointed for my second race,
Or taught my soul to fancy aught
But a white, celestial thought;
When yet I had not walked above
A mile or two from my first love,
And looking back, at that short space
Could see a glimpse of his bright face;   10
When on some gilded cloud or flower
My gazing soul would dwell an hour,
And in those weaker glories spy
Some shadows of eternity;
Before I taught my tongue to wound
My conscience with a sinful sound,
Or had the black art to dispense
A several[1] sin to every sense,
But felt through all this fleshly dress
Bright shoots of everlastingness.   20
    Oh, how I long to travel back,
And tread again that ancient track!
That I might once more reach that plain,
Where first I left my glorious train;
From whence the enlightened spirit sees
That shady city of palm trees;[2]
But ah! my soul with too much stay
Is drunk, and staggers in the way.
Some men a forward motion love,
But I by backward steps would move;   30
And when this dust falls to the urn,
In that state I came, return.

1 different.
2 as Moses was permitted a vision of the Promised Land, "the valley of Jericho, the
city of palm trees" (Deuteronomy, 34. 3).

They Are All
Gone into
the World of Light

They are all gone into the world of light!
    And I alone sit ling'ring here;

Their very memory is fair and bright,
      And my sad thoughts doth clear.

It glows and glitters in my cloudy breast,
      Like stars upon some gloomy grove,
Or those faint beams in which this hill is dressed,
      After the sun's remove.

I see them walking in an air of glory,
      Whose light doth trample on my days: 10
My days, which are at best but dull and hoary,
      Mere glimmering and decays.

O holy Hope! and high Humility,
      High as the heavens above!
These are your walks, and you have showed them me,
      To kindle my cold love.

Dear, beauteous Death! the jewel of the just,
      Shining nowhere, but in the dark;
What mysteries do lie beyond thy dust,
      Could man outlook that mark!   20

He that hath found some fledged bird's nest, may know
      At first sight if the bird be flown;
But what fair well or grove he sings in now,
      That is to him unknown.

And yet, as angels in some brighter dreams
      Call to the soul when man doth sleep,
So some strange thoughts transcend our wonted themes,
      And into glory peep.

If a star were confin'd into a tomb,
      Her captive flames must needs burn there;   30
But when the hand that locked her up, gives room,
      She'll shine through all the sphere.

O Father of eternal life, and all
      Created glories under Thee!
Resume Thy spirit from this world of thrall
      Into true liberty.

Either disperse these mists, which blot and fill
      My perspective,[1] still, as they pass:
Or else remove me hence unto that hill
      Where I shall need no glass.   40

1   telescope.

JOHN DRYDEN   [1631–1700]

To the Memory of Mr. Oldham[1]

Fare well, too little and too lately known,
Whom I began to think and call my own:
For sure our souls were near allied, and thine
Cast in the same poetic mold with mine.
One common note on either lyre did strike,
And knaves and fools we both abhorred alike.
To the same goal did both our studies drive:
The last set out the soonest did arrive.
Thus Nisus[2] fell upon the slippery place,
Whilst his young friend performed and won the race.
O early ripe! to thy abundant store
What could advancing age have added more?
It might (what nature never gives the young)
Have taught the numbers of thy native tongue.
But satire needs not those, and wit will shine
Through the harsh cadence of a rugged line.
A noble error, and but seldom made,
When poets are by too much force betrayed.
Thy gen'rous fruits, though gathered ere their prime,
Still showed a quickness; and maturing time
But mellows what we write to the dull sweets of rhyme.
Once more, hail, and farewell! farewell, thou young,
But ah! too short, Marcellus[3] of our tongue!
Thy brows with ivy and with laurels bound;
But fate and gloomy night encompass thee around.

1   John Oldham, a satiric poet, died at the age of 30.
2   In Virgil's *Aeneid*, 5. 315–39, Nisus slipped in the blood of a slain steer but tripped the runner-up and thus helped his friend Euryalus win the race.
3   nephew and heir to the emperor Augustus. He died at the age of 20.

A Song for St. Cecilia's Day[1]

1

From harmony, from heavenly harmony
    This universal frame began:
    When Nature underneath a heap
      Of jarring atoms lay,
    And could not heave her head,

1   St. Cecilia is the patron saint of music.

The tuneful voice was heard from high:
   "Arise, ye more than dead."
Then cold, and hot, and moist, and dry,
In order to their stations leap,
     And Music's power obey.   10
From harmony, from heavenly harmony
   This universal frame began:
   From harmony to harmony
Through all the compass of the notes it ran,
The diapason closing full in man.

2

What passion cannot Music raise and quell!
   When Jubal[2] struck the corded shell,
   His listening brethren stood around,
   And, wondering, on their faces fell
   To worship that celestial sound.   20
Less than a god they thought there could not dwell
   Within the hollow of that shell
   That spoke so sweetly and so well.
What passion cannot Music raise and quell!

3

   The trumpet's loud clangor
     Excites us to arms,
   With shrill notes of anger,
     And mortal alarms.
   The double double double beat
     Of the thundering drum   30
Cries: "Hark! the foes come;
Charge, charge, 'tis too late to retreat."

4

   The soft complaining flute
   In dying notes discovers
   The woes of hopeless lovers,
Whose dirge is whispered by the warbling lute.

5

   Sharp violins proclaim
Their jealous pangs, and desperation,
Fury, frantic indignation,
Depth of pains, and height of passion,   40
   For the fair, disdainful dame.

2   a descendant of Cain and "father of all those who play the lyre and pipe" (Genesis, 4. 21).

6

But O! what art can teach,
What human voice can reach,
   The sacred organ's praise?
   Notes inspiring holy love,
Notes that wing their heavenly ways
   To mend the choirs above.

7

Orpheus[3] could lead the savage race;
And trees unrooted left their place,
   Sequacious[4] of the lyre;   50
But bright Cecilia raised the wonder higher:
When to her organ vocal breath was given,
An angel heard, and straight appeared,
   Mistaking earth for heaven.

GRAND CHORUS
As from the power of sacred lays
   The spheres began to move,
And sung the great Creator's praise
   To all the blest above;
So, when the last and dreadful hour
This crumbling pageant shall devour,   60
The trumpet shall be heard on high,
The dead shall live, the living die,
And Music shall untune the sky.

3   in Greek mythology, a wonderfully gifted musician.
4   subservient, tractable (archaic).

All, All of a Piece[1]

All, all of a piece throughout;
Thy chase had a beast in view;
Thy wars brought nothing about;
Thy lovers were all untrue.
'Tis well an old age is out,
And time to begin a new.

1   from Dryden's *The Secular Masque*, written to celebrate New Year's Day, March 25, 1700, and given in an adaptation by Vanbrugh of Fletcher's comedy, *The Pilgrim*, designed for that date but postponed until April 29. The song was introduced in the madhouse scene that concludes Act 3.

JONATHAN SWIFT [1667–1745]

A Description
of the Morning

Now hardly here and there an hackney coach
Appearing, showed the ruddy morn's approach.
Now Betty from her master's bed had flown,
And softly stole to discompose her own;
The slipshod 'prentice from his master's door
Had pared the dirt, and sprinkled round the floor.
Now Moll had whirled her mop with dextrous airs,
Prepared to scrub the entry and the stairs.
The youth with broomy stumps began to trace
The kennel's edge,[1] where wheels had worn the place.
The small-coal man was heard with cadence deep,
Till drowned in shriller notes of chimney sweep:
Duns at his lordship's gate began to meet;
And brickdust Moll had screamed through half the street.
The turnkey now his flock returning sees,
Duly let out a-nights to steal for fees:
The watchful bailiffs take their silent stands,
And schoolboys lag with satchels in their hands.

1 edge of the gutter.

ALEXANDER POPE [1688–1744]

Epistle to
Dr. Arbuthnot[1]

Advertisement TO THE FIRST PUBLICATION OF THIS EPISTLE

This paper is a sort of bill of complaint, begun many years since, and
drawn up by snatches, as the several occasions offered. I had no thoughts
of publishing it, till it pleased some persons of rank and fortune (the au-
thors of *Verses to the Imitator of Horace*, and of an *Epistle to a Doctor of
Divinity from a Nobleman at Hampton Court*) to attack, in a very ex-
traordinary manner, not only my writings (of which, being public, the
public is judge) but my person, morals, and family, whereof, to those who
know me not, a truer information may be requisite. Being divided be-
tween the necessity to say something of myself, and my own laziness to
undertake so awkward a task, I thought it the shortest way to put the last
hand to this Epistle. If it have anything pleasing, it will be that by which

1 John Arbuthnot was a close and faithful friend of Pope, and, like Pope and Swift, a
member of the "Scriblerus Club," which produced satiric verse and prose. Arbuthnot
was Queen Anne's favorite physician.

I am most desirous to please, the truth and the sentiment; and if anything offensive, it will be only to those I am least sorry to offend, the vicious or the ungenerous.

Many will know their own pictures in it, there being not a circumstance but what is true; but I have, for the most part, spared their names, and they may escape being laughed at, if they please.

I would have some of them know, it was owing to the request of the learned and candid friend to whom it is inscribed, that I make not as free use of theirs as they have done of mine. However, I shall have this advantage, and honor, on my side, that whereas, by their proceeding, any abuse may be directed at any man, no injury can possibly be done by mine, since a nameless character can never be found out, but by its truth and likeness.

p. Shut, shut the door, good John! (fatigued, I said),
Tie up the knocker, say I'm sick, I'm dead.
The Dog Star[2] rages! nay 'tis past a doubt
All Bedlam, or Parnassus,[3] is let out:
Fire in each eye, and papers in each hand,
They rave, recite, and madden round the land.
    What walls can guard me, or what shades can hide?
They pierce my thickets, through my grot they glide,
By land, by water, they renew the charge,
They stop the chariot, and they board the barge.   10
No place is sacred, not the church is free;
Even Sunday shines no Sabbath day to me:
Then from the Mint[4] walks forth the man of rhyme,
Happy to catch me just at dinner time.
    Is there a parson, much bemused in beer,
A maudlin poetess, a rhyming peer,
A clerk foredoomed his father's soul to cross,
Who pens a stanza when he should engross?
Is there who, locked from ink and paper, scrawls
With desperate charcoal round his darkened walls?   20
All fly to Twit'nam,[5] and in humble strain
Apply to me to keep them mad or vain.
Arthur,[6] whose giddy son neglects the laws,
Imputes to me and my damned works the cause:
Poor Cornus[7] sees his frantic wife elope,
And curses wit, and poetry, and Pope.
    Friend to my life (which did not you prolong,
The world had wanted many an idle song)

2 Sirius, which is prominent in the heavens in late summer. In ancient Rome this was the customary time for rehearsing poetry.
3 Bedlam is the oldest English insane asylum; Parnassus is a mountain sacred to Apollo and the Muses.
4 a sanctuary for insolvent debtors.
5 Pope's home, Twickenham, a suburb of London.
6 Arthur Moore's son James, who adopted the name Smythe, wrote a comedy in which he incorporated some unpublished verses by Pope, with Pope's permission. The permission was later withdrawn, but Moore Smythe refused to take out the verses.
7 horn, caricatural name for cuckold.

What drop or nostrum can this plague remove?
Or which must end me, a fool's wrath or love?   30
A dire dilemma! either way I'm sped,
If foes, they write, if friends, they read me dead.
Seized and tied down to judge, how wretched I!
Who can't be silent, and who will not lie.
To laugh were want of goodness and of grace,
And to be grave exceeds all power of face.
I sit with sad civility, I read
With honest anguish and an aching head,
And drop at last, but in unwilling ears,
This saving counsel, "Keep your piece nine years."   40
    "Nine years!" cries he, who high in Drury Lane,[8]
Lulled by soft zephyrs through the broken pane,
Rhymes ere he wakes, and prints before term[9] ends
Obliged by hunger and request of friends:
"The piece, you think, is incorrect? why, take it,
I'm all submission, what you'd have it, make it."
    Three things another's modest wishes bound,
My friendship, and a prologue, and ten pound.
    Pitholeon[10] sends to me: "You know his Grace,
I want a patron; ask him for a place."   50
Pitholeon libeled me—"but here's a letter
Informs you, sir, 'twas when he knew no better.
Dare you refuse him? Curll[11] invites to dine,
He'll write a *Journal*, or he'll turn Divine."
Bless me! a packet—"'Tis a stranger sues,
A virgin tragedy, an orphan Muse."
If I dislike it, "Furies, death, and rage!"
If I approve, "Commend it to the stage."
There (thank my stars) my whole commission ends,
The players and I are, luckily, no friends.   60
Fired that the house reject him, "'Sdeath, I'll print it,
And shame the fools—Your interest, sir, with Lintot!"
Lintot, dull rogue, will think your price too much.
"Not, sir, if you revise it, and retouch."
All my demurs but double his attacks;
At last he whispers, "Do; and we go snacks."
Glad of a quarrel, straight I clap the door,
"Sir, let me see your works and you no more."
    'Tis sung, when Midas' ears began to spring
(Midas, a sacred person and a king),   70
His very minister who spied them first,
(Some say his queen) was forced to speak, or burst.[12]

8   London street and theater district.
9   *Terms* were judicial sessions, with which the publishing *seasons* were synchronized.
10 "A foolish poet at Rhodes who pretended much to Greek" (Pope).
11 Edmund Curll and Bernard Lintot (who is mentioned in the following lines) were
booksellers.
12 Midas, king of Phrygia, judged a musical contest between Pan and Apollo; when
Midas favored Pan, Apollo changed Midas' ears into those of an ass.

And is not mine, my friend, a sorer case,
When every coxcomb perks them in my face?
   A. Good friend, forbear! you deal in dangerous things.
I'd never name queens, ministers, or kings;
Keep close to ears, and those let asses prick;
'Tis nothing——P. Nothing? if they bite and kick?
Out with it, *Dunciad!*[13] let the secret pass,
That secret to each fool, that he's an ass: 80
The truth once told (and wherefore should we lie?)
The queen of Midas slept, and so may I.
   You think this cruel? take it for a rule,
No creature smarts so little as a fool.
Let peals of laughter, Codrus![14] round thee break,
Thou unconcerned canst hear the mighty crack.
Pit, box, and gallery in convulsions hurled,
Thou stand'st unshook amidst a bursting world.
Who shames a scribbler? break one cobweb through,
He spins the slight, self-pleasing thread anew: 90
Destroy his fib or sophistry, in vain;
The creature's at his dirty work again,
Throned in the center of his thin designs,
Proud of a vast extent of flimsy lines.
Whom have I hurt? has poet yet or peer
Lost the arched eyebrow or Parnassian sneer?
And has not Colley still his lord and whore?
His butchers Henley? his freemasons Moore?
Does not one table Bavius still admit?
Still to one bishop Philips seem a wit?   100
Still Sappho[15]——A. Hold! for God's sake—you'll offend.
No names—be calm—learn prudence of a friend.
I too could write, and I am twice as tall;
But foes like these!——P. One flatterer's worse than all.
Of all mad creatures, if the learn'd are right,
It is the slaver kills, and not the bite.
A fool quite angry is quite innocent:
Alas! 'Tis ten times worse when they repent.
   One dedicates in high heroic prose,
And ridicules beyond a hundred foes;   110
One from all Grub Street[16] will my fame defend,
And, more abusive, calls himself my friend.
This prints my letters, that expects a bribe,
And others roar aloud, "Subscribe, subscribe!"
   There are, who to my person pay their court:
I cough like Horace, and, though lean, am short;

13   Pope's mock heroic poem celebrating the triumph of dullness.
14   a poet ridiculed by Virgil and Juvenal.
15   Colley Cibber was a contemporary poet laureate; Henley preached on the uses of
the butcher's calling; Bavius was an enemy of the Roman poet Virgil; Philips, a rival of
Pope and secretary to an Irish archbishop. Sappho was a Greek poet of the seventh
century B.C.; the reference is to Lady Mary Wortley Montagu.
16   satiric name for Fleet Street, the publishing center of London.

Ammon's great son[17] one shoulder had too high,
Such Ovid's nose, and "Sir! you have an eye—"
Go on, obliging creatures, make me see
All that disgraced my betters met in me.   120
Say for my comfort, languishing in bed,
"Just so immortal Maro[18] held his head":
And when I die, be sure you let me know
Great Homer died three thousand years ago.
    Why did I write? what sin to me unknown
Dipped me in ink, my parents', or my own?
As yet a child, not yet a fool to fame,
I lisped in numbers, for the numbers came.
I left no calling for this idle trade,
No duty broke, no father disobeyed.   130
The Muse but served to ease some friend, not wife,
To help me through this long disease, my life,
To second, Arbuthnot! thy art and care,
And teach the being you preserved, to bear.
    A. But why then publish? P. Granville the polite,
And knowing Walsh, would tell me I could write;
Well-natured Garth inflamed with early praise,
And Congreve loved, and Swift endured my lays;
The courtly Talbot, Somers, Sheffield, read;
Even mitered Rochester would nod the head,   140
And St. John's self (great Dryden's friends before)
With open arms received one poet more.[19]
Happy my studies, when by these approved!
Happier their author, when by these beloved!
From these the world will judge of men and books,
Not from the Burnets, Oldmixons, and Cookes.[20]
    Soft were my numbers; who could take offense
While pure description held the place of sense?
Like gentle Fanny's[21] was my flowery theme,
A painted mistress, or a purling stream.   150
Yet then did Gildon draw his venal quill;
I wished the man a dinner, and sat still.
Yet then did Dennis[22] rave in furious fret;
I never answered, I was not in debt.
If I want provoked, or madness made them print,
I waged no war with Bedlam or the Mint.
    Did some more sober critic come abroad?
If wrong, I smiled; if right, I kissed the rod.
Pains, reading, study are their just pretense,

17 Alexander the Great.
18 Virgil.
19 Granville, Walsh, Garth, poets, and Congreve, the playwright, were contemporary
with Pope; and Talbot, Somers, Sheffield, the Bishop of Rochester, and Henry St. John
were statesmen and patrons of the arts.
20 "Authors of secret and scandalous history" (Pope).
21 reference to a poem by Thomas Parnell.
22 authors who had censured some of Pope's poetry.

And all they want is spirit, taste, and sense.   160
Commas and points they set exactly right,
And 'twere a sin to rob them of their mite.
Yet ne'er one sprig of laurel graced these ribalds,
From slashing Bentley down to piddling Tibbalds.[23]
Each wight who reads not, and but scans and spells,
Each word-catcher that lives on syllables,
Even such small critics some regard may claim,
Preserved in Milton's or in Shakespeare's name.
Pretty! in amber to observe the forms
Of hairs, or straws, or dirt, or grubs, or worms!   170
The things, we know, are neither rich nor rare,
But wonder how the devil they got there.
　　Were others angry? I excused them too;
Well might they rage; I gave them but their due.
A man's true merit 'tis not hard to find;
But each man's secret standard in his mind,
That casting weight pride adds to emptiness,
This, who can gratify? for who can guess?
The bard whom pilfered pastorals renown,
Who turns a Persian tale for half a crown,   180
Just writes to make his barrenness appear,
And strains from hard-bound brains eight lines a year:
He, who still wanting, though he lives on theft,
Steals much, spends little, yet has nothing left;
And he who now to sense, now nonsense leaning,
Means not, but blunders round about a meaning:
And he whose fustian's so sublimely bad,
It is not poetry, but prose run mad:
All these, my modest satire bade translate,
And owned that nine such poets made a Tate.[24]   190
How did they fume, and stamp, and roar, and chafe!
And swear, not Addison[25] himself was safe.
　　Peace to all such! but were there one whose fires
True Genius kindles, and fair Fame inspires;
Blessed with each talent and each art to please,
And born to write, converse, and live with ease:
Should such a man, too fond to rule alone,
Bear, like the Turk, no brother near the throne;
View him with scornful, yet with jealous eyes,
And hate for arts that caused himself to rise;   200
Damn with faint praise, assent with civil leer,
And without sneering, teach the rest to sneer;
Willing to wound, and yet afraid to strike,

23 Bentley had meddled with the text of Milton's *Paradise Lost*; Tibbald with Shakespeare's plays.
24 an inferior British poet who became poet laureate.
25 Joseph Addison, to whom Pope gives the name Atticus, was the author of a tragedy, *Cato*, but more important, reformed English taste and manners through his articles in *The Tatler* and *The Spectator*.

Just hint a fault, and hesitate dislike;
Alike reserved to blame or to commend,
A timorous foe, and a suspicious friend;
Dreading even fools; by flatterers besieged,
And so obliging that he ne'er obliged;
Like Cato, give his little senate laws,
And sit attentive to his own applause;   210
While wits and Templars every sentence raise,
And wonder with a foolish face of praise—
Who but must laugh, if such a man there be?
Who would not weep, if Atticus were he?
    What though my name stood rubric on the walls
Or plastered posts, with claps, in capitals?
Or smoking forth, a hundred hawkers' load,
On wings of winds came flying all abroad?
I sought no homage from the race that write;
I kept, like Asian monarchs, from their sight: 220
Poems I heeded (now berhymed so long)
No more than thou, great George![26] a birthday song.
I ne'er with wits or witlings passed my days
To spread about the itch of verse and praise;
Nor like a puppy daggled through the town
To fetch and carry sing-song up and down;
Nor at rehearsals sweat, and mouthed, and cried,
With handkerchief and orange at my side;
But sick of fops, and poetry, and prate,
To Bufo left the whole Castalian state.[27]   230
    Proud as Apollo on his forkéd hill,
Sat full-blown Bufo, puffed by every quill;
Fed with soft dedication all day long,
Horace and he went hand in hand in song.
His library (where busts of poets dead
And a true Pindar stood without a head)
Received of wits an undistinguished race,
Who first his judgment asked, and then a place:
Much they extolled his pictures, much his seat,
And flattered every day, and some days eat: 240
Till grown more frugal in his riper days,
He paid some bards with port, and some with praise;
To some a dry rehearsal was assigned,
And others (harder still) he paid in kind.
Dryden alone (what wonder?) came not nigh;
Dryden alone escaped this judging eye:
But still the great have kindness in reserve;
He helped to bury whom he helped to starve.

26   George II, King of England, 1727–1760.
27   Bufo, caricatural name for a patron; Castalia, a spring on Mt. Parnassus, sacred to
Apollo and the Muses, and hence a source of poetic inspiration.

May some choice patron bless each gray goose quill!
May every Bavius have his Bufo still!   250
So when a statesman wants a day's defense,
Or Envy holds a whole week's war with Sense,
Or simple Pride for flattery makes demands,
May dunce by dunce be whistled off my hands!
Blessed be the great! for those they take away,
And those they left me—for they left me Gay;[28]
Left me to see neglected genius bloom,
Neglected die, and tell it on his tomb;
Of all thy blameless life the sole return
My verse, and Queensberry weeping o'er thy urn!   260
Oh, let me live my own, and die so too!
("To live and die is all I have to do")
Maintain a poet's dignity and ease,
And see what friends, and read what books I please;
Above a patron, though I condescend
Sometimes to call a minister my friend.
I was not born for courts or great affairs;
I pay my debts, believe, and say my prayers,
Can sleep without a poem in my head,
Nor know if Dennis be alive or dead.   270
    Why am I asked what next shall see the light?
Heavens! was I born for nothing but to write?
Has life no joys for me? or (to be grave)
Have I no friend to serve, no soul to save?
"I found him close with Swift"—"Indeed? no doubt"
Cries prating Balbus, "something will come out."
'Tis all in vain, deny it as I will.
"No, such a genius never can lie still,"
And then for mine obligingly mistakes
The first lampoon Sir Will or Bubo makes.[29]   280
Poor guiltless I! and can I choose but smile,
When every coxcomb knows me by my style?
    Cursed be the verse, how well soe'er it flow,
That tends to make one worthy man my foe,
Give Virtue scandal, Innocence a fear,
Or from the soft-eyed virgin steal a tear!
But he who hurts a harmless neighbor's peace,
Insults fallen worth, or Beauty in distress,
Who loves a lie, lame Slander helps about,
Who writes a libel, or who copies out: 290
That fop whose pride affects a patron's name,
Yet absent, wounds an author's honest fame;
Who can your merit selfishly approve,

28 John Gay, close friend of Pope and author of the *Beggar's Opera*, had a monument
erected to him by the Duke of Queensberry.
29 Sir William Yonge and Bubb Dodington, Whig politicians and patrons of the arts.

And show the sense of it without the love;
Who has the vanity to call you friend,
Yet wants the honor, injured, to defend;
Who tells whate'er you think, whate'er you say,
And, if he lie not, must at least betray:
Who to the dean and silver bell can swear,
And sees at Cannons what was never there:[30]   300
Who reads but with a lust to misapply,
Make satire a lampoon, and fiction, lie:
A lash like mine no honest man shall dread,
But all such babbling blockheads in his stead.
Let Sporus[31] tremble——A. What? that thing of silk,
Sporus, that mere white curd of ass's milk?
Satire or sense, alas! can Sporus feel?
Who breaks a butterfly upon a wheel?
  P. Yet let me flap this bug with gilded wings,
This painted child of dirt, that stinks and stings;   310
Whose buzz the witty and the fair annoys,
Yet wit ne'er tastes, and beauty ne'er enjoys;
So well-bred spaniels civilly delight
In mumbling of the game they dare not bite.
Eternal smiles his emptiness betray,
As shallow streams run dimpling all the way.
Whether in florid impotence he speaks,
And, as the prompter breathes, the puppet squeaks;
Or at the ear of Eve, familiar toad,
Half froth, half venom, spits himself abroad,   320
In puns, or politics, or tales, or lies,
Or spite, or smut, or rhymes, or blasphemies.
His wit all seesaw between *that* and *this*,
Now high, now low, now master up, now miss,
And he himself one vile antithesis.
Amphibious thing! that acting either part,
The trifling head or the corrupted heart,
Fop at the toilet, flatterer at the board,
Now trips a lady, and now struts a lord.
Eve's tempter thus the rabbins[32] have expressed,   330
A cherub's face, a reptile all the rest;
Beauty that shocks you, parts that none will trust,
Wit that can creep, and pride that licks the dust.
  Not Fortune's worshiper, nor Fashion's fool,
Not Lucre's madman, nor Ambition's tool,
Not proud, nor servile, be one poet's praise,
That if he pleased, he pleased by manly ways:
That flattery, even to kings, he held a shame,

30 Pope's enemies unjustly accused him of satirizing the estate of the Duke of Chandos
at Cannons.
31 name for Lord Hervey, who had collaborated with Lady Mary Wortley Montagu in
attacks on Pope.
32 rabbis, Jewish theologians and scholars.

And thought a lie in verse or prose the same:
That not in fancy's maze he wandered long,   340
But stooped to truth, and moralized his song:
That not for fame, but Virtue's better end,
He stood the furious foe, the timid friend,
The damning critic, half approving wit,
The coxcomb hit, or fearing to be hit;
Laughed at the loss of friends he never had,
The dull, the proud, the wicked, and the mad;
The distant threats of vengeance on his head,
The blow unfelt, the tear he never shed;
The tale revived, the lie so oft o'erthrown,   350
The imputed trash, and dullness not his own;
The morals blackened when the writings 'scape,
The libeled person, and the pictured shape;[33]
Abuse on all he loved, or loved him, spread,
A friend in exile, or a father dead;
The whisper, that to greatness still too near,
Perhaps yet vibrates on his Sovereign's ear—
Welcome for thee, Fair Virtue! all the past!
For thee, fair Virtue! welcome even the last!
    A. But why insult the poor, affront the great?   360
    P. A knave's a knave to me in every state:
Alike my scorn, if he succeed or fail,
Sporus at court, or Japhet[34] in a jail,
A hireling scribbler, or a hireling peer,
Knight of the post corrupt, or of the shire,
If on a pillory, or near a throne,
He gain his prince's ear, or lose his own.
    Yet soft by nature, more a dupe than wit,
Sappho can tell you how this man was bit:
This dreaded satirist Dennis will confess   370
Foe to his pride, but friend to his distress:
So humble, he has knocked at Tibbald's door,
Has drunk with Cibber, nay, has rhymed for Moore.
Full ten years slandered, did he once reply?
Three thousand suns went down on Welsted's lie.[35]
To please a mistress one aspersed his life;
He lashed him not, but let her be his wife.
Let Budgell charge low Grub Street on his quill,
And write whate'er he pleased, except his will,
Let the two Curlls of town and court,[36] abuse   380
His father, mother, body, soul, and muse.
Yet why? that father held it for a rule,

33 Hervey ridiculed Pope's deformed back by an illustration in a book he published.
34 Japhet Crook, a forger.
35 "This man had the impudence to tell in print that Mr. P. had occasioned a Lady's death, and to name a person he never heard of" (Pope).
36 Budgell, poet and miscellaneous writer, was thought to have forged a will in order to obtain property; the two Curlls are the bookseller and Hervey.

It was a sin to call our neighbor fool;
That harmless mother thought no wife a whore:
Hear this, and spare his family, James Moore!
Unspotted names, and memorable long,
If there be force in virtue, or in song.
    Of gentle blood (part shed in honor's cause,
While yet in Britain honor had applause)
Each parent sprung——A. What fortune, pray?——P. Their own,   390
And better got than Bestia's[37] from the throne.
Born to no pride, inheriting no strife,
Nor marrying discord in a noble wife,
Stranger to civil and religious rage,
The good man walked innoxious through his age.
No courts he saw, no suits would ever try,
Nor dared an oath, nor hazarded a lie.
Unlearn'd, he knew no schoolman's subtle art,
No language but the language of the heart.
By nature honest, by experience wise,   400
Healthy by temperance, and by exercise;
His life, though long, to sickness passed unknown,
His death was instant, and without a groan.
Oh, grant me thus to live, and thus to die!
Who sprung from kings shall know less joy than I.
    O friend! may each domestic bliss be thine!
Be no unpleasing melancholy mine:
Me, let the tender office long engage,
To rock the cradle of reposing Age,
With lenient arts extend a mother's breath,   410
Make Languor smile, and smooth the bed of Death,
Explore the thought, explain the asking eye,
And keep a while one parent from the sky!
On cares like these if length of days attend,
May heaven, to bless those days, preserve my friend,
Preserve him social, cheerful, and serene,
And just as rich as when he served a Queen!
A. Whether that blessing be denied or given,
Thus far was right—the rest belongs to Heaven.

37   a Roman consul who was bribed to make a dishonorable peace.

SAMUEL JOHNSON   [1709–1784]

A Short Song
of Congratulation

Long-expected one and twenty,
Lingering year, at last is flown;

Pomp and pleasure, pride and plenty,
Great Sir John,[1] are all your own.

Loosen'd from the minor's tether,
Free to mortgage or to sell,
Wild as wind, and light as feather,
Bid the slaves of thrift farewell.

Call the Bettys, Kates, and Jennys,
Every name that laughs at care,
Lavish of your grandsire's guineas,
Show the spirit of an heir.

All that prey on vice and folly
Joy to see their quarry fly,
Here the gamester light and jolly,
There the lender grave and sly.

Wealth, Sir John, was made to wander,
Let it wander as it will:
See the jockey, see the pander,
Bid them come, and take their fill.

When the bonny blade carouses,
Pockets full, and spirits high,
What are acres? What are houses?
Only dirt, or wet or dry.

If the guardian or the mother
Tell the woes of wilful waste,
Scorn their counsel and their pother,
You can hang or drown at last.

1   The poem is addressed to the nephew of Henry Thrale, whose wife was a friend of
Johnson.

On the Death of Dr. Robert Levet[1]

Condemned to hope's delusive mine,
    As on we toil from day to day,
By sudden blasts, or slow decline,
    Our social comforts drop away.

Well tried through many a varying year,
    See LEVET to the grave descend;

1   Levet, a humble doctor, was a member of Johnson's household of poor dependents.

Officious,[2] innocent, sincere,
Of ev'ry friendless name the friend.

Yet still he fills affection's eye,
Obscurely wise, and coarsely kind;   10
Nor, lettered arrogance, deny
Thy praise to merit unrefined.

When fainting nature called for aid,
And hov'ring death prepared the blow,
His vig'rous remedy displayed
The power of art without the show.

In misery's darkest caverns known,
His useful care was ever nigh,
Where hopeless anguish poured his groan,
and lonely want retired to die.   20

No summons mocked by chill delay,
No petty gain disdained by pride,
The modest wants of ev'ry day
The toil of ev'ry day supplied.

His virtues walked their narrow round,
Nor made a pause, nor left a void;
And sure th'Eternal Master found
The single talent well employed.[3]

The busy day, the peaceful night,
Unfelt, uncounted, glided by;   30
His frame was firm, his powers were bright,
Tho' now his eightieth year was nigh.

Then with no throbbing fiery pain,
No cold gradations of decay,
Death broke at once the vital chain,
And freed his soul the nearest way.

2   kind.
3   a reference to the parable of the talents (Matthew, 25. 14–30). The servant who
multiplied the talent (a sum of money) left in his care was praised by the master; the
servant who merely hid the talent safely was blamed.

THOMAS GRAY   [1716–1771]

Ode
On the Death of a Favorite Cat,
Drowned in a Tub of Goldfishes

'Twas on a lofty vase's side,
Where China's gayest art had dyed
    The azure flowers, that blow;
Demurest of the tabby kind,
The pensive Selima reclined,
    Gazed on the lake below.

Her conscious tail her joy declared;
The fair round face, the snowy beard,
    The velvet of her paws,
Her coat, that with the tortoise vies,   10
Her ears of jet, and emerald eyes,
    She saw; and purred applause.

Still had she gazed; but 'midst the tide
Two angel forms were seen to glide,
    The Genii of the stream:
Their scaly armor's Tyrian hue
Thro' richest purple to the view
    Betrayed a golden gleam.

The hapless Nymph with wonder saw:
A whisker first and then a claw,   20
    With many an ardent wish,
She stretched in vain to reach the prize.
What female heart can gold despise?
    What Cat's averse to fish?

Presumptuous Maid! with looks intent
Again she stretched, again she bent,
    Nor knew the gulf between.
(Malignant Fate sat by, and smiled)
The slippery verge her feet beguiled,
    She tumbled headlong in.   30

Eight times emerging from the flood
She mewed to every watery God,
    Some speedy aid to send.
No Dolphin came, no Nereid stirred:
Nor cruel *Tom*, nor *Susan* heard.
    A Favorite has no friend!

From hence, ye Beauties, undeceived,
Know, one false step is ne'er retrieved,
    And be with caution bold.
Not all that tempts your wandering eyes   40
And heedless hearts, is lawful prize;
    Nor all, that glisters, gold.

Elegy

Written in a Country Churchyard

The curfew tolls the knell of parting day,
   The lowing herd wind slowly o'er the lea,
The plowman homeward plods his weary way,
   And leaves the world to darkness and to me.

Now fades the glimmering landscape on the sight,
   And all the air a solemn stillness holds,
Save where the beetle wheels his droning flight,
   And drowsy tinklings lull the distant folds;

Save that from yonder ivy-mantled tower
   The moping owl does to the moon complain   10
Of such, as wandering near her secret bower,
   Molest her ancient solitary reign.

Beneath those rugged elms, that yew-tree's shade,
   Where heaves the turf in many a mouldering heap,
Each in his narrow cell for ever laid,
   The rude forefathers of the hamlet sleep.

The breezy call of incense-breathing Morn,
   The swallow twittering from the straw-built shed,
The cock's shrill clarion, or the echoing horn,
   No more shall rouse them from their lowly bed.   20

For them no more the blazing hearth shall burn,
   Or busy housewife ply her evening care:
No children run to lisp their sire's return,
   Or climb his knees the envied kiss to share.

Oft did the harvest to their sickle yield,
   Their furrow oft the stubborn glebe[1] has broke;
How jocund did they drive their team afield!
   How bowed the woods beneath their sturdy stroke!

Let not Ambition mock their useful toil,
   Their homely joys, and destiny obscure;   30
Nor Grandeur hear with a disdainful smile
   The short and simple annals of the poor.

The boast of heraldry, the pomp of power,
   And all that beauty, all that wealth e'er gave,
Awaits alike the inevitable hour.
   The paths of glory lead but to the grave.

1 soil.

Nor you, ye proud, impute to these the fault,
    If Memory o'er their tomb no trophies raise,
Where through the long-drawn aisle and fretted vault
    The pealing anthem swells the note of praise.   40

Can storied urn or animated bust
    Back to its mansion call the fleeting breath?
Can honor's voice provoke the silent dust,
    Or flattery sooth the dull cold ear of death?

Perhaps in this neglected spot is laid
    Some heart once pregnant with celestial fire;
Hands, that the rod of empire might have swayed,
    Or waked to ecstasy the living lyre.

But Knowledge to their eyes her ample page
    Rich with the spoils of time did ne'er unroll;   50
Chill Penury repressed their noble rage,
    And froze the genial current of the soul.

Full many a gem of purest ray serene,
    The dark unfathomed caves of ocean bear:
Full many a flower is born to blush unseen,
    And waste its sweetness on the desert air.

Some village Hampden,[2] that with dauntless breast
    The little Tyrant of his fields withstood;
Some mute inglorious Milton here may rest,
    Some Cromwell guiltless of his country's blood.   60

The applause of listening senates to command,
    The threats of pain and ruin to despise,
To scatter plenty o'er a smiling land,
    And read their history in a nation's eyes,

Their lot forbade: nor circumscribed alone
    Their growing virtues, but their crimes confined;
Forbade to wade through slaughter to a throne,
    And shut the gates of mercy on mankind,

The struggling pangs of conscious truth to hide,
    To quench the blushes of ingenuous shame,   70
Or heap the shrine of Luxury and Pride
    With incense kindled at the Muse's flame.

Far from the madding crowd's ignoble strife,
    Their sober wishes never learned to stray;

2 John Hampden opposed Charles I's taxes, which were unconstitutionally imposed.

Along the cool sequestered vale of life
    They kept the noiseless tenor of their way.

Yet even these bones from insult to protect,
    Some frail memorial still erected nigh,
With uncouth rhymes and shapeless sculpture decked,
    Implores the passing tribute of a sigh.   80

Their name, their years, spelt by the unlettered muse,
    The place of fame and elegy supply:
And many a holy text around she strews,
    That teach the rustic moralist to die.

For who to dumb Forgetfulness a prey,
    This pleasing anxious being e'er resigned,
Left the warm precincts of the cheerful day,
    Nor cast one longing lingering look behind?

On some fond breast the parting soul relies,
    Some pious drops the closing eye requires;   90
Ev'n from the tomb the voice of Nature cries,
    Ev'n in our ashes live their wonted fires.

For thee, who mindful of the unhonored dead
    Dost in these lines their artless tale relate,
If chance, by lonely contemplation led,
    Some kindred spirit shall inquire thy fate,

Haply some hoary-headed swain may say,
    "Oft have we seen him at the peep of dawn
Brushing with hasty steps the dews away
    To meet the sun upon the upland lawn.   100

"There at the foot of yonder nodding beech
    That wreathes its old fantastic roots so high,
His listless length at noontide would he stretch,
    And pore upon the brook that babbles by.

"Hard by yon wood, now smiling as in scorn,
    Muttering his wayward fancies he would rove,
Now drooping, woeful wan, like one forlorn,
    Or crazed with care, or crossed in hopeless love.

"One morn I missed him on the customed hill,
    Along the heath and near his favorite tree;   110
Another came; nor yet beside the rill,
    Nor up the lawn, nor at the wood was he;

"The next with dirges due in sad array
    Slow through the church-way path we saw him borne.

Approach and read (for thou can'st read) the lay,
　Graved on the stone beneath yon agéd thorn."

THE EPITAPH
Here rests his head upon the lap of earth
　A youth to fortune and to fame unknown.
Fair Science frowned not on his humble birth,
　And Melancholy marked him for her own.　　　　　　　　　*120*

Large was his bounty, and his soul sincere,
　Heaven did a recompense as largely send:
He gave to Misery all he had, a tear,
　He gained from Heaven ('twas all he wished) a friend.

No farther seek his merits to disclose,
　Or draw his frailities from their dread abode,
(There they alike in trembling hope repose)
　The bosom of his Father and his God.

CHRISTOPHER SMART　[1722–1771]

from *Jubilate Agno*[1]

For I bless the PRINCE of PEACE and pray that all the guns may be nailed
　　up, save such are for the rejoicing days.
For I have abstained from the blood of the grape and that even at the
　　Lord's table.
For I have glorified God in GREEK and LATIN, the consecrated languages
　　spoken by the Lord on earth.
For I meditate the peace of Europe amongst family bickerings and domes-
　　tic jars.
For the HOST is in the WEST—The Lord make us thankful unto salvation.
For I preach the very GOSPEL of CHRIST without comment & with this
　　weapon shall I slay envy.
For I bless God in the rising generation, which is on my side.
For I have translated in the charity, which makes things better & I shall
　　be translated[2] myself at the last.
For he that walked upon the sea, hath prepared the floods with the Gos-
　　pel of peace.
For the merciful man is merciful to his beast, and to the trees that give
　　them shelter.　　　　　　　　　　　　　　　　　　　　　　　　10
For he hath turned the shadow of death into the morning, the Lord is his
　　name.

1　These lines are taken from a fragment of manuscript. Each line beginning with the
word *For* is in some manner a response to a line beginning with *Let*. But, as W. H. Bond
has said, Smart "intended the *Let* and *For* sections to be physically distinct." Therefore,
I have felt justified in omitting the corresponding *Let* passage—which is much inferior.
2　transformed, conveyed to heaven.

For I am come home again, but there is nobody to kill the calf or to play the musick.[3]

For the hour of my felicity, like the womb of Sarah,[4] shall come at the latter end.

For I shou'd have availed myself of waggery,[5] had not malice been multitudinous.

For there are still serpents that can speak—God bless my head, my heart & my heel.

For I bless God that I am of the same seed with Ehud, Mutius Scaevola and Colonel Draper.[6]

For the word of God is a sword on my side—no matter what other weapon a stick or a straw.

For I have adventured myself in the name of the Lord, and he hath marked me for his own.

For I bless God for the Postmaster general & all conveyancers of letters under his care especially Allen & Shevlock.[7]

For my grounds in New Canaan shall infinitely compensate for the flats & maynes of Staindrop Moor.[8]   20

For the praise of God can give to a mute fish the notes of a nightingale.

For I have seen the White Raven & Thomas Hall of Willingham & am myself a greater curiosity than both.[9]

For I look up to heaven which is my prospect to escape envy by surmounting it.

For if Pharaoh had known Joseph,[10] he would have blessed God & me for the illumination of the people.

For I pray God to bless improvements in gardening till London be a city of palm-trees.

For I pray to give his grace to the poor of England, that Charity be not offended & that benevolence may increase.

For in my nature I quested for beauty, but God, God hath sent me to sea for pearls.

For there is a blessing from the STONE of JESUS[11] which is founded upon hell to the precious jewell on the right hand of God.

For the nightly Visitor is at the window of the impenitent, while I sing a psalm of my own composing.

For there is a note added to the scale, which the Lord hath made fuller, stronger & more glorious.   30

---

3   a reference to the parable of the Prodigal Son (Luke, 15. 11–32).
4   Sarah, wife of Abraham, conceived in old age.
5   joking.
6   Ehud delivered the Israelites by killing the King of Moab; Mutius Scaevola delivered the Romans from tyranny by attempted murder of Porsena. Colonel Draper was a soldier and patron of Smart.
7   Ralph Allen began a system of cross-country posts. George Shevlock was Secretary to the Postmaster General.
8   Staindrop Moor lay adjacent to Raby Castle, the seat of the Vane family. Smart's father had been the Vanes' steward. Maynes: a wide expanse.
9   Albino ravens were displayed as curiosities. Thomas Hall was a "gigantic boy," a freak who died young.
10   The story of Joseph is told in Genesis, 37.50.
11   the White Stone of the Apocalypse (Revelations, 2.17).

WILLIAM BLAKE [1757–1827]

from *Songs of Innocence*

Introduction

Piping down the valleys wild,
Piping songs of pleasant glee,
On a cloud I saw a child,
And he laughing said to me:

"Pipe a song about a Lamb!"
So I piped with merry cheer.
"Piper, pipe that song again";
So I piped: he wept to hear.

"Drop thy pipe, thy happy pipe;
Sing thy songs of happy cheer":
So I sung the same again,
While he wept with joy to hear.

"Piper, sit thee down and write
In a book that all may read."
So he vanished from my sight,
And I plucked a hollow reed,

And I made a rural pen,
And I stained the water clear,
And I wrote my happy songs
Every child may joy to hear.

The Lamb

Does thou know who made thee?
Little Lamb, who made thee?
Gave thee life, and bid thee feed
By the stream and o'er the mead;
Gave thee clothing of delight,
Softest clothing, woolly, bright;
Gave thee such a tender voice,
Making all the vales rejoice?
   Little Lamb, who made thee?
   Dost thou know who made thee?

   Little Lamb, I'll tell thee,
   Little Lamb, I'll tell thee:

He is calléd by thy name,
For he calls himself a Lamb.
He is meek, and he is mild;
He became a little child.
I a child, and thou a lamb,
We are calléd by his name.
   Little Lamb, God bless thee!
   Little Lamb, God bless thee!

Holy Thursday

'Twas on a Holy Thursday, their innocent faces clean,
The children walking two and two, in red and blue and green,
Gray-headed beadles walked before, with wands as white as snow,
Till into the high dome of Paul's[1] they like Thames' waters flow.

O what a multitude they seemed, these flowers of London town!
Seated in companies they sit with radiance all their own.
The hum of multitudes was there, but multitudes of lambs,
Thousands of little boys and girls raising their innocent hands.

Now like a mighty wind they raise to heaven the voice of song,
Or like harmonious thunderings the seats of Heavens among.
Beneath them sit the aged men, wise guardians of the poor;
Then cherish pity, lest you drive an angel from your door.

1   St. Paul's Cathedral in London.

from *Songs of Experience*

Introduction

Hear the voice of the Bard!
Who Present, Past, and Future sees;
Whose ears have heard
The Holy Word
That walked among the ancient trees,

Calling the lapséd Soul,
And weeping in the evening dew;
That might control
The starry pole,
And fallen, fallen light renew!

"O Earth, O Earth, return!
Arise from out the dewy grass;
Night is worn,
And the morn
Rises from the slumberous mass.

"Turn away no more;
Why wilt thou turn away?
The starry floor,
The watery shore,
Is given thee till the break of day."

Earth's Answer

Earth raised up her head
From the darkness dread and drear.
Her light fled,
Stony dread!
And her locks covered with gray despair.

"Prisoned on watery shore,
Starry Jealousy does keep my den:
Cold and hoar,
Weeping o'er,
I hear the Father of the ancient men.

"Selfish Father of men!
Cruel, jealous, selfish fear!
Can delight,
Chained in night,
The virgins of youth and morning bear?

"Does spring hide its joy
When buds and blossoms grow?
Does the sower
Sow by night,
Or the plowman in darkness plow?

"Break this heavy chain
That does freeze my bones around.
Selfish! vain!
Eternal bane!
That free Love with bondage bound."

The Clod
and the Pebble

"Love seeketh not Itself to please,
Nor for itself hath any care,
But for another gives its ease,
And builds a Heaven in Hell's despair."

So sang a little Clod of Clay
Trodden with the cattle's feet,
But a Pebble of the brook
Warbled out these meters meet:

"Love seeketh only Self to please,
To bind another to Its delight,
Joys in another's loss of ease,
And builds a Hell in Heaven's despite."

Holy Thursday

Is this a holy thing to see
In a rich and fruitful land,
Babes reduced to misery,
Fed with cold and usurous hand?

Is that trembling cry a song?
Can it be a song of joy?
And so many children poor?
It is a land of poverty!

And their sun does never shine,
And their fields are bleak and bare,
And their ways are filled with thorns:
It is eternal winter there.

For where'er the sun does shine,
And where'er the rain does fall,
Babe can never hunger there,
Nor poverty the mind appall.

The Sick Rose

O Rose, thou art sick!
The invisible worm
That flies in the night,
In the howling storm,

Has found out thy bed
Of crimson joy:
And his dark secret love
Does thy life destroy.

The Tiger

Tiger! Tiger! burning bright
In the forests of the night,
What immortal hand or eye
Could frame thy fearful symmetry?

In what distant deeps or skies
Burnt the fire of thine eyes?
On what wings dare he aspire?[1]
What the hand dare seize the fire?

And what shoulder, and what art,
Could twist the sinews of thy heart?
And when thy heart began to beat,
What dread hand? and what dread feet?

What the hammer? what the chain?
In what furnace was thy brain?
What the anvil? what dread grasp
Dare its deadly terrors clasp?

When the stars threw down their spears,[2]
And watered heaven with their tears,
Did he smile his work to see?
Did he who made the Lamb make thee?

Tiger! Tiger! burning bright
In the forests of the night,
What immortal hand or eye
Dare frame thy fearful symmetry?

1 fly upward.
2 allusion to the fallen angels who rebelled against heaven.

London

I wander through each chartered[1] street,
Near where the chartered Thames does flow,

1 *to charter*: originally, to grant privileges or concede rights; in commercial usage, to
let or to hire by contract.

And mark in every face I meet
Marks of weakness, marks of woe.

In every cry of every Man,
In every Infant's cry of fear,
In every voice, in every ban,
The mind-forged manacles I hear.

How the Chimney-sweeper's cry
Every blackening Church appalls;
And the hapless Soldier's sigh
Runs in blood down Palace walls.

But most through midnight streets I hear
How the youthful Harlot's curse
Blasts the new born Infant's tear,
And blights with plagues the Marriage hearse.

Infant Sorrow

My mother groaned, my father wept;
Into the dangerous world I leapt:
Helpless, naked, piping loud,
Like a fiend hid in a cloud.

Struggling in my father's hands,
Striving against my swaddling bands,
Bound and weary I thought best
To sulk upon my mother's breast.

from Milton:
And Did Those Feet
in Ancient Time

And did those feet in ancient time
Walk upon England's mountains green?
And was the holy Lamb of God
On England's pleasant pastures seen?

And did the Countenance Divine
Shine forth upon our clouded hills?
And was Jerusalem builded here
Among these dark Satanic Mills?

Bring me my Bow of burning gold!
Bring me my Arrows of desire!

Bring me my Spear! O clouds unfold!
Bring me my Chariot of fire!

I will not cease from Mental Fight,
Nor shall my Sword sleep in my hand,
Till we have built Jerusalem
In England's green and pleasant Land.

Never Seek to Tell Thy Love

Never seek to tell thy love
Love that never told can be;
For the gentle wind does move
Silently, invisibly.

I told my love, I told my love,
I told her all my heart;
Trembling, cold, in ghastly fears,
Ah! she doth depart.

Soon as she was gone from me
A traveler came by
Silently, invisibly—
He took her with a sigh.

ROBERT BURNS [1759–1796]

Holy Willie's Prayer

And send the godly in a pet to pray—POPE.

ARGUMENT

Holy Willie was a rather oldish bachelor elder, in the parish of Mauchline,
and much and justly famed for that polemical chattering which ends in
tippling orthodoxy, and for that spiritualized bawdry which refines to li-
quorish devotion. In a sessional process with a gentleman in Mauchline—
a Mr. Gavin Hamilton—Holy Willie and his priest, Father Auld, after full
hearing in the Presbytery of Ayr, came off but second best, owing partly
to the oratorical powers of Mr. Robert Aiken, Mr. Hamilton's counsel; but
chiefly to Mr. Hamilton's being one of the most irreproachable and truly
respectable characters in the country. On losing his process, the muse
overheard him at his devotions as follows—

O Thou, wha in the Heavens dost dwell,
Wha, as it pleases best Thysel',
Sends ane to heaven and ten to hell,

A' for Thy glory,
And no for ony guid or ill
        They've done afore Thee!

I bless and praise Thy matchless might,
Whan thousands Thou has left in night,
That I am here afore Thy sight,
        For gifts an' grace   10
A burnin' an' a shinin' light,
        To a' this place.

What was I, or my generation,
That I should get sic° exaltation?   *such*
I, wha deserve most just damnation,
        For broken laws,
Sax° thousand years 'fore my creation   *six*
        Thro' Adam's cause.

When frae° my mither's womb I fell,   *from*
Thou might hae plunged me in Hell,   20
To gnash my gums, to weep and wail,
        In burnin' lakes,
Where damnéd devils roar and yell,
        Chained to their stakes;

Yet I am here a chosen sample,
To show Thy grace is great and ample;
I'm here a pillar in Thy temple,
        Strong as a rock,
A guide, a buckler, an example
        To a' Thy flock.   30

O Lord, Thou kens° what zeal I bear,   *knows*
When drinkers drink, and swearers swear,
And singin' there and dancing' here,
        Wi' great an' sma':
For I am keepit by thy fear
        Free frae them a'.

But yet, O Lord! confess I must
At times I'm fashed° wi' fleshly lust;   *plagued*
An' sometimes too, in warldly trust,
        Vile self gets in;   40
But Thou remembers we are dust,
        Defiled in sin.

O Lord! yestreen, Thou kens, wi' Meg—
Thy pardon I sincerely beg—
O! may't ne'er be a livin' plague

174

                To my dishonor,
An' I'll ne'er lift a lawless leg
                Again upon her.

Besides I farther maun° allow,   *must*
Wi' Lizzie's lass, three times I trow°—   *believe*
But, Lord, that Friday I was fou,°   *drunk*
                When I cam near her,
Or else Thou kens Thy servant true
                Wad never steer° her.   *touch*

May be Thou lets this fleshly thorn
Beset Thy servant e'en and morn
Lest he owre high and proud should turn,
                That he's sae gifted;
If sae, Thy hand maun e'en be borne,
                Until Thou lift it.   60

Lord, bless Thy chosen in this place,
For here Thou hast a chosen race;
But God confound their stubborn face,
                An' blast their name,
Wha bring Thy elders to disgrace
                An' public shame.

Lord, mind Gawn Hamilton's deserts,
He drinks, an' swears, an' plays at cartes,
Yet has sae mony takin' arts
                Wi' grit an' sma',   70
Frae God's ain priest the people's hearts
                He steals awa'.

An' when we chastened him therefor,
Thou kens how he bred sic a splore°   *disturbance*
As set the warld in a roar
                O' laughin' at us;
Curse Thou his basket and his store,
                Kail° and potatoes.   *cabbage*

Lord, hear my earnest cry an' pray'r,   80
Against that Presbyt'ry o' Ayr;
Thy strong right hand, Lord, make it bare
                Upo' their heads;
Lord, weigh it down, an' dinna spare,
                For their misdeeds.

O Lord my God, that glib-tongued Aiken,
My very heart and flesh are quakin',
To think how I sat sweatin', shakin',

An' pissed wi' dread,
While Auld wi' hingin' lip gaed sneakin',   90
    An' hid his head.

Lord, in the day o' vengeance try him;
Lord, visit them wha did employ him,
And pass not in Thy mercy by them,
    Nor hear their prayer:
But, for Thy people's sake, destroy them,
    And dinna spare.

But, Lord, remember me and mine
Wi' mercies temp'ral and divine,
That I for gear an' grace may shine   100
    Excelled by nane,
And a' the glory shall be Thine,
    Amen, Amen!

To a Mouse

On Turning Her Up in Her Nest, with the Plough, November, 1785

Wee, sleeket,° cowran, tim'rous beastie,	*smooth*
O, what a panic's in thy breastie!	
Thou need na start awa sae hasty,	
Wi' bickering brattle!°	*scurrying hurry*
I wad be laith° to rin an' chase thee,	*loath*
Wi' murd'ring pattle!°	*spade*

I'm truly sorry Man's dominion
Has broken Nature's social union,
An' justifies that ill opinion,
    Which makes thee startle,   10
At me, thy poor, earth-born companion,
    An' fellow-mortal!

I doubt na, whyles,° but thou may thieve;	*now and then*
What then? poor beastie, thou maun° live!	*must*
A daimen-icker in a thrave°	*occasional ear of corn in a sheaf*
'S a sma' request:	
I'll get a blessin wi' the lave,°	*remainder*
An' never miss 't!	

Thy wee-bit housie, too, in ruin!	
It's silly wa's the win's are strewin!	20
An' naething, now, to big° a new ane,	*build*
O' foggage° green!	*grass*
An' bleak December's winds ensuin,	
Baith snell° an' keen!	*bitter*

Thou saw the fields laid bare an' wast,
An' weary Winter comin fast,
An' cozie here, beneath the blast,
　　　　Thou thought to dwell,
Till crash! the cruel coulter° past　　　　*plough-blade*
　　　　Out thro' thy cell.　　　　30

That wee-bit heap o' leaves an' stibble,
Has cost thee monie a weary nibble!
Now thou's turn'd out, for a' thy trouble,
　　　　But° house or hald,　　　　*without*
To thole° the Winter's sleety dribble,　　　　*endure*
　　　　An' cranreuch° cauld!　　　　*hoar-frost*

But Mousie, thou art no thy-lane,°　　　　*alone*
In proving foresight may be vain:
The best laid schemes o' Mice an' Men
　　　　Gang aft agley,°　　　　*often go wrong*
An' lea'e us nought but grief an' pain,　　　　41
　　　　For promis'd joy!

Still, thou art blest, compar'd wi' me!
The present only toucheth thee:
But Och! I backward cast my e'e,
　　　　On prospects drear!
An' forward, tho' I canna see,
　　　　I guess an' fear!

O Whistle, and I'll Come to You, My Lad

O whistle, and I'll come to you, my lad;
O whistle, and I'll come to you, my lad;
Tho' father and mither and a' should gae mad,
O whistle, and I'll come to you, my lad.

But warily tent,° when ye come to court me,　　　　*heed*
And come na unless the back-yett° be a-jee°;　　　　*gate / ajar*
Syne up the back-stile, and let naebody see,
And come as ye were na comin' to me.
And come as ye were na comin' to me.

At kirk,° or at market, whene'er ye meet me,　　　　*church*
Gang° by me as tho' that ye car'd na a flee;　　　　*go*
But steal me a blink o' your bonnie black e'e,
Yet look as ye were na lookin' at me.
Yet look as ye were na lookin' at me.

Aye vow and protest that ye care na for me,
And whiles° ye may lightly my beauty a wee°;   *sometimes / little*
But court na anither, tho' jokin' ye be,
For fear that she wyle your fancy frae me.
For fear that she wyle your fancy frae me.

O, My Luve
Is Like
a Red, Red Rose

O, my luve is like a red, red rose
   That's newly sprung in June.
O, my luve is like the melodie
   That's sweetly played in tune.

As fair art thou, my bonnie lass,
   So deep in luve am I,
And I will luve thee still, my dear,
   Till a' the seas gang dry.

Till a' the seas gang dry, my dear,
   And the rocks melt wi' the sun:
And I will luve thee still, my dear,
   While the sands o' life shall run.

And fare thee weel, my only luve,
   And fare thee weel a while!
And I will come again, my luve,
   Though it were ten thousand mile.

WILLIAM WORDSWORTH   [1770–1850]

Lines Composed
a Few Miles
Above Tintern Abbey

   Five years have passed; five summers, with the length
Of five long winters! and again I hear
These waters, rolling from their mountain-springs
With a soft inland murmur. Once again
Do I behold these steep and lofty cliffs,
That on a wild secluded scene impress
Thoughts of more deep seclusion; and connect
The landscape with the quiet of the sky.

The day is come when I again repose
Here, under this dark sycamore, and view   10
These plots of cottage ground, these orchard tufts,
Which at this season, with their unripe fruits,
Are clad in one green hue, and lose themselves
'Mid groves and copses. Once again I see
These hedgerows, hardly hedgerows, little lines
Of sportive wood run wild; these pastoral farms,
Green to the very door; and wreaths of smoke
Sent up, in silence, from among the trees!
With some uncertain notice, as might seem
Of vagrant dwellers in the houseless woods,   20
Or of some Hermit's cave, where by his fire
The Hermit sits alone.

              These beauteous forms,
Through a long absence, have not been to me
As is a landscape to a blind man's eye;
But oft, in lonely rooms, and 'mid the din
Of towns and cities, I have owed to them,
In hours of weariness, sensations sweet,
Felt in the blood, and felt along the heart;
And passing even into my purer mind,
With tranquil restoration—feelings too   30
Of unremembered pleasure; such, perhaps,
As have no slight or trivial influence
On that best portion of a good man's life,
His little, nameless, unremembered, acts
Of kindness and of love. Nor less, I trust,
To them I may have owed another gift,
Of aspect more sublime; that blessed mood,
In which the burthen of the mystery,
In which the heavy and the weary weight
Of all this unintelligible world,   40
Is lightened—that serene and blessed mood,
In which the affections gently lead us on—
Until, the breath of this corporeal frame
And even the motion of our human blood
Almost suspended, we are laid asleep
In body, and become a living soul;
While with an eye made quiet by the power
Of harmony, and the deep power of joy,
We see into the life of things.

              If this
Be but a vain belief, yet, oh! how oft—   50
In darkness and amid the many shapes
Of joyless daylight; when the fretful stir
Unprofitable, and the fever of the world,

Have hung upon the beatings of my heart—
How oft, in spirit, have I turned to thee,
O sylvan Wye! thou wanderer through the woods,
How often has my spirit turned to thee!

And now, with gleams of half-extinguished thought,
With many recognitions dim and faint,
And somewhat of a sad perplexity,   60
The picture of the mind revives again;
While here I stand, not only with the sense
Of present pleasure, but with pleasing thoughts
That in this moment there is life and food
For future years. And so I dare to hope,
Though changed, no doubt, from what I was when first
I came among these hills; when like a roe
I bounded o'er the mountains, by the sides
Of the deep rivers, and the lonely streams,
Wherever nature led—more like a man   70
Flying from something that he dreads than one
Who sought the thing he loved. For nature then
(The coarser pleasures of my boyish days,
And their glad animal movements all gone by)
To me was all in all.—I cannot paint
What then I was. The sounding cataract
Haunted me like a passion; the tall rock,
The mountain, and the deep and gloomy wood,
Their colors and their forms, were then to me
An appetite; a feeling and a love,   80
That had no need of a remoter charm,
By thought supplied, nor any interest
Unborrowed from the eye.—That time is past,
And all its aching joys are now no more,
And all its dizzy raptures. Not for this
Faint I, nor mourn nor murmur; other gifts
Have followed; for such loss, I would believe,
Abundant recompense. For I have learned
To look on nature, not as in the hour
Of thoughtless youth; but hearing often times   90
The still, sad music of humanity,
Nor harsh nor grating, though of ample power
To chasten and subdue. And I have felt
A presence that disturbs me with the joy
Of elevated thoughts; a sense sublime
Of something far more deeply interfused,
Whose dwelling is the light of setting suns,
And the round ocean and the living air,
And the blue sky, and in the mind of man:
A motion and a spirit, that impels   100
All thinking things, all objects of all thought,
And rolls through all things. Therefore am I still

A lover of the meadows and the woods,
And mountains; and of all that we behold
From this green earth; of all the mighty world
Of eye, and ear—both what they half create,
And what perceive; well pleased to recognize
In nature and the language of the sense
The anchor of my purest thoughts, the nurse,
The guide, the guardian of my heart, and soul   110
Of all my moral being.

     Nor perchance,
If I were not thus taught, should I the more
Suffer my genial spirits to decay:
For thou art with me here upon the banks
Of this fair river; thou my dearest Friend,[1]
My dear, dear Friend; and in thy voice I catch
The language of my former heart, and read
My former pleasures in the shooting lights
Of thy wild eyes. Oh! yet a little while
May I behold in thee what I was once,   120
My dear, dear Sister! and this prayer I make,
Knowing that Nature never did betray
The heart that loved her; 'tis her privilege,
Through all the years of this our life, to lead
From joy to joy: for she can so inform
The mind that is within us, so impress
With quietness and beauty, and so feed
With lofty thoughts, that neither evil tongues,
Rash judgments, nor the sneers of selfish men,
Nor greetings where no kindness is, nor all   130
The dreary intercourse of daily life,
Shall e'er prevail against us, or disturb
Our cheerful faith, that all which we behold
Is full of blessings. Therefore let the moon
Shine on thee in thy solitary walk;
And let the misty mountain winds be free
To blow against thee: and, in after years,
When these wild ecstasies shall be matured
Into a sober pleasure; when thy mind
Shall be a mansion for all lovely forms,   140
Thy memory be as a dwelling place
For all sweet sounds and harmonies; oh! then,
If solitude, or fear, or pain, or grief
Should be thy portion, with what healing thoughts
Of tender joy wilt thou remember me,
And these my exhortations! Nor, perchance—
If I should be where I no more can hear
Thy voice, nor catch from thy wild eyes these gleams

1 his sister Dorothy.

Of past existence—wilt thou then forget
That on the banks of this delightful stream
We stood together; and that I, so long
A worshiper of Nature, hither came
Unwearied in that service; rather say
With warmer love—oh! with far deeper zeal
Of holier love. Nor wilt thou then forget,
That after many wanderings, many years
Of absence, these steep woods and lofty cliffs,
And this green pastoral landscape, were to me
More dear, both for themselves and for thy sake!

A Slumber
Did My Spirit Seal

A slumber did my spirit seal;
   I had no human fears;
She seemed a thing that could not feel
   The touch of earthly years.

No motion has she now, no force;
   She neither hears nor sees;
Rolled round in earth's diurnal course,
   With rocks, and stones, and trees.

My Heart
Leaps Up

My heart leaps up when I behold
   A rainbow in the sky:
So was it when my life began;
So is it now I am a man;
So be it when I shall grow old,
   Or let me die!
The Child is father of the Man;
And I could wish my days to be
Bound each to each by natural piety.

Resolution
and Independence

1

There was a roaring in the wind all night;
The rain came heavily and fell in floods;

But now the sun is rising calm and bright;
The birds are singing in the distant woods;
Over his own sweet voice the Stock-dove broods;
The Jay makes answer as the Magpie chatters;
And all the air is filled with pleasant noise of waters.

2

All things that love the sun are out of doors;
The sky rejoices in the morning's birth;
The grass is bright with rain-drops;—on the moors   10
The hare is running races in her mirth;
And with her feet she from the plashy earth
Raises a mist; that, glittering in the sun,
Runs with her all the way, wherever she doth run.

3

I was a Traveller then upon the moor;
I saw the hare that raced about with joy;
I heard the woods and distant waters roar;
Or heard them not, as happy as a boy:
The pleasant season did my heart employ;
My old remembrances went from me wholly;   20
And all the ways of men, so vain and melancholy.

4

But, as it sometimes chanceth, from the might
Of joy in minds that can no further go,
As high as we have mounted in delight
In our dejection do we sink as low;
To me that morning did it happen so;
And fears and fancies thick upon me came;
Dim sadness—and blind thoughts, I knew not, nor could name.

5

I heard the sky-lark warbling in the sky;
And I bethought me of the playful hare: 30
Even such a happy Child of earth am I;
Even as these blissful creatures do I fare;
Far from the world I walk, and from all care;
But there may come another day to me—
Solitude, pain of heart, distress, and poverty.

6

My whole life I have lived in pleasant thought,
As if life's business were a summer mood;
As if all needful things would come unsought
To genial faith, still rich in genial good;
But how can He expect that others should   40

Build for him, sow for him, and at his call
Love him, who for himself will take no heed at all?

7

I thought of Chatterton, the marvellous Boy,[1]
The sleepless Soul that perished in his pride;
Of Him who walked in glory and in joy[2]
Following his plough, along the mountain-side:
By our own spirits are we deified:
We Poets in our youth begin in gladness;
But thereof come in the end despondency and madness.

8

Now, whether it were by peculiar grace,   50
A leading from above, a something given,
Yet it befell that, in this lonely place,
When I with these untoward thoughts had striven,
Beside a pool bare to the eye of heaven
I saw a Man before me unawares:
The oldest man he seemed that ever wore grey hairs.

9

As a huge stone is sometimes seen to lie
Couched on the bald top of an eminence;
Wonder to all who do the same espy,
By what means it could thither come, and whence;   60
So that it seems a thing endued with sense:
Like a sea-beast crawled forth, that on a shelf
Of rock or sand reposeth, there to sun itself;

10

Such seemed this Man, not all alive nor dead,
Nor all asleep—in his extreme old age:
His body was bent double, feet and head
Coming together in life's pilgrimage;
As if some dire constraint of pain, or rage
Of sickness felt by him in times long past,
A more than human weight upon his frame had cast.   70

11

Himself he propped, limbs, body, and pale face,
Upon a long grey staff of shaven wood:
And, still as I drew near with gentle pace,
Upon the margin of that moorish flood
Motionless as a cloud the old Man stood,
That heareth not the loud winds when they call;
And moveth all together, if it move at all.

1 Thomas Chatteron (1752–1770) killed himself by taking arsenic.
2 Robert Burns (1759–1796), who tried to make a living at farming, but succumbed
to poverty and illness.

12

At length, himself unsettling, he the pond
Stirred with his staff, and fixedly did look
Upon the muddy water, which he conned,³   80
As if he had been reading in a book;
And now a stranger's privilege I took;
And, drawing to his side, to him did say,
"This morning gives us promise of a glorious day."

13

A gentle answer did the old Man make,
In courteous speech which forth he slowly drew:
And him with further words I thus bespake,
"What occupation do you there pursue?
This is a lonesome place for one like you."
Ere he replied, a flash of mild surprise   90
Broke from the sable orbs of his yet-vivid eyes.

14

His words came feebly, from a feeble chest,
But each in solemn order followed each,
With something of a lofty utterance drest—
Choice word and measured phrase, above the reach
Of ordinary men; a stately speech;
Such as grave Livers do in Scotland use,
Religious men, who give to God and man their dues.

15

He told, that to these waters he had come
To gather leeches,⁴ being old and poor: 100
Employment hazardous and wearisome!
And he had many hardships to endure:
From pond to pond he roamed, from moor to moor;
Housing, with God's good help, by choice or chance;
And in this way he gained an honest maintenance.

16

The old Man still stood talking by my side;
But now his voice to me was like a stream
Scarce heard; nor word from word could I divide;
And the whole body of the Man did seem
Like one whom I had met with in a dream;   110
Or like a man from some far region sent,
To give me human strength, by apt admonishment.

17

My former thoughts returned: the fear that kills;
And hope that is unwilling to be fed;

3 studied.
4 Leeches were used in medical treatment, for drawing blood.

Cold, pain, and labor, and all fleshly ills;
And might Poets in their misery dead.
—Perplexed, and longing to be comforted,
My question eagerly did I renew,
"How is it that you live, and what is it you do?"

18

He with a smile did then his words repeat;   120
And said that, gathering leeches, far and wide
He travelled; stirring thus about his feet
The waters of the pools where they abide.
"Once I could meet with them on every side;
But they have dwindled long by slow decay;
Yet still I persevere, and find them where I may."

19

While he was talking thus, the lonely place,
The old Man's shape, and speech—all troubled me:
In my mind's eye I seemed to see him pace
About the weary moors continually,   130
Wandering about alone and silently.
While I these thoughts within myself pursued,
He, having made a pause, the same discourse renewed.

20

And soon with this he other matter blended,
Cheerfully uttered, with demeanor kind,
But stately in the main; and when he ended,
I could have laughed myself to scorn to find
In that decrepit Man so firm a mind.
"God," said I, "be my help and stay secure;
I'll think of the Leech-gatherer on the lonely moor!"   140

Composed Upon Westminster Bridge

Earth has not anything to show more fair:
Dull would he be of soul who could pass by
A sight so touching in its majesty:
This city now doth, like a garment, wear
The beauty of the morning: silent, bare,
Ships, towers, domes, theaters, and temples lie
Open unto the fields, and to the sky;
All bright and glittering in the smokeless air.
Never did sun more beautifully steep
In his first splendor, valley, rock, or hill;
Ne'er saw I, never felt, a calm so deep!

The river glideth at his own sweet will:
Dear God! the very houses seem asleep;
And all that mighty heart is lying still!

The World Is
Too Much With Us

The world is too much with us; late and soon,
Getting and spending, we lay waste our powers:
Little we see in Nature that is ours;
We have given our hearts away, a sordid boon!
This Sea that bares her bosom to the moon;
The winds that will be howling at all hours,
And are up-gathered now like sleeping flowers;
For this, for everything, we are out of tune;
It moves us not—Great God! I'd rather be
A Pagan suckled in a creed outworn;
So might I, standing on this pleasant lea,
Have glimpses that would make me less forlorn;
Have sight of Proteus rising from the sea;
Or hear old Triton blow his wreathéd horn.

I Wandered
Lonely as a Cloud

I wandered lonely as a cloud
That floats on high o'er vales and hills,
When all at once I saw a crowd,
A host, of golden daffodils;
Beside the lake, beneath the trees,
Fluttering and dancing in the breeze.

Continuous as the stars that shine
And twinkle on the milky way,
They stretched in never-ending line
Along the margin of a bay:
Ten thousand saw I at a glance,
Tossing their heads in sprightly dance.

The waves beside them danced; but they
Out-did the sparkling waves in glee:
A poet could not but be gay,
In such a jocund company:
I gazed—and gazed—but little thought
What wealth the show to me had brought:

For oft, when on my couch I lie
In vacant or in pensive mood,
They flash upon that inward eye
Which is the bliss of solitude;
And then my heart with pleasure fills,
And dances with the daffodils.

Ode:

*Intimations of Immortality from
Recollections of Early Childhood*

1

There was a time when meadow, grove, and stream,
The earth, and every common sight,
    To me did seem
    Apparelled in celestial light,
The glory and the freshnesss of a dream.
It is not now as it hath been of yore;—
    Turn wheresoe'er I may,
    By night or day,
The things which I have seen I now can see no more.

2

    The Rainbow comes and goes,   10
    And lovely is the Rose;
    The Moon doth with delight
Look round her when the heavens are bare;
    Waters on a starry night
    Are beautiful and fair;
    The sunshine is a glorious birth;
    But yet I know, where'er I go,
That there hath past away a glory from the earth.

3

Now, while the birds thus sing a joyous song,
    And while the young lambs bound   20
    As to the tabor's sound,
To me alone there came a thought of grief:
A timely utterance gave that thought relief,
    And I again am strong:
The cataracts blow their trumpets from the steep;
No more shall grief of mine the season wrong;
I hear the Echoes through the mountains throng,
The Winds come to me from the fields of sleep,
    And all the earth is gay;   30
    Land and sea
    Give themselves up to jollity,

And with the heart of May
Doth every Beast keep holiday;—
Thou Child of Joy,
Shout round me, let me hear thy shouts, thou
happy Shepherd-boy!

4

Ye blessed Creatures, I have heard the call
Ye to each other make; I see
The heavens laugh with you in your jubilee;
My heart is at your festival,   40
My head hath its coronal,
The fulness of your bliss, I feel—I feel it all.
Oh evil day! if I were sullen
While Earth herself is adorning,
This sweet May-morning,
And the Children are culling
On every side,
In a thousand valleys far and wide,
Fresh flowers; while the sun shines warm,
And the Babe leaps up on his Mother's arm:—   50
I hear, I hear, with joy I hear!
—But there's a Tree, of many, one,
A single Field which I have looked upon,
Both of them speak of something that is gone;
The Pansy at my feet
Doth the same tale repeat:
Whither is fled the visionary gleam?
Where is it now, the glory and the dream?

5

Our birth is but a sleep and a forgetting:
The Soul that rises with us, our life's Star,   60
Hath had elsewhere its setting,
And cometh from afar:
Not in entire forgetfulness,
And not in utter nakedness,
But trailing clouds of glory do we come
From God, who is our home:
Heaven lies about us in our infancy!
Shades of the prison-house begin to close
Upon the growing Boy,
But He beholds the light, and whence it flows,   70
He sees it in his joy;
The Youth, who daily farther from the east
Must travel, still is Nature's Priest,
And by the vision splendid
Is on his way attended;
At length the Man perceives it die away,
And fade into the light of common day.

6

Earth fills her lap with pleasures of her own;
Yearnings she hath in her own natural kind,
And, even with something of a Mother's mind,   80
    And no unworthy aim,
    The homely Nurse doth all she can
To make her Foster-child, her Inmate Man,
    Forget the glories he hath known,
And that imperial palace whence he came.

7

Behold the Child among his new-born blisses,
A six years' Darling of a pigmy size!
See, where 'mid work of his own hand he lies,
Fretted by sallies of his mother's kisses,
With light upon him from his father's eyes!   90
See, at his feet, some little plan or chart,
Some fragment from his dream of human life,
Shaped by himself with newly-learnéd art;
    A wedding or a festival,
    A mourning or a funeral;
      And this hath now his heart,
    And unto this he frames his song:
      Then will he fit his tongue
To dialogues of business, love, or strife;
    But it will not be long   100
    Ere this be thrown aside,
    And with new joy and pride
The little Actor cons another part;
Filling from time to time his "humorous stage"
With all the Persons, down to palsied Age,
That Life brings with her in her equipage;
    As if his whole vocation
    Were endless imitation.

8

Thou, whose exterior semblance doth belie
    Thy Soul's immensity;   110
Thou best Philosopher, who yet dost keep
Thy heritage, thou Eye among the blind,
That, deaf and silent, read'st the eternal deep,
Haunted for ever by the eternal mind, —
    Mighty Prophet! Seer blest!
    On whom those truths do rest,
Which we are toiling all our lives to find,
In darkness lost, the darkness of the grave;
Thou, over whom thy Immortality
Broods like the Day, a Master o'er a Slave,   120
A Presence which is not to be put by;

To whom the grave
Is but a lonely bed without the sense or sight
Of day or the warm light,
A place of thought where we in waiting lie;
Thou little Child, yet glorious in the might
Of heaven-born freedom on thy being's height,
Why with such earnest pains dost thou provoke
The years to bring the inevitable yoke,
Thus blindly with thy blessedness at strife?   130
Full soon thy Soul shall have her earthly freight,
And custom lie upon thee with a weight,
Heavy as frost, and deep almost as life!

9

O joy! that in our embers
Is something that doth live,
That nature yet remembers
What was so fugitive!
The thought of our past years in me doth breed
Perpetrual benediction: not indeed
For that which is most worthy to be blest—   140
Delight and liberty, the simple creed
Of Childhood, whether busy or at rest,
With new-fledged hope still fluttering in his breast:—
Not for these I raise
The song of thanks and praise;
But for those obstinate questionings
Of sense and outward things,
Fallings from us, vanishings;
Blank misgivings of a Creature
Moving about in worlds not realised,   150
High instincts before which our mortal Nature
Did tremble like a guilty Thing surprised:
But for those first affections,
Those shadowy recollections,
Which, be they what they may,
Are yet the fountain-light of all our day,
Are yet a master-light of all our seeing;
Uphold us, cherish, and have power to make
Our noisy years seem moments in the being
Of the eternal Silence: truths that wake,   160
To perish never:
Which neither listlessness, nor mad endeavour,
Nor Man nor Boy,
Nor all that is at enmity with joy,
Can utterly abolish or destroy!
Hence in a season of calm weather
Though inland far we be,
Our Souls have sight of that immortal sea

Which brought us hither,
    Can in a moment travel thither,   170
And see the Children sport upon the shore,
And hear the mighty waters rolling evermore.

        10

Then sing, ye Birds, sing, sing a joyous song!
    And let the young Lambs bound
    As to the tabor's sound!
We in thought will join your throng,
    Ye that pipe and ye that play,
    Ye that through your hearts to-day
    Feel the gladness of the May!
What though the radiance which was once so bright   180
Be now for ever taken from my sight,
    Though nothing can bring back the hour
Of splendor in the grass, of glory in the flower;
    We will grieve not, rather find
    Strength in what remains behind;
    In the primal sympathy
    Which having been must ever be;
    In the soothing thoughts that spring
    Out of human suffering;
    In the faith that looks through death,   190
In years that bring the philosophic mind.

        11

And O, ye Fountains, Meadows, Hills, and Groves,
Forebode not any severing of our loves!
Yet in my heart of hearts I feel your might;
I only have relinquished one delight
To live beneath your more habitual sway.
I love the Brooks which down their channels fret,
Even more than when I tripped lightly as they;
The innocent brightness of a new-born Day
    Is lovely yet;   200
The Clouds that gather round the setting sun
Do take a sober coloring from an eye
That hath kept watch o'er man's mortality;
Another race hath been, and other palms are won.
Thanks to the human heart by which we live,
Thanks to its tenderness, its joys, and fears,
To me the meanest flower that blows can give
Thoughts that do often lie too deep for tears.

The Solitary Reaper

Behold her, single in the field,
Yon solitary Highland lass!

Reaping and singing by herself;
Stop here, or gently pass!
Alone she cuts and binds the grain,
And sings a melancholy strain;
O listen! for the vale profound
Is overflowing with the sound.

No nightingale did ever chaunt
More welcome notes to weary bands   10
Or travelers in some shady haunt,
Among Arabian sands:
A voice so thrilling ne'er was heard
In springtime from the cuckoo-bird,
Breaking the silence of the seas
Among the farthest Hebrides.

Will no one tell me what she sings?—
Perhaps the plaintive numbers flow
For old, unhappy, far-off things,
And battles long ago: 20
Or is it some more humble lay,
Familiar matter of today?
Some natural sorrow, loss, or pain,
That has been, and may be again?

Whate'er the theme, the maiden sang
As if her song could have no ending;
I saw her singing at her work,
And o'er the sickle bending;—
I listened, motionless and still;
And, as I mounted up the hill   30
The music in my heart I bore,
Long after it was heard no more.

SAMUEL TAYLOR COLERIDGE [1772–1834]

Kubla Khan

In Xanadu did Kubla Khan[1]
   A stately pleasure dome decree:
Where Alph, the sacred river, ran
Through caverns measureless to man
   Down to a sunless sea.
So twice five miles of fertile ground
With walls and towers were girdled round:

1 Kubla Khan founded the Mongol empire in the thirteenth century. Xanadu, Alph, and Mount Abora are modifications of exotic geographical names that Coleridge read of in books of travel and exploration.

And here were gardens bright with sinuous rills,
Where blossomed many an incense-bearing tree,
And here were forests ancient as the hills,   10
Enfolding sunny spots of greenery.

But oh! that deep romantic chasm which slanted
Down the green hill athwart a cedarn cover!
A savage place; as holy and enchanted
As e'er beneath a waning moon was haunted
By woman wailing for her demon lover!
And from this chasm, with ceaseless turmoil seething,
As if this earth in fast thick pants were breathing,
A mighty fountain momently was forced,
Amid whose swift half-intermitted burst   20
Huge fragments vaulted like rebounding hail,
Or chaffy grain beneath the thresher's flail:
And 'mid these dancing rocks at once and ever
It flung up momently the sacred river.
Five miles meandering with a mazy motion
Through wood and dale the sacred river ran,
Then reached the caverns measureless to man,
And sank in tumult to a lifeless ocean:
And 'mid this tumult Kubla heard from far
Ancestral voices prophesying war!   30

      The shadow of the dome of pleasure
      Floated midway on the waves;
      Where was heard the mingled measure
      From the fountain and the caves.
It was a miracle of rare device,
A sunny pleasure dome with caves of ice!

      A damsel with a dulcimer
      In a vision once I saw:
      It was an Abyssinian maid,
      And on her dulcimer she played,   40
      Singing of Mount Abora.
      Could I revive within me
      Her symphony and song,
      To such a deep delight 'twould win me,
That with music loud and long,
I would build that dome in air,
That sunny dome! those caves of ice!
And all who heard should see them there,
And all should cry, Beware! Beware!
His flashing eyes, his floating hair!
Weave a circle round him thrice,
And close your eyes with holy dread,
For he on honey-dew hath fed,
And drunk the milk of Paradise.

The Rime of
the Ancient Mariner

IN SEVEN PARTS

Facile credo, plures esse Naturas invisibiles quam visibiles in rerum universitate. Sed horum omnium familiam quis nobis enarrabit? et gradus et cognationes et discrimina et singulorum munera? Quid agunt? quae loca habitant? Harum rerum notitiam semper ambivit ingenium humanum, nunquam attigit. Juvat, interea, non diffiteor, quandoque in animo, tanquam in tabula, majoris et melioris mundi imaginem contemplari: ne mens assuefacta hodiernae vitae minutiis se contrahat nimis, et tota subsidat in pusillas cogitationes. Sed veritati interea in vigilandum est, modusque servandus, ut certa ab incertis, diem a nocte, distinguamus.

—*T. Burnet*, Archæol. Phil. *P. 68*

[I readily believe that there are more invisible than visible beings in the universe. But who will tell us the family, the ranks, the relationships, the differences, the respective functions of all these beings? What do they do? Where do they dwell? The human mind has circled around this knowledge, but has never reached it. Still, it is pleasant, I have no doubt, to contemplate sometimes in one's mind, as in a picture, the image of a bigger and better world; lest the mind, accustomed to the details of daily life, be too narrowed and settle down entirely on trifling thoughts. Meanwhile, however, we must be on the lookout for truth and observe restraint, in order that we may distinguish the certain from the uncertain, day from night.]

ARGUMENT

How a Ship having passed the Line was driven by storms to the cold Country towards the South Pole; and how from thence she made her course to the tropical Latitude of the Great Pacific Ocean; and of the strange things that befell: and in what manner the Ancyent Marinere came back to his own Country.

PART I

An ancient Mariner meeteth three Gallants bidden to a wedding-feast, and detaineth one.

It is an ancient Mariner,
And he stoppeth one of three.
"By thy long gray beard and glittering eye,
Now wherefore stopp'st thou me?

The Bridegroom's doors are opened wide,
And I am next of kin;
The guests are met, the feast is set:
May'st hear the merry din."

He holds him with his skinny hand,
"There was a ship," quoth he. 10

195

"Hold off! unhand me, graybeard loon!"
Eftsoons[1] his hand dropped he.

*The Wedding
Guest is spellbound
by the eye of the
old seafaring man,
and constrained to
hear his tale.*

He holds him with his glittering eye—
The Wedding Guest stood still,
And listens like a three years' child:
The Mariner hath his will.

The Wedding Guest sat on a stone:
He cannot choose but hear;
And thus spake on that ancient man,
The bright-eyed Mariner.   20

*The Mariner tells
how the ship sailed
southward with a
good wind and fair
weather, till it
reached the line.*[2]

"The ship was cheered,the habor cleared,
Merrily did we drop
Below the kirk, below the hill,
Below the lighthouse top.

The Sun came up upon the left,
Out of the sea came he!
And he shone bright, and on the right
Went down into the sea.

Higher and higher every day,
Till over the mast at noon—"   30
The Wedding Guest here beat his breast,
For he heard the loud bassoon.

*The Wedding
Guest heareth the
bridal music; but
the Mariner
continueth his tale.*

The bride hath paced into the hall,
Red as a rose is she;
Nodding their heads before her goes
The merry minstrelsy.

The Wedding Guest he beat his breast,
Yet he cannot choose but hear;
And thus spake on that ancient man,
The bright-eyed Mariner.   40

*The ship driven by
a storm towards the
south pole.*

"And now the STORM-BLAST came, and he
Was tyrannous and strong:
He struck with his o'ertaking wings,
And chased us south along.

With sloping masts and dipping prow,
As who pursued with yell and blow
Still treads the shadow of his foe,
And forward bends his head,
The ship drove fast, loud roared the blast,
And southward aye we fled.   50

1 at once.
2 equator.

196

And now there came both mist and snow,
And it grew wondrous cold:
And ice, mast-high, came floating by,
As green as emerald.

The land of ice, and of fearful sounds where no living thing was to be seen.

And through the drifts the snowy clifts
Did send a dismal sheen:
Nor shapes of men nor beasts we ken—
The ice was all between.

The ice was here, the ice was there,
The ice was all around: 60
It cracked and growled, and roared and howled,
Like noises in a swound!

Till a great sea-bird, called the Albatross, came through the snow-fog, and was received with great joy and hospitality.

At length did cross an Albatross,
Through the fog it came;
As if it had been a Christian soul,
We hailed it in God's name.

It ate the food it ne'er had eat,
And round and round it flew.
The ice did split with a thunder-fit;
The helmsman steered us through! 70

And lo! the Albatross proveth a bird of good omen, and followeth the ship as it returned northward through fog and floating ice.

And a good south wind sprung up behind;
The Albatross did follow,
And every day, for food or play,
Came to the mariner's hollo!

In mist or cloud, on mast or shroud,[3]
It perched for vespers nine;
Whiles all the night, through fog-smoke white,
Glimmered the white Moon-shine."

The ancient Mariner inhospitably killeth the pious bird of good omen.

"God save thee, ancient Mariner!
From the fiends, that plague thee thus!— 80
Why look'st thou so?"—"With my cross-bow
I shot the ALBATROSS.

PART II

The Sun now rose upon the right:
Out of the sea came he,
Still hid in mist, and on the left
Went down into the sea.

And the good south wind still blew behind,
But no sweet bird did follow,

3   rope extending from masthead to the side of the ship.

Nor any day for food or play
Came to the mariners' hollo!   90

*His shipmates cry
out against the
ancient Mariner,
for killing the bird
of good luck.*

And I had done a hellish thing,
And it would work 'em woe:
For all averred, I had killed the bird
That made the breeze to blow.
Ah wretch! said they, the bird to slay,
That made the breeze to blow!

*But when the fog
cleared off, they
justify the same,
and thus make
themselves accom-
plices in the crime.*

Nor dim nor red, like God's own head,
The glorious Sun uprist:
Then all averred, I had killed the bird
That brought the fog and mist,   100
'Twas right, said they, such birds to slay,
That bring the fog and mist.

*The fair breeze
continues; the ship
enters the Pacific
Ocean, and sails
northward, even
till it reaches the
Line.*

The fair breeze blew, the white foam flew,
The furrow followed free;
We were the first that ever burst
Into that silent sea.

*The ship hath been
suddenly
becalmed.*

Down dropped the breeze, the sails dropped down,
'Twas sad as sad could be;
And we did speak only to break
The silence of the sea!   110

All in a hot and copper sky,
The bloody Sun, at noon,
Right up above the mast did stand,
No bigger than the Moon.

Day after day, day after day,
We stuck, nor breath nor motion;
As idle as a painted ship
Upon a painted ocean.

*And the Albatross
begins to be
avenged.*

Water, water, every where
And all the boards did shrink;   120
Water, water, every where,
Nor any drop to drink.

The very deep did rot: O Christ!
That ever this should be!
Yea, slimy things did crawl with legs
Upon the slimy sea.

About, about, in reel and rout
The death-fires[4] danced at night;

4   phosphorescent light on the ship's rigging, an omen of disaster to sailors.

198

The water, like a witch's oils,
Burned green, and blue and white.   130

*A Spirit had
followed them; one
of the invisible
inhabitants of this
planet, neither
departed souls nor
angels; concerning*
whom the learned Jew, Josephus, and the Platonic Constantino-
politan, Michael Psellus, may be consulted. They are very
numerous, and there is no climate or element without one or more.

And some in dreams assuréd were
Of the Spirit that plagued us so;
Nine fathom deep he had followed us
From the land of mist and snow.

And every tongue, through utter drought,
Was withered at the root;
We could not speak, no more than if
We had been choked with soot.

*The shipmates, in
their sore distress,
would fain throw
the whole guilt on
the ancient
Mariner: in sign
whereof they hang
the dead sea bird round his neck.*

Ah! well a-day! what evil looks
Had I from old and young!   140
Instead of the cross, the Albatross
About my neck was hung.

PART III

There passed a weary time. Each throat
Was parched, and glazed each eye.
A weary time! a weary time!
How glazed each weary eye,
*The ancient
Mariner beholdeth
a sign in the
element afar off.*
When looking westward, I beheld
A something in the sky.

At first it seemed a little speck,   150
And then it seemed a mist;
It moved and moved, and took at last
A certain shape, I wist. [5]

A speck, a mist, a shape, I wist!
And still it neared and neared:
As if it dodged a water-sprite,
It plunged and tacked and veered.

*At its nearer
approach, it
seemeth him to be a
ship; and at a dear
ransom he freeth
his speech from the
bonds of thirst.*

With throats unslaked, with black lips baked,
We could nor laugh nor wail;
Through utter drought all dumb we stood!
I bit my arm, I sucked the blood,   160
And cried, A sail! a sail!

With throats unslaked, with black lips baked,
Agape they heard me call:
A flash of joy;
Gramercy! they for joy did grin,

5   knew.

And all at once their breath drew in,
As they were drinking all.

See! see! (I cried) she tacks no more!
Hither to work us weal;
Without a breeze, without a tide,
She steadies with upright keel!   170

The western wave was all aflame.
The day was well nigh done!
Almost upon the western wave
Rested the broad bright Sun;
When that strange shape drove suddenly
Betwixt us and the Sun.

And straight the Sun was flecked with bars,
(Heaven's Mother send us grace!)
As if through a dungeon-grate he peered
With broad and burning face.   180

Alas! (thought I, and my heart beat loud)
How fast she nears and nears!
Are those *her* sails that glance in the Sun,
Like restless gossameres?

Are those *her* ribs through which the Sun
Did peer, as through a grate?
And is that Woman all her crew?
Is that a DEATH? and are there two?
Is DEATH that woman's mate?

Her lips were red, *her* looks were free,   190
Her locks were yellow as gold:
Her skin was as white as leprosy,
The Night-mare LIFE-IN-DEATH was she,
Who thicks man's blood with cold.

The naked hulk alongside came,
And the twain were casting dice;
'The game is done! I've won! I've won!'
Quoth she, and whistles thrice.

The Sun's rim dips; the stars rush out:
At one stride comes the dark;   200
With far-heard whisper, o'er the sea,
Off shot the specter bark.

We listened and looked sideways up!
Fear at my heart, as at a cup,
My life-blood seemed to sip!

The stars were dim, and thick the night,
The steersman's face by his lamp gleamed white;
From the sails the dew did drip—
Till clomb above the eastern bar
The hornéd Moon, with one bright star   210
Within the nether tip.

One after one, by the star-dogged Moon,[6]
Too quick for groan or sigh,
Each turned his face with a ghastly pang,
And cursed me with his eye.

*His shipmates drop
down dead.*

Four times fifty living men,
(And I heard nor sigh nor groan)
With heavy thump, a lifeless lump,
They dropped down one by one.

*But Life-in-Death
begins her work on
the ancient
Mariner.*

The souls did from their bodies fly,—   220
They fled to bliss or woe!
And every soul, it passed me by,
Like the whizz of my cross-bow!"

PART IV

*The Wedding
Guest feareth that
a Spirit is talking to
him;*

"I fear thee, ancient Mariner!
I fear thy skinny hand!
And thou art long, and lank, and brown,
As is the ribbed sea-sand.

I fear thee and thy glittering eye,
And thy skinny hand, so brown."—

*But the ancient
Mariner assureth
him of his bodily
life, and
proceedeth to relate
his horrible
penance.*

"Fear not, fear not, thou Wedding Guest!   230
This body dropped not down.

Alone, alone, all, all alone,
Alone on a wide wide sea!
And never a saint took pity on
My soul in agony.

*He despiseth the
creatures of the
calm,*

The many men, so beautiful!
And they all dead did lie:
And a thousand thousand slimy things
Lived on; and so did I.

*And envieth that
they should live,
and so many be
dead.*

I looked upon the rotting sea,   240
And drew my eyes away;
I looked upon the rotting deck,
And there the dead men lay.

6   an omen of evil when a star "dogs the moon."

I looked to heaven, and tried to pray; ,
But or ever a prayer had gushed,
A wicked whisper came, and made
My heart as dry as dust.

I closed my lids, and kept them close,
And the balls like pulses beat;
For the sky and the sea, and the sea and the sky   250
Lay like a load on my weary eye,
And the dead were at my feet.

*But the curse liveth
for him in the eye
of the dead men.*
The cold sweat melted from their limbs.
Nor rot nor reek did they:
The look with which they looked on me
Had never passed away.

An orphan's curse would drag to hell
A spirit from on high;
But oh! more horrible than that
Is the curse in a dead man's eye!   260
Seven days, seven nights, I saw that curse,
And yet I could not die.

*In his loneliness
and fixedness he
yearneth towards
the journeying
Moon, and the stars
that still sojourn,
yet still move
onward; and every
where the blue sky
belong to them,
and is their
appointed rest,
and their native
country and their
own natural
homes, which they
enter unannounced, as lords that are certainly expected and yet
there is a silent joy at their arrival.*
The moving Moon went up the sky,
And no where did abide:
Softly she was going up,
And a star or two beside—

Her beams bemocked the sultry main,
Like April hoar-frost spread;
But where the ship's huge shadow lay,
The charméd water burnt alway   270
A still and awful red.

*By the light of the
Moon he beholdeth
God's creatures of
the great calm.*
Beyond the shadow of the ship,
I watched the water-snakes:
They moved in tracks of shining white,
And when they reared, the elfish light
Fell off in hoary flakes.

Within the shadow of the ship
I watched their rich attire:
Blue, glossy green, and velvet black,
They coiled and swam; and every track   280
Was a flash of golden fire.

O happy living things! no tongue
Their beauty might declare:

A spring of love gushed from my heart,
And I blessed them unaware:
Sure my kind saint took pity on me,
And I blessed them unaware.

The self-same moment I could pray;
And from my neck so free
The Albatross fell off, and sank   290
Like lead into the sea.

PART V

Oh sleep! it is a gentle thing,
Beloved from pole to pole!
To Mary Queen the praise be given!
She send the gentle sleep from Heaven,
That slid into my soul.

The silly[7] buckets on the deck,
That had so long remained,
I dreamt that they were filled with dew;
And when I awoke, it rained.   300

My lips were wet, my throat was cold,
My garments all were dank;
Sure I had drunken in my dreams,
And still my body drank.

I moved, and could not feel my limbs:
I was so light—almost
I thought that I had died in sleep,
And was a blessèd ghost.

And soon I heard a roaring wind:
It did not come anear;   310
But with its sound it shook the sails,
That were so thin and sere.

The upper air burst into life!
And a hundred fire-flags sheen,[8]
To and fro they were hurried about!
And to and fro, and in and out,
The wan stars danced between.

And the coming wind did roar more loud,
And the sails did sigh like sedge;
And the rain poured down from one black cloud;   320
The Moon was at its edge.

7 useless (because empty).
8 gleaming.

The thick black cloud was cleft, and still
The Moon was at its side:
Like waters shot from some high crag,
The lightning fell with never a jag,
A river steep and wide.

The bodies of the ship's crew are inspired and the ship moves on;

The loud wind never reached the ship,
Yet now the ship moved on!
Beneath the lightning and the Moon
The dead men gave a groan.   330

They groaned, they stirred, they all uprose,
Nor spake, nor moved their eyes;
It had been strange, even in a dream,
To have seen those dead men rise.

The helmsman steered, the ship moved on;
Yet never a breeze up-blew;
The mariners all 'gan work the ropes,
Where they were wont to do;
They raised their limbs like lifeless tools—
We were a ghastly crew.   340

The body of my brother's son
Stood by me, knee to knee:
The body and I pulled at one rope,
But he said nought to me."

"I fear thee, ancient Mariner!"
"Be calm, thou Wedding Guest!

But not by the souls of the men, nor by demons of earth or middle air, but by a blessed troop of angelic spirits, sent down by the invocation of the guardian saint.

'Twas not those souls that fled in pain,
Which to their corses came again,
But a troop of spirits blessed:

For when it dawned—they dropped their arms,   350
And clustered round the mast;
Sweet sounds rose slowly through their mouths,
And from their bodies passed.

Around, around, flew each sweet sound,
Then darted to the Sun;
Slowly the sounds came back again,
Now mixed, now one by one.

Sometimes adropping from the sky
I heard the skylark sing;
Sometimes all little birds that are,   360
How they seemed to fill the sea and air
With their sweet jargoning!

And now 'twas like all instruments,
Now like a lonely flute;
And now it is an angel's song,
That makes the heavens be mute.

It ceased; yet still the sails made on
A pleasant noise till noon,
A noise like of a hidden brook
In the leafy month of June,   370
That to the sleeping woods all night
Singeth a quiet tune.

Till noon we quietly sailed on,
Yet never a breeze did breathe:
Slowly and smoothly went the ship,
Moved onward from beneath.

*The lonesome
Spirit from the
south pole carries
on the ship as far as
the Line, in
obedience to the
angelic troop, but
still requireth
vengeance.*

Under the keel nine fathom deep,
From the land of mist and snow,
The spirit slid: and it was he
That made the ship to go.   380
The sails at noon left off their tune,
And the ship stood still also.

The Sun, right up above the mast,
Had fixed her to the ocean:
But in a minute she 'gan stir,
With a short uneasy motion—
Backwards and forwards half her length
With a short uneasy motion.

Then like a pawing horse let go,
She made a sudden bound: 390
It flung the blood into my head,
And I fell down in a swound.

*The Polar Spirit's
fellow demons, the
invisible inhab-
itants of the
element, take part
in his wrong; and
two of them relate,
one to the other,
that penance long
and heavy for the
ancient Mariner
hath been accorded
to the Polar Spirit,
who returneth
southward.*

How long in that same fit I lay,
I have not to declare;
But ere my living life returned,
I heard and in my soul discerned
Two voices in the air.

'Is it he?' quoth one, 'Is this the man?
By him who died on cross,
With his cruel bow he laid full low   400
The harmless Albatross.

The spirit who bideth by himself
In the land of mist and snow,

He loved the bird that loved the man
Who shot him with his bow.'

The other was a softer voice,
As soft as honey dew:
Quoth he, 'The man hath penance done,
And penance more will do.'

PART VI

First Voice
'But tell me, tell me! speak again,   410
Thy soft response renewing—
What makes that ship drive on so fast?
What is the ocean doing?'

Second Voice
'Still as a slave before his lord,
The ocean hath no blast;
His great bright eye most silently
Up to the Moon is cast—

If he may know which way to go;
For she guides him smooth or grim.
See, brother, see! how graciously   420
She looketh down on him.'

First Voice
'But why drive on that ship so fast,
Without or wave or wind?'

Second Voice
'The air is cut away before,
And closes from behind.

Fly, brother, fly! more high, more high!
Or we shall be belated:
For slow and slow that ship will go,
When the Mariner's trance is abated.'

I woke, and we were sailing on   430
As in a gentle weather:
'Twas night, calm night, the moon was high;
The dead men stood together.

All stood together on the deck,
For a charnel-dungeon fitter:
All fixed on me their stony eyes,
That in the Moon did glitter.

The Mariner hath been cast into a trance; for the angelic power causeth the vessel to drive northward faster than human life could endure.

The supernatural motion is retarded; the Mariner awakes, and his penance begins anew.

The pang, the curse, with which they died,
Had never passed away:
I could not draw my eyes from theirs,   440
Nor turn them up to pray.

And now this spell was snapped: once more
I viewed the ocean green,
And looked far forth, yet little saw
Of what had else been seen—

Like one, that on a lonesome road
Doth walk in fear and dread,
And having once turned round walks on,
And turns no more his head;
Because he knows, a frightful fiend   450
Doth close behind him tread.

But soon there breathed a wind on me,
Nor sound nor motion made:
Its path was not upon the sea,
In ripple or in shade.

It raised my hair, it fanned my cheek
Like a meadow-gale of spring—
It mingled strangely with my fears,
Yet it felt like a welcoming.

Swiftly, swiftly flew the ship,   460
Yet she sailed softly too:
Sweetly, sweetly blew the breeze—
On me alone it blew.

Oh! dream of joy! is this indeed
The lighthouse top I see?
Is this the hill? Is this the kirk?
Is this mine own countree?

We drifted o'er the harbor-bar,
And I with sobs did pray—
O let me be awake, my God!   470
Or let me sleep alway.

The harbor-bay was clear as glass,
So smoothly it was strewn!
And on the bay the moonlight lay,
And the shadow of the Moon.

The rock shone bright, the kirk no less,
That stands above the rock:

The moonlight steeped in silentness
The steady weathercock.

The angelic spirits leave the dead bodies,
And the bay was white with silent light,   480
Till rising from the same,
Full many shapes, that shadows were,
In crimson colors came.

And appear in their own forms of light.
A little distance from the prow
Those crimson shadows were:
I turned my eyes upon the deck—
Oh, Christ! what saw I there!

Each corse lay flat, lifeless and flat,
And, by the holy rood!
A man all light, a seraph-man,   490
On every corse there stood.

This seraph-band, each waved his hand:
It was a heavenly sight!
They stood as signals to the land,
Each one a lovely light;

This seraph-band, each waved his hand,
No voice did they impart—
No voice; but oh! the silence sank
Like music on my heart.

But soon I heard the dash of oars,   500
I heard the Pilot's cheer;
My head was turned perforce away
And I saw a boat appear.

The Pilot and the Pilot's boy,
I heard them coming fast:
Dear Lord in Heaven! it was a joy
The dead men could not blast.

I saw a third—I heard his voice:
It is the Hermit good!
He singeth loud his godly hymns   510
That he makes in the wood.
He'll shrieve my soul, he'll wash away
The Albatross's blood.

PART VII

The Hermit of the Wood,
This Hermit good lives in that wood
Which slopes down to the sea.
How loudly his sweet voice he rears!

He loves to talk with marineres
That come from a far countree.

He kneels at morn, and noon, and eve—
He hath a cushion plump: 520
It is the moss that wholly hides
The rotted old oak-stump.

The skiff-boat neared: I heard them talk,
'Why, this is strange, I trow!
Where are those lights so many and fair,
That signal made but now?'

'Strange, by my faith!' the Hermit said—
'And they answered not our cheer!
The planks looked warped! and see those sails,
How thin they are and sere!   530
I never saw aught like to them,
Unless perchance it were

Brown skeletons of leaves that lag
My forest-brook along;
When the ivy-tod⁹ is heavy with snow,
And the owlet whoops to the wolf below,
That eats the she-wolf's young.'

'Dear Lord! it hath a fiendish look—'
(The Pilot made reply)
'I am a-feared'—'Push on, push on!'   540
Said the Hermit cheerily.

The boat came closer to the ship,
But I nor spake nor stirred;
The boat came close beneath the ship,
And straight a sound was heard.

Under the water it rumbled on,
Still louder and more dread:
It reached the ship, it split the bay;
The ship went down like lead.

Stunned by that loud and dreadful sound,   550
Which sky and ocean smote,
Like one that hath been seven days drowned
My body lay afloat;
But swift as dreams, myself I found
Within the Pilot's boat.

9   ivy bush.

Upon the whirl, where sank the ship,
The boat spun round and round;
And all was still, save that the hill
Was telling of the sound.

I moved my lips—the Pilot shrieked   560
And fell down in a fit;
The holy Hermit raised his eyes,
And prayed where he did sit.

I took the oars: the Pilot's boy,
Who now doth crazy go,
Laughed loud and long, and all the while
His eyes went to and fro.
'Ha! ha!' quoth he, 'full plain I see,
The Devil knows how to row.'

And now, all in my own countree,   570
I stood on the firm land!
The Hermit stepped forth from the boat,
And scarcely he could stand.

The ancient mariner earnestly entreateth the Hermit to shrieve him; and the penance of life falls on him.

'O shrieve me, shrieve[10] me, holy man!'
The Hermit crossed his brow.
'Say quick,' quoth he, 'I bid thee say—
What manner of man art thou?'

Forthwith this frame of mine was wrenched
With a woeful agony,
Which forced me to begin my tale;   580
And then it left me free.

And ever and anon throughout his future life an agony constraineth him to travel from land to land;

Since then, at an uncertain hour,
That agony returns:
And till my ghastly tale is told,
This heart within me burns.

I pass, like night, from land to land;
I have strange power of speech;
That moment that his face I see,
I know the man that must hear me:
To him my tale I teach.   590

What loud uproar bursts from that door!
The wedding guests are there:
But in the garden bower the bride
And bride-maids singing are:
And hark the little vesper bell,
Which biddeth me to prayer!

10   *shrieve*: hear confession and grant absolution.

O Wedding Guest! this soul hath been
Alone on a wide wide sea:
So lonely 'twas, that God himself
Scarce seeméd there to be.   600

O sweeter than the marriage feast,
'Tis sweeter far to me,
To walk together to the kirk
With a goodly company!—

To walk together to the kirk,
And all together pray,
While each to his great Father bends,
Old men, and babes, and loving friends
And youth and maidens gay!

And to teach, by
his own example,
love and reverence
to all things that
God made and
loveth.

Farewell, farewell! but this I tell   610
To thee, thou Wedding Guest!
He prayeth well, who loveth well
Both man and bird and beast.

He prayeth best, who loveth best
All things both great and small;
For the dear God who loveth us,
He made and loveth all."

The Mariner, whose eye is bright,
Whose beard with age is hoar,
Is gone: and now the Wedding Guest   620
Turned from the bridegroom's door.

He went like one that hath been stunned,
And is of sense forlorn:
A sadder and a wiser man,
He rose the morrow morn.

GEORGE GORDON, LORD BYRON   [1788–1824]

She Walks in Beauty

She walks in Beauty, like the night
   Of cloudless climes and starry skies;
And all that's best of dark and bright
   Meet in her aspect and her eyes:
Thus mellowed to that tender light
   Which Heaven to gaudy day denies.

One shade the more, one ray the less,
    Had half impaired the nameless grace
Which waves in every raven tress,
    Or softly lightens o'er her face;
Where thoughts serenely sweet express,
    How pure, how dear their dwelling-place.

And on that cheek, and o'er that brow,
    So soft, so calm, yet eloquent,
The smiles that win, the tints that glow,
    But tell of days in goodness spent,
A mind at peace with all below,
    A heart whose love is innocent!

The Destruction of Sennacherib[1]

The Assyrian came down like the wolf on the fold,
And his cohorts were gleaming in purple and gold;
And the sheen of their spears was like stars on the sea,
When the blue wave rolls nightly on deep Galilee.

Like the leaves of the forest when Summer is green,
That host with their banners at sunset were seen:
Like the leaves of the forest when Autumn hath blown,
That host on the morrow lay withered and strown.

For the Angel of Death spread his wings on the blast,
And breathed in the face of the foe as he passed;
And the eyes of the sleepers waxed deadly and chill,
And their hearts but once heaved, and for ever grew still!

And there lay the steed with his nostril all wide,
But through it there rolled not the breath of his pride:
And the foam of his gasping lay white on the turf,
And cold as the spray of the rock-beating surf.

And there lay the rider distorted and pale,
With the dew on his brow and the rust on his mail;
And the tents were all silent, the banners alone,
The lances unlifted, the trumpet unblown.

And the widows of Ashur are loud in their wail,
And the idols are broke in the temple of Baal;
And the might of the Gentile, unsmote by the sword,
Hath melted like snow in the glance of the Lord!

1 See Ogden Nash's "Very Like a Whale."

Prometheus[1]

1

Titan! to whose immortal eyes
  The sufferings of mortality,
  Seen in their sad reality,
Were not as things that gods despise;
What was thy pity's recompense?
A silent suffering, and intense;
The rock, the vulture, and the chain,
All that the proud can feel of pain,
The agony they do not show,
The suffocating sense of woe,
  Which speaks but in its loneliness,   10
And then is jealous lest the sky
Should have a listener, nor will sigh
  Until its voice is echoless.

2

Titan! to thee the strife was given
  Between the suffering and the will,
  Which torture where they cannot kill;
And the inexorable Heaven,
And the deaf tyranny of Fate,
The ruling principle of Hate,   20
Which for its pleasure doth create
The things it may annihilate,
Refused thee even the boon to die:
The wretched gift Eternity
Was thine—and thou hast borne it well.
All that the Thunderer[2] wrung from thee
Was but the menace which flung back
On him the torments of thy rack;
The fate thou didst so well foresee,
But would not to appease him tell;   30
And in thy Silence was his Sentence,
And in his Soul a vain repentance,
And evil dread so ill dissembled,
That in his hand the lightnings trembled.

3

Thy Godlike crime was to be kind,
  To render with thy precepts less
  The sum of human wretchedness,

1 in Greek mythology, a Titan—one of the race of giants. Prometheus was employed
by Zeus, ruler of the gods, to make men out of mud and water. Out of pity for men's
suffering Prometheus stole fire from heaven and brought it to earth. For this he was
punished by Zeus who had him chained to Mt. Caucasus where an eagle fed on his liver.
2 Zeus.

And strengthen Man with his own mind;
But baffled as thou wert from high,
Still in thy patient energy,   40
In the endurance, and repulse
    Of thine impenetrable Spirit,
Which Earth and Heaven could not convulse,
    A mighty lesson we inherit:
Thou art a symbol and a sign
    To Mortals of their fate and force;
Like thee, Man is in part divine,
    A troubled stream from a pure source;
And Man in portions can foresee
His own funereal destiny;   50
His wretchedness, and his resistance,
And his sad unallied existence:
To which his Spirit may oppose
Itself—an equal to all woes—
    And a firm will, and a deep sense,
Which even in torture can descry
    Its own concentered recompense,
Triumphant where it dares defy,
And making Death a Victory.

from *Childe Harold's Pilgrimage, Canto III*

17

Stop!—for thy tread is on an Empire's dust![1]
    An Earthquake's spoil is sepulchred below!
    Is the spot marked with no colossal bust?
    Nor column trophied for triumphal show?
    None; but the moral's truth tells simpler so.—
As the ground was before, thus let it be;—   150
    How that red rain hath made the harvest grow!
    And is this all the world has gained by thee,
Thou first and last of fields! king-making Victory?

18

And Harold stands upon this place of skulls,
    The grave of France, the deadly Waterloo![2]
    How in an hour the power which gave annuls
    Its gifts, transferring fame as fleeting too!—

1   The third canto of *Childe Harold's Pilgrimage* was published on November 18,
1816. The battle of Waterloo had been fought on June 18, 1815. In this canto Byron
brings his hero to the battlefield, twelve miles south of Brussels; here Byron is addressing
both Childe Harold and the reader.
2   At Waterloo the combined armies of Britain and Prussia defeated the French army
of Napoleon. The victory was "king-making" in that it restored the Bourbons to the
throne of France. Napoleon was banished to St. Helena.

In "pride of place" here last the Eagle[3] flew,
    Then tore with bloody talon the rent plain,
    Pierced by the shaft of banded nations through;   160
    Ambition's life and labors all were vain—
He wears the shattered links of the world's broken chain.

19

Fit retribution! Gaul[4] may champ the bit
    And foam in fetters;—but is Earth more free?
    Did nations combat to make *One* submit?
    Or league to teach all Kings true sovereignty?
    What! shall reviving Thraldom again be
    The patched-up Idol of enlightened days?
    Shall we, who struck the Lion down, shall we
    Pay the Wolf homage? proffering lowly gaze   170
And servile knees to thrones? No! *prove* before ye praise!

20

If not, o'er one fallen despot boast no more!
    In vain fair cheeks were furrowed with hot tears
    For Europe's flowers long rooted up before
    The trampler of her vineyards; in vain, years
    Of death, depopulation, bondage, fears,
    Have all been borne, and broken by the accord
    Of roused-up millions: all that most endears
    Glory, is when the myrtle wreathes a sword,
Such as Harmodius[5] drew on Athens' tyrant Lord.   180

21

There was a sound of revelry by night,[6]
    And Belgium's Capital had gathered then
    Her Beauty and her Chivalry—and bright
    The lamps shone o'er fair women and brave men;
    A thousand hearts beat happily; and when
    Music arose with its voluptuous swell,
    Soft eyes looked love to eyes which spake again,
    And all went merry as a marriage bell;
But hush! hark! a deep sound strikes like a rising knell!

22

Did ye not hear it?—No—'twas but the wind,   190
    Or the car rattling o'er the stony street;
    On with the dance! let joy be unconfined;

3   The Old Guard, Napoleon's elite battalions, carried standards topped with bronze eagles.
4   The French.
5   an Athenian youth, executed in 514 B.C. after assassinating the tyrant Hipparchus. Hipparchus had insulted Harmodius' sister.
6   On the night of June 15 the Duchess of Richmond gave a ball in Brussels, attended by officers of the Allied armies. This was on the eve of the battle of Quatre Bras, which preceded the battle of Waterloo.

No sleep till morn, when Youth and Pleasure meet
To chase the glowing Hours with flying feet—
But hark!—that heavy sound breaks in once more,
As if the clouds its echo would repeat;
And nearer—clearer—deadlier than before!
Arm! Arm! it is—it is—the cannon's opening roar!

23

Within a windowed niche of that high hall
Sate Brunswick's fated Chieftain;[7] he did hear   200
That sound the first amidst the festival,
And caught its tone with Death's prophetic ear;
And when they smiled because he deemed it near,
His heart more truly knew that peal too well
Which stretched his father on a bloody bier,[8]
And roused the vengeance blood alone could quell;
He rushed into the field, and, foremost fighting, fell.

24

Ah! then and there was hurrying to and fro—
And gathering tears, and tremblings of distress,
And cheeks all pale, which but an hour ago   210
Blushed at the praise of their own loveliness—
And there were sudden partings, such as press
The life from out young hearts, and choking sighs
Which ne'er might be repeated; who could guess
If ever more should meet those mutual eyes,
Since upon night so sweet such awful morn could rise!

25

And there was mounting in hot haste—the steed,
The mustering squadron, and the clattering car,
Went pouring forward with impetuous speed,
And swiftly forming in the ranks of war—   220
And the deep thunder peal on peal afar;
And near, the beat of the alarming drum
Roused up the soldier ere the morning star;
While thronged the citizens with terror dumb,
Or whispering, with white lips—"The foe! they come! they come!"

26

And wild and high the "Cameron's Gathering" rose!
The war-note of Lochiel,[9] which Albyn's[10] hills
Have heard, and heard, too, have her Saxon foes:—

7   Frederick William, Duke of Brunswick and nephew of George III, was killed in the front lines at the battle of Quatre Bras.
8   The Duke of Brunswick's father had been killed at Auerbach in 1806, fighting against the army of the French Empire.
9   head of the Clan Cameron.
10   Albion, Roman name of Britain, meaning "the white land"—a reference to the white cliffs.

How in the noon of night that pibroch thrills,
Savage and shrill! But with the breath which fills 230
Their mountain-pipe, so fill the mountaineers
With the fierce native daring which instils
The strirring memory of a thousand years,
And Evan's, Donald's[11] fame rings in each clansman's ears!

27

And Ardennes[12] waves above them her green leaves,
    Dewy with Nature's tear-drops, as they pass,
Grieving, if aught inanimate e'er grieves,
    Over the unreturning brave,—alas!
Ere evening to be trodden like the grass
    Which now beneath them, but above shall grow 240
In its next verdure, when this fiery mass
    Of living valor, rolling on the foe
And burning with high hope, shall moulder cold and low.

28

Last noon beheld them full of lusty life;—
    Last eve in Beauty's circle proudly gay:
The midnight brought the signal-sound of strife,
    The morn the marshalling in arms,—the day
Battle's magnificently stern array!
    The thunder-clouds close o'er it, which when rent
The earth is covered thick with other clay, 250
    Which her own clay shall cover, heaped and pent,
Rider and horse,—friend, foe,—in one red burial blent!

11   heroes of the clan.
12   forest in Belgium.

from *Don Juan,*
Canto XI

7

To our theme.[1]—The man who has stood on the Acropolis,
    And looked down over Attica; or he 50
Who has sailed where picturesque Constantinople is,
    Or seen Timbuctoo, or hath taken tea
In small-eyed China's crockery-ware metropolis,
    Or sat amidst the bricks of Nineveh,
May not think much of London's first appearance—
But ask him what he thinks of it a year hence!

1   Byron's hero, Juan, is approaching London for the first time. Juan was born in
Spain. He has been shipwrecked in Greece, sold as a slave to the Turks, has taken part in
the siege of Ismail, and lived at the court of Catherine the Great of Russia, where he was
one of the queen's favorites. He is now being sent by Catherine on a diplomatic mission
to England, to negotiate a treaty.

8

Don Juan had got out on Shooter's Hill;
    Sunset the time, the place the same declivity
Which looks along that vale of Good and Ill
    Where London streets ferment in full activity,   60
While everything around was calm and still,
    Except the creak of wheels, which on their pivot he
Heard,—and that bee-like, bubbling, busy hum
Of cities, that boil over with their scum:—

9

I say, Don Juan, wrapped in contemplation,
    Walked on behind his carriage, o'er the summit,
And lost in wonder of so great a nation,
    Gave way to 't, since he could not overcome it.
"And here," he cried, "is Freedom's chosen station;
    Here peals the People's voice, nor can entomb it   70
Racks—prisons—inquisitions; Resurrection
Awaits it, each new meeting or election.

10

"Here are chaste wives, pure lives; here people pay
    But what they please; and if that things be dear,
'T is only that they love to throw away
    Their cash, to show how much they have a-year.
Here laws are all inviolate—none lay
    Traps for the traveller—every highway's clear—
Here"—he was interrupted by a knife,
With—"Damn your eyes! your money or your life!"—   80

11

These free-born sounds proceeded from four pads
    In ambush laid, who had perceived him loiter
Behind his carriage; and, like handy lads,
    Had seized the lucky hour to reconnoitre,
In which the heedless gentleman who gads
    Upon the road, unless he prove a fighter,
May find himself within that isle of riches
Exposed to lose his life as well as breeches.

12

Juan, who did not understand a word
    Of English, save their shibboleth, "God damn!"   90
And even that he had so rarely heard,
    He sometimes thought 't was only their "Salām,"
Or "God be with you!"—and 't is not absurd
    To think so,—for half English as I am
(To my misfortune), never can I say
I heard them wish "God with you," save that way;—

13

Juan yet quickly understood their gesture,
   And being somewhat choleric and sudden,
Drew forth a pocket pistol from his vesture,
   And fired it into one assailant's pudding—   100
Who fell, as rolls an ox o'er in his pasture,
   And roared out, as he writhed his native mud in,
Unto his nearest follower or henchman,
"Oh Jack! I'm floored by that 'ere bloody Frenchman!"

14

On which Jack and his train set off at speed,
   And Juan's suite, late scattered at a distance,
Came up, all marvelling at such a deed,
   And offering, as usual, late assistance.
Juan, who saw the moon's late minion bleed
   As if his veins would pour out his existence,   110
Stood calling out for bandages and lint,
And wished he had been less hasty with his flint.

15

"Perhaps," thought he, "it is the country's wont
   To welcome foreigners in this way: now
I recollect some innkeepers who don't
   Differ, except in robbing with a bow,
In lieu of a bare blade and brazen front—
   But what is to be done? I can't allow
The fellow to lie groaning on the road:
So take him up—I'll help you with the load."   120

16

But ere they could perform this pious duty,
   The dying man cried, "Hold! I've got my gruel!
Oh! for a glass of *max*![2] We've missed our booty;
   Let me die where I am! And as the fuel
Of Life shrunk in his heart, and thick and sooty
   The drops fell from his death-wound, and he drew ill
His breath—he from his swelling throat untied
A kerchief, crying, "Give Sal that!"—and died.

17

The cravat stained with bloody drops fell down
   Before Don Juan's feet: he could not tell   130
Exactly why it was before him thrown,
   Nor what the meaning of the man's farewell.
Poor Tom was once a kiddy upon town,
   A thorough varmint, and a *real* swell,

2 gin.

Full flash, all fancy,[3] until fairly diddled,
His pockets first and then his body riddled.

18

Don Juan, having done the best he could
   In all the circumstances of the case,
As soon as "Crowner's quest"[4] allowed, pursued
   His travels to the capital apace;—   140
Esteeming it a little hard he should
   In twelve hours' time, and very little space,
Have been obliged to slay a free-born native
In self-defence: this made him meditative.

19

He from the world had cut off a great man,
   Who in his time had made heroic bustle.
Who in a row like Tom could lead the van,
   Booze in the ken, or at the spellken hustle?
Who queer a flat? Who (spite of Bow-street's ban)
   On the high toby-spice so flash the muzzle?   150
Who on a lark with black-eyed Sal (his blowing),
So prime—so swell—so nutty—and so knowing?[5]

20

But Tom's no more—and so no more of Tom.
   Heroes must die; and by God's blessing 'tis
Not long before the most of them go home.
   Hail! Thamis, hail! Upon thy verge it is
That Juan's chariot, rolling like a drum
   In thunder, holds the way it can't well miss,
Through Kennington and all the other "tons,"
Which make us wish ourselves in town at once;—   160

21

Through Groves, so called as being void of trees,
   (Like *lucus* from *no* light); through prospects named
Mount Pleasant, as containing nought to please,
   Nor much to climb; through little boxes framed
Of bricks, to let the dust in at your ease,
With "To be let," upon their doors proclaimed;

3   *flash*: knowing; *fancy*: a sport.
4   coroner's inquest.
5   *ken*: thieves' lodging house; *spellken*: a play house; *queer a flat*: cheat a simpleton;
Bow street: the first London police were stationed in Bow Street; *high toby-spice*:
robbery on horseback; *flash the muzzle*: show off the face, swagger; *blowing (or
blowen)*: piece; *nutty*: amorous, fascinating.

Through "Rows" most modestly called "Paradise,"[6]
Which Eve might quit without much sacrifice;—

22

Through coaches, drays, choked turnpikes, and a whirl
   Of wheels, and roar of voices, and confusion;   170
Here taverns wooing to a pint of "purl,"
   There mails fast flying off like a delusion;
There barbers' blocks with periwigs in curl
   In windows; here the lamplighter's infusion
Slowly distilled into the glimmering glass
(For in those days we had not got to gas—);

23

Through this, and much, and more, is the approach
   Of travellers to mighty Babylon:
Whether they come by horse, or chaise, or coach,
   With slight exceptions, all the ways seem one.   180
I could say more, but do not choose to encroach
   Upon the Guide-book's privilege. The sun
Had set some time, and night was on the ridge
Of twilight, as the party crossed the bridge.

6 Juan has driven by Pleasant Row and Paradise Row on the way from Kennington to Westminister Bridge.

PERCY BYSSHE SHELLEY [1792–1822]

Mont Blanc

1

The everlasting universe of things
Flows through the mind, and rolls its rapid waves,
Now dark—now glittering—now reflecting gloom—
Now lending splendor, where from secret springs
The source of human thought its tribute brings
Of waters,—with a sound but half its own,
Such as a feeble brook will oft assume
In the wild woods, among the mountains lone,
Where waterfalls around it leap for ever,
Where woods and winds contend, and a vast river   10
Over its rocks ceaselessly bursts and raves.

2

Thus thou, Ravine of Arve—dark, deep Ravine—
Thou many-colored, many-voicèd vale,

Over whose pines, and crags, and caverns sail
Fast cloud-shadows and sunbeams: awful scene,
Where Power in likeness of the Arve comes down
From the ice-gulfs that gird his secret throne,
Bursting through these dark mountains like the flame
Of lightning through the tempest;—thou dost lie,
Thy giant brood of pines around thee clinging,   20
Children of elder time, in whose devotion
The chainless winds still come and ever came
To drink their odors, and their mighty swinging
To hear—an old and solemn harmony;
Thine earthly rainbows stretched across the sweep
Of the aethereal waterfall, whose veil
Robes some unsculptured image; the stange sleep
Which when the voices of the desert fail
Wraps all in its own deep eternity;—
Thy caverns echoing to the Arve's commotion,   30
A loud, lone sound no other sound can tame;
Thou art pervaded with that ceaseless motion,
Thou art the path of that unresting sound—
Dizzy Ravine! and when I gaze on thee
I seem as in a trance sublime and strange
To muse on my own separate fantasy,
My own, my human mind, which passively
Now renders and receives fast influencings,
Holding an unremitting interchange
With the clear universe of things around;   40
One legion of wild thoughts, whose wandering wings
Now float above thy darkness, and now rest
Where that or thou art no unbidden guest,
In the still cave of the witch Poesy,
Seeking among the shadows that pass by
Ghosts of all things that are, some shade of thee,
Some phantom, some faint image; till the breast
From which they fled recalls them, thou art there!

3

Some say that gleams of a remoter world
Visit the soul in sleep,—that death is slumber,   50
And that its shapes the busy thoughts outnumber
Of those who wake and live.—I look on high;
Has some unknown omnipotence unfurled
The veil of life and death? or do I lie
In dream, and does the mightier world of sleep
Spread far around and inaccessibly
Its circles? For the very spirit fails,
Driven like a homeless cloud from steep to steep
That vanishes among the viewless gales!
Far, far above, piercing the infinite sky,   60

Mont Blanc appears,—still, snowy, and serene—
Its subject mountains their unearthly forms
Pile around it, ice and rock; broad vales between
Of frozen floods, unfathomable deeps,
Blue as the overhanging heaven, that spread
And wind among the accumulated steeps;
A desert peopled by the storms alone,
Save when the eagle brings some hunter's bone,
And the wolf tracks her there—how hideously
Its shapes are heaped around! rude, bare, and high,   70
Ghastly, and scarred, and riven.—Is this the scene
Where the old Earthquake-dæmon taught her young
Ruin? Were these their toys? or did a sea
Of fire envelop once this silent snow?
None can reply—all seems eternal now.
The wilderness has a mysterious tongue
Which teaches awful doubt, or faith so mild,
So solemn, so serene, that man may be,
But for such faith, with nature reconciled;
Thou hast a voice, great Mountain, to repeal   80
Large codes of fraud and woe; not understood
By all, but which the wise, and great, and good
Interpret, or make felt, or deeply feel.

                    4
The fields, the lakes, the forests, and the streams,
Ocean, and all the living things that dwell
Within the daedal[1] earth; lightning, and rain,
Earthquake, and fiery flood, and hurricane,
The torpor of the year when feeble dreams
Visit the hidden buds, or dreamless sleep
Holds every future leaf and flower;—the bound   90
With which from that detested trance they leap;
The works and ways of man, their death and birth,
And that of him and all that his may be;
All things that move and breathe with toil and sound
Are born and die; revolve, subside, and swell.
Power dwells apart in its tranquillity,
Remote, serene, and inaccessible:
And *this*, the naked countenance of earth,
On which I gaze, even these primaeval mountains
Teach the adverting mind. The glaciers creep   100
Like snakes that watch their prey, from their far fountains,
Slow rolling on; there, many a precipice,
Frost and the Sun in scorn of mortal power

    1 ingeniously formed.

Have piled: dome, pyramid, and pinnacle,
A city of death, distinct with many a tower
And wall impregnable of beaming ice.
Yet not a city, but a flood of ruin
Is there, that from the boundaries of the sky
Rolls its perpetual stream; vast pines are strewing
Its destined path, or in the mangled soil   110
Branchless and shattered stand; the rocks, drawn down
From yon remotest waste, have overthrown
The limits of the dead and living world,
Never to be reclaimed. The dwelling-place
Of insects, beasts, and birds, becomes its spoil
Their food and their retreat for ever gone,
So much of life and joy is lost. The race
Of man flies far in dread; his work and dwelling
Vanish, like smoke before the tempest's stream,
And their place is not known. Below, vast caves   120
Shine in the rushing torrents' restless gleam,
Which from those secret chasms in tumult welling
Meet in the vale, and one majestic River,
The breath and blood of distant lands, for ever
Rolls its loud waters to the ocean-waves,
Breathes its swift vapors to the circling air.

5

Mont Blanc yet gleams on high:—the power is there,
The still and solemn power of many sights,
And many sounds, and much of life and death.
In the calm darkness of the moonless nights,   130
In the lone glare of day, the snows descend
Upon that Mountain; none beholds them there,
Nor when the flakes burn in the sinking sun,
Or the star-beams dart through them:—Winds contend
Silently there, and heap the snow with breath
Rapid and strong, but silently! Its home
The voiceless lightning in these solitudes
Keeps innocently, and like vapor broods
Over the snow. The secret Strength of things
Which governs thought, and to the infinite dome   140
Of Heaven is as a law, inhabits thee!
And what were thou, and earth, and stars, and sea,
If to the human mind's imaginings
Silence and solitude were vacancy?

Ozymandias

I met a traveller from an antique land
Who said: Two vast and trunkless legs of stone

Stand in the desert . . . Near them, on the sand,
Half sunk, a shattered visage lies, whose frown,
And wrinkled lip, and sneer of cold command,
Tell that its sculptor well those passions read
Which yet survive, stamped on these lifeless things,
The hand that mocked them, and the heart that fed:
And on the pedestal these words appear:
"My name is Ozymandias, king of kings:
Look on my works, ye Mighty, and despair."
Nothing beside remains. Round the decay
Of that colossal wreck, boundless and bare
The lone and level sands stretch far away.

Song to the Men of England

Men of England, wherefore plough
For the lords who lay ye low?
Wherefore weave with toil and care
The rich robes your tyrants wear?

Wherefore feed, and clothe, and save,
From the cradle to the grave,
Those ungrateful drones who would
Drain your sweat—nay, drink your blood?

Wherefore, Bees of England, forge
Many a weapon, chain, and scourge,   10
That these stingless drones may spoil
The forced produce of your toil?

Have ye leisure, comfort, calm,
Shelter, food, love's gentle balm?
Or what is it ye buy so dear
With your pain and with your fear?

The seed ye sow, another reaps;
The wealth ye find, another keeps;
The robes ye weave, another wears;
The arms ye forge, another bears.   20

Sow seed—but let no tyrant reap;
Find wealth—let no impostor heap;
Weave robes—let not the idle wear;
Forge arms—in your defense to bear.

Shrink to your cellars, holes, and cells:
In halls ye deck another dwells.

Why shake the chains ye wrought? Ye see
The steel ye tempered glance on ye.

With plough and spade, and hoe and loom,
Trace your grave, and build your tomb,   30
And weave your winding-sheet, till fair
England be your sepulcher.

Ode to the West Wind

1

O wild West Wind, thou breath of Autumn's being,
Thou, from whose unseen presence the leaves dead
Are driven, like ghosts from an enchanter fleeing,

Yellow, and black, and pale, and hectic red,
Pestilence-stricken multitudes: O thou,
Who chariotest to their dark wintry bed

The wingéd seeds, where they lie cold and low,
Each like a corpse within its grave, until
Thine azure sister of the Spring shall blow

Her clarion o'er the dreaming earth, and fill   10
(Driving sweet buds like flocks to feed in air)
With living hues and odors plain and hill:

Wild Spirit, which art moving everywhere;
Destroyer and preserver; hear, oh, hear!

2

Thou on whose stream, mid the steep sky's commotion,
Loose clouds like earth's decaying leaves are shed,
Shook from the tangled boughs of Heaven and Ocean,

Angels of rain and lightning: there are spread
On the blue surface of thine aery surge,
Like the bright hair uplifted from the head   20

Of some fierce Maenad,[1] even from the dim verge
Of the horizon to the zenith's height,
The locks of the approaching storm. Thou dirge

1 A female attendant of Bacchus, the god of wine.

226

Of the dying year, to which this closing night
Will be the dome of a vast sepulcher,
Vaulted with all thy congregated might

Of vapors, from whose solid atmosphere
Black rain, and fire, and hail will burst: oh, hear!

3

Thou who didst waken from his summer dreams
The blue Mediterranean, where he lay,   30
Lulled by the coil of his crystálline streams,

Beside a pumice isle in Baiae's bay,[2]
And saw in sleep old palaces and towers
Quivering within the wave's intenser day,

All overgrown with azure moss and flowers
So sweet, the sense faints picturing them! Thou
For whose path the Atlantic's level powers

Cleave themselves into chasms, while far below
The sea-blooms and the oozy woods which wear
The sapless foliage of the ocean, know   40

Thy voice, and suddenly grow gray with fear,
And tremble and despoil themselves: oh, hear!

4

If I were a dead leaf thou mightest bear;
If I were a swift cloud to fly with thee;
A wave to pant beneath thy power, and share

The impulse of thy strength, only less free
Than thou, O uncontrollable! If even
I were as in my boyhood, and could be

The comrade of thy wanderings over Heaven
As then, when to outstrip thy skiey speed   50
Scarce seemed a vision; I would ne'er have striven

As thus with thee in prayer in my sore need.
Oh, lift me as a wave, a leaf, a cloud!
I fall upon the thorns of life! I bleed!

A heavy weight of hours has chained and bowed
One too like thee; tameless, and swift, and proud.

2 near Naples, the site of the palaces of Julius Caesar, Pompey, and Nero.

5

Make me thy lyre, even as the forest is:
What if my leaves are falling like its own!
The tumult of thy mighty harmonies

Will take from both a deep, autumnal tone,   60
Sweet though in sadness. Be thou, Spirit fierce,
My spirit! Be thou me, impetuous one!

Drive my dead thoughts over the universe
Like withered leaves to quicken a new birth!
And, by the incantation of this verse,

Scatter, as from an unextinguished hearth
Ashes and sparks, my words among mankind!
Be through my lips to unawakened earth

The trumpet of a prophecy! O, Wind,
If Winter comes, can Spring be far behind?   70

To a Skylark

Hail to thee, blithe Spirit!
    Bird thou never wert,
That from Heaven, or near it,
    Pourest thy full heart
In profuse strains of unpremeditated art.

Higher still and higher
    From the earth thou springest
Like a cloud of fire;
    The blue deep thou wingest,
And singing still dost soar, and soaring ever singest.   10

In the golden lightning
    Of the sunken sun,
O'er which clouds are bright'ning,
    Thou dost float and run;
Like an unbodied joy whose race is just begun.

The pale purple even
    Melts around thy flight;
Like a star of Heaven,
    In the broad daylight
Thou art unseen, but yet I hear thy shrill delight,   20

Keen as are the arrows
    Of that silver sphere,

Whose intense lamp narrows
   In the white dawn clear
Until we hardly see—we feel that it is there.

All the earth and air
   With thy voice is loud,
As, when night is bare,
   From one lonely cloud
The moon rains out her beams, and Heaven is overflowed.   30

What thou art we know not;
   What is most like thee?
From rainbow clouds there flow not
   Drops so bright to see
As from thy presence showers a rain of melody.

Like a Poet hidden
   In the light of thought,
Singing hymns unbidden,
   Till the world is wrought
To sympathy with hopes and fears it heeded not: 40

Like a high-born maiden
   In a palace-tower,
Soothing her love-laden
   Soul in secret hour
With music sweet as love, which overflows her bower:

Like a glow-worm golden
   In a dell of dew,
Scattering unbeholden
   Its aereal hue
Among the flowers and grass, which screen it from the view!   50

Like a rose embowered
   In its own green leaves,
By warm winds deflowered,
   Till the scent it gives
Makes faint with too much sweet those heavy-wingéd thieves:

Sound of vernal showers
   On the twinkling grass,
Rain-awakened flowers,
   All that ever was
Joyous, and clear, and fresh, thy music doth surpass: 60

Teach us, Sprite or Bird,
   What sweet thoughts are thine:
I have never heard

Praise of love or wine
That panted forth a flood of rapture so divine.

Chorus Hymeneal,[1]
   Or triumphal chant,
Matched with thine would be all
   But an empty vaunt,
A thing wherein we feel there is some hidden want.   70

What objects are the fountains
   Of thy happy strain?
What fields, or waves, or mountains?
   What shapes of sky or plain?
What love of thine own kind? what ignorance of pain?

With thy clear keen joyance
   Languor cannot be:
Shadow of annoyance
   Never came near thee:
Thou lovest—but ne'er knew love's sad satiety.   80

Waking or asleep,
   Thou of death must deem
Things more true and deep
   Than we mortals dream,
Or how could thy notes flow in such a crystal stream?

We look before and after,
   And pine for what is not:
Our sincerest laughter
   With some pain is fraught;
Our sweetest songs are those that tell of saddest thought.   90

Yet if we could scorn
   Hate, and pride, and fear;
If we were things born
   Not to shed a tear,
I know not how thy joy we ever should come near.

Better than all measures
   Of delightful sound,
Better than all treasures
   That in books are found,
Thy skill to poet were, thou scorner of the ground!   100

Teach me half the gladness
   That thy brain must know,

1 marriage song.

Such harmonious madness
      From my lips would flow
The world should listen then—as I am listening now.

JOHN CLARE   [1793–1864]

Badger

When midnight comes a host of dogs and men
Go out and track the badger to his den,
And put a sack within the hole, and lie
Till the old grunting badger passes by.
He comes and hears—they let the strongest loose.
The old fox hears the noise and drops the goose.
The poacher shoots and hurries from the cry,
And the old hare half wounded buzzes by.
They get a forkèd stick to bear him down
And clap the dogs and bear him to the town,   10
And bait him all the day with many dogs,
And laugh and shout and fright the scampering hogs.
He runs along and bites at all he meets:
They shout and hollo down the noisy streets.

He turns about to face the loud uproar
And drives the rebels to their very door.
The frequent stone is hurled where'er they go;
When badgers fight, then everyone's a foe.
The dogs are clapt¹ and urged to join the fray;
The badger turns and drives them all away.   20
Though scarcely half as big, demure² and small,
He fights with dogs for hours and beats them all.
The heavy mastiff, savage in the fray,
Lies down and licks his feet and turns away.
The bulldog knows his match and waxes cold,
The badger grins and never leaves his hold.
He drives the crowd and follows at their heels
And bites them through—the drunkard swears and reels.

The frightened women take the boys away,
The blackguard laughs and hurries on the fray.   30
He tries to reach the woods, an awkward race,
But sticks and cudgels quickly stop the chase.
He turns again and drives the noisy crowd

1   placed in position.
2   a variant of *diminute*, meaning "diminished."

And beats the many dogs in noises loud.
He drives away and beats them everyone,
And then they loose them all and set them on.
He falls as dead and kicked by boys and men,
Then starts and grins and drives the crowd again;
Till kicked and torn and beaten out he lies
And leaves his hold and cackles, groans, and dies.   40

JOHN KEATS [1795–1821]

When I
Have Fears

When I have fears that I may cease to be
  Before my pen has gleaned my teeming brain,
Before high-piled books, in charactery,
  Hold like rich garners the full ripened grain;
When I behold, upon the night's starred face,
  Huge cloudy symbols of a high romance,
And think that I may never live to trace
  Their shadows, with the magic hand of chance;
And when I feel, fair creature of an hour,
  That I shall never look upon thee more,
Never have relish in the faery power
  Of unreflecting love;—then on the shore
Of the wide world I stand alone, and think
Till love and fame to nothingness do sink.

Bright Star

Bright star, would I were steadfast as thou art—
Not in lone splendor hung aloft the night,
And watching, with eternal lids apart,
Like nature's patient sleepless Eremite,[1]
The moving waters at their priestlike task
Of pure ablution round earth's human shores,
Or gazing on the new soft fallen mask
Of snow upon the mountains and the moors:
No—yet still steadfast, still unchangeable,
Pillowed upon my fair love's ripening breast
To feel for ever its soft fall and swell,
Awake for ever in a sweet unrest;
Still, still to hear her tender-taken breath,
And so live ever—or else swoon to death.

1 hermit.

La Belle Dame
Sans Merci[1]

O what can ail thee, knight at arms,
    Alone and palely loitering?
The sedge has withered from the lake,
    And no birds sing.

O what can ail thee, knight at arms,
    So haggard and so woebegone?
The squirrel's granary is full,
    And the harvest's done.

I see a lily on the thy brow
    With anguish moist and fever dew,   10
And on thy cheeks a fading rose
    Fast withereth too.

I met a lady in the meads,
    Full beautiful, a faery's child:
Her hair was long, her foot was light,
    And her eyes were wild.

I made a garland for her head,
    And bracelets too, and fragrant zone;[2]
She looked at me as she did love,
    And made sweet moan.   20

I set her on my pacing steed,
    And nothing else saw all day long;
For sidelong would she bend and sing
    A faery's song.

She found me roots of relish sweet,
    And honey wild, and manna dew,
And sure in language strange she said,
    "I love thee true!"

She took me to her elfin grot,
    And there she wept and sighed full sore;   30
And there I shut her wild, wild eyes
    With kisses four.

And there she lulléd me asleep,
    And there I dreamed—Ah! woe betide!
The latest dream I ever dreamed
    On the cold hill side.

1   The Beautiful Lady Without Pity.
2   belt.

I saw pale kings, and princes too,
    Pale warriors, death-pale were they all;
Who cried—"La Belle Dame Sans Merci
    Hath thee in thrall!"   40

I saw their starved lips in the gloam,
    With horrid warming gapéd wide,
And I awoke and found me here,
    On the cold hill's side.

And this is why I sojourn here,
    Alone and palely loitering,
Though the sedge is withered from the lake,
    And no birds sing.

Ode to Psyche[1]

O Goddess! hear these tuneless numbers, wrung
    By sweet enforcement and remembrance dear,
And pardon that thy secrets should be sung
    Even into thine own soft-conchèd[2] ear:
Surely I dreamt to-day, or did I see
    The wingèd Psyche with awakened eyes?
I wandered in a forest thoughtlessly,
    And, on the sudden, fainting with surprise,
Saw two fair creatures, couched side by side
    In deepest grass, beneath the whisp'ring roof   10
    Of leaves and trembled blossoms, where there ran
        A brooklet, scarce espied:
'Mid hushed, cool-rooted flowers, fragrant-eyed,
    Blue, silver-white, and budded Tyrian,[3]
They lay calm-breathing on the bedded grass;
    Their arms embraced, and their pinions too;
    Their lips touched not, but had not bade adieu,
As if disjoined by soft-handed slumber,
And ready still past kisses to outnumber
    At tender eye-dawn of aurorean love: 20
        The wingèd boy I knew;
But who wast thou, O happy, happy dove?
        His Psyche true!

O latest born and loveliest vision far
    Of all Olympus'[4] faded hierarchy!

1   Psyche was a nymph who married Cupid, god of love ("the winged boy"). In later mythology the word came to signify the soul.
2   shell-like.
3   purple.
4   a mountain where the Greek gods lived.

Fairer than Phœbe's sapphire-regioned star,[5]
   Or Vesper,[6] amorous glow-worm of the sky;
Fairer than these, though temple thou hast none,
     Nor altar heaped with flowers;
Nor virgin-choir to make delicious moan   30
     Upon the midnight hours;
No voice, no lute, no pipe, no incense sweet
   From chain-swung censer teeming;
No shrine, no grove, no oracle, no heat
     Of pale-mouthed prophet dreaming.

O brightest! though too late for antique vows,
   Too, too late for the fond believing lyre,
When holy were the haunted forest boughs,
   Holy the air, the water, and the fire;
Yet even in these days so far retired   40
   From happy pieties, thy lucent fans,[7]
   Fluttering among the faint Olympians,
I see, and sing, by my own eyes inspired.
So let me be thy choir, and make a moan
     Upon the midnight hours;
Thy voice, thy lute, thy pipe, thy incense sweet
   From swinged censer teeming;
Thy shrine, thy grove, thy oracle, thy heat
     Of pale-mouthed prophet dreaming.

Yes, I will be thy priest, and build a fane   50
   In some untrodden region of my mind,
Where branched thoughts, new grown with pleasant pain,
   Instead of pines shall murmur in the wind:
Far, far around shall those dark-clustered trees
   Fledge the wild-ridged mountains steep by steep;
And there by zephyrs, streams, and birds, and bees,
   The moss-lain Dryads[8] shall be lulled to sleep;
And in the midst of this wide quietness
A rosy sanctuary will I dress
With the wreathed trellis of a working brain,   60
   With buds, and bells, and stars without a name,
With all the gardener Fancy e'er could feign,
   Who breeding flowers, will never breed the same:
And there shall be for thee all soft delight
   That shadowy thought can win,
A bright torch, and a casement ope at night,
   To let the warm Love in!

5   Phoebe is another name for Diana, goddess of the moon.
6   the evening star.
7   wings.
8   wood nymphs.

Ode to a Nightingale

1

My heart aches, and a drowsy numbness pains
  My sense, as though of hemlock I had drunk
Or emptied some dull opiate to the drains
  One minute past, and Lethe-wards[1] had sunk:
'Tis not through envy of thy happy lot,
  But being too happy in thine happiness,—
     That thou, light-winged Dryad[2] of the trees,
      In some melodious plot
  Of beechen green, and shadows numberless,
     Singest of summer in full-throated ease.   10

2

O, for a draught of vintage! that hath been
  Cooled a long age in the deep-delved earth,
Tasting of Flora[3] and the country green,
  Dance, and Provençal song, and sunburnt mirth!
O for a beaker full of the warm South,
  Full of the true, the blushful Hippocrene,[4]
     With beaded bubbles winking at the brim,
      And purple-stained mouth;
  That I might drink, and leave the world unseen,
     And with thee fade away into the forest dim: 20

3

Fade far away, dissolve, and quite forget
  What thou among the leaves hast never known,
The weariness, the fever, and the fret
  Here, where men sit and hear each other groan;
Where palsy shakes a few, sad, last gray hairs,
  Where youth grows pale, and specter-thin, and dies;
     Where but to think is to be full of sorrow
      And leaden-eyed despairs,
  Where Beauty cannot keep her lustrous eyes,
     Or new Love pine at them beyond tomorrow.   30

4

Away! away! for I will fly to thee,
  Not charioted by Bacchus[5] and his pards,
But on the viewless wings of Poesy,
  Though the dull brain perplexes and retards:

1 Lethe is the river of forgetfulness.
2 wood nymph.
3 goddess of flowers.
4 a spring sacred to the Muses.
5 god of wine.

Already with thee! tender is the night,
　　And haply the Queen-Moon is on her throne,
　　　　Clustered around by all her starry Fays;[6]
　　　　　　But here there is no light,
　　Save what from heaven is with the breezes blown
　　　　Through verdurous glooms and winding mossy ways.　　　40

5

I cannot see what flowers are at my feet,
　　Nor what soft incense hangs upon the boughs,
But, in embalmed darkness, guess each sweet
　　Wherewith the seasonable month endows
The grass, the thicket, and the fruit-tree wild;
　　White hawthorn, and the pastoral eglantine;
　　　　Fast fading violets covered up in leaves;
　　　　　　And mid-May's eldest child,
The coming musk-rose, full of dewy wine,
　　　　The murmurous haunt of flies on summer eves.　　　50

6

Darkling I listen; and, for many a time
　　I have been half in love with easeful Death,
Called him soft names in many a muséd rhyme,
　　To take into the air my quiet breath;
Now more than ever seems it rich to die,
　　To cease upon the midnight with no pain,
　　　　While thou art pouring forth thy soul abroad
　　　　　　In such an ecstasy!
Still wouldst thou sing, and I have ears in vain—
　　　　To thy high requiem become a sod.　　　60

7

Thou wast not born for death, immortal Bird!
　　No hungry generations tread thee down;
The voice I hear this passing night was heard
　　In ancient days by emperor and clown:
Perhaps the self-same song that found a path
　　Through the sad heart of Ruth,[7] when, sick for home,
　　　　She stood in tears amid the alien corn;
　　　　　　The same that oft-times hath
Charmed magic casements, opening on the foam
　　　　Of perilous seas, in faery lands forlorn.　　　70

8

Forlorn! the very word is like a bell
　　To toll me back from thee to my sole self!

6　fairies.
7　After her husband's death, Ruth left her native land and lived in Palestine with her
mother-in-law Naomi. See the Book of Ruth in the Old Testament.

Adieu! the fancy cannot cheat so well
    As she is famed to do, deceiving elf.
Adieu! adieu! thy plaintive anthem fades
    Past the near meadows, over the still stream,
        Up the hill-side; and now 'tis buried deep
            In the next valley-glades:
    Was it a vision, or a waking dream?
        Fled is that music:—Do I wake or sleep?   80

Ode on a Grecian Urn

1

Thou still unravished bride of quietness,
    Thou foster child of silence and slow time,
Sylvan historian, who canst thus express
    A flowery tale more sweetly than our rhyme:
What leaf-fringed legend haunts about thy shape
    Of deities or mortals, or of both,
        In Tempe or the dales of Arcady?[1]
    What men or gods are these? What maidens loth?
What mad pursuit? What struggle to escape?
        What pipes and timbrels? What wild ecstasy?   10

2

Heard melodies are sweet, but those unheard
    Are sweeter; therefore, ye soft pipes, play on;
Not to the sensual ear, but, more endeared,
    Pipe to the spirit ditties of no tone:
Fair youth, beneath the trees, thou canst not leave
    Thy song, nor ever can those trees be bare;
        Bold Lover, never, never canst thou kiss,
Though winning near the goal—yet, do not grieve;
    She cannot fade, though thou hast not thy bliss,
        For ever wilt thou love, and she be fair!   20

3

Ah, happy, happy boughs! that cannot shed
    Your leaves, nor ever bid the Spring adieu;
And, happy melodist, unwearied,
    For ever piping songs for ever new;
More happy love! more happy, happy love!
    For ever warm and still to be enjoyed,

1 Tempe is a valley sacred to Apollo, god of music and poetry. Arcady is a region in
Greece frequently presented as an idyllic pastoral scene.

For ever panting, and for ever young,
All breathing human passion far above,
   That leaves a heart high-sorrowful and cloyed,
     A burning forehead, and a parching tongue.   30

4

Who are these coming to the sacrifice?
   To what green altar, O mysterious priest,
Lead'st thou that heifer lowing at the skies,
   And all her silken flanks with garlands drest?
What little town by river or sea shore,
   Or mountain-built with peaceful citadel,
     Is emptied of this folk, this pious morn?
And, little town, thy streets for evermore
   Will silent be; and not a soul to tell
     Why thou art desolate, can e'er return.   40

5

O Attic[2] shape! Fair attitude! with brede[3]
Of marble men and maidens overwrought,
With forest branches and the trodden weed;
   Thou, silent form, dost tease us out of thought
As doth eternity: Cold Pastoral!
   When old age shall this generation waste,
     Thou shalt remain, in midst of other woe
Than ours, a friend to man, to whom thou say'st,
   "Beauty is truth, truth beauty,"—that is all
     Ye know on earth, and all ye need to know.   50

2   belonging to Attica, or ancient Athens, and connoting elegance.
3   embroidery.

To Autumn

1

Season of mists and mellow fruitfulness,
   Close bosom-friend of the maturing sun;
Conspiring with him how to load and bless
   With fruit the vines that round the thatch-eves run;
To bend with apples the mossed cottage-trees,
   And fill all fruit with ripeness to the core;
     To swell the gourd, and plump the hazel shells
   With a sweet kernel; to set budding more,
And still more, later flowers for the bees,
Until they think warm days will never cease,   10
     For Summer has o'er-brimmed their clammy cells.

2

Who hath not seen thee oft amid thy store?
   Sometimes whoever seeks abroad may find
Thee sitting careless on a granary floor,
   Thy hair soft-lifted by the winnowing wind;
Or on a half-reaped furrow sound asleep,
   Drowsed with the fume of poppies, while thy hook
    Spares the next swath and all its twined flowers:
And sometimes like a gleaner thou dost keep
   Steady thy laden head across a brook;   20
   Or by a cyder-press, with patient look,
    Thou watchest the last oozings hours by hours.

3

Where are the songs of Spring? Ay, where are they?
   Think not of them, thou hast thy music too,—
While barred clouds bloom the soft-dying day,
   And touch the stubble-plains with rosy hue;
Then in a wailful choir the small gnats mourn
   Among the river sallows,[1] borne aloft
    Or sinking as the light wind lives or dies;
And full-grown lambs loud bleat from hilly bourn;   30
   Hedge-crickets sing; and now with treble soft
   The red-breast whistles from a garden-croft;[2]
    And gathering swallows twitter in the skies.

1   broad-leaved willows.
2   *croft*: a small enclosed field usually adjoining a house.

This Living Hand

This living hand, now warm and capable
Of earnest grasping, would, if it were cold
And in the icy silence of the tomb,
So haunt thy days and chill thy dreaming nights
That thou wouldst wish thine own heart dry of blood
So in my veins red life might stream again,
And thou be conscience-calmed—see here it is—
I hold it towards you.

ELIZABETH BARRETT BROWNING [1806–1861]

14   If Thou
Must Love Me[1]

If thou must love me, let it be for nought
Except for love's sake only. Do not say
"I love her for her smile—her look—her way
Of speaking gently,—for a trick of thought
That falls in well with mine, and certes brought
A sense of pleasant ease on such a day"—
For these things in themselves, Belovèd, may
Be changed, or change for thee,—and love, so wrought,
May be unwrought so. Neither love me for
Thine own dear pity's wiping my cheeks dry,—
A creature might forget to weep, who bore
Thy comfort long, and lose thy love thereby!
But love me for love's sake, that evermore
Thou mayst love on, through love's eternity.

1   from *Sonnets from the Portuguese.*

EDGAR ALLAN POE   [1809–1849]

To Helen[1]

Helen, thy beauty is to me
   Like those Nicean[2] barks of yore
That gently, o'er a perfumed sea,
   The weary way-worn wanderer bore
   To his own native shore.

On desperate seas long wont to roam,
   Thy hyacinth hair, thy classic face,
Thy Naiad[3] airs have brought me home
   To the glory that was Greece,
And the grandeur that was Rome.

Lo, in yon brilliant window-niche
   How statue-like I see thee stand,
   The agate lamp within thy hand,
Ah! Psyche,[4] from the regions which
   Are holy land!

1   Helen of Troy.
2   pertaining to Nicaea, an ancient city in Asia Minor.
3   water nymph.
4   a beautiful princess with whom Cupid fell in love.

ALFRED, LORD TENNYSON   [1809–1892]

Mariana[1]

Mariana in the moated grange (Measure for Measure)

With blackest moss the flower-plots
    Were thickly crusted, one and all:
The rusted nails fell from the knots
    That held the pear to the gable-wall.
The broken sheds looked sad and strange:
    Unlifted was the clinking latch;
    Weeded and worn the ancient thatch
Upon the lonely moated grange.
      She only said, "My life is dreary,
        He cometh not," she said;   10
      She said, "I am aweary, aweary,
        I would that I were dead!"

Her tears fell with the dews at even;
    Her tears fell ere the dews were dried;
She could not look on the sweet heaven,
    Either at morn or eventide.
After the flitting of the bats,
    When thickest dark did trance the sky,
    She drew her casement-curtain by,
And glanced athwart the glooming flats.   20
      She only said, "The night is dreary,
        He cometh not," she said;
      She said, "I am aweary, aweary,
        I would that I were dead!"

Upon the middle of the night,
    Waking she heard the night-fowl crow:
The cock sung out an hour ere light:
    From the dark fen the oxen's low
Came to her: without hope of change,
    In sleep she seemed to walk forlorn,   30
    Till cold winds woke the gray-eyed morn
About the lonely moated grange.
      She only said, "The day is dreary,
        He cometh not," she said:
      She said, "I am aweary, aweary,
        I would that I were dead!"

About a stone-cast from the wall
    A sluice with blackened waters slept,
And o'er it many, round and small,

---

1   Mariana, a character in Shakespeare's *Measure for Measure*, had been jilted by Angelo and lived in great unhappiness in the "moated grange." A grange is an isolated farmhouse.

The clustered marish[2]-mosses crept.   40
Hard by a poplar shook alway,
   All silver-green with gnarléd bark:
   For leagues no other tree did mark
The level waste, the rounding gray.
     She only said, "My life is dreary,
       He cometh not," she said;
     She said, "I am aweary, aweary,
       I would that I were dead!"

And ever when the moon was low,
   And the shrill winds were up and away,   50
In the white curtain, to and fro,
   She saw the gusty shadow sway.
But when the moon was very low,
   And wild winds bound within their cell,
   The shadow of the poplar fell
Upon her bed, across her brow.
     She only said, "The night is dreary,
       He cometh not," she said;
     She said, "I am aweary, aweary,
       I would that I were dead!"   60

All day within the dreamy house,
   The doors upon their hinges creaked;
The blue fly sung in the pane; the mouse
   Behind the mouldering wainscot shrieked,
Or from the crevice peered about.
   Old faces glimmered through the doors,
   Old footsteps trod the upper floors,
Old voices called her from without.
     She only said, "My life is dreary,
       He cometh not," she said;   70
     She said, "I am aweary, aweary,
       I would that I were dead!"

The sparrow's chirrup on the roof,
   The slow clock ticking, and the sound
Which to the wooing wind aloof
   The poplar made, did all confound
Her sense; but most she loathed the hour
   When the thick-moted sunbeam lay
   Athwart the chambers, and the day
Was sloping toward his western bower.   80
     Then, said she, "I am very dreary,
       He will not come," she said;
     She wept, "I am aweary, aweary,
       Oh God, that I were dead!"

2 marsh.

The Lady
of Shalott

PART I

On either side the river lie
Long fields of barley and of rye,
That clothe the wold[1] and meet the sky;
And thro' the field the road runs by
      To many-towered Camelot;[2]
And up and down the people go,
Gazing where the lilies blow
Round an island there below,
      The island of Shalott.

Willows whiten, aspens quiver,   10
Little breezes dusk and shiver
Thro' the wave that runs for ever
By the island in the river
      Flowing down to Camelot.
Four gray walls, and four gray towers,
Overlook a space of flowers,
And the silent isle imbowers
      The Lady of Shalott.

By the margin, willow-veiled,
Slide the heavy barges trailed   20
By slow horses; and unhailed
The shallop[3] flitteth silken-sailed
      Skimming down to Camelot:
But who hath seen her wave her hand?
Or at the casement seen her stand?
Or is she known in all the land,
      The Lady of Shalott?

Only reapers, reaping early
In among the bearded barley,
Hear a song that echoes cheerly   30
From the river winding clearly,
      Down to towered Camelot:
And by the moon the reaper weary,
Piling sheaves in uplands airy,
Listening, whispers, " 'Tis the fairy
      Lady of Shalott."

1   an upland area of open country.
2   in Arthurian legend, the site of King Arthur's palace and court.
3   a small open boat propelled by oars or sails.

PART II

There she weaves by night and day
A magic web with colors gay.
She has heard a whisper say,
A curse is on her if she stay   40
        To look down to Camelot.
She knows not what the curse may be,
And so she weaveth steadily,
And little other care hath she,
        The Lady of Shalott.

And moving thro' a mirror clear
That hangs before her all the year,
Shadows of the world appear.
There she sees the highway near
        Winding down to Camelot: 50
There the river eddy whirls,
And there the surly village-churls,
And the red cloaks of market girls,
        Pass onward from Shalott.

Sometimes a troop of damsels glad,
An abbot on an ambling pad,
Sometimes a curly shepherd-lad,
Or long-haired page in crimson clad,
        Goes by to towered Camelot;
And sometimes thro' the mirror blue   60
The knights come riding two and two:
She hath no loyal knight and true,
        The Lady of Shalott.

But in her web she still delights
To weave the mirror's magic sights,
For often thro' the silent nights
A funeral, with plumes and lights
        And music, went to Camelot:
Or when the moon was overhead,
Came two young lovers lately wed;   70
"I am half sick of shadows," said
        The Lady of Shalott.

PART III

A bow-shot from her bower-eaves,
He rode between the barley-sheaves,
The sun came dazzling thro' the leaves,
And flamed upon the brazen greaves[4]

4 armor for the leg below the knee.

Of bold Sir Lancelot.
A red-cross knight for ever kneeled
To a lady in his shield,
That sparkled on the yellow field,   80
    Beside remote Shalott.

The gemmy bridle glittered free,
Like to some branch of stars we see
Hung in the golden Galaxy.
The bridle bells rang merrily
    As he rode down to Camelot:
And from his blazoned baldric slung
A mightly silver bugle hung,
And as he rode his armor rung,
    Beside remote Shalott.   90

All in the blue unclouded weather
Thick-jewelled shone the saddle-leather,
The helmet and the helmet-feather
Burned like one burning flame together,
    As he rode down to Camelot.
As often thro' the purple night,
Below the starry clusters bright,
Some bearded meteor, trailing light,
    Moves over still Shalott.

His broad clear brow in sunlight glowed;   100
On burnished hooves his war-horse trode;
From underneath his helmet flowed
His coal-black curls as on he rode,
    As he rode down to Camelot.
From the bank and from the river
He flashed into the crystal mirror,
"Tirra lirra," by the river
    Sang Sir Lancelot.

She left the web, she left the loom,
She made three paces thro' the room,   110
She saw the water-lily bloom,
She saw the helmet and the plume,
    She looked down to Camelot.
Out flew the web and floated wide;
The mirror cracked from side to side;
"The curse is come upon me," cried
    The Lady of Shalott.

PART IV

In the stormy east-wind straining,
The pale yellow woods were waning,

The broad stream in his banks complaining,   120
Heavily the low sky raining
        Over towered Camelot;
Down she came and found a boat
Beneath a willow left afloat,
And round about the prow she wrote
        The Lady of Shalott.

And down the river's dim expanse
Like some bold seer in a trance,
Seeing all his own mischance—
With a glassy countenance   130
        Did she look to Camelot.
And at the closing of the day
She loosed the chain, and down she lay;
The broad stream bore her far away,
        The Lady of Shalott.

Lying, robed in snowy white
That loosely flew to left and right—
The leaves upon her falling light—
Thro' the noises of the night
        She floated down to Camelot: 140
And as the boat-head wound along
The willowy hills and fields among,
They heard her singing her last song,
        The Lady of Shalott.

Heard a carol, mournful, holy,
Chanted loudly, chanted lowly,
'Till her blood was frozen slowly,
And her eyes were darkened wholly,
        Turn'd to towered Camelot.
For ere she reached upon the tide   150
The first house by the water-side,
Singing in her song she died,
        The Lady of Shalott.

Under tower and balcony,
By garden-wall and gallery,
A gleaming shape she floated by,
Dead-pale between the houses high,
        Silent into Camelot.
Out upon the wharfs they came,
Knight and burgher, lord and dame,   160
And round the prow they read her name,
        The Lady of Shalott.

Who is this? and what is here?
And in the lighted palace near

Died the sound of royal cheer;
And they crossed themselves for fear,
    All the knights at Camelot:
But Lancelot mused a little space;
He said, "She has a lovely face;
God in his mercy lend her grace,   170
    The Lady of Shalott."

Ulysses

It little profits that an idle king,
By this still hearth, among these barren crags,
Matched with an aged wife, I mete and dole
Unequal laws unto a savage race,
That hoard, and sleep, and feed, and know not me.
I cannot rest from travel: I will drink
Life to the lees: all times I have enjoyed
Greatly, have suffered greatly, both with those
That loved me, and alone; on shore, and when
Through scudding drifts the rainy Hyades[1]   10
Vext the dim sea. I am become a name;
For always roaming with a hungry heart
Much have I seen and known: cities of men
And manners, climates, councils, governments,
Myself not least, but honored of them all, —
And drunk delight of battle with my peers,
Far on the ringing plains of windy Troy.
I am a part of all that I have met;
Yet all experience is an arch wherethrough
Gleams that untraveled world, whose margin fades   20
For ever and for ever when I move.
How dull it is to pause, to make an end,
To rust unburnished, not to shine in use!
As though to breathe were life. Life piled on life
Were all too little, and of one to me
Little remains: but every hour is saved
For that eternal silence, something more,
A bringer of new things; and vile it were
From some three suns to store and hoard myself,
And this gray spirit yearning in desire   30
To follow knowledge, like a sinking star,
Beyond the utmost bound of human thought.
    This is my son, mine own Telemachus,
To whom I leave the scepter and the isle—
Well-loved of me, discerning to fulfill

1   a group of stars believed to bring rain.

This labor, by slow prudence to make mild
A rugged people, and through soft degrees
Subdue them to the useful and the good.
Most blameless is he, centered in the sphere
Of common duties, decent not to fail   40
In offices of tenderness, and pay
Meet adoration to my household gods,
When I am gone. He works his work, I mine.
    There lies the port: the vessel puffs her sail:
There gloom the dark broad seas. My mariners,
Souls that have toiled, and wrought, and thought with me—
That ever with a frolic welcome took
The thunder and the sunshine, and opposed
Free hearts, free foreheads—you and I are old;
Old age hath yet his honor and his toil;   50
Death closes all: but something ere the end,
Some work of noble note, may yet be done,
Not unbecoming men that strove with Gods.
The lights begin to twinkle from the rocks:
The long day wanes: the slow moon climbs: the deep
Moans round with many voices. Come, my friends,
'Tis not too late to seek a newer world.
Push off, and sitting well in order smite
The sounding furrows; for my purpose holds
To sail beyond the sunset, and the baths   60
Of all the western stars, until I die.
It may be that the gulfs will wash us down:
It may be we shall touch the Happy Isles,[2]
And see the great Achilles, whom we knew.
Though much is taken, much abides; and though
We are not now that strength which in old days
Moved earth and heaven, that which we are, we are,—
One equal temper of heroic hearts,
Made weak by time and fate, but strong in will
To strive, to seek, to find, and not to yield.   70

2   the home of the blessed after death.

Tears, Idle Tears[1]

    Tears, idle tears, I know not what they mean,
Tears from the depth of some divine despair
Rise in the heart, and gather to the eyes,
In looking on the happy autumn-fields,
And thinking of the days that are no more.

1   From *The Princess*.

Fresh as the first beam glittering on a sail,
That brings our friends up from the underworld,
Sad as the last which reddens over one
That sinks with all we love below the verge;
So sad, so fresh, the days that are no more.

Ah, sad and strange as in dark summer dawns
The earliest pipe of half-awakened birds
To dying ears, when unto dying eyes
The casement slowly grows a glimmering square;
So sad, so strange, the days that are no more.

Dear as remembered kisses after death,
And sweet as those by hopeless fancy feigned
On lips that are for others; deep as love,
Deep as first love, and wild with all regret;
O Death in Life, the days that are no more!

"Frater Ave Atque Vale"[1]

Row us out from Desenzano, to your Sirmione[2] row!
So they rowed, and there we landed—"'O venusta Sirmio!'"[3]
There to me through all the groves of olive in the summer glow,
There beneath the Roman ruin where the purple flowers grow,
Came that "Ave atque Vale" of the poet's hopeless woe,
Tenderest of Roman poets nineteen hundred years ago,
"Frater Ave atque Vale"—as we wandered to and fro
Gazing at the Lydian[4] laughter of the Garda Lake below
Sweet Catullus's all-but-island, olive-silvery Sirmio!

1 "Brother, Hail and Farewell," a quotation from Catullus, a Latin poet of the first
century B.C. Catullus's poem is a last farewell to his brother.
2 Desenzano is a town on Lake Garda in northern Italy. Sirmione, known as Sirmio in
antiquity, is the peninsula on Lake Garda where the villa of Catullus once stood.
3 "O beautiful Sirmio," a quotation from Catullus.
4 The Etruscans, who lived near Lake Garda, were believed to have come from Lydia
in Asia Minor.

ROBERT BROWNING   [1812–1889]

My Last Duchess
Ferrara

That's my last Duchess painted on the wall,
Looking as if she were alive. I call

That piece a wonder, now: Frà Pandolf's hands
Worked busily a day, and there she stands.
Will't please you sit and look at her? I said
"Frà Pandolf" by design, for never read
Strangers like you that pictured countenance,
The depth and passion of its earnest glance,
But to myself they turned (since none puts by
The curtain I have drawn for you, but I)   10
And seemed as they would ask me, if they durst,
How such a glance came there; so, not the first
Are you to turn and ask thus. Sir, 'twas not
Her husband's presence only, called that spot
Of joy into the Duchess' cheek; perhaps
Frà Pandolf chanced to say, "Her mantle laps
Over my lady's wrist too much," or "Paint
Must never hope to reproduce the faint
Half-flush that dies along her throat": such stuff
Was courtesy, she thought, and cause enough   20
For calling up that spot of joy. She had
A heart—how shall I say?—too soon made glad,
Too easily impressed: she liked whate'er
She looked on, and her looks went everywhere.
Sir, 'twas all one! My favor at her breast,
The dropping of the daylight in the West,
The bough of cherries some officious fool
Broke in the orchard for her, the white mule
She rode with round the terrace—all and each
Would draw from her alike the approving speech,   30
Or blush, at least. She thanked men,—good! but thanked
Somehow—I know not how—as if she ranked
My gift of a nine-hundred-years-old name
With anybody's gift. Who'd stoop to blame
This sort of trifling? Even had you skill
In speech—(which I have not)—to make your will
Quite clear to such an one, and say, "Just this
Or that in you disgusts me; here you miss,
Or there exceed the mark"—and if she let
Herself be lessoned so, nor plainly set   40
Her wits to yours, forsooth, and made excuse,
—E'en then would be some stooping; and I choose
Never to stoop. Oh sir, she smiled, no doubt,
Whene'er I passed her; but who passed without
Much the same smile? This grew; I gave commands;
Then all smiles stopped together. There she stands
As if alive. Will't please you rise? We'll meet
The company below, then. I repeat,
The Count your master's known munificence
Is ample warrant that no just pretence   50
Of mine for dowry will be disallowed;

Though his fair daughter's self, as I avowed
At starting, is my object. Nay, we'll go
Together down, sir. Notice Neptune, though,
Taming a sea-horse, thought a rarity,
Which Claus of Innsbruck cast in bronze for me!

Meeting at Night

1

The gray sea and the long black land;
And the yellow half-moon large and low;
And the startled little waves that leap
In fiery ringlets from their sleep,
As I gain the cove with pushing prow,
And quench its speed i' the slushy sand.

2

Then a mile of warm sea-scented beach;
Three fields to cross till a farm appears;
A tap at the pane, the quick sharp scratch
And blue spurt of a lighted match,
And a voice less loud, thro' its joys and fears,
Than the two hearts beating each to each!

Parting at Morning

Round the cape of a sudden came the sea,
And the sun looked over the mountain's rim:
And straight was a path of gold for him,
And the need of a world of men for me.

Up at a Villa—
Down in the City
(as distinguished by an Italian person of quality)

1

Had I but plenty of money, money enough and to spare,
The house for me, no doubt, were a house in the city-square;
Ah, such a life, such a life, as one leads at the window there!

2

Something to see, by Bacchus, something to hear, at least!
There, the whole day long, one's life is a perfect feast;
While up at a villa one lives, I maintain it, no more than a beast.

3

Well now, look at our villa! stuck like the horn of a bull
Just on a mountain-edge as bare as the creature's skull,
Save a mere shag of a bush with hardly a leaf to pull!
—I scratch my own, sometimes, to see if the hair's turned wool.   10

4

But the city, oh the city—the square with the houses! Why?
They are stone-faced, white as a curd, there's something to take the eye!
Houses in four straight lines, not a single front awry;
You watch who crosses and gossips, who saunters, who hurries by;
Green blinds, as a matter of course, to draw when the sun gets high;
And the shops with fanciful signs which are painted properly.

5

What of a villa? Though winter be over in March by rights,
'Tis May perhaps ere the snow shall have withered well off the heights:
You've the brown ploughed land before, where the oxen steam and
    wheeze,
And the hills over-smoked behind by the faint gray olive-trees.   20

6

Is it better in May, I ask you? You've summer all at once;
In a day he leaps complete with a few strong April suns.
'Mid the sharp short emerald wheat, scarce risen three fingers well,
The wild tulip, at end of its tube, blows out its great red bell
Like a thin clear bubble of blood, for the children to pick and sell.

7

Is it ever hot in the square? There's a fountain to spout and splash!
In the shade it sings and springs; in the shine such foam-bows flash
On the horses with curling fish-tails, that prance and paddle and pash
Round the lady atop in her conch—fifty gazers do not abash,
Though all that she wears is some weeds round her waist in a sort of
    sash.   30

8

All the year long at the villa, nothing to see though you linger,
Except yon cypress that points like death's lean lifted forefinger.
Some think fireflies pretty, when they mix i' the corn and mingle,
Or thrid the stinking hemp till the stalks of it seem a-tingle.
Late August or early September, the stunning cicala is shrill,
And the bees keep their tiresome whine round the resinous firs on the hill.
Enough of the seasons,—I spare you the months of the fever and chill.

9

Ere you open your eyes in the city, the blessed church-bells begin:
No sooner the bells leave off than the diligence rattles in:
You get the pick of the news, and it costs you never a pin.   40

By-and-by there's the traveling doctor gives pills, lets blood, draws teeth;
Or the Pulcinello-trumpet breaks up the market beneath.
At the post-office such a scene-picture—the new play, piping hot!
And a notice how, only this morning, three liberal thieves were shot.
Above it, behold the Archbishop's most fatherly of rebukes,
And beneath, with his crown and his lion, some little new law of the
    Duke's!
Or a sonnet with flowery marge, to the Reverend Don So-and-so
Who is Dante, Boccaccio, Petrarca, Saint Jerome and Cicero,[1]
"And moreover," (the sonnet goes rhyming,) "the skirts of Saint Paul has
    reached,
Having preached us those six Lent-lectures more unctuous than ever he
    preached."   50
Noon strikes,—here sweeps the procession! our Lady borne smiling and
    smart
With a pink gauze gown all spangles, and seven swords stuck in her heart!
Bang-whang-whang goes the drum, *tootle-te-tootle* the fife;
No keeping one's haunches still: it's the greatest pleasure in life.

10

But bless you, it's dear—it's dear! fowls, wine, at double the rate.
They have clapped a new tax upon salt, and what oil pays passing the gate
It's a horror to think of. And so, the villa for me, not the city!
Beggars can scarcely be choosers: but still—ah, the pity, the pity!
Look, two and two go the priests, then the monks with cowls and sandals,
And the penitents dressed in white shirts, a-holding the yellow
    candles;   60
One, he carries a flag up straight, and another a cross with handles,
And the Duke's guard brings up the rear, for the better prevention of
    scandals:
Bang-whang-whang goes the drum, *tootle-te-tootle* the fife.
Oh, a day in the city-square, there is no such pleasure in life!

1   *Dante, Boccaccio, Petrarca*: poets of Italy; *Saint Jerome*: Christian scholar and
Father of the Church; *Cicero*: Roman orator.

EDWARD LEAR [1812–1888]

By Way
of Preface

"How pleasant to know Mr. Lear!"
    Who has written such volumes of stuff!
Some think him ill-tempered and queer,
    But a few think him pleasant enough.

His mind is concrete and fastidious,
    His nose is remarkably big;

His visage is more or less hideous,
  His beard it resembles a wig.

He has ears, and two eyes, and ten fingers,
  Leastways if you reckon two thumbs;   10
Long ago he was one of the singers,
  But now he is one of the dumbs.

He sits in a beautiful parlor,
  With hundreds of books on the wall;
He drinks a great deal of Marsala,[1]
  But never gets tipsy at all.

He has many friends, laymen and clerical,
  Old Foss is the name of his cat;
His body is perfectly spherical,
  He weareth a runcible[2] hat.   20

When he walks in a waterproof white,
  The children run after him so!
Calling out, "He's come out in his night-
  Gown, that crazy old Englishman, oh!"

He weeps by the side of the ocean,
  He weeps on the top of the hill;
He purchases pancakes and lotion,
  And chocolate shrimps from the mill.

He reads but he cannot speak Spanish,
  He cannot abide ginger-beer: 30
Ere the days of his pilgrimage vanish,
  How pleasant to know Mr. Lear!

1   a kind of Italian wine.
2   a nonsense word invented by Lear.

WALT WHITMAN   [1819–1892]

Crossing
Brooklyn Ferry

1

Flood-tide below me! I see you face to face!
Clouds of the west—sun there half an hour high—I see you also face to
  face.

Crowds of men and women attired in the usual costumes, how curious
  you are to me!

On the ferry-boats the hundreds and hundreds that cross, returning
    home, are more curious to me than you suppose,
And you that shall cross from shore to shore years hence are more to me,
    and more in my meditations, than you might suppose.

2

The impalpable sustenance of me from all things at all hours of the day,
The simple, compact, well-joined scheme, myself disintegrated, every
    one disintegrated yet part of the scheme,
The similitudes of the past and those of the future,
The glories strung like beads on my smallest sights and hearings, on the
    walk in the street and the passage over the river,
The current rushing so swiftly and swimming with me far away,   10
The others that are to follow me, the ties between me and them,
The certainty of others, the life, love, sight, hearing of others.

Others will enter the gates of the ferry and cross from shore to shore,
Others will watch the run of the flood-tide,
Others will see the shipping of Manhattan north and west, and the heights
    of Brooklyn to the south and east,
Others will see the islands large and small;
Fifty years hence, others will see them as they cross, the sun half an hour
    high,
A hundred years hence, or ever so many hundred years hence, others will
    see them,
Will enjoy the sunset, the pouring-in of the flood-tide, the falling-back to
    the sea of the ebb-tide.

3

It avails not, time nor place—distance avails not,   20
I am with you, you men and women of a generation, or ever so many gen-
    erations hence,
Just as you feel when you look on the river and sky, so I felt,
Just as any of you is one of a living crowd, I was one of a crowd,
Just as you are refreshed by the gladness of the river and the bright flow, I
    was refreshed,
Just as you stand and lean on the rail, yet hurry with the swift current, I
    stood yet was hurried,
Just as you look on the numberless masts of ships and the thick-stemmed
    pipes of steamboats, I looked.

I too many and many a time crossed the river of old,
Watched the Twelfth-month sea-gulls, saw them high in the air floating
    with motionless wings, oscillating their bodies,
Saw how the glistening yellow lit up parts of their bodies and left the rest
    in strong shadow,
Saw the slow-wheeling circles and the gradual edging toward the south, 30
Saw the reflection of the summer sky in the water,
Had my eyes dazzled by the shimmering track of beams,

Looked at the fine centrifugal spokes of light round the shape of my head
    in the sunlit water,
Looked on the haze on the hills southward and south-westward,
Looked on the vapor as it flew in fleeces tinged with violet,
Looked toward the lower bay to notice the vessels arriving,
Saw their approach, saw aboard those that were near me,
Saw the white sails of schooners and sloops, saw the ships at anchor,
The sailors at work in the rigging or out astride the spars,
The round masts, the swinging motion of the hulls, the slender serpentine
    pennants,   40
The large and small steamers in motion, the pilots in their pilothouses,
The white wake left by the passage, the quick tremulous whirl of the
    wheels,
The flags of all nations, the falling of them at sunset,
The scallop-edged waves in the twilight, the ladled cups, the frolicsome
    crests and glistening,
The stretch afar growing dimmer and dimmer, the gray walls of the gran-
    ite storehouses by the docks,
On the river the shadowy group, the big steam-tug closely flanked on
    each side by the barges, the hay-boat, the belated lighter,
On the neighboring shore the fires from the foundry chimneys burning
    high and glaringly into the night,
Casting their flicker of black contrasted with wild red and yellow light
    over the tops of houses, and down into the clefts of streets.

4
These and all else were to me the same as they are to you,
I loved well those cities, loved well the stately and rapid river,   50
The men and women I saw were all near to me,
Others the same—others who look back on me because I looked forward
    to them,
(The time will come, though I stop here today and tonight.)

5
What is it then between us?
What is the count of the scores or hundreds of years between us?

Whatever it is, it avails not—distance avails not, and place avails not,
I too lived, Brooklyn of ample hills was mine,
I too walked the streets of Manhattan island, and bathed in the waters
    around it,
I too felt the curious abrupt questionings stir within me,
In the day among crowds of people sometimes they came upon me,   60
In my walks home late at night or as I lay in my bed they came upon me,
I too had been struck from the float[1] forever held in solution,
I too had received identity by my body,
That I was I knew was of my body, and what I should be I knew I should
    be of my body.

---

1 the flux or flood of the tide; a floating object.

6

It is not upon you alone the dark patches fall,
The dark threw its patches down upon me also,
The best I had done seemed to me blank and suspicious,
My great thoughts as I supposed them, were they not in reality meagre?
Nor is it you alone who know what it is to be evil,
I am he who knew what it was to be evil, 70
I too knitted the old knot of contrariety,[2]
Blabbed, blushed, resented, lied, stole, grudged,
Had guile, anger, lust, hot wishes I dared not speak,
Was wayward, vain, greedy, shallow, sly, cowardly, malignant,
The wolf, the snake, the hog, not wanting in me,
The cheating look, the frivolous word, the adulterous wish, not wanting,
Refusals, hates, postponements, meanness, laziness, none of these want-
      ing,
Was one with the rest, the days and haps[3] of the rest,
Was called by my nighest name by clear loud voices of young men as they
      saw me approaching or passing,
Felt their arms on my neck as I stood, or the negligent leaning of their
      flesh against me as I sat, 80
Saw many I loved in the street or ferry-boat or public assembly, yet never
      told them a word,
Lived the same life with the rest, the same old laughing, gnawing, sleep-
      ing,
Played the part that still looks back on the actor or actress,
The same old role, the role that is what we make it, as great as we like,
Or as small as we like, or both great and small.

7

Closer yet I approach you,
What thought you have of me now, I had as much of you—I laid in my
      stores in advance,
I considered long and seriously of you before you were born.

Who was to know what should come home to me?
Who knows but I am enjoying this? 90
Who knows, for all the distance, but I am as good as looking at you now,
      for all you cannot see me?

8

Ah, what can ever be more stately and admirable to me than mast-
      hemmed Manhattan?
River and sunset and scallop-edged waves of flood-tide?
The sea-gulls oscillating their bodies, the hay-boat in the twilight, and the
      belated lighter?

---

2 opposites; diametrical difference.
3 happenings; accidents.

What gods can exceed these that clasp me by the hand, and with voices I
    love call me promptly and loudly by my nighest name as I ap-
    proach?
What is more subtle than this which ties me to the woman or man that
    looks in my face?
Which fuses me into you now, and pours my meaning into you?

We understand then do we not?
What I promised without mentioning it, have you not accepted?
What the study could not teach—what the preaching could not accom-
    plish is accomplished, is it not?   100

9
Flow on, river! flow with the flood-tide, and ebb with the ebb-tide!
Frolic on, crested and scallop-edged waves!
Gorgeous clouds of the sunset! drench with your splendor me, or the men
    and women generations after me!
Cross from shore to shore, countless crowds of passengers!
Stand up, tall masts of Mannahatta! stand up, beautiful hills of Brooklyn!
Throb, baffled and curious brain! throw out questions and answers!
Suspend here and everywhere, eternal float of solution!
Gaze, loving and thirsting eyes, in the house or street or public assembly!
Sound out, voices of young men! loudly and musically call me by my
    nighest name!
Live, old life! play the part that looks back on the actor or actress!   110
Play the old role, the role that is great or small according as one makes it!
Consider, you who peruse me, whether I may not in unknown ways be
    looking upon you;
Be firm, rail over the river, to support those who lean idly, yet haste with
    the hasting current;
Fly on, sea-birds! fly sideways, or wheel in large circles high in the air;
Receive the summer sky, you water, and faithfully hold it till all downcast
    eyes have time to take it from you!
Diverge, fine spokes of light, from the shape of my head, or any one's
    head, in the sunlit water!
Come on, ships from the lower bay! pass up or down, white-sailed
    schooners, sloops, lighters!
Flaunt away, flags of all nations! be duly lowered at sunset!
Burn high your fires, foundry chimneys! cast black shadows at nightfall!
    cast red and yellow light over the tops of the houses!
Appearances, now or henceforth, indicate what you are,   120
You necessary film, continue to envelop the soul,
About my body for me, and your body for you, be hung our divinest
    aromas,
Thrive, cities—bring your freight, bring your shows, ample and sufficient
    rivers,
Expand, being than which none else is perhaps more spiritual,
Keep your places, objects than which none else is more lasting.

You have waited, you always wait, you dumb, beautiful ministers,
We receive you with free sense at last, and are insatiate henceforward,
Not you any more shall be able to foil us, or withhold yourselves from us,
We use you, and do not cast you aside—we plant you permanently with-
    in us,   ·
We fathom you not—we love you—there is perfection in you also,   130
You furnish your parts toward eternity,
Great or small, you furnish your parts toward the soul.

I Saw in Louisiana
a Live-Oak Growing

I saw in Louisiana a live-oak growing,
All alone stood it and the moss hung down from the branches,
Without any companion it grew there uttering joyous leaves of dark
    green,
And its look, rude, unbending, lusty, made me think of myself,
But I wondered how it could utter joyous leaves standing alone there
    without its friend near, for I knew I could not,
And I broke off a twig with a certain number of leaves upon it, and
    twined around it a little moss,
And brought it away, and I have placed it in sight in my room.
It is not needed to remind me as of my own dear friends,
(For I believe lately I think of little else than of them,)
Yet it remains to me a curious token, it makes me think of manly love;
For all that, and though the live-oak glistens there in Louisiana solitary in
    a wide flat space,
Uttering joyous leaves all its life without a friend a lover near,
I know very well I could not.

Beat! Beat! Drums!

1

Beat! beat! drums!—blow! bugles! blow!
Through the windows—through doors—burst like a ruthless force,
Into the solemn church, and scatter the congregation;
Into the school where the scholar is studying;
Leave not the bridegroom quiet—no happiness must he have now with his
    bride;
Nor the peaceful farmer any peace, ploughing his field or gathering his
    grain;
So fierce you whirr and pound, you drums—so shrill you bugles blow.

2

Beat! beat! drums!—blow! bugles! blow!
Over the traffic of cities—over the rumble of wheels in the streets:

Are beds prepared for sleepers at night in the houses? No sleepers must
    sleep in those beds;
No bargainers' bargains by day—no brokers or speculators—would they
    continue?
Would the talkers be talking? would the singer attempt to sing?
Would the lawyer rise in the court to state his case before the judge?
Then rattle quicker, heavier drums–you bugles wilder blow.

3

Beat! beat! drums!—blow! bugles! blow!
Make no parley—stop for no expostulation;
Mind not the timid—mind not the weeper or prayer;
Mind not the old man beseeching the young man;
Let not the child's voice be heard, nor the mother's entreaties;
Make even the trestles to shake the dead, where they lie awaiting the
    hearses,
So strong you thump, O terrible drums—so loud you bugles blow.

A Farm Picture

Through the ample open door of the peaceful country barn,
A sunlit pasture field, with cattle and horses feeding;
And haze, and vista, and the far horizon, fading away.

Cavalry Crossing a Ford

A line in long array, where they wind betwixt green islands;
They take a serpentine course—their arms flash in the sun—hark to the
    musical clank;
Behold the silvery river—in it the splashing horses, loitering, stop to
    drink;
Behold the brown-faced men—each group, each person, a picture—the
    negligent rest on the saddles;
Some emerge on the opposite bank—others are just entering the ford—
    while,
Scarlet, and blue, and snowy white,
The guidon[1] flags flutter gaily in the wind.

1 A guidon is a guide-flag carried by a cavalry troop.

An Army Corps on the March

With its cloud of skirmishers in advance,
With now the sound of a single shot snapping like a whip, and now an
      irregular volley,
The swarming ranks press on and on, the dense brigades press on;
Glittering dimly, toiling under the sun—the dust-covered men,
In columns rise and fall to the undulations of the ground,
With artillery interspersed—the wheels rumble, the horses sweat,
As the army corps advances.

When Lilacs Last in the Dooryard Bloomed

1

When lilacs last in the dooryard bloomed,
And the great star early drooped in the western sky in the night,
I mourned, and yet shall mourn with ever-returning spring.

Ever-returning spring, trinity sure to me you bring,
Lilac blooming perennial and drooping star in the west,
And thought of him I love.

2

O powerful western fallen star!
O shades of night—O moody, tearful night!
O great star disappeared—O the black murk that hides the star!
O cruel hands that hold me powerless—O helpless soul of me!   10
O harsh surrounding cloud that will not free my soul.

3

In the dooryard fronting an old farm-house near the white-washed pal-
      ings,
Stands the lilac-bush tall-growing with heart-shaped leaves of rich green,
With many a pointed blossom rising delicate, with the perfume strong I
      love,
With every leaf a miracle—and from this bush in the dooryard,
With delicate-colored blossoms and heart-shaped leaves of rich green,
A sprig with its flower I break.

4

In the swamp in secluded recesses,
A shy and hidden bird is warbling a song.

Solitary the thrush,   20
The hermit withdrawn to himself, avoiding the settlements,
Sings by himself a song.

Song of the bleeding throat,
Death's outlet song of life, (for well dear brother I know,
If thou wast not granted to sing thou would'st surely die.)

                    5
Over the breast of the spring, the land, amid cities,
Amid lanes and through old woods, where lately the violets peeped from
        the ground, spotting the gray debris,
Amid the grass in the fields each side of the lanes, passing the endless
        grass,
Passing the yellow-speared wheat, every grain from its shroud in the dark-
        brown fields uprisen,
Passing the apple-tree blows of white and pink in the orchards,   30
Carrying a corpse to where it shall rest in the grave,
Night and day journeys a coffin.

                    6
Coffin that passes through lanes and streets,
Through day and night with the great cloud darkening the land,
With the pomp of the inlooped flags with the cities draped in black,
With the show of the States themselves as of crape-veiled women stand-
        ing,
With processions long and winding and the flambeaus of the night,
With the countless torches lit, with the silent sea of faces and the unbared
        heads,
With the waiting depot, the arriving coffin, and the sombre faces,
With dirges through the night, with the thousand voices rising strong and
        solemn,   40
With all the mournful voices of the dirges poured around the coffin,
The dim-lit churches and the shuddering organs—where amid these you
        journey,
With the tolling tolling bells' perpetual clang,
Here, coffin that slowly passes,
I give you my sprig of lilac.

                    7
(Nor for you, for one alone,
Blossoms and branches green to coffins all I bring,
For fresh as the morning, thus would I chant a song for you O sane and
        sacred death.

All over bouquets of roses,
O death, I cover you over with roses and early lilies,   50
But mostly and now the lilac that blooms the first,

Copious I break, I break the sprigs from the bushes,
With loaded arms I come, pouring for you,
For you and the coffins all of you O death.)

8

O western orb sailing the heaven,
Now I know what you must have meant as a month since I walked,
As I walked in silence the transparent shadowy night,
As I saw you had something to tell as you bent to me night after night,
As you drooped from the sky low down as if to my side, (while the other
    stars all looked on,)
As we wandered together the solemn night, (for something I know not
    what kept me from sleep,)   60
As the night advanced, and I saw on the rim of the west how full you were
    of woe,
As I stood on the rising ground in the breeze in the cool transparent night,
As I watched where you passed and was lost in the netherward black of
    the night,
As my soul in its trouble dissatisfied sank, as where you sad orb,
Concluded, dropt in the night, and was gone.

9

Sing on there in the swamp,
O singer bashful and tender, I hear your notes, I hear your call,
I hear, I come presently, I understand you,
But a moment I linger, for the lustrous star has detained me,
The star my departing comrade holds and detains me.   70

10

O how shall I warble myself for the dead one there I loved?
And how shall I deck my song for the large sweet soul that has gone?
And what shall my perfume be for the grave of him I love?

Sea-winds blown from east and west,
Blown from the Eastern sea and blown from the Western sea, till there on
    the prairies meeting,
These and with these and the breath of my chant,
I'll perfume the grave of him I love.

11

O what shall I hang on the chamber walls?
And what shall the pictures be that I hang on the walls,
To adorn the burial-house of him I love?   80

Pictures of growing spring and farms and homes,
With the Fourth-month[1] eve at sundown, and the gray smoke lucid and
    bright,

1   April. Whitman's mother was a Quaker, and the Quakers named the months in this
fashion, by numbers.

With floods of the yellow gold of the gorgeous, indolent, sinking sun,
    burning, expanding the air,
With the fresh sweet herbage under foot, and the pale green leaves of the
    trees prolific,
In the distance the flowing glaze, the breast of the river, with a wind-
    dapple here and there,
With ranging hills on the banks, with many a line against the sky, and
    shadows,
And the city at hand with dwellings so dense, and stacks of chimneys,
And all the scenes of life and the workshops, and the workmen homeward
    returning.

12

Lo, body and soul—this land,
My own Manhattan with spires, and the sparkling and hurrying tides,
    and the ships,   90
The varied and ample land, the South and the North in the light, Ohio's
    shores and flashing Missouri,
And ever the far-spreading prairies covered with grass and corn.

Lo, the most excellent sun so calm and haughty,
The violet and purple morn with just-felt breezes,
The gentle soft-born measureless light,
The miracle spreading bathing all, the fulfilled noon,
The coming eve delicious, the welcome night and the stars,
Over my cities shining all, enveloping man and land.

13

Sing on, sing on you gray-brown bird,
Sing from the swamps, the recesses, pour your chant from the bushes,   100
Limitless out of the dusk, out of the cedars and pines.

Sing on dearest brother, warble your reedy song,
Loud human song, with voice of uttermost woe.

O liquid and free and tender!
O wild and loose to my soul—O wondrous singer!
You only I hear—yet the star holds me, (but will soon depart,)
Yet the lilac with mastering odor holds me.

14

Now while I sat in the day and looked forth,
In the close of the day with its light and the fields of spring, and the
    farmers preparing their crops,
In the large unconscious scenery of my land with its lakes and forests,   110
In the heavenly aerial beauty, (after the perturbed winds and the storms,)
Under the arching heavens of the afternoon swift passing, and the voices
    of children and women,

The many-moving sea-tides, and I saw the ships how they sailed,
And the summer approaching with richness, and the fields all busy with
    labor,
And the infinite separate houses, how they all went on, each with its
    meals and minutia of daily usages,
And the streets how their throbbings throbbed, and the cities pent—lo,
    then and there,
Falling upon them all and among them all, enveloping me with the rest,
Appeared the cloud, appeared the long black trail,
And I knew death, its thought, and the sacred knowledge of death.

Then with the knowledge of death as walking one side of me,   120
And the thought of death close-walking the other side of me,
And I in the middle as with companions, and as holding the hands of
    companions,
I fled forth to the hiding receiving night that talks not,
Down to the shores of the water, the path by the swamp in the dimness,
To the solemn shadowy cedars and ghostly pines so still.

And the singer so shy to the rest received me,
The gray-brown bird I know received us comrades three,
And he sang the carol of death, and a verse for him I love.

From deep secluded recesses,
From the fragrant cedars and the ghostly pines so still,   130
Came the carol of the bird.

And the charm of the carol rapt me,
As I held as if by their hands my comrades in the night,
And the voice of my spirit tallied the song of the bird.

Come lovely and soothing death,
Undulate round the world, serenely arriving, arriving,
In the day, in the night, to all, to each,
Sooner or later delicate death.

Praised be the fathomless universe,
For life and joy, and for objects and knowledge curious,   140
And for love, sweet love—but praise! praise! praise!
For the sure-enwinding arms of cool-enfolding death.

Dark mother always gliding near with soft feet,
Have none chanted for thee a chant of fullest welcome?
Then I chant it for thee, I glorify thee above all,
I bring thee a song that when thou must indeed come, come unfalter-
    ingly.

Approach strong deliveress,
When it is so, when thou hast taken them I joyously sing the dead,

Lost in the loving floating ocean of thee,
Laved in the flood of thy bliss O death. 150

From me to thee glad serenades,
Dances for thee I propose saluting thee, adornments and feastings for
       thee,
And the sights of the open landscape and the high-spread sky are fitting,
And life and the fields, and the huge and thoughtful night.

The night in silence under many a star,
The ocean shore and the husky whispering wave whose voice I know,
And the soul turning to thee O vast and well-veiled death,
And the body gratefully nestling close to thee.

Over the tree-tops I float thee a song,
Over the rising and sinking waves, over the myriad fields and the prairies
       wide, 160
Over the dense-packed cities all and the teeming wharves and ways,
I float this carol with joy, with joy to thee O death.

     15
To the tally of my soul,
Loud and strong kept up the gray-brown bird,
With pure deliberate notes spreading filling the night.

Loud in the pines and cedars dim,
Clear in the freshness moist and the swamp-perfume,
And I with my comrades there in the night.

While my sight that was bound in my eyes unclosed,
As to long panoramas of visions. 170

And I saw askant[2] the armies,
I saw as in noiseless dreams hundreds of battle-flags,
Borne through the smoke of the battles and pierced with missiles I saw
       them,
And carried hither and yon through the smoke, and torn and bloody,
And at last but a few shreds left on the staffs, (and all in silence,)
And the staffs all splintered and broken.

I saw battle-corpses, myriads of them,
And the white skeletons of young men, I saw them,
I saw the debris and debris of all the slain soldiers of the war,
But I saw they were not as was thought, 180
They themselves were fully at rest, they suffered not,
The living remained and suffered, the mother suffered,
And the wife and the child and the musing comrade suffered,
And the armies that remained suffered.

2 obliquely; with distrust.

16

Passing the visions, passing the night,
Passing, unloosing the hold of my comrades' hands,
Passing the song of the hermit bird and the tallying song of my soul,
Victorious song, death's outlet song, yet varying ever-altering song,
As low and wailing, yet clear the notes, rising and falling, flooding the
    night,
Sadly sinking and fainting, as warning and warning, and yet again burst-
    ing with joy,   190
Covering the earth and filling the spread of the heaven,
As that powerful psalm in the night I heard from recesses,
Passing, I leave thee lilac with heart-shaped leaves,
I leave thee there in the door-yard, blooming, returning with spring.

I cease from my song for thee,
From my gaze on thee in the west, fronting the west, communing with
    thee,
O comrade lustrous with silver face in the night.

Yet each to keep and all, retrievements out of the night,
The song, the wondrous chant of the gray-brown bird,
And the tallying chant, the echo aroused in my soul,   200
With the lustrous and drooping star with the countenance full of woe,
With the holders holding my hand nearing the call of the bird,
Comrades mine and I in the midst, and their memory ever to keep, for the
    dead I loved so well,
For the sweetest, wisest soul of all my days and lands—and this for his
    dear sake,
Lilac and star and bird twined with the chant of my soul,
There in the fragrant pines and the cedars dusk and dim.

The Runner

On a flat road runs the well-trained runner;
He is lean and sinewy, with muscular legs;
He is thinly clothed—he leans forward as he runs,
With lightly closed fists, and arms partially raised.

A Noiseless
Patient Spider

A noiseless patient spider,
I marked where on a little promontory it stood isolated,
Marked how to explore the vacant vast surrounding,

It launched forth filament, filament, filament, out of itself,
Ever unreeling down, ever tirelessly speeding them.

And you O my soul where you stand,
Surrounded, detached, in measureless oceans of space,
Ceaselessly musing, venturing, throwing, seeking the spheres to connect
    them,
Till the bridge you will need be formed, till the ductile anchor hold,
Till the gossamer thread you fling catch somewhere, O my soul.

Sparkles from the Wheel

Where the city's ceaseless crowd moves on the livelong day,
Withdrawn I join a group of children watching, I pause aside with them.

By the curb toward the edge of the flagging,
A knife-grinder works at his wheel sharpening a great knife,
Bending over he carefully holds it to the stone, by foot and knee,
With measured tread he turns rapidly, as he presses with light but firm
    hand,
Forth issue then in copious golden jets,
Sparkles from the wheel.

The scene and all its belongings, how they seize and affect me,
The sad sharp-chinned old man with worn clothes and broad shoulder-
    band of leather,
Myself effusing and fluid, a phantom curiously floating, now here ab-
    sorbed and arrested,
The group, (an unminded point set in a vast surrounding,)
The attentive, quiet children, the loud, proud, restive base of the streets,
The low hoarse purr of the whirling stone, the light-pressed blade,
Diffusing, dropping, sideways-darting, in tiny showers of gold,
Sparkles from the wheel.

MATTHEW ARNOLD [1822–1888]

Dover Beach

The sea is calm tonight,
The tide is full, the moon lies fair
Upon the straits;—on the French coast the light
Gleams and is gone; the cliffs of England stand,
Glimmering and vast out in the tranquil bay.
Come to the window, sweet is the night-air!

Only, from the long line of spray
Where the sea meets the moon-blanched land,
Listen! you hear the grating roar
Of pebbles which the waves draw back,and fling,   10
At their return, up the high strand,
Begin, and cease, and then again begin,
With tremulous cadence slow, and bring
The eternal note of sadness in.

Sophocles long ago
Heard it on the Aegean, and it brought
Into his mind the turbid ebb and flow
Of human misery; we
Find also in the sound a thought,
Hearing it by this distant northern sea.   20

The Sea of Faith
Was once, too, at the full, and round earth's shore
Lay like the folds of a bright girdle furled.
But now I only hear
Its melancholy, long, withdrawing roar,
Retreating, to the breath
Of the night-wind, down the vast edges drear
And naked shingles of the world.

Ah, love, let us be true
To one another! for the world, which seems   30
To lie before us like a land of dreams,
So various, so beautiful, so new,
Hath really neither joy, nor love, nor light,
Nor certitude, nor peace, nor help for pain;
And we are here as on a darkling plain
Swept with confused alarms of struggle and flight,
Where ignorant armies clash by night.

CHRISTINA ROSSETTI   [1830–1894]

Song

When I am dead, my dearest,
    Sing no sad songs for me;
Plant thou no roses at my head,
    Nor shady cypress tree:
Be the green grass above me
    With showers and dewdrops wet;
And if thou wilt, remember,
    And if thou wilt, forget,

I shall not see the shadows,
    I shall not feel the rain;
I shall not hear the nightingale
    Sing on, as if in pain:
And dreaming through the twilight
    That doth not rise nor set,
Haply I may remember,
    And haply may forget.

A Christmas Carol

In the bleak mid-winter
    Frosty wind made moan,
Earth stood hard as iron,
    Water like a stone;
Snow had fallen, snow on snow,
    Snow on snow,
In the bleak mid-winter
    Long ago.

Our God, Heaven cannot hold Him
    Nor earth sustain;   10
Heaven and earth shall flee away
    When He comes to reign:
In the bleak mid-winter
    A stable-place sufficed
The Lord God Almighty
    Jesus Christ.

Enough for Him whom cherubim
    Worship night and day,
A breastful of milk
    And a mangerful of hay;   20
Enough for Him whom angels
    Fall down before,
The ox and ass and camel
    Which adore.

Angels and archangels
    May have gathered there,
Cherubim and seraphim
    Thronged the air,
But only His mother
    In her maiden bliss   30
Worshipped the Beloved
    With a kiss.

What can I give Him,
   Poor as I am?
If I were a shepherd
   I would bring a lamb,
If I were a wise man,
   I would do my part,—
Yet what I can I give Him,
   Give my heart.

40

Spring Quiet

Gone were but the Winter,
   Come were but the Spring,
I would go to a covert
   Where the birds sing;

Where in the white-thorn
   Singeth a thrush,
And a robin sings
   In the holly-bush.

Full of fresh scents
   Are the budding boughs,
Arching high over
   A cool green house:

Full of sweet scents,
   And whispering air
Which sayeth softly:
   "We spread no snare;

Here dwell in safety,
   Here dwell alone,
With a clear stream
   And a mossy stone.

Here the sun shineth
   More shadily;
Here is heard an echo
   Of the far sea,
Though far off it be."

EMILY DICKINSON [1830–1884]

Success Is
Counted Sweetest

Success is counted sweetest
By those who ne'er succeed.
To comprehend a nectar
Requires sorest need.

Not one of all the purple Host
Who took the Flag today
Can tell the definition
So clear of Victory

As he defeated—dying—
On whose forbidden ear
The distant strains of triumph
Burst agonized and clear!

I Like a
Look of Agony

I like a look of Agony,
Because I know it's true—
Men do not sham Convulsion,
Nor simulate, a Throe—

The Eyes glaze once—and that is Death—
Impossible to feign
The Beads upon the Forehead
By homely Anguish strung.

The Soul Selects
Her Own Society

The Soul selects her own Society—
Then—shuts the Door—
To her divine Majority—
Present no more—

Unmoved—she notes the Chariots—pausing—
At her low Gate—
Unmoved—an Emperor be kneeling
Upon her Mat—

I've known her—from an ample nation—
Choose One—
Then—close the Valves of her attention—
Like Stone—

After Great Pain,
a Formal Feeling Comes

After great pain, a formal feeling comes—
The Nerves sit ceremonious, like Tombs—
The stiff Heart questions was it He, that bore,
And Yesterday, or Centuries before?

The Feet, mechanical, go round—
Of Ground, or Air, or Ought—
A Wooden way
Regardless grown,
A Quartz contentment, like a stone—

This is the Hour of Lead—
Remembered, if outlived,
As Freezing persons, recollect the Snow—
First—Chill—then Stupor—then the letting go—

There's Been a Death,
in the Opposite House

There's been a Death, in the Opposite House,
As lately as Today—
I know it, by the numb look
Such Houses have—alway—

The Neighbors rustle in and out—
The Doctor—drives away—
A Window opens like a Pod—
Abrupt—mechanically—

Somebody flings a Mattrass out—
The Children hurry by—
They wonder if it died—on that—
I used to—when a Boy—

The Minister—goes stiffly in—
As if the House were His—
And He owned all the Mourners—now—
And little Boys—besides—

And then the Milliner—and the Man
Of the Appalling Trade—
To take the measure of the House—
There'll be that Dark Parade—

Of Tassels—and of Coaches—soon—
It's easy as a Sign—
The Intuition of the News—
In just a Country Town—

They Shut Me Up
in Prose

They shut me up in Prose—
As when a little Girl
They put me in the Closet—
Because they liked me "still"—

Still! Could themself have peeped—
And seen my Brain—go round—
They might as wise have lodged a Bird
For Treason—in the Pound—

Himself has but to will
And easy as a Star
Look down upon Captivity—
And laugh—No more have I—

The Way I Read
a Letter's—This

The Way I read a Letter's—this—
'Tis first—I lock the Door—
And push it with my fingers—next—
For transport it be sure—

And then I go the furthest off
To counteract a knock—
Then draw my little Letter forth
And slowly pick the lock—

Then—glancing narrow, at the Wall—
And narrow at the floor
For Firm Conviction of a Mouse
Not exorcised before—

Peruse how infinite I am
To no one that You—know—
And sigh for lack of Heaven—but not
The Heaven God bestow—

The Name—
of It—Is "Autumn"

The name—of it—is "Autumn"—
The hue—of it—is Blood—
An Artery—upon the Hill—
A Vein—along the Road—

Great Globules—in the Alleys—
And Oh, the Shower of Stain—
When Winds—upset the Basin—
And spill the Scarlet Rain—

It sprinkles Bonnets—far below—
It gathers ruddy Pools—
Then—eddies like a Rose—away—
Upon Vermilion Wheels—

Ah, Teneriffe![1]

Ah, Teneriffe!
Retreating Mountain!
Purples of Ages—pause for *you*—

Sunset—reviews her Sapphire Regiment—
Day—drops you her Red Adieu!

Still—clad in your Mail of ices—
Thigh of Granite—and thew—of Steel—
Heedless—alike—of pomp—or parting

Ah, Teneriffe!
I'm kneeling—still—

1 *Teneriffe*: one of the Canary Islands, a chain of mountainous islands in the Atlantic, off the west coast of Africa.

A Drunkard Cannot
Meet a Cork

A Drunkard cannot meet a Cork
Without a Revery—
And so encountering a Fly
This January Day
Jamaicas of Remembrance stir
That send me reeling in—
The moderate drinker of Delight
Does not deserve the spring—
Of juleps, part are in the Jug
And more are in the joy—
Your connoisseur in Liquors
Consults the Bumble Bee—

LEWIS CARROLL   [1832–1898]

The White
Knight's Song[1]

"I'll tell thee everything I can:
    There's little to relate.
I saw an aged aged man,
    A-sitting on a gate.
'Who are you, aged man?' I said,
    'And how is it you live?'
And his answer trickled through my head
    Like water through a sieve.

"He said, 'I look for butterflies,
    That sleep among the wheat;   10
I make them into mutton pies,
    And sell them in the street.
I sell them unto men,' he said,
    'Who sail on stormy seas;
And that's the way I get my bread—
    A trifle, if you please!'

"But I was thinking of a plan
    To dye one's whiskers green,
And always use so large a fan

1   a parody of Wordworth's "Resolution and Independence."

That they could not be seen.
So, having no reply to give
   To what the old man said,
I cried, 'Come, tell me how you live!'
   And thumped him on the head.

"His accents mild took up the tale:
   He said, 'I go my ways,
And when I find a mountain rill,
   I set it in a blaze;
And there they make a stuff they call
   Rowland's Macassar oil—[2]
Yet twopence halfpenny is all
   They give me for my toil.'

"But I was thinking of a way
   To feed oneself on batter
And so go on from day to day
   Getting a little fatter.
I shook him well from side to side,
   Until his face was blue:
'Come, tell me how you live,' I cried,
   'And what it is you do?'

"He said, 'I hunt for haddocks' eyes
   Among the heather bright,
I work them into waistcoat buttons
   In the silent night.
And these I do not sell for gold
   Or coin of silvery shine,
But for a copper halfpenny,
   And that will purchase nine.

"'I sometimes dig for buttered rolls,
   Or set limed twigs for crabs:
I sometimes search the grassy knolls
   For wheels of hansom cabs;
And that's the way' (he gave a wink)
   'By which I get my wealth—
And very gladly will I drink
   Your honor's noble health.'

"I heard him then, for I had just
   Completed my design
To keep the Menai Bridge[3] from rust
   By boiling it in wine.

2   hair oil.
3   The Menai Strait separates Wales from the Isle of Anglesey and is crossed by two
famous bridges, one by Telford and one by Robert Stephenson.

I thanked him much for telling me
    The way he got his wealth,
But chiefly for his wish that he
    Might drink my noble health.

"And now, if e'er by chance I put
    My fingers into glue,
Or madly squeeze a right-hand foot
    Into a left-hand shoe,
Or if I drop upon my toe
    A very heavy weight,   70
I weep, for it reminds me so
Of that old man I used to know—
Whose look was mild, whose speech was slow,
Whose hair was whiter than the snow,
Whose face was very like a crow,
    With eyes, like cinders, all aglow,
Who seemed distracted with his woe,
Who rocked his body to and fro,
And muttered mumblingly and low,
As if his mouth were full of dough,   80
Who snorted like a buffalo—
That summer evening long ago,
    A-sitting on a gate."

Jabberwocky

'Twas brillig, and the slithy toves
    Did gyre and gimble in the wabe:
All mimsy were the borogoves,
    And the mome raths outgrabe.

"Beware the Jabberwock, my son!
    The jaws that bite, the claws that catch!
Beware the Jubjub bird, and shun
    The frumious Bandersnatch!"

He took his vorpal sword in hand:
    Long time the manxome foe he sought—
So rested he by the Tumtum tree
    And stood awhile in thought.

And, as in uffish thought he stood,
    The Jabberwock, with eyes of flame,
Came whiffling through the tulgey wood,
    And burbled as it came!

One, two! One, two! and through and through
    The vorpal blade went snicker snack!
He left it dead and with his head
    He went galumphing back.

"And hast thou slain the Jabberwock?
    Come to my arms, my beamish boy!
O frabjous day! Callooh! Callay!"
    He chortled in his joy.

'Twas brillig, and the slithy toves
    Did gyre and gimble in the wabe:
All mimsy were the borogoves,
    And the mome raths outgrabe.[1]

1   "You seem very clever at explaining words, Sir," said Alice. "Would you kindly tell me the meaning of the poem called '*Jabberwocky*?'"

"Let's hear it," said Humpty Dumpty. "I can explain all the poems that ever were invented—and a good many that haven't been invented just yet."

This sounded very hopeful, so Alice repeated the first verse:—

> *" 'Twas brillig, and the slithy toves*
> *Did gyre and gimble in the wabe:*
> *All mimsy were the borogoves,*
> *And the mome raths outgrabe. "*

"That's enough to begin with," Humpty Dumpty interrupted: "there are plenty of hard words there. '*Brillig*' means four o'clock in the afternoon—the time when you begin *broiling* things for dinner."

"That'll do very well," said Alice: "and '*slithy*'?"

"Well, '*slithy*' means 'lithe and slimy.' 'Lithe' is the same as 'active.' You see it's like a portmanteau—there are two meanings packed up into one word."

"I see it now," Alice remarked thoughtfully: "and what are '*toves*'?"

"Well, '*toves*' are something like badgers—they're something like lizards—and they're something like corkscrews."

"They must be very curious-looking creatures."

"They are that," said Humpty Dumpty: "also they make their nest under sun-dials—also they live on cheese."

"And what's '*gyre*' and to '*gimble*'?"

"To '*gyre*' is to go round and round like a gyroscope. To '*gimble*' is to make holes like a gimblet."

"And '*the wabe*' is the grass-plot round a sun-dial, I suppose?" said Alice, surprised at her own ingenuity.

"Of course it is. It's called '*wabe*,' you know, because it goes a long way before it, and a long way behind it—"

"And a long way beyond it on each side," Alice added.

"Exactly so. Well then, '*mimsy*' is 'flimsy and miserable' (there's another portmanteau for you). And a '*borogove*' is a thin shabby-looking bird with its feathers sticking out all round—something like a live mop."

"And then '*mome raths*'?" said Alice. "I'm afraid I'm giving you a great deal of trouble."

"Well, a '*rath*' is a sort of green pig; but '*mome*' I'm not certain about. I think it's short for 'from home'—meaning that they'd lost their way, you know."

"And what does '*outgrabe*' mean?"

"Well, '*outgribing*' is something between bellowing and whistling, with a kind of sneeze in the middle: however, you'll hear it done, maybe—down in the wood yonder—and, when you've once heard it, you'll be *quite* content. Who's been repeating all that hard stuff to you?"

THOMAS HARDY [1840–1928]

Neutral Tones

We stood by a pond that winter day,
And the sun was white, as though chidden of God,
And a few leaves lay on the starving sod;
    —They had fallen from an ash, and were gray.

Your eyes on me were as eyes that rove
Over tedious riddles of years ago;
And some words played between us to and fro
    On which lost the more by our love.

The smile on your mouth was the deadest thing
Alive enough to have strength to die;
And a grin of bitterness swept thereby
    Like an ominous bird a-wing. . . .

Since then, keen lessons that love deceives,
And wrings with wrong, have shaped to me
Your face, and the God-curst sun, and a tree,
    And a pond edged with grayish leaves.

Drummer Hodge

They throw in Drummer Hodge, to rest
    Uncoffined—just as found:
His landmark is a kopje-crest
    That breaks the veldt around;[1]
And foreign constellations west
    Each night above his mound.

Young Hodge the Drummer never knew—
    Fresh from his Wessex home—
The meaning of the broad Karoo,
    The Bush,[2] the dusty loam,
And why uprose to nightly view
    Strange stars amid the gloam.

Yet portion of that unknown plain
    Will Hodge for ever be;
His homely Northern breast and brain
    Grow to some Southern tree,
And strange-eyed constellations reign
    His stars eternally.

1 A kopje is a hillock in South African dialect; veldt is grassland.
2 Karoo is a region of dry flatland in South Africa; bush is uncleared land.

The Darkling Thrush

I leant upon a coppice gate
    When Frost was specter-gray,
And Winter's dregs made desolate
    The weakening eye of day.
The tangled bine-stems scored the sky
    Like strings of broken lyres,
And all mankind that haunted nigh
    Had sought their household fires.

The land's sharp features seemed to be
    The Century's corpse outleant,   10
His crypt the cloudy canopy,
    The wind his death-lament.
The ancient pulse of germ and birth
    Was shrunken hard and dry,
And every spirit upon earth
    Seemed fervorless as I.

At once a voice arose among
    The bleak twigs overhead
In a full-hearted evensong
    Of joy illimited;   20
An aged thrush, frail, gaunt, and small,
    In blast-beruffled plume,
Had chosen thus to fling his soul
    Upon the growing gloom.

So little cause for carolings
    Of such ecstatic sound
Was written on terrestrial things
    Afar or nigh around,
That I could think there trembled through
    His happy good-night air   30
Some blessed Hope, whereof he knew
    And I was unaware.

The Convergence of the Twain

(*Lines on the loss of the "Titanic"*)

1

In a solitude of the sea
Deep from human vanity,
And the Pride of Life that planned her, stilly couches she.

2

Steel chambers, late the pyres
Of her salamandrine fires,
Cold currents thrid, and turn to rhythmic tidal lyres.

3

Over the mirrors meant
To glass the opulent
The sea-worm crawls—grotesque, slimed, dumb, indifferent.

4

Jewels in joy designed   10
To ravish the sensuous mind
Lie lightless, all their sparkles bleared and black and blind.

5

Dim moon-eyed fishes near
Gaze at the gilded gear
And query: "What does this vaingloriousness down here?" . . .

6

Well: while was fashioning
This creature of cleaving wing,
The Immanent Will that stirs and urges everything

7

Prepared a sinister mate
For her—so gaily great—   20
A Shape of Ice, for the time far and dissociate.

8

And as the smart ship grew
In stature, grace, and hue,
In shadowy silent distance grew the Iceberg too.

9

Alien they seemed to be:
No mortal eye could see
The intimate welding of their later history,

10

Or sign that they were bent
By paths coincident
On being anon twin halves of one august event,   30

11

Till the Spinner of the Years
Said "Now!" And each one hears,
And consummation comes, and jars two hemispheres.

When I Set Out
for Lyonnesse[1]

When I set out for Lyonnesse,
    A hundred miles away,
    The rime was on the spray,
And starlight lit my lonesomeness
When I set out for Lyonnesse
    A hundred miles away.

What would bechance at Lyonnesse
    While I should sojourn there
    No prophet durst declare,
Nor did the wisest wizard guess
What would bechance at Lyonnesse
    While I should sojourn there.

When I came back from Lyonnesse
    With magic in my eyes,
    All marked with mute surmise
My radiance rare and fathomless,
When I came back from Lyonnesse
    With magic in my eyes.

1 legendary country off the south coast of Cornwall, England—scene of Arthurian romance. It is said to have disappeared suddenly beneath the sea.

The Voice

Woman much missed, how you call to me, call to me,
Saying that now you are not as you were
When you had changed from the one who was all to me,
But as at first, when our day was fair.

Can it be you that I hear? Let me view you, then,
Standing as when I drew near to the town
Where you would wait for me: yes, as I knew you then,
Even to the original air-blue gown!

Or is it only the breeze, in its listlessness
Travelling across the wet mead to me here,
You being ever dissolved to wan wistlessness,
Heard no more again far or near?

    Thus I; faltering forward,
    Leaves around me falling,
Wind oozing thin through the thorn from norward,
    And the woman calling.

Afterwards

When the Present has latched its postern behind my tremulous stay,
　　And the May month flaps its glad green leaves like wings,
Delicate-filmed as new-spun silk, will the neighbors say,
　　"He was a man who used to notice such things"?

If it be in the dusk when, like an eyelid's soundless blink,
　　The dewfall-hawk comes crossing the shades to alight
Upon the wind-warped upland thorn, a gazer may think,
　　"To him this must have been a familiar sight."

If I pass during some nocturnal blackness, mothy and warm,
　　When the hedgehog travels furtively over the lawn,
One may say, "He strove that such innocent creatures should come to no
　　　　harm,
　　But he could do little for them; and now he is gone."

If, when hearing that I have been stilled at last, they stand at the door,
　　Watching the full-starred heavens that winter sees,
Will this thought rise on those who will meet my face no more,
　　"He was one who had an eye for such mysteries"?

And will any say when my bell of quittance is heard in the gloom,
　　And a crossing breeze cuts a pause in its outrollings,
Till they rise again, as they were a new bell's boom,
　　"He hears it not now, but used to notice such things"?

from *The Dynasts*

The Eve of Waterloo[1]
(*Chorus of Phantoms*)

The eyelids of eve fall together at last,
And the forms so foreign to field and tree
Lie down as though native, and slumber fast!

Sore are the thrills of misgiving we see
In the artless champaign at this harlequinade,
Distracting a vigil where calm should be!

The green seems opprest, and the Plain afraid
Of a Something to come, whereof these are the proofs,—
Neither earthquake, nor storm, nor eclipse's shade!

---

1 See the description of the battle of Waterloo by Byron in *Childe Harold's Pilgrimage, Canto III.*

Yea, the coneys are scared by the thud of hoofs,   10
And their white scuts flash at their vanishing heels,
And swallows abandon the hamlet-roofs.

The mole's tunnelled chambers are crushed by wheels,
The lark's eggs scattered, their owners fled;
And the hedgehog's household the sapper[2] unseals.

The snail draws in at the terrible tread,
But in vain; he is crushed by the felloe-rim;[3]
The worm asks what can be overhead,

And wriggles deep from a scene so grim,
And guesses him safe; for he does not know   20
What a foul red flood will be soaking him!

Beaten about by the heel and toe
Are butterflies, sick of the day's long rheum,[4]
To die of a worse than the weather-foe.

Trodden and bruised to a miry tomb
Are ears that have greened but will never be gold,
And flowers in the bud that will never bloom.

So the season's intent, ere its fruit unfold,
Is frustrate, and mangled, and made succumb,
Like a youth of promise struck stark and cold! . . .   30

And what of these who tonight have come?
—The young sleep sound; but the weather awakes
In the veterans, pains from the past that numb;

Old stabs of Ind, old Peninsular aches,
Old Friedland chills, haunt their moist mud bed,
Cramps from Austerlitz; till their slumber breaks.[5]

And each soul shivers as sinks his head
On the loam he's to lease with the other dead
From tomorrow's mist-fall till Time be sped!

2   (a) a military specialist in field fortifications; (b) a military specialist in placing and removing mines.
3   wheel rim.
4   watery discharge of mucous membrane, especially of the eyes and nose. Here used figuratively of the weather.
5   *Ind*: India; *Peninsular*: pertaining to Portugal and Spain; *Friedland*: town in Eastern Prussia; *Austerlitz*: in Czechoslovakia. These were the scenes of battles between the French and the Allies during the Napoleonic Wars.

GERARD MANLEY HOPKINS [1844–1889]

The Starlight Night

Look at the stars! look, look up at the skies!
  O look at all the fire-folk sitting in the air!
  The bright boroughs, the circle-citadels there!
Down in dim woods the diamond delves! the elves'-eyes!
The grey lawns cold where gold, where quickgold lies!
  Wind-beat whitebeam! airy abeles[1] set on a flare!
  Flake-doves sent floating forth at a farmyard scare!—
Ah well! it is all a purchase, all is a prize.

Buy then! bid then!—What?—Prayer, patience, alms, vows.
Look, look: a May-mess, like on orchard boughs!
  Look! March-bloom, like on mealed-with-yellow sallows![2]
These are indeed the barn; withindoors house
The shocks. This piece-bright paling shuts the spouse
  Christ home, Christ and his mother and all his hallows.[3]

1   white poplars.
2   willows.
3   saints.

The Windhover[1]

TO CHRIST OUR LORD

I caught this morning morning's minion,[2] king-
    dom of daylight's dauphin,[3] dapple-dawn-drawn Falcon, in his
    riding
  Of the rolling level underneath him steady air, and striding
High there, how he rung[4] upon the rein of a wimpling[5] wing
In his ecstasy! then off, off forth on swing,
  As a skate's heel sweeps smooth on a bow-bend: the hurl and gliding
  Rebuffed the big wind. My heart in hiding
Stirred for a bird,—the achieve of, the mastery of the thing!

Brute beauty and valor and act, oh, air, pride, plume, here
  Buckle![6] AND the fire that breaks from thee then, a billion
Times told lovelier, more dangerous, O my chevalier![7]

1   European falcon.
2   darling.
3   heir to the throne.
4   In falconry to ring is to rise in the air spirally; to ring a horse is to guide it in a circle
on a long rein.
5   rippling; turning.
6   gather together (and dive).
7   knight.

No wonder of it: shéer plód makes plough down sillion[8]
Shine, and blue-bleak embers, ah my dear,
   Fall, gall themselves, and gash gold-vermilion.

8   the ridge between plowed furrows.

Pied Beauty

Glory be to God for dappled things—
   For skies of couple-color as a brinded[1] cow;
      For rose-moles all in stipple[2] upon trout that swim;
Fresh-firecoal chestnut-falls;[3] finches' wings;
   Landscape plotted and pieced—fold, fallow, and plough;
      And all trades, their gear and tackle and trim.

All things counter,[4] original, spare,[5] strange;
   Whatever is fickle, freckled (who knows how?)
      With swift, slow; sweet, sour; adazzle, dim;
He fathers-forth whose beauty is past change:
         Praise him.

1   archaic form of *brindled*.
2   painted in small touches of color.
3   chestnuts without their husks.
4   opposite, contrary.
5   rare.

Binsey Poplars

   My aspens dear, whose airy cages quelled,
   Quelled or quenched in leaves the leaping sun,
   All felled, felled, are all felled;
      Of a fresh and following folded rank
            Not spared, not one
            That dandled a sandalled
         Shadow that swam or sank
On meadow and river and wind-wandering weed-winding bank.

   O if we but knew what we do
         When we delve or hew—
      Hack and rack the growing green!
         Since country is so tender
      To touch, her being só slender,
      That, like this sleek and seeing ball
      But a prick will make no eye at all,
      Where we, even where we mean
            To mend her we end her,

288

When we hew or delve:
After-comers cannot guess the beauty been.
   Ten or twelve, only ten or twelve
      Strokes of havoc unselve
         The sweet especial scene,
      Rural scene, a rural scene,
      Sweet especial rural scene.

Felix Randal

Felix Randal the farrier, O is he dead then? my duty all ended,
Who have watched his mould of man, big-boned and hardy-handsome
Pining, pining, till time when reason rambled in it and some
Fatal four disorders, fleshed there, all contended?

Sickness broke him. Impatient, he cursed at first, but mended
Being anointed and all; though a heavenlier heart began some
Months earlier, since I had our sweet reprieve and ransom
Tendered to him. Ah well, God rest him all road ever he offended!

This seeing the sick endears them to us, us too it endears.
My tongue had taught thee comfort, touch had quenched thy tears,
Thy tears that touched my heart, child, Felix, poor Felix Randal;

How far from then forethought of, all thy more boisterous years,
When thou at the random grim forge, powerful amidst peers,
Didst fettle for the great gray drayhorse his bright and battering sandal!

Spring and Fall

To a Young Child

Márgarét, are you gríeving
Over Goldengrove unleaving?
Leáves, like the things of man, you
With your fresh thoughts care for, can you?
Áh! ás the heart grows older
It will come to such sights colder
By and by, nor spare a sigh
Though worlds of wanwood leafmeal lie;
And yet you wíll weep and know why.
Now no matter, child, the name:
Sórrow's spríngs áre the same.
Nor mouth had, no nor mind, expressed
What heart heard of, ghost guessed:
It ís the blight man was born for,
It is Margaret you mourn for.

No Worst,
There is None

No worst, there is none. Pitched past pitch of grief,
More pangs will, schooled at forepangs, wilder wring.
Comforter, where, where is your comforting?
Mary, mother of us, where is your relief?
My cries heave, herds-long; huddle in a main, a chief
Woe, world-sorrow; on an age-old anvil wince and sing—
Then lull, then leave off. Fury had shrieked "No ling-
      ering! Let me be fell: force I must be brief."

   O the mind, mind has mountains; cliffs of fall
Frightful, sheer, no-man-fathomed. Hold them cheap
May who ne'er hung there. Nor does long our small
Durance deal with that steep or deep. Here! creep,
Wretch, under a comfort serves in a whirlwind: all
Life death does end and each day dies with sleep.

My Own Heart
Let Me More
Have Pity On

My own heart let me more have pity on; let
Me live to my sad self hereafter kind,
Charitable; not live this tormented mind
With this tormented mind tormenting yet.
   I cast for comfort I can no more get
By groping round my comfortless, than blind
Eyes in their dark can day or thirst can find
Thirst's all-in-all in all a world of wet.

Soul, self; come, poor Jackself, I do advise
You, jaded, let be; call off thoughts awhile
Elsewhere; leave comfort root-room; let joy size
At God knows when to God knows what; whose smile
's not wrung, see you; unforeseen times rather—as skies
Between pie mountains—lights a lovely mile.

A. E. HOUSMAN [1859–1936]

Loveliest of Trees, the Cherry Now

Loveliest of trees, the cherry now
Is hung with bloom along the bough,
And stands about the woodland ride
Wearing white for Eastertide.

Now, of my threescore years and ten,
Twenty will not come again,
And take from seventy springs a score,
It only leaves me fifty more.

And since to look at things in bloom
Fifty springs are little room,
About the woodlands I will go
To see the cherry hung with snow.

Lancer

I 'listed at home for a lancer,
   Oh who would not sleep with the brave?
I 'listed at home for a lancer
   To ride on a horse to my grave.

And over the seas we were bidden
   A country to take and to keep;
And far with the brave I have ridden,
   And now with the brave I shall sleep.

For round me the men will be lying
   That learned me the way to behave,
And showed me my business of dying:
   Oh who would not sleep with the brave?

They ask and there is not an answer;
Says I, I will 'list for a lancer,
   Oh who would not sleep with the brave?

And I with the brave shall be sleeping
   At ease on my mattress of loam,
When back from their taking and keeping
   The squadron is riding at home.

The wind with the plumes will be playing,
    The girls will stand watching them wave,
And eyeing my comrades and saying
    Oh who would not sleep with the brave?

They ask and there is not an answer;
Says you, I will 'list for a lancer,
    Oh who would not sleep with the brave?

Tell Me Not Here,
It Needs Not Saying

Tell me not here, it needs not saying,
    What tune the enchantress plays
In aftermaths of soft September
    Or under blanching mays,
For she and I were long acquainted
    And I knew all her ways.

On russet floors, by waters idle,
    The pine lets fall its cone;
The cuckoo shouts all day at nothing
    In leafy dells alone;   10
And traveller's joy beguiles in autumn
    Hearts that have lost their own.

On acres of the seeded grasses
    The changing burnish heaves;
Or marshalled under moons of harvest
    Stand still all night the sheaves;
Or beeches strip in storms for winter
    And stain the wind with leaves.

Possess, as I possessed a season,
    The countries I resign,   20
Where over elmy plains the highway
    Would mount the hills and shine,
And full of shade the pillared forest
    Would murmur and be mine.

For nature, heartless, witless nature,
    Will neither care nor know
What stranger's feet may find the meadow
    And trespass there and go,
Nor ask amid the dews of morning
    If they are mine or no.   30

RUDYARD KIPLING   [1865–1936]

Danny Deever

"What are the bugles blowin' for?" said Files-on-Parade.
"To turn you out, to turn you out," the Color-Sergeant said.
"What makes you look so white, so white?" said Files-on-Parade.
"I'm dreadin' what I've got to watch," the Color-Sergeant said.
> For they're hangin' Danny Deever, you can hear the Dead March
> > play,
> The Regiment's in 'ollow square—they're hangin' him today;
> They've taken of his buttons off an' cut his stripes away,
> An' they're hangin' Danny Deever in the mornin'.

"What makes the rear-rank breathe so 'ard?" said Files-on-Parade.
"It's bitter cold, it's bitter cold," the Color-Sergeant said.   10
"What makes that front-rank man fall down?" said Files-on-Parade.
"A touch o' sun, a touch o' sun," the Color-Sergeant said.
> They are hangin' Danny Deever, they are marchin' of 'im round.
> They 'ave 'alted Danny Deever by 'is coffin on the ground;
> And 'e'll swing in 'arf a minute for a sneakin' shootin' hound—
> O they're hangin' Danny Deever in the mornin'!

"'Is cot was right-'and cot to mine," said Files-on-Parade.
"'E's sleepin' out an' far tonight," the Color-Sergeant said.
"I've drunk 'is beer a score o' times," said Files-on-Parade.   20
"'E's drinkin' bitter beer alone," the Color-Sergeant said.
> They are hangin' Danny Deever, you must mark 'im to 'is place,
> For 'e shot a comrade sleepin'—you must look 'im in the face;
> Nine 'undred of 'is county an' the Regiment's disgrace,
> While they're hangin' Danny Deever in the mornin'.

"What's that so black agin the sun?" said Files-on-Parade.
"It's Danny fightin' 'ard for life," the Color-Sergeant said.
"What's that that whimpers over'ead?" said Files-on-Parade.
"It's Danny's soul that's passin' now," the Color-Sergeant said.
> For they're done with Danny Deever, you can 'ear the quickstep play,
> The Regiment's in column, an' they're marchin' us away;   30
> Ho! the young recruits are shakin', an' they'll want their beer today,
> After hangin' Danny Deever in the mornin'!

WILLIAM BUTLER YEATS   [1865–1939]

The Lake Isle
of Innisfree

I will arise and go now, and go to Innisfree,
And a small cabin build there, of clay and wattles[1] made:
Nine bean rows will I have there, a hive for the honey bee,
And live alone in the bee-loud glade.

And I shall have some peace there, for peace comes dropping slow,
Dropping from the veils of the morning to where the cricket sings;
There midnight's all a glimmer, and noon a purple glow,
And evening full of the linnet's wings.

I will arise and go now, for always night and day
I hear lake water lapping with low sounds by the shore;
While I stand on the roadway, or on the pavements gray,
I hear it in the deep heart's core.

1   *wattles*: poles interwoven with light branches or reeds.

The Wild Swans
at Coole

The trees are in their autumn beauty,
The woodland paths are dry,
Under the October twilight the water
Mirrors a still sky;
Upon the brimming water among the stones
Are nine-and-fifty swans.

The nineteenth autumn has come upon me
Since I first made my count;
I saw, before I had well finished,
All suddenly mount   10
And scatter wheeling in great broken rings
Upon their clamorous wings.

I have looked upon those brilliant creatures,
And now my heart is sore.
All's changed since I, hearing at twilight,
The first time on this shore,
The bell-beat of their wings above my head,
Trod with a lighter tread.

Unwearied still, lover by lover,
They paddle in the cold   20
Companionable streams or climb the air;
Their hearts have not grown old;
Passion or conquest, wander where they will,
Attend upon them still.

But now they drift on the still water,
Mysterious, beautiful;
Among what rushes will they build,
By what lake's edge or pool
Delight men's eyes when I awake some day
To find they have flown away?   30

Easter 1916[1]

I have met them at close of day
Coming with vivid faces
From counter or desk among gray
Eighteenth-century houses.
I have passed with a nod of the head
Or polite meaningless words,
Or have lingered awhile and said
Polite meaningless words,
And thought before I had done
Of a mocking tale or a gibe   10
To please a companion
Around the fire at the club,
Being certain that they and I
But lived where motley is worn:
All changed, changed utterly:
A terrible beauty is born.

That woman's[2] days were spent
In ignorant good-will,
Her nights in argument
Until her voice grew shrill.   20
What voice more sweet than hers
When, young and beautiful,

1 On Easter Monday, 1916, Irish rebels against the English government occupied
several buildings in Dublin, including the Post Office. Troops were brought to Dublin
and after bitter fighting the rebels surrendered. The leaders of the rebellion were tried
by court martial; fifteen were executed and others were sentenced to penal servitude.
Among those executed were Padraic Pearse, Thomas MacDonagh, and James Connolly,
whom Yeats names. Constance Markievicz, for "using a revolver with great skill," was
given a life sentence.
2 Constance Markievicz. She came of an Anglo-Irish family, the Gore-Booths of Sligo
where Yeats spent much of his boyhood.

She rode to harriers?
This man[3] had kept a school
And rode our wingéd horse;
This other[4] his helper and friend
Was coming into his force;
He might have won fame in the end,
So sensitive his nature seemed,
So daring and sweet his thought.   30
This other man[5] I had dreamed
A drunken, vainglorious lout.
He had done most bitter wrong
To some who are near my heart,
Yet I number him in the song;
He, too, has resigned his part
In the casual comedy;
He, too, has been changed in his turn,
Transformed utterly:
A terrible beauty is born.   40

Hearts with one purpose alone
Through summer and winter seem
Enchanted to a stone
To trouble the living stream.
The horse that comes from the road,
The rider, the birds that range
From cloud to tumbling cloud,
Minute by minute they change;
A shadow of cloud on the stream
Changes minute by minute;   50
A horse-hoof slides on the brim,
And a horse plashes within it;
The long-legged moor-hens dive,
And hens to moor-cocks call;
Minute by minute they live:
The stone's in the midst of all.

Too long a sacrifice
Can make a stone of the heart.
O when may it suffice?
That is Heaven's part, our part   60
To murmur name upon name,
As a mother names her child
When sleep at last has come
On limbs that had run wild.
What is it but nightfall?

3   Padraic Pearse, who was a strong supporter of the Irish language movement.
4   the poet Thomas MacDonagh.
5   John MacBride, husband of Maud Gonne. Yeats had been in love with her and had
written about it in his poems.

No, no, not night but death;
Was it needless death after all?
For England may keep faith[6]
For all that is done and said.
We know their dream; enough   70
To know they dreamed and are dead;
And what if excess of love
Bewildered them till they died?
I write it out in a verse—
MacDonagh and MacBride
And Connolly[7] and Pearse
Now and in time to be,
Wherever green is worn,
Are changed, changed utterly:
A terrible beauty is born.   80

   September 25, 1916

6 Yeats means: England may grant Ireland Home Rule. In 1914 the Liberal party in
England proposed a bill in Parliament granting Home Rule to Ireland. In spite of Tory
opposition and the opposition of Unionists in Northern Ireland who were preparing to
resist Home Rule with armed force, the bill passed and was in the statute book, waiting
to be put into effect. Then Britain went to war with Germany, and Home Rule was
deferred for the duration.
7   James Connolly, one of the executed rebels. A Marxist labor organizer, his ideas are
still influential in Irish politics.

The Second Coming

Turning and turning in the widening gyre[1]
The falcon cannot hear the falconer;
Things fall apart; the centre cannot hold;
Mere anarchy is loosed upon the world,
The blood-dimmed tide is loosed, and everywhere
The ceremony of innocence is drowned;
The best lack all conviction, while the worst
Are full of passionate intensity.

Surely some revelation is at hand;
Surely the Second Coming is at hand.
The Second Coming! Hardly are those words out
When a vast image out of *Spiritus Mundi*[2]
Troubles my sight: somewhere in sands of the desert
A shape with lion body and the head of a man,
A gaze blank and pitiless as the sun,
Is moving its slow thighs, while all about it

1   a circling, spiraling motion.
2   "What spiritualists call the subliminal mind, what Jung considers the racial uncon-
scious, and what Henry More called *Anima Mundi.*"—Richard Ellmann, *The Identity
of Yeats.*

Reel shadows of the indignant desert birds.
The darkness drops again; but now I know
That twenty centuries of stony sleep
Were vexed to nightmare by a rocking cradle,
And what rough beast, its hour come round at last,
Slouches towards Bethlehem to be born?

Sailing to Byzantium[1]

1

That is no country for old men. The young
In one another's arms, birds in the trees
—Those dying generations—at their song,
The salmon-falls, the mackerel-crowded seas,
Fish, flesh, or fowl, commend all summer long
Whatever is begotten, born, and dies.
Caught in that sensual music all neglect
Monuments of unageing intellect.

2

An aged man is but a paltry thing,
A tattered coat upon a stick, unless   10
Soul clap its hands and sing, and louder sing
For every tatter in its mortal dress,
Nor is there singing school but studying
Monuments of its own magnificence;
And therefore I have sailed the seas and come
To the holy city of Byzantium.

3

O sages standing in God's holy fire
As in the gold mosaic of a wall,
Come from the holy fire, perne in a gyre,[2]
And be the singing-masters of my soul.   20
Consume my heart away; sick with desire
And fastened to a dying animal
It knows not what it is; and gather me
Into the artifice of eternity.

4

Once out of nature I shall never take
My bodily form from any natural thing,

1 ancient Greek city, renamed Constantinople by the Roman emperor Constantine I,
which became the capital of the Eastern Roman or Byzantine Empire after the fall of
Rome in 476 A.D. The city is famous for its mosaics and other works of art.
2 *To perne* is a verb invented by Yeats. He had been told that the noun *pern* was an
Irish name for a spool on which thread is wound; hence, to turn, spin; *gyre* (pronounced
with a hard g) is a pattern formed by a circling or spiraling motion.

But such a form as Grecian goldsmiths make
Of hammered gold and gold enameling
To keep a drowsy Emperor awake;
Or set upon a golden bough to sing   30
To lords and ladies of Byzantium
Of what is past, or passing, or to come.

Among School Children

1

I walk through the long schoolroom questioning;
A kind old nun in a white hood replies;
The children learn to cipher and to sing,
To study reading-books and history,
To cut and sew, be neat in everything
In the best modern way—the children's eyes
In momentary wonder stare upon
A sixty-year-old smiling public man.

2

I dream of a Ledaean body,[1] bent
Above a sinking fire, a tale that she   10
Told of a harsh reproof, or trivial event
That changed some childish day to tragedy—
Told, and it seemed that our two natures blent
Into a sphere from youthful sympathy,
Or else, to alter Plato's parable,[2]
Into the yolk and white of the one shell.

3

And thinking of that fit of grief or rage
I look upon one child or t'other there
And wonder if she stood so at that age—
For even daughters of the swan can share   20
Something of every paddler's heritage—
And had that color upon cheek or hair,
And thereupon my heart is driven wild:
She stands before me as a living child.

4

Her present image floats into the mind—
Did Quattrocento[3] finger fashion it

1 In Greek mythology, Zeus assumed the shape of a swan and had intercourse with
Leda. She brought forth two eggs, out of one of which came Helen, and out of the other
Castor and Pollux.
2 In Plato's "Symposium," Aristophanes relates that "the primeval man was round,
his back and sides forming a circle; and he had four hands and four feet, one head with
two faces, looking opposite ways."
3 the fifteenth century, especially with reference to Italian literature and art.

Hollow of cheek as though it drank the wind
And took a mess of shadows for its meat?
And I though never of Ledaean kind
Had pretty plumage once—enough of that,   30
Better to smile on all that smile, and show
There is a comfortable kind of old scarecrow.

5

What youthful mother, a shape upon her lap
Honey of generation had betrayed,
And that must sleep, shriek, struggle to escape
As recollection or the drug decide,
Would think her son, did she but see that shape
With sixty or more winters on its head,
A compensation for the pang of his birth,
Or the uncertainty of his setting forth?   40

6

Plato thought nature but a spume that plays
Upon a ghostly paradigm[4] of things;
Solider Aristotle played the taws[5]
Upon the bottom of a king of kings;
World-famous golden-thighed Pythagoras[6]
Fingered upon a fiddle-stick or strings
What a star sang and careless Muses heard:
Old clothes upon old sticks to scare a bird.

7

Both nuns and mothers worship images,
But those the candles light are not as those   50
That animate a mother's reveries,
But keep a marble or a bronze repose.
And yet they too break hearts—O Presences
That passion, piety or affection knows,
And that all heavenly glory symbolise—
O self-born mockers of man's enterprise;

8

Labor is blossoming or dancing where
The body is not bruised to pleasure soul,
Nor beauty born out of its own despair,
Nor blear-eyed wisdom out of midnight oil.   60

4   pattern.
5   leather strap slit into strips at the end.
6   born on the island of Samos about 580 B.C. Said to have been the first man who
called himself a "philosopher" or lover of wisdom. The *Golden Sayings* attributed to
him—hence "golden-thighed"—are not genuine. We can only ascribe to him with
certainty the doctrine of the transmigration of souls, and of number as the principle of
the harmony of the universe and of moral life; and, further, certain religious and moral
precepts.

O chestnut-tree, great-rooted blossomer,
Are you the leaf, the blossom or the bole?
O body swayed to music, O brightening glance,
How can we know the dancer from the dance?

Byzantium

The unpurged images of day recede;
The Emperor's drunken soldiery are abed;
Night resonance recedes, night-walkers' song
After great cathedral gong;
A starlit or a moonlit dome disdains
All that man is,
All mere complexities,
The fury and the mire of human veins.

Before me floats an image, man or shade,
Shade more than man, more image than a shade;   10
For Hades' bobbin bound in mummy-cloth
May unwind the winding path;
A mouth that has no moisture and no breath
Breathless mouths may summon;
I hail the superhuman;
I call it death-in-life and life-in-death.

Miracle, bird or golden handiwork,
More miracle than bird or handiwork,
Planted on the star-lit golden bough,
Can like the cocks of Hades crow,   20
Or, by the moon embittered, scorn aloud
In glory of changeless metal
Common bird or petal
And all complexities of mire or blood.

At midnight on the Emperor's pavement flit
Flames that no fagot feeds, nor steel has lit,
Nor storm disturbs, flames begotten of flame,
Where blood-begotten spirits come
And all complexities of fury leave,
Dying into a dance,   30
An agony of trance,
An agony of flame that cannot singe a sleeve.

Astraddle on the dolphin's mire and blood,
Spirit after spirit! The smithies break the flood,
The golden smithies of the Emperor!

Marbles of the dancing floor
Break bitter furies of complexity,
Those images that yet
Fresh images beget,
That dolphin-torn, that gong-tormented sea.   40

Lapis Lazuli[1]

FOR HARRY CLIFTON[2]

I have heard that hysterical women say
They are sick of the palette and fiddle-bow,
Of poets that are always gay,
For everybody knows or else should know
That if nothing drastic is done
Aeroplane and Zeppelin will come out,
Pitch like King Billy bomb-balls[3] in
Until the town lie beaten flat.

All perform their tragic play,
There struts Hamlet, there is Lear,   10
That's Ophelia, that Cordelia;
Yet they, should the last scene be there,
The great stage curtain about to drop,
If worthy their prominent part in the play,
Do not break up their lines to weep.
They know that Hamlet and Lear are gay;
Gaiety transfiguring all that dread.
All men have aimed at, found and lost;
Black out; Heaven blazing into the head:
Tragedy wrought to its uttermost.   20
Though Hamlet rambles and Lear rages,
And all the drop-scenes drop at once
Upon a hundred thousand stages,
It cannot grow by an inch or an ounce.

On their own feet they came, or on shipboard,
Camel-back, horse-back, ass-back, mule-back,
Old civilizations put to the sword.
Then they and their wisdom went to rack:
No handiwork of Callimachus,[4]

1 a deep-blue stone used chiefly for ornament.
2 friend of Yeats, who had given him a lapis lazuli medallion, on which were carved
the figures of an old man and a servant.
3 William III, King of England from 1689 to 1702. He made war with cannon balls
that exploded on impact. "King Billy" also refers to Kaiser Wilhelm II, whose zeppelins
and airplanes harried the English in World War I.
4 Greek sculptor of the fifth century B.C.

Who handled marble as if it were bronze,   30
Made draperies that seemed to rise
When sea-wind swept the corner, stands;
His long lamp-chimney shaped like the stem
Of a slender palm, stood but a day;
All things fall and are built again,
And those that build them again are gay.

Two Chinamen, behind them a third,
Are carved in lapis lazuli,
Over them flies a long-legged bird,
A symbol of longevity;   40
The third, doubtless a serving-man,
Carries a musical instrument.

Every discoloration of the stone,
Every accidental crack or dent,
Seems a water-course or an avalanche,
Or lofty slope where it still snows
Though doubtless plum or cherry-branch
Sweetens the little half-way house
Those Chinamen climb towards, and I
Delight to imagine them seated there;   50
There, on the mountain and the sky,
On all the tragic scene they stare.
One asks for mournful melodies;
Accomplished fingers begin to play.
Their eyes mid many wrinkles, their eyes,
Their ancient, glittering eyes, are gay.

Long-Legged Fly

That civilization may not sink,
Its great battle lost,
Quiet the dog, tether the pony
To a distant post;
Our master Caesar is in the tent
Where the maps are spread,
His eyes fixed upon nothing,
A hand under his head.
Like a long-legged fly upon the stream
His mind moves upon silence.   10

That the topless towers be burnt
And men recall that face,
Move most gently if move you must
In this lonely place.

She thinks, part woman, three parts a child,
That nobody looks; her feet
Practise a tinker shuffle
Picked up on a street.
Like a long-legged fly upon the stream
Her mind moves upon silence.   20

That girls at puberty may find
The first Adam in their thought,
Shut the door of the Pope's chapel,
Keep those children out.
There on that scaffolding reclines
Michael Angelo.
With no more sound than the mice make
His hand moves to and fro.
Like a long-legged fly upon the stream
His mind moves upon silence.   30

Politics

> In our time the destiny of man presents its meaning in
> *political terms*—THOMAS MANN[1]

How can I, that girl standing there,
My attention fix
On Roman or on Russian
Or on Spanish politics?
Yet here's a travelled man that knows
What he talks about,
And there's a politician
That has read and thought,
And maybe what they say is true
Of war and war's alarms,
But O that I were young again
And held her in my arms!

1 German novelist (1875–1955).

ROBERT FROST [1875–1963]

Mending Wall

Something there is that doesn't love a wall,
That sends the frozen-ground-swell under it
And spills the upper boulders in the sun,
And makes gaps even two can pass abreast.
The work of hunters is another thing:

I have come after them and made repair
Where they have left not one stone on a stone,
But they would have the rabbit out of hiding,
To please the yelping dogs. The gaps I mean,
No one has seen them made or heard them made,   10
But at spring mending-time we find them there.
I let my neighbor know beyond the hill;
And on a day we meet to walk the line
And set the wall between us once again.
We keep the wall between us as we go.
To each the boulders that have fallen to each.
And some are loaves and some so nearly balls
We have to use a spell to make them balance:
"Stay where you are until our backs are turned!"
We wear our fingers rough with handling them.   20
Oh, just another kind of outdoor game,
One on a side. It comes to little more:
There where it is we do not need the wall:
He is all pine and I am apple orchard.
My apple trees will never get across
And eat the cones under his pines, I tell him.
He only says, "Good fences make good neighbors."
Spring is the mischief in me, and I wonder
If I could put a notion in his head:
"*Why* do they make good neighbors? Isn't it   30
Where there are cows? But here there are no cows.
Before I built a wall I'd ask to know
What I was walling in or walling out,
And to whom I was like to give offense.
Something there is that doesn't love a wall,
That wants it down." I could say "Elves" to him,
But it's not elves exactly, and I'd rather
He said it for himself. I see him there,
Bringing a stone grasped firmly by the top
In each hand, like an old-stone savage armed.   40
He moves in darkness as it seems to me,
Not of woods only and the shade of trees.
He will not go behind his father's saying,
And he likes having thought of it so well
He says again, "Good fences make good neighbors."

After Apple Picking

My long two-pointed ladder's sticking through a tree
Toward heaven still,
And there's a barrel that I didn't fill
Beside it, and there may be two or three
Apples I didn't pick upon some bough.

But I'am done with apple-picking now.
Essence of winter sleep is on the night,
The scent of apples: I am drowsing off.
I cannot rub the strangeness from my sight
I got from looking through a pane of glass 10
I skimmed this morning from the drinking trough
And held against the world of hoary grass.
It melted, and I let it fall and break.
But I was well
Upon my way to sleep before it fell,
And I could tell
What form my dreaming was about to take.
Magnified apples appear and disappear,
Stem end and blossom end,
And every fleck of russet showing clear. 20
My instep arch not only keeps the ache,
It keeps the pressure of a ladder-round.
I feel the ladder sway as the boughs bend.
And I keep hearing from the cellar bin
The rumbling sound
Of load on load of apples coming in.
For I have had too much
Of apple-picking: I am overtired
Of the great harvest I myself desired.
There were ten thousand thousand fruit to touch, 30
Cherish in hand, lift down, and not let fall.
For all
That struck the earth,
No matter if not bruised or spiked with stubble,
Went surely to the cider-apple heap
As of no worth.
One can see what will trouble
This sleep of mine, whatever sleep it is.
Were he not gone,
The woodchuck could say whether it's like his 40
Long sleep, as I describe its coming on,
Or just some human sleep.

The Hill Wife

I. LONELINESS

Her Word

One ought not to have to care
    So much as you and I
Care when the birds come round the house
    To seem to say good-by;

Or care so much when they come back
   With whatever it is they sing;
The truth being we are as much
   Too glad for the one thing

As we are too sad for the other here—
   With birds that fill their breasts   10
But with each other and themselves
   And their built or driven nests.

II. HOUSE FEAR

Always—I tell you this they learned—
Always at night when they returned
To the lonely house from far away,
To lamps unlighted and fire gone gray,
They learned to rattle the lock and key
To give whatever might chance to be,
Warning and time to be off in flight:
And preferring the out- to the indoor night,   20
They learned to leave the house door wide
Until they had lit the lamp inside.

III. THE SMILE

Her Word

I didn't like the way he went away.
That smile! It never came of being gay.
Still he smiled—did you see him?—I was sure!
Perhaps because we gave him only bread
And the wretch knew from that that we were poor.
Perhaps because he let us give instead
Of seizing from us as he might have seized.
Perhaps he mocked at us for being wed,   30
Or being very young (and he was pleased
To have a vision of us old and dead).
I wonder how far down the road he's got.
He's watching from the woods as like as not.

IV. THE OFT-REPEATED DREAM

She had no saying dark enough
   For the dark pine that kept
Forever trying the window latch
   Of the room where they slept.

The tireless but ineffectual hands
   That with every futile pass   40
Made the great tree seem as a little bird
   Before the mystery of glass!

It never had been inside the room,
   And only one of the two
Was afraid in an oft-repeated dream
   Of what the tree might do.

V. THE IMPULSE

It was too lonely for her there,
   And too wild,
And since there were but two of them,
   And no child,   50

And work was little in the house,
   She was free,
And followed where he furrowed field,
   Or felled tree.

She rested on a log and tossed
   The fresh chips,
With a song only to herself
   On her lips.

And once she went to break a bough
   Of black alder.   60
She strayed so far she scarcely heard
   When he called her—

And didn't answer—didn't speak—
   Or return.
She stood, and then she ran and hid
   In the fern.

He never found her, though he looked
   Everywhere,
And he asked at her mother's house
   Was she there.   70

Sudden and swift and light as that
   The ties gave,
And he learned of finalities
   Besides the grave.

The Witch of Coös

I staid the night for shelter at a farm
Behind the mountain, with a mother and son,
Two old-believers. They did all the talking.

Mother.   Folks think a witch who has familiar spirits
She could call up to pass a winter evening,
But won't, should be burned at the stake or something.
Summoning spirits isn't "Button, button,
Who's got the button," I would have them know.

Son.   Mother can make a common table rear
And kick with two legs like an army mule.   10

Mother.   And when I've done it, what good have I done?
Rather than tip a table for you, let me
Tell you what Ralle the Sioux Control[1] once told me.
He said the dead had souls, but when I asked him
How could that be—I thought the dead were souls,
He broke my trance. Don't that make you suspicious
That there's something the dead are keeping back?
Yes, there's something the dead are keeping back.

Son.   You wouldn't want to tell him what we have
Up attic, mother?   20

Mother.   Bones—a skeleton.

Son.   But the headboard of mother's bed is pushed
Against the attic door: the door is nailed.
It's harmless. Mother hears it in the night
Halting perplexed behind the barrier
Of door and headboard. Where it wants to get
Is back into the cellar where it came from.

Mother.   We'll never let them, will we, son? We'll never!

Son.   It left the cellar forty years ago
And carried itself like a pile of dishes   30
Up one flight from the cellar to the kitchen,
Another from the kitchen to the bedroom,
Another from the bedroom to the attic,
Right past both father and mother, and neither stopped it.
Father had gone upstairs; mother was downstairs.
I was a baby: I don't know where I was.

Mother.   The only fault my husband found with me—
I went to sleep before I went to bed,
Especially in winter when the bed
Might just as well be ice and the clothes snow.   40
The night the bones came up the cellar-stairs

---

1 *Sioux*: a member of the North American peoples who spoke Siouan languages;
control: a personality or spirit believed to control the utterances of a spiritualist medium.

Toffile had gone to bed alone and left me,
But left an open door to cool the room off
So as to sort of turn me out of it.
I was just coming to myself enough
To wonder where the cold was coming from,
When I heard Toffile upstairs in the bedroom
And thought I heard him downstairs in the cellar.
The board we had laid down to walk dry-shod on
When there was water in the cellar in spring   50
Struck the hard cellar bottom. And then someone
Began the stairs, two footsteps for each step,
The way a man with one leg and a crutch,
Or a little child, comes up. It wasn't Toffile:
It wasn't anyone who could be there.
The bulkhead double-doors were double-locked
And swollen tight and buried under snow.
The cellar windows were banked up with sawdust
And swollen tight and buried under snow.
It was the bones. I knew them—and good reason.   60
My first impulse was to get to the knob
And hold the door. But the bones didn't try
The door; they halted helpless on the landing,
Waiting for things to happen in their favor.
The faintest restless rustling ran all through them.
I never could have done the thing I did
If the wish hadn't been too strong in me
To see how they were mounted for this walk.
I had a vision of them put together
Not like a man, but like a chandelier.   70
So suddenly I flung the door wide on him.
A moment he stood balancing with emotion,
And all but lost himself. (A tongue of fire
Flashed out and licked along his upper teeth.
Smoke rolled inside the sockets of his eyes.)
Then he came at me with one hand outstretched,
The way he did in life once; but this time
I struck the hand off brittle on the floor,
And fell back from him on the floor myself.
The finger-pieces slid in all directions.   80
(Where did I see one of those pieces lately?
Hand me my button-box—it must be there.)
I sat up on the floor and shouted, "Toffile,
It's coming up to you." It had its choice
Of the door to the cellar or the hall.
It took the hall door for the novelty,
And set off briskly for so slow a thing,
Still going every which way in the joints, though,
So that it looked like lightning or a scribble,
From the slap I had just now given its hand.   90

I listened till it almost climbed the stairs
From the hall to the only finished bedroom,
Before I got up to do anything;
Then ran and shouted, "Shut the bedroom door,
Toffile, for my sake!" "Company," he said,
"Don't make me get up; I'm too warm in bed."
So lying forward weakly on the handrail
I pushed myself upstairs, and in the light
(The kitchen had been dark) I had to own
I could see nothing. "Toffile, I don't see it. 100
It's with us in the room though. It's the bones."
"What bones?" "The cellar bones—out of the grave."
That made him throw his bare legs out of bed
And sit up by me and take hold of me.
I wanted to put out the light and see
If I could see it, or else mow the room,
With our arms at the level of our knees,
And bring the chalk-pile down. "I'll tell you what—
It's looking for another door to try.
The uncommonly deep snow has made him think 110
Of his old song, *The Wild Colonial Boy*,
He always used to sing along the tote-road.
He's after an open door to get out-doors.
Let's trap him with an open door up attic."
Toffile agreed to that, and sure enough,
Almost the moment he was given an opening,
The steps began to climb the attic stairs.
I heard them. Toffile didn't seem to hear them.
"Quick!" I slammed to the door and held the knob.
"Toffile, get nails." I made him nail the door shut, 120
And push the headboard of the bed against it.
Then we asked was there anything
Up attic that we'd ever want again.
The attic was less to us than the cellar.
If the bones liked the attic, let them have it,
Let them stay in the attic. When they sometimes
Come down the stairs at night and stand perplexed
Behind the door and headboard of the bed,
Brushing their chalky skull with chalky fingers,
With sounds like the dry rattling of a shutter, 130
That's what I sit up in the dark to say—
To no one any more since Toffile died.
Let them stay in the attic since they went there.
I promised Toffile to be cruel to them
For helping them be cruel once to him.

    Son.   We think they had a grave down in the cellar.

    Mother.   We know they had a grave down in the cellar.

Son.   We never could find out whose bones they were.

Mother.   Yes, we could too, son. Tell the truth for once.
They were a man's his father killed for me.   140
I mean a man he killed instead of me.
The least I could do was to help dig their grave.
We were about it one night in the cellar.
Son knows the story: but 'twas not for him
To tell the truth, suppose the time had come.
Son looks surprised to see me end a lie
We'd kept all these years between ourselves
So as to have it ready for outsiders.
But tonight I don't care enough to lie—
I don't remember why I ever cared.   150
Toffile, if he were here, I don't believe
Could tell you why he ever cared himself . . .

She hadn't found the finger-bone she wanted
Among the buttons poured out in her lap.
I verified the name next morning: Toffile.
The rural letter-box said Toffile Lajway.

Stopping by Woods
on a Snowy Evening

Whose woods these are I think I know.
His house is in the village though;
He will not see me stopping here
To watch his woods fill up with snow.

My little horse must think it queer
To stop without a farmhouse near
Between the woods and frozen lake
The darkest evening of the year.

He gives his harness bells a shake
To ask if there is some mistake.
The only other sound's the sweep
Of easy wind and downy flake.

The woods are lovely, dark and deep,
But I have promises to keep,
And miles to go before I sleep,
And miles to go before I sleep.

Design

I found a dimpled spider, fat and white,
On a white heal-all,[1] holding up a moth
Like a white piece of rigid satin cloth—
Assorted characters of death and blight
Mixed ready to begin the morning right,
Like the ingredients of a witch's broth—
A snow-drop spider, a flower like froth,
And dead wings carried like a paper kite.

What had that flower to do with being white,
The wayside blue and innocent heal-all?
What brought the kindred spider to that height,
Then steered the white moth thither in the night?
What but design of darkness to appall?—
If design govern in a thing so small.

1   a blue flower.

Directive

Back out of all this now too much for us,
Back in a time made simple by the loss
Of detail, burned, dissolved, and broken off
Like graveyard marble sculpture in the weather,
There is a house that is no more a house
Upon a farm that is no more a farm
And in a town that is no more a town.
The road there, if you'll let a guide direct you
Who only has at heart your getting lost,
May seem as if it should have been a quarry—   10
Great monolithic knees the former town
Long since gave up pretense of keeping covered.
And there's a story in a book about it:
Besides the wear of iron wagon wheels
The ledges show lines ruled southeast-northwest,
The chisel work of an enormous Glacier
That braced his feet against the Arctic Pole.
You must not mind a certain coolness from him
Still said to haunt this side of Panther Mountain.
Nor need you mind the serial ordeal   20
Of being watched from forty cellar holes
As if by eye pairs out of forty firkins.
As for the woods' excitement over you
That sends light rustle rushes to their leaves,
Charge that to upstart inexperience.

Where were they all not twenty years ago?
They think too much of having shaded out
A few old pecker-fretted apple trees.
Make yourself up a cheering song of how
Someone's road home from work this once was,   30
Who may be just ahead of you on foot
Or creaking with a buggy load of grain.
The height of the adventure is the height
Of country where two village cultures faded
Into each other. Both of them are lost.
And if you're lost enough to find yourself
By now, pull in your ladder road behind you
And put a sign up CLOSED to all but me.
Then make yourself at home. The only field
Now left's no bigger than a harness gall.   40
First there's the children's house of make-believe,
Some shattered dishes underneath a pine,
The playthings in the playhouse of the children.
Weep for what little things could make them glad.
Then for the house that is no more a house,
But only a belilaced cellar hole,
Now slowly closing like a dent in dough.
This was no playhouse but a house in earnest.
Your destination and your destiny's
A brook that was the water of the house,   50
Cold as a spring as yet so near its source,
Too lofty and original to rage.
(We know the valley streams that when aroused
Will leave their tatters hung on barb and thorn.)
I have kept hidden in the instep arch
Of an old cedar at the waterside
A broken drinking goblet like the Grail
Under a spell so the wrong ones can't find it,
So can't get saved, as Saint Mark says they mustn't.[1]
(I stole the goblet from the children's playhouse.)   60
Here are your waters and your watering place.
Drink and be whole again beyond confusion.

1 Mark, 4.11, 12: "That seeing they may see, and not perceive . . . lest at any time
they should be converted, and their sins should be forgiven them."

EDWARD THOMAS   [1878–1917]

The Gallows

There was a weasel lived in the sun
With all his family,

Till a keeper shot him with his gun
And hung him up on a tree,
Where he swings in the wind and rain,
In the sun and in the snow,
Without pleasure, without pain,
On the dead oak tree bough.

There was a crow who was no sleeper,
But a thief and a murderer   10
Till a very late hour; and this keeper
Made him one of the things that were,
To hang and flap in rain and wind
In the sun and in the snow.
There are no more sins to be sinned
On the dead oak tree bough.

There was a magpie, too,
He had a long tongue and a long tail;
He could both talk and do—
But what did that avail?   20
He, too, flaps in the wind and rain
Alongside weasel and crow,
Without pleasure, without pain,
On the dead oak tree bough.

And many other beasts
And birds, skin, bone, and feather,
Have been taken from their feasts
And hung up there together.
To swing and have endless leisure
In the sun and in the snow,   30
Without pain, without pleasure,
On the dead oak tree bough.

Aspens

All day and night, save winter, every weather,
Above the inn, the smithy, and the shop,
The aspens at the cross-roads talk together
Of rain, until their last leaves fall from the top.

Out of the blacksmith's cavern comes the ringing
Of hammer, shoe, and anvil; out of the inn
The clink, the hum, the roar, the random singing—
The sounds that for these fifty years have been.

The whisper of the aspens is not drowned,
And over lightless pane and footless road,

Empty as sky, with every other sound
Not ceasing, calls their ghosts from their abode,

A silent smithy, a silent inn, nor fails
In the bare moonlight or the thick-furred gloom,
In tempest or the night of nightingales,
To turn the cross-roads to a ghostly room.

And it would be the same were no house near.
Over all sorts of weather, men, and times,
Aspens must shake their leaves and men may hear
But need not listen, more than to my rhymes.

Whatever wind blows, while they and I have leaves
We cannot other than an aspen be
That ceaselessly, unreasonably grieves,
Or so men think who like a different tree.

WALLACE STEVENS   [1879–1955]

Hibiscus on the Sleeping Shores

I say now, Fernando, that on that day
The mind roamed as a moth roams,
Among the blooms beyond the open sand;

And that whatever noise the motion of the waves
Made on the sea-weeds and the covered stones
Disturbed not even the most idle ear.

Then it was that that monstered moth
Which had lain folded against the blue
And the colored purple of the lazy sea,

And which had drowsed along the bony shores,
Shut to the blather that the water made,
Rose up besprent and sought the flaming red

Dabbled with yellow pollen—red as red
As the flag above the old café—
And roamed there all the stupid afternoon.

Disillusionment
of Ten O'Clock

The houses are haunted
By white night-gowns.
None are green,
Or purple with green rings,
Or green with yellow rings,
Or yellow with blue rings.
None of them are strange,
With socks of lace
And beaded ceintures.
People are not going
To dream of baboons and periwinkles.
Only, here and there, an old sailor,
Drunk and asleep in his boots,
Catches tigers
In red weather.

Sunday Morning

1

Complacencies of the peignoir, and late
Coffee and oranges in a sunny chair,
And the green freedom of a cockatoo
Upon a rug mingle to dissipate
The holy hush of ancient sacrifice.
She dreams a little, and she feels the dark
Encroachment of that old catastrophe,
As a calm darkens among water-lights.
The pungent oranges and bright, green wings
Seem things in some procession of the dead,   10
Winding across wide water, without sound.
The day is like wide water, without sound,
Stilled for the passing of her dreaming feet
Over the seas, to silent Palestine,
Dominion of the blood and sepulchre.

2

Why should she give her bounty to the dead?
What is divinity if it can come
Only in silent shadows and in dreams?
Shall she not find in comforts of the sun,
In pungent fruit and bright, green wings, or else   20
In any balm or beauty of the earth,
Things to be cherished like the thought of heaven?
Divinity must live within herself:

Passions of rain, or moods in falling snow;
Grievings in loneliness, or unsubdued
Elations when the forest blooms; gusty
Emotions on wet roads on autumn nights;
All pleasures and all pains, remembering
The bough of summer and the winter branch.
These are the measures destined for her soul.   30

3

Jove in the clouds had his inhuman birth.
No mother suckled him, no sweet land gave
Large-mannered motions to his mythy mind.
He moved among us, as a muttering king,
Magnificent, would move among his hinds,
Until our blood, commingling, virginal,
With heaven, brought such requital to desire
The very hinds discerned it, in a star.
Shall our blood fail? Or shall it come to be
The blood of paradise? And shall the earth   40
Seem all of paradise that we shall know?
The sky will be much friendlier then than now,
A part of labor and a part of pain,
And next in glory to enduring love,
Not this dividing and indifferent blue.

4

She says, "I am content when wakened birds,
Before they fly, test the reality
Of misty fields, by their sweet questionings;
But when the birds are gone, and their warm fields
Return no more, where, then, is paradise?"   50
There is not any haunt of prophecy,
Nor any old chimera of the grave,
Neither the golden underground, nor isle
Melodious, where spirits gat them home,
Nor visionary south, nor cloudy palm
Remote on heaven's hill, that has endured
As April's green endures; or will endure
Like her remembrance of awakened birds,
Or her desire for June and evening, tipped
By the consummation of the swallow's wings.   60

5

She says, "But in contentment I still feel
The need of some imperishable bliss."
Death is the mother of beauty; hence from her,
Alone, shall come fulfilment to our dreams
And our desires. Although she strews the leaves
Of sure obliteration on our paths,

The path sick sorrow took, the many paths
Where triumph rang its brassy phrase, or love
Whispered a little out of tenderness,
She makes the willow shiver in the sun   70
For maidens who were wont to sit and gaze
Upon the grass, relinquished to their feet.
She causes boys to pile new plums and pears
On disregarded plate. The maidens taste
And stray impassioned in the littering leaves.

6

Is there no change of death in paradise?
Does ripe fruit never fall? Or do the boughs
Hang always heavy in that perfect sky,
Unchanging, yet so like our perishing earth,
With rivers like our own that seek for seas   80
They never find, the same receding shores
That never touch with inarticulate pang?
Why set the pear upon those river-banks
Or spice the shores with odors of the plum?
Alas, that they should wear our colors there,
The silken weavings of our afternoons,
And pick the strings of our insipid lutes!
Death is the mother of beauty, mystical,
Within whose burning bosom we devise
Our earthly mothers waiting, sleeplessly.   90

7

Supple and turbulent, a ring of men
Shall chant in orgy on a summer morn
Their boisterous devotion to the sun,
Not as a god, but as a god might be,
Naked among them, like a savage source.
Their chant shall be a chant of paradise,
Out of their blood, returning to the sky;
And in their chant shall enter, voice by voice,
The windy lake wherein their lord delights,
The trees, like serafin, and echoing hills,   100
That choir among themselves long afterward.
They shall know well the heavenly fellowship
Of men that perish and of summer morn.
And whence they came and whither they shall go
The dew upon their feet shall manifest.

8

She hears, upon that water without sound,
A voice that cries, "The tomb in Palestine
Is not the porch of spirits lingering.
It is the grave of Jesus, where he lay."

We live in an old chaos of the sun,   110
Or old dependency of day and night,
Or island solitude, unsponsored, free,
Of that wide water, inescapable.
Deer walk upon our mountains, and the quail
Whistle about us their spontaneous cries;
Sweet berries ripen in the wilderness;
And, in the isolation of the sky,
At evening, casual flocks of pigeons make
Ambiguous undulations as they sink,
Downward to darkness, on extended wings.   120

Bantams
in Pine-Woods

Chieftain Iffucan of Azcan in caftan
Of tan with henna hackles, halt!

Damned universal cock, as if the sun
Was blackamoor to bear your blazing tail.

Fat! Fat! Fat! Fat! I am the personal.
Your world is you. I am my world.

You ten-foot poet among inchlings. Fat!
Begone! An inchling bristles in these pines,

Bristles, and points their Appalachian tangs,
And fears not portly Azcan nor his hoos.

Peter Quince[1]
at the Clavier

1
Just as my fingers on these keys
Make music, so the selfsame sounds
On my spirit make a music, too.

Music is feeling, then, not sound;
And thus it is that what I feel,
Here in this room, desiring you,

1   the carpenter who directed the play before the Duke of Athens in Shakespeare's *A Midsummer Night's Dream*.

Thinking of your blue-shadowed silk,
Is music. It is like the strain
Waked in the elders by Susanna.[2]

Of a green evening, clear and warm, 10
She bathed in her still garden, while
The red-eyed elders watching, felt

The basses of their beings throb
In witching chords, and their thin blood
Pulse pizzicati of Hosanna.[3]

                2
In the green water, clear and warm,
Susanna lay.
She searched
The touch of springs, 20
And found
Concealed imaginings.
She sighed,
For so much melody.

Upon the bank, she stood
In the cool
Of spent emotions.
She felt, among the leaves,
The dew
Of old devotions.

She walked upon the grass, 30
Still quavering.
The winds were like her maids,
On timid feet,
Fetching her woven scarves,
Yet wavering.

A breath upon her hand
Muted the night.
She turned—
A cymbal crashed,
And roaring horns. 40

                3
Soon, with a noise like tambourines,
Came her attendant Byzantines.

2 In the apocryphal Old Testament story, Susanna, the faithful wife, was spied on by
two elders while her husband was away. When she rejected their advances, they accused
her of adultery, but she was saved from death by the prophet Daniel.
3 *Pizzicati:* plucking of strings instead of bowing; *Hosanna:* song of praise to God.

They wondered why Susanna cried
Against the elders by her side;

And as they whispered, the refrain
Was like a willow swept by rain.

Anon, their lamps' uplifted flame
Revealed Susanna and her shame.

And then, the simpering Byzantines
Fled, with a noise like tambourines.   50

4

Beauty is momentary in the mind—
The fitful tracing of a portal;
But in the flesh it is immortal.

The body dies; the body's beauty lives.
So evenings die, in their green going,
A wave, interminably flowing.
So gardens die, their meek breath scenting
The cowl of winter, done repenting.
So maidens die, to the auroral
Celebration of a maiden's choral.   60
Susanna's music touched the bawdy strings
Of those white elders; but, escaping,
Left only Death's ironic scraping.
Now, in its immortality, it plays
On the clear viol of her memory,
And makes a constant sacrament of praise.

Thirteen Ways
of Looking at
a Blackbird

1

Among twenty snowy mountains,
The only moving thing
Was the eye of the blackbird.

2

I was of three minds,
Like a tree
In which there are three blackbirds.

3

The blackbird whirled in the autumn winds.
It was a small part of the pantomime.

4

A man and a woman
Are one.
A man and a woman and a blackbird
Are one.

5

I do not know which to prefer,
The beauty of inflections
Or the beauty of innuendoes,
The blackbird whistling
Or just after.

6

Icicles filled the long window
With barbaric glass.
The shadow of the blackbird
Crossed it, to and fro.
The mood
Traced in the shadow
An indecipherable cause.

7

O thin men of Haddam,
Why do you imagine golden birds?
Do you not see how the blackbird
Walks around the feet
Of the women about you?

8

I know noble accents
And lucid, inescapable rhythms;
But I know, too,
That the blackbird is involved
In what I know.

9

When the blackbird flew out of sight,
It marked the edge
Of one of many circles.

10

At the sight of blackbirds
Flying in a green light,
Even the bawds of euphony
Would cry out sharply.

11

He rode over Connecticut
In a glass coach.

10

20

30

40

Once, a fear pierced him,
In that he mistook
The shadow of his equipage
For blackbirds.

12
The river is moving.
The blackbird must be flying.

13
It was evening all afternoon.
It was snowing
And it was going to snow.
The blackbird sat
In the cedar-limbs.

50

Study
of Two Pears

1
Opusculum pædagogum.[1]
The pears are not viols,
Nudes or bottles.
They resemble nothing else.

2
They are yellow forms
Composed of curves
Bulging toward the base.
They are touched red.

3
They are not flat surfaces
Having curved outlines.
They are round
Tapering toward the top.

4
In the way they are modeled
There are bits of blue.
A hard dry leaf hangs
From the stem.

5
The yellow glistens.
It glistens with various yellows,

1   "a little pedagogical work."

Citrons, oranges and greens
Flowering over the skin.

6

The shadows of the pears
Are blobs on the green cloth.
The pears are not seen
As the observer wills.

Song of
Fixed Accord

Rou-cou spoke the dove,
Like the sooth lord of sorrow,
Of sooth love and sorrow,
And a hail-bow, hail-bow,
To this morrow.

She lay upon the roof,
A little wet of wing and woe,
And she rou-ed there,
Softly she piped among the suns
And their ordinary glare,

The sun of five, the sun of six,
Their ordinariness,
And the ordinariness of seven,
Which she accepted,
Like a fixed heaven,

Not subject to change . . .
Day's invisible beginner,
The lord of love and of sooth sorrow,
Lay on the roof
and made much within her.

WILLIAM CARLOS WILLIAMS [1883–1963]

January Morning

SUITE:

1

I have discovered that most of
the beauties of travel are due to
the strange hours we keep to see them:

the domes of the Church of
the Paulist Fathers in Weehawken
against a smoky dawn—the heart stirred—
are beautiful as Saint Peters
approached after years of anticipation.

2

Though the operation was postponed
I saw the tall probationers   10
in their tan uniforms
                   hurrying to breakfast!

3

—and from basement entries
neatly coiffed, middle aged gentlemen
with orderly moustaches and
well-brushed coats

4

—and the sun, dipping into the avenues
streaking the tops of
the irregular red houselets,
                       and   20
the gay shadows dropping and dropping.

5

—and a young horse with a green bed-quilt
on his withers shaking his head:
bared teeth and nozzle high in the air!

6

—and a semicircle of dirt-colored men
about a fire bursting from an old
ash can,

7

        —and the worn,
blue car rails (like the sky!)
gleaming among the cobbles!   30

8

—and the rickety ferry-boat "Arden"![1]
What an object to be called "Arden"
among the great piers—on the
ever new river!
                "Put me a Touchstone[2]

1   named after the Forest of Arden in Shakespeare's *As You Like it*.
2   the clown in *As You Like It*.

at the wheel, white gulls, and we'll
follow the ghost of the *Half Moon*[3]
to the North West Passage—and through!
(at Albany!) for all that!"

9

Exquisite brown waves—long   40
circlets of silver moving over you!
enough with crumbling ice crusts among you!
The sky has come down to you,
lighter than tiny bubbles, face to
face with you!
                    His spirit is
a white gull with delicate pink feet
and a snowy breast for you to
hold to your lips delicately!

10

The young doctor is dancing with happiness   50
in the sparkling wind, alone
at the prow of the ferry! He notices
the curdy barnacles and broken ice crusts
left at the ship's base by the low tide
and thinks of summer and green
shell-crusted ledges among
                    the emerald eel-grass!

11

Who knows the Palisades[4] as I do
know the river breaks east from them
above the city—but they continue south   60
—under the sky—to bear a crest of
little peering houses that brighten
with dawn behind the moody
water-loving giants of Manhattan.

12

Long yellow rushes bending
above the white snow patches;
purple and gold ribbon
of the distant wood:
                    what an angle
you make with each other as   70
you lie there in contemplation.

3   the name of Henry Hudson's ship on his third voyage of discovery. Looking for a
new route to China, in 1609 Hudson sailed from Holland to New York and ascended the
river now called Hudson to the vicinity of the present Albany. On the fourth voyage,
1610, looking for a northwest passage, he reached what is now called Hudson's Bay.
4   cliffs on the New Jersey side of the Hudson River.

13

Work hard all your young days
and they'll find you too, some morning
staring up under
your chiffonier at its warped
bass-wood bottom and your soul—
out!
—among the little sparrows
behind the shutter.

14

—and the flapping flags are at   80
half mast for the dead admiral.

15

All this—
            was for you, old woman.
I wanted to write a poem
that you would understand.
For what good is it to me
if you can't understand it?
                  But you got to try hard—
But—
       Well, you know how   90
the young girls run giggling
on Park Avenue after dark
when they ought to be home in bed?
Well,
that's the way it is with me somehow.

Spring and All

By the road to the contagious hospital
under the surge of the blue
mottled clouds driven from the
northeast—a cold wind. Beyond, the
waste of broad, muddy fields
brown with dried weeds, standing and fallen

patches of standing water
the scattering of tall trees

All along the road the reddish
purplish, forked, upstanding, twiggy
stuff of bushes and small trees
with dead, brown leaves under them
leafless vines—

Lifeless in appearance, sluggish
dazed spring approaches—

They enter the new world naked,
cold, uncertain of all
save that they enter. All about them
the cold, familiar wind—

Now the grass, tomorrow
the stiff curl of wildcarrot leaf
One by one objects are defined—
It quickens: clarity, outline of leaf

But now the stark dignity of
entrance—Still, the profound change
has come upon them: rooted, they
grip down and begin to awaken

To Elsie

The pure products of America
go crazy—
mountain folk from Kentucky

or the ribbed north end of
Jersey
with its isolate lakes and

valleys, its deaf-mutes, thieves
old names
and promiscuity between

devil-may-care men who have taken   10
to railroading
out of sheer lust of adventure—

and young slatterns, bathed
in filth
from Monday to Saturday

to be tricked out that night
with gauds
from imaginations which have no

peasant traditions to give them
character   20
but flutter and flaunt

sheeer rags—succumbing without
emotion
save numbed terror

under some hedge of choke-cherry
or viburnum—
which they cannot express—

Unless it be that marriage
perhaps
with a dash of Indian blood

30

will throw up a girl so desolate
so hemmed round
with disease or murder

that she'll be rescued by an
agent—
reared by the state and

sent out at fifteen to work in
some hard-pressed
house in the suburbs—

some doctor's family, some Elsie—
voluptuous water
expressing with broken

40

brain the truth about us—
her great
ungainly hips and flopping breasts

addressed to cheap
jewelry
and rich young men with fine eyes

as if the earth under our feet
were
an excrement of some sky

50

and we degraded prisoners
destined
to hunger until we eat filth

while the imagination strains
after deer
going by fields of goldenrod in

the stifling heat of September
Somehow
it seems to destroy us

It is only in isolate flecks that
something
is given off

No one
to witness
and adjust, no one to drive the car

The Red Wheelbarrow

so much depends
upon

a red wheel
barrow

glazed with rain
water

beside the white
chickens.

Poem

As the cat
climbed over
the top of

the jamcloset
first the right
forefoot

carefully
then the hind
stepped down

into the pit of
the empty
flowerpot

This Is
Just To Say

I have eaten
the plums
that were in
the icebox

and which
you were probably
saving
for breakfast

Forgive me
they were delicious
so sweet
and so cold

Iris

a burst of iris so that
come down for
breakfast

we searched through the
rooms for
that

sweetest odor and at
first could not
find its

source then a blue as
of the sea
struck

startling us from among
those trumpeting
petals

The Artist

Mr. T.
      bareheaded
            in a soiled undershirt

his hair standing out
       on all sides
                 stood on his toes
heels together
       arms gracefully
                 for the moment
curled above his head.
       Then he whirled about
                 bounded
into the air
       and with an *entrechat*[1]
                 perfectly achieved
completed the figure.
       My mother
                 taken by surprise
where she sat
       in her invalid's chair
                 was left speechless.
Bravo! she cried at last
       and clapped her hands.
                 The man's wife
came from the kitchen:
       What goes on here? she said.
                 But the show was over.

1 a leap made by the ballet dancer during which he crosses his legs, sometimes with a beating motion.

The Sparrow

TO MY FATHER

This sparrow
       who comes to sit at my window
                 is a poetic truth
more than a natural one.
       His voice,
                 his movements,
his habits—
       how he loves to
                 flutter his wings
in the dust—   10
       all attest it;
                 granted he does it
to rid himself of lice
       but the relief he feels
                 makes him

cry out lustily—
        which is a trait
                more related to music
than otherwise.
        Wherever he finds himself   20
                in early spring,
on back streets
        or beside palaces,
                he carries on
unaffectedly
        his amours.
                It begins in the egg,
his sex genders it:
        What is more pretentiously
                useless   30
or about which
        we more pride ourselves?
                It leads as often as not
to our undoing.
        The cockerel, the crow
                with their challenging voices
cannot surpass
        the insistence
                of his cheep!
Once   40
        at El Paso
                toward evening,
I saw—and heard!—
        ten thousand sparrows
                who had come in from
the desert
        to roost. They filled the trees
                of a small park. Men fled
(with ears ringing!)
        from their droppings,   50
                leaving the premises
to the alligators
        who inhabit
                the fountain. His image
is familiar
        as that of the artistocratic
                unicorn, a pity
there are not more oats eaten
        nowadays
                to make living easier   60
for him.
        At that,
                his small size,

keen eyes,
　　　　serviceable beak
　　　　　　and general truculence
assure his survival—
　　　　to say nothing
　　　　　　of his innumerable
brood.　　　　　　　　　　　　　　　　　　　　　70
　　　　Even the Japanese
　　　　　　know him
and have painted him
　　　　sympathetically,
　　　　　　with profound insight
into his minor
　　　　characteristics.
　　　　　　Nothing even remotely
subtle
　　　　about his lovemaking.　　　　　　　　80
　　　　　　He crouches
before the female,
　　　　drags his wings,
　　　　　　waltzing,
throws back his head
　　　　and simply—
　　　　　　yells! The din
is terrific.
　　　　The way he swipes his bill
　　　　　　across a plank　　　　　　　　90
to clean it,
　　　　is decisive.
　　　　　　So with everything
he does. His coppery
　　　　eyebrows
　　　　　　give him the air
of being always
　　　　a winner—and yet
　　　　　　I saw once,
the female of his species　　　　　　　　100
　　　　clinging determinedly
　　　　　　to the edge of
a waterpipe,
　　　　catch him
　　　　　　by his crown-feathers
to hold him
　　　　silent,
　　　　　　subdued,
hanging above the city streets
　　　　until　　　　　　　　　　　　110
　　　　　　she was through with him.

What was the use
        of that?
                        She hung there
herself,
        puzzled at her success.
                        I laughed heartily.
Practical to the end,
        it is the poem
                of his existence   120
that triumphed
        finally;
                        a wisp of feathers
flattened to the pavement,
        wings spread symmetrically
                        as if in flight,
the head gone,
        the black escutcheon of the breast
                        undecipherable,
an effigy of a sparrow,   130
        a dried wafer only,
                        left to say
and it says it
        without offense,
                        beautifully;
This was I,
        a sparrow.
                        I did my best;
farewell.

D. H. LAWRENCE   [1885–1930]

The Song of a Man Who Has Come Through

Not I, not I, but the wind that blows through me!
A fine wind is blowing the new direction of Time.
If only I let it bear me, carry me, if only it carry me!
If only I am sensitive, subtle, oh, delicate, a winged gift!
If only, most lovely of all, I yield myself and am borrowed
By the fine, fine wind that takes its course through the chaos of the world
Like a fine, an exquisite chisel, a wedge-blade inserted;
If only I am keen and hard like the sheer tip of a wedge
Driven by invisible blows,

The rock will split, we shall come at the wonder, we shall find the Hes-
    perides.[1]

Oh, for the wonder that bubbles into my soul,
I would be a good fountain, a good well-head,
Would blur no whisper, spoil no expression.

What is the knocking?
What is the knocking at the door in the night?
It is somebody wants to do us harm.

No, no, it is the three strange angels.
Admit them, admit them.

1 in Greek mythology, a garden producing golden apples.

Humming-bird

I can imagine, in some otherworld
Primeval-dumb, far back
In that most awful stillness, that only gasped and hummed,
Humming-birds raced down the avenues.

Before anything had a soul,
While life was a heave of Matter, half inanimate,
This little bit chipped off in brilliance
And went whizzing through the slow, vast, succulent stems.

I believe there were no flowers then,
In the world where the humming-bird flashed ahead of creation.
I believe he pierced the slow vegetable veins with his long beak.

Probably he was big
As mosses, and little lizards, they say, were once big.
Probably he was a jabbing, terrifying monster.

We look at him through the wrong end of the long telescope of Time,
Luckily for us.

Kangaroo

In the northern hemisphere
Life seems to leap at the air, or skim under the wind
Like stags on rocky ground, or pawing horses, or springy scut-tailed
    rabbits.

Or else rush horizontal to charge at the sky's horizon,
Like bulls or bisons or wild pigs.

Or slip like water slippery towards its ends,
As foxes, stoats, and wolves, and prairie dogs.

Only mice, and moles, and rats, and badgers, and beavers, and perhaps
    bears
Seem belly-plumbed to the earth's mid-navel.
Or frogs that when they leap come flop, and flop to the center of the
    earth.   10

But the yellow antipodal Kangaroo, when she sits up,
Who can unseat her, like a liquid drop that is heavy, and just touches
    earth.

The downward drip
The down-urge.
So much denser than cold-blooded frogs.

Delicate mother Kangaroo
Sitting up there rabbit-wise, but huge, plumb-weighted,
And lifting her beautiful slender face, oh! so much more gently and finely
    lined than a rabbit's, or than a hare's,
Lifting her face to nibble at a round white peppermint drop which she
    loves, sensitive mother Kangaroo.

Her sensitive, long, pure-bred face.   20
Her full antipodal eyes, so dark,
So big and quiet and remote, having watched so many empty dawns in si-
    lent Australia.

Her little loose hands, and drooping Victorian shoulders.
And then her great weight below the waist, her vast pale belly
With a thin young yellow little paw hanging out, and straggle of a long
    thin ear, like ribbon,
Like a funny trimming to the middle of her belly, thin little dangle of an
    immature paw, and one thin ear.

Her belly, her big haunches
And, in addition, the great muscular python-stretch of her tail.

There, she shan't have any more peppermint drops.
So she wistfully, sensitively sniffs the air, and then turns, goes off in slow
    sad leaps   30

On the long flat skis of her legs,
Steered and propelled by that steel-strong snake of a tail.

Stops again, half turns, inquisitive to look back.
While something stirs quickly in her belly, and a lean little face comes
    out, as from a window,
Peaked and a bit dismayed,
Only to disappear again quickly away from the sight of the world, to
    snuggle down in the warmth,
Leaving the trail of a different paw hanging out.

Still she watches with eternal, cocked wistfulness!
How full her eyes are, like the full, fathomless, shining eyes of an Austra-
    lian black-boy
Who has been lost so many centuries on the margins of existence!   40

She watches with insatiable wistfulness.
Untold centuries of watching for something to come,
For a new signal from life, in that silent lost land of the South.

Where nothing bites but insects and snakes and the sun, small life.
Where no bull roared, no cow ever lowed, no stag cried, no leopard
    screeched, no lion coughed, no dog barked,
But all was silent save for parrots occasionally, in the haunted blue bush.

Wistfully watching, with wonderful liquid eyes.
And all her weight, all her blood, dripping sack-wise down towards the
    earth's center,
And the live little-one taking in its paw at the door of her belly.

Leap then, and come down on the line that draws to the earth's deep,
    heavy center.   50

Energetic Women

Why are women so energetic?
prancing their knees under their tiny skirts
like war-horses; or war-ponies at last!

Why are they so centrifugal?
Why are they so bursting, flinging themselves about?
Why, as they grow older, do they suffer from blood-pressure?

Why are they never happy to be still?
Why did they cut off their long hair
which they could comb by the hour in luxurious quiet?

I suppose when the men all started being Willy wet-legs
women felt it was no longer any use being a linger-longer-Lucy.

Volcanic Venus

What has happened in the world?
the women are like little volcanoes
all more or less in eruption.

It is very unnerving, moving in a world of smouldering volcanoes.
It is rather agitating, sleeping with a little Vesuvius.

And exhausting, penetrating the lava-crater of a tiny Ixtaccihuatl
and never knowing when you'll provoke an earthquake.

It's No Good!

It's no good, the women are in eruption,
and those that have been good so far
now begin to steam ominously,
and if they're over forty-five, hurl great stones into the air
which are very like to hit you on the head as you sit
on the very slopes of the matrimonial mountain
where you've sat peacefully all these years.

Venegeance is mine, saith the Lord,
but the women are my favorite vessels of wrath.

Bavarian Gentians

Not every man has gentians in his house
in Soft September, at slow, sad Michaelmas.[1]

Bavarian gentians, big and dark, only dark
darkening the day-time, torch-like with the smoking blueness of Pluto's[2]
        gloom,
ribbed and torch-like, with their blaze of darkness spread blue
down flattening into points, flattened under the sweep of white day
torch-flower of the blue-smoking darkness, Pluto's dark-blue daze,
black lamps from the halls of Dis, burning dark blue,
giving off darkness, blue darkness, as Demeter's pale lamps give off light,
lead me then, lead the way.

1   feast of the archangel Michael, September 29.
2   Pluto ("Dis") was god of the underworld. He came upon Persephone—daughter of
Zeus and Demeter, the corn goddess—as she was gathering flowers and carried her off.
Demeter searched for her daughter in vain; in her grief she caused a famine, and
humankind would have died had Zeus not persuaded Pluto to let Persephone return to
earth for a part of the year.

Reach me a gentian, give me a torch!
let me guide myself with the blue, forked torch of this flower
down the darker and darker stairs, where blue is darkened on blueness
even where Persephone goes, just now, from the frosted September
to the sightless realm where darkness is awake upon the dark
and Persephone herself is but a voice
or a darkness invisible enfolded in the deeper dark
of the arms Plutonic, and pierced with the passion of dense gloom,
among the splendor of torches of darkness, shedding darkness on the lost
    bride and her groom.

EZRA POUND [1885–1972]

Portrait d'une Femme[1]

Your mind and you are our Sargasso Sea,[2]
London has swept about you this score years
And bright ships left you this or that in fee:
Ideas, old gossip, oddments of all things,
Strange spars of knowledge and dimmed wares of price.
Great minds have sought you—lacking someone else.
You have been second always. Tragical?
No. You preferred it to the usual thing:
One dull man, dulling and uxorious,
One average mind—with one thought less, each year.   10
Oh, you are patient, I have seen you sit
Hours, where something might have floated up.
And now you pay one. Yes, you richly pay.
You are a person of some interest, one comes to you
And takes strange gain away:
Trophies fished up; some curious suggestion;
Fact that leads nowhere; and a tale or two,
Pregnant with mandrakes,[3] or with something else
That might prove useful and yet never proves,
That never fits a corner or shows use,   20
Or finds its hour upon the loom of days:
The tarnished, gaudy, wonderful old work;
Idols and ambergris[4] and rare inlays,
These are your riches, your great store; and yet
For all this sea-hoard of deciduous[5] things,

1 Portrait of a Lady
2 area of the north Atlantic covered with floating vegetation. Legend has it that ships
are entangled and held in the mass.
3 *mandrake*: a Mediterranean herb of the nightshade family having a large forked
root traditionally credited with human attributes.
4 waxy substance found in tropical waters, believed to come from the intestines of the
sperm whale. It is used as a fixative in perfume.
5 falling off or shedding seasonally at a certain stage in the life cycle.

Strange woods half sodden, and new brighter stuff:
In the slow float of differing light and deep,
No! there is nothing! In the whole and all,
Nothing that's quite your own.
          Yet this is you.   30

The River-Merchant's Wife: a Letter

While my hair was still cut straight across my forehead
I played about the front gate, pulling flowers.
You came by on bamboo stilts, playing horse,
You walked about my seat, playing with blue plums.
And we went on living in the village of Chōkan:
Two small people, without dislike or suspicion.

At fourteen I married My Lord you.
I never laughed, being bashful.
Lowering my head, I looked at the wall.
Called to, a thousand times, I never looked back.

At fifteen I stopped scowling,
I desired my dust to be mingled with yours
Forever and forever and forever.
Why should I climb the look out?

At sixteen you departed,
You went into far Ku-tō-en, by the river of swirling eddies,
And you have been gone five months.
The monkeys make sorrowful noise overhead.

You dragged your feet when you went out.
By the gate now, the moss is grown, the different mosses,
Too deep to clear them away!
The leaves fall early this autumn, in wind.
The paired butterflies are already yellow with August
Over the grass in the West garden;
They hurt me. I grow older.
If you are coming down through the narrows of the river Kiang,
Please let me know beforehand,
And I will come out to meet you
          As far as Chō-fū-Sa.
              By Rihaku (Li T'ai Po)[1]

---

1 *Li Po*: eighth-century Chinese poet whose name in Japanese—from which Pound is translating—is Rihaku.

from *Hugh Selwyn Mauberley*

(LIFE AND CONTACTS)

"Vocat Aestus in Umbram," Nemesianus, Ec. IV[1]

I

E. P. ODE POUR L'ELECTION
DE SON SEPULCHRE[1]

For three years, out of key with his time,
He strove to resuscitate the dead art
Of poetry; to maintain "the sublime"
In the old sense. Wrong from the start—

No, hardly, but seeing he had been born
In a half savage country, out of date;
Bent resolutely on wringing lilies from the acorn;
Capaneus;[2] trout for factitious bait;

Ἴδμεν γάρ τοι πάνθ' ὄσ' ἐνὶ Τροίη[3]
Caught in the unstopped ear;   10
Giving the rocks small lee-way
The chopped seas held him, therefore, that year.

His true Penelope was Flaubert,
He fished by obstinate isles;
Observed the elegance of Circe's[4] hair
Rather than the mottoes on sun-dials.

Unaffected by "the march of events,"
He passed from men's memory in *l'an trentiesme*
De son eage,[5] the case presents
No adjunct to the Muses' diadem.   20

II

The age demanded an image
Of its accelerated grimace,
Something for the modern stage,
Not, at any rate, an Attic grace;

1 *"Vocat Aestus . . ."*: "the heats calls us into the shade." *"E. P. Ode . . ."*: "Ezra
Pound: ode for the election of his sepulcher," adapted from Pierre Ronsard's "Ode de
l'élection de son sépulchre" (1550).
2 one of the seven heroes who marched against Thebes. He defied Zeus and was struck
down by a thunderbolt as he was climbing the Theban walls.
3 "For we know all the things that in Troy [the Greeks and Trojans endured by the
will of the gods]," *Odyssey*, 12.189.
4 Penelope was Odysseus' faithful wife, and a symbol of devotion; Flaubert was a
nineteenth-century French novelist who aimed at perfection of form and precision of
words; Circe is the goddess who bewitched the followers of Odysseus.
5 "the thirtieth year of his age"; paraphrased from François Villon's *Grand
Testament.*

343

Not, not certainly, the obscure reveries
Of the inward gaze;
Better mendacities
Than the classics in paraphrase!

The "age demanded" chiefly a mould in plaster,
Made with no loss of time,   30
A prose kinema,[6] not, not assuredly, alabaster
Or the "sculpture" of rhyme.

III

The tea-rose tea-gown, etc.
Supplants the mousseline of Cos,
The pianola "replaces"
Sappho's barbitos.[7]

Christ follows Dionysus,[8]
Phallic and ambrosial
Made way for macerations;[9]
Caliban casts out Ariel.[10]   40

All things are a flowing,
Sage Heracleitus[11] says;
But a tawdry cheapness
Shall outlast our days.

Even the Christian beauty
Defects—after Samothrace;
We see τὸ καλὸν[12]
Decreed in the market place.

Faun's flesh is not to us,
Nor the saint's vision.   50
We have the press for wafer;
Franchise for circumcision.

All men, in law, are equals.
Free of Pisistratus,[13]
We choose a knave or an eunuch
To rule over us.

---

6   movement.
7   Sappho was a Greek poet of Lesbos, and the barbitos was her lyre; Cos is a Greek island famous for its silks.
8   the wine god.
9   *macerate*: to soften, waste away.
10   Caliban the bestial, and Ariel the ethereal man in Shakespeare's *The Tempest*.
11   pre-Socratic philosopher who emphasized the doctrine that all is in flux.
12   "the beautiful"; Samothrace is the Greek island where the statue of the Winged Victory was found.
13   Athenian tyrant.

344

O bright Apollo,
τὶν᾽ ἄνδρα, τὶν ἥρωα, τινα θεὸν,[14]
What god, man, or hero
Shall I place a tin wreath upon!   60

IV

These fought in any case,
and some believing,
                    pro domo,[15] in any case . . .

Some quick to arm,
some for adventure,
some from fear of weakness,
some from fear of censure,
some for love of slaughter, in imagination,
learning later . . .
some in fear, learning love of slaughter;   70

Died some, pro patria,
                    non "dulce" non "et decor"[16]. . . .
walked eye-deep in hell
believing in old men's lies, then unbelieving
came home, home to a lie,
home to many deceits,
home to old lies and new infamy;
usury age-old and age-thick
and liars in public places.

Daring as never before, wastage as never before.   80
Young blood and high blood,
fair cheeks, and fine bodies;

fortitude as never before

frankness as never before,
disillusions as never told in the old days,
hysterias, trench confessions,
laughter out of dead bellies.

V

There died a myriad,
And of the best, among them,
For an old bitch gone in the teeth,   90
For a botched civilization,

14   "what man, what hero, what god [shall we praise]?"—Pindar, "Second Olympian
Ode."
15   "for home."
16   referring to Horace's line *Dulce et decorum est pro patria mori*, "It is sweet and
proper to die for one's country."

Charm, smiling at the good mouth,
Quick eyes gone under earth's lid,

For two gross of broken statues,
For a few thousand battered books.

YEUX GLAUQUES[17]

Gladstone was still respected,
When John Ruskin produced
"King's Treasuries";[18] Swinburne
And Rossetti still abused.

Fœtid Buchanan lifted up his voice   100
When that faun's head of hers[19]
Became a pastime for
Painters and adulterers.

The Burne-Jones cartons
Have preserved her eyes;
Still, at the Tate, they teach
Cophetua[20] to rhapsodize;

Thin like brook-water,
With a vacant gaze.
The English Rubaiyat was still-born   110
In those days.

The thin, clear gaze, the same
Still darts out faun-like from the half-ruin'd face,
Questing and passive. . . .
"Ah, poor Jenny's[21] case" . . .

Bewildered that a world
Shows no surprise
At her last maquero's[22]
Adulteries.

17   sea-green eyes. Pound's French translation of the title of a poem by Théophile
Gautier, *Caerulei Oculi*.
18   Ruskin's "Of Kings' Treasuries," the opening lecture in *Sesame and Lilies*.
19   Buchanan attacked Rossetti and Swinburne in an article titled "The Fleshly School
of Poetry"; "faun's head of hers" refers to Elizabeth Siddal, a painter's model whom
Rossetti married. Two years later she killed herself.
20   "Cophetua and the Beggar Maid" is a painting by Burne-Jones now at the Tate
Gallery.
21   the prostitute in a poem by Rossetti. Also, in Shakespeare's *Merry Wives of
Windsor*, Mistress Quickly says, "Vengeance of Jinny's case. Fie on her! Never name her,
child, if she be a whore."
22   pimp's.

Among the pickled fœtuses and bottled bones,   120
Engaged in perfecting the catalogue,
I found the last scion of the
Senatorial families of Strasbourg, Monsieur Verog.[24]

For two hours he talked of Gallifet;
Of Dowson; of the Rhymers' Club;[25]
Told me how Johnson (Lionel) died
By falling from a high stool in a pub . . .

But showed no trace of alcohol
At the autopsy, privately performed—
Tissue preserved—the pure mind   130
Arose toward Newman[26] as the whiskey warmed.

Dowson found harlots cheaper than hotels;
Headlam for uplift; Image impartially imbued
With raptures for Bacchus, Terpsichore and the Church.
So spoke the author of "The Dorian Mood,"[27]

M. Verog, out of step with the decade,
Detached from his contemporaries,
Neglected by the young,
Because of these reveries.

BRENNBAUM[28]

The sky-like limpid eyes,   140
The circular infant's face,
The stiffness from spats to collar
Never relaxing into grace;

The heavy memories of Horeb, Sinai and the forty years,
Showed only when the daylight fell

23   "Siena made me; Maremma undid me." Dante, *Purgatorio*, 5.135. Dante's line is
spoken by Pia de' Tolomei of Siena, whose husband, in order to marry another woman,
murdered her at his castle in the Tuscan Maremma.
24   Dr. Victor Gustave Plarr was born in Strasbourg but lived in England, where he was
a friend of Dowson and Lionel Johnson, and was librarian to the Royal College of
Surgeons.
25   a literary club, whose members included Ernest Dowson, Lionel Johnson, and W.
B. Yeats. Galliffet was a French general.
26   Cardinal John Henry Newman, English theologian and writer.
27   The Reverend Steward Headlam was an associate of the Rhymers' Club and gave
parties where churchmen and theater people mixed. Professor Selwyn Image was a
friend of Lionel Johnson and Plarr; Plarr wrote a book of verse called *In the Dorian
Mood*.
28   the English writer and caricaturist, Max Beerbohm.

Level across the face
Of Brennbaum "The Impeccable."

MR. NIXON[29]

In the cream gilded cabin of his steam yacht
Mr. Nixon advised me kindly, to advance with fewer
Dangers of delay. "Consider   150
        "Carefully the reviewer.

"I was as poor as you are;
"When I began I got, of course,
"Advance on royalties, fifty at first," said Mr. Nixon,
"Follow me, and take a column,
"Even if you have to work free.

"Butter reviewers. From fifty to three hundred
"I rose in eighteen months;
"The hardest nut I had to crack
"Was Dr. Dundas.   160

"I never mentioned a man but with the view
"Of selling my own works.
"The tip's a good one, as for literature
"It gives no man a sinecure.

"And no one knows, at sight, a masterpiece.
"And give up verse, my boy,
"There's nothing in it."

        .   .   .   .   .

Likewise a friend of Bloughram's[30] once advised me:
Don't kick against the pricks,
Accept opinion. The "Nineties" tried your game   170
And died, there's nothing in it.

                x
Beneath the sagging roof
The stylist[31] has taken shelter,
Unpaid, uncelebrated,
At last from the world's welter

Nature receives him;
With a placid and uneducated mistress

29 Arnold Bennett, to whom Pound refers in his letters as an author who frankly
declared that his real interest in literature was financial.
30 Blougram is a bishop in a poem by Robert Browning.
31 Ford Madox Ford, novelist.

He exercises his talents
And the soil meets his distress.

The haven from sophistications and contentions   180
Leaks through its thatch;
He offers succulent cooking;
The door has a creaking latch.

                    XI
"Conservatrix of Milésien"[32]
Habits of mind and feeling,
Possibly. But in Ealing
With the most bank-clerkly of Englishmen?

No, "Milésian" is an exaggeration.
No instinct has survived in her
Older than those her grandmother   190
Told her would fit her station.

                    XII
"Daphne[33] with her thighs in bark
Stretches toward me her leafy hands,"—
Subjectively. In the stuffed-satin drawing-room
I await The Lady Valentine's commands,

Knowing my coat has never been
Of precisely the fashion
To stimulate, in her,
A durable passion;

Doubtful, somewhat, of the value   200
Of well-gowned approbation
Of literary effort,
But never of The Lady Valentine's vocation:

Poetry, her border of ideas,
The edge, uncertain, but a means of blending
With other strata
Where the lower and higher have ending;

A hook to catch the Lady Jane's attention,
A modulation toward the theatre,

---

32   Pound's adaptation of a phrase from a story by Rémy de Goncourt: *Femmes,
conservatrices des traditions milésiennes*, "Women, conservators of Milesian traditions."
The *Milesian Tales* were a collection of short stories of love and adventure, by Aristides of
Miletus (second century b.c.).
33   Daphne was loved by Apollo, from whom she escaped by being transformed into a
laurel tree. The two lines quoted are a translation from a poem byThéophile Gautier, *Le
Château du Souvenir*.

Also, in the case of revolution,   210
A possible friend and comforter.

              .   .   .   .   .

Conduct, on the other hand, the soul
"Which the highest cultures have nourished"
To Fleet St.³⁴ where
Dr. Johnson flourished;

Beside this thoroughfare
The sale of half-hose has
Long since superseded the cultivation
Of Pierian roses.³⁵

Go, dumb-born book,³⁶   220
Tell her that sang me once that song of Lawes:
Hadst thou but song
As thou hast subjects known,
Then were there cause in thee that should condone
Even my faults that heavy upon me lie,
And build her glories their longevity.

Tell her that sheds
Such treasure in the air,
Recking naught else but that her graces give
Life to the moment,   230
I would bid them live
As roses might, in magic amber laid,
Red overwrought with orange and all made
One substance and one color
Braving time.

Tell her that goes
With song upon her lips
But sings not out the song, nor knows
The maker of it, some other mouth,
May be as fair as hers,   240
Might, in new ages, gain her worshippers,
When our two dusts with Waller's shall be laid,
Siftings on siftings in oblivion,
Till change hath broken down
All things save Beauty alone.

34   a street in London of printers and publishers, now taken over by haberdashers.
35   One of Sappho's poems addresses a woman of no culture who will "have no share in
the roses from Pieria." Pieria was a part of ancient Macedonia where the Muses were
worshipped.
36   based on Edmund Waller's "Go, Lovely Rose," which was set to music by Henry
Lawes, a seventeenth-century composer.

Canto XVII

So that the vines burst from my fingers
And the bees weighted with pollen
Move heavily in the vine-shoots:
          chirr—chirr—chir-rikk—a purring sound,
And the birds sleepily in the branches.
          ZAGREUS![1] IO[2] ZAGREUS!
With the first pale-clear of the heaven
And the cities set in their hills,
And the goddess[3] of the fair knees
Moving there, with the oak-woods behind her,   10
The green slope, with white hounds
          leaping about her;
And thence down to the creek's mouth, until evening,
Flat water before me,
          and the trees growing in water,
Marble trunks out of stillness,
Or past the palazzi,[4]
            in the stillness,
The light now, not of the sun.
          Chrysophrase,[5]   20
And the water green clear, and blue clear;
On, to the great cliffs of amber.
            Between them,
Cave of Nerea,[6]
          she like a great shell curved,
And the boat drawn without sound,
Without odor of ship-work,
Nor bird-cry, nor any noise of wave moving,
Nor splash of porpoise, nor any noise of wave moving,
Within her cave, Nerea,   30
            she like a great shell curved
In the suavity of the rock,
            cliff green-gray in the far,
In the near, the gate-cliffs of amber,
And the wave
          green clear, and blue clear,
And the cave salt-white, and glare-purple,
          cool, porphyry[7] smooth,
          the rock sea-worn.

1 Dionysos, god of wine, ecstasy, and tragedy.
2 Hail.
3 Artemis (Diana), goddess of the hunt, virginal and chaste.
4 palaces in Venice.
5 light green semiprecious stone.
6 "a Poundian composite of Thetis, daughter of Nereus, whose sea-cave was at Thessaly, and Aphrodite (Venus), born of the sea-foam, whom Botticelli depicts being borne to shore on a great curved shell." Christine Froula, *A Guide to Ezra Pound's Selected Poems.*
7 purple semiprecious stone.

No gull-cry, no sound of porpoise,   40
Sand as of malachite,[8] and no cold there,
        the light not of the sun.

Zagreus, feeding his panthers,
        the turf clear as on hills under light.
And under the almond-trees, gods,
        with them, *choros nympharum*.[9] Gods,
Hermes[10] and Athene,[11]
        As shaft of compass,
Between them, trembled—
To the left is the place of fauns,   50
        sylva nympharum;[12]
The low wood, moor-scrub,
        the doe, the young spotted deer,
        leap up through the broom-plants,
            as dry leaf amid yellow.
And by one cut of the hills,
        the great alley of Memnons.[13]
Beyond sea, crests seen over dune
Night sea churning shingle,
To the left, the alley of cypress.   60
            A boat came,
One man holding her sail,
Guiding her with oar caught over gunwale, saying:
"   There, in the forest of marble,
"   the stone trees—out of water—
"   the arbors of stone—
"   marble leaf, over leaf,
"   silver, steel over steel,
"   silver beaks rising and crossing,
"   prow set against prow,   70
"   stone, ply over ply,
"   the gilt beams flare of an evening"
Borso,[14] Carmagnola,[15] the men of craft, *i vitrei*,[16]
Thither, at one time, time after time,
And the waters richer than glass,
Bronze gold, the blaze over the silver,
Dye-pots in the torch-light,
The flash of wave under prows,

8   green semiprecious stone.
9   chorus of nymphs.
10   Greek god who served as messenger and herald. Honored as the god of roads, guide
to the underworld, patron of tradespeople and thieves, inventor of music, et cetera.
11   Greek goddess, the daughter of Zeus. Together with Zeus and Apollo honored as the
embodiment of divine authority.
12   wood of nymphs.
13   probably Memnon, son of Eon and Tithonus.
14   Borso d'Este (1431–1471), son of the lord of Ferrara and a patron of the arts.
15   Francesco da Carmagnola (1380–1431). Executed in Venice for treason.
16   the glassmakers.

And the silver beaks rising and crossing.
      Stone trees, white and rose-white in the darkness,   80

Cypress there by the towers,
      Drift under hulls in the night.

      "In the gloom the gold
Gathers the light about it" . . . [17]

Now supine in burrow, [18] half over-arched bramble,
One eye for the sea, through that peek-hole,
Gray light, with Athene.
Zothar [19] and her elephants, the gold loin-cloth,
The sistrum, [20] shaken, shaken,
      the cohorts of her dancers.   90
And Aletha, [21] by bend of the shore,
      with her eyes seaward,
      and in her hands sea-wrack
Salt-bright with the foam.
Koré [22] through the bright meadow,
      with green-gray dust in the grass:
"For this hour, brother of Circe." [23]
Arm laid over my shoulder,
Saw the sun for three days, the sun fulvid, [24]
As a lion lift over sand-plain;   100
      and that day,
And for three days, and none after,
Splendor, as the splendor of Hermes,
And shipped thence
      to the stone place,
Pale white, over water,
      known water,

17 slightly altered version of a line in "Canto XI": "In the gloom, the gold gathers the light against it." In that canto Pound describes the efforts of Sigismondo Malatesta, a fifteenth-century captain of mercenaries, to carry forward the building of the Tempio at Rimini while taking part in the wars between city states.
18 reference to the *Odyssey* of Homer. Odysseus is washed up on the shore of Paiakia. He makes a bed in a burrow and falls asleep. There he is discovered by a princess, Nausikaa, and her maidservants.
19 probably an invented name.
20 an Egyptian metal rattle.
21 probably an invented name.
22 Persephone, daughter of Zeus and Demeter, the goddess of fertility. While plucking flowers near Enna in Sicily, Persephone was carried off into the lower world by Hades, with the consent of her father. Demeter then made the earth barren. To appease her wrath, Zeus sent Hermes to bring Persephone back. But since she had eaten part of a pomegranate given to her by Hades (i.e., had already become his wife), she could only spend two-thirds of the year in the upper world with her mother. During this time the earth would again be fertile.
23 in Greek mythology a celebrated magician, daughter of the sun and an ocean nymph. She lived on the island of Aeaea. In the *Odyssey* she turns part of Odysseus's crew into swine, but with the help of Hermes he compels her to turn them back again into men. Then Odysseus spends a whole year with her in love-making and other pleasures.
24 tawny.

And the white forest of marble, bent bough over bough,
The pleached arbor of stone,
Thither Borso, when they shot the barbed arrow at him,   110
And Carmagnola, between the two columns,
Sigismundo,[25] after that wreck in Dalmatia.[26]
    Sunset like the grasshopper flying.

25 Sigismondo Malatesta. See footnote 17.
26 Adriatic shore east of Venice.

H. D. (HILDA DOOLITTLE) [1886–1961]

Oread[1]

Whirl up, sea—
whirl your pointed pines,
splash your great pines
on our rocks,
hurl your green over us,
cover us with your pools of fir.

1   mountain nymph.

Heat

O wind, rend open the heat,
cut apart the heat,
rend it to tatters.
Fruit cannot drop
through this thick air—
fruit cannot fall into heat
that presses up and blunts
the points of pears
and rounds the grapes.

Cut the heat—
plough through it,
turning it on either side
of your path.

from Tribute to the Angels

21
This is no rune nor riddle,
it is happening everywhere;

what I mean is—it is so simple
yet no trick of the pen or brush

could capture that impression;
music could do nothing with it,

nothing whatever; what I mean is—   300
but you have seen for yourself

that burnt-out wood crumbling . . .
you have seen for yourself.

22
A new sensation
is not granted to everyone,

not to everyone everywhere,
but to us here, a new sensation

strikes paralysing,
strikes dumb,

strikes the senses numb,   310
sets the nerves quivering;

I am sure you see
what I mean;

it was an old tree
such as we see everywhere,

anywhere here—and some barrel staves
and some bricks

and an edge of the wall
uncovered and the naked ugliness

and then . . . music? O, what I meant   320
by music when I said music, was—

music sets up ladders,
it makes us invisible,

it sets us apart,
it lets us escape;

but from the visible
there is no escape;

there is no escape from the spear
that pierces the heart.

23

We are part of it;   330
we admit the transubstantiation,[1]

not God merely in bread
but God in the other-half of the tree

that looked dead—
did I bow my head?

did I weep? my eyes saw,
it was not a dream

yet it was vision,
it was a sign,

it was *the Angel which redeemed me*,   340
it was the Holy Ghost—

a half-burnt-out apple-tree
blossoming;

this is the flowering of the rood,
this is the flowering of the wood

where Annael, we pause to give
thanks that we rise again from death and live.

24

Every hour, every moment
has its specific attendant Spirit;

the clock-hand, minute by minute,   350
ticks round its prescribed orbit;

but this curious mechanical perfection
should not separate but relate rather,

our life, this temporary eclipse
to that other . . .

25

. . . of the *no need*
of the moon to shine in it,

for it was ticking minute by minute
(the clock at my bed-head,

1 in Roman Catholic and Eastern Orthodox dogma, the miraculous change by which
the eucharistic elements at their consecration become the body and blood of Christ while
keeping the appearance of bread and wine.

with its dim, luminous disc)
when the Lady knocked;

I was talking casually
with friends in the other room,

when we saw the outer hall
grow lighter—then we saw where the door was,

there was no door
(this was a dream of course),

and she was standing there,
actually, at the turn of the stair.

26
one of us said, how odd,
she is actually standing there,

I wonder what brought her?
another of us said,

have we some power between us,
we three together,

that acts as a sort of magnet,
that attracts the super-natural?

(yet it was all natural enough,
we agreed);

I do not know what I said
or if I said anything,

for before I had time to speak,
I realized I had been dreaming,

that I lay awake now on my bed,
that the luminous light

was the phosphorescent face
of my little clock

and the faint knocking
was the clock ticking.

27
And yet in some very subtle way,
she was there more than ever,

as if she had miraculously
related herself to time here,

which is no easy trick, difficult
even for the experienced stranger,

of whom we must *be not forgetful*
for *some have entertained angels unawares.*

                    28
I had been thinking of Gabriel,[2]
of the moon-cycle, of the moon-shell,

of the moon-crescent   400
and the moon at full:

I had been thinking of Gabriel,
the moon-regent, the Angel,

and I had intended to recall him
in the sequence of candle and fire

and the law of the seven;
I had not forgotten

his special attribute
of annunciator; I had thought

to address him as I had the others,   410
Uriel, Annael;[3]

how could I imagine
the Lady herself would come instead?

                    29
We have seen her
the world over,

Our Lady of the Goldfinch,[4]
Our Lady of the Candelabra,

Our Lady of the Pomegranate,
Our Lady of the Chair;

we have seen her, an empress,   420
magnificent in pomp and grace,

2   an archangel.
3   archangels.
4   "Our Lady of the Goldfinch," et cetera, are the names given to paintings of the
Virgin Mary.

and we have seen her
with a single flower

or a cluster of garden-pinks
in a glass beside her;

we have seen her snood
drawn over her hair,

or her face set in profile
with the blue hood and stars;

we have seen her head bowed down   430
with the weight of a domed crown,

or we have seen her, a wisp of a girl
trapped in a golden halo;

we have seen her with arrow, with doves
and a heart like a valentine;

we have seen her in fine silks imported
from all over the Levant,[5]

and hung with pearls brought
from the city of Constantine;[6]

we have seen her sleeve   440
of every imaginable shade

of damask and figured brocade;
it is true,

the painters did very well by her;
it is true, they missed never a line

of the suave turn of the head
or subtle shade of lowered eye-lid

or eye-lids half-raised; you find
her everywhere (or did find),

in cathedral, museum, cloister,   450
at the turn of the palace stair.

30
We see her hand in her lap,
smoothing the apple-green

5   countries bordering on the East Mediterranean.
6   Constantinople.

or the apple-russet silk;
we see her hand at her throat,

fingering a talisman
brought by a crusader from Jerusalem;

we see her hand unknot a Syrian veil
or lay down a Venetian shawl

on a polished table that reflects   460
half a miniature broken column;

we see her stare past a mirror
through an open window,

where boat follows slow boat on the lagoon;
there are white flowers on the water.

                    31
But none of these, none of these
suggest her as I saw her,

though we approach possibly
something of her cool beneficence

in the gracious friendliness   470
of the marble sea-maids in Venice,

who climb the altar-stair
at *Santa Maria dei Miracoli*,[7]

or we acclaim her in the name
of another in Vienna,

Maria von dem Schnee,
Our Lady of the Snow.

                    32
For I can say truthfully,
her veils were *white as snow*,

so as no fuller[8] *on earth*   480
can white them; I can say

she looked beautiful, she looked lovely,
she was *clothed with a garment*

7 Saint Mary of the Miracles, a church in Venice.
8 A fuller is one who shrinks and thickens woolen cloth by moistening, heating, and pressing (Webster's *Collegiate Dictionary*). It is hard to see how this could apply to whitening veils.

down to the foot, but it was not
girt about with a golden girdle,

there was no gold, no color
there was no gleam in the stuff

nor shadow of hem and seam,
as it fell to the floor; she bore

none of her usual attributes;   490
the Child was not with her.

MARIANNE MOORE   [1887–1972]

The Steeple-Jack

Revised, 1961

Dürer[1] would have seen a reason for living
      in a town like this, with eight stranded whales
to look at; with the sweet sea air coming into your house
on a fine day, from water etched
      with waves as formal as the scales
on a fish.

One by one in two's and three's, the seagulls keep
      flying back and forth over the town clock,
or sailing around the lighthouse without moving their wings
rising steadily with a slight   10
      quiver of the body—or flock
mewing where

a sea the purple of the peacock's neck is
      paled to greenish azure as Dürer changed
the pine green of the Tyrol to peacock blue and guinea
gray. You can see a twenty-five-
      pound lobster; and fish nets arranged
to dry. The

whirlwind fife-and-drum of the storm bends the salt
      marsh grass, disturbs stars in the sky and the   20
star on the steeple; it is a privilege to see so
much confusion. Disguised by what
      might seem the opposite, the sea-
side flowers and

1   Albrecht Dürer, 1471–1528, German painter and engraver.

trees are favored by the fog so that you have
    the tropics at first hand: the trumpet vine,
foxglove, giant snapdragon, a salpiglossis that has
spots and stripes; morning-glories, gourds,
    or moon-vines trained on fishing twine
at the back door: 30

cattails, flags, blueberries and spiderwort,
    striped grass, lichens, sunflowers, asters, daisies—
yellow and crab-claw ragged sailors with green bracts—toad-plant,
petunias, ferns; pink lilies, blue
    ones, tigers; poppies; black sweet-peas.
The climate

is not right for the banyan, frangipani, or
    jack-fruit trees; or for exotic serpent
life. Ring lizard and snakeskin for the foot, if you see fit;
but here they've cats, not cobras, to 40
    keep down the rats. The diffident
little newt

with white pin-dots on black horizontal spaced-
    out bands lives here; yet there is nothing that
ambition can buy or take away. The college student
named Ambrose sits on the hillside
    with his not-native books and hat
and sees boats

at sea progress white and rigid as if in
    a groove. Liking an elegance of which 50
the source is not bravado, he knows by heart the antique
sugar-bowl shaped summerhouse of
    interlacing slats, and the pitch
of the church

spire, not true, from which a man in scarlet lets
    down a rope as a spider spins a thread;
he might be part of a novel, but on the sidewalk a
sign says C. J.Poole, Steeple Jack,
    in black and white; and one in red
and white says 60

Danger. The church portico has four fluted
    columns, each a single piece of stone, made
modester by whitewash. This would be a fit haven for
waifs, children, animals, prisoners,
    and presidents who have repaid
sin-driven

senators by not thinking about them. The
    place has a schoolhouse, a post-office in a

store, fish-houses, hen-houses, a three-masted
        schooner on   70
the stocks. The hero, the student,
        the steeple jack, each in his way,
is at home.

It could not be dangerous to be living
        in a town like this, of simple people,
who have a steeple-jack placing danger signs by the church
while he is gilding the solid-
        pointed star, which on a steeple
stands for hope.

Silence

My father used to say,
"Superior people never make long visits,
have to be shown Longfellow's grave
or the glass flowers at Harvard.
Self-reliant like the cat—
that takes its prey to privacy,
the mouse's limp tail hanging like a shoelace from its mouth—
they sometimes enjoy solitude,
and can be robbed of speech
by speech which has delighted them.
The deepest feeling always shows itself in silence;
not in silence, but restraint."
Nor was he insincere in saying, "Make my house your inn."
Inns are not residences.

The Animals Sick of the Plague[1]

        A malady smote the earth one year,
        Felling beasts and infecting all with fear,
To prove to them what grave offenders they were;
Although plague was the name by which it was known,
For it literally congested Acheron,[2]
        Warring on creatures everywhere,
It did not bear off all but all were endangered.
        Any that lingered barely stirred—
Could merely breathe and that diseasedly.
        Nothing aroused their energy.   10
        Neither wolf nor fox disappeared

1 adaptation of a fable by the French poet Jean de La Fontaine (1621–1695).
2 river of the infernal regions.

To stalk young prey as it sunned.
The demoralized doves scattered
And love starved; life was moribund.

When the lion had called his constituency
He said, "Dear friends, this is heaven's remedy
For the sins we have thought a boon.
So he who is guiltiest
Should sacrifice his good to that of the rest
And possibly most of us will then be immune.   20
In accord with the past, history suggests to one,
Penance as atoning for evil done.
So without subterfuge, braving the consequence,
Let each search his conscience.
As for me, I have preyed on flocks of sheep so often
That I have become a glutton.
Because they had wronged me? not once.
Moreover I would devour him when I mastered
The shepherd.
Therefore let me be sacrificed in recompense,   30
But first make a clean breast, not just *I* say how I offend:
We must have justice and detect the trespass,
Then rend the culprit's carcass."
The fox said, "Sire, you are too good to rend;
Your sense of honor is excessively nice.
Eat sheep, Sire! Poor dolts, their loss is no sacrifice.
A sinful king? Oh no. You prove when you devour
The beasts that you thought them superior.
As for the shepherd, one would swear
That he went where he ought to go,   40
Having become to any of us, high or low,
A monster none can endure."
When the fox said this, applause deafened the cur
And no one dared to consider
A tiger, bear, or other beast of prominence
Guilty of any offense.
In fact, quarrelers of evident spleen
Were canonized for their innocent mien.
When his turn came the ass said, "To take a backward glance,
I recall passing clerical domain,   50
The herbs and grass and hunger close to sustenance.
Fiend take me, how could I refrain?
I nipped off as much grass as would lie on my tongue;
So sinned, if what we say must be disinterested."
They made too much noise to hear what the donkey said.
A wolf pronounced the verdict, to which he clung,
Convinced they had found the animal they must kill—
The battered rapscallion who had made the world ill.
He deserved to be hung as an example.

Eat another's grass! What could be more horrible.   60
        Death, only death was suitable
For the criminal—inflicted at once by spite.
And so, as you are weak or are invincible,
The court says white is black or that black crimes are white.

ROBINSON JEFFERS [1887–1962]

Birds

The fierce musical cries of a couple of sparrowhawks hunting on the
        headland,
Hovering and darting, their heads northwestward,
Prick like silver arrows shot through a curtain the noise of the ocean
Trampling its granite; their red backs gleam
Under my window around the stone corners; nothing gracefuller, nothing
Nimbler in the wind. Westward the wave-gleaners,
The old gray sea-going gulls are gathered together, the northwest wind
        wakening
Their wings to the wild spirals of the wind-dance.
Fresh as the air, salt as the foam, play birds in the bright wind, fly falcons
Forgetting the oak and the pinewood, come gulls
From the Carmel[1] sands and the sands at the river-mouth, from Lobos[2]
        and out of the limitless
Power of the mass of the sea, for a poem
Needs multitude, multitudes of thoughts, all fierce, all flesh-eaters, musi-
        cally clamorous
Bright hawks that hover and dart headlong, and ungainly
Gray hungers fledged with desire of transgression, salt slimed beaks, from
        the sharp
Rock-shores of the world and the secret waters.

1   town on the coast of northern California.
2   promontory southwest of Monterey.

Hurt Hawks

                1
The broken pillar of the wing jags from the clotted shoulder,
The wing trails like a banner in defeat,
No more to use the sky forever but live with famine
And pain a few days: cat nor coyote
Will shorten the week of waiting for death, there is game
        without talons.
He stands under the oak-bush and waits
The lame feet of salvation; at night he remembers freedom
And flies in a dream, the dawns ruin it.

He is strong and pain is worse to the strong, incapacity is
    worse.
The curs of the day come and torment him
At distance, no one but death the redeemer will humble
    that head,
The intrepid readiness, the terrible eyes.
The wild God of the world is sometimes merciful to those
That ask mercy, not often to the arrogant.
You do not know him, you communal people, or you have
    forgotten him;
Intemperate and savage, the hawk remembers him;
Beautiful and wild, the hawks, and men that are dying,
    remember him.

2

I'd sooner, except the penalties, kill a man than a hawk; but
    the great redtail
Had nothing left but unable misery
From the bone too shattered for mending, the wing that
    trailed under his talons when he moved.
We had fed him six weeks, I gave him freedom,
He wandered over the foreland hill and returned in the
    evening, asking for death,
Not like a beggar, still eyed with the old
Implacable arrogance. I gave him the lead gift in the twilight.
    What fell was relaxed,
Owl-downy, soft feminine feathers; but what
Soared: the fierce rush: the night-herons by the flooded river
    cried fear at its rising
Before it was quite unsheathed from reality.

New Mexican Mountain

I watch the Indians dancing to help the young corn at Taos pueblo. The
    old men squat in a ring
And make the song, the young women with fat bare arms, and a few
    shame-faced young men, shuffle the dance.

The lean-muscled young men are naked to the narrow loins, their breasts
    and backs daubed with white clay,
Two eagle-feathers plume the black heads. They dance with reluctance,
    they are growing civilized; the old men persuade them.

Only the drum is confident, it thinks the world has not changed; the beat-
    ing heart, the simplest of rhythms,
It thinks the world has not changed at all; it is only a dreamer, a brainless
    heart, the drum has no eyes.

These tourists have eyes, the hundred watching the dance, white Americans, hungrily too, with reverence, not laughter;
Pilgrims from civilization, anxiously seeking beauty, religion, poetry; pilgrims from the vacuum.

People from cities, anxious to be human again. Poor show how they suck you empty! The Indians are emptied,
And certainly there was never religion enough, nor beauty nor poetry here . . . to fill Americans.

Only the drum is confident, it thinks the world has not changed. Apparently only myself and the strong
Tribal drum, and the rockhead of Taos mountain, remember that civilization is a transient sickness.

T. S. ELIOT   [1888–1965]

The Love Song
of J. Alfred Prufrock

S'io credesse che mia riposta fosse
A persona che mai tornasse al mondo,
Questa fiamma staria senza piu scosse.
Ma perciocche giammai di questo fondo
Non torno vivo alcun, s'i'odo il vero,
Senza tema d'infamia ti rispondo.[1]

Let us go then, you and I,
When the evening is spread out against the sky
Like a patient etherized upon a table;
Let us go, though certain half-deserted streets,
The muttering retreats
Of restless nights in one-night cheap hotels
And sawdust restaurants with oyster-shells:
Streets that follow like a tedious argument
Of insidious intent
To lead you to an overwhelming question . . .   10
Oh, do not ask, "What is it?"
Let us go and make our visit.

In the room the women come and go
Talking of Michelangelo.

The yellow fog that rubs its back upon the window-panes,
The yellow smoke that rubs its muzzle on the window-panes

1 "If I believed that my answer would be to one who would ever return to the world, this flame would shake no more; but since no one ever returns alive from this depth, if what I hear is true, I answer you without fear of infamy." This is Guido da Montefeltro's answer to Dante when asked why he is being punished in hell (Dante's *Inferno* 27, 61–66).

Licked its tongue into the corners of the evening,
Lingered upon the pools that stand in drains,
Let fall upon its back the soot that falls from chimneys,
Slipped by the terrace, made a sudden leap,   20
And seeing that it was a soft October night,
Curled once about the house, and fell asleep.

And indeed there will be time
For the yellow smoke that slides along the street,
Rubbing its back upon the window-panes;
There will be time, there will be time
To prepare a face to meet the faces that you meet;
There will be time to murder and create,
And time for all the works and days[2] of hands
That lift and drop a question on your plate;   30
Time for you and time for me,
And time yet for a hundred indecisions,
And for a hundred visions and revisions,
Before the taking of a toast and tea.

In the room the women come and go
Talking of Michelangelo.

And indeed there will be time
To wonder, "Do I dare?" and, "Do I dare?"
Time to turn back and descend the stair,
With a bald spot in the middle of my hair—   40
[They will say: "How his hair is growing thin!"]
My morning coat, my collar mounting firmly to the chin,
My necktie rich and modest, but asserted by a simple pin—
[They will say: "But how his arms and legs are thin!"]
Do I dare
Disturb the universe?
In a minute there is time
For decisions and revisions which a minute will reverse.

For I have known them all already, known them all:—
Have known the evenings, mornings, afternoons,   50
I have measured out my life with coffee spoons;
I know the voices dying with a dying fall
Beneath the music from a farther room.
   So how should I presume?

And I have known the eyes already, known them all—
The eyes that fix you in a formulated phrase,
And when I am formulated, sprawling on a pin,
When I am pinned and wriggling on the wall,
Then how should I begin

2   an allusion to Hesiod's *Works and Days*, a poem praising hard work in the fields.

To spit out all the butt-ends of my days and ways?   60
    And how should I presume?

And I have known the eyes already, known them all—
The eyes that fix you in a formulated phrase,
And when I am formulated, sprawling on a pin,
When I am pinned and wriggling on the wall,
Then how should I begin
To spit out all the butt-ends of my days and ways?   60
    And how should I presume?

And I have known the arms already, known them all—
Arms that are braceleted and white and bare
[But in the lamplight, downed with light brown hair!]
Is it perfume from a dress
That makes me so digress?
Arms that lie along a table, or wrap about a shawl.
    And should I then presume?
    And how should I begin?

       .   .   .   .   .

Shall I say, I have gone at dusk through narrow streets   70
And watched the smoke that rises from the pipes
Of lonely men in shirt-sleeves, leaning out of windows? . . .

I should have been a pair of ragged claws
Scuttling across the floors of silent seas.

       .   .   .   .   .

And the afternoon, the evening, sleeps so peacefully!
Smoothed by long fingers,
Asleep . . . tired . . . or it malingers,
Stretched on the floor, here beside you and me.
Should I, after tea and cakes and ices,
Have the strength to force the moment to its crisis?   80
But though I have wept and fasted, wept and prayed,
Though I have seen my head [grown slightly bald] brought in upon a plat-
    ter,[3]
I am no prophet—and here's no great matter;
I have seen the moment of my greatness flicker,
And I have seen the eternal Footman hold my coat, and snicker,
And in short, I was afraid.

And would it have been worth it, after all,
After the cups, the marmalade, the tea,
Among the porcelain, among some talk of you and me,
Would it have been worth while,   90

3   like the head of John the Baptist. At the request of Salome he was executed, and his
head was brought in to Herod on a platter (Matthew, 14.1–11).

To have bitten off the matter with a smile,
To have squeezed the universe into a ball
To roll it toward some overwhelming question,
To say: "I am Lazarus, come from the dead,[4]
Come back to tell you all, I shall tell you all"—
If one, settling a pillow by her head,
　　Should say: "That is not what I meant at all.
　　That is not it, at all."

And would it have been worth it, after all,
Would it have been worth while　　　　　　　　　　100
After the sunsets and the dooryards and the sprinkled streets,
After the novels, after the teacups, after the skirts that trail along the
　　　　floor—
And this, and so much more?—
It is impossible to say just what I mean!
But as if a magic lantern threw the nerves in patterns on a screen:
Would it have been worth while,
If one, settling a pillow or throwing off a shawl,
And turning toward the window, should say:
　　"That is not it at all,
　　That is not what I meant, at all."　　　　　　　　　110

　　　　　　.　　　.　　　.　　　.　　　.

No! I am not Prince Hamlet, nor was meant to be;
Am an attendant lord, one that will do
To swell a progress, start a scene or two,
Advise the prince; no doubt, an easy tool,
Deferential, glad to be of use,
Politic, cautious, and meticulous;
Full of high sentence, but a bit obtuse;
At times, indeed, almost ridiculous—
Almost, at times, the Fool.

I grow old . . . I grow old . . .　　　　　　　　　　120
I shall wear the bottoms of my trousers rolled.[5]

Shall I part my hair behind? Do I dare to eat a peach?
I shall wear white flannel trousers, and walk upon the beach.
I have heard the mermaids singing, each to each.

I do not think that they will sing to me.

I have seen them riding seaward on the waves
Combing the white hair of the waves blown back
When the wind blows the water white and black.

4　the brother of Mary and Martha, who was raised from death by Christ (John, 11.
1–44).
5　trousers with cuffs, a new fashion then.

370

We have lingered in the chambers of the sea
By sea-girls wreathed with seaweed red and brown   130
Till human voices wake us, and we drown.

Rhapsody on
a Windy Night

Twelve o'clock.
Along the reaches of the street
Held in a lunar synthesis,
Whispering lunar incantations
Dissolve the floors of memory
And all its clear relations,
Its divisions and precisions.
Every street lamp that I pass
Beats like a fatalistic drum,
And through the spaces of the dark   10
Midnight shakes the memory
As a madman shakes a dead geranium.

Half-past one,
The street-lamp sputtered,
The street-lamp muttered,
The street-lamp said, "Regard that woman
Who hesitates toward you in the light of the door
Which opens on her like a grin.
You see the border of her dress
Is torn and stained with sand,   20
And you see the corner of her eye
Twists like a crooked pin."

The memory throws up high and dry
A crowd of twisted things;
A twisted branch upon the beach
Eaten smooth, and polished
As if the world gave up
The secret of its skeleton,
Stiff and white.
A broken spring in a factory yard,   30
Rust that clings to the form that the strength has left
Hard and curled and ready to snap.

Half-past two,
The street-lamp said,
"Remark the cat which flattens itself in the gutter,
Slips out its tongue
And devours a morsel of rancid butter."

So the hand of the child, automatic,
Slipped out and pocketed a toy that was running along the quay.
I could see nothing behind that child's eye.   40
I have seen eyes in the street
Trying to peer through lighted shutters,
And a crab one afternoon in a pool,
An old crab with barnacles on his back,
Gripped the end of a stick which I held him.

Half-past three,
The lamp sputtered,
The lamp muttered in the dark.
The lamp hummed:
"Regard the moon,   50
La lune ne garde aucune rancune,[1]
She winks a feeble eye,
She smiles into corners.
She smooths the hair of the grass.
The moon has lost her memory.
A washed-out smallpox cracks her face,
Her hand twists a paper rose,
That smells of dust and eau de Cologne,
She is alone
With all the old nocturnal smells   60
That cross and cross across her brain."
The reminiscence comes
Of sunless dry geraniums
And dust in crevices,
Smells of chestnuts in the streets,
And female smells in shuttered rooms,
And cigarettes in corridors
And cocktail smells in bars.

The lamp said,
"Four o'clock,   70
Here is the number on the door.
Memory!
You have the key,
The little lamp spreads a ring on the stair.
Mount.
The bed is open; the tooth-brush hangs on the wall,
Put your shoes at the door, sleep, prepare for life."

The last twist of the knife.

1 The moon doesn't hold a grudge.

Gerontion[1]

Thou hast nor youth nor age
But as it were an after dinner sleep
Dreaming of both.[2]

Here I am, an old man in a dry month,
Being read to by a boy, waiting for rain.[3]
I was neither at the hot gates[4]
Nor fought in the warm rain
Nor knee deep in the salt marsh,[5] heaving a cutlass,
Bitten by flies, fought.
My house is a decayed house,
And the jew squats on the window sill, the owner,
Spawned in some estaminet[6] of Antwerp,
Blistered in Brussels, patched and peeled in London.   10
The goat coughs at night in the field overhead;
Rocks, moss, stonecrop, iron, merds.
The woman keeps the kitchen, makes tea,
Sneezes at evening, poking the peevish gutter.
                                        I an old man,
A dull head among windy spaces.

Signs are taken for wonders. "We would see a sign!"[7]
The word within a word, unable to speak a word,
Swaddled with darkness. In the juvescence of the year
Came Christ the tiger   20
In depraved May, dogwood and chestnut, flowering judas,[8]
To be eaten, to be divided, to be drunk
Among whispers; by Mr. Silvero
With caressing hands, at Limoges
Who walked all night in the next room;

By Hakagawa, bowing among the Titians;
By Madame de Tornquist, in the dark room
Shifting the candles; Fräulein von Kulp
Who turned in the hall, one hand on the door.[9] Vacant shuttles
Weave the wind. I have no ghosts,   30

1 little old man.
2 Shakespeare, *Measure for Measure*, Act 3, Scene 1.
3 from a life of Edward Fitzgerald: "in a dry month, old and blind, being read to by a country boy, longing for rain."
4 *hot gates*: translation of the Greek place name Thermopylae.
5 Sigismondo Malatesta, fifteenth-century Italian mercenary soldier, writes of fighting in the marshes. See also Ezra Pound's *Cantos*.
6 café.
7 Matthew 16 and John 6: Jesus has been asked for a sign that he is the son of God. In Matthew he replies that no sign shall be given; in John he says that he is the sign.
8 This description is taken from *The Education of Henry Adams*. Adams compares the rank growth and depravity of the spring in Washington with the strict moral tone of New England.
9 Mr. Silvero, Hakagawa, Madame de Tornquist, and Fräulein von Kulp seem to be imaginary characters.

An old man in a draughty house
Under a windy knob.

After such knowledge, what forgiveness? Think now
History has many cunning passages, contrived corridors[10]
And issues, deceives with whispering ambitions,
Guides us by vanities. Think now
She gives when our attention is distracted
And what she gives, gives with such supple confusions
That the giving famishes the craving. Gives too late
What's not believed in, or if still believed,   40
In memory only, reconsidered passion. Gives too soon
Into weak hands, what's thought can be dispensed with
Till the refusal propagates a fear. Think
Neither fear nor courage saves us. Unnatural vices
Are fathered by our heroism. Virtues
Are forced upon us by our impudent crimes.
These tears are shaken from the wrath-bearing tree.

The tiger springs in the new year. Us he devours. Think at last
We have not reached conclusion, when I
Stiffen in a rented house. Think at last   50
I have not made this show purposelessly
And it is not by any concitation
Of the backward devils.
I would meet you upon this honestly.
I that was near your heart was removed therefrom
To lose beauty in terror, terror in inquisition.
I have lost my passion: why should I need to keep it
Since what is kept must be adulterated?
I have lost my sight, smell, hearing, taste and touch:
How should I use them for your closer contact?   60

These with a thousand small deliberations
Protract the profit of their chilled delirium,
Excite the membrane, when the sense has cooled,
With pungent sauces, multiply variety
In a wilderness of mirrors. What will the spider do,
Suspend its operations, will the weevil
Delay? De Bailhache, Fresca, Mrs. Cammel,[11] whirled
Beyond the circuit of the shuddering Bear
In fractured atoms. Gull against the wind, in the windy straits
Of Belle Isle, or running on the Horn,   70
White feathers in the snow, the Gulf claims,
And an old man driven by the Trades

10   In 1919, shortly before this poem was written, the leaders of the victorious Allied
powers meeting at Versailles had "contrived" a corridor from Poland to the sea. This
same corridor would be one of the matters of dispute that brought on the Second World
War.
11   Again, these are apparently imaginary characters.

To a sleepy corner.
                              Tenants of the house,
Thoughts of a dry brain in a dry season.

The Hollow Men

Mistah Kurtz—he dead.
A penny for the Old Guy[1]

1

We are the hollow men
We are the stuffed men
Leaning together
Headpiece filled with straw. Alas!
Our dried voices, when
We whisper together
Are quiet and meaningless
As wind in dry grass
Or rats' feet over broken glass
In our dry cellar   10

Shape without form, shade without color,
Paralyzed force, gesture without motion;

Those who have crossed
With direct eyes, to death's other Kingdom
Remember us—if at all—not as lost
Violent souls, but only
As the hollow men
The stuffed men.

2

Eyes I dare not meet in dreams
In death's dream kingdom   20
These do not appear:
There, the eyes are
Sunlight on a broken column
There, is a tree swinging
And voices are
In the wind's singing
More distant and more solemn
Than a fading star.

Let me be no nearer
In death's dream kingdom   30

1 The first epigraph is the cabin boy announcing Kurtz's death in Joseph Conrad's
story, *Heart of Darkness*. The second is the cry of children collecting on Guy Fawkes
Day, celebrating the discovery of a plot to blow up the House of Parliament.

Let me also wear
Such deliberate disguises
Rat's coat, crowskin, crossed staves
In a field
Behaving as the wind behaves
No nearer—

Not that final meeting
In the twilight kingdom

3

This is the dead land
This is cactus land   40
Here the stone images
Are raised, here they receive
The supplication of a dead man's hand
Under the twinkle of a fading star.

Is it like this
In death's other kingdom
Waking alone
At the hour when we are
Trembling with tenderness
Lips that would kiss   50
Form prayers to broken stone.

4

The eyes are not here
There are no eyes here
In this valley of dying stars
In this hollow valley
This broken jaw of our lost kingdoms

In this last of meeting places
We grope together
And avoid speech
Gathered on this beach of the tumid river[2]   60

Sightless, unless
The eyes reappear
As the perpetual star
Multifoliate rose[3]
Of death's twilight kingdom
The hope only
Of empty men.

2 the river Acheron in the underworld.
3 an emblem of Christ and the Virgin.

5

Here we go round the prickly pear
Prickly pear prickly pear
Here we go round the prickly pear   70
At five o'clock in the morning.

Between the idea
And the reality
Between the motion
And the act
Falls the Shadow
                    For Thine is the Kingdom

Between the conception
And the creation
Between the emotion   80
And the response
Falls the Shadow
                        Life is very long

Between the desire
And the spasm
Between the potency
And the existence
Between the essence
And the descent
Falls the Shadow   90
                    For Thine is the Kingdom

For Thine is
Life is
For Thine is the

This is the way the world ends
This is the way the world ends
This is the way the world ends
Not with a bang but a whimper.

Macavity:
the Mystery Cat

Macavity's a Mystery Cat: he's called the Hidden Paw—
For he's the master criminal who can defy the Law.
He's the bafflement of Scotland Yard, the Flying Squad's despair:
For when they reach the scene of crime—*Macavity's not there!*

Macavity, Macavity, there's no one like Macavity,
He's broken every human law, he breaks the law of gravity.
His powers of levitation would make a fakir stare,
And when you reach the scene of crime—*Macavity's not there!*
You may seek him in the basement, you may look up in the air—
But I tell you once and once again, *Macavity's not there!*   10

Macavity's a ginger cat, he's very tall and thin;
You would know him if you saw him, for his eyes are sunken in.
His brow is deeply lined with thought, his head is highly domed;
His coat is dusty from neglect, his whiskers are uncombed.
He sways his head from side to side, with movements like a snake;
And when you think he's half asleep, he's always wide awake.

Macavity, Macavity, there's no one like Macavity,
For he's a fiend in feline shape, a monster of depravity.
You may meet him in a by-street, you may see him in the square—
But when a crime's discovered, then *Macavity's not there!*   20

He's outwardly respectable. (They say he cheats at cards.)
And his footprints are not found in any file of Scotland Yard's.
And when the larder's looted, or the jewel-case is rifled,
Or when the milk is missing, or another Peke's been stifled,
Or the greenhouse glass is broken, and the trellis past repair—
Ay, there's the wonder of the thing! *Macavity's not there!*

And when the Foreign Office find a Treaty's gone astray,
Or the Admiralty lose some plans and drawings by the way,
There may be a scrap of paper in the hall or on the stair—
But it's useless to investigate—*Macavity's not there!*   30
And when the loss has been disclosed, the Secret Service say:
"It *must* have been Macavity!"—but he's a mile away.
You'll be sure to find him resting, or a-licking of his thumbs,
Or engaged in doing complicated long division sums.

Macavity, Macavity, there's no one like Macavity,
There never was a Cat of such deceitfulness and suavity.
He always has an alibi, and one or two to spare:
At whatever time the deed took place—MACAVITY WASN'T THERE!
And they say that all the Cats whose wicked deeds are widely known
(I might mention Mungojerrie, I might mention Griddlebone)   40
Are nothing more than agents for the Cat who all the time
Just controls their operations: the Napoleon of Crime!

Bells for John Whiteside's Daughter

There was such speed in her little body,
And such lightness in her footfall,
It is no wonder her brown study
Astonishes us all.

Her wars were bruited in our high window.
We looked among orchard trees and beyond
Where she took arms against her shadow,
Or harried unto the pond

The lazy geese, like a snow cloud
Dripping their snow on the green grass,
Tricking and stopping, sleepy and proud,
Who cried in goose, Alas,

For the tireless heart within the little
Lady with rod that made them rise
From their noon apple-dreams and scuttle
Goose-fashion under the skies!

But now go the bells and we are ready,
In one house we are sternly stopped
To say we are vexed at her brown study,
Lying so primly propped.

Dog

Cock-a-doodle-doo the brass-lined rooster goes,
Brekekekex intones the fat Greek frog,
These fantasies do not worry me as does
The bow-wow-wow of dog.

I had a doggie who used to sit and beg,
A pretty little creature with tears in his eyes
And anomalous hand extended on a leg.
Housebroken was my Huendchen, and so wise.

Booms a big dog's voice like a fireman's bell.
But Fido sits at dusk on Madame's lap   10
And bored beyond his tongue's poor skill to tell
Rehearses his pink paradigm, To yap.

However. Up the lane the tender bull
Proceeds unto his kine; he yearns for them,
Whose eyes adore him and are beautiful,
Love speeds him, and no treason or mayhem.

But having come to the gateway in the fence,
Listen! again the hateful barking dog,
Like a numerous army rattling the battlements
With shout, though it is but his monologue,   20
With lion's courage and sting-bee's virulence
Though he is but one dog.

Shrill is the fury of the royal bull,
His knees quiver, and the honeysuckle vine
Expires with anguish as his voice, dreadful,
Cries, "What do you want of my bonded lady kine?"

Now the air trembles to the sorrowing Moo
Of twenty blameless ladies of the mead
Who fear their lord's precarious set-to.
It is the sunset and the heavens bleed.   30

The hooves of the brave bull slither the claybank
And cut the green tendrils of the vine; the horn
Slices the young birch into splinter and shank
But lunging leaves the bitch's boy untorn.

Across the late sky comes master, Hodge by name,
Upright, two-legged, tall-browed, and self-assured,
In his hand a cudgel, in his blue eye a flame:
"Have I beat my dog so sore and he is not cured?"

Old Hodge stays not his hand, but whips to kennel
The renegade, God's peace betide the souls   40
Of the pure in heart! But from the box in the fennel.
Blaze two red eyes as hot as cooking-coals.

EDNA ST. VINCENT MILLAY [1892–1950]

Love Is
Not All

Love is not all: it is not meat nor drink
Nor slumber nor a roof against the rain;
Nor yet a floating spar to men that sink
And rise and sink and rise and sink again;

Love can not fill the thickened lung with breath,
Nor clean the blood, nor set the fractured bone;
Yet many a man is making friends with death
Even as I speak, for lack of love alone.
It well may be that in a difficult hour,
Pinned down by pain and moaning for release,
Or nagged by want past resolution's power,
I might be driven to sell your love for peace,
Or trade the memory of this night for food.
It well may be. I do not think I would.

HUGH MacDIARMID   [1892–1978]

The Bonnie Broukit° Bairn°

dirty / child

Mars is braw° in crammasy,°	*gaily dressed / crimson*
Venus in a green silk goun,	
The auld mune shak's her gowden° feathers,	*golden*
Their starry talk's a wheen° o' blethers,°	*a good deal / nonsense*
Nane for thee a thochtie° sparin',	*a little thought*
Earth, thou bonnie broukit bairn!	
—But greet,° an' in your tears ye'll drown	*cry*
The haill° clanjamfrie!°	*whole / worthless bunch*

Crowdieknowe

Oh to be at Crowdieknowe	
When the last trumpet blaws,	
An' see the deid° come loupin' owre	*dead*
The auld grey wa's.°	*walls*
Muckle° men wi' tousled beards.	*large*
I grat° as a bairn°	*wept / child*
'll scramble frae the croodit° clay	*thickened*
Wi' feck° o' swearin'.	*plenty*
An' glower° at God an' a' his gang	*stare*
O' angels i' the lift°	*sky*
—Thae trashy bleezin° French-like folk	*drunk*
Wha gar'd° them shift!	*forced*
Fain° the weemun-folk'll seek	*gladly*
To mak' them haud° their row	*hold*
—Fegs,° God's no blate° gin he stirs up	*Truly / not shy*
The men o' Crowdieknowe!	

from *In Memoriam James Joyce*

In the Fall

Let the only consistency
In the course of my poetry
Be like that of the hawthorn tree
Which in early Spring breaks
Fresh emerald, then by nature's law
Darkens and deepens and takes
Tints of purple-maroon, rose-madder and straw.

Sometimes these hues are found
Together, in pleasing harmony bound.
Sometimes they succeed each other. But through   10
All the changes in which the hawthorn is dight,[1]
No matter in what order, one thing is sure
—The haws[2] shine ever the more ruddily bright!

And when the leaves have passed
Or only in a few tatters remain
The tree to the winter condemned
        Stands forth at last
     Not bare and drab and pitiful,
But a candelabrum of oxidised silver gemmed
By innumerable points of ruby   20
Which dominate the whole and are visible
Even at considerable distance
As flame-points of living fire.
That so it may be
With my poems too at last glance
Is my only desire.
All else must be sacrificed to this great cause.
I fear no hardships. I have counted the cost.
I with my heart's blood as the hawthorn with its haws
Which are sweetened and polished by the frost!   30

See how these haws burn, there down the drive,
In this autumn air that feels like cotton wool,
When the earth has the gelatinous limpness of a body dead as a
    whole
While its tissues are still alive!

Poetry is human existence come to life,
The glorious energy that once employed
Turns all else in creation null and void,

1   adorned.
2   hawthorn berries.

382

The flower and fruit, the meaning and goal,
Which won all else is needs removed by the knife   40
Even as a man who rises high
Kicks away the ladder he has come up by.

This single-minded zeal, this fanatic devotion to art
Is alien to the English poetic temperament no doubt,
"This narrowing intensity" as the English say,
But I have it even as you had it, Yeats, my friend,
And would have it with me as with you at the end,
I who am infinitely more un-English than you
And turn Scotland to poetry like those women who
In their passion secrete and turn to   50
Musk through and through!

So I think of you, Joyce, and of Yeats and others who are dead
As I walk this Autumn and observe
The birch tremulously pendulous in jewels of cairngorm,3
The sauch, the osier, and the crack-willow4
Of the beaten gold of Australia;
The sycamore in rich straw-gold;
The elm bowered in saffron;
The oak in flecks of salmon gold;
The beeches huge torches of living orange.   60
Billow upon billow of autumnal foliage
From the sheer high bank glass themselves
Upon the ebon and silver current that floods freely
Past the shingle shelves.
I linger where a crack willow slants across the stream,
Its olive leaves slashed with fine gold.
Beyond the willow a young beech
Blazes almost blood-red,
Vying in intensity with the glowing cloud of crimson
That hangs about the purple bole of a gean5   70
Higher up the brae6 face.

And yonder, the lithe green-grey bole of an ash, with its boughs
Draped in the cinnamon-brown lace of samara.7
(And I remember how in April upon its bare twigs
The flowers came in ruffs like the unshorn ridges
Upon a French poodle—like a dull mulberry at first,
Before the first feathery fronds
Of the long-stalked, finely-poised, seven-fingered leaves)—
Even the robin hushes his song
In these gold pavilions.   80

3   a yellow or smoky brown crystalline quartz.
4   kinds of trees.
5   wild cherry tree.
6   a hillside that is usually along a river.
7   a dry, one-seeded, winged fruit that remains closed at maturity.

Other masters may conceivably write
Even yet in C major
But we—we take the perhaps "primrose path"
To the dodecaphonic[8] bonfire.

They are not endless these variations of form
Though it is perhaps impossible to see them all.
It is certainly impossible to conceive one that doesn't exist.
But I keep trying in our forest to do both of these,
And though it is a long time now since I saw a new one
I am by no means weary yet of my concentration   90
On phyllotaxis[9] here in preference to all else,
All else—but my sense of sny![10]

The gold edging of a bough at sunset, its pantile[11] way
Forming a double curve, tegula and imbrex[12] in one,
Seems at times a movement on which I might be borne
Happily to infinity; but again I am glad
When it suddenly ceases and I find myself
Pursuing no longer a rhythm of duramen[13]
But bouncing on the diploe[14] in a clearing between earth and air
Or headlong in dewy dallops[15] or a moon-spairged fernshaw[16]   100
Or caught in a dark dumosity,[17] or even
In open country again watching an aching spargosis[18] of stars.

8   twelve-tone.
9   the arrangement of leaves on a stem and in relation to one another.
10   the upward curve of the edge of a plank, expecially toward the bow or stern.
11   a longitudinally curved roofing tile.
12   *tegula and imbrex*: technical descriptions of tiles.
13   heartwood.
14   porous bony tissue between the external and internal layers of the skull.
15   doolloups. A doolloup is "A steep *shank*, or glen, where two *haughs* are exactly opposite to each other" (*Jamieson's Scottish Dictionary*). A haugh is "Low-lying flat ground, properly on the border of a river."
16   *shaw*: "A piece of ground which becomes suddenly flat at the bottom of a hill or steep bank."
17   *dumosity*: I cannot find this word, even in Jamieson. I think MacDiarmid is playing here—it sounds like a made-up word, probably meaning "darkness." A dark dumosity would be very dark.
18   sprinkling.

WILFRED OWEN   [1893–1918]

Anthem for
Doomed Youth

What passing-bells for these who die as cattle?
  Only the monstrous anger of the guns.
  Only the stuttering rifles' rapid rattle

Can patter out their hasty orisons.[1]
No mockeries now for them; no prayers nor bells,
   Nor any voice of mourning save the choirs,—
The shrill, demented choirs of wailing shells;
   And bugles calling for them from sad shires.

What candles may be held to speed them all?
   Not in the hands of boys, but in their eyes
Shall shine the holy glimmers of good-byes.
   The pallor of girls' brows shall be their pall;
Their flowers the tenderness of patient minds,
And each slow dusk a drawing-down of blinds.

1 prayers.

Exposure

Our brains ache, in the merciless iced east winds that knive us . . .
Wearied we keep awake because the night is silent . . .
Low, drooping flares confuse our memory of the salient . . .
Worried by silence, sentries whisper, curious, nervous,
         But nothing happens.

Watching, we hear the mad gusts tugging on the wire,
Like twitching agonies of men among its brambles.
Northward, incessantly, the flickering gunnery rumbles,
Far off, like a dull rumor of some other war.
         What are we doing here?   10

The poignant misery of dawn begins to grow . . .
We only know war lasts, rain soaks, and clouds sag stormy.
Dawn massing in the east her melancholy army
Attacks once more in ranks on shivering ranks of gray,
         But nothing happens.

Sudden successive flights of bullets streak the silence.
Less deadly than the air that shudders black with snow,
With sidelong flowing flakes that flock, pause, and renew;
We watch them wandering up and down the wind's nonchalance,
         But nothing happens.   20

Pale flakes with fingering stealth come feeling for our faces—
We cringe in holes, back on forgotten dreams, and stare, snow-dazed,
Deep into grassier ditches. So we drowse, sun-dozed,
Littered with blossoms trickling where the blackbird fusses.
         Is it that we are dying?

Slowly our ghosts drag home: glimpsing the sunk fires, glozed
With crusted dark-red jewels; crickets jingle there;

For hours the innocent mice rejoice: the house is theirs;
Shutters and doors, all closed: on us the doors are closed,—
      We turn back to our dying. 30

Since we believe not otherwise can kind fires burn;
Nor even suns smile true on child, or field, or fruit.
For God's invincible spring our love is made afraid;
Therefore, not loath, we lie out here; therefore were born,
      For love of God seems dying.

To-night, His frost will fasten on this mud and us,
Shriveling many hands, puckering foreheads crisp.
The burying-party, picks and shovels in their shaking grasp,
Pause over half-known faces. All their eyes are ice,
      But nothing happens. 40

Disabled

He sat in a wheeled chair, waiting for dark,
And shivered in his ghastly suit of gray,
Legless, sewn short at elbow. Through the park
Voices of boys rang saddening like a hymn,
Voices of play and pleasures after day,
Till gathering sleep had mothered them from him.

About this time Town used to swing so gay
When glow-lamps budded in the light blue trees,
And girls glanced lovelier as the air grew dim,—
In the old times, before he threw away his knees. 10
Now he will never feel again how slim
Girls' waists are, or how warm their subtle hands,
All of them touch him like some queer disease.

There was an artist silly for his face,
For it was younger than his youth, last year.
Now, he is old; his back will never brace;
He's lost his color very far from here,
Poured it down shell-holes till the veins ran dry,
And half his lifetime lapsed in the hot race,
And leap of purple spurted from his thigh. 20

One time he liked a blood-smear down his leg,
After the matches, carried shoulder-high.
It was after football, when he'd drunk a peg,
He thought he'd better join.—He wonders why.
Someone had said he'd look a god in kilts,
That's why; and may be, too, to please his Meg;
Aye, that was it, to please the giddy jilts

386

He asked to join. He didn't have to beg;
Smiling they wrote his lie; aged nineteen years.
Germans he scarcely thought of; all their guilt,
And Austria's, did not move him. And no fears
Of Fear came yet. He thought of jeweled hilts
For daggers in plaid socks; of smart salutes;
And care of arms; and leave; and pay arrears;
Esprit de corps, and hints for young recruits.
And soon he was drafted out with drums and cheers.

Some cheered him home, but not as crowds cheer Goal.
Only a solemn man who brought him fruits
Thanked him; and then inquired about his soul.

Now, he will spend a few sick years in Institutes,
And do what things the rules consider wise,
And take whatever pity they may dole.
Tonight he noticed how the women's eyes
Passed from him to the strong men that were whole.
How cold and late it is! Why don't they come
And put him into bed? Why don't they come?

E. E. CUMMINGS [1894–1963]

Portrait

Buffalo Bill's
defunct
        who used to
        ride a watersmooth-silver
                        stallion
and break onetwothreefourfive pigeonsjustlikethat
                                Jesus
he was a handsome man
                        and what i want to know is
how do you like your blueeyed boy
Mister Death

Poem, or Beauty Hurts Mr. Vinal

take it from me kiddo
believe me
my country, 'tis of

you, land of the Cluett
Shirt Boston Garter and Spearmint
Girl With the Wrigley Eyes (of you
land of the Arrow Ide
and Earl &
Wilson
Collars) of you i   10
sing:land of Abraham Lincoln and Lydia E. Pinkham,
land above all of Just Add Hot Water And Serve—
from every B. V. D.

let freedom ring

amen. i do however protest, anent the un
-spontaneous and otherwise scented merde which
greets one (Everywhere Why) as divine poesy per
that and this radically defunct periodical. i would

suggest that certain ideas gestures
rhymes, like Gillette Razor Blades   20
having been used and reused
to the mystical moment of dullness emphatically are
Not To Be Resharpened. (Case in point

if we are to believe these gently O sweetly
melancholy trillers amid the thrillers
these crepuscular violinists among my and your
skyscrapers—Helen & Cleopatra were Just Too Lovely,
The Snail's On The Thorn enter Morn and God's
In His andsoforth

do you get me?) according   30
to such supposedly indigenous
throstles Art is O World O Life
a formula: example, Turn Your Shirttails Into
Drawers and If It Isn't An Eastman It Isn't A
Kodak therefore my friends let
us now sing each and all fortissimo A-
mer
i
ca, I
love,   40
You. And there're a
hun-dred-mil-lion-oth-ers, like
all of you successfully if
delicately gelded (or spaded)
gentlemen (and ladies)—pretty

littleliverpill-
hearted-Nujolneeding-There's-A-Reason

americans (who tensetendoned and with
upward vacant eyes, painfully
perpetually crouched, quivering, upon the   50
sternly allotted sandpile
—how silently
emit a tiny violetflavored nuisance: Odor?

ono.
comes out like a ribbon lies flat on the brush

my sweet
old etcetera

my sweet old etcetera
aunt lucy during the recent

war could and what
is more did tell you just
what everybody was fighting

for,
my sister

isabel created hundreds
(and
hundreds) of socks not to
mention shirts fleaproof earwarmers

etcetera wristers etcetera, my
mother hoped that

i would die etcetera
bravely of course my father used
to become hoarse talking about how it was
a privilege and if only he
could meanwhile my

self etcetera lay quietly
in the deep mud et

cetera
(dreaming,
et
   cetera, of
Your smile
eyes knees and of your Etcetera)

somewhere i have
never travelled,
gladly beyond

somewhere i have never travelled,gladly beyond
any experience,your eyes have their silence:
in your most frail gesture are things which enclose me,
or which i cannot touch because they are too near

your slightest look easily will unclose me
though i have closed myself as fingers,
you open always petal by petal myself as Spring opens
(touching skilfully,mysteriously) her first rose

or if your wish be to close me,i and
my life will shut very beautifully,suddenly,
as when the heart of this flower imagines
the snow carefully everywhere descending;

nothing which we are to perceive in this world equals
the power of your intense fragility:whose texture
compels me with the color of its countries,
rendering death and forever with each breathing

(i do not know what it is about you that closes
and opens;only something in me understands
the voice of your eyes is deeper than all roses)
nobody,not even the rain,has such small hands

a he as o

a he as o
ld as who stag
geri
ng up some streetfu

l of peopl
e lurche
s viv
idly

from ti(& d
esperate
ly)m
e to ti

me shru
gg

ing as if to say b
ut for chreyesake how ca

n
i s
ell drunk if i
be pencils

old age sticks

old age sticks
up Keep
Off
signs)&

youth yanks them
down(old
age
cries No

Tres)&(pas)
youth laughs
(sing
old age

scolds Forbid
den Stop
Must
n't Don't

&)youth goes
right on
gr
owing old

HART CRANE   [1899–1932]

Legend

As silent as a mirror is believed
Realities plunge in silence by . . .

I am not ready for repentance;
Nor to match regrets. For the moth
Bends no more than the still
Imploring flame. And tremorous
In the white falling flakes

Kisses are,—
The only worth all granting.

It is to be learned—
This cleaving and this burning,
But only by the one who
Spends out himself again.

Twice and twice
(Again the smoking souvenir,
Bleeding eidolon!) and yet again.
Until the bright logic is won
Unwhispering as a mirror
Is believed.

Then, drop by caustic drop, a perfect cry
Shall string some constant harmony,—
Relentless caper for all those who step
The legend of their youth into the noon.

Black Tambourine

The interests of a black man in a cellar
Mark tardy judgment on the world's closed door.
Gnats toss in the shadow of a bottle,
And a roach spans a crevice in the floor.

Æsop, driven to pondering, found
Heaven with the tortoise and the hare;
Fox brush and sow ear top his grave
And mingling incantations on the air.

The black man, forlorn in the cellar,
Wanders in some mid-kingdom, dark, that lies,
Between his tambourine, stuck on the wall,
And, in Africa, a carcass quick with flies.

from *The Bridge*

To Brooklyn Bridge

How many dawns, chill from his rippling rest
The seagull's wings shall dip and pivot him,
Shedding white rings of tumult, building high
Over the chained bay waters Liberty—

Then, with inviolate curve, forsake our eyes
As apparitional as sails that cross
Some page of figures to be filed away;
—Till elevators drop us from our day . . .

I think of cinemas, panoramic sleights
With multitudes bent toward some flashing scene   10
Never disclosed, but hastened to again,
Foretold to other eyes on the same screen;

And Thee, across the harbor, silver-paced
As though the sun took step of thee, yet left
Some motion ever unspent in thy stride,—
Implicitly thy freedom staying thee!

Out of some subway scuttle, cell or loft
A bedlamite speeds to thy parapets,
Tilting there momently, shrill shirt ballooning,
A jest falls from the speechless caravan.   20

Down Wall, from girder into street noon leaks,
A rip-tooth of the sky's acetylene;
All afternoon the cloud-flown derricks turn . . .
Thy cables breathe the North Atlantic still.

And obscure as that heaven of the Jews,
Thy guerdon . . . Accolade thou dost bestow
Of anonymity time cannot raise:
Vibrant reprieve and pardon thou dost show.

O harp and altar, of the fury fused,
(How could mere toil align thy choiring strings!)   30
Terrific threshold of the prophet's pledge,
Prayer of pariah, and the lover's cry,—

Again the traffic lights that skim thy swift
Unfractioned idiom, immaculate sigh of stars,
Beading thy path—condense eternity:
And we have seen night lifted in thine arms.

Under thy shadow by the piers I waited;
Only in darkness is thy shadow clear.
The City's fiery parcels all undone,
Already snow submerges an iron year . . .   40

O Sleepless as the river under thee,
Vaulting the sea, the prairies' dreaming sod,
Unto us lowliest sometimes sweep, descend
And of the curveship lend a myth to God.

Cape Hatteras[1]

The seas all crossed, weathered the capes, the voyage
done . . . —WALT WHITMAN

Imponderable the dinosaur
        sinks slow,
            the mammoth saurian[2]
            ghoul, the eastern
                  Cape . . .
While rises in the west the coastwise range,
                 slowly the hushed land—
Combustion at the astral core—the dorsal change
Of energy—convulsive shift of sand . . .
But we, who round the capes, the promontories   10
Where strange tongues vary messages of surf
Below grey citadels, repeating to the stars
The ancient names—return home to our own
Hearths, there to eat an apple and recall
The songs that gypsies dealt us at Marseille
Or how the priests walked—slowly through Bombay—
Or to read you, Walt,[3]—knowing us in thrall

To that deep wonderment, our native clay
Whose depth of red, eternal flesh of Pocahontus—
Those continental folded æons, surcharged   20
With sweetness below derricks, chimneys, tunnels—
Is veined by all that time has really pledged us . . .
And from above, thin squeaks of radio static,
The captured fume of space foams in our ears—
What whisperings of far watches on the main
Relapsing into silence, while time clears
Our lenses, lifts a focus, resurrects
A periscope to glimpse what joys or pain
Our eyes can share or answer—then deflects
Us, shunting to a labyrinth submersed   30
Where each sees only his dim past reversed . . .

But that star-glistered salver[4] of infinity,
The circle, blind crucible of endless space,
Is sluiced by motion,—subjugated never.
Adam and Adam's answer in the forest
Left Hesperus[5] mirrored in the lucid pool.
Now the eagle dominates our days, is jurist
Of the ambiguous cloud. We know the strident rule
Of wings imperious . . . Space, instantaneous,

1   on Hatteras Island, between Pamlico Sound and the Atlantic Ocean.
2   any of a group of reptiles including some lizards, crocodiles, and extinct dinosaurs.
3   Walt Whitman.
4   a tray for serving foods or beverages.
5   evening star.

Flickers a moment, consumes us in its smile: 40
A flash over the horizon—shifting gears—
And we have laughter, or more sudden tears.
Dream cancels dream in this new realm of fact
From which we wake into the dream of act;
Seeing himself an atom in a shroud—
Man hears himself an engine in a cloud!

"—Recorders ages hence"—ah, syllables of faith!
Walt, tell me, Walt Whitman, if infinity
Be still the same as when you walked the beach
Near Paumanok[6]—your lone patrol—and heard the   50
    wraith
Through surf, its bird note there a long time falling . . .
For you, the panoramas and this breed of towers,
Of you—the theme that's statured in the cliff.
O Saunterer on free ways still ahead!
Not this our empire yet, but labyrinth
Wherein your eyes, like the Great Navigator's[7] without ship,
Gleam from the great stones of each prison crypt
Of canyoned traffic . . . Confronting the Exchange,
Surviving in a world of stocks,—they also range   60
Across the hills where second timber strays
Back over Connecticut farms, abandoned pastures,—
Sea eyes and tidal, undenying, bright with myth!

The nasal whine of power whips a new universe . . .
Where spouting pillars spoor the evening sky,
Under the looming stacks of the gigantic power house
Stars prick the eyes with sharp ammoniac proverbs,
New verities, new inklings in the velvet hummed
Of dynamos, where hearing's leash is strummed . . .
Power's script,—wound, bobbin-bound, refined—   70
Is stropped to the slap of belts on booming spools, spurred
Into the bulging bouillon, harnessed jelly of the stars.
Towards what? The forked crash of split thunder parts
Our hearing momentwise; but fast in whirling armatures,[8]
As bright as frogs' eyes, giggling in the girth
Of steely gizzards—axle-bound, confined
In coiled precision, bunched in mutual glee
The bearings glint,—O murmurless and shined
In oilrinsed circles of blind ecstasy!

Stars scribble on our eyes the frosty sagas,   80
The gleaming cantos of unvanquished space . . .

6 *Paumanok*: Indian name for Long Island. Whitman wasn't near Paumanok, as Crane has it—he was on Paumanok.
7 Christopher Columbus.
8 *armature*: coils of wire around a metal core in which electric current is induced in a generator or the input current interacts with a magnetic field to produce torque in a motor.

O sinewy silver biplane, nudging the wind's withers!
There, from Kill Devils Hill at Kitty Hawk[9]
Two brothers in their twinship left the dune;
Warping the gale, the Wright windwrestlers veered
Capeward, then blading the wind's flank, banked and spun
What ciphers risen from prophetic script,
What marathons new-set between the stars!
The soul, by naphtha[10] fledged into new reaches,
Already knows the closer clasp of Mars,—   90
New latitudes, unknotting, soon give place
To what fierce schedules, rife of doom apace!

Behold the dragon's covey—amphibian, ubiquitous
To hedge the seaboard, wrap the headland, ride
The blue's cloud-templed districts unto ether . . .
While Iliads[11] glimmer through eyes raised in pride
Hell's belt springs wider into heaven's plumed side.
O bright circumferences, heights employed to fly
War's fiery kennel masked in downy offings,—
This tournament of space, the threshed and chiselled height,   100
Is baited by marauding circles, bludgeon flail
Of rancorous grenades whose screaming petals carve us
Wounds that we wrap with theorems sharp as hail!

Wheeled swiftly, wings emerge from larval-silver hangars.
Taut motors surge, space-gnawing, into flight;
Through sparkling visibility, outspread, unsleeping,
Wings clip the last peripheries of light . . .
Tellurian[12] wind-sleuths on dawn patrol,
Each plane a hurtling javelin of winged ordnance,
Bristle the heights above a screeching gale to hover;   110
Surely no eye that Sunward Escadrille[13] can cover!
There, meaningful, fledged as the Pleiades[14]
With razor sheen they zoom each rapid helix![15]
Up-chartered choristers of their own speeding
They, cavalcade on escapade, shear Cumulus[16]—
Lay siege and hurdle Cirrus[17] down the skies!
While Cetus-like,[18] O thou Dirigible, enormous Lounger
Of pendulous auroral beaches,—satellited wide
By convoy planes, moonferrets that rejoin thee

9   where the Wright brothers, Wilbur and Orville, made the first powered flight.
10   any of various volatile and often flammable liquid hydro-carbon mixtures used
chiefly as solvents and dilutents.
11   reference to Homer's *Iliad* that tells of the siege of Troy.
12   characteristic of the earth.
13   unit of a European air command usually containing six airplanes.
14   a visible cluster of six stars in the constellation Taurus.
15   something spiral in form.
16   a cloud formation.
17   a cloud formation.
18   *Cetus*: equatorial constellation south of Pisces and Aries.

On fleeing balconies as thou dost glide,
—Hast splintered space!

                    Low, shadowed of the Cape,
Regard the moving turrets! From grey decks
See scouting griffons[19] rise through gaseous crepe
Hung low . . . until a conch of thunder answers
Cloud-belfries, banging, while searchlights, like fencers,
Slit the sky's pancreas of foaming anthracite
Toward thee, O Corsair[20] of the typhoon,—pilot, hear!
Thine eyes bicarbonated white by speed, O Skygak,[21] see
How from thy path above the levin's[22] lance   130
Thou sowest doom thou hast nor time nor chance
To reckon—as thy stilly eyes partake
What alcohol of space . . . ! Remember, Falcon-Ace,
Thou hast there in thy wrist a Sanskrit[23] charge
To conjugate infinity's dim marge—
Anew . . . !

                    But first, here at this height receive
The benediction of the shell's deep, sure reprieve!
Lead-perforated fuselage, escutcheoned[24] wings
Lift agonized quittance, tilting from the invisible brink   140
Now eagle-bright, now
                    quarry-hid, twist-
                              -ing, sink with
Enormous repercussive list-
                              -ings down
Giddily spiralled
                    gauntlets, upturned, unlooping
In guerrilla sleights, trapped in combustion gyr-
Ing, dance the curdled depth
                              down whizzing   150
Zodiacs,[25] dashed
                    (now nearing fast the Cape!)
                              down gravitation's
                                        vortex into crashed
. . . dispersion . . . into mashed and shapeless débris . . .
By Hatteras bunched the beached heap of high bravery!

                              ♦

The stars have grooved our eyes with old persuasions
Of love and hatred, birth,—surcease of nations . . .

19 *griffon:* a fabulous animal with head, foreparts, and wings like those of an eagle,
hind legs and tail like those of a lion.
20 pirate.
21 apparently an invented name.
22 *levin:* lightning (archaic).
23 ancient Indian language.
24 shielded.
25 signs of the zodiac.

But who has held the heights more sure than thou,
O Walt!—Ascensions of thee hover in me now   160
As thou at junctions elegiac, there, of speed
With vast eternity, dost wield the rebound seed!
The competent loam, the probable grass,—travail
Of tides awash the pedestal of Everest, fail
Not less than thou in pure impulse inbred
To answer deepest soundings! O, upward from the dead
Thou bringest tally, and a pact, new bound,
Of living brotherhood!

                Thou, there beyond—
Glacial sierras and the flight of ravens,   170
Hermetically past condor zones, through zenith havens
Past where the albatross has offered up
His last wing-pulse, and downcast as a cup
That's drained, is shivered back to earth—thy wand
Has beat a song, O Walt,—there and beyond!
And this, thine other hand, upon my heart
Is plummet ushered of those tears that start
What memories of vigils, bloody, by that Cape,—
Ghoul-mound of man's perversity at balk
And fraternal massacre! Thou, pallid there as chalk,   180
Hast kept of wounds, O Mourner, all that sum
That then from Appomattox stretched to Somme![26]

Cowslip and shad-blow,[27] flaked like tethered foam
Around bared teeth of stallions, bloomed that spring
When first I read thy lines, rife as the loam
Of prairies, yet like breakers cliffward leaping!
O, early following thee, I searched the hill
Blue-writ and odor-firm with violets, 'til
With June the mountain laurel broke through green
And filled the forest with what clustrous sheen!   190
Potomac lilies,—then the Pontiac rose,
And Klondike edelweiss[28] of occult snows!
White banks of moonlight came descending valleys—
How speechful on oak-vizored palisades,
As vibrantly I following down Sequoia alleys
Heard thunder's eloquence through green arcades
Set trumpets breathing in each clump and grass tuft—'til
Gold autumn, captured, crowned the trembling hill!

Panis Angelicus![29] Eyes tranquil with the blaze
Of love's own diametric gaze, of love's amaze!   200

26 *Appomattox*: place in Virginia where Lee surrendered to Grant. *Somme*: in France,
scene of battles in the First World War.
27 serviceberry, a North American tree or shrub of the rose family.
28 a perennial herb that grows high in the Alps.
29 angelic bread, from a hymn by Thomas Aquinas referring to the Eucharist: "The
angelic bread becomes the bread of man."

Not greatest, thou,—not first, nor last,—but near
And onward yielding past my utmost year.
Familiar, thou, as mendicants[30] in public places;
Evasive—too—as dayspring's spreading arc to trace is:—
Our Meistersinger,[31] thou set breath in steel;
And it was thou who on the boldest heel
Stood up and flung the span on even wing
Of that great Bridge,[32] our Myth, whereof I sing!

Years of the Modern! Propulsions toward what capes?   210
But thou, *Panis Angelicus*, hast thou not seen
And passed that Barrier that none escapes—
But knows it leastwise as death-strife?—O, something green,
Beyond all sesames of science was thy choice
Wherewith to bind us throbbing with one voice,
New integers of Roman, Viking, Celt—
Thou, Vedic[33] Caesar, to the greensward knelt!

And now, as launched in abysmal cupolas of space,
Toward endless terminals, Easters of speeding light—   220
Vast engines outward veering with seraphic grace
On clarion cylinders pass out of sight
To course that span of consciousness thou'st named
The Open Road—thy vision is reclaimed!
What heritage thou'st signalled to our hands!

And see! the rainbow's arch—how shimmeringly stands
Above the Cape's ghoul-mound, O joyous seer!
Recorders ages hence, yes, they shall hear
In their own veins uncancelled thy sure tread
And read thee by the aureole 'round thy head   230
Of pasture-shine, *Panis Angelicus*!
                                        Yes, Walt,
Afoot again, and onward without halt,—
Not soon, nor suddenly,—No, never to let go
        My hand
                in yours,
                        Walt Whitman—
                                so—

30 beggars.
31 *meistersinger*: a member of any of various German guilds formed chiefly in the
fifteenth and sixteenth centuries by workmen and craftsmen for the cultivation of poetry
and music.
32 Brooklyn Bridge.
33 relating to the four canonical collections of hymns, prayers, and liturgical formulas
that comprise the Veda, the earliest Hindu sacred writings.

OGDEN NASH [1902–1971]

Portrait of the
Artist as a
Prematurely Old Man

It is common knowledge to every schoolboy and even
    every Bachelor of Arts,
That all sin is divided into two parts.
One kind of sin is called a sin of commission, and that
    is very important,
And it is what you are doing when you are doing some-
    thing you ortant,
And the other kind of sin is just the opposite and is
    called a sin of omission and is equally bad in the
    eyes of all right-thinking people, from Billy Sunday   10
    to Buddha,
And it consists of not having done something you
    shuddha.
I might as well give you my opinion of these two kinds
    of sin as long as, in a way, against each other we
    are pitting them,
And that is, don't bother your head about sins of com-
    mission because however sinful, they must at least
    be fun or else you wouldn't be committing them.
It is the sin of omission, the second kind of sin,   20
That lays eggs under your skin.
The way you get really painfully bitten
Is by the insurance you haven't taken out and the checks
    you haven't added up the stubs of and the ap-
    pointments you haven't kept and the bills you
    haven't paid and the letters you haven't written.
Also, about sins of omission there is one particularly
    painful lack of beauty,
Namely, it isn't as though it had been a riotous red-
    letter day or night every time you neglected to do   30
    your duty;
You didn't get a wicked forbidden thrill
Every time you let a policy lapse or forgot to pay a
    bill;
You didn't slap the lads in the tavern on the back and
    loudly cry Whee,
Let's all fail to write just one more letter before we go
    home, and this round of unwritten letters is on me.
No, you never get any fun
Out of the things you haven't done,   40
But they are the things that I do not like to be amid,
Because the suitable things you didn't do give you a

lot more trouble than the unsuitable things you
    did.
The moral is that it is probably better not to sin at all,
    but if some kind of sin you must be pursuing,
Well, remember to do it by doing rather than by not
    doing.

Very Like
a Whale

One thing that literature would be greatly the better for
Would be a more restricted employment by authors of
    simile and metaphor.
Authors of all races, be they Greeks, Romans, Teutons
    or Celts,
Can't seem just to say that anything is the thing it is
    but have to go out of their way to say that it is like
    something else.
What does it mean when we are told
That the Assyrian came down like a wolf on the fold?[1]   10
In the first place, George Gordon Byron had had enough
    experience
To know that it probably wasn't just one Assyrian, it
    was a lot of Assyrians.
However, as too many arguments are apt to induce
    apoplexy and thus hinder longevity,
We'll let it pass as one Assyrian for the sake of brevity.
Now then, this particular Assyrian, the one whose co-
    horts were gleaming in purple and gold,
Just what does the poet mean when he says he came   20
    down like a wolf on the fold?
In heaven and earth more than is dreamed of in our
    philosophy there are a great many things,
But I don't imagine that among them there is a wolf
    with purple and gold cohorts or purple and gold
    anythings.
No, no, Lord Byron, before I'll believe that this As-
    syrian was actually like a wolf I must have some
    kind of proof;
Did he run on all fours and did he have a hairy tail and   30
    a big red mouth and big white teeth and did he
    say Woof woof?
Frankly I think it very unlikely, and all you were en-
    titled to say, at the very most,
Was that the Assyrian cohorts came down like a lot of

---

1   See "The Destruction of Sennacherib" on page 212.

Assyrian cohorts about to destroy the Hebrew host.
But that wasn't fancy enough for Lord Byron, oh dear
    me no, he had to invent a lot of figures of speech
    and then interpolate them,
With the result that whenever you mention Old Testa-   40
    ment soldiers to people they say Oh yes, they're
    the ones that a lot of wolves dressed up in gold
    and purple ate them.
That's the kind of thing that's being done all the time
    by poets, from Homer to Tennyson;
They're always comparing ladies to lilies and veal to
    venison,
And they always say things like that the snow is a white
    blanket after a winter storm.
Oh it is, is it, all right then, you sleep under a six-inch   50
    blanket of snow and I'll sleep under a half-inch
    blanket of unpoetical blanket material and we'll
    see which one keeps warm,
And after that maybe you'll begin to comprehend dimly
What I mean by too much metaphor and simile.

The Purist

I give you now Professor Twist,
A conscientious scientist.
Trustees exclaimed, "He never bungles!"
And sent him off to distant jungles.
Camped on a tropic riverside,
One day he missed his loving bride.
She had, the guide informed him later,
Been eaten by an alligator.
Professor Twist could not but smile.
"You mean," he said, "a crocodile."

Old Men

People expect old men to die,
They do not really mourn old men.
Old men are different. People look
At them with eyes that wonder when . . .
People watch with unshocked eyes;
But the old men know when an old man dies.

LANGSTON HUGHES [1902–1967]

Children's Rhymes

When I was a chile we used to play,
"One—two—buckle my shoe!"
and things like that. But now, Lord,
listen at them little varmits!

> *By what sends*
> *the white kids*
> *I ain't sent:*
> *I know I can't*
> *be President.*

There is two thousand children
in this block, I do believe!

> *What don't bug*
> *them white kids*
> *sure bugs me:*
> *We knows everybody*
> *ain't free!*

Some of these young ones is cert'ly bad—
One batted a hard ball right through my window
And my gold fish et the glass.

> *What's written down*
> *for white folks*
> *ain't for us a-tall:*
> *"Liberty and Justice—*
> *Huh—For All."*

> *Oop-pop-a-da!*
> *Skee! Daddle-de-do!*
> *Be-bop!*
Salt'peanuts!
> *De-dop!*

Night Funeral
in Harlem

Night funeral
in Harlem:

Where did they get
Them two fine cars?

Insurance man, he did not pay—
His insurance lapsed the other day—
Yet they got a satin box
For his head to lay.

   Night funeral
   in Harlem: 10

   Who was it sent
   That wreath of flowers?

Them flowers came
from that poor boy's friends—
They'll want flowers, too,
When they meet their ends.

   Night funeral
   in Harlem:

   Who preached that
   Black boy to his grave?   20

Old preacher-man
Preached that boy away—
Charged Five Dollars
His girl friend had to pay:

   Night funeral
   in Harlem.

When it was all over
And the lid shut on his head
and the organ had done played
and the last prayers been said   30
and six pallbearers
Carried him out for dead
And off down Lenox Avenue
That long black hearse sped,
   The street light
   At his corner
   Shined just like a tear—

That boy that they was mournin'
Was so dear, so dear
To them folks that brought the flowers,   40

To that girl who paid the preacher-man—
It was all their tears that made
   That poor boy's
   Funeral grand.

   Night funeral
   in Harlem.

Harlem

What happens to a dream deferred?

   Does it dry up
   like a raisin in the sun?
   Or fester like a sore—
   And then run?
   Does it stink like rotten meat?
   Or crust and sugar over—
   like a syrupy sweet?

   Maybe it just sags
   like a heavy load.

   Or does it explode?

Same in Blues

I said to my baby,
Baby, take it slow.
I can't, she said, I can't!
I got to go!

   There's a certain
   amount of traveling
   in a dream deferred.

Lulu said to Leonard,
I want a diamond ring.
Leonard said to Lulu,
You won't get a goddam thing!

   A certain
   amount of nothing
   in a dream deferred.

Daddy, daddy, daddy,
All I want is you.

10

You can have me, baby—
But my lovin' days is through.

>*A certain*
>*amount of impotence*
>*in a dream deferred.*

Three parties
On my party line—
But that third party,
Lord, ain't mine!

>*There's liable*
>*to be confusion*
>*in a dream deferred.*

From river to river
Uptown and down,
There's liable to be confusion
when a dream gets kicked around.

CARL RAKOSI [1903–   ]

Americana IX

Your correspondent must be kidding when he says
that OK came to us from Obediah Kelly, a freight agent
who used to sign his initials on bills of lading.

Why, there are a dozen explanations more intriguing,
such as, an invention of the early telegraphers;

or, variant of **okeh**, a Choctaw word meaning "IT IS SO"
(which may account
                for Mrs. Nicholas Murray Butler's[1] *horror*
at finding it in English drawing rooms by 1935
and, worse still, in The Oxford Dictionary);

or, a corruption of the harvest word, **hoacky**,
the last load brought in from the fields;

or, the identification letters for the outer keel
which used to be laid first by the early shipbuilders.

At one time it was even used as an incantation
against fleas,

---

1 wife of the president of Columbia University.

which may explain why some people thought
it had its origin in a sign: THE PEOPLE IS OLL KORRECT

painted by Thomas Daniels, a local handyman,
on a farm wagon drawn by twenty-four horses   20
carrying thirty-six young women dressed in white
to a Whig rally in a grove in Champaign County, Ohio.

Another possibility is that OK stood
for Old Kinderhook, the birthplace of Martin Van Buren,
known to his supporters as The Sage of Kinderhook
and to his enemies as The Kinderhook Fox

but after five hundred of his loyal rowdies
using OK as a rallying cry were thrown out
                              of a Whig meeting,
the *Daily Express* suggested that the word was Arabic   30
which read backwards meant Kicked Out.

The possibility I like best, however, is that OK stood
for Aux Quais where the French sailors
used to date American girls during the Revolutionary War.

At any rate, OK is the first word
                              learned by immigrants
and makes them instant
                    democrats.

PATRICK KAVANAGH   [1904–1967]

Gold Watch

Engraved on the case
House and mountain
And a far mist
Rising from faery fountain.

On inner case
No. 2244
Elgin Nath. . . .
Sold by a guy in a New York store.

Dates of repairs
1914 M.Y., 1918 H.J.,
She has had her own cares.

Slender hands
Of blue steel,

And within the precious
Platinum balance wheel.

Delicate mechanism
Counting out in her counting-house
My pennies of time.

Tinker's Wife

I saw her amid the dunghill debris
Looking for things
Such as an old pair of shoes or gaiters.
She was a young woman,
A tinker's wife.
Her face had streaks of care
Like wires across it,
But she was supple
As a young goat
On a windy hill.

She searched on the dunghill debris,
Tripping gingerly
Over tin canisters
And sharp-broken
Dinner plates.

Memory of
My Father

Every old man I see
Reminds me of my father
When he had fallen in love with death
One time when sheaves were gathered.

That man I saw in Gardner Street
Stumble on the kerb was one,
He stared at me half-eyed,
I might have been his son.

And I remember the musician
Faltering over his fiddle
In Bayswater, London,
He too set me the riddle.

Every old man I see
In October-colored weather
Seems to say to me:
"I was once your father."

If Ever You Go
to Dublin Town

If ever you go to Dublin town
In a hundred years or so
Inquire for me in Baggot Street
And what I was like to know.
O he was a queer one,
Fol dol the di do,
He was a queer one
I tell you.

My great-grandmother knew him well,
He asked her to come and call   10
On him in his flat and she giggled at the thought
Of a young girl's lovely fall.
O he was dangerous,
Fol dol the di do,
He was dangerous
I tell you.

On Pembroke Road look out for my ghost,
Dishevelled with shoes untied,
Playing through the railings with little children
Whose children have long since died.   20
O he was a nice man,
Fol dol the di do,
He was a nice man
I tell you.

Go into a pub and listen well
If my voice still echoes there,
Ask the men what their grandsires thought
And tell them to answer fair.
O he was eccentric,
Fol dol the di do,   30
He was eccentric
I tell you.

He had the knack of making men feel
As small as they really were
Which meant as great as God had made them
But as males they disliked his air.
O he was a proud one,
Fol dol the di do,
He was a proud one
I tell you.   40

If ever you go to Dublin town
In a hundred years or so

Sniff for my personality,
Is it Vanity's vapor now?
O he was a vain one,
Fol dol the di do,
He was a vain one
I tell you.

I saw his name with a hundred others
In a book in the library,   50
It said he had never fully achieved
His potentiality.
O he was slothful,
Fol dol the di do,
He was slothful
I tell you.

He knew that posterity has no use
For anything but the soul,
The lines that speak the passionate heart,
The spirit that lives alone.   60
O he was a lone one,
Fol dol the di do
Yet he lived happily
I tell you.

Lines Written on
a Seat on the
Grand Canal, Dublin
"Erected to the Memory of
Mrs. Dermot O'Brien"

O commemorate me where there is water,
Canal water preferably, so stilly
Greeny at the heart of summer. Brother
Commemorate me thus beautifully.
Where by a lock Niagariously roars
The falls for those who sit in the tremendous silence
Of mid-July. No one will speak in prose
Who finds his way to these Parnassian[1] islands.
A swan goes by head low with many apologies,
Fantastic light looks through the eyes of bridges—
And look! a barge comes bringing from Athy
And other far-flung towns mythologies.
O commemorate me with no hero-courageous
Tomb—just a canal-bank seat for the passer-by.

1 Parnassus is a mountain in Greece sacred to Apollo and the Muses. *Parnassian:* of or
relating to poetry.

W. H. AUDEN   [1907–1973]

Get There If You
Can and See the Land

Get there if you can and see the land you once were proud to own
Though the roads have almost vanished and the expresses never run:

Smokeless chimneys, damaged bridges, rotting wharves and choked
                                canals,
Tramlines buckled, smashed trucks lying on their side across the
                                rails;

Power-stations locked, deserted, since they drew the boiler fires;
Pylons fallen or subsiding, trailing dead high-tension wires;

Head-gears gaunt on grass-grown pit-banks, seams abandoned years
                                ago;   10
Drop a stone and listen for its splash in flooded dark below.

Squeeze into the works through broken windows or through damp-
                                sprung doors;
See the rotted shafting, see holes gaping in the upper floors;

Where the Sunday lads come talking motor-bicycle and girl,
Smoking cigarettes in chains until their heads are in a whirl.

Far from there we spent the money, thinking we could well afford,
While they quietly undersold us with their cheaper trade abroad;

At the theatre, playing tennis, driving motor-cars we had,
In our continental villas, mixing cocktails for a cad.   20

These were boon companions who devised the legends for our tombs,
These who have betrayed us nicely while we took them to our rooms.

Newman, Ciddy, Plato, Fronny, Pascal, Bowdler, Baudelaire,
Doctor Frommer, Mrs. Allom, Freud, the Baron, and Flaubert.[1]

Lured with their compelling logic, charmed with beauty of their
                                verse,
With their loaded sideboards whispered "Better join us, life is worse."

1   John Henry Newman, English cardinal and writer; Plato, Greek philosopher;
Blaise Pascal, French mathematician and philosopher; Thomas Bowdler, English editor
whose name has given the word *bowdlerize* to the language, meaning to edit out all
possibly scatological references; Charles Baudelaire, French poet; Sigmund Freud,
Austrian neurologist, the founder of psychoanalysis; Gustave Flaubert, French novelist.
The Baron, possibly Baron Charlus, a character in Marcel Proust's novel, *A La
Recherche du Temps Perdu*. Ciddy, Fronny, Doctor Frommer, and Mrs. Allom are either
invented names or names known privately to Auden and his friends.

Taught us at the annual camps arranged by the big business men
"Sunbathe, pretty till you're twenty. You shall be our servants then."

Perfect pater.[2] Marvellous mater.[3] Knock the critic down who dares—   30
Very well, believe it, copy, till your hair is white as theirs.

Yours you say were parents to avoid, avoid then if you please
Do the reverse on all occasions till you catch the same disease.

When we asked the way to Heaven, these directed us ahead
To the padded room, the clinic and the hangman's little shed.

Intimate as war-time prisoners in an isolation camp,
Living month by month together, nervy, famished, lousy, damp.

On the sopping esplanade[4] or from our dingy lodgings we
Stare out dully at the rain which falls for miles into the sea.

Lawrence, Blake and Homer Lane,[5] once healers in our English land;   40
These are dead as iron for ever; these can never hold our hand.

Lawrence was brought down by smut-hounds, Blake went dotty as
                                                            he sang,
Homer Lane was killed in action by the Twickenham[6] Baptist gang.

Have things gone too far already? Are we done for? Must we wait
Hearing doom's approaching footsteps regular down miles of
                                                            straight;

Run the whole night through in gumboots, stumble on and gasp for
                                                            breath,
Terrors drawing close and closer, winter landscape, fox's death;   50

Or, in friendly fireside circle, sit and listen for the crash
Meaning that the mob has realised something's up, and start to
                                                            smash;

Engine-drivers with their oil-cans, factory girls in overalls
Blowing sky-high monster stores, destroying intellectuals?

Hope and fear are neck and neck: which is it near the course's end
Crashes, having lost his nerve; is overtaken on the bend?

Shut up talking, charming in the best suits to be had in town,
Lecturing on navigation while the ship is going down.

2 father.
3 mother.
4 a level, open stretch of paved or grassy ground.
5 D. H. Lawrence, novelist; William Blake, poet; Homer Lane, psychologist.
6 residential municipal borough of Middlesex, England, eleven miles southwest of
London.

412

Drop those priggish ways for ever, stop behaving like a stone:
Throw the bath-chairs right away, and learn to leave ourselves alone.

If we really want to live, we'd better start at once to try;
If we don't it doesn't matter, but we'd better start to die.

At Last the Secret Is Out

At last the secret is out, as it always must come in the end,
The delicious story is ripe to tell to the intimate friend;
Over the tea-cups and in the square the tongue has its desire;
Still waters run deep, my dear, there's never smoke without fire.

Behind the corpse in the reservoir, behind the ghost on the links,
Behind the lady who dances and the man who madly drinks,
Under the look of fatigue, the attack of migraine and the sigh
There is always another story, there is more than meets the eye.

For the clear voice suddenly singing, high up in the convent wall,
The scent of elder bushes, the sporting prints in the hall,
The croquet matches in summer, the handshake, the cough, the kiss,
There is always a wicked secret, a private reason for this.

On This Island

Look, stranger, on this island now
The leaping light for your delight discovers,
Stand stable here
And silent be,
That through the channels of the ear
May wander like a river
The swaying sound of the sea.

Here at a small field's ending pause
When the chalk wall falls to the foam and its tall ledges
Oppose the pluck
And knock of the tide,
and the shingle scrambles after the suck-
-ing surf,
And a gull lodges
A moment on its sheer side.

Far off like floating seeds the ships
Diverge on urgent voluntary errands,
And this full view
Indeed may enter

And move in memory as now these clouds do,
That pass the harbor mirror
And all the summer through the water saunter.

Musée
des Beaux Arts[1]

About suffering they were never wrong,
The Old Masters: how well they understood
Its human position; how it takes place
While someone else is eating or opening a window or just walking dully
    along;
How, when the aged are reverently, passionately waiting
For the miraculous birth, there always must be
Children who did not specially want it to happen, skating
On a pond at the edge of the wood:
They never forgot
That even the dreadful martyrdom must run its course
Anyhow in a corner, some untidy spot
Where the dogs go on with their doggy life and the torturer's horse
Scratches its innocent behind on a tree.

In Brueghel's *Icarus*,[2] for instance: how everything turns away
Quite leisurely from the disaster; the ploughman may
Have heard the splash, the foresaken cry,
But for him it was not an important failure; the sun shone
As it had to on the white legs disappearing into the green
Water; and the expensive delicate ship that must have seen
Something amazing, a boy falling out of the sky,
Had somewhere to get to and sailed calmly on.

1   Museum of Fine Arts.
2   "The Fall of Icarus," a sixteenth-century painting by Pieter Brueghel. Daedalus
constructed wings of wax. His son, Icarus, flew too near the sun, the wax melted, and he
fell into the sea and drowned.

LOUIS MacNEICE   [1907–1963]

The sunlight
on the garden

The sunlight on the garden
Hardens and grows cold,
We cannot cage the minute
Within its nets of gold,
When all is told
We cannot beg for pardon.

Our freedom as free lances
Advances towards its end;
The earth compels, upon it
Sonnets and birds descend;
And soon, my friend,
We shall have no time for dances.

The sky was good for flying
Defying the church bells
And every evil iron
Siren and what it tells:
The earth compels,
We are dying, Egypt, dying

And not expecting pardon,
Hardened in heart anew,
But glad to have sat under
Thunder and rain with you,
And grateful too
For sunlight on the garden.

THEODORE ROETHKE   [1908–1963]

My Papa's Waltz

The whiskey on your breath
Could make a small boy dizzy;
But I hung on like death:
Such waltzing was not easy.

We romped until the pans
Slid from the kitchen shelf;
My mother's countenance
Could not unfrown itself.

The hand that held my wrist
Was battered on one knuckle;
At every step you missed
My right ear scraped a buckle.

You beat time on my head
With a palm caked hard by dirt,
Then waltzed me off to bed
Still clinging to your shirt.

The Waking

I wake to sleep, and take my waking slow.
I feel my fate in what I cannot fear.
I learn by going where I have to go.

We think by feeling. What is there to know?
I hear my being dance from ear to ear.
I wake to sleep, and take my waking slow.

Of those so close beside me, which are you?
God bless the Ground! I shall walk softly there,
And learn by going where I have to go.

Light takes the Tree; but who can tell us how?
The lowly worm climbs up a winding stair;
I wake to sleep, and take my waking slow.

Great Nature has another thing to do
To you and me; so take the lively air,
And, lovely, learn by going where to go.

This shaking keeps me steady. I should know.
What falls away is always. And is near.
I wake to sleep, and take my waking slow.
I learn by going where I have to go.

Praise to the End!

1

It's dark in this wood, soft mocker.
For whom have I swelled like a seed?
What a bone-ache I have.
Father of tensions, I'm down to my skin at last.

It's a great day for the mice.
Prickle-me, tickle-me, close stems.
Bumpkin, he can dance alone.
Ooh, ooh, I'm a duke of eels.

Arch my back, pretty-bones, I'm dead at both ends.
Softly, softly, you'll wake the clams.   10
I'll feed the ghost alone.
Father, forgive my hands.

The rings have gone from the pond.
The river's alone with its water.
All risings
Fall.

416

2

Where are you now, my bonny beating gristle,
My blue original dandy, numb with sugar?
Once I fished from the banks, leaf-light and happy:
On the rocks south of quiet, in the close regions of kissing,   20
I romped, lithe as a child, down the summery streets of my veins,
Strict as a seed, nippy and twiggy.
Now the water's low. The weeds exceed me.
It's necessary, among the flies and bananas, to keep a constant vigil,
For the attacks of false humility take sudden turns for the worse.
Lacking the candor of dogs, I kiss the departing air;
I'm untrue to my own excesses.

Rock me to sleep, the weather's wrong.
Speak to me, frosty beard.
Sing to me, sweet.   30

Mips and ma the mooly moo,
The likes of him is biting who,
A cow's a care and who's a coo?—
What footie does is final.

My dearest dear my fairest fair,
Your father tossed a cat in air,
Though neither you nor I was there,—
What footie does is final.

Be large as an owl, be slick as a frog,
Be good as a goose, be big as a dog,   40
Be sleek as a heifer, be long as a hog,—
What footie will do will be final.

I conclude! I conclude!
My dearest dust, I can't stay here.
I'm undone by the flip-flap of odious pillows.
An exact fall of waters has rendered me impotent.
I've been asleep in a bower of dead skin.
It's a piece of a prince I ate.
This salt can't warm a stone.
These lazy ashes.   50

3

The stones were sharp,
The wind came at my back;
Walked along the highway,
Mincing like a cat.

The sun came out;
The lake turned green;
Romped upon the goldy grass,
Aged thirteen.

The sky cracked open
The world I knew;   60
Lay like the cats do
Sniffing the dew.

　　I dreamt I was all bones;
　　The dead slept in my sleeve;
　　Sweet Jesus tossed me back:
　　I wore the sun with ease.

　　The several sounds were low;
　　The river ebbed and flowed:
　　Desire was winter-calm,
　　A moon away.   70

Such owly pleasures! Fish come first, sweet bird.
Skin's the least of me. Kiss this.
Is the eternal near, fondling?
I hear the sound of hands.

Can the bones breathe? This grave has an ear.
It's still enough for the knock of a worm.
I feel more than a fish.
Ghost, come closer.

　　　　　4
Arch of air, my heart's original knock,
I'm awake all over: 80
I've crawled from the mire, alert as a saint or a dog;
I know the back-stream's joy, and the stone's eternal pulseless longing.
Felicity I cannot hoard.
My friend, the rat in the wall, brings me the clearest messages;
I bask in the bower of change;
The plants wave me in, and the summer apples;
My palm-sweat flashes gold;
Many astounds before, I lost my identity to a pebble;
The minnows love me, and the humped and spitting creatures.

I believe! I believe! —   90
In the sparrow, happy on gravel;
In the winter-wasp, pulsing its wings in the sunlight;
I have been somewhere else; I remember the sea-faced uncles.
I hear, clearly, the heart of another singing,
Lighter than bells,
Softer then water.

Wherefore, O birds and small fish, surround me.
Lave me, ultimate waters.
The dark showed me a face.
My ghosts are all gay.   100
The light becomes me.

418

Elegy for Jane

My Student, Thrown by a Horse

I remember the neckcurls, limp and damp as tendrils;
And her quick look, a sidelong pickerel smile;
And how, once startled into talk, the light syllables leaped for her,
And she balanced in the delight of her thought,
A wren, happy, tail into the wind,
Her song trembling the twigs and small branches.
The shade sang with her;
The leaves, their whispers turned to kissing;
And the mold sang in the bleached valleys under the rose.

Oh, when she was sad, she cast herself down into such a pure depth,
Even a father could not find her:
Scraping her cheek against straw;
Stirring the clearest water.

My sparrow, you are not here,
Waiting like a fern, making a spiny shadow.
The sides of wet stones cannot console me,
Nor the moss, wound with the last light.

If only I could nudge you from this sleep,
My maimed darling, my skittery pigeon.
Over this damp grave I speak the words of my love:
I, with no rights in this matter,
Neither father nor lover.

CHARLES OLSON [1910–1970]

The Kingfishers[1]

I

1

What does not change / is the will to change

He woke, fully clothed, in his bed. He
remembered only one thing, the birds, how
when he came in, he had gone around the rooms
and got them back in their cage, the green one first,
she with the bad leg, and then the blue,
the one they had hoped was a male

1 any of numerous non-passerine birds, usually crested and brightly colored, with a short tail and long, stout, sharp bill.

Otherwise? Yes, Fernand, who had talked lispingly of Albers[2] & Angkor
    Vat.[3]
He had left the party without a word. How he got up, got into his coat,
I do not know. When I saw him, he was at the door, but it did not mat-
    ter,   10
he was already sliding along the wall of the night, losing himself
in some crack of the ruins. That it should have been he who said, "The
    kingfishers!
who cares
for their feathers
now?"[4]

His last words had been, "The pool is slime." Suddenly everyone,
ceasing their talk, sat in a row around him, watched
they did not so much hear, or pay attention, they
wondered, looked at each other, smirked, but listened,
he repeated and repeated, could not go beyond his thought   20
"The pool   the kingfishers' feathers were wealth   why
did the export stop?"

It was then he left

2

I thought of the E on the stone,[5] and of what Mao said[6]
la lumiere"
               but the kingfisher
de l'aurore"
               but the kingfisher flew west
est devant nous![7]
               he got the color of his breast   30
               from the heat of the setting sun!

The features are, the feebleness of the feet (syndactylism[8] of the 3rd & 4th
    digit)
the bill, serrated, sometimes a pronounced beak, the wings
where the color is, short and round, the tail
inconspicuous.

But not these things were the factors. Not the birds.
The legends are
legends. Dead, hung up indoors, the kingfisher

2 Josef Albers, (1888–1976), American painter, born in Germany.
3 ruins of an ancient city in Cambodia.
4 The feathers of the kingfisher were once bartered in trade.
5 symbol found by Plutarch in the temple at Delphi, an ancient town in Greece. The
oracle at Delphi was consulted on important occasions.
6 Mao-Tse-tung (1893–1976), Chinese Communist, leader of the People's Republic of
China (1949–1976). *what Mao said*: in a speech in 1948 to the Chinese Communist
party, shortly before the Communists defeated the forces of Chiang Kai-shek.
7 *la lumière . . . devant nous*: the light of dawn is before us.
8 union of two or more digits, normal in many birds.

will not indicate a favoring wind,
or avert the thunderbolt. Nor, by its nesting,   40
still the waters, with the new year, for seven days.
It is true, it does nest with the opening year, but not on the waters.
It nests at the end of a tunnel bored by itself in a bank. There,
six or eight white and translucent eggs are laid, on fishbones
not on bare clay, on bones thrown up in pellets by the birds.

                              On these rejectamenta[9]
(as they accumulate they form a cup-shaped structure) the young are
        born.
And, as they are fed and grow, this nest of excrement and decayed fish be-
        comes

                        a dripping, fetid mass

Mao concluded: 50
                nous devons

                        nous lever

                              et agir![10]

        3
When the attentions change / the jungle
leaps in
            even the stones are split
                        they rive

Or,
enter
that other conqueror we more naturally recognize   60
he so resembles ourselves

But the E
cut so rudely on the oldest stone
sounded otherwise,
was differently heard

as, in another time, were treasures used:

(and, later, much later, a fine ear thought
a scarlet coat)

                    "of green feathers feet, beaks and eyes
                        of gold[11]   70

                    "animals likewise,
                        resembling snails

9   rejected things.
10 *nous devons . . . et agir*: we must rise and act.
11 This and the following items are from a list of the treasures given by Montezuma,
king of the Aztecs, to Cortez, leader of the Spanish conquistadors.

"a large wheel, gold, with figures of unknown four-foots,
and worked with tufts of leaves, weight
3800 ounces

"last, two birds, of thread and freatherwork, the quills
gold, the feet
gold, the two birds perched on two reeds
gold, the reeds arising from two embroidered mounds,
one yellow, the other   80
white.

"And from each reed hung
seven feathered tassels.

In this instance, the priests
(in dark cotton robes, and dirty,
their dishevelled hair matted with blood, and flowing wildly
over their shoulders)
rush in among the people, calling on them
to protect their gods

And all now is war   90
where so lately there was peace,
and the sweet brotherhood, the use
of tilled fields.

                    4
Not one death but many,
not accumulation but change, the feed-back proves, the feed-back is
the law

            Into the same river no man steps twice
            when fire dies air dies
            No one remains, nor is, one

Around an appearance, one common model, we grow up   100
many. Else how is it,
if we remain the same,
we take pleasure now
in what we did not take pleasure before? love
contrary objects? admire and/or find fault? use
other words, feel other passions, have
nor figure, appearance, disposition, tissue
the same?
            To be in different states without a change
            is not a possibility   110

We can be precise. The factors are
in the animal and/or the machine the factors are

    422

communication and/or control, both involve
the message. And what is the message? The message is
a discrete or continuous sequence of measurable events distributed in
       time

is the birth of air, is
the birth of water, is
a state between
the origin and
the end, between   120
birth and the beginning of
another fetid nest

is change, presents
no more than itself

And the too strong grasping of it,
when it is pressed together and condensed,
loses it

This very thing you are

II

    They buried their dead in a sitting posture[12]
    serpent   cane   razor   ray of the sun   130

    And she sprinkled water on the head of the child, crying
    "Cioa-coatl! Cioa-coatl!"[13]
    with her face to the west

    Where the bones are found, in each personal heap
    with what each enjoyed, there is always
    the Mongolian louse

The light is in the east. Yes. And we must rise, act. Yet
in the west, despite the apparent darkness (the whiteness
which covers all), if you look, if you can bear, if you can, long enough

              as long as it was necessary for him, my guide   140
              to look into the yellow of that longest-lasting rose

so you must, and, in that whiteness, into that face, with what candor,
    look

and considering the dryness of the place
    the long absence of an adequate race

12   the speaker is touring an Aztec burial ground with a guide who speaks Italian.
13   *Cioa*: apparently a misspelling of *Ciao*: Hello, Hi, or So long! *Coatl*: probably
Quetzalcoatl, the plumed serpent god of the Aztecs, god of the wind and the west.

        (of the two who first came, each a conquistador, one healed, the
                other
        tore the eastern idols down, toppled
        the temple walls, which, says the excuser
        were black from human gore)

hear
hear, where the dry blood talks   150
        where the old appetite walks

                        la piu saporita et migliore
                        che si possa truovar al mondo[14]

        where it hides, look
        in the eye how it runs
        in the flesh / chalk

                but under these petals
                in the emptiness
                regard the light, contemplate
                the flower   160

        whence it arose

                with what violence benevolence is bought
                what cost in gesture justice brings
                what wrongs domestic rights involve
                what stalks
                this silence

                what pudor pejorocracy[15] affronts
                how awe, night-rest and neighborhood can rot
                what breeds where dirtiness is law
                what crawls   170
                below

                                III

I am no Greek, hath not th' advantage.
And of course, no Roman:[16]
he can take no risk that matters,
the risk of beauty least of all.

But I have my kin, if for no other reason than
(as he said, next of kin) I commit myself, and,

14   the most savory and best that can be found in the world.
15   *pudor*: shame. *pejorocracy*: a neologism based on the Latin *pejor* meaning "worse."
A *pejorocracy* would be a democracy in a state of decline.
16   "he rejects the Greco-Roman heritage in favor of the Indian" (Paul Christensen,
Charles Olson: Call Him Ishmael. I recommend this book to anyone who wishes to learn
more about Olson and the "projectivist poetic").

given my freedom, I'd be a cad
if I didn't. Which is most true.

It works out this way, despite the disadvantage.
I offer, in explanation, a quote:
si j'ai du goût, ce n'est guères
que pour la terre et les pierres.[17]

Despite the discrepancy (an ocean   courage   age)
this is also true: if I have any taste
it is only because I have interested myself
in what was slain in the sun

    I pose you your question:

shall you uncover honey / where maggots are?

    I hunt among stones

17   "If I have any taste, it is hardly anything more than a taste for the earth and stones"
(Arthur Rimbaud, French poet).

ELIZABETH BISHOP   [1911–1979]

Cirque d'Hiver[1]

Across the floor flits the mechanical toy,
fit for a king of several centuries back.
A little circus horse with real white hair.
His eyes are glossy black.
He bears a little dancer on his back.

She stands upon her toes and turns and turns.
A slanting spray of artificial roses
is stitched across her skirt and tinsel bodice.
Above her head she poses
another spray of artificial roses.

His mane and tail are straight from Chirico.[2]
He has a formal, melancholy soul.
He feels her pink toes dangle toward his back
along the little pole
that pierces both her body and her soul

and goes through his, and reappears below,
under his belly, as a big tin key.
He canters three steps, then he makes a bow,

1   winter circus.
2   Giorgio Di Chirico, Italian painter.

canters again, bows on one knee,
canters, then clicks and stops, and looks at me.

The dancer, by this time, has turned her back.
He is the more intelligent by far.
Facing each other rather desperately—
his eye is like a star—
we stare and say, "Well, we have come this far."

Cape Breton[1]

Out on the high "bird islands," Ciboux and Hertford,
the razorbill auks[2] and the silly-looking puffins[3] all stand
with their backs to the mainland
in solemn, uneven lines along the cliff's brown grass-frayed edge,
while the few sheep pastured there go "Baaa, baaa."
(Sometimes, frightened by aeroplanes, they stampede
and fall over into the sea or onto the rocks.)
The silken water is weaving and weaving,
disappearing under the mist equally in all directions,
lifted and penetrated now and then   10
by one shag's[4] dripping serpent-neck,
and somewhere the mist incorporates the pulse,
rapid but unurgent, of a motorboat.

The same mist hangs in thin layers
among the valleys and gorges of the mainland
like rotting snow-ice sucked away
almost to spirit; the ghosts of glaciers drift
among those folds and folds of fir: spruce and hackmatack[5]—
dull, dead, deep peacock-colors,
each riser distinguished from the next   20
by an irregular nervous saw-tooth edge,
alike, but certain as a stereoscopic view.

The wild road clambers along the brink of the coast.
On it stand occasional small yellow bulldozers,
but without their drivers, because today is Sunday.
The little white churches have been dropped into the matted hills
like lost quartz arrowheads.

1 Canadian island.
2 a black and white short-necked diving sea bird.
3 a sea bird with a short neck and a "deep grooved parti-colored laterally compressed bill" (*Webster's Collegiate Dictionary*).
4 possibly a misprint for *snag*: a tree embedded in water that constitutes a hazard to navigation. A "shag" is a shaggy tangled mass or covering—it is hard to visualize this as having a "serpent-neck."
5 tamarack, or balsam poplar.

426

The road appears to have been abandoned.
Whatever the landscape had of meaning appears to have been
                                            abandoned,   30
unless the road is holding it back, in the interior,
where we cannot see,
where deep lakes are reputed to be,
and disused trails and mountains of rock
and miles of burnt forests standing in gray scratches
like the admirable scriptures made on stones by stones—
and these regions now have little to say for themselves
except in thousands of light song-sparrow songs floating upward
freely, dispassionately, through the mist, and meshing
in brown-wet, fine, torn fish-nets.   40

A small bus comes along, in up-and-down rushes,
packed with people, even to its step.
(On weekdays with groceries, spare automobile parts, and pump
                                            parts,
but today only two preachers extra, one carrying his frock coat on a
                                            hanger.)
It passes the closed roadside stand, the closed schoolhouse,
where today no flag is flying
from the rough-adzed[6] pole topped with a white china doorknob.
It stops, and a man carrying a baby gets off,   50
climbs over a stile, and goes down through a small steep meadow,
which establishes its poverty in a snowfall of daisies,
to his invisible house beside the water.

The birds keep on singing, a calf bawls, the bus starts.
The thin mist follows
the white mutations of its dream;
an ancient chill is rippling the dark brooks.

6 *adze*: a cutting tool with a thin arched blade set at right angles to the handle, used
for shaping wood.

The Burglar
of Babylon

On the fair green hills of Rio
    There grows a fearful stain:
The poor who come to Rio
    And can't go home again.

On the hills a million people,
    A million sparrows, nest,
Like a confused migration
    That's had to light and rest,

Building its nests, or houses,
    Out of nothing at all, or air.   10
You'd think a breath would end them,
    They perch so lightly there.

But they cling and spread like lichen,
    And the people come and come.
There's one hill called the Chicken,
    And one called Catacomb;

There's the hill of Kerosene,
    And the hill of the Skeleton,
The hill of Astonishment,
    And the hill of Babylon.   20

Micuçú[1] was a burglar and killer,
    An enemy of society.
He had escaped three times
    From the worst penitentiary.

They don't know how many he murdered
    (Though they say he never raped),
And he wounded two policemen
    This last time he escaped.

They said, "He'll go to his auntie,
    Who raised him like a son.   30
She has a little drink shop
    On the hill of Babylon."

He did go straight to his auntie,
    And he drank a final beer.
He told her, "The soldiers are coming,
    And I've got to disappear.

"Ninety years they gave me.
    Who wants to live that long?
I'll settle for ninety hours,
    On the hill of Babylon.   40

"Don't tell anyone you saw me.
    I'll run as long as I can.
You were good to me, and I love you,
    But I'm a doomed man."

Going out, he met a *mulata*[2]
    Carrying water on her head.

1 Micuçú (mē-coo-soo) is the folk name of a deadly snake, in the north (author's note).
2 feminine of *mulatto*, which *Webster's* defines as "1: the first generation offspring of
a Negro and a white 2: a person of mixed Caucasian and Negro ancestry."

"If you say you saw me, daughter,
    You're just as good as dead."

There are caves up there, and hideouts,
    And an old fort, falling down.   50
They used to watch for Frenchmen
    From the hill of Babylon.

Below him was the ocean.
    It reached far up the sky,
Flat as a wall, and on it
    Were freighters passing by,

Or climbing the wall, and climbing
    Till each looked like a fly,
And then fell over and vanished;
    And he knew he was going to die.   60

He could hear the goats *baa-baa*-ing,
    He could hear the babies cry;
Fluttering kites strained upward;
    And he knew he was going to die.

A buzzard flapped so near him
    He could see its naked neck.
He waved his arms and shouted,
    "Not yet, my son, not yet!"

An Army helicopter
    Came nosing around and in.   70
He could see two men inside it,
    But they never spotted him.

The soldiers were all over,
    On all sides of the hill,
And right against the skyline
    A row of them, small and still.

Children peeked out of windows,
    And men in the drink shop swore,
And spat a little *cachaça*[3]
    At the light cracks in the floor.   80

But the soldiers were nervous, even
    With tommy guns in hand,
And one of them, in a panic,
    Shot the officer in command.

3   Brazilian white rum.

He hit him in three places;
    The other shots went wild.
The soldier had hysterics
    And sobbed like a little child.

The dying man said, "Finish
    The job we came here for."   90
He committed his soul to God
    And his sons to the Governor.

They ran and got a priest,
    And he died in hope of Heaven
—A man from Pernambuco,[4]
    The youngest of eleven.

They wanted to stop the search,
    But the Army said, "No, go on,"
So the soldiers swarmed again
    Up the hill of Babylon.   100

Rich people in apartments
    Watched through binoculars
As long as the daylight lasted.
    And all night, under the stars,

Micuçú hid in the grasses
    Or sat in a little tree,
Listening for sounds, and staring
    At the lighthouse out at sea.

And the lighthouse stared back at him,
    Till finally it was dawn.   110
He was soaked with dew, and hungry,
    On the hill of Babylon.

The yellow sun was ugly,
    Like a raw egg on a plate—
Slick from the sea. He cursed it,
    For he knew it sealed his fate.

He saw the long white beaches
    And people going to swim,
With towels and beach umbrellas,
    But the soldiers were after him.   120

Far, far below, the people
    Were little colored spots,

4   state in northeastern Brazil.

And the heads of those in swimming
    Were floating coconuts.

He heard the peanut vendor
    Go *peep-peep* on his whistle,
And the man that sells umbrellas
    Swinging his watchman's rattle.

Women with market baskets
    Stood on the corners and talked,   130
Then went on their way to market,
    Gazing up as they walked.

The rich with their binoculars
    Were back again, and many
Were standing on the rooftops,
    Among TV antennae.

It was early, eight or eight-thirty.
    He saw a soldier climb,
Looking right at him. He fired,
    And missed for the last time.   140

He could hear the soldier panting,
    Though he never got very near.
Micuçú dashed for shelter.
    But he got it, behind the ear.

He heard the babies crying
    Far, far away in his head,
And the mongrels barking and barking.
    Then Micuçú was dead.

He had a Taurus revolver,
    And just the clothes he had on,   150
With two contos⁵ in the pockets,
    On the hill of Babylon.

The police and the populace
    Heaved a sigh of relief,
But behind the counter his auntie
    Wiped her eyes in grief.

"We have always been respected.
    My shop is honest and clean.
I loved him, but from a baby
    Micuçú was always mean.   160

5   Brazilian coins. 1 conto = 1000 escudos.

"We have always been respected.
    His sister has a job.
Both of us gave him money.
    Why did he have to rob?"

"I raised him to be honest,
    Even here, in Babylon slum."
The customers had another,
    Looking serious and glum.

But one of them said to another,
    When he got outside the door,   170
"He wasn't much of a burglar,
    He got caught six times—or more."

This morning the little soldiers
    Are on Babylon hill again;
Their gun barrels and helmets
    Shine in a gentle rain.

Micuçú is buried already.
    They're after another two,
But they say they aren't as dangerous
    As the poor Micuçú.   180

On the fair green hills of Rio
    There grows a fearful stain:
The poor who come to Rio
    And can't go home again.

There's the hill of Kerosene,
    And the hill of the Skeleton,
The hill of Astonishment,
    And the hill of Babylon.

In the
Waiting Room

In Worcester, Massachusetts,
I went with Aunt Consuelo
to keep her dentist's appointment
and sat and waited for her
in the dentist's waiting room.
It was winter. It got dark
early. The waiting room
was full of grown-up people,

432

arctics and overcoats,
lamps and magazines.   10
My aunt was inside
what seemed like a long time
and while I waited I read
the *National Geographic*
(I could read) and carefully
studied the photographs:
the inside of a volcano,
black, and full of ashes;
then it was spilling over
in rivulets of fire.   20
Osa and Martin Johnson[1]
dressed in riding breeches,
laced boots, and pith helmets.
A dead man slung on a pole
—"Long Pig," the caption said.
Babies with pointed heads
wound round and round with string;
black, naked women with necks
wound round and round with wire
like the necks of light bulbs.   30
Their breasts were horrifying.
I read it right straight through.
I was too shy to stop.
And then I looked at the cover:
the yellow margins, the date.

Suddenly, from inside,
came an *oh!* of pain
—Aunt Consuelo's voice—
not very loud or long.
I wasn't at all surprised;   40
even then I knew she was
a foolish, timid woman.
I might have been embarrassed,
but wasn't. What took me
completely by surprise
was that it was *me:*
my voice, in my mouth.
Without thinking at all
I was my foolish aunt,
I—we—were falling, falling,   50
our eyes glued to the cover
of the *National Geographic*,
February, 1918.

1 Martin and Osa Johnson were explorers, writers, and film producers. They produced and appeared in numerous travelogues.

I said to myself: three days
and you'll be seven years old.
I was saying it to stop
the sensation of falling off
the round, turning world
into cold, blue-black space.
But I felt: you are an *I*,   60
you are an *Elizabeth*,
you are one of *them*.
Why should you be one, too?
I scarcely dared to look
to see what it was I was.
I gave a sidelong glance
—I couldn't look any higher—
at shadowy gray knees,
trousers and skirts and boots
and different pairs of hands   70
lying under the lamps.
I knew that nothing stranger
had ever happened, that nothing
stranger could ever happen.
Why should I be my aunt,
or me, or anyone?
What similarities—
boots, hands, the family voice
I felt in my throat, or even
the *National Geographic*   80
and those awful hanging breasts—
held us all together
or made us all just one?
How—I didn't know any
word for it—how "unlikely" . . .
How had I come to be here,
like them, and overhear
a cry of pain that could have
got loud and worse but hadn't?

The waiting room was bright   90
and too hot. It was sliding
beneath a big black wave,
another, and another.

Then I was back in it.
The War was on. Outside,
in Worcester, Massachusetts,
were night and slush and cold,
and it was still the fifth
of February, 1918.

ROBERT HAYDEN   [1913–1980]

Middle Passage

1

Jesús, Estrella, Esperanza, Mercy:

Sails flashing to the wind like weapons,
sharks following the moans the fever and the dying;
horror the corposant[1] and compass rose.[2]

Middle Passage:
      voyage through death
             to life upon these shores.

"10 April 1800—
Blacks rebellious. Crew uneasy. Our linguist says
their moaning is a prayer for death,   10
ours and their own. Some try to starve themselves.
Lost three this morning leaped with crazy laughter
to the waiting sharks, sang as they went under."

Desire, Adventure, Tartar, Ann:

Standing to America, bringing home
black gold, black ivory, black seed.

      Deep in the festering hold thy father lies,
      of his bones New England pews are made,
      those are altar lights that were his eyes.

Jesus   Saviour   Pilot   Me   20
Over   Life's   Tempestuous   Sea

We pray that Thou wilt grant, O Lord,
safe passage to our vessels bringing
heathen souls unto Thy chastening.

Jesus Saviour

      "8 bells. I cannot sleep, for I am sick
with fear, but writing eases fear a little
since still my eyes can see these words take shape
upon the page & so I write, as one
would turn to exorcism. 4 days scudding,   30
but now the sea is calm again. Misfortune
follows in our wake like sharks (our grinning

1 holy body.
2 compass card.

435

tutelary gods). Which one of us
has killed an albatross? A plague among
our blacks—Ophthalmia:[3] blindness—& we
have jettisoned the blind to no avail.
It spreads, the terrifying sickness spreads.
Its claws have scratched sight from the Capt.'s eyes
& there is blindness in the fo'c'sle
& we must sail 3 weeks before we come   40
to port."

       What port awaits us, Davy Jones'[4]
       or home? I've heard of slavers drifting, drifting,
       playthings of wind and storm and chance, their crews
       gone blind, the jungle hatred
       crawling up on deck.

Thou Who Walked on Galilee

    "Deponent[5] further sayeth *The Bella J*
    left the Guinea Coast
    with cargo of five hundred blacks and odd   50
    for the barracoons[6] of Florida:

    "That there was hardly room 'tween-decks for half
    the sweltering cattle stowed spoon-fashion there;
    that some went mad of thirst and tore their flesh
    and sucked the blood:

    "That Crew and Captain lusted with the comeliest
    of the savage girls kept naked in the cabins;
    that there was one they called The Guinea Rose
    and they cast lots and fought to lie with her:

    "That when the Bo's'n piped all hands, the flames   60
    spreading from starboard already were beyond
    control, the negroes howling and their chains
    entangled with the flames:

    "That the burning blacks could not be reached,
    that the Crew abandoned ship,
    leaving their shrieking negresses behind,
    that the Captain perished drunken with the wenches:

    "Further Deponent sayeth not."

Pilot Oh Pilot Me

3   inflammation of the eyeball.
4   the bottom of the sea personified.
5   one who gives evidence.
6   enclosures or barracks used for holding slaves.

2

Aye, lad, and I have seen those factories,   70
Gambia, Rio Pongo, Calabar;[7]
have watched the artful mongos[8] baiting traps
of war wherein the victor and the vanquished

Were caught as prizes for our barracoons.
Have seen the nigger kings whose vanity
and greed turned wild black hides of Fellatah,
Mandingo, Ibo, Kru[9] to gold for us.

And there was one—King Anthracite[10] we named him—
fetish face beneath French parasols
of brass and orange velvet, impudent mouth   80
whose cups were carven skulls of enemies:

He'd honor us with drum and feast and conjo[11]
and palm-oil glistening wenches deft in love,
and for tin crowns that shone with paste,
red calico and German-silver trinkets

Would have the drums talk war and send
his warriors to burn the sleeping villages
and kill the sick and old and lead the young
in coffles[12] to our factories.

Twenty years a trader, twenty years,   90
for there was wealth aplenty to be harvested
from those black fields, and I'd be trading still
but for the fevers melting down my bones.

3

Shuttles in the rocking loom of history,
the dark ships move, the dark ships move,
their bright ironical names
like jests of kindness on a murderer's mouth;
plough through thrashing glister toward
fata morgana's[13] lucent melting shore,
weave toward New World littorals that are   100
mirage and myth and actual shore.

Voyage through death,
              voyage whose chartings are unlove.

7   *Gambia*: West African country; *Rio Pongo*: West African river; *Calabar*: a port in Nigeria.
8   slave-traders.
9   *Fellatah*: a Muslim people; *Mandingo*: a West African people; *Ibo*: people of southwestern Nigeria; *Kru*: tribesmen in Liberia.
10   a hard natural coal of high luster.
11   magic.
12   *coffle*: a train of animals fastened together.
13   *fata morgana*: a fate foretold by means of magic. Perhaps an illusion.

A charnel stench, effluvium of living death
spreads outward from the hold,
where the living and the dead, the horribly dying,
lie interlocked, lie foul with blood and excrement.

> *Deep in the festering hold thy father lies,*
> *the corpse of mercy rots with him,*   110
> *rats eat love's rotten gelid eyes.*

> *But, oh, the living look at you*
> *with human eyes whose suffering accuses you,*
> *whose hatred reaches through the swill of dark*
> *to strike you like a leper's claw.*

> *You cannot stare that hatred down*
> *or chain the fear that stalks the watches*
> *and breathes on you its fetid scorching breath;*
> *cannot kill the deep immortal human wish,*
> *the timeless will.*

    "But for the storm that flung up barriers   120
of wind and wave, *The Armistad*,[14] señores,
would have reached the port of Principe[15] in two,
three days at most; but for the storm we should
have been prepared for what befell.
Swift as the puma's leap it came. There was
that interval of moonless calm filled only
with the water's and the rigging's usual sounds,
then sudden movement, blows and snarling cries
and they had fallen on us with machete
and marlinspike.[16] It was as though the very   130
air, the night itself were striking us.
Exhausted by the rigors of the storm,
we were no match for them. Our men went down
before the murderous Africans. Our loyal
Celestino ran from below with gun
and lantern and I saw, before the cane-
knife's wounding flash, Cinquez,
that surly brute who calls himself a prince,
directing, urging on the ghastly work.
He hacked the poor mulatto down, and then   140
he turned on me. The decks were slippery
when daylight finally came. It sickens me

14 *The Amistad*: a case before the U.S. Supreme Court in 1841 involving the legal status of blacks who had been sold into slavery in Africa and were being transported abroad by ship. The defendants, i.e., the blacks, had seized the ship, which was then seized by a U.S. warship. The court ruled that the blacks, having been originally kidnapped and made slaves, were, by international law, free men.
15 island in western Africa in the Gulf of Guinea.
16 *marlinspike*: an iron tool that tapers to a point and is used to separate strands of rope and wire.

to think of what I saw, of how these apes
threw overboard the butchered bodies of
our men, true Christians all, like so much jetsam.[17]
Enough, enough. The rest is quickly told:
Cinquez was forced to spare the two of us
you see to steer the ship to Africa,
and we like phantoms doomed to rove the sea
voyaged east by day and west by night,   150
deceiving them, hoping for rescue,
prisoners on our own vessel, till
at length we drifted to the shores of this
your land, America, where we were freed
from our unspeakable misery. Now we
demand, good sirs, the extradition of
Cinquez and his accomplices to La
Havana. And it distresses us to know
there are so many here who seem inclined
to justify the mutiny of these blacks.   160
We find it paradoxical indeed
that you whose wealth, whose tree of liberty
are rooted in the labor of your slaves
should suffer the august John Quincy Adams
to speak with so much passion of the right
of chattel slaves to kill their lawful masters
and with his Roman rhetoric weave a hero's
garland for Cinquez. I tell you that
we are determined to return to Cuba
with our slaves and there see justice done. Cinquez—   170
or let us say 'the Prince'—Cinquez shall die."

The deep immortal human wish,
the timeless will:

　　Cinquez its deathless primaveral image,
　　life that transfigures many lives.

Voyage through death
　　　　　　　　to life upon these shores.

17　the part of a ship, its equipment or cargo, that is cast overboard to lighten the load
in times of distress.

Runagate Runagate[1]

1

Runs falls rises stumbles on from darkness into darkness
and the darkness thicketed with shapes of terror
and the hunters pursuing and the hounds pursuing

1　*runagate*: a fugitive or runaway.

and the night cold and the night long and the river
to cross and the jack-muh-lanterns[2] beckoning beckoning
and blackness ahead and when shall I reach that somewhere
morning and keep on going and never turn back and keep on going

                    Runagate
                        Runagate
                            Runagate   10

Many thousands rise and go
many thousands crossing over

                                        O mythic North
                                O star-shaped yonder Bible city

Some go weeping and some rejoicing
some in coffins and some in carriages
some in silks and some in shackles

            Rise and go or fare you well

No more auction block for me
no more driver's lash for me   20

        If you see my Pompey, 30 yrs of age,
        new breeches, plain stockings, negro shoes;
        if you see my Anna, likely young mulatto
        branded E on the right cheek, R on the left,
        catch them if you can and notify subscriber.
        Catch them if you can, but it won't be easy.
        They'll dart underground when you try to catch them,
        plunge into quicksand, whirlpools, mazes,
        turn into scorpions when you try to catch them.

And before I'll be a slave
I'll be buried in my grave   30

        North star and bonanza gold
        I'm bound for the freedom, freedom-bound
        and oh Susyanna don't you cry for me

            Runagate

            Runagate

        2
Rises from their anguish and their power,

            Harriet Tubman,[3]

2 jack-o'-lanterns, lights caused by marsh gas.
3 black woman who led slaves to freedom on the Underground Railroad.

440

woman of earth, whipscarred,
a summoning, a shining 40

Mean to be free

And this was the way of it, brethren brethren,
way we journeyed from Can't to Can.
Moon so bright and no place to hide,
the cry up and the patterollers riding,
hound dogs belling in bladed air.
And fear starts a-murbling, Never make it,
we'll never make it. *Hush that now,*
and she's turned upon us, levelled pistol
glinting in the moonlight: 50
Dead folks can't jaybird-talk,[4] she says;
you keep on going now or die, she says.

Wanted   Harriet Tubman   alias The General
alias Moses   Stealer of Slaves

In league with Garrison   Alcott   Emerson
Garrett   Douglass   Thoreau   John Brown[5]

Armed and known to be Dangerous

Wanted   Reward   Dead or Alive

Tell me, Ezekiel,[6] oh tell me do you see
mailed Jehovah coming to deliver me? 60

Hoot-owl calling in the ghosted air,
five times calling to the hants in the air.
Shadow of a face in the scary leaves,
shadow of a voice in the talking leaves:

Come ride-a my train

Oh that train, ghost-story train
through swamp and savanna movering movering,
over trestles of dew, through caves of the wish,
Midnight Special on a sabre track movering movering,
first stop Mercy and the last Hallelujah. 70

Come ride-a my train

Mean mean mean to be free.

4   to *jaybird-talk* would be to chatter like a jay.
5   names of American abolitionists.
6   Hebrew prophet of the sixth century B.C.

DYLAN THOMAS [1914–1953]

The Force That
Through the Green Fuse
Drives the Flower

The force that through the green fuse drives the flower
Drives my green age; that blasts the roots of trees
Is my destroyer.
And I am dumb to tell the crooked rose
My youth is bent by the same wintry fever.

The force that drives the water through the rocks
Drives my red blood; that dries the mouthing streams
Turns mine to wax.
And I am dumb to mouth unto my veins
How at the mountain spring the same mouth sucks.

The hand that whirls the water in the pool
Stirs the quicksand; that ropes the blowing wind
Hauls my shroud sail.
And I am dumb to tell the hanging man
How of my clay is made the hangman's lime.

The lips of time leech to the fountain head;
Love drips and gathers, but the fallen blood
Shall calm her sores.
And I am dumb to tell a weather's wind
How time has ticked a heaven round the stars.

And I am dumb to tell the lover's tomb
How at my sheet goes the same crooked worm.

Fern Hill

Now as I was young and easy under the apple boughs
About the lilting house and happy as the grass was green,
    The night above the dingle starry,
        Time let me hail and climb
      Golden in the heydays of his eyes,
And honored among wagons I was prince of the apple towns
And once below a time I lordly had the trees and leaves
        Trail with daisies and barley
      Down the rivers of the windfall light.

And as I was green and carefree, famous among the barns
About the happy yard and singing as the farm was home,

10

In the sun that is young once only,
    Time let me play and be
Golden in the mercy of his means,
And green and golden I was huntsman and herdsman, the calves
Sang to my horn, the foxes on the hills barked clear and cold,
    And the sabbath rang slowly
In the pebbles of the holy streams.

All the sun long it was running, it was lovely, the hay
Fields high as the house, the tunes from the chimneys, it was air   20
    And playing, lovely and watery
        And fire green as grass.
    And nightly under the simple stars
As I rode to sleep the owls were bearing the farm away,
All the moon long I heard, blessed among stables, the nightjars
    Flying with the ricks, and the horses
        Flashing into the dark.

And then to awake, and the farm, like a wanderer white
With the dew, come back, the cock on his shoulder: it was all
    Shining, it was Adam and maiden,   30
        The sky gathered again
    And the sun grew round that very day.
So it must have been after the birth of the simple light
In the first, spinning place, the spellbound horses walking warm
    Out of the whinnying green stable
        On to the fields of praise.

And honored among foxes and pheasants by the gay house
Under the new made clouds and happy as the heart was long,
    In the sun born over and over,
        I ran my heedless ways,   40
    My wishes raced through the house high hay
And nothing I cared, at my sky blue trades, that time allows
In all his tuneful turning so few and such morning songs
    Before the children green and golden
        Follow him out of grace,

Nothing I cared, in the lamb white days, that time would take me
Up to the swallow thronged loft by the shadow of my hand,
    In the moon that is always rising,
        Nor that riding to sleep
    I should hear him fly with the high fields   50
And wake to the farm forever fled from the childless land.
Oh as I was young and easy in the mercy of his means,
    Time held me green and dying
        Though I sang in my chains like the sea.

Do Not
Go Gentle into
That Good Night

Do not go gentle into that good night,
Old age should burn and rave at close of day;
Rage, rage against the dying of the light.

Though wise men at their end know dark is right,
Because their words had forked no lightning they
Do not go gentle into that good night.

Good men, the last wave by, crying how bright
Their frail deeds might have danced in a green bay,
Rage, rage against the dying of the light.

Wild men who caught and sang the sun in flight,
And learn, too late, they grieved it on its way,
Do not go gentle into that good night.

Grave men, near death, who see with blinding sight
Blind eyes could blaze like meteors and be gay,
Rage, rage against the dying of the light.

And you, my father, there on the sad height,
Curse, bless, me now with your fierce tears, I pray.
Do not go gentle into that good night.
Rage, rage against the dying of the light.

DUDLEY RANDALL [1914–   ]

Blackberry Sweet

Black girl black girl
lips as curved as cherries
full as grape bunches
sweet as blackberries

Black girl black girl
when you walk you are
magic as a rising bird
or a falling star

Black girl black girl
what's your spell to make
the heart in my breast
jump   stop   shake

444

HENRY REED [1914–   ]

Naming of Parts

Today we have naming of parts. Yesterday,
We had daily cleaning. And tomorrow morning,
We shall have what to do after firing. But today,
Today we have naming of parts. Japonica
Glistens like coral in all of the neighboring gardens,
    And today we have naming of parts.

This is the lower sling swivel. And this
Is the upper sling swivel, whose use you will see,
When you are given your slings. And this is the piling swivel,
Which in your case you have not got. The branches   10
Hold in the gardens their silent, eloquent gestures,
    Which in our case we have not got.

This is the safety-catch, which is always released
With an easy flick of the thumb. And please do not let me
See anyone using his finger. You can do it quite easy
If you have any strength in your thumb. The blossoms
Are fragile and motionless, never letting anyone see
    Any of them using their finger.

And this you can see is the bolt. The purpose of this
Is to open the breech, as you see. We can slide it   20
Rapidly backwards and forwards: we call this
Easing the spring. And rapidly backwards and forwards
The early bees are assaulting and fumbling the flowers:
    They call it easing the Spring.

They call it easing the Spring: it is perfectly easy
If you have any strength in your thumb: like the bolt,
And the breech, and the cocking-piece, and the point of balance,
Which in our case we have not got; and the almond-blossom
Silent in all of the gardens and the bees going backwards and forwards,
    For today we have naming of parts.   30

JOHN MANIFOLD [1915–   ]

Fife Tune
(6/8) for Sixth Platoon, 308th I.T.C.

One morning in spring
We marched from Devizes
All shapes and all sizes

Like beads on a string,
But yet with a swing
We trod the bluemetal
And full of high fettle
We started to sing.

She ran down the stair
A twelve-year-old darling
And laughing and calling
She tossed her bright hair;
Then silent to stare
At the men flowing past her—
There were all she could master
Adoring her there.

It's seldom I'll see
A sweeter or prettier;
I doubt we'll forget her
In two years or three,
And lucky he'll be
She takes for a lover
While we are far over
The treacherous sea.

RUTH STONE [1915–   ]

Green Apples

In August we carried the old horsehair mattress
To the back porch
And slept with our children in a row.
The wind came up the mountain into the orchard
Telling me something;
Saying something urgent.
I was happy.
The green apples fell on the sloping roof
And rattled down.
The wind was shaking me all night long;
Shaking me in my sleep
Like a definition of love,
Saying, this is the moment,
Here, now.

I Have Three Daughters

I have three daughters
Like greengage plums.
They sat all day
Sucking their thumbs.
And more's the pity,
They cried all day,
Why doesn't our mother's brown hair
Turn gray?

I have three daughters
Like three cherries.   10
They sat at the window
The boys to please.
And they couldn't wait
For their mother to grow old.
Why doesn't our mother's brown hair
Turn to snow?

I have three daughters
In the apple tree
Singing Mama send Daddy
With three young lovers   20
To take them away from me.

I have three daughters
Like greengage plums,
Sitting all day
And sighing all day
And sucking their thumbs;
Singing, Mama won't you fetch and carry,
And Daddy, won't you let us marry,
Singing, sprinkle snow down on Mama's hair
And lordy, give us our share.   30

Hunger

I have been up and down the town
Looking for I don't know what.
The doors of houses are all shut.
Along the streets the hedges grow
Neatly between the houses, row
After row, all leafless now and brown.

What do I want, says eye to ear.
Whatever it is, it's guarded here;
Clipped and kept and the price is dear.
Are they all beautiful there inside?
Is what I want to be inside?

Past February and brilliant days
Burn pools of water in the snow.
Telltale visible breath and words;
Saw-toothed icicles crack their glaze;
I walk between the houses row after row
Pierced by the sounds of winter-crazed birds.

ROBERT LOWELL [1917–1977]

Mr. Edwards¹
and the Spider

I saw the spiders marching through the air,
Swimming from tree to tree that mildewed day
   In latter August when the hay
   Came creaking to the barn. But where
     The wind is westerly,
Where gnarled November makes the spiders fly
Into the apparitions of the sky,
   They purpose nothing but their ease and die
Urgently beating east to sunrise and the sea;

What are we in the hands of the great God?   10
It was in vain you set up thorn and briar
   In battle array against the fire
   And treason crackling in your blood;
     For the wild thorns grow tame
And will do nothing to oppose the flame;
Your lacerations tell the losing game
   You play against a sickness past your cure.
How will the hands be strong? How will the heart endure?

A very little thing, a little worm,
Or hourglass-blazoned spider, it is said,   20
   Can kill a tiger. Will the dead
   Hold up his mirror and affirm
     To the four winds the smell
And flash of his authority? It's well

1 Jonathan Edwards, eighteenth-century Calvinist theologian, born in East Windsor, Connecticut.

448

If God who holds you to the pit of hell,
Much as one holds a spider, will destroy,
Baffle and dissipate your soul. As a small boy

On Windsor Marsh, I saw the spider die
When thrown into the bowels of fierce fire:
　　There's no long struggle, no desire　　　　　　　　30
　　　　To get up on its feet and fly—
　　　　　　It stretches out its feet
And dies. This is the sinner's last retreat;
Yes, and no strength exerted on the heat
Then sinews the abolished will, when sick
And full of burning, it will whistle on a brick.

But who can plumb the sinking of that soul?
Josiah Hawley,[2] picture yourself cast
　　Into a brick-kiln where the blast
　　　　Fans your quick vitals to a coal—　　　　　　40
　　　　　　If measured by a glass,
How long would it seem burning! Let there pass
A minute, ten, ten trillion; but the blaze
Is infinite, eternal: this is death,
To die and know it. This is the Black Widow, death.

2　Edwards' cousin, who opposed his revivalist preachings.

Memories
of West Street
and Lepke

Only teaching on Tuesdays, book-worming
in pajamas fresh from the washer each morning,
I hog a whole house on Boston's
"hardly passionate Marlborough Street,"[1]
where even the man
scavenging filth in the back alley trash cans,
has two children, a beach wagon, a helpmate,
and is a "young Republican."
I have a nine months' daughter,
young enough to be my granddaughter.　　　　　　　　10
Like the sun she rises in her flame-flamingo infants' wear.

These are the tranquillized *Fifties*,
and I am forty. Ought I to regret my seedtime?
I was a fire-breathing Catholic C.O.,[2]

1　Henry James said an example of extreme understatement would be that
Marlborough Street was hardly passionate.
2　conscientious objector.

449

and made my manic statement,
telling off the state and president, and then
sat waiting sentence in the bull pen
beside a Negro boy with curlicues
of marijuana in his hair.

Given a year,   20
I walked on the roof of the West Street Jail,[3] a short
enclosure like my school soccer court,
and saw the Hudson River once a day
through sooty clothesline entanglements
and bleaching khaki tenements.
Strolling, I yammered metaphysics with Abramowitz,[4]
a jaundice-yellow ("it's really tan")
and fly-weight pacifist,
so vegetarian,
he wore rope shoes and preferred fallen fruit.   30
He tried to convert Bioff and Brown,
the Hollywood pimps, to his diet.
Hairy, muscular, suburban,
wearing chocolate double-breasted suits,
they blew their tops and beat him black and blue.

I was so out of things, I'd never heard
of the Jehovah's Witnesses.
"Are you a C.O.?" I asked a fellow jailbird.
"No," he answered, "I'm a J.W."
He taught me the "hospital tuck,"   40
and pointed out the T shirted back
of *Murder Incorporated's* Czar Lepke,[5]
there piling towels on a rack,
or dawdling off to his little segregated cell full
of things forbidden the common man:
a portable radio, a dresser, two toy American
flags tied together with a ribbon of Eastern palm.
Flabby, bald, lobotomized,
he drifted in a sheepish calm,
where no agonizing reappraisal   50
jarred his concentration on the electric chair—
hanging like an oasis in his air
of lost connections. . . .

3   jail in New York from which prisoners were sent elsewhere. Lowell says that "all
sorts of people were there, including German bundists and Jehovah's Witnesses."
4   Robert Lowell recounts that "Abramowitz didn't eat meat—or fruit, unless fallen
from the tree; his clothes were made of fallen vegetables. Bioff and Brown attacked
him."
5   Lou (Lepke) Buchalter, one of the leaders of New York's labor and industrial
rackets, and a member of the ruling board of Murder, Inc. He went to the electric chair
in 1944. Lowell says, "He was a mild soul—looked like an art critic I knew but less
dangerous. Lepke was evil as a negative reality."

Skunk Hour

(For Elizabeth Bishop)

Nautilus Island's[1] hermit
heiress still lives through winter in her Spartan cottage;
her sheep still graze above the sea.
Her son's a bishop. Her farmer
is first selectman in our village;
she's in her dotage.

Thirsting for
the hierarchic privacy
of Queen Victoria's century,
she buys up all   10
the eyesores facing her shore,
and lets them fall.

The season's ill—
we've lost our summer millionaire,
who seemed to leap from an L. L. Bean
catalogue. His nine-knot yawl
was auctioned off to lobstermen.
A red fox stain covers Blue Hill.[2]

And now our fairy
decorator brightens his shop for fall;   20
his fishnet's filled with orange cork,
orange, his cobbler's bench and awl;
there is no money in his work,
he'd rather marry.

One dark night,
my Tudor Ford climbed the hill's skull;
I watched for love-cars. Lights turned down,
they lay together, hull to hull,
where the graveyard shelves on the town. . . .
My mind's not right.   30

A car radio bleats,
"Love, O careless Love. . . ." I hear
my ill-spirit sob in each blood cell,
as if my hand were at its throat. . . .
I myself am hell;
nobody's here—

---

1 *Nautilus Island*: apparently a small, privately owned island off the coast of Maine,
in Blue Hill Bay.
2   town in Hancock County, Maine.

only skunks, that search
in the moonlight for a bite to eat.
They march on their soles up Main Street:
white stripes, moonstruck eyes' red fire
under the chalk-dry and spar spire
of the Trinitarian Church.

I stand on top
of our back steps and breathe the rich air—
a mother skunk with her column of kittens swills the garbage
　　　　pail.
She jabs her wedge-head in a cup
of sour cream, drops her ostrich tail,
and will not scare.

For the
Union Dead

"Relinquunt Omnia Servare Rem Publicam."[1]

The old South Boston Aquarium stands
in a Sahara of snow now. Its broken windows are boarded.
The bronze weathervane cod has lost half its scales.
The airy tanks are dry.

Once my nose crawled like a snail on the glass;
my hand tingled
to burst the bubbles
drifting from the noses of the cowed, compliant fish.

My hand draws back. I often sigh still
for the dark downward and vegetating kingdom
of the fish and reptile. On a morning last March,
I pressed against the new barbed and galvanized

fence on the Boston Common. Behind their cage,
yellow dinosaur steamshovels were grunting
as they cropped up tons of mush and grass
to gouge their underworld garage.

Parking spaces luxuriate like civic
sandpiles in the heart of Boston.
A girdle of orange, Puritan-pumpkin colored girders
braces the tingling Statehouse,

40

10

20

1　"They gave up everything to serve the State."

shaking over the excavations, as it faces Colonel Shaw[2]
and his bell-cheeked Negro infantry
on St. Gaudens'[3] shaking Civil War relief,
propped by a plank splint against the garage's earthquake.

Two months after marching through Boston,
half the regiment was dead;
at the dedication,
William James[4] could almost hear the bronze Negroes breathe.

Their monument sticks like a fishbone
in the city's throat.   30
Its Colonel is as lean
as a compass-needle.

He has an angry wrenlike vigilance,
a greyhound's gentle tautness;
he seems to wince at pleasure,
and suffocate for privacy.

He is out of bounds now. He rejoices in man's lovely,
peculiar power to choose life and die—
when he leads his black soldiers to death,
he cannot bend his back.   40

On a thousand small town New England greens,
the old white churches hold their air
of sparse, sincere rebellion; frayed flags
quilt the graveyards of the Grand Army of the Republic.

The stone statues of the abstract Union Soldier
grow slimmer and younger each year—
wasp-waisted, they doze over muskets
and muse through their sideburns . . .

Shaw's father wanted no monument
except the ditch,   50
where his son's body was thrown
and lost with his "niggers."

The ditch is nearer.
There are no statues for the last war here;

2   Robert Gould Shaw, born in Boston in 1837 and killed at Fort Wagner, South
Carolina in 1863. Shaw enlisted as a private in the Union Army in 1861, was promoted to
captain, and in 1863 became colonel of the 54th Massachusetts, the first regiment of
Negro troops from a free state mustered into the U.S. service. A statue by Saint-Gaudens
of Shaw stands on Boston Common.
3   Augustus Saint-Gaudens, American sculptor, 1848–1907.
4   American psychologist and philosopher, 1842–1910.

on Boylston Street, a commercial photograph
shows Hiroshima boiling

over a Mosler Safe, the "Rock of Ages"
that survived the blast. Space is nearer.
When I crouch to my television set,
the drained faces of Negro school-children rise like balloons.   60

Colonel Shaw
is riding on his bubble,
he waits
for the blesséd break.

The Aquarium is gone. Everywhere,
giant finned cars nose forward like fish;
a savage servility
slides by on grease.

KEITH DOUGLAS   [1920–1944]

Vergissmeinicht[1]

Three weeks gone and the combatants gone,
returning over the nightmare ground
we found the place again, and found
the soldier sprawling in the sun.

The frowning barrel of his gun
overshadowing. As we came on
that day, he hit my tank with one
like the entry of a demon.

Look. Here in the gunpit spoil
the dishonored picture of his girl
who has put: *Steffi. Vergissmeinicht*
in a copybook gothic script.

We see him almost with content
abased, and seeming to have paid
and mocked at by his own equipment
that's hard and good when he's decayed.

But she would weep to see today
how on his skin the swart flies move;
the dust upon the paper eye
and the burst stomach like a cave.

1   "forget me not."

454

For here the lover and killer are mingled
who had one body and one heart.
And death who had the soldier singled
has done the lover mortal hurt.

RICHARD WILBUR   [1921–   ]

The Beautiful
Changes

One wading a Fall meadow finds on all sides
The Queen Anne's Lace lying like lilies
On water; it glides
So from the walker, it turns
Dry grass to a lake, as the slightest shade of you
Valleys my mind in fabulous blue Lucernes.[1]

The beautiful changes as a forest is changed
By a chameleon's tuning his skin to it;
As a mantis, arranged
On a green leaf, grows
Into it, makes the leaf leafier, and proves
Any greenness is deeper than anyone knows.

Your hands hold roses always in a way that says
They are not only yours; the beautiful changes
In such kind ways,
Wishing ever to sunder
Things and things' selves for a second finding, to lose
For a moment all that it touches back to wonder.

1   Lucerne, a lake in Switzerland.

Love Calls Us
to the Things
of This World

The eyes open to a cry of pulleys,
And spirited from sleep, the astounded soul
Hangs for a moment bodiless and simple
As false dawn.
                    Outside the open window
The morning air is all awash with angels.

Some are in bed-sheets, some are in blouses,
Some are in smocks: but truly there they are.

Now they are rising together in calm swells
Of halcyon feeling, filling whatever they wear   10
With the deep joy of their impersonal breathing;

　　Now they are flying in place, conveying
The terrible speed of their omnipresence, moving
And staying like white water; and now of a sudden
They swoon down into so rapt a quiet
That nobody seems to be there.
　　　　　　　　　　　　The soul shrinks

　　From all that it is about to remember,
From the punctual rape of every bléssed day,
And cries,   20
　　　　　　"Oh, let there be nothing on earth but laundry,
Nothing but rosy hands in the rising steam
And clear dances done in the sight of heaven."

　　Yet, as the sun acknowledges
With a warm look the world's hunks and colors,
The soul descends once more in bitter love
To accept the waking body, saying now
In a changed voice as the man yawns and rises,

　　"Bring them down from their ruddy gallows;
Let there be clean linen for the backs of thieves;   30
Let lovers go fresh and sweet to be undone,
And the heaviest nuns walk in a pure floating
Of dark habits,
　　　　　　keeping their difficult balance."

Piazza di Spagna,
Early Morning[1]

　　　　　　I can't forget
　How she stood at the top of that long marble stair
Amazed, and then with a sleepy pirouette
Went dancing slowly down to the fountain-quieted square;

　　　　Nothing upon her face
But some impersonal loneliness,—not then a girl,
　　But as it were a reverie of the place,
　　　A called-for falling glide and whirl;

　　　As when a leaf, petal, or thin chip
Is drawn to the falls of a pool and, circling a moment above it,

1　a square in Rome with a flight of stairs and a fountain at the bottom.

456

Rides on over the lip—
Perfectly beautiful, perfectly ignorant of it.

PHILIP LARKIN   [1922–1985]

Within
the Dream
You Said

Within the dream you said:
Let us kiss then,
In this room, in this bed,
But when all's done
We must not meet again.

Hearing this last word,
There was no lambing-night,
No gale-driven bird
Nor frost-encircled root
As cold as my heart.

Night-Music

At one the wind rose,
And with it the noise
Of the black poplars.

Long since had the living
By a thin twine
Been led into their dreams
Where lanterns shine
Under a still veil
Of falling streams;
Long since had the dead
Become untroubled
In the light soil.
There were no mouths
To drink of the wind,
Nor any eyes
To sharpen on the stars'
Wide heaven-holding,
Only the sound
Long sibilant-muscled trees
Were lifting up, the black poplars.

And in their blazing solitude
The stars sang in their sockets through the night:
"Blow bright, blow bright
The coal of this unquickened world."

Mr Bleaney

"This was Mr Bleaney's room. He stayed
The whole time he was at the Bodies,[1] till
They moved him." Flowered curtains, thin and frayed,
Fall to within five inches of the sill,

Whose window shows a strip of building land,
Tussocky, littered. "Mr Bleaney took
My bit of garden properly in hand."
Bed, upright chair, sixty-watt bulb, no hook

Behind the door, no room for books or bags—
"I'll take it." So it happens that I lie
Where Mr Bleaney lay, and stub my fags
On the same saucer-souvenir, and try

Stuffing my ears with cotton-wool, to drown
The jabbering set he egged her on to buy.
I know his habits—what time he came down,
His preference for sauce to gravy, why

He kept on plugging at the four aways[2]—
Likewise their yearly frame: the Frinton folk
Who put him up for summer holidays,
And Christmas at his sister's house in Stoke.

But if he stood and watched the frigid wind
Tousling the clouds, lay on the fusty bed
Telling himself that this was home, and grinned,
And shivered, without shaking off the dread

That how we live measures our own nature,
And at his age having no more to show
Than one hired box should make him pretty sure
He warranted no better, I don't know.

1 automobile factory (slang).
2 The "four aways" section of British football-pool forms requires competitors to
gamble on a prediction of four Association Football teams winning matches "away" from
their home grounds—more difficult, supposedly, than predicting "home" wins, but
attracting some gamblers because they need make fewer predictions. Mr. Bleaney might
argue that persistence in this limited field would be more likely to bring prizes.—Alan
Brownjohn

Wild Oats

About twenty years ago
Two girls came in where I worked—
A bosomy English rose
And her friend in specs I could talk to.
Faces in those days sparked
The whole shooting-match off, and I doubt
If ever one had like hers:
But it was the friend I took out,

And in seven years after that
Wrote over four hundred letters,
Gave a ten-guinea ring
I got back in the end, and met
At numerous cathedral cities
Unknown to the clergy. I believe
I met beautiful twice. She was trying
Both times (so I thought) not to laugh.

Parting, after about five
Rehearsals, was an agreement
That I was too selfish, withdrawn,
And easily bored to love.
Well, useful to get that learnt.
In my wallet are still two snaps
Of bosomy rose with fur gloves on.
Unlucky charms, perhaps.

JAMES DICKEY [1923–   ]

Cherrylog Road

Off Highway 106
At Cherrylog Road I entered
The '34 Ford without wheels,
Smothered in kudzu,
With a seat pulled out to run
Corn whiskey down from the hills,

And then from the other side
Crept into an Essex
With a rumble seat of red leather
And then out again, aboard   10
A blue Chevrolet, releasing
The rust from its other color,

Reared up on three building blocks.
None had the same body heat;
I changed with them inward, toward
The weedy heart of the junkyard,
For I knew that Doris Holbrook
Would escape from her father at noon

And would come from the farm
To seek parts owned by the sun   20
Among the abandoned chassis,
Sitting in each in turn
As I did, leaning forward
As in a wild stock-car race

In the parking lot of the dead.
Time after time, I climbed in
And out the other side, like
An envoy or movie star
Met at the station by crickets.
A radiator cap raised its head,   30

Become a real toad or a kingsnake
As I neared the hub of the yard,
Passing through many states,
Many lives, to reach
Some grandmother's long Pierce-Arrow
Sending platters of blindness forth

From its nickel hubcaps
And spilling its tender upholstery
On sleepy roaches,
The glass panel in between   40
Lady and colored driver
Not all the way broken out,

The back-seat phone
Still on its hook.
I got in as though to exclaim,
"Let us go to the orphan asylum,
John; I have some old toys
For children who say their prayers."

I popped with sweat as I thought
I heard Doris Holbrook scrape   50
Like a mouse in the southern-state sun
That was eating the paint in blisters
From a hundred car tops and hoods.
She was tapping like code,

Loosening the screws,
Carrying off headlights,
Sparkplugs, bumpers,
Cracked mirrors and gear-knobs,
Getting ready, already,
To go back with something to show   60

Other than her lips' new trembling
I would hold to me soon, soon,
Where I sat in the ripped back seat
Talking over the interphone,
Praying for Doris Holbrook
To come from her father's farm

And to get back there
With no trace of me on her face
To be seen by her red-haired father
Who would change, in the squalling barn,   70
Her back's pale skin with a strop,
Then lay for me

In a bootlegger's roasting car
With a string-triggered 12-gauge shotgun
To blast the breath from the air.
Not cut by the jagged windshields,
Through the acres of wrecks she came
With a wrench in her hand,

Through dust where the blacksnake dies
Of boredom, and the beetle knows   80
The compost has no more life.
Someone outside would have seen
The oldest car's door inexplicably
Close from within:

I held her and held her and held her,
Convoyed at terrific speed
By the stalled, dreaming traffic around us,
So the blacksnake, stiff
With inaction, curved back
Into life, and hunted the mouse   90

With deadly overexcitement,
The beetles reclaimed their field
As we clung, glued together,
With the hooks of the seat springs
Working through to catch us red-handed
Amidst the gray breathless batting

That burst from the seat at our backs.
We left by separate doors
Into the changed, other bodies
Of cars, she down Cherrylog Road   100
And I to my motorcycle
Parked like the soul of the junkyard

Restored, a bicycle fleshed
With power, and tore off
Up Highway 106, continually
Drunk on the wind in my mouth,
Wringing the handlebar for speed,
Wild to be wreckage forever.

DENISE LEVERTOV [1923–   [

Brass Tacks

1

The old wooden house a soft
almost-blue faded green
embowered in southern autumn's
nearly-yellow green leaves,
the air damp after a night of rain.

2

The black girl sitting alone in the back row
smiled at me.

3

Yes, in strange kitchens
I know where to find the forks,

and among another woman's perfume bottles   10
I can find the one that suits me,

and in the bedrooms
of children I have not met
I have galloped the island
of Chincoteague[1] at 3 a.m., too tired to sleep—

but beyond that

at how many windows I have listened
to the cricket-quivering of borrowed moonlight.

1 an island off the coast of Maryland and Virginia.

4

Brass tacks that glint
                    illumination of dailiness   20
        and hold down feet to earth
                    ears to the rush and whisper of
                              the ring and rattle of
                              the Great Chain—[2]
brass tacks that rivet
the eyes to Consolation,
              that *are* Consolation.

5

Weighed down by two shopping bags she trudges
uphill diagonally across the nameless (but grassy)
East Boston square—Fort Something,   30
it was once. Her arms ache, she wonders
if some items she is carrying deserve to be classed
as conspicuous consumption. It would be nice
if a gray pet donkey came by magic
to meet her now, panniers[3] ready
for her burdens . . . She looks up,
and the weight
lifts: behind the outstretched eager
bare limbs and swaying twigs of two
still-living elms   40

in moonstone blue of dusk
the new moon itself is swinging
back and forth on a cloud-trapeze!

6

The spring snow
is flying
          aslant
                    over the crocus gold
                    and into evening.

7

Returning tired towards his temporary
lodging, wondering again   50
if his workday was useful at all

the human being saw the rose-colored leaves
of a small plant growing among
the stones of a low wall

2   probably a reference to the Great Chain of Being, a concept of the universe as
composed of contiguous hierarchies of spirit and matter, descending from God to the
lowest parts of creation.
3   baskets.

unobtrusively, and found himself
standing quite still, gazing,
and found himself
smiling.

Like Loving Chekhov

Loving this man who is far away
is like loving Anton Chekhov.[1]
It is true, I do love Anton Chekhov,
I have loved him longer than I have known this man.
I love all the faces of Chekhov in my collection
of photos that show him in different years of his life,
alone, or with brothers and sisters, with actors,
                                        with Gorki,[2]
with Tolstoi,[3] with his wife, with his undistinguished
endearing pet dogs; from beardless student to pince-nez'd   10
famous and ailing man.
                    I have no photo
of the man I love.

I love Chekhov for travelling alone
to the prison island[4] without being asked.
For writing of the boiling, freezing, terrible seas
around the island and around the lives of its people
that they "resembled the scared dreams
of a small boy who's been reading
                        Lost in the Ocean Wastes   20
before going to sleep, and whose blanket has fallen off,
so he huddles shivering
and can't wake up."
For treasuring the ugly inkstand a penniless seamstress
gave him in thanks for his doctoring.
If there's an afterlife,
I hope to meet Anton Chekhov there.

                Loving the man I love
is like that, because he is far away,
and because he is scrupulous, and because surely   30
nothing he says or does can bore me.
But it's different too. Chekhov had died
long before I was born. This man is alive.

1 Russian dramatist and story-writer.
2 Russian writer.
3 Russian novelist.
4 Sakhalin Island in the North Pacific, where criminals were sent to hard labor. In
1890 Chekhov travelled to Sakhalin to study the conditions under which prisoners lived.
He wrote a book about his experiences, *The Island*, that showed the need for penal
reform.

He is alive and not here.
This man has shared my bed, our bodies
have warmed each other and given each other
delight, our bodies
are getting angry with us for giving them to each other
                                          and then
allowing something they don't understand to   40
                              pry them apart,
                                    a metallic
cruel wedge that they hear us call
necessity.
              Often it seems unreal to love
a man who is far away, or only real to the mind,
the mind teasing the body. But it's real,
he's alive, and it's not in the afterlife
I'm looking to see him,
but in this here and now, before I'm a month older,   50
before one more gray hair has grown on my head.
If he makes me think about Chekhov it's not because
he resembles him the least but because the ache
of distance between me and a living man I know and
                                          don't know
grips me with pain and fear, a pain and fear
familiar in the love of the unreachable dead.

The Pilots

Because they were prisoners,
because they were polite and friendly and lonesome and homesick,
because they said Yes, they knew
                        the names of the bombs they dropped
        but didn't say whether they understood what these bombs
                              are designed to do
                              to human flesh, and because
        I didn't ask them, being unable to decide
        whether to ask would serve
        any purpose other than cruelty, and   10
because since then I met Mrs. Brown, the mother of one of
                              their fellow prisoners,
and loved her, for she has the same lovingkindness in her
that I saw in Vietnamese women (and men too)
and because my hostility left the room and wasn't there
                        when I thought I needed it
while I was drinking tea with the POW's,

because of all these reasons I hope
they were truly as ignorant,
                as unawakened,   20
                        as they seemed,

I hope their chances in life up to this point
have been poor,
I hope they can truly be considered
victims of the middle America they come from,
their American Legionnaire fathers, their macho high schools,
their dull skimped Freshman English courses,

for if they did understand precisely
what they were doing, and did it anyway, and would do it again,

then I must learn to distrust   30
my own preference for trusting people,

then I must learn to question
my own preference for liking people,

then I must learn to keep
my hostility chained to me
so it won't leave me when I need it.

And if it is proved to me
that these men understood their acts,

how shall I ever again
be able to meet the eyes of Mrs. Brown?   40

The Dragonfly-Mother[1]

I was setting out from my house
to keep my promise

but the Dragonfly-Mother stopped me.

I was to speak to a multitude
for a good cause, but at home

the Dragonfly-Mother was listening
not to a speech but to the creak of
                    stretching tissue,
tense hum of leaves unfurling.

Who is the Dragonfly-Mother?   10
What does she do?

She is the one who hovers
on stairways of air,

1 Readers may be interested to read "The Earthwoman and the Waterwoman"
(*Collected Earlier Poems*, p. 31), a poem written in 1957, to which this 1979 poem
makes some allusions. (author's note).

                        sometimes almost
grazing your cheekbone,
she is the one who darts unforeseeably
into unsuspected dimensions,

who sees in water
her own blue fire zigzag, and lifts
her self in laughter   20
into the tearful pale sky

that sails blurred clouds in the stream.

                              ♦

She sat at my round table,
we told one another dreams,
I stayed home breaking my promise.

When she left I slept
three hours, and arose

and wrote. I remember the cold
Waterwoman, in dragonfly dresses

and blue shoes, long ago.   30
She is the same,

whose children were thin,
left at home when she went out dancing.
She is the Dragonfly-Mother,

that cold
is only the rush of air

swiftness brings.
There is a summer
over the water, over

the river mirrors   40
where she hovers, a summer
fertile, abundant, where dreams
grow into acts and journeys.

Her children
are swimmers, nymphs and newts, metamorphic.
                        When she tells
her stories she listens; when she listens
she tells you the story you utter.

                              ♦

When I broke my promise,
and slept, and later   50

cooked and ate the food she had bought
and left in my kitchen,

I kept a tryst with myself,
a long promise that can be fulfilled
only poem by poem,
broken over and over.

                    I too,
a creature, grow among reeds,
            in mud, in air,
in sunbright cold, in fever   60
of blue-gold zenith, winds
of passage.

            Dragonfly-Mother's
a messenger,
if I don't trust her
I can't keep faith.

                There is a summer
in the sleep
of broken promises, fertile dreams,
acts of passage, hovering   70
journeys over the fathomless waters.

Williams: An Essay[1]

His theme
over and over:

the twang of plucked
catgut
from which struggles
music,

the tufted swampgrass
quicksilvering
dank meadows,

a baby's resolute fury—metaphysic   10
of appetite and tension.

1 The reference is to the poet William Carlos Williams. See pages 325–336.

Not
the bald image, but always—
undulant, elusive, beyond reach
of any dull
staring eye—lodged

among the words, beneath
the skin of image: nerves,

muscles, rivers
of urgent blood, a mind   20

secret, disciplined, generous and
unfathomable.
                    Over

and over,
his theme
            hid itself and
smilingly reappeared.

                        He loved
persistence—but it must
be linked to invention: landing   30
backwards, "facing
into the wind's teeth,"
                        to please him.

He loved
the lotus cup, fragrant
upon the swaying water, loved

the wily mud
pressing swart riches into its roots,

and the long stem of connection.

LOUIS SIMPSON [1923–   ]

The Battle

Helmet and rifle, pack and overcoat
Marched through a forest. Somewhere up ahead
Guns thudded. Like the circle of a throat
The night on every side was turning red.

They halted and they dug. They sank like moles
Into the clammy earth between the trees.
And soon the sentries, standing in their holes,
Felt the first snow. Their feet began to freeze.

At dawn the first shell landed with a crack.
Then shells and bullets swept the icy woods.
This lasted many days. The snow was black.
The corpses stiffened in their scarlet hoods.

Most clearly of that battle I remember
The tiredness in eyes, how hands looked thin
Around a cigarette, and the bright ember
Would pulse with all the life there was within.

Chocolates

Once some people were visiting Chekhov.
While they made remarks about his genius
the Master fidgeted. Finally
he said, "Do you like chocolates?"

They were astonished, and silent.
He repeated the question,
whereupon one lady plucked up her courage
and murmured shyly, "Yes."

"Tell me," he said, leaning forward,
light glinting from his spectacles,
"what kind? The light, sweet chocolate
or the dark, bitter kind?"

The conversation became general.
They spoke of cherry centers,
of almonds and Brazil nuts.
Losing their inhibitions
they interrupted one another.
For people may not know what they think
about politics in the Balkans,
or the vexed question of men and women,

but everyone has a definite opinion
about the flavor of shredded coconut.
Finally someone spoke of chocolates filled with liqueur,
and everyone, even the author of *Uncle Vanya*,
was at a loss for words.

As they were leaving he stood by the door
and took their hands.
                    In the coach returning to Petersburg
they agreed that it had been a most
unusual conversation.

Why Do You Write about Russia?

When I was a child
my mother told stories about the country
she came from. Wolves were howling,
snow fell, the drunken Cossack
shouted in the snow.

Rats prowled the floor of the cellar
where the children slept.
Once, after an illness, she was sent
to Odessa, on the sea. There were battleships
painted white, and ladies and gentlemen   10
walking the esplanade . . . white naval uniforms
and parasols.

These stories were told
against a background of tropical night . . .
a sea breeze stirring the flowers
that open at dusk, smelling like perfume.
The voice that spoke of freezing cold
itself was warm and infinitely comforting.

So it is with poetry: whatever numbing horrors
it may speak of, the voice itself   20
tells of love and infinite wonder.

Later, when I came to New York,
I used to go to my grandmother's
in Brooklyn. The names of stations
return in their order like a charm:
Franklin, Nostrand, Kingston.
And members of the family gather:
the three sisters, the one brother,
one of the cousins from Washington,
and myself . . . a "student at Columbia."   30
But what am I really?

For when my grandmother says, "Eat!
People who work with their heads have to eat more. . . ."

Work? Does it deserve a name
so full of seriousness and high purpose?
Gazing across Amsterdam Avenue
at the windows opposite, letting my mind
wander where it will, from the page
to Malaya, or some street in Paris . . .
Drifting smoke. The end will be as fatal   40
as an opium-eater's dream.

◆

The view has changed—to evergreens,
a hedge, and my neighbor's roof.
This too is like a dream, the way we live
with our cars and power-mowers . . .
a life that shuns emotion
and the violence that goes with it,
the object being to live quietly
and bring up children to be happy.

Yes, but what are you going to tell them   50
of what lies ahead?
That the better life seems
the more it goes sour? The child no longer
a child, his happiness all of a sudden
behind him. And he in turn
expected to bring up his children
to be happy . . .

What then do I want?
A life in which there are depths
beyond happiness. As one of my friends,   60
Grigoryev, says, "Two things
constantly cry out in creation,
the sea and man's soul."

Reaching from where we are
to where we came from . . . *Thalassa*!
a view of the sea.

◆

I sit listening to the rasp
of a power-saw, the puttering of a motorboat.
The whole meaningless life around me
affirming a positive attitude . . .   70

When a hat appears, a black felt hat,
gliding along the hedge . . .

then a long, black overcoat
that falls beneath the knee.

He produces a big, purple handkerchief,
brushes off a chair, and sits.

"It's hot," he says, "but I like to walk,
that way you get to see the world.
And so, what are you reading now?"

Chekhov, I tell him.   80

"Of course. But have you read Leskov?
There are sentences that will stay in your mind
a whole lifetime.
For instance, in the 'Lady Macbeth,'
when the woman says to her lover,
'You couldn't be nearly as desirous
as you say you are, for I heard you singing'. . .
he answers, 'What about gnats?
They sing all their lives, but it's not for joy.'"

So my imaginary friend tells stories   90
of the same far place the soul comes from.

When I think about Russia
it's not that area of the earth's surface
with Leningrad to the West and Siberia
to the East—I don't know anything
about the continental mass.

It's a sound, such as you hear
in a sea breaking along a shore.

My people came from Russia,   100
bringing with them nothing
but that sound.

Physical Universe

He woke at five and, unable
to go back to sleep,
went downstairs.

A book was lying on the table
where his son had done his homework.
He took it into the kitchen,

made coffee, poured himself a cup,
and settled down to read.

"There was a local eddy in the swirling gas
of the primordial galaxy,   10
and a cloud was formed, the protosun,
as wide as the present solar system.

This contracted. Some of the gas
formed a diffuse, spherical nebula,
a thin disk, that cooled and flattened.
Pulled one way by its own gravity,
the other way by the sun,
it broke, forming smaller clouds,
the protoplanets. Earth
was 2000 times as wide as it is now."   20

The earth was without form, and void,
and darkness was upon the face of the deep.

                              ♦

"Then the sun began to shine,
dispelling the gases and vapors,
shrinking the planets, melting earth,
separating iron and silicate
to form the core and mantle.
Continents appeared . . . "
history, civilisation,
the discovery of America   30
and the settling of Green Harbor,
bringing us to Tuesday, the seventh of July.

Tuesday, the day they pick up the garbage!
He leaped into action,
took the garbage bag out of its container,
tied it with a twist of wire,
and carried it out to the tool-shed,
taking care not to let the screen-door slam,
and put it in the large garbage-can
that was three-quarters full.   40
He kept it in the tool-shed so the raccoons
couldn't get at it.

He carried the can out to the road,
then went back into the house
and walked around, picking up newspapers
and fliers for: "Thompson Seedless Grapes,
California's finest sweet eating";

"Scott Bathroom Tissue";

"Legislative report from Senator Ken LaValle."

He put all this paper in a box,   50
and emptied the waste baskets in the two
downstairs bathrooms,
and the basket in the study.

He carried the box out to the road,
taking care not to let the screen-door slam,
and placed the box next to the garbage.

Now let the garbage men come!

◆

He went back upstairs.
Susan said, "Did you put out the garbage?"
But her eyes were closed.   60
She was sleeping, yet could speak in her sleep,
ask a question, even answer one.

"Yes," he said, and climbed into bed.
She turned around to face him,
with her eyes still closed.

He thought, perhaps she's an oracle,
speaking from the Collective Unconscious.
He said to her, "Do you agree with Darwin
that people and monkeys have a common ancestor?
Or should we stick to the Bible?"   70

She said, "Did you take out the garbage?"

"Yes," he said, for the second time.
Then thought about it. Her answer
had something in it of the sublime.
Like a *koan* . . . the kind of irrelevance
a Zen-master says to the disciple
who is asking riddles of the universe.

He put his arm around her,
and she continued to breathe evenly
from the depths of sleep.   80

CAROLYN KIZER   [1925–   ]

Semele Recycled[1]

After you left me forever,
I was broken into pieces,
and all the pieces flung into the river.
Then the legs crawled ashore
and aimlessly wandered the dusty cow-track.
They became, for a while, a simple roadside shrine:
A tiny table set up between the thighs
held a dusty candle, weed, and fieldflower chains
placed reverently there by children and old women.
My knees were hung with tin triangular medals   10
to cure all forms of hysterical disease.

After I died forever in the river,
my torso floated, bloated in the stream,
catching on logs or stones among the eddies.
White water foamed around it, then dislodged it;
after a whirlwind trip, it bumped ashore.
A grizzled old man who scavenged along the banks
had already rescued my arms and put them by,
knowing everything has its uses, sooner or later.

When he found my torso, he called it his canoe,   20
and, using my arms as paddles,
he rowed me up and down the scummy river.
When catfish nibbled my fingers, he scooped them up
and blessed his re-usable bait.
Clumsy but serviceable, that canoe!
The trail of blood that was its wake
attracted the carp and eels, and the river turtle,
easily landed, dazed by my tasty red.

A young lad found my head among the rushes
and placed it on a dry stone.   30
He carefully combed my hair with a bit of shell
and set small offerings before it
which the birds and rats obligingly stole at night,
so it seemed I ate.
And the breeze wound through my mouth and empty sockets
so my lungs would sigh and my dead tongue mutter.

1   *Semele*: In Greek mythology, daughter of Cadmus and Harmonia, beloved of Zeus.
Hera, jealous of Semele, disguised herself as her nurse and persuaded her to obtain a
promise from Zeus to grant her wish, then to request him to show himself to her in all his
divine splendor. When Zeus appeared with thunder and lightning Semele was consumed
by the flames and, dying, gave birth to a six months' child, Dionysus. Zeus saved the
child from the fire and hid him in his thigh until the time of birth. When Dionysus
became a god he raised his mother from the underworld and set her in the heavens under
the name of Thyone.

Attached to my throat like a sacred necklace
was a circlet of small snails.
Soon the villagers came to consult my oracular head
with its waterweed crown.   40
Seers found occupation, interpreting sighs,
and their papyrus rolls accumulated.

Meanwhile, young boys retrieved my eyes
they used for marbles in a simple game
—till somebody's pretty sister snatched at them
and set them, for luck, in her bridal diadem.
Poor girl! When her future groom caught sight of her,
all eyes, he crossed himself in horror,
and stumbled away in haste
through her dowered meadows.   50

What then of my heart and organs,
my sacred slit
which loved you best of all?
They were caught in a fisherman's net
and tossed at night into a pen for swine.
But they shone so by moonlight that the sows stampeded,
trampled each other in fear, to get away.
And the fisherman's wife, who had 13 living children
and was contemptuous of holy love,
raked the rest of me onto the compost heap.   60

Then in their various places and helpful functions,
the altar, oracle, offal, canoe, and oars
learned the wild rumor of your return.
The altar leapt up and ran to the canoe,
scattering candle grease and wilted grasses.
Arms sprang to their sockets, blind hands with nibbled nails
groped their way, aided by loud lamentation,
to the bed of the bride, snatched up those unlucky eyes
from her discarded veil and diadem,
and rammed them home. O what a bright day it was!   70
This empty body danced on the river bank.
Hollow, it called and searched among the fields
for those parts that steamed and simmered in the sun,
and never would have found them.

But then your great voice rang out under the skies
my name!—and all those private names
for the parts and places that had loved you best.
And they stirred in their nest of hay and dung.
The distraught old ladies chasing their lost altar,
and the seers pursuing my skull, their lost employment,   80
and the tumbling boys, who wanted the magic marbles,
and the runaway groom, and the fisherman's 13 children

set up such a clamor with their cries of "Miracle!"
that our two bodies met like a thunderclap
in mid-day—right at the corner of that wretched field
with its broken fenceposts and startled, skinny cattle.
We fell in a heap on the compost heap
and all our loving parts made love at once,
while the bystanders cheered and prayed and hid their eyes
and then went decently about their business.   90

And here it is, moonlight again; we've bathed in the river
and are sweet and wholesome once more.
We kneel side by side in the sand;
we worship each other in whispers.
But the inner parts remember fermenting hay,
the comfortable odor of dung, the animal incense,
and passion, its bloody labor,
its birth and rebirth and decay.

FRANK O'HARA   [1926–1966]

Sleeping
on the Wing

Perhaps it is to avoid some great sadness,
as in a Restoration tragedy the hero cries "Sleep!
O for a long sound sleep and so forget it!"
that one flies, soaring above the shoreless city,
veering upward from the pavement as a pigeon
does when a car honks or a door slams, the door
of dreams, life perpetuated in parti-colored loves
and beautiful lies all in different languages.

Fear drops away too, like the cement, and you
are over the Atlantic. Where is Spain? where is   10
who? The Civil War was fought to free the slaves,
was it? A sudden down-draught reminds you of gravity
and your position in respect to human love. But
here is where the gods are, speculating, bemused.
Once you are helpless, you are free, can you believe
that? Never to waken to the sad struggle of a face?
to travel always over some impersonal vastness,
to be out of, forever, neither in nor for!

The eyes roll asleep as if turned by the wind
and the lids flutter open slightly like a wing.   20
The world is an iceberg, so much is invisible!
and was and is, and yet the form, it may be sleeping

too. Those features etched in the ice of someone
loved who died, you are a sculptor dreaming of space
and speed, your hand alone could have done this.
Curiosity, the passionate hand of desire. Dead,
or sleeping? Is there speed enough? And, swooping,
you relinquish all that you have made your own,
the kingdom of your self sailing, for you must awake
and breathe your warmth in this beloved image   30
whether it's dead or merely disappearing,
as space is disappearing and your singularity.

A Step Away
from Them

It's my lunch hour, so I go
for a walk among the hum-colored
cabs. First, down the sidewalk
where laborers feed their dirty
glistening torsos sandwiches
and Coca-Cola, with yellow helmets
on. They protect them from falling
bricks, I guess. Then onto the
avenues where skirts are flipping
above heels and blow up over   10
grates. The sun is hot, but the
cabs stir up the air. I look
at bargains in wristwatches. There
are cats playing in sawdust.
                      On
to Times Square, where the sign
blows smoke over my head, and higher
the waterfall pours lightly. A
Negro stands in a doorway with a
toothpick, languorously agitating.   20
A blonde chorus girl clicks: he
smiles and rubs his chin. Everything
suddenly honks: it is 12:40 of
a Thursday.
              Neon in daylight is a
great pleasure, as Edwin Denby[1] would
write, as are light bulbs in daylight.
I stop for a cheeseburger at JULIET'S
CORNER. Giulietta Masina, wife of
Federico Fellini, è bell' attrice.[2]   30

1   American architect (1872–1957). Denby designed a type face and a new kind of
genealogical chart. He also composed songs to poetry.
2   Federico Fellini, Italian movie director. e bell' attrice: "is a fine actress."

And chocolate malted. A lady in
foxes on such a day puts her poodle
in a cab.
    There are several Puerto
Ricans on the avenue today, which
makes it beautiful and warm. First
Bunny[3] died, then John Latouche,[4]
then Jackson Pollock.[5] But is the
earth as full as life was full, of them?
And one has eaten and one walks,   40
past the magazines with nudes
and the posters for BULLFIGHT and
the Manhattan Storage Warehouse,
which they'll soon tear down. I
used to think they had the Armory
Show[6] there.
        A glass of papaya juice
and back to work. My heart is in my
pocket, it is Poems by Pierre Reverdy.[7]

3   Violet Ranney Lang (1924–1956), known as "Bunny" Lang. She wrote poetry and
plays. In the early 1950s she acted in and directed plays at the Poets' Theatre in
Cambridge, Massachusetts.
4   John Treville Latouche (1917–1956), playwright and lyricist. He wrote the long
poem "Ballad for Americans" which was performed as a radio cantata, and the book and
lyrics for *Cabin in the Sky* and other Broadway shows. He also wrote a book, *Congo*,
about his travels in Africa.
5   American painter (1912–1956).
6   An exhibition of Futurist and other avant-garde art that took place in New York
City in 1913. Marcel Duchamp's "Nude Descending a Staircase" caused a sensation.
7   French Surrealist poet (1889–1960).

ROBERT BLY [1926–   ]

Late at Night
During a Visit
of Friends

1
We spent all day fishing and talking.
At last, late at night, I sit at my desk alone,
And rise and walk out in the summery night.
A dark thing hopped near me in the grass.

2
The trees were breathing, the windmill slowly pumped.
Overhead the rain clouds that rained on Ortonville
Covered half the stars.
The air was still cool from their rain.

3

It is very late.
I am the only one awake.
Men and women I love are sleeping nearby.

4

The human face shines as it speaks of things
Near itself, thoughts full of dreams.
The human face shines like a dark sky
As it speaks of those things that oppress the living.

Hearing Men
Shout at Night
on Macdougal Street

How strange to awake in a city,
And hear grown men shouting in the night!
On the farm the darkness wins,
And the small ones nestle in their graves of cold:
Here is a boiling that only exhaustion subdues,
A bitter moiling of muddy waters
At which the voices of white men feed!

The street is a sea, and mud boils up
When the anchor is lifted, for now at midnight there is about to sail
The first New England slave-ship with the Negroes in the hold.

For My Son Noah,
Ten Years Old

Night and day arrive, and day after day goes by,
and what is old remains old, and what is young
        remains young, and grows old.
The lumber pile does not grow younger, nor the
        two-by-fours lose their darkness,
but the old tree goes on, the barn stands without help
        so many years;
the advocate of darkness and night is not lost.

The horse steps up, swings on one leg, turns its body,
the chicken flapping claws onto the roost, its wings
        whelping and walloping,
but what is primitive is not to be shot out into the
        night and the dark.
And slowly the kind man comes closer, loses his rage,
        sits down at table.

My Father's
Wedding
1924

Today, lonely for my father, I saw
a log, or branch,
long, bent, ragged, bark gone.
I felt lonely for my father when I saw it.
It was the log
that lay near my uncle's old milk wagon.

Some men live with an invisible limp,
stagger, or drag
a leg. Their sons are often angry.
Only recently I thought: 10
Doing what you want . . .
Is that like limping? Tracks of it show in sand.

Have you seen those giant bird-
men of Bhutan?[1]
Men in bird masks, with pig noses, dancing,
teeth like a dog's, sometimes
dancing on one bad leg!
They do what they want, the dog's teeth say that!

But I grew up without dogs' teeth,
showed a whole body,   20
left only clear tracks in sand.
I learned to walk swiftly, easily,
no trace of a limp.
I even leaped a little. Guess where my defect is!

Then what? If a man, cautious,
hides his limp,
Somebody has to limp it! Things
do it; the surroundings limp.
House walls get scars,
the car breaks down; matter, in drudgery, takes it up.   30

On my father's wedding day,
no one was there
to hold him. Noble loneliness
held him. Since he never asked for pity
his friends thought he
was whole. Walking alone, he could carry it.

He came in limping. It was a simple
wedding, three

1 a protectorate of India, on the northeast border.

482

or four people. The man in black,
lifting the book, called for order.   40
And the invisible bride
stepped forward, before his own bride.

He married the invisible bride, not his own.
In her left
breast she carried the three drops
that wound and kill. He already had
his barklike skin then,
made rough especially to repel the sympathy

he longed for, didn't need, and wouldn't accept.
They stopped. So   50
the words are read. The man in black
speaks the sentence. When the service
is over, I hold him
in my arms for the first time and the last.

After that he was alone
and I was alone.
No friends came; he invited none.
His two-story house he turned
into a forest,
where both he and I are the hunters.   60

ROBERT CREELEY [1926-   ]

I Know
a Man

As I sd to my
friend, because I am
always talking,—John, I

sd, which was not his
name, the darkness sur-
rounds us, what

can we do against
it, or else, shall we &
why not, buy a goddamn big car,

drive, he sd, for
christ's sake, look
out where yr going.

Kore[1]

As I was walking
   I came upon
chance walking
   the same road upon.

As I sat down
   by chance to move
later
   if and as I might,

light the wood was,
   light and green,
and what I saw
   before I had not seen.

It was a lady
   accompanied
by goat men
   leading her.

Her hair held earth.
   Her eyes were dark.
A double flute
   made her move.

"O love,
   where are you
leading
   me now?"

1   Persephone. In Greek mythology, daughter of Zeus and Demeter, wife of Hades, ruler of the underworld. She spent two-thirds of the year in the underworld as the goddess of death, the rest in the upper world with her mother who presided over the fertility of the earth.

ALLEN GINSBERG [1926–   ]

A Supermarket
in California

What thoughts I have of you tonight, Walt Whitman, for I walked down the sidestreets under the trees with a headache self-conscious looking at the full moon.

In my hungry fatigue, and shopping for images, I went into the neon fruit supermarket, dreaming of your enumerations!

What peaches and what penumbras![1] Whole familes shopping at night! Aisles full of husbands! Wives in the avocados, babies in the tomatoes!—and you, Garcia Lorca,[2] what were you doing down by the watermelons?

I saw you, Walt Whitman, childless, lonely old grubber, poking among the meats in the refrigerator and eyeing the grocery boys.

I heard you asking questions of each: Who killed the pork chops? What price bananas? Are you my Angel?

I wandered in and out of the brilliant stacks of cans following you, and followed in my imagination by the store detective.

We strode down the open corridors together in our solitary fancy tasting artichokes, possessing every frozen delicacy, and never passing the cashier.

Where are we going, Walt Whitman? The doors close in an hour. Which way does your beard point tonight?

(I touch your book and dream of our odyssey[3] in the supermarket and feel absurd.)

Will we walk all night through solitary streets? The trees add shade to shade, lights out in the houses, we'll both be lonely.

Will we stroll dreaming of the lost America of love past blue automobiles in driveways, home to our silent cottage?

Ah, dear father, graybeard, lonely old courage-teacher, what America did you have when Charon quit poling his ferry and you got out on a smoking bank and stood watching the boat disappear on the black waters of Lethe?[4]

Berkeley 1955

1 *penumbra*: a space of partial illumination (as in an eclipse) between the shadow and the light.
2 Spanish poet and playwright.
3 wandering journey—from the *Odyssey* of Homer, an epic that describes the wanderings of Odysseus.
4 In Greek mythology, Charon is the ferryman who brings souls across the river Lethe (forgetfulness) to the underworld.

Sunflower Sutra[1]

I walked on the banks of the tincan banana dock and sat down under the huge shade of a Southern Pacific locomotive to look at the sunset over the box house hills and cry.

Jack Kerouac sat beside me on a busted rusty iron pole, companion, we thought the same thoughts of the soul, bleak and blue and sad-eyed, surrounded by the gnarled steel roots of trees of machinery.

The oily water on the river mirrored the red sky, sun sank on top of final Frisco peaks, no fish in that stream, no hermit in these mounts,

1 *sutra*: (a) a precept summarizing Vedic teaching (Hindu history and culture); (b) a discourse of the Buddha.

just ourselves rheumy-eyed and hungover like old bums on the riverbank, tired and wily.

Look at the Sunflower, he said, there was a dead gray shadow against the sky, big as a man, sitting dry on top of a pile of ancient sawdust—

—I rushed up enchanted—it was my first sunflower, memories of Blake—my visions—Harlem

and Hells of the Eastern rivers, bridges clanking Joes Greasy Sandwiches, dead baby carriages, black treadless tires forgotten and unretreaded, the poem of the riverbank, condoms & pots, steel knives, nothing stainless, only the dank muck and the razor sharp artifacts passing into the past—

and the gray Sunflower poised against the sunset, crackly bleak and dusty with the smut and smog and smoke of olden locomotives in its eye—

corolla of bleary spikes pushed down and broken like a battered crown, seeds fallen out of its face, soon-to-be-toothless mouth of sunny air, sunrays obliterated on its hairy head like a dried wire spiderweb,

leaves stuck out like arms out of the stem, gestures from the sawdust root, broke pieces of plaster fallen out of the black twigs, a dead fly in its ear,

Unholy battered old thing you were, my sunflower O my soul, I loved you then!

The grime was no man's grime but death and human locomotives,

all that dress of dust, that veil of darkened railroad skin, that smog of cheek, that eyelid of black mis'ry, that sooty hand or phallus or protuberance of artifical worse-than-dirt—industrial—modern— all that civilization spotting your crazy golden crown—

and those blear thoughts of death and dusty loveless eyes and ends and withered roots below, in the home-pile of sand and sawdust, rubber dollar bills, skin of machinery, the guts and innards of the weeping coughing car, the empty lonely tincans with their rusty tongues alack, what more could I name, the smoked ashes of some cock cigar, the cunts of wheelbarrows and the milky breasts of cars, wornout asses out of chairs & sphincters of dynamos—all these

entangled in your mummied roots—and you there standing before me in the sunset, all your glory in your form!

A perfect beauty of a sunflower! a perfect excellent lovely sunflower existence! a sweet natural eye to the new hip moon, woke up alive and excited grasping in the sunset shadow sunrise golden monthly breeze!

How many flies buzzed round you innocent of your grime, while you cursed the heavens of the railroad and your flower soul?

Poor dead flower? when did you forget you were a flower? when did you look at your skin and decide you were an impotent dirty old locomotive? the ghost of a locomotive? the specter and shade of a once powerful mad American locomotive?

You were never no locomotive, Sunflower, you were a sunflower!

And you Locomotive, you are a locomotive, forget me not!

So I grabbed up the skeleton thick sunflower and stuck it at my side like a
    scepter,

and deliver my sermon to my soul, and Jack's soul too, and anyone who'll
    listen,

—We're not our skin of grime, we're not our dread bleak dusty imageless
    locomotive, we're all beautiful golden sunflowers inside, we're
    blessed by our own seed & golden hairy naked accomplishment-
    bodies growing into mad black formal sunflowers in the sunset,
    spied on by our eyes under the shadow of the mad locomotive riv-
    erbank sunset Frisco hilly tincan evening sitdown vision.

Berkeley 1955

America

America I've given you all and now I'm nothing.

America two dollars and twentyseven cents January 17, 1956.

I can't stand my own mind.

America when will we end the human war?

Go fuck yourself with your atom bomb.

I don't feel good don't bother me.

I won't write my poem till I'm in my right mind.

America when will you be angelic?

When will you take off your clothes?

When will you look at yourself through the grave?   10

When will you be worthy of your million Trotskyites?[1]

America why are your libraries full of tears?

America when will you send your eggs to India?

I'm sick of your insane demands.

When can I go into the supermarket and buy what I need with my good
    looks?

America after all it is you and I who are perfect not the next world.

Your machinery is too much for me.

You made me want to be a saint.

There must be some other way to settle this argument.

Burroughs[2] is in Tangiers I don't think he'll come back it's sinister.   20

Are you being sinister or is this some form of practical joke?

I'm trying to come to the point.

I refuse to give up my obsession.

America stop pushing I know what I'm doing.

America the plum blossoms are falling.

---

1 *Trotskyite*: a follower of Leon Trotksy, one of the Bolsheviks who came to power in
Russia following the revolution of 1917. Trotsky's writings on communist theory were
widely read. Stalin had him murdered.

2 William Burroughs, novelist.

I haven't read the newspapers for months, everyday somebody goes on
    trial for murder.
America I feel sentimental about the Wobblies.[3]
America I used to be a communist when I was a kid I'm not sorry.
I smoke marijuana every chance I get.
I sit in my house for days on end and stare at the roses in the closet.   30
When I go to Chinatown I get drunk and never get laid.
My mind is made up there's going to be trouble.
You should have seen me reading Marx.[4]
My psychoanalyst thinks I'm perfectly right.
I won't say the Lord's Prayer.
I have mystical visions and cosmic vibrations.
America I still haven't told you what you did to Uncle Max after he came
    over from Russia.
I'm addressing you.
Are you going to let your emotional life be run by Time Magazine?
I'm obsessed by Time Magazine.   40
I read it every week.
Its cover stares at me every time I slink past the corner candystore.
I read it in the basement of the Berkeley Public Library.
It's always telling me about responsibility. Businessmen are serious.
    Movie producers are serious. Everybody's serious but me.
It occurs to me that I am America.
I am talking to myself again.

Asia is rising against me.
I haven't got a chinaman's chance.
I'd better consider my national resources.   50
My national resources consist of two joints of marijuana millions of geni-
    tals an unpublishable private literature that goes 1400 miles an
    hour and twentyfive-thousand mental institutions.
I say nothing about my prisons nor the millions of underprivileged who
    live in my flowerpots under the light of five hundred suns.
I have abolished the whorehouses of France, Tangiers is the next
    to go.
My ambition is to be President despite the fact that I'm a Catholic.

America how can I write a holy litany in your silly mood?
I will continue like Henry Ford my strophes are as individual as his auto-
    mobiles more so they're all different sexes.
America I will sell you strophes $2500 apiece $500 down on your old
    strophe
America free Tom Mooney[5]

---

3 *Wobbly*: a member of the Industrial Workers of the World.
4 Karl Marx (1818–1883), German political philosopher and socialist, the author of
Das Kapital.
5 Thomas Joseph Mooney, American labor leader. During a parade in San Francisco
on July 22, 1916, a bomb explosion caused numerous deaths and injuries. Mooney was
charged with complicity in the bombing and sentenced to death. The sentence was
commuted to life imprisonment and in 1939 he was pardoned and released.

America save the Spanish Loyalists[6]
America Sacco & Vanzetti[7] must not die   60
America I am the Scottsboro[8] boys.
America when I was seven momma took me to Communist Cell meetings
     they sold us garbanzos[9] a handful per ticket a ticket costs a nickel
     and the speeches were free everybody was angelic and sentimental
     about the workers it was all so sincere you have no idea what a
     good thing the party was in 1835 Scott Nearing was a grand old
     man a real mensch Mother Bloor made me cry I once saw Israel
     Amter plain.[10] Everybody must have been a spy.
America you don't really want to go to war.
America it's them bad Russians.
Them Russians them Russians and them Chinamen. And them Russians.
The Russia wants to eat us alive. The Russia's power mad. She wants to
     take our cars from out our garages.
Her wants to grab Chicago. Her needs a Red Readers' Digest. Her wants
     our auto plants in Siberia. Him big bureaucracy running our fil-
     lingstations.
That no good. Ugh. Him make Indians learn read. Him need big black
     niggers. Hah. Her make us all work sixteen hours a day. Help.
America this is quite serious.
America this is the impression I get from looking in the television set.   70
America is this correct?
I'd better get right down to the job.
It's true I don't want to join the Army or turn lathes in precision parts fac-
     tories, I'm nearsighted and psychopathic anyway.
America I'm putting my queer shoulder to the wheel.

6 supporters of the Republic in the Spanish Civil War (1936–1939).
7 anarchists charged with killing a watchman in Braintree, Massachusetts, in the
course of a robbery. They were executed in 1927. Many believed them to be innocent.
8 In Alabama, in April, 1931, nine black men were arrested and charged with raping
two white women. Eight were condemned to death, the ninth to life imprisonment.
There were appeals and new trials, and in April, 1935, the convictions were reversed by
the U.S. Supreme Court. Thirty years later, information came to light that proved the
defendants' innocence conclusively.
9 Spanish name for chickpeas.
10 *Scott Nearing*: social scientist and farmer, blacklisted in university circles for his
radical ideas; *Mother Bloor*: feminist and foremost female communist; *Israel Amter*:
communist leader.

GALWAY KINNELL [1927–   ]

The Bear

1

In late winter
I sometimes glimpse bits of steam
coming up from
some fault in the old snow

and bend close and see it is lung-colored
and put down my nose
and know
the chilly, enduring odor of bear.

2

I take a wolf's rib and whittle
it sharp at both ends   10
and coil it up
and freeze it in blubber and place it out
on the fairway of the bears.

And when it has vanished
I move out on the bear tracks,
roaming in circles
until I come to the first, tentative, dark
splash on the earth.

And I set out
running, following the splashes   20
of blood wandering over the world.
At the cut, gashed resting places
I stop and rest,
at the crawl-marks
where he lay out on his belly
to overpass some stretch of bauchy ice
I lie out
dragging myself forward with bear-knives in my fists.

3

On the third day I begin to starve,
at nightfall I bend down as I knew I would   30
at a turd sopped in blood,
and hesitate, and pick it up,
and thrust it in my mouth, and gnash it down,
and rise
and go on running.

4

On the seventh day,
living by now on bear blood alone,
I can see his upturned carcass far out ahead, a scraggled,
steamy hulk,
the heavy fur riffling in the wind.   40

I come up to him
and stare at the narrow-spaced, petty eyes,
the dismayed
face laid back on the shoulder, the nostrils

flared, catching
perhaps the first taint of me as he
died.

I hack
a ravine in his thigh, and eat and drink,
and tear him down his whole length   50
and open him and climb in
and close him up after me, against the wind,
and sleep.

5

And dream
of lumbering flatfooted
over the tundra,
stabbed twice from within,
splattering a trail behind me,
splattering it out no matter which way I lurch,
no matter which parabola of bear-transcendence,   60
which dance of solitude I attempt,
which gravity-clutched leap,
which trudge, which groan.

6

Until one day I totter and fall—
fall on this
stomach that has tried so hard to keep up,
to digest the blood as it leaked in,
to break up
and digest the bone itself: and now the breeze
blows over me, blows off   70
the hideous belches of ill-digested bear blood
and rotted stomach
and the ordinary, wretched odor of bear,

blows across
my sore, lolled tongue a song
or screech, until I think I must rise up
and dance. And I lie still.

7

I awaken I think. Marshlights
reappear, geese
come trailing again up the flyway.   80
In her ravine under old snow the dam-bear
lies, licking
lumps of smeared fur
and drizzly eyes into shapes
with her tongue. And one

hairy-soled trudge stuck out before me,
the next groaned out,
the next,
the next,
the rest of my days I spend   90
wandering: wondering
what, anyway,
was that sticky infusion, that rank flavor of blood, that
    poetry, by which I lived?

Little Sleep's-Head
Sprouting Hair
in the Moonlight

1
You cry, waking from a nightmare.

When I sleepwalk
into your room, and pick you up,
and hold you up in the moonlight, you cling to me
hard,
as if clinging could save us. I think
you think
I will never die, I think I exude
to you the permanence of smoke or stars,
even as   10
my broken arms heal themselves around you.

2
I have heard you tell
the sun, *don't go down*, I have stood by
as you told the flower, *don't grow old,*
don't die. Little Maud,

I would blow the flame out of your silver cup,
I would suck the rot from your fingernail,
I would brush your sprouting hair of the dying light,
I would scrape the rust off your ivory bones,
I would help death escape through the little ribs of your body,   20
I would alchemize the ashes of your cradle back into wood,
I would let nothing of you go, ever,

until washerwomen
feel the clothes fall asleep in their hands,
and hens scratch their spell across hatchet blades,
and rats walk away from the cultures of the plague,
and iron twists weapons toward the true north,

and grease refuses to slide in the machinery of progress,
and men feel as free on earth as fleas on the bodies of men,
and lovers no longer whisper to the one beside them in the   30
    dark, O *you-who-will-no-longer-be* . . .

And yet perhaps this is the reason you cry,
this the nightmare you wake crying from:
being forever
in the pre-trembling of a house that falls.

       3
In a restaurant once, everyone
quietly eating, you clambered up
on my lap: to all
the mouthfuls rising toward
all the mouths, at the top of your voice   40
you cried
your one word, *caca! caca! caca!*
and each spoonful
stopped, a moment, in midair, in its withering
steam.

Yes,
you cling because
I, like you, only sooner
than you, will go down
the path of vanished alphabets,   50
the roadlessness
to the other side of the darkness,
your arms
like the shoes left behind,
like the adjectives in the halting speech
of very old men,
which used to be able to call up the forgotten nouns.

      4
And you yourself,
some impossible Tuesday
in the year Two Thousand and Nine, will walk out   60
among the black stones
of the field, in the rain,
and the stones saying
over their one word, *ci-gît, ci-gît, ci-gît,*[1]

and the raindrops
hitting you on the fontanel[2]

1 here lies.
2 membrane-covered opening in bone or between bones.

over and over, and you standing there
unable to let them in.

5

If one day it happens
you find yourself with someone you love   70
in a café at one end
of the Pont Mirabeau,[3] at the zinc bar
where white wine stands in upward opening glasses,

and if you commit then, as we did, the error
of thinking,
one day all this will only be memory,

learn to reach deeper
into the sorrows
to come—to touch
the almost imaginary bones   80
under the face, to hear under the laughter
the wind crying across the stones. Kiss
the mouth
which tells you, *here,*
here is the world. This mouth. This laughter. These temple bones.

The still undanced cadence of vanishing.

6

In the light the moon
sends back, I can see in your eyes

the hand that waved once
in my father's eyes, a tiny kite   90
wobbling far up in the twilight of his last look,
and the angel
of all mortal things lets go the string.

7

Back you go, into your crib.

The last blackbird lights up his gold wings: *farewell.*
Your eyes close inside your head,
in sleep. Already
in your dreams the hours begin to sing.

Little sleep's-head sprouting hair in the moonlight,
when I come back   100
we will go out together,

3   bridge in Paris.

we will walk out together among
the ten thousand things,
each scratched in time with such knowledge, *the wages
of dying is love.*

After Making Love
We Hear Footsteps

For I can snore like a bullhorn
or play loud music
or sit up talking with any reasonably sober Irishman
and Fergus will only sink deeper
into his dreamless sleep, which goes by all in one flash,
but let there be that heavy breathing
or a stifled come-cry anywhere in the house
and he will wrench himself awake
and make for it on the run—as now, we lie together,
after making love, quiet, touching along the length of our bodies,
familiar touch of the long-married,
and he appears—in his baseball pajamas, it happens,
the neck opening so small
he has to screw them on, which one day may make him wonder
about the mental capacity of baseball players—
and flops down between us and hugs us and snuggles himself to sleep,
his face gleaming with satisfaction at being this very child.

In the half darkness we look at each other
and smile
and touch arms across his little, startlingly muscled body—
this one whom habit of memory propels to the ground of his making,
sleeper only the mortal sounds can sing awake,
this blessing love gives again into our arms.

JOHN ASHBERY [1927–   ]

The Instruction Manual

As I sit looking out of a window of the building
I wish I did not have to write the instruction manual on the uses of a new
    metal.
I look down into the street and see people, each walking with an inner
    peace,
And envy them—they are so far away from me!
Not one of them has to worry about getting out this manual on schedule.

And, as my way is, I begin to dream, resting my elbows on the desk and
　　leaning out of the window a little,
Of dim Guadalajara! City of rose-colored flowers!
City I wanted most to see, and most did not see, in Mexico!
But I fancy I see, under the press of having to write the instruction manual,
Your public square, city, with its elaborate little bandstand!　　　　　10
The band is playing *Scheherazade* by Rimsky- Korsakov.
Around stand the flower girls, handing out rose- and lemon-colored
　　flowers,
Each attractive in her rose-and-blue striped dress (Oh! such shades of rose
　　and blue),
And nearby is the little white booth where women in green serve you
　　green and yellow fruit.
The couples are parading; everyone is in a holiday mood.
First, leading the parade, is a dapper fellow
Clothed in deep blue. On his head sits a white hat
And he wears a mustache, which has been trimmed for the occasion.
His dear one, his wife, is young and pretty; her shawl is rose, pink, and
　　white.
Her slippers are patent leather, in the American fashion,　　　　　20
And she carries a fan, for she is modest, and does not want the crowd to
　　see her face too often.
But everybody is so busy with his wife or loved one
I doubt they would notice the mustachioed man's wife.
Here come the boys! They are skipping and throwing little things on the
　　sidewalk
Which is made of gray tile. One of them, a little older, has a toothpick in
　　his teeth.
He is silenter than the rest, and affects not to notice the pretty young girls
　　in white.
But his friends notice them, and shout their jeers at the laughing girls.
Yet soon all this will cease, with the deepening of their years,
And love bring each to the parade grounds for another reason.
But I have lost sight of the young fellow with the toothpick.　　　　　30
Wait—there he is—on the other side of the bandstand,
Secluded from his friends, in earnest talk with a young girl
Of fourteen or fifteen. I try to hear what they are saying
But it seems they are just mumbling something—shy words of love, prob-
　　ably.
She is slightly taller than he, and looks quietly down into his sincere eyes.
She is wearing white. The breeze ruffles her long fine black hair against
　　her olive cheek.
Obviously she is in love. The boy, the young boy with the toothpick, he is
　　in love too;
His eyes show it. Turning from this couple,
I see there is an intermission in the concert.
The paraders are resting and sipping drinks through straws　　　　　40
(The drinks are dispensed from a large glass crock by a lady in dark blue),

496

And the musicians mingle among them, in their creamy white uniforms, and talk
About the weather, perhaps, or how their kids are doing at school.

Let us take this opportunity to tiptoe into one of the side streets.
Here you may see one of those white houses with green trim
That are so popular here. Look—I told you!
It is cool and dim inside, but the patio is sunny.
An old woman in gray sits there, fanning herself with a palm leaf fan.
She welcomes us to her patio, and offers us a cooling drink.
"My son is in Mexico City," she says. "He would welcome you too 50
If he were here. But his job is with a bank there.
Look, here is a photograph of him."
And a dark-skinned lad with pearly teeth grins out at us from the worn leather frame.
We thank her for her hospitality, for it is getting late
And we must catch a view of the city, before we leave, from a good high place.
That church tower will do—the faded pink one, there against the fierce blue of the sky. Slowly we enter.
The caretaker, an old man dressed in brown and gray, asks us how long we have been in the city, and how we like it here.
His daughter is scrubbing the steps—she nods to us as we pass into the tower.
Soon we have reached the top, and the whole network of the city extends before us.
There is the rich quarter, with its houses of pink and white, and its crumbling, leafy terraces. 60
There is the poorer quarter, its homes a deep blue.
There is the market, where men are selling hats and swatting flies
And there is the public library, painted several shades of pale green and beige.
Look! There is the square we just came from, with the promenaders.
There are fewer of them, now that the heat of the day has increased,
But the young boy and girl still lurk in the shadows of the bandstand.
And there is the home of the little old lady—
She is still sitting in the patio, fanning herself.
How limited, but how complete withal, has been our experience of Guadalajara!
We have seen young love, married love, and the love of an aged mother for her son. 70
We have heard the music, tasted the drinks, and looked at colored houses.
What more is there to do, except stay? And that we cannot do.
And as a last breeze freshens the top of the weathered old tower, I turn my gaze
Back to the instruction manual which has made me dream of Guadalajara.

And Ut Pictura Poesis[1]
Is Her Name

You can't say it that way any more.
Bothered about beauty you have to
Come out into the open, into a clearing,
And rest. Certainly whatever funny happens to you
Is OK. To demand more than this would be strange
Of you, you who have so many lovers,
People who look up to you and are willing
To do things for you, but you think
It's not right, that if they really knew you . . .
So much for self-analysis. Now,   10
About what to put in your poem-painting:
Flowers are always nice, particularly delphinium.
Names of boys you once knew and their sleds,
Skyrockets are good—do they still exist?
There are a lot of other things of the same quality
As those I've mentioned. Now one must
Find a few important words, and a lot of low-keyed,
Dull-sounding ones. She approached me
About buying her desk. Suddenly the street was
Bananas and the clangor of Japanese instruments.   20
Humdrum testaments were scattered around. His head
Locked into mine. We were a seesaw. Something
Ought to be written about how this affects
You when you write poetry:
The extreme austerity of an almost empty mind
Colliding with the lush, Rousseau-like[2] foliage of its desire to
    communicate
Something between breaths, if only for the sake
Of others and their desire to understand you and desert you
For other centers of communication, so that understanding
May begin, and in doing so be undone.   30

1 *Ut Pictura Poesis*: *As a Painting, Poetry*, from Horace's *Ars Poetica*.
2 Henri Rousseau (1844–1910), French painter.

But What Is
the Reader
to Make
of This?

A lake of pain, an absence
Leading to a flowering sea? Give it a quarter-turn
And watch the centuries begin to collapse
Through each other, like floors in a burning building,
Until we get to this afternoon:

498

Those delicious few words spread around like jam
Don't matter, nor does the shadow.
We have lived blasphemously in history
And nothing has hurt us or can.
But beware of the monstrous tenderness, for out of it
The same blunt archives loom. Facts seize hold of the web
And leave it ash. Still, it is the personal,
Interior life that gives us something to think about.
The rest is only drama.

Meanwhile the combinations of every extendable circumstance
In our lives continue to blow against it like new leaves
At the edge of a forest a battle rages in and out of
For a whole day. It's not the background, we're the background,
On the outside looking out. The surprises history has
For us are nothing compared to the shock we get
From each other, though time still wears
The colors of meanness and melancholy, and the general life
Is still many sizes too big, yet
Has style, woven of things that never happened
With those that did, so that a mood survives
Where life and death never could. Make it sweet again!

Around the Rough and Rugged Rocks the Ragged Rascal Rudely Ran

I think a lot about it,
Think quite a lot about it—
The omnipresent possibility of being interrupted
While what I stand for is still almost a bare canvas:
A few traceries, that may be fibers, perhaps
Not even these but shadows, hallucinations. . . .

And it is well then to recall
That this track is the outer rim of a flat crust,
Dimensionless, except for its poor, parched surface,
The face one raises to God,
Not the rich dark composite
We keep to ourselves,
Carpentered together any old way,
Coffee from an old tin can, a belch of daylight,
People leaving the beach.
If I could write it
And also write about it—

The interruption—
Rudeness on the face of it, but who
Knows anything about our behavior?

Forget what it is you're coming out of,
Always into something like a landscape
Where no one has ever walked
Because they're too busy.
Excitedly you open your rhyming dictionary.
It has begun to snow.

Never Seek
to Tell Thy Love[1]

Many colors will take you to themselves
But now I want someone to tell me how to get home.
The way back there is streaked and stippled,
A shaded place. It belongs where it is going

Not where it is. The flowers don't talk to Ida now.
They speak only the language of flowers,
Saying things like, How hard I tried to get there.
It must mean I'm not here yet. But you,
You seem so formal, so serious. You can't read poetry,
Not the way they taught us back in school.

Returning to the point was always the main thing, then.
Did we ever leave it? I don't think so. It was our North Pole.
We skulked and hungered there for years, and now,
Like dazzled insects skimming the bright airs,
You are back on the road again, the path leading
Vigorously upward, through intelligent and clear spaces.
They don't make rocks like us any more.

And holding on to the thread, fine as a cobweb, but incredibly strong,
Each of us advances into his own labyrinth.
The gift of invisibility
Has been granted to all but the gods, so we say such things,
Filling the road up with colors, faces,
Tender speeches, until they feed us to the truth.

1 See the poem by William Blake with this title.

JAMES WRIGHT [1927–1980]

Autumn Begins
in Martins Ferry, Ohio

In the Shreve High football stadium,
I think of Polacks nursing long beers in Tiltonsville,
And gray faces of Negroes in the blast furnace at Benwood,
And the ruptured night watchman of Wheeling Steel,
Dreaming of heroes.

All the proud fathers are ashamed to go home.
Their women cluck like starved pullets,
Dying for love.

Therefore,
Their sons grow suicidally beautiful
At the beginning of October,
And gallop terribly against each other's bodies.

A Blessing

Just off the highway to Rochester, Minnesota,
Twilight bounds softly forth on the grass.
And the eyes of those two Indian ponies
Darken with kindness.
They have come gladly out of the willows
To welcome my friend and me.
We step over the barbed wire into the pasture
Where they have been grazing all day, alone.
They ripple tensely, they can hardly contain their happiness
That we have come.
They bow shyly as wet swans. They love each other.
There is no loneliness like theirs.
At home once more,
They begin munching the young tufts of spring in the darkness.
I would like to hold the slenderer one in my arms,
For she has walked over to me
And nuzzled my left hand.
She is black and white,
Her mane falls wild on her forehead,
And the light breeze moves me to caress her long ear
That is delicate as the skin over a girl's wrist.
Suddenly I realize
That if I stepped out of my body I would break
Into blossom.

A Winter Daybreak above Vence[1]

The night's drifts
Pile up below me and behind my back,
Slide down the hill, rise again, and build
Eerie little dunes on the roof of the house.
In the valley below me,
Miles between me and the town of St.-Jeannet,
The road lamps glow.
They are so cold, they might as well be dark.
Trucks and cars
Cough and drone down there between the golden   10
Coffins of greenhouses, the startled squawk
Of a rooster claws heavily across
A grove, and drowns.
The gumming snarl of some grouchy dog sounds,
And a man bitterly shifts his broken gears.
True night still hands on,
Mist cluttered with a racket of its own.

Now on the mountainside,
A little way downhill among turning rocks,
A square takes form in the side of a dim wall.   20
I hear a bucket rattle or something, tinny,
No other stirring behind the dim face
Of the goatherd's house. I imagine
His goats are still sleeping, dreaming
Of the fresh roses
Beyond the walls of the greenhouse below them
And of lettuce leaves opening in Tunisia.

I turn, and somehow
Impossibly hovering in the air over everything,
The Mediterranean, nearer to the moon   30
Than this mountain is,
Shines. A voice clearly
Tells me to snap out of it. Galway
Mutters out of the house and up the stone stairs
To start the motor. The moon and the stars
Suddenly flicker out, and the whole mountain
Appears, pale as a shell.

Look, the sea has not fallen and broken
Our heads. How can I feel so warm
Here in the dead center of January? I can   40
Scarcely believe it, and yet I have to, this is

1   village of France situated in the Maritime Alps, northwest of Nice.

The only life I have. I get up from the stone.
My body mumbles something unseemly
And follows me. Now we are all sitting here strangely
On top of the sunlight.

ANNE SEXTON   [1928–1974]

Cinderella

You always read about it:
the plumber with twelve children
who wins the Irish Sweepstakes.
From toilets to riches.
That story.

Or the nursemaid,
some luscious sweet from Denmark
who captures the oldest son's heart.
From diapers to Dior.
That story.   10

Or a milkman who serves the wealthy,
eggs, cream, butter, yogurt, milk,
the white truck like an ambulance
who goes into real estate
and makes a pile.
From homogenized to martinis at lunch.

Or the charwoman
who is on the bus when it cracks up
and collects enough from the insurance.
From mops to Bonwit Teller.   20
That story.

Once
the wife of a rich man was on her deathbed
and she said to her daughter Cinderella:
Be devout. Be good. Then I will smile
down from heaven in the seam of a cloud.
The man took another wife who had
two daughters, pretty enough
but with hearts like blackjacks.
Cinderella was their maid.   30
She slept on the sooty hearth each night
and walked around looking like Al Jolson.
Her father brought presents home from town,
jewels and gowns for the other women

but the twig of a tree for Cinderella.
She planted that twig on her mother's grave
and it grew to a tree where a white dove sat.
Whenever she wished for anything the dove
would drop it like an egg upon the ground.
The bird is important, my dears, so heed him.   40

Next came the ball, as you all know.
It was a marriage market.
The prince was looking for a wife.
All but Cinderella were preparing
and gussying up for the big event.
Cinderella begged to go too.
Her stepmother threw a dish of lentils
into the cinders and said: Pick them
up in an hour and you shall go.
The white dove brought all his friends;   50
all the warm wings of the fatherland came,
and picked up the lentils in a jiffy.
No, Cinderella, said the stepmother,
you have no clothes and cannot dance.
That's the way with stepmothers.

Cinderella went to the tree at the grave
and cried forth like a gospel singer:
Mama! Mama! My turtledove,
send me to the prince's ball!
The bird dropped down a golden dress   60
and delicate little gold slippers.
Rather a large package for a simple bird.
So she went. Which is no surprise.
Her stepmother and sisters didn't
recognize her without her cinder face
and the prince took her hand on the spot
and danced with no other the whole day.

As nightfall came she thought she'd better
get home. The prince walked her home
and she disappeared into the pigeon house   70
and although the prince took an axe and broke
it open she was gone. Back to her cinders.
These events repeated themselves for three days.
However on the third day the prince
covered the palace steps with cobbler's wax
and Cinderella's gold shoe stuck upon it.
Now he would find whom the shoe fit
and find his strange dancing girl for keeps.
He went to their house and the two sisters
were delighted because they had lovely feet.   80

The eldest went into a room to try the slipper on
but her big toe got in the way so she simply
sliced it off and put on the slipper.
The prince rode away with her until the white dove
told him to look at the blood pouring forth.
That is the way with amputations.
They don't just heal up like a wish.
The other sister cut off her heel
but the blood told as blood will.
The prince was getting tired.   90
He began to feel like a shoe salesman.
But he gave it one last try.
This time Cinderella fit into the shoe
like a love letter into its envelope.

At the wedding ceremony
the two sisters came to curry favor
and the white dove pecked their eyes out.
Two hollow spots were left
like soup spoons.

Cinderella and the prince   100
lived, they say, happily ever after,
like two dolls in a museum case
never bothered by diapers or dust,
never arguing over the timing of an egg,
never telling the same story twice,
never getting a middle-aged spread,
their darling smiles pasted on for eternity.
Regular Bobbsey Twins.
That story.

Hansel and Gretel

Little plum,
said the mother to her son,
I want to bite,
I want to chew,
I will eat you up.
Little child,
little nubkin,
sweet as fudge,
you are my blitz.
I will spit on you for luck   10
for you are better than money.
Your neck as smooth
as a hard-boiled egg;

soft cheeks, my pears,
let me buzz you on the neck
and take a bite.
I have a pan that will fit you.
Just pull up your knees like a game hen.
Let me take your pulse
and set the oven for 350.   20
Come, my pretender, my fritter,
my bubbler, my chicken biddy!
Oh succulent one,
it is but one turn in the road
and I would be a cannibal!

Hansel and Gretel
and their parents
had come upon evil times.
They had cooked the dog
and served him up like lamb chops.   30
There was only a loaf of bread left.
The final solution,
their mother told their father,
was to lose the children in the forest.
We have enough bread for ourselves
but none for them.
Hansel heard this
and took pebbles with him
into the forest.
He dropped a pebble every fifth step   40
and later, after their parents had left them,
they followed the pebbles home.
The next day their mother gave them
each a hunk of bread
like a page out of the Bible
and sent them out again.
This time Hansel dropped bits of bread.
The birds, however, ate the bread
and they were lost at last.
They were blind as worms.   50
They turned like ants in a glove
not knowing which direction to take.
The sun was in Leo
and water spouted from the lion's head
but still they did not know their way.

So they walked for twenty days
and twenty nights
and came upon a rococo house
made all of food from its windows
to its chocolate chimney.   60
A witch lived in that house

and she took them in.
She gave them a large supper
to fatten them up
and then they slept,
z's buzzing from their mouths like flies.
Then she took Hansel,
the smarter, the bigger,
the juicier, into the barn
and locked him up.   70
Each day she fed him goose liver
so that he would fatten,
so that he would be as larded
as a plump coachman,
that knight of the whip.
She was planning to cook him
and then gobble him up
as in a feast
after a holy war.

She spoke to Gretel   80
and told her how her brother
would be better than mutton;
how a thrill would go through her
as she smelled him cooking;
how she would lay the table
and sharpen the knives
and neglect none of the refinements.
Gretel
who had said nothing so far
nodded her head and wept.   90
She who neither dropped pebbles or bread
bided her time.

The witch looked upon her
with new eyes and thought:
Why not this saucy lass
for an hors d'oeuvre?
She explained to Gretel
that she must climb into the oven
to see if she would fit.
Gretel spoke at last: 100
Ja, Fräulein, show me how it can be done.
The witch thought this fair
and climbed in to show the way.
It was a matter of gymnastics.
Gretel,
seeing her moment in history,
shut fast the oven,
locked fast the door,
fast as Houdini,

and turned the oven on to bake.   110
The witch turned as red
as the Jap flag.
Her blood began to boil up
like Coca-Cola.
Her eyes began to melt.
She was done for.
Altogether a memorable incident.

As for Hansel and Gretel,
they escaped and went home to their father.
Their mother,   120
you'll be glad to hear, was dead.
Only at suppertime
while eating a chicken leg
did our children remember
the woe of the oven,
the smell of the cooking witch,
a little like mutton,
to be served only with burgundy
and fine white linen
like something religious.   130

DONALD HALL [1928–   ]

Ox Cart Man

In October of the year,
he counts potatoes dug from the brown field,
counting the seed, counting
the cellar's portion out,
and bags the rest on the cart's floor.

He packs wool sheared in April, honey
in combs, linen, leather
tanned from deerhide,
and vinegar in a barrel
hooped by hand at the forge's fire.

He walks by his ox's head, ten days
to Portsmouth Market, and sells potatoes,
and the bag that carried potatoes,
flaxseed, birch brooms, maple sugar, goose
feathers, yarn.

When the cart is empty he sells the cart.
When the cart is sold he sells the ox,
harness and yoke, and walks

home, his pockets heavy
with the year's coin for salt and taxes,

and at home by fire's light in November cold
stitches new harness
for next year's ox in the barn,
and carves the yoke, and saws planks
building the cart again.

ADRIENNE RICH [1929–   ]

Diving into
the Wreck

First having read the book of myths,
and loaded the camera,
and checked the edge of the knife-blade,

I put on
the body-armor of black rubber
the absurd flippers
the grave and awkward mask.
I am having to do this
not like Cousteau[1] with his
assiduous team   10
aboard the sun-flooded schooner
but here alone.

There is a ladder.
The ladder is always there
hanging innocently
close to the side of the schooner.
We know what it is for,
we who have used it.
Otherwise
it's a piece of maritime floss   20
some sundry equipment.

I go down.
Rung after rung and still
the oxygen immerses me
the blue light
the clear atoms
of our human air.
I go down.
My flippers cripple me,

_____
1 Jacques Yves Cousteau (1910–   ), French underwater explorer and author.

I crawl like an insect down the ladder
and there is no one
to tell me when the ocean
will begin.

First the air is blue and then
it is bluer and then green and then
black I am blacking out and yet
my mask is powerful
it pumps my blood with power
the sea is another story
the sea is not a question of power
I have to learn alone
to turn my body without force
in the deep element.

And now: it is easy to forget
what I came for
among so many who have always
lived here
swaying their crenellated² fans
between the reefs
and besides
you breathe differently down here.

I came to explore the wreck.
The words are purposes.
The words are maps.
I came to see the damage that was done
and the treasures that prevail.
I stroke the beam of my lamp
slowly along the flank
of something more permanent
than fish or weed

the thing I came for:
the wreck and not the story of the wreck
the thing itself and not the myth

the drowned face³ always staring
toward the sun
the evidence of damage
worn by salt and sway into this threadbare beauty
the ribs of the disaster
curving their assertion
among the tentative haunters.

2   notched.
3   the figurehead of a ship.

This is the place.
And I am here, the mermaid whose dark hair
streams black, the merman in his armored body
We circle silently
about the wreck
we dive into the hold.
I am she: I am he

whose drowned face sleeps with open eyes
whose breasts still bear the stress
whose silver, copper, vermeil[4] cargo lies
obscurely inside barrels
half-wedged and left to rot
we are the half-destroyed instruments
that once held to a course
the water-eaten log
the fouled compass

We are, I am, you are
by cowardice or courage
the one who find our way
back to this scene
carrying a knife, a camera
a book of myths
in which
our names do not appear.

80

90

4   gilded silver, bronze or copper.

Upper Broadway

The leafbud straggles forth
toward the frigid light of the airshaft   this is faith
this pale extension of a day
when looking up   you know   something is changing
winter has turned   though the wind is colder
Three streets away   a roof collapses   onto people
who thought they still had time   Time out of mind

I have written so many words
wanting to live inside you
to be of use to you

Now I must write for myself   for this blind
woman scratching the pavement   with her wand of thought
this slippered crone   inching on icy streets
reaching into wire trashbaskets   pulling out
what was thrown away   and infinitely precious

I look at my hands and see   they are still unfinished
I look at the vine and see the leafbud
inching toward life

I look at my face in the glass   and see
a halfborn woman

GARY SNYDER [1930–   ]

Hay for
the Horses

He had driven half the night
From far down San Joaquin
Through Mariposa, up the
Dangerous mountain roads,
And pulled in at eight a.m.,
With his big truckload of hay
        behind the barn.
With winch and ropes and hooks
We stacked the bales up clean
To splintery redwood rafters
High in the dark, flecks of alfalfa
Whirling through shingle-cracks of light,
Itch of haydust in the
        sweaty shirt and shoes.
At lunchtime under black oak
Out in the hot corral,
—The old mare nosing lunchpails,
Grasshoppers crackling in the weeds—
"I'm sixty-eight" he said,
"I first bucked hay when I was seventeen.
I thought, that day I started,
I sure would hate to do this all my life.
And dammit, that's just what
I've gone and done."

December[1]

Three a.m.—a far bell
    coming closer:
fling up useless futon[2] on the shelf;
outside, ice-water in the hand & wash the face.

1 This poem describes the day of a monk or layman in a Zen Buddhist monastery.
2 cushion.

Ko the bird-head, silent, skinny,
swiftly cruise the room with
salt plum tea.

Bell from the hondo[3] chanting sutras.[4] Gi:[5]
deep bell, small bell, wooden drum.
    sanzen[6] at four   10
    kneel on icy polisht boards in line;

Shukuza rice and pickles
barrel and bucket
dim watt bulb.
    till daybreak nap upright.
                sweep
    garden and hall.
    frost outside
                wind through walls.

At eight the lecture bell. high chair,   20
Ke helps the robe—red, gold,
    black lacquer in the shadow
    sun and cold

Saiza[7] a quarter to ten
soup and rice dab on the bench
feed the hungry ghosts
    back in the hall by noon.
two o clock sanzen
three o clock bellywarmer
    boild up soup-rice mush.   30
dinging and scuffing. out back smoke,
                and talk.

At dusk, at five,
black robes draw into the hall.
    stiff joints, sore knees bend
        the jiki[8] pads by with his incense lit,
                bells,
    wood block crack
  & stick slips round the room
on soft straw sandals.   40

seven, sanzen
    tea, and a leaf-shaped candy.

3   main hall, usually a separate building, in a Japanese monastery, used principally for lectures and meals.
4   part of the Canon containing the dialogue or discourses of the Buddha.
5   temple.
6   interview between Zen master (roshi) and the monk or layman undergoing Zen training.
7   break.
8   person who presides over sessions of meditation.

kinhin[9] at eight with folded hands—
    single-file racing in flying robes leaning
        to wake—

nine o clock one more sanzen
ten, hot noodles,
three bowls each.

Sit until midnight. chant.
    make three bows and pull the futon down.   50
    roll in the bed—
    black.

A far bell coming closer.

  9   pacing and meditating.

The Dead
by the Side
of the Road

How did a great Red-tailed Hawk
    come to lie—all stiff and dry—
    on the shoulder of
        Interstate 5?

Her wings for dance fans

Zac skinned a skunk with a crushed head
    washed the pelt in gas; it hangs,
      tanned, in his tent

Fawn stew on Hallowe'en
    hit by a truck on highway forty-nine   10
    offer cornmeal by the mouth;
        skin it out.

Log trucks run on fossil fuel

I never saw a Ringtail til I found one in the road:
    case-skinned it with the toenails
      footpads, nose, and whiskers on;
        it soaks in salt and water
        sulphuric acid pickle;

she will be a pouch for magic tools.

The Doe was apparently shot   20
    lengthwise and through the side—

        shoulder and out the flank
            belly full of blood

Can save the other shoulder maybe,
    if she didn't lie too long—
Pray to their spirits. Ask them to bless us:
    our ancient sisters' trails
        the roads were laid across and kill them:
            night-shining eyes

The dead by the side of the road.   30

By Frazier
Creek Falls

Standing up on lifted, folded rock
looking out and down—

The creek falls to a far valley.
hills beyond that
facing, half-forested, dry
—clear sky
strong wind in the
stiff glittering needle clusters
of the pine—their brown
round trunk bodies
straight, still;
rustling trembling limbs and twigs

listen.

This living flowing land
is all there is, forever

We *are* it
it sings through us—

We could live on this Earth
without clothes or tools!

TED HUGHES [1930–   ]

The Thought-Fox

I imagine this midnight moment's forest:
Something else is alive

Beside the clock's loneliness
And this blank page where my fingers move.

Through the window I see no star:
Something more near
Though deeper within darkness
Is entering the loneliness:

Cold, delicately as the dark snow
A fox's nose touches twig, leaf;
Two eyes serve a movement, that now
And again now, and now, and now

Sets neat prints into the snow
Between trees, and warily a lame
Shadow lags by stump and in hollow
Of a body that is bold to come

Across clearings, an eye,
A widening deepening greenness,
Brilliantly, concentratedly,
Coming about its own business

Till, with a sudden sharp hot stink of fox,
It enters the dark hole of the head.
The window is starless still; the clock ticks,
The page is printed.

Pike

Pike, three inches long, perfect
Pike in all parts, green tigering the gold.
Killers from the egg: the malevolent aged grin.
They dance on the surface among the flies.

Or move, stunned by their own grandeur,
Over a bed of emerald, silhouette
Of submarine delicacy and horror.
A hundred feet long in their world.

In ponds, under the heat-struck lily pads—
Gloom of their stillness: 10
Logged on last year's black leaves, watching upwards.
Or hung in an amber cavern of weeds

The jaws' hooked clamp and fangs
Not to be changed at this date;
A life subdued to its instrument;
The gills kneading quietly, and the pectorals.

Three we kept behind glass,
Jungled in weed: three inches, four,
And four and a half: fed fry to them—
Suddenly there were two. Finally one.   20

With a sag belly and the grin it was born with.
And indeed they spare nobody.
Two, six pounds each, over two feet long,
High and dry and dead in the willow-herb—

One jammed past its gills down the other's gullet:
The outside eye stared: as a vice locks—
The same iron in this eye
Though its film shrank in death.

A pond I fished, fifty yards across,
Whose lilies and muscular tench   30
Had outlasted every visible stone
Of the monastery that planted them—

Stilled legendary depth:
It was as deep as England. It held
Pike too immense to stir, so immense and old
That past nightfall I dared not cast

But silently cast and fished
With the hair frozen on my head
For what might move, for what eye might move.
The still splashes on the dark pond,   40

Owls hushing the floating woods
Frail on my ear against the dream
Darkness beneath night's darkness had freed,
That rose slowly toward me, watching.

Heptonstall
Old Church

A great bird landed here.

Its song drew men out of rock,
Living men out of bog and heather.

Its song put a light in the valleys
And harness on the long moors.

Its song brought a crystal from space
And set it in men's heads.

Then the bird died.

Its giant bones
Blackened and became a mystery.

The crystal in men's heads
Blackened and fell to pieces.

The valleys went out.
The moorland broke loose.

Ravens

As we came through the gate to look at the few new lambs
On the skyline of lawn smoothness,
A raven bundled itself into air from midfield
And slid away under hard glistenings, low and guilty.
Sheep nibbling, kneeling to nibble the reluctant nibbled grass.
Sheep staring, their jaws pausing to think, then chewing again,
Then pausing. Over there a new lamb
Just getting up, bumping its mother's nose
As she nibbles the sugar coating off it
While the tattered banners of her triumph swing and drip from her rear
    end.   10
She sneezes and a glim of water flashes from her rear end.
She sneezes again and again, till she's emptied.
She carries on investigating her new present and seeing how it works.
Over here is something else. But you are still interested
In that new one, and its new spark of voice,
And its tininess.
Now over here, where the raven was,
Is what interests you next. Born dead,
Twisted like a scarf, a lamb of an hour or two,
Its insides, the various jellies and crimsons and transparencies   20
And threads and tissues pulled out
In straight lines, like tent ropes
From its upward belly opened like a lamb-wool slipper,
The fine anatomy of silvery ribs on display and the cavity,
The head also emptied through the eye sockets,
The woolly limbs swathed in birth-yolk and impossible
To tell now which in all this field of quietly nibbling sheep
Was its mother. I explain
That it died being born. We should have been here, to help it.

So it died being born. "And did it cry?" you cry.   30
I pick up the dangling greasy weight by the hooves soft as dogs' pads
That had trodden only womb water
And its raven-drawn strings dangle and trail,

Its loose head joggles, and "Did it cry?" you cry again.
Its two-fingered feet splay in their skin between the pressures
Of my finger and thumb. And there is another,
Just born, all black, splaying its tripod, inching its new points
Toward its mother, and testing the note
It finds in its mouth. But you have eyes now
Only for the tattered bundle of throwaway lamb.   40
"Did it cry?" you keep asking, in a three-year-old field-wide
Piercing persistence. "Oh, yes," I say, "it cried,"

Though this one was lucky insofar
As it made the attempt into a warm wind
And its first day of death was blue and warm
The magpies gone quiet with domestic happiness
And skylarks not worrying about anything
And the blackthorn budding confidently
And the skyline of hills, after millions of hard years,
Sitting soft.   50

A Motorbike

We had a motorbike all through the war
In an outhouse—thunder, flight, disruption
Cramped in rust, under washing, abashed, outclassed
By the Brens, the Bombs, the Bazookas elsewhere.

The war ended, the explosions stopped.
The men surrendered their weapons
And hung around limply.
Peace took them all prisoner.
They were herded into their home towns.
A horrible privation began   10
Of working a life up out of the avenues
And the holiday resorts and the dance halls.

Then the morning bus was as bad as any labor truck,
The foreman, the boss, as bad as the S.S.
And the ends of the street and the bends of the road
And the shallowness of the shops and the shallowness of the beer
And the sameness of the next town
Were as bad as electrified barbed wire.
The shrunk-back war ached in their testicles
And England dwindled to the size of a dog track.   20

So there came this quiet young man
And he bought our motorbike for twelve pounds.
And he got it going, with difficulty.
He kicked it into life—it erupted
Out of the six year sleep, and he was delighted.

A week later, astride it, before dawn,
A misty frosty morning,
He escaped

Into a telegraph pole
On the long straight west of Swinton. 30

ETHERIDGE KNIGHT   [1931–   ]

Hard Rock Returns to Prison from the Hospital for the Criminal Insane

Hard Rock was "known not to take no shit
From nobody," and he had the scars to prove it:
Split purple lips, lumped ears, welts above
His yellow eyes, and one long scar that cut
Across his temple and plowed through a thick
Canopy of kinky hair.

The WORD was that Hard Rock wasn't a mean nigger
Anymore, that the doctors had bored a hole in his head,
Cut out part of his brain, and shot electricity
Through the rest. When they brought Hard Rock back, 10
Handcuffed and chained, he was turned loose,
Like a freshly gelded stallion, to try his new status.
And we all waited and watched, like indians at a corral,
To see if the WORD was true.

As we waited we wrapped ourselves in the cloak
Of his exploits: "Man, the last time, it took eight
Screws to put him in the Hole." "Yeah, remember when he
Smacked the captain with his dinner tray?" "He set
The record for time in the Hole—67 straight days!"
"Ol Hard Rock! man, that's one crazy nigger." 20
And then the jewel of a myth that Hard Rock had once bit
A screw on the thumb and poisoned him with syphilitic spit.

The testing came, to see if Hard Rock was really tame.
A hillbilly called him a black son of a bitch
And didn't lose his teeth, a screw who knew Hard Rock
From before shook him down and barked in his face.
And Hard Rock did *nothing*. Just grinned and looked silly,
His eyes empty like knot holes in a fence.

And even after we discovered that it took Hard Rock
Exactly 3 minutes to tell you his first name,   30
We told ourselves that he had just wised up,
Was being cool; but we could not fool ourselves for long,
And we turned away, our eyes on the ground. Crushed.
He had been our Destroyer, the doer of things
We dreamed of doing but could not bring ourselves to do,
The fears of years, like a biting whip,
Had cut grooves too deeply across our backs.

SYLVIA PLATH   [1932–1963]

Morning Song

Love set you going like a fat gold watch.
The midwife slapped your footsoles, and your bald cry
Took its place among the elements.

Our voices echo, magnifying your arrival. New statue.
In a drafty museum, your nakedness
Shadows our safety. We stand round blankly as walls.

I'm no more your mother
Than the cloud that distils a mirror to reflect its own slow
Effacement at the wind's hand.

All night your moth-breath
Flickers among the flat pink roses. I wake to listen:
A far sea moves in my ear.

One cry, and I stumble from bed, cow-heavy and floral
In my Victorian nightgown.
Your mouth opens clean as a cat's. The window square

Whitens and swallows its dull stars. And now you try
Your handful of notes;
The clear vowels rise like balloons.

Daddy

You do not do, you do not do
Any more, black shoe
In which I have lived like a foot
For thirty years, poor and white,
Barely daring to breathe or Achoo.

Daddy, I have had to kill you.
You died before I had time—
Marble-heavy, a bag full of God,
Ghastly statue with one grey toe
Big as a Frisco seal   10

And a head in the freakish Atlantic
Where it pours bean green over blue
In the waters off beautiful Nauset.
I used to pray to recover you.
Ach, du.[1]

In the German tongue, in the Polish town
Scraped flat by the roller
Of wars, wars, wars.
But the name of the town is common.
My Polack friend   20

Says there are a dozen or two.
So I never could tell where you
Put your foot, your root,
I never could talk to you.
The tongue stuck in my jaw.

It stuck in a barb wire snare.
Ich,[2] ich, ich, ich,
I could heardly speak.
I thought every German was you.
And the language obscene   30

An engine, an engine
Chuffing me off like a Jew.
A Jew to Dachau, Auschwitz, Belsen.
I began to talk like a Jew.
I think I may well be a Jew.

The snows of the Tyrol, the clear beer of Vienna
Are not very pure or true.
With my gypsy ancestress and my weird luck
And my Taroc[3] pack and my Taroc pack
I may be a bit of a Jew.   40

I have always been scared of *you*,
With your Luftwaffe, your gobbledygoo.
And your neat moustache

1 you.
2 I.
3 cards used in fortune telling.

522

And your Aryan eye, bright blue.
Panzer-man, panzer-man, O You—

Not God but a swastika[4]
So black no sky could squeak through.
Every woman adores a Fascist,
The boot in the face, the brute
Brute heart of a brute like you.   50

You stand at the blackboard, daddy,
In the picture I have of you,
A cleft in your chin instead of your foot
But no less a devil for that, no not
Any less the black man who

Bit my pretty red heart in two.
I was ten when they buried you.
At twenty I tried to die
And get back, back, back to you.
I thought even the bones would do.   60

But they pulled me out of the sack,
And they stuck me together with glue.
And then I knew what to do.
I made a model of you,
A man in black with a Meinkampf[5] look

And a love of the rack and the screw.
And I said I do, I do.
So daddy, I'm finally through.
The black telephone's off at the root,
The voices just can't worm through.   70

If I've killed one man, I've killed two——
The vampire who said he was you
And drank my blood for a year,
Seven years, if you want to know.
Daddy, you can lie back now.

There's a stake in your fat black heart
And the villagers never liked you.
They are dancing and stamping on you.
They always *knew* it was you.
Daddy, daddy, you bastard, I'm through.   80

4 emblem of the German Nazis.
5 Hitler wrote an autobiography titled *Mein Kampf (My Struggle)*.

The Bee Meeting

Who are these people at the bridge to meet me? They are the
       villagers————
The rector, the midwife, the sexton, the agent for bees.
In my sleeveless summery dress I have no protection,
And they are all gloved and covered, why did nobody tell me?
They are smiling and taking out veils tacked to ancient hats.

I am nude as a chicken neck, does nobody love me?
Yes, here is the secretary of bees with her white shop smock,
Buttoning the cuffs at my wrists and the slit from my neck to my knees.
Now I am milkweed silk, the bees will not notice.
They will not smell my fear, my fear, my fear.   10

Which is the rector now, is it that man in black?
Which is the midwife, is that her blue coat?
Everybody is nodding a square black head, they are knights in visors,
Breastplates of cheesecloth knotted under the armpits.
Their smiles and their voices are changing. I am led through a beanfield.

Strips of tinfoil winking like people,
Feather dusters fanning their hands in a sea of bean flowers,
Creamy bean flowers with black eyes and leaves like bored hearts.
Is it blood clots the tendrils are dragging up that string?
No, no, it is scarlet flowers that will one day be edible.   20

Now they are giving me a fashionable white straw Italian hat
And a black veil that moulds to my face, they are making me one of them.
They are leading me to the shorn grove, the circle of hives.
Is it the hawthorn that smells so sick?
The barren body of hawthorn, etherizing its children.

Is it some operation that is taking place?
It is the surgeon my neighbors are waiting for,
This apparition in a green helmet,
Shining gloves and white suit.
Is it the butcher, the grocer, the postman, someone I know?   30

I cannot run, I am rooted, and the gorse hurts me
With its yellow purses, its spiky armory.
I could not run without having to run forever.
The white hive is snug as a virgin,
Sealing off her brood cells, her honey, and quietly humming.

Smoke rolls and scarves in the grove.
The mind of the hive thinks this is the end of everything.
Here they come, the outriders, on their hysterical elastics.
If I stand very still, they will think I am cow parsley,
A gullible head untouched by their animosity,   40

Not even nodding, a personage in a hedgerow.
The villagers open the chambers, they are hunting the queen.
Is she hiding, is she eating honey? She is very clever.
She is old, old, old, she must live another year, and she knows it.
While in their fingerjoint cells the new virgins

Dream of a duel they will win inevitably,
A curtain of wax dividing them from the bride flight,
The upflight of the murderess into a heaven that loves her.
The villagers are moving the virgins, there will be no killing.
The old queen does not show herself, is she so ungrateful?   50

I am exhausted, I am exhausted———
Pillar of white in a blackout of knives.
I am the magician's girl who does not flinch.
The villagers are untying their disguises, they are shaking hands.
Whose is that long white box in the grove, what have they accomplished,
    why am I cold?

MARY OLIVER   [1935-   ]

Sleeping in the Forest

I thought the earth
remembered me, she
took me back so tenderly, arranging
her dark skirts, her pockets
full of lichens and seeds. I slept
as never before, a stone
on the riverbed, nothing
between me and the white fire of the stars
but my thoughts, and they floated
light as moths among the branches
of the perfect trees. All night
I heard the small kingdoms breathing
around me, the insects, and the birds
who do their work in the darkness. All night
I rose and fell, as if in water, grappling
with a luminous doom. By morning
I had vanished at least a dozen times
into something better.

Strawberry Moon

1

My great-aunt Elizabeth Fortune
stood under the honey locust trees,

the white moon over her and a young man near.
The blossoms fell down like white feathers,
the grass was warm as a bed, and the young man
full of promises, and the face of the moon
a white fire.

Later,
when the young man went away and came back with a
        bride,   10
Elizabeth
climbed into the attic.

2
Three women came in the night
to wash the blood away,
and burn the sheets,
and take away the child.

Was it a boy or girl?
No one remembers.

3
Elizabeth Fortune was not seen again
for forty years.   20

Meals were sent up,
laundry exchanged.

It was considered a solution
more proper than shame
showing itself to the village.

4
Finally, name by name, the downstairs died
or moved away,
and she had to come down,
so she did.

At sixty-one, she took in boarders,   30

washed their dishes,
made their beds,
spoke whatever had to be spoken,
and no more.

5
I asked my mother:
what happened to the man? She answered:

Nothing.
They had three children.
He worked in the boatyard.

I asked my mother: did they ever meet again?   40
No, she said,
though sometimes he would come
to the house to visit.
Elizabeth, of course, stayed upstairs.

6

Now the women are gathering
in smoke-filled rooms,
rough as politicians,
scrappy as club fighters.
And should anyone be surprised

if sometimes, when the white moon rises,   50
women want to lash out
with a cutting edge?

Poem for My Father's Ghost

Now is my father
A traveler, like all the bold men
He talked of, endlessly
And with boundless admiration,
Over the supper table,
Or gazing up from his white pillow—
Book on his lap always, until
Even that grew too heavy to hold.

Now is my father free of all binding fevers.
Now is my father   10
Traveling where there is no road.

Finally, he could not lift a hand
To cover his eyes.
Now he climbs to the eye of the river,
He strides through the Dakotas,
He disappears into the mountains. And though he looks
Cold and hungry as any man
At the end of a questing season,

He is one of *them* now:
He cannot be stopped.   20

Now is my father
Walking the wind,
Sniffing the deep Pacific
That begins at the end of the world.

Vanished from us utterly,
Now is my father circling the deepest forest—
Then turning in to the last red campfire burning
In the final hills,

Where chieftains, warriors and heroes
Rise and make him welcome,   30
Recognizing, under the shambles of his body,
A brother who has walked his thousand miles.

LUCILLE CLIFTON [1936–   ]

The 1st

What I remember about that day
is boxes stacked across the walk
and couch springs curling through the air
and drawers and tables balanced on the curb
and us, hollering,
leaping up and around
happy to have a playground;

nothing about the emptied rooms
nothing about the emptied family

Still

still
it was nice
when the scissors man come round
running his wheel
rolling his wheel
and the sparks shooting
out in the dark
across the lot
and over to the white folks section

still
it was nice
in the light of Maizie's store
to watch the wheel

and catch the wheel—
fire spinning in the air
and our edges
and our points
sharpening good as anybodys'[1]

1 See Whitman's "Sparkles from the Wheel," page 269.

Good Times

My Daddy has paid the rent
and the insurance man is gone
and the lights is back on
and my uncle Brud has hit
for one dollar straight
and they is good times
good times
good times

My Mama has made bread
and Grampaw has come
and everybody is drunk
and dancing in the kitchen
and singing in the kitchen
oh these is good times
good times
good times

oh children think about the
good times

CHARLES SIMIC [1938–   ]

Stone

Go inside a stone
That would be my way.
Let somebody else become a dove
Or gnash with a tiger's tooth.
I am happy to be a stone.

From the outside the stone is a riddle:
No one knows how to answer it.
Yet within, it must be cool and quiet
Even though a cow steps on it full weight,
Even though a child throws it in a river;

The stone sinks, slow, unperturbed
To the river bottom
Where the fishes come to knock on it
And listen.

I have seen sparks fly out
When two stones are rubbed,
So perhaps it is not dark inside after all;
Perhaps there is a moon shining
From somewhere, as though behind a hill—
Just enough light to make out
The strange writings, the star-charts
On the inner walls.

SEAMUS HEANEY [1939–   ]

Digging

Between my finger and my thumb
The squat pen rests; snug as a gun.

Under my window, a clean rasping sound
When the spade sinks into gravelly ground:
My father, digging. I look down

Till his straining rump among the flowerbeds
Bends low, comes up twenty years away
Stooping in rhythm through potato drills
Where he was digging.

The coarse boot nestled on the lug, the shaft   10
Against the inside knee was levered firmly.
He rooted out tall tops, buried the bright edge deep
To scatter new potatoes that we picked
Loving their cool hardness in our hands.

By God, the old man could handle a spade.
Just like his old man.

My grandfather cut more turf in a day
Than any other man on Toner's bog.
Once I carried him milk in a bottle
Corked sloppily with paper. He straightened up   20
To drink it, then fell to right away

Nicking and slicing neatly, heaving sods
Over his shoulder, going down and down
For the good turf. Digging.

The cold smell of potato mould, the squelch and slap
Of soggy peat, the curt cuts of an edge
Through living roots awaken in my head.
But I've no spade to follow men like them.

Between my finger and my thumb
The squat pen rests.   30
I'll dig with it.

Mid-Term Break

I sat all morning in the college sick bay
Counting bells knelling classes to a close.
At two o'clock our neighbors drove me home.

In the porch I met my father crying—
He had always taken funerals in his stride—
And Big Jim Evans saying it was a hard blow.

The baby cooed and laughed and rocked the pram
When I came in, and I was embarrassed
By old men standing up to shake my hand

And tell me they were "sorry for my trouble."
Whispers informed strangers I was the eldest,
Away at school, as my mother held my hand

In hers and coughed out angry tearless sighs.
At ten o'clock the ambulance arrived
With the corpse, stanched and bandaged by the nurses.

Next morning I went up into the room. Snowdrops
And candles soothed the bedside; I saw him
For the first time in six weeks. Paler now,

Wearing a poppy bruise on his left temple,
He lay in the four foot box as in his cot.
No gaudy scars, the bumper knocked him clear.

A four foot box, a foot for every year.

Girls Bathing,
Galway 1965[1]

The swell foams where they float and crawl,
A catherine wheel[2] of arm and hand;
Each head bobs curtly as a football.
The yelps are faint here on the strand.

No milk-limbed Venus ever rose
Miraculous on this western shore.
A pirate queen in battle clothes
Is our sterner myth. The breakers pour

Themselves into themselves, the years
Shuttle through space invisibly.
Where crests unfurl like creamy beer
The queen's clothes melt into the sea

And generations sighing in
The salt suds where the wave has crashed
Labor in fear of flesh and sin
For the time has been accomplished

As through the shallows in swimsuits,
Bare-legged, smooth-shouldered and long-backed
They wade ashore with skips and shouts.
So Venus comes, matter-of-fact.

1 *Galway*: a county of western Ireland bordering on the Atlantic.
2 a firework device that revolves, named after the saint who was martyred on a wheel.

North

I returned to a long strand,
the hammered shod of a bay,
and found only the secular
powers of the Atlantic thundering.

I faced the unmagical
invitations of Iceland,
the pathetic colonies
of Greenland, and suddenly

those fabulous raiders,
those lying in Orkney[1] and Dublin[2]   10

1 islands of northern Scotland that constitute a county.
2 a county in eastern Ireland.

measured against
their long swords rusting,

those in the solid
belly of stone ships,
those hacked and glinting
in the gravel of thawed streams

were ocean-deafened voices
warning me, lifted again   20
in violence and epiphany.
The longship's swimming tongue

was buoyant with hindsight—
it said Thor's[3] hammer swung
to geography and trade,
thick-witted couplings and revenges,

the hatreds and behindbacks
of the althing, lies and women,
exhaustions nominated peace,
memory incubating the spilled blood.   30

It said, "Lie down
in the word-hoard, burrow
the coil and gleam
of your furrowed brain.

Compose in darkness.
Expect aurora borealis[4]
in the long foray
but no cascade of light.

Keep your eye clear
as the bleb[5] of the icicle,   40
trust the feel of what nubbed treasure
your hands have known."

3   the Scandinavian god of war, son of Odin.
4   a luminous phenomenon that consists of streamers or arches of light in the sky at
night. It is said to be of electrical origin and is most visible in the arctic regions.
5   a bubble or small blister.

Punishment

I can feel the tug
of the halter at the nape
of her neck, the wind
on her naked front.

It blows her nipples
to amber beads,
it shakes the frail rigging
of her ribs.

I can see her drowned
body in the bog,   10
the weighing stone,
the floating rods and boughs.

Under which at first
she was a barked sapling
that is dug up
oak-bone, brain-firkin:

her shaved head
like a stubble of black corn,
her blindfold a soiled bandage,
her noose a ring   20

to store
the memories of love.
Little adulteress,
before they punished you

you were flaxen-haired,
undernourished, and your
tar-black face was beautiful.
My poor scapegoat,

I almost love you
but would have cast, I know,   30
the stones of silence.
I am the artful voyeur

of your brain's exposed
and darkened combs,
your muscles' webbing
and all your numbered bones:

I who have stood dumb
when your betraying sisters,
cauled in tar,
wept by the railings,   40

who would connive
in civilized outrage
yet understand the exact
and tribal, intimate revenge.

Singing School[1]

Fair seedtime had my soul, and I grew up
Fostered alike by beauty and by fear;
Much favored in my birthplace, and no less
In that beloved Vale to which, erelong,
I was transplanted . . .
WILLIAM WORDSWORTH: THE PRELUDE

He [the stable-boy] had a book of Orange[2]
rhymes, and the days when we read them
together in the hay-loft gave me the
pleasure of rhyme for the first time. Later
on I can remember being told, when there
was a rumour of a Fenian[3] rising, that
rifles were being handed out to the
Orangemen; and presently, when I began
to dream of my future life, I thought I
would like to die fighting the Fenians.
W. B. YEATS: AUTOBIOGRAPHIES

1. THE MINISTRY OF FEAR
For Seamus Deane

Well, as Kavanagh said, we have lived
In important places. The lonely scarp
Of St. Columb's College, where I billeted
For six years, overlooked your Bogside.[4]
I gazed into new worlds: the inflamed throat
Of Brandywell, its floodlit dogtrack,
The throttle of the hare. In the first week
I was so homesick I couldn't even eat
The biscuits left to sweeten my exile.
I threw them over the fence one night   10
In September 1951
When the lights of houses in the Lecky Road
Were amber in the fog. It was an act
Of stealth.
        Then Belfast,[5] and then Berkeley.[6]
Here's two on's are sophisticated,
Dabbling in verses till they have become
A life: from bulky envelopes arriving

---

1 for the source of this title see the poem, "Sailing to Byzantium," by W. B. Yeats.
2 Protestant Irish, especially of Ulster.
3 *Fenian:* a member of a secret 19th century Irish and Irish-American organization
dedicated to the overthrow of British rule in Ireland.
4 Catholic section of Derry City in northern Ireland.
5 city and port in northern Ireland.
6 town in northern California, site of a university.

In vacation time to slim volumes
Despatched "with the author's compliments".   20
Those poems in longhand, ripped from the wire spine
Of your exercise book, bewildered me—
Vowels and ideas bandied free
As the seed-pods blowing off our sycamores.
I tried to write about the sycamores
And innovated a South Derry[7] rhyme
With *hushed* and *lulled* full chimes for *pushed* and *pulled*.
Those hobnailed boots from beyond the mountain
Were walking, by God, all over the fine
Lawns of elocution.   30
                 Have our accents
Changed? "Catholics, in general, don't speak
As well as students from the Protestant schools."
Remember that stuff? Inferiority
Complexes, stuff that dreams were made on.
"What's your name, Heaney?"
                     "Heaney, Father."
                              "Fair
Enough."
             On my first day, the leather strap   40
Went epileptic in the Big Study,
Its echoes plashing over our bowed heads,
But I still wrote home that a boarder's life
Was not so bad, shying as usual.

On long vacations, then, I came to life
In the kissing seat of an Austin Sixteen[8]
Parked at a gable, the engine running,
My fingers tight as ivy on her shoulders,
A light left burning for her in the kitchen.
And heading back for home, the summer's   50
Freedom dwindling night by night, the air
All moonlight and a scent of hay, policemen
Swung their crimson flashlamps, crowding round
The car like black cattle, snuffing and pointing
The muzzle of a sten-gun in my eye:
"What's your name, driver?"
                   "Seamus . . ."
                     Seamus?

They once read my letters at a roadblock
And shone their torches on your hieroglyphics,   60
"Svelte dictions" in a very florid hand.

---

7   county in the north of Ireland.
8   small British automobile.

Ulster[9] was British, but with no rights on
The English lyric: all around us, though
We hadn't named it, the ministry of fear.

2. A CONSTABLE CALLS

His bicycle stood at the window-sill,
The rubber cowl of a mud-splasher
Skirting the front mudguard,
Its fat black handlegrips

Heating in sunlight, the "spud"   70
Of the dynamo gleaming and cocked back,
The pedal treads hanging relieved
Of the boot of the law.

His cap was upside down
On the floor, next his chair.
The line of its pressure ran like a bevel[10]
In his slightly sweating hair.

He had unstrapped
The heavy ledger, and my father
Was making tillage[11] returns
In acres, roods, and perches.   80

Arithmetic and fear.
I sat staring at the polished holster
With its buttoned flap, the braid cord
Looped into the revolver butt.

"Any other root crops?
Mangolds? Marrowstems? Anything like that?"
"No." But was there not a line
Of turnips where the seed ran out

In the potato field? I assumed
Small guilts and sat   90
Imagining the black hole in the barracks.
He stood up, shifted the baton-case

Further round on his belt,
Closed the domesday book,[12]

9   Northern Ireland, comprising counties Antrim, Armagh, Down, Fermanagh,
Londonderry, and Tyrone.
10   the angle that one surface or line makes with another when they are not at right
angles. The slant or inclination of such a surface or line.
11   cultivated land.
12   the Domesday Book was a record of a survey of English lands made by order of
William the Conqueror in 1085–1086.

Fitted his cap back with two hands,
And looked at me as he said goodbye.

A shadow bobbed in the window.
He was snapping the carrier spring
Over the ledger. His boot pushed off
And the bicycle ticked, ticked, ticked.   100

3. ORANGE DRUMS, TYRONE,[13] 1966

The lambeg[14] balloons at his belly, weighs
Him back on his haunches, lodging thunder
Grossly there between his chin and his knees.
He is raised up by what he buckles under.

Each arm extended by a seasoned rod,
He parades behind it. And though the drummers
Are granted passage through the nodding crowd
It is the drums preside, like giant tumors.

To every cocked ear, expert in its greed,
His battered signature subscribes "No Pope."   110
The goatskins sometimes plastered with his blood.
The air is pounding like a stethoscope.

4. SUMMER 1969

While the Constabulary covered the mob
Firing into the Falls,[15] I was suffering
Only the bullying sun of Madrid.
Each afternoon, in the casserole heat
Of the flat, as I sweated my way through
The life of Joyce,[16] stinks from the fishmarket
Rose like the reek off a flax-dam.
At night on the balcony, gules of wine,   120
A sense of children in their dark corners,
Old women in black shawls near open windows,
The air a canyon rivering in Spanish.
We talked our way home over starlit plains
Where patent leather of the Guardia Civil[17]
Gleamed like fish-bellies in flax-poisoned waters.

"Go back," one said, "try to touch the people."
Another conjured Lorca[18] from his hill.

---

13   county of northern Ireland.
14   drum.
15   Catholic area of Belfast, the scene of violent incidents between Protestants and
Catholics.
16   James Joyce, Irish novelist.
17   Spanish constabulary.
18   Garcia Lorca, Spanish poet and playwright.

We sat through death counts and bullfight reports
On the television, celebrities   130
Arrived from where the real thing still happened.

I retreated to the cool of the Prado.[19]
Goya's "Shootings of the Third of May"[20]
Covered a wall—the thrown-up arms
And spasm of the rebel, the helmeted
And knapsacked military, the efficient
Rake of the fusillade. In the next room
His nightmares, grafted to the palace wall—
Dark cyclones, hosting, breaking; Saturn[21]
Jewelled in the blood of his own children,   140
Gigantic Chaos turning his brute hips
Over the world. Also, that holmgang[22]
Where two berserks club each other to death
For honor's sake, greaved in a bog, and sinking.

He painted with his fists and elbows, flourished
The stained cape of his heart as history charged.

5. FOSTERAGE[23]
   For Michael McLaverty

"Description is revelation!" Royal
Avenue, Belfast, 1962,
A Saturday afternoon, glad to meet
Me, newly cubbed in language, he gripped   160
My elbow. "Listen. Go your own way.
Do your own work. Remember
Katherine Mansfield[24]—*I will tell*
How the laundry basket squeaked . . . that note of exile."
But to hell with overstating it:
"Don't have the veins bulging in your biro."[25]
And then, "Poor Hopkins!"[26] I have the *Journals*
He gave me, underlined, his buckled self
Obeisant to their pain. He discerned
The lineaments of patience everywhere   170
And fostered me and sent me out, with words
Imposing on my tongue like obols.[27]

19   museum in Madrid famous for its collection of paintings.
20   painting by Francisco Goya showing the execution of Spaniards by a French firing squad.
21   an ancient Italian god of seedtime and harvest, later identified with the Greek Kronos who, thrust out by Zeus, came across the sea to Latium. Saturn was compelled to eat his children but Jupiter, with the help of his mother, Cybele, managed to escape.
22   *holm*: a small inland or inshore island.
23   (a) the act of fostering (b) a custom once prevalent in Ireland, Wales, and Scotland of entrusting one's child to foster parents to be brought up.
24   short-story writer. Born in New Zealand, she lived in England.
25   ball-point pen (a Bic).
26   the English poet, Gerard Manley Hopkins.
27   *obol*: ancient Greek coin.

6. EXPOSURE

It is December in Wicklow:[28]
Alders dripping, birches
Inheriting the last light,
The ash tree cold to look at.

A comet that was lost
Should be visible at sunset,
Those million tons of light
Like a glimmer of haws and rose-hips,[29]   180

And I sometimes see a falling star.
If I could come on meteorite!
Instead I walk through damp leaves,
Husks, the spent flukes of autumn,

Imagining a hero
On some muddy compound,
His gift like a slingstone
Whirled for the desperate.

How did I end up like this?
I often think of my friends'   190
Beautiful prismatic counselling
And the anvil brains of some who hate me

As I sit weighing and weighing
My responsible *tristia*.[30]
For what? For the ear? For the people?
For what is said behind-backs?

Rain comes down through the alders,
Its low conducive voices
Mutter about let-downs and erosions
And yet each drop recalls   200

The diamond absolutes.
I am neither internee nor informer;
An inner émigré, grown long-haired
And thoughtful; a wood-kerne[31]

Escaped from the massacre,
Taking protective coloring
From bole and bark, feeling
Every wind that blows;

28 county of eastern Ireland.
29 *haw*: hawthorn berry; *rose-hip*: the ripened accessory fruit of a rose.
30 sadness (from Ovid).
31 *kern*: a light-armed foot soldier of medieval Ireland or Scotland.

Who, blowing up these sparks
For their meagre heat, have missed   210
The once-in-a-lifetime portent,
The comet's pulsing rose.

TOI DERRICOTTE [1941–   ]

Fears of the Eighth Grade

when i ask what things they fear,
their arms raise like soldiers volunteering for battle:
fear to go into a dark room, my murderer is waiting;
fear of taking a shower, someone will stab me;
fear of being kidnapped, raped;
fear of dying in war.
when i ask how many fear this,
all the children raise their hands.

i think of this little box of consecrated land,
the bombs somewhere else,
the dead children in their mothers' arms,
women crying at the gates of the palace.

how thin the veneer!
the paper towels, napkins, toilet paper—everything
burned up in a day.

these children see the city after armageddon;
the demons stand visible in the air
between their friends talking;
they see fires in a spring day
the instant before conflagration:
they feel blood through closed faucets
& touch sharks crawling at the bottom of the sea.

Hamtramck: The Polish Women[1]

what happens to the beautiful girls with slender hips and bright round
        dresses?
one day they disappear without leaving a trace of themselves,
and the next they appear again, dragging a heavy shopping cart from the

---

1 Hamtramck: Polish settlement in Detroit.

bakery to the pork store with packages of greasy sausage and pota-
toes.
Like old nuns they waddle down the main street, past the gaudy cathe-
dral with the little infant of prague[2]—in real clothes—linens they
tend lovingly, starch in steamy buckets (their hands thick as pota-
toes, white), and iron with dignity.

2   carved wooden statue of the Christ child in the Church of Our Lady of Victory in
Prague. This must be a copy.

The Good
Old Dog

i will lay down my silk robe
beside me near the old bed,
for the good old dog;
                    she loves the feel
of it under her, and she will
push it and pull it, knead
and scrape until she has it right;
                    then she'll drop down,
heavy, silver and black in the moonlight,
on it and a couple of pillows (not
bothering the cat who has taken over
                    her real bed)
                              and breathe out deeply.
gorgeously fat,
her face
like the face of a seal.

On Stopping Late
in the Afternoon
for Steamed Dumplings

The restaurant is empty
except for the cooks and waiters.
One makes a pillow of linens and sleeps,
putting his feet up in a booth;
another folds paper tablecloths. Why
have I stopped to eat alone on this rainy
day? Why savor the wet meat of the
steamed dumpling? As I pick it up,
the waiter appraises me. Am I one
of those lonely women who must stop
for treats along the way—am I that starved?
The white dough burns—much too hot, yet,

I stick it in my mouth, quickly,
as if to destroy the evidence.
The waiter still watches. Suddenly
I am sorry to be here—sad
that my little pleasure has been stolen.

SHARON OLDS [1942–   ]

The Victims

When Mother divorced you, we were glad. She took it and
took it, in silence, all those years and then
kicked you out, suddenly, and her
kids loved it. Then you were fired, and we
grinned inside, the way people grinned when
Nixon's helicopter lifted off the South
Lawn for the last time. We were tickled
to think of your office taken away,
your secretaries taken away,
your lunches with three double bourbons,
your pencils, your reams of paper. Would they take your
suits back, too, those dark
carcasses hung in your closet, and the black
noses of your shoes with their large pores?
She had taught us to take it, to hate you and take it
until we pricked with her for your
annihilation, Father. Now I
pass the bums in doorways, the white
slugs of their bodies gleaming through slits in their
suits of compressed silt, the stained
flippers of their hands, the underwater
fire of their eyes, ships gone down with the
lanterns lit, and I wonder who took it and
took it from them in silence until they had
given it all away and had nothing
left but this.

The Sign
of Saturn[1]

Sometimes my daughter looks at me with an
amber black look, like my father
about to pass out from disgust, and I remember

1 Saturn, an Italian god—in Greek, Kronos—was said to have eaten his children.

she was born under the sign of Saturn,
the father who ate his children. Sometimes
the dark, silent back of her head
reminds me of him unconscious on the couch
every night, his face turned away.
Sometimes I hear her talking to her brother
with that coldness that passed for reason in him,
that anger hardened by will, and when she rages
into her room, and slams the door,
I can see his vast blank back
when he passed out to get away from us
and lay while the bourbon turned, in his brain,
to coal. Sometimes I see that coal
ignite in her eyes. As I talk to her,
trying to persuade her toward the human, her little
clear face tilts as if she can
not hear me, as if she were listening
to the blood in her own ear, instead,
her grandfather's voice.

Armor

Just about at the triple-barreled pistol
I can't go on. I sink down
as if shot, beside the ball of its butt
larded with mother-of-pearl. My son
leaves me on the bench, and goes on. Hand on
hip, he gazes at a suit of armor,
blue eyes running over the silver,
looking for a slit. He shakes his head,
hair greenish as the gold velvet
cod-skirt hanging before him in volutes   10
at a metal groin. Next, I see him
facing a case of shields, fingering
the sweater over his heart, and then
for a long time I don't see him, as a mother will
lose her son in war. I sit
and think about men. Finally Gabe
comes back, sated, so fattened with gore
his eyelids bulge. We exit under the
huge tumescent jousting irons,
their pennants a faded rose, like the mist   20
before his eyes. He slips his hand
lightly in mine, and says *Not one of those
suits is really safe.* But when we
get to the wide museum steps
railed with gold like the descent from heaven,
he can't resist,

and before my eyes, down the stairs,
over and over, clutching his delicate
unprotected chest, Gabriel
dies, and dies.   30

ALICE WALKER   [1944–   ]

from *African Images*
Glimpses from a Tiger's Back

1
Beads around
my neck
Mt. Kenya away
over pineappled hills
Kikuyuland.

2
A book of poems
Mt. Kenya's
Bluish peaks
"Wangari!"[1]
My new name.

5
A strange noise!
"Perhaps an elephant
is eating our roof"
In the morning
much blue.

7
Elephant legs
In a store
To hold
Umbrellas.

9
The clear Nile
A fat crocodile
Scratches his belly
And yawns.

1 Kikuyu clan name indicating honorary acceptance into the Leopard clan (author's note).

10

The rain forest
Red orchids—glorious!
And near one's eyes
The spinning cobra.

13

See! through the trees!
A leopard in
the branches—
No, only a giraffe
Munching his dinner.

18

Very American
I want to eat
The native food—
But a whole goat!

21

"America!?" "Yes."
"But you are like
my aunt's cousin
who married so-and-so."
"Yes, (I say), I know."

24

Unusual things amuse us
A little African girl
Sees my white friend
And runs
She thinks he wants her
For his dinner.

25

The fresh corpse
Of a white rhinoceros
His horn gone
Some Indian woman
Will be approached
Tonight.

29

That you loved me
I felt sure
Twice you asked
me gently
if I liked the

strange
gray
stew.

30
Pinching both my legs
the old man kneels
before me on the
ground
his head white
Ah! Africa's mountain
peaks
Snow to grace
eternal spring!

38
An African girl
Gives me a pineapple
Her country's national
Flower
How proudly she
Blinks the eye
Put out
By a sharp pineapple
Frond.
I wonder if I should
Kneel
At her bare little
Feet?

45
in my journal
I thought I could
capture
everything. . . .
Listen!
the soft wings of cranes
sifting the salt sea
air.

Chic Freedom's Reflection

(for Marilyn Pryce)

One day
Marilyn marched

beside me (demon-
stration)
and we ended up
at county farm
no phone
no bail
something about
"traffic vio-
lation"
which irrelevance
Marilyn dismissed
with a shrug
    She
had just got
      back
from
    Paris France
        In
      the
      Alabama
        hell
      she
    smell-
        ed
    so
    wonderful
like spring
& love
   &
freedom

    She
    wore a
SNCC pin
right between
  her breasts
    near her
      heart
& with a chic
    (on "jail?")
accent
   & nod of
condescent
    to frumpy
    work-house
      hags
powdered her nose
    tip-
        toe
in a badge.

In These
Dissenting Times

> *To acknowledge our ancestors means*
> *we are aware that we did not make*
> *ourselves, that the line stretches*
> *all the way back, perhaps, to God; or*
> *to Gods. We remember them because it*
> *is an easy thing to forget: that we*
> *are not the first to suffer, rebel,*
> *fight, love and die. The grace with*
> *which we embrace life, in spite of*
> *the pain, the sorrows, is always a*
> *measure of what has gone before.*
> —ALICE WALKER, "FUNDAMENTAL DIFFERENCE"

IN THESE DISSENTING TIMES

I shall write of the old men I knew
And the young men
I loved
And of the gold toothed women
Mighty of arm
Who dragged us all
To church.

1
THE OLD MEN USED TO SING

The old men used to sing
And lifted a brother
Carefully   10
Out the door
I used to think they
Were born
Knowing how to
Gently swing
A casket
They shuffled softly
Eyes dry
        More awkward
With the flowers   20
Than with the widow
After they'd put the
Body in
And stood around waiting
In their
Brown suits.

2

Those were the days
Of winking at a
Funeral
Romance blossomed   30
In the pews
Love signaled
Through the
Hymns
What did we know?

Who smelled the flowers
Slowly fading
Knew the arsonist
Of the church?

3

WOMEN

They were women then   40
My mama's generation
Husky of voice—Stout of
Step
With fists as well as
Hands
How they battered down
Doors
And ironed
Starched white
Shirts   50
How they led
Armies
Headragged Generals
Across mined
Fields
Booby-trapped
Ditches
To discover books
Desks
A place for us   60
How they knew what we
Must know
Without knowing a page
Of it
Themselves.

550

4
THREE DOLLARS CASH

Three dollars cash
For a pair of catalog shoes
Was what the midwife charged
My mama
For bringing me.   70
"We wasn't so country then," says Mom,
"You being the last one—
And we couldn't, like
We done
When she brought your
Brother,
Send her out to the
Pen
And let her pick
Out   80
A pig."

5
YOU HAD TO GO
TO FUNERALS

You had to go to funerals
Even if you didn't know the
People
Your Mama always did
Usually your Pa.
In new patent leather shoes
It wasn't so bad
And if it rained
The graves dropped open   90
And if the sun was shining
You could take some of the
Flowers home
In your pocket
book. At six and seven
The face in the gray box
Is always your daddy's
Old schoolmate
Mowed down before his
Time.   100
You don't even ask
After a while
What makes them lie so
Awfully straight

And still. If there's a picture of
Jesus underneath
The coffin lid
You might, during a boring sermon,
Without shouting or anything,
Wonder who painted it;   110

And how *he* would like
All eternity to stare
It down.

6

They had broken teeth
And billy club scars
But we didn't notice
Or mind
They were uncles.
It was their *job*
To come home every summer   120
From the North
And tell my father
He wasn't no man
And make my mother
Cry and long
For Denver, Jersey City,
Philadelphia.
They were uncles.
Who noticed how
Much   130
They drank
And acted womanish
With they do-rags
We were nieces.
And they were almost
Always good
For a nickel
Sometimes
a dime.

7

THEY TAKE A LITTLE NIP

They take a little nip   140
Now and then
Do the old folks

Now they've moved to
Town
You'll sometimes
See them sitting
Side by side
On the porch

Straightly
As in church   150

Or working diligently
Their small
City stand of
Greens

Serenely pulling
Stalks and branches
Up
Leaving all
The weeds

8
SUNDAY SCHOOL, CIRCA 1950

"Who made you?" was always   160
The question
The answer was always
"God."
Well, there we stood
Three feet high
Heads bowed
Leaning into
Bosoms.

Now
I no longer recall   170
The Catechism
Or brood on the Genesis
Of life
No.

I ponder the exchange
Itself
And salvage mostly
The leaning.

In Uganda
an Early King

In Uganda an early king chose
his wives
from among the straight and lithe
who natural as birds of paradise
and the wild poinsettias
grow

(Did you ever see Uganda women? Dainty
are their fingers
genteel their footsteps on the sand)
and he brought them behind   10
the palace to a place constructed
like a farmer's fattening pen
with slats raised off the ground
and nothing for
an escapable door
he force-fed them bran and milk
until the milk ran down their
chins
off the bulging mounds that filled
their skins   20

their eyes quite disappeared
they grew too fat to stand
but slithered to the hole
that poured their dinner
enormous seals

Because? *He liked fat wives*
they showed him prosperous!
and if they up and burst
or tore their straining skins
across the splintered floor,   30
why, like balloons,
he bought some more.

PHILIP SCHULTZ [1945–   ]

My Guardian
Angel Stein

In our house every floor was a wailing wall
& each sideward glance a history of insult.
Nightly Grandma bolted the doors believing God

had a personal grievance to settle on our heads.
Not Atreus[1] exactly but we had furies (Uncle Jake
banged the tables demanding respect from fate) & enough

outrage to impress Aristotle[2] with the prophetic unity
of our misfortune. No wonder I hid behind the sofa sketching
demons to identify the faces in my dreams & stayed under

bath water until my lungs split like pomegranate seeds.
Stein arrived one New Year's Eve fresh from a salvation in Budapest.
Nothing in his 6,000 years prepared him for our nightly bacchanal[3]

of immigrant indignity except his stint in the Hundred Years' War
where he lost his eyesight & faith both. This myopic angel knew
everything about calamity (he taught King David the art of hubris

& Moses the price of fame) & quoted Dante to prove others
had it worse. On winter nights we memorized the Dead Sea Scrolls
until I could sleep without a night light & he explained why

the stars appear only at night ("Insomniacs, they study the Torah[4]
all day"). Once I asked him outright, "Stein, why is our house
so unhappy?" Adjusting his rimless glasses, he said: "Boychick,

life is a comedy salted with despair. All humans are disappointed.
Laugh yourself to sleep each night & with luck, pluck & credit cards
you'll beat them at their own game. Catharsis is necessary in this house!"

Ah, Stein, bless your outsized wings & balding pate & while I'm at it
why not bless the imagination's lonely fray with time, which, yes,
like love & family romance, has neither beginning, middle nor end.

1   in Greek legend, king of Mycenae and father of Agamemnon and Menelaus. The
story of the house of Atreus is filled with murder, incest, and revenge.
2   Greek philosopher, 384–322 B.C.
3   revel (from Bacchus, god of wine).
4   the body of wisdom and law contained in Jewish Scripture and other sacred liter-
ature and oral tradition.

JANE KENYON [1945–   ]

November Calf

She calved in the ravine, beside
the green-scummed pond.
Full clouds and mist hung low—
it was unseasonably warm. Steam
rose from her head as she pushed
and called; her cries went out
over the still-lush fields.

First came the front feet, then
the blossom-nose, shell-pink
and glistening; and then the broad
forehead, flopping black ears,
and neck . . . She worked
until the steaming length of him
rushed out onto the ground, then
turned and licked him with her wide
pink tongue. He lifted up his head
and looked around.

The herd pressed close to see, then
frolicked up the bank, flicking
their tails. It looked like revelry.
The farmer set off for the barn,
swinging in a widening arc
a frayed and knotted scrap of rope.

KATHA POLLITT [1949–   ]

Of the Scythians[1]

who came whirling out of the North
like a locust swarm, storm-darkening the sky,
their long hair whipping in the wind like the manes of horses,
no one remembers anything now but I:

how they screamed to the slaughter, as the skirl[2] of a thousand flutes
fashioned from enemies' thighbones shrilled them on.
Naked they rode. We stood by our huts, stunned mute:
gold flashed from each spear, gold glittered on each arm.

1 nomadic people inhabiting Scythia, an ancient region of Eurasia.
2 the shrill, high sound of a bagpipe.

I was a child in the temple. The old priest
hid me in a secret cellar with the images.
Above my head I heard him chant a last
prayer to the god. Since then

I scorn to mix with those who have come after.
Fat farmers, milky scribblers! What do they know
who have never heard the Scythians' terrible laughter
or seen in the wind their glittering wild hair flow?

Turning Thirty

This spring, you'd swear it actually gets dark earlier.
At the elegant new restaurants downtown
your married friends lock glances over the walnut torte:
it's ten o'clock. They have important jobs
and go to bed before midnight. Only you
walking alone up the dazzling avenue
still feel a girl's excitement, for the thousandth time
you enter your life as though for the first time,
as an immigrant enters a huge, mysterious capital:
Paris, New York. So many wide plazas, so many marble addresses!   10
Home, you write feverishly
in all five notebooks at once, then faint into bed
dazed with ambition and too many cigarettes.

Well, what's wrong with that? Nothing, except
really you don't believe wrinkles mean character
and know it's an ominous note
that the Indian skirts flapping on the sidewalk racks
last summer looked so gay you wanted them all
but now are marked clearer than price tags: not for you.
Oh, what were you doing, why weren't you paying attention   20
that piercingly blue day, not a cloud in the sky,
when suddenly "choices"
ceased to mean "infinite possibilities"
and became instead "deciding what to do without"?
No wonder you're happiest now
riding on trains from one lover to the next.
In those black, night-mirrored windows
a wild white face, operatic, still enthralls you:
a romantic heroine,
suspended between lives, suspended between destinations.   30

Woman Asleep on
a Banana Leaf
from a Chinese painting

Who wouldn't want such a bed?
In the heat of the afternoon, in a private shade,
she has hidden herself away
like a long, translucent, emerald-spotted snake
her skin a ripple, her spine
curved against the long green spine of this leaf.
Now let the ladies call from their silk pavilion,
and let Lord X compare someone else's skin
to the petals of peonies and other
appropriate seasonal flowers.
She dreams of skin that is cool and green and secret.
When she wakes up she will be completely happy.

CAROLYN FORCHÉ [1950–   ]

The Colonel

What you have heard is true. I was in his house. His wife carried
a tray of coffee and sugar. His daughter filed her nails, his son went
out for the night. There were daily papers, pet dogs, a pistol on the
cushion beside him. The moon swung bare on its black cord over
the house. On the television was a cop show. It was in English.
Broken bottles were embedded in the walls around the house to
scoop the kneecaps from a man's legs or cut his hands to lace. On
the windows there were gratings like those in liquor stores. We had
dinner, rack of lamb, good wine, a gold bell was on the table for
calling the maid. The maid brought green mangoes, salt, a type of
bread. I was asked how I enjoyed the country. There was a brief
commercial in Spanish. His wife took everything away. There was
some talk then of how difficult it had become to govern. The parrot
said hello on the terrace. The colonel told it to shut up, and pushed
himself from the table. My friend said to me with his eyes: say
nothing. The colonel returned with a sack used to bring groceries
home. He spilled many human ears on the table. They were like
dried peach halves. There is no other way to say this. He took one
of them in his hands, shook it in our faces, dropped it into a water
glass. It came alive there. I am tired of fooling around he said. As
for the rights of anyone, tell your people they can go fuck them-
selves. He swept the ears to the floor with his arm and held the last
of his wine in the air. Something for your poetry, no? he said. Some
of the ears on the floor caught this scrap of his voice. Some of the
ears on the floor were pressed to the ground.

May 1978

GARRETT KAORU HONGO   [1951–   ]

Yellow Light

One arm hooked around the frayed strap
of a tar-black patent-leather purse,
the other cradling something for dinner:
fresh bunches of spinach from a J-Town *yaoya*,[1]
sides of split Spanish mackerel from Alviso's,
maybe a loaf of Langendorf; she steps
off the hissing bus at Olympic and Fig,
begins the three-block climb up the hill,
passing gangs of schoolboys playing war,
Japs against Japs, Chicanas chalking sidewalks   10
with the holy double-yoked crosses of hopscotch,
and the Korean grocer's wife out for a stroll
around this neighborhood of Hawaiian apartments
just starting to steam with cooking
and the anger of young couples coming home
from work, yelling at kids, flicking on
TV sets for the Wednesday Night Fights.

If it were May, hydrangeas and jacaranda
flowers in the streetside trees would be
blooming through the smog of late spring.   20
Wisteria in Masuda's front yard would be
shaking out the long tresses of its purple hair.
Maybe mosquitoes, moths, a few orange butterflies
settling on the lattice of monkey flowers
tangled in chain-link fences by the trash.

But this is October, and Los Angeles
seethes like a billboard under twilight.
From used-car lots and the movie houses uptown,
long silver sticks of light probe the sky.
From the Miracle Mile, whole freeways away,   30
a brilliant fluorescence breaks out
and makes war with the dim squares
of yellow kitchen light winking on
in all the side streets of the Barrio.

She climbs up the two flights of flagstone
stairs to 201-B, the spikes of her high heels
clicking like kitchen knives on a cutting board,
props the groceries against the door,
fishes through memo pads, a compact,
empty packs of chewing gum, and finds her keys.   40

1   greengrocery.

The moon then, cruising from behind
a screen of eucalyptus across the street,
covers everything, everything in sight,
in a heavy light like yellow onions.

Who Among
You Knows the
Essence of Garlic?

Can your foreigner's nose smell mullets
roasting in a glaze of brown bean paste
and sprinkled with novas of sea salt?

Can you hear my grandmother
chant the mushroom's sutra?[1]

Can you hear the papayas crying
as they bleed in porcelain plates?

I'm telling you that the bamboo
slips the long pliant shoots
of its myriad soft tongues   10
into your mouth that is full of oranges.

I'm saying that the silver waterfalls
of bean threads will burst in hot oil
and stain your lips like zinc.

The marbled skin of the blue mackerel
works good for men. The purple oils
from its flesh perfume the tongues of women.

If you swallow them whole, the rice cakes
soaking in a broth of coconut milk and brown sugar
will never leave the bottom of your stomach.   20

Flukes of giant black mushrooms
leap from their murky tubs
and strangle the toes of young carrots.

Broiling chickens ooze grease,
yellow tears of fat collect
and spatter in the smoking pot.

Soft ripe pears, blushing
on the kitchen window sill,
kneel like plump women

1   (a) a precept summarizing Vedic teaching; (b) a discourse of the Buddha.

taking a long, luxurious shampoo,   30
and invite you to bite their hips.

Why not grab basketfuls of steaming noodles,
lush and slick as the hair of a fine lady,
and squeeze?

The shrimps, big as Portuguese thumbs,
stew among cut guavas, red onions,
ginger root, and rosemary in lemon juice,
the palm oil bubbling to the top,
breaking through layers and layers
of shredded coconut and sliced cashews.   40

Who among you knows the essence
of garlic and black lotus root,
of red and green peppers sizzling
among squads of oysters in the skillet,
of crushed ginger, fresh green onions,
and pale-blue rice wine simmering
in the stomach of a big red fish?

Something Whispered
in the Shakuhachi[1]

No one knew the secret of my flutes,
and I laugh now
because some said
I was enlightened.
But the truth is
I'm only a gardener
who before the War
was a dirt farmer and learned
how to grow the bamboo
in ditches next to the fields,   10
how to leave things alone
and let the silt build up
until it was deep enough to stink
bad as night soil, bad
as the long, witch-grey
hair of a ghost.

No secret in that.

My land was no good, rocky,
and so dry I had to sneak
water from the whites,   20

1 Japanese end-blown bamboo flute of Chinese origin.

hacksaw the locks off the chutes at night,
and blame Mexicans, Filipinos,
or else some wicked spirit
of a migrant, murdered in his sleep
by sheriffs and wanting revenge.
Even though they never believed me,
it didn't matter—no witnesses,
and my land was never thick with rice,
only the bamboo
growing lush as old melodies   30
and whispering like brush strokes
against the fine scroll of wind.

I found some string in the shed
or else took a few stalks
and stripped off their skins,
wove the fibers, the floss,
into cords I could bind
around the feet, ankles, and throats
of only the best bamboos.
I used an ice pick for an awl,   40
a fish knife to carve finger holes,
and a scythe to shape the mouthpiece.

I had my flutes.

◆

When the War came,
I told myself I lost nothing.

My land, which was barren,
was not actually mine but leased
(we could not own property)
and the shacks didn't matter.

What did were the power lines nearby   50
and that sabotage was suspected.

What mattered to me
were the flutes I burned
in a small fire
by the bath house.

◆

All through Relocation,
in the desert where they put us,
at night when the stars talked
and the sky came down
and drummed against the mesas,   60

I could hear my flutes
wail like fists of wind
whistling through the barracks.
I came out of Camp,
a blanket slung over my shoulder,
found land next to this swamp,
planted strawberries and beanplants,
planted the dwarf pines and tended them,
got rich enough to quit
and leave things alone,   70
let the ditches clog with silt again
and the bamboo grow thick as history.

                                        ◆

So, when it's bad now,
when I can't remember what's lost
and all I have for the world to take
means nothing,
I go out back of the greenhouse
at the far end of my land
where the grasses go wild
and the arroyos come up   80
with cat's-claw and giant dahlias,
where the children of my neighbors
consult with the wise heads
of sunflowers, huge against the sky,
where the rivers of weather
and the charred ghosts of old melodies
converge to flood my land
and sustain the one thicket
of memory that calls for me
to come and sit   90
among the tall canes
and shape full-throated songs
out of wind, out of bamboo,
out of a voice
that only whispers.

JIMMY SANTIAGO BACA   [1952–   ]

Cloudy Day

It is windy today. A wall of wind crashes against,
windows clunk against, iron frames
as wind swings past broken glass
and seethes, like a frightened cat
in empty spaces of the cellblock.

In the exercise yard
we sat huddled in our prison jackets,
on our haunches against the fence,
and the wind carried our words
over the fence,   10
while the vigilant guard on the tower
held his cap at the sudden gust.

I could see the main tower from where I sat,
and the wind in my face
gave me the feeling I could grasp
the tower like a cornstalk,
and snap it from its roots of rock.

The wind plays it like a flute,
this hollow shoot of rock.
The brim girded with barbwire   20
with a guard sitting there also,
listening intently to the sounds
as clouds cover the sun.

I thought of the day I was coming to prison,
in the back seat of a police car,
hands and ankles chained, the policeman pointed,
    "See that big water tank? The big
    silver one out there, sticking up?
    That's the prison."

And here I am, I cannot believe it.   30
Sometimes it is such a dream, a dream,
where I stand up in the face of the wind,
like now, it blows at my jacket,
and my eyelids flick a little bit,
while I stare disbelieving. . . .

The third day of spring,
and four years later, I can tell you,
how a man can endure, how a man
can become so cruel, how he can die
or become so cold. I can tell you this,   40
I have seen it every day, every day,
and still I am strong enough to love you,
love myself and feel good;
even as the earth shakes and trembles,
and I have not a thing to my name,
I feel as if I have everything, everything.

There Are Black

There are black guards slamming cell gates
on black men,
And brown guards saying hello to brown men
with numbers on their backs,
And white guards laughing with white cons,
and red guards, few, say nothing
to red inmates as they walk by to chow and cells.

There you have it, the little antpile . . .
convicts marching in straight lines, guards flying
on badged wings, permits to sting, to glut themselves
at the cost of secluding themselves from their people . . .
Turning off their minds like watertaps
wrapped in gunnysacks that insulate the pipes
carrying the pale weak water to their hearts.

It gets bad when you see these same guards
carrying buckets of blood out of cells,
see them puking at the smell, the people,
their own people slashing their wrists,
hanging themselves with belts from light outlets;
it gets bad to see them clean up the mess,
carry the blue cold body out under sheets,
and then retake their places in guard cages,
watching their people maul and mangle themselves,

And over this blood-rutted land,
the sun shines, the guards talk of horses and guns,
go to the store and buy new boots,
and the longer they work here the more powerful they become,
taking on the presence of some ancient mummy,
down in the dungeons of prison, a mummy
that will not listen, but has a strange power
in this dark world, to be so utterly disgusting in ignorance,
and yet so proudly command so many men. . . .

And the convicts themselves, at the mummy's
feet, blood-splattered leather, at this one's feet,
they become cobras sucking life out of their brothers,
they fight for rings and money and drugs,
in this pit of pain their teeth bare fangs,
to fight for what morsels they can. . . .

And the other convicts, guilty
of nothing but their born color, guilty of being innocent,
they slowly turn to dust in the nightly winds here,

10

20

30

40

565

flying in the wind back to their farms and cities.
From the gash in their hearts, sand flies up spraying
over houses and through trees,

                      look at the sand blow over this deserted place,
you are looking at them.

GLOSSARY

ACATALECTIC   Not catalectic; not lacking a syllable in the last foot. Acatalectic verse has the full number of syllables required by the pattern of meter. See CATALEXIS, HYPERMETER.

ACCENT (SYNONYM FOR STRESS)   The emphasis given to certain syllables in a line of verse. *Word accent* is the normally spoken pattern of stressed and unstressed syllables. *Rhetorical accent* is the emphasis given to a word because of its importance in a sentence. *Metrical accent* is the stress pattern set up by a regular verse meter. *Wrenched accent*: the meter forces a shift in the normal word accent, as in ballads. *Hovering accent*: it is difficult to decide which of two adjacent syllables should receive greater stress.

ACEPHALOUS   See HEADLESS LINE.

AESTHETICISM (AESTHETIC MOVEMENT)   A literary movement in the nineteenth century whose motto was "art for art's sake." It arose in opposition to the utilitarian doctrine that everything, including art, must be "useful" and contribute to the material progress of society; in practice this ideology had led to cynical materialism and self-righteous middle class morality. Led by Walter Pater and Oscar Wilde, the Aesthetic Movement insisted that art was independent of any didactic end and of any theory of what was morally good or useful. Later, however, the movement deteriorated to interest merely in stylistic polish and unusual subject matter. The term *fin de siècle* ("end of the century"), which had once connoted "Progress," came to connote "decadence." If capitalized, "Decadence" often refers to the Aesthetic Movement itself.

AFFECTIVE FALLACY   In the New Criticism, the alleged error of judging a literary work according to the emotional effect it produces in the reader. *Affect* is the technical term in psychology meaning "feeling or emotion"; it is related to the word *affection*.

ALBA   Provençal, a song by lovers when they part at dawn. In French, *aubade*; German, *Tagelied*.

ALEXANDRINE   In English, a line of iambic hexameter. The line conventionally has a *caesura*, or pause, in the middle, dividing it into symmetrical halves called *hemistiches*:

A needless Alexandrine ends the song
That, like a wounded snake, | | drags its slow length along.
                                              Pope, *An Essay on Criticism*

The Alexandrine has been common in French poetry since the twelfth century, and is used in elevated verse such as the tragedies of Racine. In English, the Spenserian stanza (q.v.) ends with an Alexandrine.

ALLEGORY   An extended metaphor, with subordinate metaphors depending from the main. In allegorical narrative, the literal action evokes another, parallel action composed of ideas. In simple allegory, there is a one-to-one correspondence of literal and abstract meanings.

Many a green isle needs must be
In the deep wide sea of Misery,
Or the mariner, worn and wan,
Never thus could voyage on—
Day and night, and night and day,
Drifting on his weary way . . .
Shelley, "Lines Written Among the Euganean Hills"

Here happiness is a green island, misery is a sea, man is a mariner, and life is a voyage. But allegorical narrative may be a great deal more complicated, with several levels of meaning. In the first book of Spenser's *Faerie Queene*, the Redcross Knight passes through actual adventures. He fights with a real fire-breathing dragon, is seduced by a real woman, suffers actual pain and imprisonment. This is the literal narrative. But at the same time the poem is an allegory of man's spiritual pilgrimage. The Redcross Knight is seeking holiness. In this he is aided by Una (Truth) and misled by Duessa (False Religion) and Archimago (Illusion). Moreover, there is an historical allegory. Redcross is an Englishman; he falls prey to the Church of Rome (the giant Orgoglio); he is rescued by Prince Arthur (the Reformation), and finally weds Una (Anglicanism).

If the story, literally told, pleases as much as the original, and in the same way, to what purpose was the allegory employed? For the function of allegory is not to hide but to reveal, and it is properly used only for that which cannot be said, or so well said, in literal speech. The inner life, and specially the life of love, religion, and spiritual adventure, has therefore always been the field of true allegory; for here there are intangibles which only allegory can fix and reticences which only allegory can overcome.
C. S. Lewis, *The Allegory of Love*, 1936

ALLITERATION (INITIAL RHYME)   Repetition of sounds, usually at the beginning of words.

Hast thou *f*orgot me then, and do I *s*eem
Now in thine eye *s*o *f*oul, once deemed *s*o *f*air
Milton, *Paradise Lost*

Alliteration unifies these lines and emphasizes the alliterated words and their relationships of unity and contrast with each other. *Hidden alliteration* is the repetition of sounds within the words, as the *s* sound above in "Ha*s*t" and "on*c*e."

   Old English poetry was written in *alliterative meter* arranged in tight patterns. Each line was divided by a pause into two verses; the verse-pairs were linked by the alliteration of one or two stressed syllables in the first verse with the first stressed syllable of the second verse. Alliterative meter was characteristic of Middle English prosody also; the patterns, however, were less regular.

A faire felde ful of folke fonde I there bytwene.

William Langland, Piers Plowman

ALLUSION A reference, usually brief, to something outside the literary text itself. In the following example, "three-days personage" refers to Christ:

He does not become a three-days personage,
Imposing his separation,
Calling for pomp.

Stevens, "The Death of a Soldier"

Addison says of the use of allusions:

It is this talent of affecting the imagination that gives an embellishment to good sense, and makes one man's compositions more agreeable than another's. It sets off all writings in general, but it is the very life and highest perfection of poetry. Where it shines in an eminent degree, it has preserved several poems for many ages, that have nothing else to recommend them; and where all the other beauties are present, the work appears dry and insipid, if this single one be wanting. It has something in it like creation; it bestows a kind of existence, and draws up to the reader's view several objects which are not to be found in being. It makes additions to nature, and gives a greater variety to God's works. In a word, it is able to beautify and adorn the most illustrious scenes in the universe, or to fill the mind with more glorious shows and apparitions, than can be found in any part of it.

Addison, The Spectator, 1711–12

AMBIGUITY (MULTIPLE MEANING) The use of language so that more than one interpretation of a word or passage is relevant to the meaning. In the following passage from Paradise Lost, the army of devils is facing the army of angels. The devils have artillery concealed in their ranks and are preparing to use it. Satan, leader of the devils, is speaking:

"Vanguard, to right and left the front unfold;
That all may see who hate us, how we seek
Peace and composure, and with open breast
Stand ready to receive them, if they like
Our overture, and turn not back perverse;
But that I doubt; however, witness Heaven,
Heaven witness thou anon, while we discharge
Freely our part. Ye who appointed stand,
Do as you have in charge, and briefly touch
What we propound, and loud that all may hear."
    So scoffing in ambiguous words, he scarce
Had ended, when . . .

"Discharge," "charge," and "touch" are puns, a form of ambiguity. They contain hidden references to the use of artillery: discharge—to shoot; charge—the load in a gun; touch—to set off gunpowder. The lines

573

That all may see who hate us, how we seek
Peace and composure . . .

are ambiguous, for the devils seek peace by making war. "Turn not back perverse" hints at what will happen to the angels when the artillery hits them, with a pun on *perverse,* meaning both wrongheaded and bowled over. "Propound" is ambiguous; the word sounds like the double thunder of cannon.

In these lines by Dylan Thomas, "grave" is ambiguous, meaning both serious and having to do with death:

I shall not murder
The mankind of her going with a grave truth . . .
      "A Refusal to Mourn the Death, by Fire, of a Child in London"

AMPHIBRACH A metrical foot of three syllables: one weak, one strong, and one weak ($\smile$ ´ $\smile$), as in the word *arrangement.*

AMPHIMACER A metrical foot of three syllables: one strong, one weak, and one strong (´ $\smile$ ´). Also called the cretic foot.

Héar mý lóve, | héar mý práyer . . .
       Plautus, *Curculio* (trans. G. E. Duckworth)

ANACREONTIC VERSE Verse written in the style of Anacreon, a Greek poet of the sixth century B.C., who sang of wine, love, and other pleasures. The regular Anacreontic meter is exemplified in Longfellow's *Hiawatha:*

Ŏn thĕ shóres ŏf | Gítchĕ Gúmĕe . . .

ANACRUSIS The addition of one or more unstressed syllables before the first word of a line whose meter normally begins with a stress, as in the second line of the following:

When the stars threw down their spears,
And watered heaven with their tears,
Did he smile his work to see?
        Blake, "The Tiger"

ANALOGY A comparison of two like relationships, e.g., the relationship of man to God is compared to the relationship of a child to his father. For an analogy in verse, see CONCEIT, the lines quoted from Donne's "A Valediction: Forbidding Mourning." Loosely, *analogy* may mean any similarity between things.

ANAPEST, ANAPESTIC A metrical foot of three syllables, with two weak stresses and one strong thus: $\smile$ $\smile$ ´. See also METER and RISING METER.

ANTISTROPHE See ODE.

APOCAPATED RHYME See RHYME.

APOLLO The Greek god of poetry—also of medicine, archery, light, youth, prophecy, and music, especially the lyre. *Apollonian* connotes a sense of classical order, moderation, reason, and culture. See DIONYSUS.

APOSTROPHE A figure of speech in which an absent person, or a personification, is addressed.

574

Come, seeling night,
Scarf up the tender eye of pitiful day.

Shakespeare, Macbeth

APPROXIMATE RHYME See RHYME.

ARCADIA, ARCADY A mountainous region of Greece which became, in the conventions of pastoral poetry, the symbol of a retreat from the complexities of the real world to a simple, happy, and uncorrupted world of singing shepherds. See PASTORAL.

ARCHAISM A word, expression, or spelling that is obsolete.

ARGUMENT OF A POEM The plot or sequence of ideas that is the poem's intellectual substructure.

ASSOCIATION A process of thinking in which a given work or image recalls, suggests, or connotes certain other images or emotions.

ASSONANCE Repetition of vowel sounds preceded and followed by different consonant sounds, as in "*time*" and "*mind*." Assonance may be described loosely as a resemblance of vowel sounds.

ATMOSPHERE The emotional setting in which a fictive world exists—its mood, as perceived by the reader: calm, humorous, mysterious, sinister, oppressive, etc.

AUBADE See ALBA.

AUGUSTAN AGE In Roman literature, the period of the reign of Caesar Augustus (27 B.C.–14 A.D.), which included the classical authors Ovid, Horace, and Virgil. In English literature, the term is applied to the early eighteenth century, when the authors Pope, Swift, Addison, and Steele were writing. Cf. CLASSICAL and NEOCLASSICAL.

BALLAD A narrative poem, originally intended to be sung. The story is told in compact dramatic scenes, with simple dialogue and concrete imagery, and often a refrain. A *folk*, or *popular ballad*, is an anonymous communal creation transmitted orally from one person to another, and therefore may exist in more than one version. See "Sir Patrick Spens," "Thomas the Rhymer," and "Edward, Edward," pp. 49–53. A *literary ballad* is a ballad written by a single author in deliberate imitation of the folk ballad. Coleridge's "Rime of the Ancient Mariner" (pp. 195–211) and Keats's "La Belle Dame Sans Merci" are well-known literary ballads (pp. 233–234). See also Elizabeth Bishop's "The Burglars of Babylon" (pp. 427–432) for a modern example.

BALLAD STANZA A quatrain that alternates tetrameter with trimeter lines, and usually rhymes *a b c b*.

The very deep did rot: O Christ!
That ever this should be!
Yea, slimy things did crawl with legs
Upon the slimy sea.

Coleridge, "The Rime of the Ancient Mariner"

BALLADE A fixed verse form having three identically rhymed 8- or 10-line stanzas and an envoy, whose refrain (*R*) is the same as that of each stanza.

575

(Rhyme scheme is *a b a b b c b R* in the octaves and *b c b R* in the envoy; or it is *a b a b b c d c R* in the 10-line stanzas and *c c d c R* in the envoy.) A *double ballade* has six regular stanzas but often no envoy. Ballades are more common in French than in English, and in English are usually employed for light verse.

BARD Originally, a Celtic minstrel-poet who entertained warriors by singing of their feats; later, any poet.

BATHOS (SINKING) A sudden and unintentional descent from the exalted in style and content to the ridiculous, often because the author is straining for sublimity.

> The Eternal heard, and from the heavenly quire
>   Chose out the cherub with the flaming sword,
> And bad him swiftly drive the approaching fire
>   From where our naval magazines were stored.
> Dryden, "Annus Mirabilis"

>   Hast thou then survived—
> Mild offspring of infirm humanity,
> Meek infant! among all forlornest things
> The most forlorn—one life of that bright star,
> The second glory of the Heavens?—Thou hast.
> Wordsworth, "Address to My Infant Daughter"

Bathos may simply mean language that is flat, dismal, or ridiculous.

> "Lord Byron" was an Englishman
>   A poet I believe,
> His first works in old England
>   Was poorly received.
> Perhaps it was "Lord Byron's" fault
>   And perhaps it was not.
> His life was full of misfortunes,
>   Ah, strange was his lot.
> Julia Moore (the Sweet Singer of Michigan), "Lord Byron's Life"

This last is bathos, but not sinking, for the Sweet Singer was sunk from the start. And whenever the subject comes up, someone will quote McGonagall. Everyone has a favorite passage from McGonagall—this is mine:

> Oh! ill-fated Bridge of the Silv'ry Tay,
> I must now conclude my lay
> By telling the world fearlessly without the least dismay,
> That your central girders would not have given way,
> At least many sensible men do say,
> Had they been supported on each side with buttresses,
> At least many sensible men confesses,
> For the stronger we our houses do build,
> The less chance we have of being killed.
> William McGonagall, "The Tay Bridge Disaster"

BEAST EPIC   A related series of tales (*beast fables*) about animals with human characteristics. The medieval beast epic was often an allegory aimed at social satire, in which Reynard the Fox could be interpreted as the Church, Noble the Lion as the king, and Ysengrim the Wolf as the aristocracy. Chauntecleer the Cock was a favorite character. The genre is as old as Aesop's fables of the sixth century B.C. See "The Animals Sick of the Plague," pp. 363–365.

BEAT POETRY   A kind of verse first written in the United States in the late 1950s. Originally *beat* may have meant "worn out," "exhausted"; it has also been said to mean "beatific." The most famous of the Beats (Beat poets) was Allen Ginsberg, whose *Howl* epitomized attitudes and techniques of the movement. Beat poetry is usually written in free verse. The language is slangy. The poet writes about personal habits, friends, experiences of sex, use of hallucinatory drugs. Frequently the beat writer expresses dislike for middle class ("square") people.

BEAUTY

The sense of beauty is intuitive, and beauty itself is all that inspires pleasure without, and aloof from, and even contrarily to, interest.

Coleridge, *Biographia Literaria*

What the imagination seizes as Beauty must be truth—whether it existed before or not—for I have the same Idea of all our passions as of Love; they are all in their sublime, creative of essential Beauty.

Keats, Letter to Benjamin Bailey

BESTIARY   A medieval collection of descriptions of animals, real and fictitious, which allegorized Christian doctrines; e.g., the phoenix, a legendary bird that rises anew from the ashes of its pyre, represents the immortal soul, and the unicorn is a metaphor for Christ.

BLANK VERSE   Unrhymed iambic pentameter. After its introduction by Surrey in the sixteenth century, blank verse was widely used in the drama. Later it was used for nondramatic poetry. The tradition includes the drama of Marlowe and Shakespeare, Milton's *Paradise Lost*, Wordsworth's *The Prelude*, and some of Browning's dramatic monologues.

But, soft! What light through yonder window breaks?
It is the east, and Juliet is the sun.

Shakespeare, *Romeo and Juliet*

BOMBAST   Originally, cotton stuffing to make bulges in garments, according to Elizabethan fashion. Bombastic language is pretentious and inflated:

Pistol. I'll see her damned first; to Pluto's damned lake, by this hand, to the infernal deep, with Erebus and tortures vile also.

Shakespeare, *Henry IV*, Part 2

BROKEN RHYME   See RHYME.

BUCOLIC   (1) referring to shepherds. (2) a pastoral poem.

BURLESQUE   Any imitation of other literary works, or of people's actions and attitudes, which aims to amuse and to ridicule by distortion or by incongruity of style and subject. *High burlesque* uses a high style and a low subject. Examples of high burlesque are the *parody* (q.v.), which mocks a specific literary work by applying its style to a trivial subject, and the *mock epic*, or *mock heroic* style, which ridicules a trivial subject by treating it with the high style of the epic, as in Pope's "Rape of the Lock." *Low burlesque*, in contrast, uses a low style with a high subject, as in a *travesty*, which ridicules a specific literary work by treating its dignified subject in a grotesque low style that exaggerates the peculiarities of the original. See also SATIRE.

BYRONIC   Referring to romantic behavior patterned on the attitudes and opinions of Lord Byron. Symptoms include veiled guilt, proud scorn of society, and rhapsodizing about nature.

CACOPHONY   A combination of sounds that is harsh, discordant, or hard to articulate, usually because of clusters of consonants. Cacophony can be used to support meaning.

> Blow, winds, and crack your cheeks! rage! blow!
>
> Shakespeare, *King Lear*

Cf. DISSONANCE.

CADENCE   (Derived from Latin *cadens*, falling.) The rising and falling rhythmic flow of spoken language, resulting from the pattern of stressed and unstressed syllables. See FREE VERSE.

CAESURA   A pause within a line of verse, dictated by speech rhythm rather than meter. In scanning verse, the caesura may be indicated by vertical bars.

> Know then thyself, | | presume not God to scan;
> The proper study of Mankind | | is Man.
>
> Pope, *An Essay on Man*

CANON (and APOCRYPHA)   A canon is a list of an author's works accepted as authentic, e.g., there are thirty-six plays in the canon of Shakespeare. Works doubtfully ascribed to an author are apocrypha.

CANTO   A subdivision of an epic or narrative poem, corresponding to a chapter in a novel.

CANZONE   A Provençal or Italian lyric, sometimes set to music. There are a number of verse forms with different metrical patterns.

CAROL   Originally, a song for a circle dance, as around the Christmas crib in the Middle Ages; later, traditional Christmas songs or drinking songs.

CAROLINE   (Derived from Latin *Carolus*, Charles.) Of the period of King Charles I of England, 1625–1649. See CAVALIER POETS.

CARPE DIEM MOTIF   The Latin words mean "Seize the day." A poetic theme as ancient as Greek and Latin lyrics: make the most of the present.

CATALEXIS (TRUNCATION)   A *catalectic* line omits the final unaccented syllables of the meter.

> Tíger! | Tíger! | búrning | bríght [˘]
> In the forests of the night
>
> Blake, "The Tiger"

See ACATALECTIC.

CAVALIER POETS Seventeenth-century poets who were sympathetic to King Charles I (1625–1649): Herrick, Carew, Suckling, Lovelace, and Waller. Much of their poetry is in the manner of a song: gallant, witty, devil-may-care.

CELTIC RENAISSANCE (IRISH LITERARY REVIVAL) The nationalistic Irish literary movement of the late nineteenth and early twentieth centuries, in which Irish intellectuals and writers asserted their cultural independence from Britain. The aim was for art rooted in the Celtic and Gaelic heritage, or in Irish life, as in the writings of Yeats and Synge.

CHANSON French for "song." *Chanson courtois*: "courtly song." *Chanson de geste*: "song of noble deeds," a type of Old French (eleventh to fourteenth century) epic tale in verse, centered on a legendary or historical hero, such as Charlemagne. The most famous is the *Chanson de Roland*, or *Song of Roland*. *Chanson populaire*: "song of the people."

CHANT ROYAL A French fixed verse form having five stanzas of eleven lines each, rhyming *a b a b c c d d e d R*—*R* being a refrain—and an envoy that rhymes *d d e d R*. Uncommon in English.

CHIASMUS (Derived from Greek *chiazein*, "to mark crosswise.") A rhetorical figure with two syntactically parallel constructions, one of which has the word order reversed:

They fall successive, and successive rise.

CHORIAMB A metrical unit consisting of a trochee (choree) and an iamb ($'\smile\smile'$). Frequent in Greek dramatic choruses and lyric poetry—rare in English.

Ah, thy | snow-coloured hands! | once they were chains, | mighty to bind | me fast.

Swinburne, "Choriambics"

CLASSIC A work generally recognized as being of enduring significance; a model or a standard of excellence.

CLASSICAL Referring to Greek and Roman literature.

CLASSICISM An aesthetic that stresses tradition, convention, form, decorum, balance, restraint, moderation, simplicity, dignity, austerity. These qualities have been thought to be attributes of ancient Greek and Roman culture, but reading Greek or Roman literature, or a little history, will dispel the illusion. See ROMANTICISM.

CLICHÉ A stale, trite figure of speech. As Pope remarked:

Where'er you find "the cooling western breeze,"
In the next line, it "whispers through the trees";
If crystal streams "with pleasing murmurs creep,"
The reader's threatened (not in vain) with "sleep."

An Essay on Criticism

CLOSED COUPLET An end-stopped, rhymed couplet that contains a complete thought.

579

Let such teach others who themselves excel,
And censure freely who have written well.

Pope, *An Essay on Criticism*

COMMONWEALTH (PURITAN INTERREGNUM)   The parliamentary government that controlled England between the execution of Charles I in 1649 and the restoration of Charles II to the throne in 1660.

COMPLAINT   Usually a lyric poem in which the speaker laments the absence or unresponsiveness of his beloved. But poets may complain about anything; for example, Chaucer's "Complaint to his Purse."

COMPLETE RHYME   See RHYME.

CONCEIT   A far-fetched comparison between things seemingly unlike. The *Petrarchan conceit*, as written by the Italian poet Petrarch (1304–1374), was a Platonic idealization—usually the poet's idealization of his mistress. He might compare her to precious stones, artifacts, beautiful birds and animals, flowers, plants, and mythical creatures. The conceits in this passage from Spenser's "Epithalamion," in which he celebrates his marriage to Elizabeth Boyle, are in the manner of Petrarch:

Tell me ye merchants daughters did ye see
So fayre a creature in your towne before,
So sweet, so lovely, and so mild as she,
Adornd with beautyes grace and vertues store,
Her goodly eyes lyke Saphyres shining bright,
Her forehead yvory white,
Her cheekes lyke apples which the sun hath rudded,
Her lips lyke cherryes charming men to byte,
Her brest like to a bowle of creame uncrudded,
Her paps lyke lyllies budded,
Her snowie necke lyke to a marble towre,
And all her body like a pallace fayre,
Ascending uppe with many a stately stayre,
To honors seat and chastities sweet bowre.
Why stand ye still ye virgins in amaze,
Upon her so to gaze,
Whiles ye forget your former lay to sing,
To which the woods did answer and your eccho ring.

Conceits such as these were satirized by Shakespeare:

My mistress' eyes are nothing like the sun;
Coral is far more red than her lips' red;
If snow be white, why then her breasts are dun;
If hairs be wires, black wires grow on her head.

Metaphysical conceits, used by John Donne and his followers, exploited all fields of knowledge for comparisons—theology, astronomy, mythology, history, commerce, geography, metallurgy, alchemy, mathematics, etc. In 1693 Dryden said that John Donne's poetry "affects the metaphysics," or resembles the abstruse terms and arguments of the scholastic philosophers. In his "Life of Cowley" (1777) Dr. Johnson finds in the metaphysical poets "a combination of dissimilar images, or discovery of occult resemblances in things apparently unlike. Of wit, thus defined, they have more than enough. The most heterogeneous ideas are yoked by violence together; nature and art are ransacked for illustrations, comparisons, and allusions; their learning instructs, and their subtilty surprises; but the reader commonly thinks his improvement dearly bought, and, though he sometimes admires, is seldom pleased."

In the nineteenth century the metaphysical poets were neglected. Then, the research of scholars and an essay by T. S. Eliot titled "The Metaphysical Poets" (1921), in which he reviewed H. J. C. Grierson's *Metaphysical Lyrics and Poems of the Seventeenth Century*, roused new interest in these poets. They have had a strong influence on modern poetry, in the kind of verse in which complex ideas and concrete images are important, as in the poems of Eliot himself.

One of the more famous metaphysical conceits is Donne's comparison of two lovers to the legs of a mathematical compass, in "A Valediction: Forbidding Mourning":

If they be two, they are two so
  As stiff twin compasses are two;
Thy soul, the fixed foot, makes no show
  To move, but doth, if th' other do.

And though it in the center sit,
  Yet when the other far doth roam,
It leans and hearkens after it,
  And grows erect, as that comes home.

Such wilt thou be to me, who must
  Like th' other foot, obliquely run;
Thy firmness makes my circle just,
  And makes me end where I begun.

In the following lines, from Crashaw's "Saint Mary Magdalene," metaphysical ingenuity falls into absurdity. The tearful eyes of the repentant Magdalene are described as

    two faithful fountains
Two walking baths, two weeping motions,
Portable and compendious oceans.

Here is a modern metaphysical conceit in Eliot's "The Love Song of J. Alfred Prufrock":

Let us go then, you and I,
When the evening is spread out against the sky
Like a patient etherised upon a table.

CONCRETE   A term applied to language that is full of images (words evoking sense perceptions); to be distinguished from language that is abstract.

Taking the hands of someone you love,
You see they are delicate cages.
                                        Robert Bly, "Taking the Hands"

Down the ravine behind the empty house,
The cowbells follow one another
Into the distances of the afternoon.

James Wright, "Lying in a Hammock on William Duffy's Farm in
Pine Island, Minnesota"

CONCRETE POETRY   Writing in which visual elements contribute essentially to
the effect. A letter of the alphabet may be printed repeatedly, like a pat-
tern in a carpet. A few words may be printed in different combinations.
The outline of the poem may resemble an object—e.g., the seventeenth-
century poems "The Altar" and "Easter Wings" by George Herbert (q.v.)
and the "pattern poem" by Reinhard Döhl, 1965, (see below). Parenthe-
ses may be scattered over the page like bird wings, or there may be splat-
ters of dots. Some critics make a distinction between the concrete poem
and the *shaped poem*: besides having a shape that represents something—
e.g., an altar—the shaped poem has literary elements: significant lan-
guage, meter, rhyme, etc.; concrete poetry, on the other hand, is "the
thing itself," purely a design, without literary attributes. When concrete
poetry consists only of visual elements, it is arguable that it is not poetry
but a form of visual art.

ping pong
    ping pong ping
    pong ping pong
        ping pong

Eugen Gomringer, 1952

pfelApfelApfelApfel
felApfelApfelApfelApfelA
felApfelApfelApfelApfelApfe
ApfelApfelApfelApfelApfelApf
pfelApfelApfelApfelApfelApfel
ApfelApfelApfelApfelApfelApfe
pfelApfelApfelApfelApfelApfelA
ApfelApfelApfelApfelApfelApfe
felApfelApfelApfelApfelApfel
pfelApfelApfelApfelApfelApf
elApfelApfelApfelWurmAp
elApfelApfelApfelApfel
pfelApfelApfelApfel
felApfelApfelA
felApfel

Reinhard Döhl, "Pattern Poem with an Elusive Intruder," 1965

582

Paul de Vree, "April in Paris," 1966

CONNOTATION   The significance of a word beyond its factual, neutral *denotation*; the associations, attitudes, and emotional meanings the word carries to or evokes from the reader by means of implication or suggestion. In the example below, instead of *boat* and *horses*, words with more specific and romantic connotations have been used:

> There is no *frigate* like a book
>   To take us lands away,
> Nor any *coursers* like a page
>   Of prancing poetry.

Emily Dickinson

See DENOTATION.

CONSONANCE   Repetition of consonant sounds where the vowels before the consonants differ, as in "stru*ts*" and "fre*ts*." Consonance may be used as a form of approximate rhyme (see RHYME). Sometimes the word *consonance* is used loosely to describe a repetition of consonant sounds.

CONSONANTAL RHYME.   See RHYME.

CONVENTION   Any generally accepted feature of style or subject matter derived from past usage or custom. Conventions in poetry include rhyme, all stanza forms, genres (such as the pastoral elegy, dramatic monologue, and literary ballad), and stock characters (the epic hero, the languishing lover, and his cruel and beautiful mistress).

COUPLET   A pair of successive lines of verse, especially when they rhyme and are of the same length; a two-line stanza. See CLOSED COUPLET and HEROIC COUPLET.

DACTYL, DACTYLIC   A metrical foot of three syllables, with one strong stress and two weak, thus: ′ ‿ ‿. See also METER and FALLING METER.

DECADENCE   See AESTHETICISM.

DECONSTRUCTION

A label for certain literary critical practices based on the writings of the contemporary French philosopher Jacques Derrida (Dér ree dä), who has tried to demonstrate that any text, however well constructed (as rigorous logical argument and/or as formally perfect literary art), can be "deconstructed" to uncover not more and more accurate meanings but the paradoxes and aporias (puzzles without solutions) inherent in all language. It is impossible for language to be a kind of window or mirror revealing meanings and the realities to which meanings supposedly refer; meanings are not constructed out of precisely definable elements such as syllables, letters, words, and simple ideas, but arise from the contrasts and comparisons among these. *P* differs from *b*; thus, there is a difference betwen *pat* and *bat*. Because of such contrasts and comparisons, there is always some delay or deferral, however brief, in any act of comprehension. Complexity or closeness of meaning usually makes the deferral longer. Derrida has coined the term "differ*a*nce" to refer to the oppositions inherent in the difference and deferral that we call comprehension. (In French, *différer* means "to differ" and "to defer.") "Differ*a*nce" is the basis of meaning; but because the differences and deferrals cannot be measured in absolute units, "differ*a*nce" is also the basis of ambiguity. Sounds blend into each other, letters are sloppily written, ideas combine and become confused both on the page and in the reader's mind.

For Derrida, there is no deconstruction*ism*, no system of theories independent of specific deconstructions of particular texts, nor is *deconstruction* a unique method with its own devices and fields of study. Derrida has "deconstructed" texts in philosophy, linguistics, psychoanalysis and literature, painstakingly applying to them equally their own techniques and those of other disciplines.

Largely through the work of Geoffrey Hartman, J. Hillis Miller, the late Paul de Man, and Harold Bloom, all at Yale, *deconstruction* has enjoyed a great vogue in recent American literary criticism although it is still very controversial. Its adherents see it as having added imagination and philosophical depth to criticism which it has liberated from the austerities of the New Critics and raised to an equal status with literature itself. Its opponents view it as wildly muddled and faddishly obscure. Derrida has had only the barest marginal impact on American philosophy.

Robert Losada

See STRUCTURALISM, POST-STRUCTURALISM, STRUCTURALIST POETICS.

DECORUM   The principle that the style and diction of a literary work should be appropriate to the genre, subject, speaker, audience, and occasion. A high (or grand or elevated) style is required for serious subjects and noble themes and characters in the epic, tragedy, elegy, and ode. A low (or plain) style, closer to everyday speech, may be used for comedy, satire, and lyrics.

Aristotle recommended that tragic poets write what is appropriate and avoid incongruities. Horace, in the *Art of Poetry*, said that a speaker's words should be in accord with his or her station: a slave should speak like a slave, an Assyrian like an Assyrian, and so on. Moreover, comic and tragic themes should never be mingled. These ideas prevailed in the theory of poetry throughout the Renaissance and long after. Neoclassic writers such as Tasso and Mazzoni went further, laying down rules for the epic poem, the dramatic, and the lyric, distinguishing one genre sharply from another and stating what style was appropriate for each. They emphasized propriety, elegance, and correct taste, excluding whatever was vulgar or unconventional.

However, medieval poets had not paid much attention to classical theory, and some Renaissance poets, influenced by the Bible and Christian literature, broke with decorum. They wrote tragical comedies, comical tragedies, histories, romances, naive lyrics, vulgar eclogues. These poets appealed to nature, and decorum has often been assaulted by poets who write out of their "feelings" rather than by rules. In 1800, in the Preface to *Lyrical Ballads*, Wordsworth attacked the decorum of the preceding age, arguing that poetry could be written about "humble and rustic" life, in a "selection of language really used by men."

DENOTATION   The dictionary definition of a word, referring to objects or facts, from which emotion is excluded. See CONNOTATION.

DIBRACH   See PYRRHIC.

DICTION   Choice of words, the vocabulary used in a literary text. The appropriateness of a particular word is determined by its context.

DIDACTIC   With intent to teach, especially to instruct in moral virtues or assert a doctrine or thesis as true, as in *Paradise Lost* where Milton's intent is to "justify the ways of God to men." *Didactic* is a neutral and descriptive, rather than a derogatory, critical term, because didactic works can be imaginative. As well as illustrating truths outside the text, they may be interesting and delightful in themselves. Some didactic poems convey practical information. The Greek poet Hesiod's *Works and Days* includes a farmer's almanac, a description of the work to be done at different seasons, advice on navigation, etc.

DIMETER   A line of two metrical feet, as the fourth line of

Tell me, where is fancy bred,
Or in the heart, or in the head?
How begot, how nourished?
        Reply, reply.

                                                Shakespeare, *The Merchant of Venice*

DIONYSUS   The Greek god of vegetation, vineyards, and wine. *Dionysian* connotes intoxication, ecstasy, frenzy, madness, and the deep irrational source of inspiration for music and poetry. See APOLLO.

DIPODIC VERSE   *Dipody* is Greek for "a combination of two feet." In dipodic verse, two metrical feet must be considered as one unit for scansion. The metrical unit is less the individual foot than a pair of feet, related but slightly different, one foot usually having a stronger stress than the other.

Táffy wăs ă | Welshman,

Táffy wăs ă | thief.

DIRGE (THRENODY)   A lyric poem or song commemorating a death and expressing grief. A *monody* is a dirge sung by one person. Cf. ELEGY.

DISSOCIATION OF SENSIBILITY   A term made famous by T. S. Eliot's use of it in his essay "The Metaphysical Poets" (1921). In the metaphysical poets, according to Eliot, there was an immediate correlation between abstract thought and concrete phenomena. However, in later poets, especially Milton, the poet's thinking process was separated from his or her sense perceptions and, as a result, verse became inflated and its images empty of tangible intellectual application. Metaphors, for example, were merely decorative, instead of embodying thought in images so that the reader could "feel" the thought. "Tennyson and Browning are poets," wrote Eliot, "and they think; but they do not feel their thought as immediately as the odor of a rose. A thought to Donne was an experience . . ."

DISSONANCE   A discord of sounds. It may be intentional or unintentional. Dissonance may be cacophony, harsh and unpleasing, or it may be an interesting variation of sounds. See CACOPHONY.

DISTICH   A couplet.

DISTRIBUTED STRESS   See HOVERING STRESS.

DITHYRAMB   In ancient Greece, an irregular and wildly passionate choral hymn or chant sung in honor of Dionysus at a sacrificial festival; forerunner of Greek tragedy. A highly emotional or wildly lyrical piece of writing may be termed *dithyrambic*.

DOGGEREL   Rhymed verse that is too clumsy to be taken seriously. It is characterized by close-recurring rhymes, monotonous meter, and trivial thoughts. But doggerel can be written intentionally to be comic and humorous, as in Samuel Butler's *Hudibras*:

More peevish, cross, and splenetic
Than dog distract or monkey sick.

DOUBLE RHYME   See RHYME.

DRAMATIC IRONY   See IRONY.

DRAMATIC MONOLOGUE   A poem consisting of words spoken by a fictional character to a silent audience. Sometimes the speaker reveals aspects of his or her own personality of which he or she is unaware. See PERSONA. Also, Robert Browning, "My Last Duchess," p. 250, and T. S. Eliot, "The Love Song of J. Alfred Prufrock," p. 367.

DUPLE METERS   Meters with feet consisting of two syllables. Iambic (⌣´) and trochaic (´⌣) are duple meters. See TRIPLE METERS.

ECLOGUE   A pastoral poem, especially a pastoral dialogue. In modern usage, any verse dialogue where the setting is important.

ELEGIAC QUATRAIN   Four lines of iambic pentameter rhyming *a b a b*.

> How perfect was the calm! it seemed no sleep;
> No mood, which season takes away, or brings:
> I could have fancied that the mighty Deep
> Was even the gentlest of all gentle Things.
>
> Wordsworth, "Elegiac Stanzas"

ELEGY   (Derived from the Greek, *E, E legein!* "To cry woe, woe!") As early as the time of Mimnermus (ca. 630 B.C.) it was the metrical form for love poetry, in couplets of a long dactylic hexameter and a shorter pentameter line. The elegiac meter was also used for martial verse, dirge and lamentation, and occasional poetry of a descriptive or topical sort. The pastoral elegy has an especially rich tradition.

In England in the sixteenth and early seventeenth centuries, the word *elegy* is used for Petrarchan love poems, laments, and essays. The elegies of Donne include witty poems on trivial topics; apparently serious defenses of outrageous propositions; dramatic situations, real or imaginary, in which elements of wit or paradox may be incidentally present (J. B. Leishman). Donne's "Anatomy of the World" (1611) applies the elegy to death—he said, "funeral elegy"—and Milton's "Lycidas" (1637) establishes the elegy as a genre, a lament for the dead.

In current usage the word *elegiac* may mean meditative. Or it may be applied to verse that expresses sorrow over the dead. See the following poems in the anthology: Milton, "Lycidas"; Dryden, "To the Memory of Mr. Oldham"; Johnson, "On the Death of Dr. Robert Levet"; Gray, "Elegy"; Whitman, "When Lilacs Last in the Dooryard Bloom'd"; Hardy, "Drummer Hodge"; Hopkins, "Felix Randal"; Ransom, "Bells for John Whiteside's Daughter"; Roethke, "Elegy for Jane"; Lowell, "For the Union Dead"; Oliver, "Poem for my Father's Ghost."

ELEVATION   Use of a high style or subject; grand or lofty writing.

ELISION   The omission of part of a word (o'er, ne'er), or the dropping of an unaccented syllable to make a line conform to a metrical pattern.

> And yet 'tis almost 'gainst my conscience.
>
> Shakespeare, *Hamlet*

ELIZABETHAN   The period of Queen Elizabeth I (1558–1603), which included Spenser, Sidney, Marlowe, and Shakespeare. The English Renaissance.

ELLIPSIS   Leaving out words that are needed to express a meaning completely.

EMOTIVE LANGUAGE   Language that expresses or evokes feelings and attitudes:

> And my poor fool is hanged! No, no, no life!
> Why should a dog, a horse, a rat, have life,
> And thou no breath at all?
>
> Shakespeare, *King Lear*

Emotive language is contrasted to *referential language*, in which neutral statements are made about facts.

EMPATHY (The equivalent word in German is *Einfuhlung,* meaning "feeling into.") A person's mental identification with an object of perception, imagining how it feels to be inside something that is outside oneself. "If a Sparrow come before my Window, I take part in its existence and pick about the Gravel."—Keats

ENCOMIASTIC VERSE A general term for poems which praise or glorify a person, object, or abstract idea, as Wordsworth's "Ode to Duty."

END RHYME See RHYME.

END-STOPPED LINE One in which the end of a syntactical unit (phrase, clause, or sentence) coincides with the end of the line.

> Good nature and good sense must ever join;
> To err is human, to forgive, divine.
>
> Pope, *An Essay on Criticism*

Cf. RUN-ON LINE.

ENJAMBMENT See RUN-ON LINE.

ENVOY (ENVOI) French for "a sending on the way"; a concluding stanza, dedicating the poem (such as a ballade) to an important person (such as a prince).

> O conquerour of Brutes Albyoun,
> Which that by lyne and free eleccioun
> Been verray kyng, this song to yow I sende;
> And ye, that mowen alle oure harmes amende,
> Have mynde upon my supplicacioun!
>
> Chaucer, "The Complaynt of Chaucer to his Purse"

EPIC A long narrative poem with an exalted style and a heroic theme. Some epics are modeled on Homer's *Iliad* and *Odyssey.*

> Homer has shown in what meter may best be written the deeds of kings and captains, and the sorrows of war.
>
> Horace, *Art of Poetry*

Homeric conventions include the poet's invocation to the Muse for her aid; the poet's asking her an epic question, the answer to which begins the narrative *in medias res*, or in the middle of things; the hero's noble deeds and adventures, such as a descent into the underworld and battles in which the gods (the "machinery") take part; and, throughout the poem, a ceremonial high style with epic similes, catalogues, and processions of characters. Virgil's *Aeneid* and Milton's *Paradise Lost* are in the Homeric tradition.

The word *epic* may also be used to describe heroic narrative poems that do not follow the Homeric conventions—e.g., *Beowulf,* Dante's *Divine Comedy, La Chanson de Roland,* the *Ramayana,* and the *Mahabharata.* (For *mock epic,* see BURLESQUE).

EPIC QUESTION Asked by the writer of an epic to the Muse; the answer reveals what started the action.

Who first seduced them to that foul revolt?
The infernal Serpent; he it was, whose guile,
Stirred up with envy and revenge, deceived
The Mother of Mankind . . .

Milton, *Paradise Lost*

EPIC SIMILE   In epics, an extended comparison in which one or both of the subjects compared are described in elaborate detail, and in which the secondary subject (the vehicle) may be developed beyond its specific likeness to the primary subject (the tenor).

[Satan] stood and called
His Legions, Angel Forms, who lay entranced
Thick as Autumnal Leaves that strow the Brooks
In Vallombrosa, where th' Etrurian shades
High overarched imbower; or scattered sedge
Afloat, when with fierce Winds Orion armed
Hath vexed the Red-Sea Coast, whose waves o'erthrew
Busiris and his Memphian Chivalry,
While with perfidious hatred they pursued
The Sojourners of Goshen, who beheld
From the safe shore thir floating Carcasses
And broken Chariot Wheels; so thick bestrown
Abject and lost lay these, covering the Flood,
Under amazement of thir hideous change.

Milton, *Paradise Lost*

EPIGRAM   A polished, terse, and often witty remark, either in prose or verse. In verse the form is usually a couplet or quatrain, but tone is what distinguishes the epigram, rather than form. In the Renaissance, epigrams were patterned on the satiric examples of Martial and other Roman writers, rather than on Greek epigrams, some of which are delicate lyrics. In England in the seventeenth and eighteenth centuries, when epigrams were fashionable, there was a variety of types: insults, compliments, and pithy sayings. Epigrams may be parts of a poem. Pope's *Essays* are a series of epigrammatic couplets, each of which is a separate, memorable saying:

A little learning is a dangerous thing;
Drink deep, or taste not the Pierian spring . . .

An Essay on Criticism

These epigrams show the range:

A petty Sneaking Knave I knew—
O Mr. Cromek, how do ye do?

William Blake

Stand close around, ye Stygian set,
    With Dirce in one boat conveyed!
Or Charon, seeing, may forget
    That he is old and she a shade.

Walter Savage Landor

589

EPILOGUE   A concluding section, separated from the main body of the literary work.

EPISTLE   A verse epistle is a poem in the form of a letter addressed to a specific person, e.g., Pope's "Epistle to Dr. Arbuthnot."

EPITAPH   Writing that could be placed on a grave, though this may not be done or intended. The epitaph sums up a life; some epitaphs are panegyrics, others are ribald. There are epitaphs that satirize a living person or an institution. Milton's poem on Shakespeare is one kind of epitaph:

What needs my Shakespeare for his honored bones
The labor of an age in piled stones . . .

Ralegh's on Leicester is another:

Here lies the noble Warrior that never blunted sword;
Here lies the noble Courtier that never kept his word;
Here lies his Excellency that governed all the state;
Here lies the Lord of Leicester that all the world did hate.

EPITHALAMION   (Greek, "at the bridal chamber.") A lyric poem, either solemn or ribald, to be sung outside the bridal chamber on the wedding night.

EPITHET   A word or phrase that describes the characteristic quality of a person or thing, as "Ethelred the Unready" or Homer's "wine-faced sea" and "fleet-footed Achilles." A *transferred epithet* is an adjective, word, or phrase that is shifted from the noun it would most obviously modify and applied to an associated but unexpected noun. In Keats's "Ode to a Nightingale," the word *embalmed*, which evokes the closeness of an overwhelming perfume of flowers, is applied to the night itself:

I cannot see what flowers are at my feet,
    Nor what soft incense hangs upon the boughs,
But, in embalmed darkness, guess each sweet
    Wherewith the seasonable month endows
The grass, the thicket, and the fruit-tree wild.

EPODE   See ODE.

EULOGY   A speech or composition in praise of a person or thing, especially a formal poem praising a dead person.

EUPHONY   A combination of sounds that is pleasant, musical, and fluent.

Full fathom five thy father lies;
    Of his bones are coral made;
Those are pearls that were his eyes.

Shakespeare, *The Tempest*

EXACT RHYME   See RHYME.

EXPLICATION   An explanation. Originally, a French classroom technique of line-by-line, word-by-word explanation. To explicate a poem is to make it clear by explaining its meaning.

EYE RHYME   See RHYME.

FABLE   A brief tale in prose or verse, intended to illustrate a moral. The characters are often talking animals, as in Aesop's fables. See "The Animals Sick of the Plague," pp. 363–365.

FABLIAU   (Plural: *fabliaux*.) Earthy, comic, medieval tales in verse or prose, which usually satirized the clergy and middle class morality, and were often obscene. Chaucer's "Miller's Tale" is a *fabliau*.

FALLING METER   Meter in which the movement falls away from the stressed syllable of each foot. The trochee ($'\ \smile$) and the dactyl ($'\ \smile\ \smile$) are falling meters.

FANCY (IMAGINATION)   Fancy is the faculty of arranging ideas and images in pleasant combinations. The creations of fancy are casual, whimsical, and often amusing; they are less profound and exciting than those of *Imagination*, which seems to be discovering new images and ideas. Until the nineteenth century the words Fancy and Imagination were often used to mean the same thing, as in this passage from Edmund Burke's "On Taste," 1757:

Besides the ideas, with their annexed pains and pleasures, which are presented by the sense, the mind of man possesses a sort of creative power of its own; either in representing at pleasure the images of things in the order and manner in which they were received by the senses, or in combining those images in a new manner, and according to a different order. This power is called imagination; and to this belongs whatever is called wit, fancy, invention, and the like. But it must be observed, that this power of the imagination is incapable of producing anything absolutely new; it can only vary the disposition of those ideas which it has received from the senses.

However some writers had begun to distinguish between Fancy and Imagination. Imagination was originality:

Original Genius . . . above all . . . is distinguished by an inventive and plastic Imagination, by which it sketches out a creation of its own, discloses truths that were formerly unknown, and exhibits a succession of scenes and events which were never before contemplated or conceived.
William Duff, *An Essay on Original Genius*, 1767

In 1817 in *Biographia Literaria*, Coleridge differentiated between Fancy and Imagination in these words:

The imagination, then, I consider either as primary, or secondary. The primary imagination I hold to be the living power and prime agent of all human perception, and as a repetition in the finite mind of the eternal act of creation in the infinite I AM. The secondary imagination I consider as an echo of the former, coexisting with the conscious will, yet still as identical with the primary in the *kind* of its agency, and differing only in *degree* and in the *mode* of its operation. It dissolves, diffuses, dissipates, in order to recreate; or where this process is rendered impossible, yet still at all events it struggles to idealize and to unify. It is essentially *vital*, even as all objects (*as* objects) are essentially fixed and dead.

Fancy, on the contrary, has no other counters to play with, but fixities and definites. The fancy is indeed no other than a mode of memory emancipated from the order of time and space; while it is blended with, and modified by that empirical phenomenon of the will, which we express by the word *choice*. But equally with the ordinary memory the fancy must receive all its materials ready made from the law of association.

See IMAGINATION.

FEMININE RHYME.   See RHYME.

FIGURATIVE LANGUAGE   Language that means something more than or other than what it literally says. See TROPE, SIMILE, METAPHOR, METONOMY, SYNECDOCHE, PERSONIFICATION, SYMBOL, ALLEGORY, PARADOX, IRONY, HYPERBOLE, and UNDERSTATEMENT.

FIGURES OF SPEECH   Rhetorical devices that depart from the ordinary meaning of words by arranging the words to achieve special effects. In figurative language, on the other hand, the meaning of the words themselves is radically changed. See APOSTROPHE, CHIASMUS, INVOCATION, RHETORICAL QUESTION, and ZEUGMA.

FIN DE SIÈCLE   See AESTHETICISM.

FIXED FORM   Any of the standard, highly structured arrangements of meter and rhyme patterns that define a poem as a sonnet, or ballade, or villanelle, etc. Other forms are: ballad stanza, double ballade, chant royal, closed couplet, elegiac quatrain, heroic quatrain, ottava rima, rime royal (or Chaucerian stanza), rondeau, rondeau redouble, rondel, rondelet, roundel, sapphic, sestina, Spenserian stanza, terza rima, triolet, and virelay.

FLYTING   An impromptu folk contest in which two contenders heap abuse on each other. This is the model for flytings in verse, such as the dispute between Beowulf and Unferth in the Old English epic *Beowulf*, and "The Flyting of Dunbar and Kennedie."

Quod Kennedy to Dunbar
Dathane devillis sone, and dragon dispitous,
    Abironis birth, and bred with Beliall;
Wod werwolf, worme, and scorpion vennemous . . .

FOLK BALLAD   See BALLAD.

FOOT   A metric unit consisting of one stressed syllable ($'$) and one or more unstressed syllables ($\smile\smile$). For those feet most commonly used in English, see pp. 31–34.

FORMS   Conventional arrangements of meter and rhyme patterns. See FIXED FORM.

FOUND POETRY   A piece of writing that is read as poetry though it was not intended to be. Usually the poem is found in a passage of prose—it may be from a news item, advertisement, handbook, travel book, or catalogue—which is then divided into lines of verse. Most found poems, though not all, are funny—like people at a masquerade.

Rising and Sinking

(from *The Beauties of Nature*, by Sir John Lubbock, F.R.S.)

The Welsh Mountains are older than the Vosges,
The Vosges than the Pyrenees,
The Pyrenees than the Alps,
And the Alps than the Andes.
Scandinavia is rising in the north,
And sinking at the south.
South America is rising on the west
And sinking in the east.
Slow subterranean movements
Are still in progress.

Shirley Kaufman

Order in the Streets

(from instructions printed on a child's toy, Christmas 1968,
as reported in the *New York Times*)

1.2.3.
Switch on.

Jeep rushes
to the scene
of riot.

Jeep goes
in all directions
by mystery action.

Jeep stops periodically
to turn hood over

machine gun appears
with realistic
shooting noise.

After putting down riot,
jeep goes
back to the headquarters.

Donald Justice

FOURTEENER Elizabethan term for heptameter (q.v.)

FREE VERSE (VERS LIBRE) Poetry in which rhythm is based not on strict meter,
but on a highly organized pattern of cadences. See poems by Whitman,
Williams, Lawrence, Pound, H.D., et al.

When this verse was first dictated to me, I consider'd a Monotonous Ca-
dence, like that used by Milton and Shakespeare & all writers of English

Blank Verse, derived from the modern bondage of Rhyming, to be a necessary and indispensible part of Verse. But I soon found that in the mouth of a true Orator such monotony was not only awkward, but as much a bondage as rhyme itself. I therefore have produced a variety in every line, both of cadences and number of syllables. Every word and every letter is studied and put into its fit place; the terrific numbers are reserved for the terrific parts, the mild & gentle for the mild & gentle parts, and the prosaic for inferior parts; all are necessary for each other. Poetry Fetter'd Fetters the Human Race.

William Blake, Jerusalem

See the discussion of free verse, pp. 4–5.

FULL RHYME See RHYME.

GENRE A certain type of literature, distinguished rather by the subject and the way the subject is usually treated than by the technical form. Drama, for example, includes the genres of tragedy, comedy, and melodrama. Poetry includes several major genres and many minor ones: folk and literary ballad, beast epic, burlesque, carol, dirge, dramatic monologue, eclogue, elegy, epic, epistle, epithalamion, hymn, idyll, lampoon, lyric, mock epic, ode, paean, parody, pastoral and pastoral elegy, prothalamion, and song.

GEORGIAN Pertaining to the reign of any king named George, but *Georgian poetry* refers to a kind of verse published in England after 1910, early in the reign of George V. The Georgian poets were collected by Sir Edward Marsh in five anthologies. They derived from the romantics, but though they wrote a great deal about nature, there was little pressure of thought. The best known of the Georgians were John Masefield, W. H. Davies, Ralph Hodgson, Rupert Brooke, and a very fine poet indeed—Walter de la Mare. For a while D. H. Lawrence was counted among the Georgians. But Hardy and Yeats were omitted. When Ezra Pound launched the Imagist movement, he ridiculed the Georgians for their triteness of thought and technique.

GEORGIC A poem about rural life, especially the labor of farming, as in Virgil's *Georgics*; to be distinguished from the pastoral idyll of happy shepherds.

GLOSS An explanation or interpretation of a difficult word or passage in a text, often by means of a footnote.

GNOMIC POETRY Poetry that makes pithy, proverbial statements. A *gnome* is the statement of a truth, an aphorism.

Success is counted sweetest
By those who ne'er succeed.

Emily Dickinson

GOTHIC Characterized by a medieval setting and an atmosphere that is mysterious, frightening, and often supernatural. Gothic influence is apparent in the poetry of the Graveyard School (q.v.) and in Romantic poetry such as Coleridge's "The Rime of the Ancient Mariner"and Byron's "Manfred."

GRAVEYARD SCHOOL A group of mid-eighteenth century poets who wrote mysterious and melancholy poems on death. Unlike their neoclassical contemporaries, they are associated with the Gothic revival, which anticipated the melancholy aspects of the romantic period. Among the poets are Thomas Parnell, Robert Blair, Edward Young, and Thomas Gray, whose "Elegy Written in a Country Churchyard" is the most famous "Grave-yard" poem.

HAIKU (HOKKU) A Japanese verse form of seventeen syllables divided into lines of five syllables, seven, and five. It is a very old form; the earliest extant examples date from the beginning of the thirteenth century. The haiku may be sad or gay, deep or frivolous, religious, humorous, or satirical. Haikus usually give an image that is a starting point for thought and emotion. The scene is only sketched; the reader infers the rest. In nearly all haiku there is a *kigo*, a word or expression that indicates the time of year.

Fallen petals rise
   back to the branch—I watch:
      oh . . . butterflies!

                                    Moritake (1452–1540)

Old pond:
   frog jump-in
      water-sound.

                                      Bashō (1644–1694)

Wild geese! I know
   that they did eat the barley;
      yet, when they go . . .

                                    Yasui (1657–1743)
                          (trans. Harold G. Henderson)

HALF RHYME See RHYME.

HARMONY The principle by which parts are blended into a unified and pleasing whole.

HEAD RHYME See RHYME and ALLITERATION.

HEADLESS LINE (ACEPHALOUS) A line with the first syllable missing, in the strict pattern of the meter. (Gr. *acephalous*, "headless").

Whán | thăt Á | prĭll wĭth | hĭs shŏur | ĕs soóte.

                                    Geoffrey Chaucer

HEMISTICH See ALEXANDRINE.

HEPTAMETER (FOURTEENER, SEPTENARY) A line of fourteen syllables, usually seven iambic feet, commonly used in England in the sixteenth century, especially for narrative. The line divides into the ballad meter of four stresses followed by three.

The God now having laide aside his borrowed shape of Bull,
Had in his likenesse showed himself: And with his pretty trull
Tane landing in the Isle of Crete. When in that while her Sire
Not knowing where she was become, sent after to enquire.

            Ovid, *Metamorphoses*, 1567 (trans. Arthur Golding)

HEROIC COUPLET   Two lines of rhymed iambic pentameter, end-stopped. Especially popular in the eighteenth century.

His fate was destined to a barren strand,
A petty fortress, and a dubious hand.

Johnson, "The Vanity of Human Wishes"

See END-STOPPED LINE and CLOSED COUPLET.

HEROIC QUATRAIN   Four lines of iambic pentameter, rhymed *a b a b*. Synonymous with *elegiac quatrain* (q.v.)

HEXAMETER   A line of six feet, as in the final line of

We look before and after,
    And pine for what is not:
Our sincerest laughter
    With some pain is fraught;
Our sweetest songs are those that tell of saddest thought.

Shelley, "To a Skylark"

See ALEXANDRINE.

HIDDEN ALLITERATION.   See ALLITERATION.

HIGH BURLESQUE.   See BURLESQUE.

HISTORICAL RHYME   See RHYME.

HORATIAN ODE   See ODE.

HOVERING STRESS (DISTRIBUTED STRESS)   In metrics, an accent that could be placed equally well on either of two adjacent syllables, so that it seems to hover between them.

There is sweet music here that softer falls
Than petals from blown roses on the grass . . .

Tennyson, "The Lotus-Eaters"

HUDIBRASTIC VERSE   Octosyllabic couplets in iambic tetrameter, as in Samuel Butler's *Hudibras*.

See DOGGEREL.

HUMOURS   The theory of "humours" is referred to by writers from Chaucer to the seventeenth century. Though the theory may not be stated explicitly, character portraits are frequently based upon it. In Medieval and Renaissance psychology there were four humours, that is, four fluids of the human body, which released their vapors to the brain and thus influenced physical and psychological health. When the four humours were in balance, the person behaved normally, but if one humour became dominant, it stereotyped the personality. Too much blood made the person sanguine: ruddy-faced, cheerful, and amorous. Too much phlegm made one phlegmatic: dull, unresponsive, and cowardly. Too much yellow bile made one choleric: irritable, obstinate, vengeful, and easily aroused to anger. Too much black bile made one melancholic: depressed, brooding, satiric, and gluttonous.

HYMN   From Greek *hymnos*, a song praising heroes or the gods. By extension, a literary hymn is a song of praise, such as Shelley's "Hymn to Intellectual Beauty."

HYPERBOLE   Overstatement or exaggeration for the sake of emphasis. Marvell's lines are hyperbolic:

> My vegetable love should grow
> Vaster than empires and more slow;
> An hundred years should go to praise
> Thine eyes, and on thy forehead gaze . . .
>
> "To His Coy Mistress"

HYPERMETER   In metrics, the addition of one or more unstressed syllables at the beginning or end of a line.

To be, or not to be; that is the ques | tion:

IAMB(US), IAMBIC   A metrical foot of two syllables, with a weak stress followed by a strong, thus: ⌣ ⁄. Iambic is the most common meter in English poetry. See also METER, BLANK VERSE, and RISING METER.

IDENTICAL RHYME   See RHYME.

IDYLL   A short picturesque poem idealizing rural life; the charming pastoral of singing shepherds, as distinguished from the mournful pastoral elegy.

> Come live with me and be my Love,
> And we will all the pleasures prove . . .
> The shepherd swains shall dance and sing
> For thy delight each May morning—
>
> Marlowe, "The Passionate Shepherd to His Love"

See also ARCADIA.

IMAGE   A word or cluster of words that evoke sense-perceptions: sight, hearing, smell, taste, or touch. Poets embody their thought in images, for we can hardly grasp an idea unless we conceive it in physical terms.

  The Imagist poets (see IMAGISM) concentrated on writing in images. In their use of the term, an image was a sense-perception that caused an intuition of some kind. "An 'image,'" said Ezra Pound, "is that which presents an intellectual and emotional complex in an instant of time." He also said, "A poem is an image or a succession of images."

> I am moved by fancies that are curled
> Around these images, and cling . . .
>
> T. S. Eliot, "Preludes"

> The hand that whirls the water in the pool
> Stirs the quicksand; that ropes the blowing wind
> Hauls my shroud sail.
> And I am dumb to tell the hanging man
> How of my clay is made the hangman's lime.
>
> Dylan Thomas, "The Force That Through
> the Green Fuse Drives the Flower"

See IMAGISM, SYMBOLISM, SURREALISM.

IMAGERY   Images considered collectively, as the imagery of light in *Oedipus Rex*.

IMAGINATION

The word is predominantly used in cases where, carried away by enthusiasm and passion, you think you see what you describe, and you place it before the eyes of your hearers.

On the Sublime, traditionally ascribed to Longinus, first or second century A.D.

The poet's eye, in a fine frenzy rolling,
Doth glance from heaven to earth, from earth to heaven;
And, as imagination bodies forth
The forms of things unknown, the poet's pen
Turns them to shapes, and gives to airy nothing
A local habitation and a name.

Shakespeare, *A Midsummer Night's Dream*

The poet . . . brings the whole soul of man into activity. . . . He diffuses a tone and spirit of unity, that blends, and (as it were) *fuses*, each into each, by the synthetic and magical power, to which we have exclusively appropriated the name of imagination. This power . . . reveals itself in the balance or reconciliation of opposite or discordant qualities: of sameness, with difference; of the general, with the concrete; the idea, with the image; the individual, with the representative; the sense of novelty and freshness, with old and familiar objects; a more than usual state of emotion, with more than usual order; judgement ever awake and steady self-possession, with enthusiasm and feeling profound or vehement; and while it blends and harmonizes the natural and the artificial, still subordinates art to nature; the manner to the matter; and our admiration of the poet to our sympathy with the poetry.

Coleridge, *Biographia Literaria*

See FANCY.

IMAGISM   A literary movement that started about 1910, including the critic T. E. Hulme and the poets Ezra Pound, T. S. Eliot, H. D. (Hilda Doolittle), John Gould Fletcher, F. S. Flint, and Richard Aldington. Amy Lowell contributed to the movement until she broke with Pound. Pound says "The tenets of the Imagist faith were published in March 1913 as follows:

1. Direct treatment of the 'thing,' whether subjective or objective.
2. To use absolutely no word that does not contribute to the presentation.
3. As regarding rhythm: to compose in sequence of the musical phrase, not in sequence of the metronome."

Pound's two-line poem "In a Station of the Metro" is often quoted as an example of Imagist writing:

The apparition of these faces in the crowd;
Petals on a wet, black bough.

This poem, Pound says, originated in a ride on the metro, when he saw beautiful faces. They obsessed him, till they became

an equation . . . not in speech, but in little splotches of color. It was just that—a "pattern," or hardly a pattern, if by "pattern" you mean something with a "repeat" in it . . . My experience in Paris should have gone into paint . . . In a poem of this sort one is trying to record the precise instant when a thing outward and objective transforms itself, or darts into a thing inward and subjective.

"Vorticism"

The ideas of the imagists have had a powerful influence on writing in the twentieth century, both verse and prose.

See IMAGE, SURREALISM, and also the discussion of Imagism on pp. 25–27.

IMITATION

The poet being an imitator, like a painter or any other artist, must of necessity imitate one of three objects—things as they were or are, things as they are said or thought to be, or things as they ought to be.

Aristotle, Poetics

As Aristotle used it, mimesis, or "imitation," meant the artistic process of selecting and arranging material in order to show its true significance. Imitation was not, as S. H. Butcher explains, mere copying; it was creation:

"Imitation" in the sense in which Aristotle applies the word to poetry, is equivalent to "producing" or "creating according to a true idea," which forms part of the definition of art in general. The "true idea" for fine art is derived from the εἶδος, the general concept which the intellect spontaneously abstracts from the details of sense. There is an ideal form which is present in each individual phenomenon but imperfectly manifested. This form impresses itself as a sensuous appearance on the mind of the artist; he seeks to give it a more complete expression, to bring to light the ideal which is only half revealed in the world of reality. His distinctive work as an artist consists in stamping the given material with the impress of the form which is universal. . . . "Imitation," so understood, is a creative act.

S. H. Butcher, Aristotle's Theory of Poetry

After Aristotle, other critics have said that poetry originates in "imitation." However, for some of them the word seems to mean not bringing forth the ideal or universal form, but a clever representation of things as they are. Such is the effect of the following statement by Vico:

Children excel in imitation; we observe them generally amuse themselves by imitating what they are able to understand. This axiom shows that the world in its infancy was composed of poetic nations, for poetry is nothing but imitation. . . . all the arts of things necessary, useful, convenient, and even in large part those of human pleasure, were invented in the poetic centuries before the philosophers came . . . the arts are nothing but imitations of nature, poems in a certain way made of things.

Vico, The New Science

The word *imitation* may be used to mean learning from other people. "The Poet," says Ben Jonson, must be able to "convert the substance, or Riches, of another Poet to his owne use" (*Timber*, 1641). And poets write *imitations*—that is, poems modeled on other poems. Johnson's "Vanity of Human Wishes" is an imitation of Juvenal's "Tenth Satire."

IMPERFECT RHYME   See RHYME.

INCREMENTAL REPETITION   A term introduced by Francis B. Gummere in 1907 to describe a device of the ballad: repeating lines with changes in certain words to show a development of the story. See the questions and answers in "Edward, Edward," p. 52.

INITIAL RHYME   See RHYME and ALLITERATION.

INSPIRATION

A man cannot say, "I will compose poetry." The greatest poet even cannot say it; for the mind in creation is as a fading coal, which some invisible influence, like an inconstant wind, awakens to transitory brightness; this power arises from within, like the colour of a flower which fades and changes as it is developed, and the conscious portions of our natures are unprophetic either of its approach or its departure. Could this influence be durable in its original purity and force, it is impossible to predict the greatness of the results; but when composition begins, inspiration is already on the decline, and the most glorious poetry that has ever been communicated to the world is probably a feeble shadow of the original conceptions of the Poet.

Shelley, *A Defense of Poetry*

INTENSITY   Concentration of meaning.

Language is a means of communication. To charge language with meaning to the utmost possible degree, we have . . . the three chief means:

1. throwing the object (fixed or moving) onto the visual imagination.
2. inducing emotional correlations by the sound and rhythm of the speech.
3. inducing both of the effects by stimulating the associations (intellectual or emotional) that have remained in the receiver's consciousness in relation to the actual words or word groups employed . . .

Incompetence will show in the use of too many words.

Pound, *ABC of Reading*

INTENTIONAL FALLACY   In the "new criticism," according to W. K. Wimsatt and M. C. Beardsley, the error of trying to judge a literary work according to the author's statement of his intention in writing it, or according to the known biographical and historical facts surrounding its production.

INTERNAL RHYME   See RHYME.

INTERREGNUM   See COMMONWEALTH.

INVENTION

Invention is nothing other than the natural virtue of an imagination, conceiving the ideas and forms of all things that can be imagined, whether of heaven or of earth, living or inanimate, for the purpose of afterwards representing, describing, imitating; for just as the aim of the orator is to persuade, so that of the poet is to imitate, invent, and represent—things which are, or which may be—in a resemblance to truth.

Ronsard, A Brief on the Art of French Poetry, 1565

INVERSION   (1) reversal of the normal order of words, for emphasis or because the rhyme or meter demands it.

Bird thou never wert.

Shelley, "To a Skylark"

(2) The use of a foot opposite from the one required by the meter. An inverted accent, foot, or stress substitutes a dactyl for an anapest or a trochee for an iamb (and vice versa).

INVOCATION   The poet's appeal to the muse for assistance at the beginning of an epic or other long work.

IRISH LITERARY REVIVAL   See CELTIC RENAISSANCE.

IRONY   A rhetorical device by which a writer implies a discrepancy or an additional meaning that is often contradictory to the literal meaning of his words. In *verbal irony*, the meaning is different from, and usually the opposite of, what is said, as in the words *pure* and *religious* in the anonymous sixteenth-century poem "Of Alphus":

No egg on Friday Alph will eat,
  But drunken will he be
On Friday still. Oh, what a pure
  Religious man is he!

In *dramatic irony*, there is a discrepancy between what a character says and what the author thinks: when Milton's Satan convinces Eve that she should eat the apple, we know that Milton is against it. Dramatic irony also may refer to the additional significance of a character's speech or action to the audience, when they know certain crucial information that he does not. In *irony of situation*, the outcome of a situation is inappropriate, or different from what was expected. In *romantic irony*, the author creates an illusion and then deliberately destroys it by a change of tone, personal comment, or contradicting statement.

ITALIAN SONNET   See SONNET.

JACOBEAN   (From the Latin *Jacobus*, James). The period of King James I (1603–1625). At this time Chapman, Bacon, Drayton, Shakespeare, Jonson, Donne, Tourneur, Webster, Beaumont, and Fletcher were writing, and the King James version of the Bible was made.

KENNING   A metaphorical compound word or phrase used in Old English and Old Norse poetry. The ocean is the "whale-road" or "the foaming fields"; a lord is "dispenser of rings." A kenning may describe complex emotion.

He bade a seaworthy
wave-cutter be fitted out for him; the warrior king
he would seek, he said, over swan's riding.

Beowulf (trans. from the Anglo-Saxon by Michael Alexander)

LAKE POETS   Wordsworth, Coleridge, and Southey were called "the Lake Poets" because they lived in Cumberland, in the Lake District.

LAMENT   A literary work, often a poem, expressing intense grief.

> I am the man that hath seen affliction by the rod of His wrath. . . .
> How is the gold become dim! how is the most fine gold changed! the stones of the sanctuary are poured out in the top of every street.
> The precious sons of Zion, comparable to fine gold, how are they esteemed as earthen pitchers, the work of the hands of the potter!
>
> *The Lamentations of Jeremiah*

LAMPOON   A satirical attack, in verse or prose, upon an individual person, such as Pope's attack on Colley Cibber in *The Dunciad*. Lampoons were common in seventeenth- and eighteenth-century England, until the introduction of libel laws.

LAY   A narrative poem of adventure. In Medieval France the *lai* was written in octosyllabic couplets—a form adopted by Walter Scott in *The Lay of the Last Minstrel* (1805).

LEONINE RHYME   See RHYME.

LIGHT VERSE   Verse written mainly to entertain or amuse. The category includes nonsense verse, limericks, nursery rhymes, witty epigrams, some lyrics, satire, parodies, occasional verse, and *vers de société*.

LIMERICK   An anapestic jingle, used for making jokes; very popular in English.

Requiem

> There was a young belle of old Natchez
> Whose garments were always in patchez.
> When comment arose
> On the state of her clothes,
> She replied, When Ah itchez, Ah scratchez.
>
> Ogden Nash, *Bed Riddance*

LINE   A row of words. In prose the lines run on; in poetry each line ends or breaks where the rhythm dictates. Prose-writers think in sentences, poets think in lines. A line of poetry may be called a verse. See END-STOPPED LINE, RUN-ON LINE.

LINKED RHYME   See RHYME.

LITERALISM   (1) Adherence to the letter, the exact words of the original: "a literal translation." (2) Understanding words only in their strict sense, in a matter-of-fact, unimaginative way.

LITERARY BALLAD   See BALLAD.

LOW BURLESQUE   See BURLESQUE.

LYRE   A musical instrument of ancient Greece, consisting of a sound box (originally a turtle shell), with two curving arms carrying a cross bar (yoke) from which strings were stretched to the body. It was used to accompany the voice in singing and recitation, and became a symbol for music and poetry.

602

. . . the lyre was invented by the Greek Mercury . . . This lyre was given him by Apollo, god of civil light or of the nobility . . . and with this lyre Orpheus, Amphion and other theological poets, who professed knowledge of laws, founded and established the humanity of Greece. . . . the lyre was the union of the cords or forces of the fathers, of which the public force was composed which is called civil authority, which finally put an end to all private force and violence. Hence the law was defined with full propriety by the poets as *lyra regnorum*, "the lyre of kingdoms". . . .

Vico, *The New Science*

LYRIC   In ancient Greece, a poem to be sung or recited accompanied by a lyre. Now, any poem expressing personal emotion rather than describing events. Sonnets, elegies, odes, hymns, etc. are lyric poems.

MACARONIC   Verse consisting of a mixture of languages, especially Latin and a modern language. It began as a burlesque of Medieval sermons in which the monks mixed Latin with the vernacular.

MADRIGAL   A short lyric poem to be sung in several (as many as eight) parts, often with elaborate counterpoint. The theme may be pastoral, satiric, or concerned with love. Writing madrigals was fashionable in England in the last quarter of the sixteenth century.

MASCULINE RHYME   See RHYME.

MEANING   The meaning of a poem is in the form, images, rhythm, and tone, as well as in those ideas which could equally well be expressed in prose. The meaning of a poem is the poem itself. *Four levels of meaning*: a medieval concept, useful for understanding Dante's *Divine Comedy* and other works; in the *Summa Theologica* Thomas Aquinas stated that works should be read for their allegorical, moral, and anagogic meanings as well as their primary, literal meaning:

So far as the things of the Old Law signify the things of the New Law, there is the allegorical sense; so far as the things done in Christ . . . are signs of what we ought to do, there is the moral sense. But so far as they signify what relates to eternal glory, there is the anagogical sense.

MEDIEVAL ROMANCE (METRICAL ROMANCE)   A verse tale of adventure with a courtly background, on themes of loyalty, bravery, honor, and especially love. The romance originated in medieval France. At first, the word was applied to vernacular French, as opposed to Latin, literature; later it came to mean imaginative, as opposed to historical, writing. Critics have distinguished between the romance and the national epic. The romance is less heroic than the epic, more fanciful and sophisticated. The ideal of "courtly love" is essential; the hero undertakes "love service" for his lady and is ennobled by it. Romance cycles are: "The Matter of Britain"—tales of King Arthur and poems derived from Breton lays; "The Matter of Rome"—tales of Alexander, the Trojan war, Thebes, and the Orient; "The Matter of France"—Charlemagne. The best-known romances in English are *Sir Gawain and the Green Knight* and Sir Thomas Malory's *Morte d'Arthur*.

MEIOSIS   See UNDERSTATEMENT.

METAPHOR   An implied comparison, omitting explicit words of comparison such as *like, as, as if,* and *than.* A metaphor is more compressed than a simile, because it identifies two things with each other or substitutes one for the other: "My love is a rose." A *dead metaphor* is one that is no longer recognized as a comparison: "the arm of a chair." A *submerged metaphor* implies, rather than states, one of the two subjects: "my winged heart" implies that "my heart is a bird." In a *mixed metaphor*, the comparison is strikingly disparate: "to take arms against a sea of troubles." See the discussion of metaphor, pp. 1–3.

Tenor and *vehicle* are terms used by I. A. Richards to explain the process of metaphor. If we take the sentence "My love is a rose," the principal subject "my love" would be called the *tenor* (because it is what we are "holding on to" or talking about), and the secondary subject "rose" would be called the *vehicle* (because it carries the weight of the comparison).

METAPHYSICAL CONCEIT   See CONCEIT.

METAPHYSICAL POETS   Seventeenth-century poets whose style of writing had a colloquial tone, tightly knit syntax, irony, devices of wit such as puns and paradoxes, and the farfetched original comparisons called metaphysical conceits. The best-known metaphysical poets are John Donne, Andrew Marvell, John Cleveland, Abraham Cowley, George Herbert, Richard Crashaw, and Henry Vaughan. See CONCEIT, and the discussion of John Donne's "The Sun Rising," pp. 14–18.

METER   The regular recurrence of patterns of accented and unaccented syllables. The basic metrical unit is the foot, which can be iambic, trochaic, anapestic, dactylic, spondaic, or pyrrhic. The number of feet per line is indicated by the terms monometer, dimeter, trimeter, tetrameter, pentameter, hexameter, heptameter, or octameter. (For examples, see individual entries, e.g., IAMBIC, HEXAMETER, etc.) A line of poetry is called a verse, and it is described by naming the kind of feet and the number of them in the line, e.g., "iambic pentameter." *Scansion* is the practice of describing the metrical patterns of a poem. See ACCENT, BLANK VERSE, CADENCE, FOOT, FREE VERSE, QUANTITATIVE VERSE, RHYTHM, SCANSION, SPRUNG RHYTHM, VERSE, and the discussion of meter, pp. 31–34.

METONYMY   A figure of speech in which the thing or idea given to the reader represents some other thing or idea that is closely associated with it. The name of a writer often means "her works," or "his works," as in the statement "I have read all of Shakespeare." "The crown" can mean "the monarch." Metonymy may be *synecdoche* (q.v.), using a part for the whole, as when "horse" is used to mean "cavalry."

METRICAL ACCENT   See ACCENT.

METRICAL ROMANCE   See MEDIEVAL ROMANCE.

MIMESIS   See IMITATION.

MIXED METAPHOR   See METAPHOR.

MOCK EPIC   See BURLESQUE.

MOCK HEROIC STYLE   See BURLESQUE.

MONODY   See DIRGE.

MONOLOGUE   See DRAMATIC MONOLOGUE.

MONOMETER   A line of one metrical foot.

> Thus I
> Passe by
> And die;
> As One,
> Unknown,
> And gon.
>
> Herrick, "Upon His Departure Hence"

MONOSYLLABIC FOOT   A foot of only one syllable:

Díng, | dóng, | béll;

Pússy̆'s | ín thĕ | wéll.

MOTIF   A recurrent image, word, phrase, theme, character, or situation in a work of literature.

MULTIPLE MEANING   See AMBIGUITY.

MUSE   In Greek mythology, any of the nine daughters of Zeus and Mnemosyne, goddess of memory, who were the goddesses presiding over the arts. Clio was the muse of history, Calliope of epic poetry, Erato of love and lyric poetry, Euterpe of music, Melpomene of tragedy, Polyhymnia of songs to the gods, Terpsichore of the dance, Thalia of comedy, and Urania of astronomy. Later "the Muse" came to mean the goddess or power that inspired poets.

MUSICAL DEVICES   A general term for ways of using language that bring out its affinities to music, by the choice and arrangement of accents to form rhythm and meter, or by the choice and arrangement of sounds to form assonance, consonance, alliteration, rhymes, stanza patterns, and refrains.

NARRATIVE   A narrative poem is a poem that tells a story. Narrative poetry may be as simple as a nursery rhyme or as sophisticated as a poem by T. S. Eliot. The subject is vast, for anything that happens may be written in a poem. See ALLEGORY, BALLAD, EPIC, POETRY.

NATURALISM   (1) A kind of art that closely imitates nature. (2) Sometimes used to describe the work of a "nature" poet, such as Wordsworth, who describes country life and scenes. (3) A late nineteenth-century movement in literature, mainly the novel, sometimes described as the extreme form of realism. Its proponents sought to record actual life, documented in scientifically accurate detail, in order to prove that all human actions are determined by heredity and environment. This meant recording dispassionately, even photographically, a "slice of life." However, the slice was usually chosen from the lower class slums, so naturalism had a definite tendency to be sordid as well as deterministic. The major figure of the movement was Emile Zola, who called his technique "naturalism" to distinguish it from the "realism" of Balzac and Flaubert. There are naturalistic influences in the poems of Thomas Hardy, E. A. Robinson, and Edgar Lee Masters.

NATURE *Nature* has been a controlling concept in Western thought since antiquity. In the Middle Ages nature was considered primarily as the entire universe created by God and sustained by Him. Beginning in the Renaissance and culminating in the eighteenth century, *nature* and *nature's laws* were increasingly separated from theological considerations and were emphasized as the universal and necessary foundation of religion, ethics, politics, law, and art. Nature was "One clear, unchanged, and universal light" (Pope, *An Essay on Criticism*).

Here are some basic definitions of *nature* as the word occurs in poetry:

1. The creative and regulative physical power which is conceived of as operating in the material world and as the immediate cause of all its phenomena.

Where Nature shall provide Green Grass,
And fat'ning Clover for their Fare.

Dryden, trans. of Virgil's *Georgic III*, 1697

2. The material world, or its collective objects and phenomena, especially those with which we, as humans, are most directly in contact; frequently the features and products of the earth itself, as contrasted with those of civilization.

But all her shows did Nature yield,
To please and win this pilgrim wise.
He saw the partridge drum in the woods;
He heard the woodcock's evening hymn;
He found the tawny thrushes' broods;
And the shy hawk did wait for him;

Ralph Waldo Emerson, *Woodnotes I*, 1840

3. *The* (or *a*) *state of nature*: (*a*) the moral state natural to humans, as opposed to a state of grace; (*b*) the human condition before the foundation of organized society; (*c*) an uncultivated or undomesticated condition.

Nor think, in NATURE'S STATE they blindly trod;
The state of Nature was the reign of God:
Self-love and Social at her birth began,
Union the bond of all things, and of Man.
Pride then was not; nor Arts, that Pride to aid;
Man walked with beast, joint tenant of the shade;

Pope, *An Essay on Man*

4. The inherent impulse, in humans or animals, by which behavior is determined and controlled.

And smale foweles maken melodye,
That slepen al the nyght with open ye
So priketh hem nature in hir corages . . .
                    Chaucer, *General Prologue to the Canterbury Tales*

Yet do I fear thy nature;
It is too full o' the milk of human kindness
To catch the nearest way.
                                        Shakespeare, *Macbeth*

NEAR RHYME   See RHYME.

NEGATIVE CAPABILITY

Several things dove-tailed in my mind, and at once it struck me what quality went to form a Man of achievement, especially in Literature, and which Shakespeare possessed so enormously—I mean *Negative Capability*, that is, when a man is capable of being in uncertainties, mysteries, doubts, without any irritable reaching after fact and reason—Coleridge, for instance, would let go by a fine isolated verisimilitude caught from the Penetralium of mystery, from being incapable of remaining content with half-knowledge.
                    John Keats, Letter to George and Thomas Keats

NEOCLASSICAL   Referring to a revival of classicism during the Augustan Age in England. See AUGUSTAN AGE.

NEW CRITICISM   A term applied to the writings of the literary critics R. P. Blackmur, Cleanth Brooks, John Crowe Ransom, Allen Tate, Robert Penn Warren, and, with less certainty, to those of Kenneth Burke, T. S. Eliot, William Empson, I. A. Richards, and Yvor Winters. In general, New Critics regard a poem as an object for rigorously empirical, objective analysis (textual criticism). The poem is treated "primarily as poetry and not another thing," without reference to the author's life or intention (the intentional fallacy), to the history of the society in which the author lived, to the traditional genre of the work, or to the effect the work has upon either the reader's emotions (the affective fallacy) or later literary history.

NONSENSE VERSE   A kind of light verse with pleasant, orderly, even jingly sounds, absurd statements, and words that are not in the dictionary. The best-known writers of nonsense verse are Edward Lear and Lewis Carroll. See "By Way of Preface," p. 254 and "Jabberwocky," p. 279.

NUMBER POEM   Numbers arranged so as to make *concrete* or *sound poetry* (q.v.). The author of the numbers printed below says that they were written to be read aloud and that the numbers have no significance beyond their sound value. Each number is to be pronounced separately, e.g., 375 as "three seven five."

```
0  9
0  4 3 1
   1 3 1 3 1 8 5
      0   5
      0   5 5 5
      3 7 5
      0   9
```

OBJECTIVE CORRELATIVE

The only way of expressing emotion in the form of art is by finding an "objective correlative"; in other words, a set of objects, a situation, a chain of events which shall be the formula of that *particular* emotion; such that when the external facts, which must terminate in sensory experience, are given, the emotion is immediately evoked.

T. S. Eliot, "Hamlet and His Problems"

OBJECTIVISTS American poets who were published together in *The "Objectivists" Anthology* (1931) edited by Louis Zukofsky. The group included Charles Reznikoff, George Oppen, Carl Rakosi, and Zukofsky. Lorine Niedecker, who was not in the anthology, must also be included. Their poems were based on Imagism as developed by Ezra Pound in 1912 and the writings of William Carlos Williams. "In my own work," said Williams, "it has always sufficed that the object of my attention be presented without further comment." From this it would appear that he required poetry to be impersonal, but other remarks by Williams indicate that the subjective response of the poet directs the creative process: "you are nature—in action . . . you are to make" ("A Beginning on the Short Story," 1950). Zukofsky says, "You live with the things as they exist and as you sense them and think them . . . put them into a shape that, apart from your having lived it, is now on its own" ("A Note" by Robert Creeley, in Zukofsky, *A 1–12*, 1967). Rakosi says, "How does one make into an object the subjective experience from which a poem is composed? By feeling the experience sincerely: by setting bounds to it and incorporating only those parts which belong together, making it something like a sculpture which one can walk around and examine from all sides and find solid and coherent . . . " ("Scenes from My Life," 1983).

Tamalpais in cloud

Mist over farmlands

Local knowledge
In the heavy hills

The great loose waves move landward
Heavysided in the wind

George Oppen, "A Morality Play: Preface"

OBJECTIVITY   See SUBJECTIVITY.

OBLIQUE RHYME   See RHYME.

OCCASIONAL POEM   A poem written to commemorate a specific event or occasion, e.g., Yeats's "Easter 1916."

OCTAMETER   A line of eight feet. Because of its awkward length, which often breaks into two tetrameters, the line is rare in English. It is used by Tennyson in *Frater Ave atque Vale*:

Row us out from Desenzano, to your Sirmione row!
So they rowed, and there we landed—"O venusta Sirmio!"

OCTAVE   The first eight lines of a Petrarchan sonnet. See SONNET.

OCTET   Synonym for *octave*.

OCTOSYLLABIC COUPLET   A stanza in which each of the two lines contains eight syllables.

ODE   In English, a serious and dignified lyric poem, usually fairly long, with an elaborate stanzaic structure for which there is no conventional fixed form (see Keats, "Ode to Psyche," "Ode to a Nightingale," "Ode on a Grecian Urn," and "To Autumn," pp. 234–240). The Greek poet Pindar modeled his odes on the choric songs of the drama, in which the chorus chanted or sang the *strophe* while dancing to the left, the *antistrophe* while retracing the pattern to the right, and the metrically different *epode* while standing still. The Pindaric or *irregular* ode in English is an imitation of this, having the strophe and antistrophe in a stanzaic form different from that of the epode. The irregular ode was introduced into England by Cowley; it became popular after the Restoration (see Dryden, "A Song for St. Cecilia's Day," p. 145). The Pindaric ode is exalted and enthusiastic. The Horatian ode, modeled on the odes of the Latin poet Horace, is simpler—often one stanzaic pattern throughout—cool and sober (see Marvell, "An Horation Ode Upon Cromwell's Return from Ireland," p. 136).

OFF RHYME   See RHYME.

ONOMATOPOEIA   The use of words that imitate sounds: *bang, buzz, hiss, scratch*.

ORNAMENT   *Poetic ornament* is a critical term—no longer used—for an image, epithet, or figure of speech.

ORPHIC   Resembling the music of Orpheus, who is said to have charmed stones and wild beasts with his lyre. Entrancing, mystic, oracular.

OTTAVA RIMA   A stanza of eight lines of iambic pentameter rhymed *a b a b a b c c*. It was used by the Italian writers of comic epics, Pulci, Berni, and Ariosto. The stanza was introduced into England in the sixteenth century by Wyatt. Byron adopted it for his "Beppo," "The Vision of Judgment," and *Don Juan*:

Yes, Don Alfonso! husband now no more,
  If ever you indeed deserved the name,
Is't worthy of your years?—you have three-score—
  Fifty, or sixty, it is all the same—
Is't wise or fitting, causeless to explore
  For facts against a virtuous woman's fame?
Ungrateful, perjured, barbarous Don Alfonso,
How dare you think your lady would go on so?

OVERSTATEMENT See HYPERBOLE.

OXYMORON A figurative use of language in which a paradox contains a direct contradiction. Milton describes hell as "no light, but rather darkness visible." See PARADOX.

PAEAN A song or hymn of praise, joy, or triumph, originally sung by Greeks in gratitude to Apollo.

PANEGYRIC A formal speech or piece of writing praising someone. Cf. ENCOMIASTIC VERSE, EULOGY.

PANTOUM A Malayan verse form introduced into French and English. It consists of any number of quatrains rhyming *a b a b*, the second and fourth lines of each stanza used as the first and third of the next. In the final stanza, the second and fourth lines are lines three and one of the opening stanza, so that the poem ends with its first line.

PARABLE A short, simple story intended to illustrate a moral lesson. Best known are the parables of Jesus, such as "The Good Samaritan" and "The Prodigal Son." If, instead of human beings, the characters in the parable are abstract qualities, then it is an *allegory* (q.v.); if they are animals, plants, or objects, then it is a *fable* (q.v.).

PARADOX An apparent contradiction that is nevertheless in some sense true and valid, as in the phrases "conspicuous by his absence" and "damn by faint praise." An *oxymoron* (q.v.) combines direct contraries, as in "living death."

PARALLELISM Correspondence of syntactical forms such as phrases, clauses, or sentences, often with repetition of words. Parallelism is particularly useful in free verse, which tends to come to a stop with the thought. The repeated phrase is like a rhyme, pulling the lines forward.

Just as you feel when you look at the river and sky, so I felt,
Just as any of you is one of a living crowd, I was one of a crowd,
Just as you are refreshed by the gladness of the river and the bright flow, I
    was refreshed,
Just as you stand and lean on the rail, yet hurry with the swift current, I
    stood yet was hurried,
Just as you look on the numberless masts of ships and the thick-stemmed
    pipes of steamboats, I looked.
                    Whitman, "Crossing Brooklyn Ferry"

PARAPHRASE A restatement of the idea of a text in words that are different but as close as possible to the meaning of the original. See PROSE PARAPHRASE.

610

PARARHYME   See RHYME.

PARNASSIANS   The *Parnassiens* were French poets, centering on Leconte de Lisle, who began publishing in the 1860s. The characteristics of their verse are "hardness," precision, clarity:

The best work is made
from hard, strong materials,
 obstinately precise—
the line of the poem, onyx, steel.
Théophile Gautier, L'Art (trans. Denise Levertov)

They wrote about history, science, nature, philosophy, and contemporary life, but some Parnassians were chiefly writers of lyrics. Rebelling against the Romantic subjectivity and social concern of Hugo, Vigny, and Lamartine, they wanted poetry to be impersonal, excluding both the personality of the author and any moral or social usefulness. In the latter, they anticipated the Aesthetic Movement, which adopted their motto, "art for art's sake." They revived the older French fixed verse forms, such as the ballade, rondeau, and villanelle. Baudelaire, Heredia, Sully-Prudhomme, François Coppée, Anatole France, and Mallarmé were associated with the movement at one time or another. In England in the 1870s, Austin Dobson, Edmund Gosse, and Andrew Lang imitated the Parnassians in form and style, though not in thought. The English poets were somewhat inhibited by Victorian conventions.

PARNASSUS   A mountain in central Greece, frequented by Apollo and the Muses. Parnassus is 8068 feet high.

PARODY   A form of *burlesque* (q.v.). Literary or critical parody is an imitation of another author's style or a particular work. Through distortion or exaggeration the parodist points out salient features of the original. Parody may be funny, or malicious, or flattering. Lewis Carroll's parody of Wordsworth's "Resolution and Independence" is funny, and also it is acute literary criticism, emphasizing Wordsworth's earnestness, the circumstantiality of the narrative, and the eccentricity of the character. See "Resolution and Independence," p. 182, and "The White Knight's Song," p. 277.

PARTIAL RHYME   See RHYME.

PASTORAL   A genre of poetry, based on classical models, that deals with rustic life, usually with shepherds. The Greek poet Theocritus (third century B.C.) wrote the first pastoral poetry, describing Sicilian shepherds, or *pastors*. After he established the conventions, pastoral became a highly artificial genre based on literary imitation, especially of Theocritus and Virgil. The setting was often *Arcadia*, a perpetual summer of meadows, trees, and flowers where shepherds and shepherdesses, who did no work, had love affairs and composed and sang songs of three major kinds: the *eclogue*, or singing match between two shepherds; the *complaint*, in which a shepherd praises his mistress's beauty and laments her cruelty; and the *pastoral elegy*, in which the shepherd bewails the death of a fellow shepherd. The Renaissance developed the *pastoral romance*—long tales of love and adventure in a pastoral setting—and *pastoral drama*. Shakespeare's *As You Like It* is derived from these. The pastoral world is often presented as simple and uncorrupted, an escape from the complexities and frustration of urban life into peace and the satisfaction of desires. Pastoral may be called *bucolic* or *idyllic*. Christian literature incorporates some features of the pastoral: the minister is the "shepherd" of his "flock," etc.

PASTORAL ELEGY   An elegy that incorporates pastoral conventions, such as representing the poet and the person for whom he mourns as shepherds, invoking the muses and making references to classical myths, having all nature join in mourning for the dead shepherd, asking the nymphs where they were when death took their beloved and why they did not save him, questioning divine justice and lamenting the world's corrupt state, having a procession of mourners and a list of appropriate flowers to deck the hearse, and closing with a tone of peaceful assurance that death leads to a better life. Milton's "Lycidas" (q.v.) and Shelley's "Adonais" are the most famous examples of pastoral elegy in English.

PATHETIC FALLACY   The attribution of human characteristics to inanimate objects, in a way less complete and less formal than full personification:

The one red leaf, the last of its clan,
That dances as often as dance it can.

Coleridge, "Christabel"

The term *pathetic fallacy* is derived from *pathelikos* (Gr. sensitive). John Ruskin introduced the term in 1856. He said that among the people who had the pathetic fallacy were those who felt strongly but reasoned weakly, and those who were inspired. The term has come to have a pejorative sense, describing literature that credits nature with human emotions. However, the objection may not be to the point of view, but to its being expressed awkwardly, for many poets—Wordsworth and Hardy, for example—have written as though nature and the human mind were in sympathy, or were controlled by the same forces. Indeed, this is one of the oldest and most widely held of beliefs.

See NATURE.

PATHOS   The quality in a work of literature which evokes pity, sorrow, or tenderness from the reader. A pathetic situation is often one where the innocent and helpless suffer. Pathos should be distinguished from *bathos* (q.v.) and from *tragedy*.

PAUSE   A moment of hesitation in the rhythm of verse. A pause within a line is called a *caesura* (q.v.). A pause at the end of a line or stanza is called a *metrical pause*. A pause for intensified poetic effect is a *rhetorical pause*. A pause is often used to compensate for a missing syllable.

PEGASUS   In classical mythology, a winged horse that sprang from the blood of Medusa when she was slain by Perseus. With his hoof Pegasus caused the spring Hippocrene, the source of poetry, to well forth on Mount Helicon. Thus Pegasus is associated with the Muses and with poetry.

PENTAMETER A line of five feet:

Rŏugh wínds | dŏ sháke | thĕ dár | lĭng búds | ŏf Máy

Shakespeare, *Sonnet 18*

PERFECT RHYME See RHYME.

PERIPHRASIS (From the Greek *periphrazein*: to speak around.) Circumlocu-
tion. Using a longer phrase or indirect, abstract way of stating ideas or
naming things in place of a shorter and plainer expression. Periphrasis
may be euphemistic—using mild words instead of strong: "passing away"
for "death"—or it may be descriptive, as in Old English *kenning* (q.v.).
Periphrasis easily degenerates into verbosity and a habitual avoidance of
plain speech:

Up springs the lark . . .
Amid the dawning clouds, and from their haunts
Calls up the *tuneful nations* . . .

James Thomson, "Spring," 1728

PERSONA The fictitious narrator imagined by the poet to speak the words of a
poem. The persona is a "voice" or "mask" which should not be confused
with the author's private personality. In "The Love Song of J. Alfred
Prufrock," the speaker is the persona, Prufrock, not T. S. Eliot. In these
lines of Browning's dramatic monologue, "Soliloquy of the Spanish Clois-
ter," the persona is not Robert Browning but a ridiculous monk:

Gr-r-r—there go, my heart's abhorrence!
    Water your damned flowerpots, do!
If hate killed men, Brother Lawrence,
    God's blood, would not mine kill you!

PERSONIFICATION A figurative use of language in which human qualities or
feelings are attributed to nonhuman organisms, inanimate objects, or ab-
stract ideas:

the farm, like a wanderer white
With the dew, come back, the cock on his shoulder.

Dylan Thomas, "Fern Hill"

Personification may be the representation of an abstract quality or
idea by a human figure. It is in this sense that Addison uses the word in
the following passage:

. . . when the Author represents any Passion, Appetite, Virtue or Vice,
under a visible Shape, and makes it a Person or an Actor in his Poem. Of
this Nature are the Descriptions of Hunger and Envy in *Ovid*, of Fame in
Virgil, and of Sin and Death in *Milton*. We find a whole Creation of the
like shadowy Persons in *Spencer* [sic], who had an admirable Talent in
Representations of this kind.

Addison, *The Spectator*, 1711–12

See ALLEGORY, PATHETIC FALLACY.

PETRARCHAN CONCEIT   See CONCEIT.

PETRARCHAN SONNET   See SONNET.

PINDARIC ODE   See ODE.

POET   One who writes poetry. The word is derived from the Greek *poiein*, "to make." The poet is traditionally regarded as a "maker" and the poem as *poiēma*, "something made."

POETIC LICENSE   The liberty taken by poets to depart from fact and to use the language in unconventional ways in order to achieve special effects.

POETICS   The branch of *rhetoric* (q.v.) that has to do with poetry.

POETRY   Many writers have tried to define poetry, describing the aim of poetry, the character of the poet, and how poems are written. Here are a few examples:

All good poets, epic as well as lyric, compose their beautiful poems not by art, but because they are inspired and possessed. . . . the lyric poets are not in their right mind when they are composing their beautiful strains . . . they are simply inspired to utter that to which the Muse impels them . . . God takes away the mind of poets and uses them as his ministers, as he also uses diviners and holy prophets, in order that we who hear them may know them to be speaking not of themselves who utter these priceless words in a state of unconsciousness, but that God himself is the speaker, and that through them He is conversing with us.

Plato, Ion, c. 390 B.C.

The aim of poets is either to be beneficial or to delight, or in their phrases to combine charm and high applicability to life. . . . By at once delighting and teaching the reader, the poet who mixes the sweet with the useful has everybody's approval.

Horace (65–8 B.C.), Epistle to the Pisos (The Art of Poetry)

Roscommon paraphrases this: "A poet should instruct, or please, or both."

The end [of poetry] is the giving of instruction in pleasurable form, for poetry teaches, and does not simply amuse, as some used to think.

Scaliger, Poetics, 1561

The aim of the poet is to imitate, invent, and represent—things which are, or which may be—in a resemblance to truth.

Ronsard, A Brief on the Art of French Poetry, 1565

[The poet] commeth to you with words sent in delightful proportion, either accompanied with, or prepared for the well inchaunting skill of Music; and with a tale forsooth he commeth unto you: with a tale which holdeth children from play, and old men from the chimney corner. And pretending no more, doth intende the winning of the mind from wickednesse to vertue . . .

Sidney, An Apologie for Poetrie, 1595

He is called a *Poet*, not he which writeth in measure only; but that fayneth and formeth a fable, and writes things like the Truth. For, the Fable and Fiction is (as it were) the form and soul of any poetical work, or poem.

Ben Jonson, Timber: or, Discoveries, 1641

Poetry is the spontaneous overflow of powerful feelings: it takes its origin from emotion recollected in tranquillity; the emotion is contemplated till, by a species of reaction, the tranquillity gradually disappears, and an emotion, kindred to that which was before the subject of contemplation, is gradually produced, and does itself actually exist in the mind. In this mood successful composition generally begins, and in a mood similar to this it is carried on; but the emotion, of whatever kind, and in whatever degree, from various causes, is qualified by various pleasures, so that in describing any passions whatsoever, which are voluntarily described, the mind will, upon the whole, be in a state of enjoyment.

Wordsworth, Preface to Lyrical Ballads, 1800

As to the poetical Character itself (I mean that sort of which, if I am any thing, I am a Member; that sort distinguished from the Wordsworthian or egotistical sublime; which is a thing per se and stands alone) it is not itself—it has no self— it is everything and nothing—It has no character— it enjoys light and shade; it lives in gusto, be it foul or fair, high or low, rich or poor, mean or elevated—It has as much delight in conceiving an Iago as an Imogen. What shocks the virtuous philosopher, delights the chameleon Poet. It does no harm from its relish of the dark side of things any more than from its taste for the bright one; because they both end in speculation. A Poet is the most unpoetical of anything in existence; because he has no Identity—he is continually informing and filling some other Body—the Sun, the Moon, the Sea and Men and Women who are creatures of impulse are poetical and have about them an unchangeable attribute—the poet has none; no identity—he is certainly the most unpoetical of all God's Creatures.

Keats, Letter to Richard Woodhouse, 1818

A poem is the very image of life expressed in its eternal truth. . . . A Poet is a nightingale, who sits in darkness and sings to cheer its own solitude with sweet sounds . . . . Poetry is the record of the best and happiest moments of the happiest and best minds. . . . Poetry turns all things to loveliness; it exalts the beauty of that which is most beautiful, and it adds beauty to that which is most deformed. . . . Poets are the hierophants of an unapprehended inspiration; the mirrors of the gigantic shadows which futurity casts upon the present; the words which express what they understand not; the trumpets which sing to battle and feel not what they inspire; the influence which is moved not, but moves. Poets are the unacknowledged legislators of the world.

Shelley, A Defence of Poetry, 1821

I would define, in brief, the Poetry of words as The Rhythmical Creation of Beauty. Its sole arbiter is Taste. With the Intellect or with the Conscience, it has only collateral relations. Unless incidentally, it has no concern whatever either with Duty or with Truth.

Poe, "The Poetic Principle," 1848

Poetry is not magic. In so far as poetry, or any other of the arts, can be said to have an ulterior purpose, it is, by telling the truth, to disenchant and disintoxicate.

Auden, The Dyer's Hand, and Other Essays, 1962

With this idea of poetry, which is about as far removed from Plato's *Ion* as it is possible to get, I'll leave the question.

POPULAR BALLAD   See BALLAD.

POULTER'S MEASURE   Rhymed lines of twelve and fourteen syllables, alternating. Named from the poultryman's practice of giving twelve eggs for the first dozen, fourteen eggs for the second. The meter was used in the sixteenth century by Wyatt, Surrey, and other English poets.

PRE-RAPHAELITE   Referring to the mid-nineteenth-century movement in art and literature known as the Pre-Raphaelite Brotherhood. They turned to the art before Raphael for inspiration, aiming to represent nature in exact detail and to depict uplifting subjects. Of the poets, Dante Gabriel Rossetti was the most famous; his "The Blessed Damozel" has often been anthologized. In 1871, Rossetti was attacked by Robert Buchanan in an article titled "The Fleshly School of Poetry."

PROJECTIVE VERSE   A movement in contemporary American poetry influenced by the work of Ezra Pound and William Carlos Williams. Its practitioners include Charles Olson, Robert Creeley, Robert Duncan, and Denise Levertov. The theories of the school are stated by Charles Olson in an article, "Projective Verse," first published in 1950. Robert Creeley summarizes Olson's ideas as follows:

He outlines . . . the premise of "composition by field" (the value of which William Carlos Williams was to emphasize by reprinting it in part in his own *Autobiography*); and defines a basis for structure in the poem in term of its '*kinetics*' ("the poem itself must, at all points, be a high energy-construct, and, at all points, an energy discharge . . . "), the '*principle*' of its writing (form is never more than an extension of content), and the '*process*' ("ONE PERCEPTION MUST IMMEDIATELY AND DIRECTLY LEAD TO A FURTHER PERCEPTION . . . "). He equally distinguishes between breathing and hearing, as these relate to the line: "And the line comes (I swear it) from the breath, from the breathing of the man who writes, at that moment that he writes . . . "

The New American Poetry, 1960

See Charles Olson, "The Kingfishers," pp. 419–425.

PROSE PARAPHRASE   A restatement in prose of the content of a poem. The use of paraphrase is to help understanding, but the music and images are lost. In fact, the poetry is lost.

PROSE POEM   As the name indicates, a prose poem is writing that has all the qualities of a poem with one exception—it is not written in lines of verse but as prose. In the nineteenth century Baudelaire, Rimbaud, and Mallarmé wrote prose poems. The form has been used by many poets in this century, including Max Jacob, Bertolt Brecht, Juan Ramón Jiménez, and Jorge Luis Borges. Among American poets Kenneth Patchen, Robert Bly,

W. S. Merwin, and Russell Edson have written prose poems. See "The Colonel" by Carolyn Forché, p. 558.

Anywhere Out of the World

Life is a hospital where every patient is obsessed by the desire of changing beds. One would like to suffer opposite the stove, another is sure he would get well beside the window.

It always seems to me that I should be happy anywhere but where I am, and this question of moving is one that I am eternally discussing with my soul.

"Tell me, my soul, poor chilly soul, how would you like to live in Lisbon? It must be warm there, and you would be as blissful as a lizard in the sun. It is a city by the sea; they say that it is built of marble, and that its inhabitants have such a horror of the vegetable kingdom that they tear up all the trees. You see it is a country after my own heart; a country entirely made of mineral and light, and with liquid to reflect them."

My soul does not reply.

"Since you are so fond of being motionless and watching the pageantry of movement, would you like to live in the beatific land of Holland? Perhaps you could enjoy yourself in that country which you have so long admired in paintings on museum walls. What do you say to Rotterdam, you who love forests of masts, and ships that are moored on the doorsteps of houses?"

My soul remains silent.

"Perhaps you would like Batavia better? There, moreover, we should find the wit of Europe wedded to the beauty of the tropics."

Not a word. Can my soul be dead?

"Have you sunk into so deep a stupor that you are happy only in your unhappiness? If that is the case, let us fly to countries that are the counterfeits of Death. I know just the place for us, poor soul. We will pack up our trunks for Torneo. We will go still farther, to the farthest end of the Baltic Sea; still farther from life if possible; we will settle at the Pole. There the sun only obliquely grazes the earth, and the slow alternations of daylight and night abolish variety and increase that other half of nothingness, monotony. There we can take deep baths of darkness, while sometimes for our entertainment, the Aurora Borealis will shoot up its rose-red sheafs like the reflections of the fireworks of hell!"

At last my soul explodes! "Anywhere! Just so it is out of the world!"

Charles Baudelaire, (trans. Louis Varèse)

PROSODY   The systematic, technical study of versification, including meter, rhyme, sound effects, and stanza patterns. *Prosody* has nothing to do with prose. See "Meter, Rhyme, Stanza, and Sound," pp. 31–38.

PROTHALAMION   A poem or song heralding a marriage. Edmund Spenser coined the word and used it as the title of one of his poems.

PSEUDO-STATEMENT   In the writings of I. A. Richards (*Science and Poetry*, 1926), a pseudo-statement is a statement that is "true" though it is contradicted by fact.

A pseudo-statement is "true" if it suits and serves some attitude or links together attitudes which on other grounds are desirable . . . A pseudo-statement is a form of words which is justified entirely by its effect in releasing or organizing our impulses and attitudes (due regard being had for the better or worse organizations of these *inter se*); a statement, on the other hand, is justified by its truth, i.e., its correspondence, in a highly technical sense, with the fact to which it points.

The following are pseudo-statements:

Machines have made their god. They walk or fly.
The towers bend like Magi, mountains weep,
Needles go mad, and metal sheds a tear.

Louis Simpson, "Outward"

PUN   A play on words, use of a word in a context where two or more of its meanings are relevant.

O Nelly Gray! O, Nelly Gray!
   Is this your love so warm?
The love that loves a scarlet coat
   Should be more uniform!

Thomas Hood, "Faithless Nelly Gray"

PURE POETRY   In contrast to didactic poetry, the aim of which is to teach moral or other truth, pure poetry aims only to delight the reader by the beauty of its language, music, and imagery. As words have meanings, however, and reflect the opinions of the author, no poetry can be absolutely *pure*.

PURITAN INTERREGNUM   See COMMONWEALTH.

PURPLE PASSAGE (or PURPLE PATCH)   A passage so heightened in style that it stands out from its context. *Purple* because this was the color of royalty, associated with gorgeous, barbaric courts.

PYRRHIC   Also called *dibrach*. A metrical foot of two unstressed syllables, thus: ˘˘. Because the pyrrhic foot has no stress, it is rarely considered a legitimate foot in modern English scansion.

Nŏr shăll | déath brág | thŏu wăn | dĕr'st ín | hĭs sháde

Prosody is not an exact science. The line could just as well be scanned:

Nór shăll | déath brág | thŏu wán | dĕr'st ĭn | hĭs sháde

QUALITATIVE VERSE   Also called *accentual verse*. Verse in which the metrical system is based on the language's having stressed (or accented) and unstressed (or unaccented) syllables. English verse is qualitative. See QUANTITATIVE VERSE.

QUANTITATIVE VERSE   Verse in which the metrical system is based on the length of time it takes to pronounce the syllables of the language, as in classical Greek and Latin. A long syllable takes twice as much time to pronounce as a short syllable. One long syllable therefore is considered equal to two short ones; the principle of substitution in classical metrics is based on this relationship. A long syllable contains either a long vowel or diphthong, or a short vowel plus two or more consonants. Stress, or accent, is irrelevant in quantitative verse.

QUATRAIN   A four-line stanza.

REALISM   (1) Said to be possessed by a work that closely imitates the details and appearances of real life, especially of commonplace middle or lower class life; often contrasted to *romance*, which invents imaginary worlds. (2) *Literary realism* was a nineteenth-century movement of writers in France, led by Champfleury. At the extreme, literary realism showed the disillusion and determinism of *naturalism* (q.v.).

REFRAIN   A line or lines repeated at regular intervals in a poem, represented by capital R in the rhyme scheme. For example, *a a a R, b b b R, c c c R*. See REPETEND.

REPETEND   A recurring word or phrase. As distinguished from a refrain (q.v.), a repetend is an irregular, or partial rather than complete, repetition. See the following repetends in "The Love Song of J. Alfred Prufrock," p. 367: "Let us go," "there will be time," "I have known," "would it have been worth it."

RESTORATION PERIOD   Dating from the end of the Puritan Commonwealth, in 1660, when the monarchy (Charles II) was restored, until about 1700. John Milton and John Dryden were the major literary figures. Other poets were Marvell, Samuel Butler, and the Earl of Rochester; prose writers, Hobbes, Bunyan, Locke, Newton, Samuel Pepys, and Sir William Temple. The Puritan ban on theater productions was revoked, and playwrights such as Dryden, Etherege, Wycherley, and Congreve wrote comedies and heroic dramas.

RHAPSODY   An unusually intense and irregular poem or piece of prose, ecstatic and enthusiastic. The writer of rhapsodies is called a rhapsodist. However, people who merely recite rhapsodic poems are also called rhapsodists, as in this definition by Scaliger:

While the poet is the imitator of things, the rhapsodist is he who acts out the imitation, and according as the poet represents, the rhapsodist can reproduce.

Poetics

RHETORIC   In the broad sense, the art of persuasion. In the narrow sense, the study of techniques used in public speaking (oratory) and in writing: figures of speech, diction, structure, and rhythm. In the medieval curriculum, grammar, logic, and rhetoric constituted the *trivium* or four-year course of undergraduate study. Music, arithmetic, geometry, and astronomy made up the *quadrivium* or three-year course from the B.A. to M.A. degree. These were the seven liberal arts.

Critics have often tried to distinguish between rhetoric and *poetics*, the theory of making and judging poetry. Aristotle said that the aim of rhetoric was to persuade, the aim of poetry to imitate. In the following stanza, Davies says that it is meter that distinguishes poetry from rhetoric:

For Rhetoric, clothing speech in rich array,
In looser numbers teacheth her to range
With twenty tropes, and turnings every way,
And various figures, and licentious change;
But poetry, with rule and order strange,
So curiously doth move each single pace,
As all is marred if she one foot misplace.

Orchestra

Attempts to distinguish between rhetoric and poetry are not conclusive, however, for rhetoric is a part of poetry.

RHETORICAL ACCENT   See ACCENT.

RHETORICAL FIGURES   See FIGURES OF SPEECH.

RHETORICAL QUESTION   A question asked for effect, to express a thought rather than to find out information.

O, Wind,
If Winter comes, can Spring be far behind?

Shelley, "Ode to the West Wind"

RHYME   The identity or similarity of sound patterns. Rhyme at the end of lines is called *end* or *terminal* rhyme. Rhyme occurring within a line is *internal* rhyme ("I conceive you may use any language you choose to indulge in . . ."). If the word before the caesura rhymes with the concluding words, the rhyme is *leonine* ("Oh! a private buffoon is a light-hearted loon . . . "). The most common rhyme in English is that of the final accented vowels and all following sounds (night—light, heaven—seven, fertility—puerility). This is called *complete, exact, full, perfect, true* rhyme, or *rime suffisante*. A rhyme that is not perfect and has only similarity rather than identity of sound patterns (once—France) can be called *approximate, half, imperfect, near, oblique, off, partial,* or *slant* rhyme. *Assonance, consonance,* and *pararhyme,* are forms of approximate rhyme. In *assonance,* the vowels in the words are identical, while the consonants coming directly before and after the vowels change (time—mind). In *consonance,* or *consonantal* rhyme, the vowels change but the consonant sounds after the vowels are identical—the consonant sounds preceding the vowels may be, but are not necessarily, identical (struts—frets, lives—loves, fleshed—flashed, tigress—progress). If the consonant sounds both before and after the changing vowels are identical (as in lives—loves), consonance may be called *pararhyme.* And *alliteration,* or *initial* or *head* rhyme (forgot—foul—fair), and *hidden alliteration* (hast—once) are sometimes considered variations of rhyme. In *masculine* rhyme, the final syllable is stressed (name—fame, support—retort, roundelay—month of May). In *feminine* rhyme, the stressed syllables are followed by unstressed ones (after—laughter); *double* rhyme rhymes two syllables (double—trouble), and *triple* rhyme—often found in comic verse—rhymes three syllables (intellectual—hen-pecked you all). *Eye* rhyme rhymes only the spellings (cough—bough—though—rough). If an eye rhyme was once pronounced as a true rhyme, it is called a *historical* rhyme. In *identical* rhyme, in contrast, the rhyming words have identical pronunciation but different spelling (to—too—two, their—there), or the same word is used twice with different meanings. This is also called *rime riche*. In *apocapated* rhyme, the final syllable of one of the rhyme words is discounted (mope—ropeless). In *broken* rhyme, one of the rhyming words is completed at the beginning of the next line. In *linked* rhyme, found in early Welsh verse, one of the rhyming words is formed by linking the final syllable of one line to the first sound of the next line:

Dame, at our *door*
*D*rowned, and among our shoals,
Remember us in the roads, the heaven-haven of the Re*ward*
        Gerard Manley Hopkins, "The Wreck of the Deutschland"

RHYME ROYAL   A seven-line stanza of iambic pentameter, having the rhyme scheme *a b a b b c c*. Rhyme royal took its name from James I of England's writing in this stanza, although he was not the first to use it. It is sometimes called the Chaucerian stanza.

Flee from the prees, and dwelle with sothfastness,
   Suffice unto thy good, though it be small;
For hord hath hate, and climbing tikelnesse,
   Prees hath envye, and well blent overall;
Savour no more than thee bihove shall;
   Reule well thyself, that other folk canst rede;
   And trouthe thee shall deliver, it is no drede.
        Geoffrey Chaucer, "Balade de Bon Conseyl"

RHYME SCHEME   The pattern formed by the terminal rhymes of all the lines in a stanza. The rhyming words are assigned letters in the order of their occurrence, and a letter is repeated to show that a later word rhymes with an earlier one. A quatrain, for instance, may have a rhyme scheme of *a b a b*, *a b c b*, or *a a b a*, etc.

RHYTHM   Repetition of stress. Regular rhythm in verse is *meter* (q.v.). Irregular rhythm is *free verse* (q.v.).

Rhythm is a form cut into time.

        Pound, *ABC of Reading*

Rhythm is the entire movement, the flow, the recurrence of stress and unstress that is related to the rhythms of the blood, the rhythms of nature. It involves certainly stress, time, pitch, the texture of the words, the total meaning of the poem.

        Theodore Roethke, "Some Remarks on Rhythm"

RIME   Alternate spelling for rhyme.

RISING METER   Meter in which the movement rises up to the stressed syllable of each foot. The iamb (⌣´) and the anapest (⌣ ⌣´) are rising meters.

ROCKING RHYTHM   A rhythmic effect that occurs when the stressed syllables in a line of verse fall between two unstressed syllables, as with anapestic and dactylic meter.

Believe me if | all those en | dearing young | charms . . .

ROMANTIC PERIOD   In British literature, the period of the late eighteenth and early nineteenth centuries when the poets Burns, Blake, Scott, Wordsworth, Coleridge, Byron, Shelley, and Keats were writing. Among prose writers there were Coleridge, Hazlitt, Lamb, De Quincey, Jane Austen, and Scott. The period is sometimes dated from the outbreak of the French Revolution (1789) to the death of Scott (1832).

ROMANTICISM   An aesthetic that stresses imagination, individualism, the visionary and mysterious, "the spontaneous overflow of powerful feelings." See CLASSICISM, NEOCLASSICAL, ROMANTIC PERIOD.

RONDEAU   A French fixed verse form of three stanzas characterized by the use of a refrain and only two rhymes in the pattern *a a b b a, a a b R, a a b b a R*. The refrain is the first half of the opening line. The lines usually contain eight syllables.

RONDEL (and ROUNDEL)   Both words are derived from the Old French *rondel*, *rond*, meaning "round," and have been used interchangeably. In English *rondel* usually refers to a poem having three stanzas and two rhymes, the rhyme scheme being *A B b a, a b A B, a b b a A (B)*—the capital letters standing for repeated lines. If there are thirteen lines, a refrain is made of the two opening lines, which are repeated as the seventh and eighth lines. If there are fourteen lines, the two-line refrain appears three times.

The *roundel* consists of eleven lines in three stanzas, rhyming *a b a R, b a b, a b a R*—R standing for the refrain. The refrain is made by taking the first word or a phrase from the opening line; if it is a phrase, the refrain usually rhymes with the second line.

RUN-ON LINE (ENJAMBMENT)   A line that completes its grammatical unity and meaning by going into the next line without a pause. Running-on is marked by an absence of punctuation between the lines. The term is also used for carrying-over from one couplet or stanza to the next.

A thing of beauty is a joy for ever:
Its loveliness increases; it will never
Pass into nothingness; but still will keep
A bower quiet for us, and a sleep
Full of sweet dreams, and health, and quiet breathing.

Keats, *Endymion*

See END-STOPPED LINE.

SAPPHIC   A quatrain written in a meter derived from that of the Greek lyric poet Sappho. Each of the first three lines has eleven syllables, of which the fourth and eleventh may be either long or short: $-\ \smile\ |\ -\ \smile\ |\ -\ \smile\ \smile\ |\ -\ \smile\ |\ -\ \smile$. The last line has only five syllables: $-\ \smile\ \smile\ |\ -\ \smile$.

All the night sleep came not upon my eyelids,
Shed not dew, nor shook nor unclosed a feather,
Yet with lips shut close and with eyes of iron,
    Stood and beheld me.

Swinburne, "Sapphics"

SATIRE   Dr. Johnson's definition is probably the best: "a poem in which wickedness or folly is censured." Satire may be Horatian or Juvenalian, after the Roman poet Horace, who was amused at human foibles and gently mocked them, and Juvenal, who attacked vice with severe ridicule. Donne's "Satire IV" is Horatian; Johnson's "Vanity of Human Wishes" is modeled on Juvenal. Frequently the satiric poet feels called upon to justify his or her art, as Pope does in "An Epistle to Dr. Arbuthnot." Satirists present themselves as mild, honest persons who are compelled by the evil around them to speak out. See BURLESQUE.

SCANSION   The process of analyzing the metrical patterns of a poem. To scan a poem, one goes through it line by line marking the accented and unaccented syllables, then grouping them into metrical feet. One identifies the kind of feet, the number of feet per line, and the stanza pattern, if there is one. The stanza pattern is described by noting the rhyme scheme, with each letter followed by a numerical exponent to indicate the number of feet in the line. A ballad stanza, for instance, which alternates tetrameter and trimeter lines, is notated $a^4 b^3 c^4 b^3$. When the formal pattern of the verse is established, it is necessary to see how the rhetorical accents counterpoint with it.

SECONDARY STRESS   An accent on a syllable weaker than the primary stress of a word, but stronger than its unstressed syllables, e.g., the stress on the first syllable of the word $èvocátion$.

SENSIBILITY   In the eighteenth century, sensibility referred to a person's capacity to respond emotionally, even tearfully, to the joy or distress of others, and to respond to beauty. In the twentieth century, sensibility has acquired a meaning closer to sensitivity, referring to a person's capacity for aesthetic understanding and enjoyment.

SENTENTIA   Aphorisms, pointed statements alleging a truth, such as Aristotle's remark that "Education is learning to take pleasure in the right things." Sententious verse aims at instructing rather than giving pleasure. At the worst it is ponderous and trite. Unfortunately, as Northrop Frye says:

> The sententious approach to literature is still the popular one, accounting for the wide appeal of such poems as Kipling's If or Longfellow's Psalm of Life.
> The Well-Tempered Critic, 1963

SENTIMENTALISM   In the eighteenth century, self-conscious indulgence in emotional tenderness, pity, and sympathy—"the sadly pleasing tear," "the luxury of grief," "dear, delicious pain."

SENTIMENTALITY   Emotion in excess of what the occasion requires.

SEPTENARY   Synonym for heptameter (q.v.).

SESTET (also spelled SEXTET)   A six-line poem or stanza. The term often refers to the final six lines of a Petrarchan sonnet. See SONNET.

SESTINA   A French fixed verse form having six unrhymed six-line stanzas with the same terminal words, in different orders, followed by a tercet using three of them, or all six if two are used per line. In the following diagram, each letter represents the terminal word of a line, and each horizontal line of letters represents one stanza:

```
a b c d e f
f a e b d c
c f d a b e
e c b f a d
d e a c f b
b d f e c a
    e c a
```

SHAKESPEAREAN SONNET   See SONNET.

SHAPED POEM   See CONCRETE POETRY.

SIMILE   An expressed comparison, often using the words *like, as, as if, than*:

My luve is *like* a red, red rose.

SINKING   See BATHOS.

SKELTONIC VERSE   Verse in the headlong, quick-rhyming, slapdash manner of John Skelton (1460?–1529).

For though my ryme be ragged,
Tattered and iagged,
Rudely rayne beaten,
Rusty and mothe eaten;
If ye take well therwith,
It hath in it some pyth.

John Skelton, "Colyn Cloute"

SLANT RHYME   See RHYME.

SLASH   See VIRGULE.

SOLILOQUY   In drama (especially Elizabethan), an extended speech by a solitary character expressing inner thoughts aloud to herself or himself and the audience. Hamlet's famous speech beginning "To be or not to be" is a soliloquy.

SONNET   A fixed verse form, having fourteen lines (occasionally twelve or sixteen) of iambic pentameter (in English) with an elaborate rhyme scheme. The *Petrarchan*, or *Italian*, sonnet is divided into an *octave* (or octet) rhyming *a b b a a b b a*, and a *sestet* usually rhyming *c d e c d e* or *c d c d c d*. Between the octet and sestet there is a significant break in meaning, a movement from question to answer, complaint to resolution, cause to effect, etc. The *Shakespearean*, or *English*, sonnet has three quatrains and a final couplet which usually contains an epigrammatic statement of the theme. The rhyme scheme is *a b a b, c d c d, e f e f, g g*, or else *a b b a, c d d c, e f f e, g g*. The *Spenserian*, or "*link*" sonnet rhymes *a b a b, b c b c, c d c d, e e*, and often has no break in meaning between the octave and sestet. Poets have felt free to make their own variations on these traditional forms. See SONNET SEQUENCE.

SONNET SEQUENCE   A series of sonnets by one author. It may have a single theme. See sonnets by Spenser, Sidney, and Shakespeare.

SOUND POETRY   Verse in which sound effects are far more important than imagery or statement. Some *sound poems* have little or no meaning in the ordinary sense of the word; therefore, as with concrete poems (q.v.) in which there are only visual elements, it is arguable that this is not poetry but another form of expression. The following "exclamation poem," according to the author, was written to be shouted aloud. It requires "voice, gesture, and soapbox."

zacoatl!   seascarnal!
        manpoise!
FERNBLEST LANGERS SNORN
    snoflects & nervequil

Neil Mills, 1970

SPENSERIAN STANZA   A nine-line stanza rhymed *a b a b b c b c c*. All of the lines are iambic pentameter, except the final one, which is iambic hexameter, an Alexandrine.

He there does now enjoy eternall rest
And happie ease, which thou dost want and crave,
And further from it daily wanderest:
What if some little paine the passage have.
That makes fraile flesh to feare the bitter wave?
Is not short paine well borne, that brings long ease,
And layes the soule to sleepe in quiet grave?
Sleepe after toyle, port after stormie seas,
Ease after warre, death after life does greatly please.

Spenser, The Faerie Queene

SPONDEE, SPONDAIC   A metrical foot of two syllables, both of which are stressed thus: ′ ′. Spondee cannot be the basic meter of a poem. Rather, it is introduced as a variant or substitute foot, especially for an iamb or trochee. Spondee neither rises nor falls. See also METER.

SPRUNG RHYTHM   A term coined by Gerard Manley Hopkins to describe a kind of rhythm between strict meter and free verse. The verse is measured according to the number of stressed syllables, which may stand alone or be followed by any number of unstressed syllables. The stressed syllables are always considered to begin the feet, so the most common feet in Hopkins' verse are the spondee, dactyl, and trochee. Hopkins pointed out that sprung rhythm is characteristic of common speech, written prose, most music, and nursery rhymes: "Little Jack Horner sat in a corner . . . "

STANZA   A group of lines considered as a unit, forming a division of a poem, and recurring in the same pattern or variations of the pattern. A stanza pattern is determined by the number of lines, the kind of feet and the number of feet per line, and the rhyme scheme. Many stanzaic forms are conventional and have their own names: See FIXED FORM. The common name for a two-line stanza is *couplet*, for a three-line stanza, *tercet*, and for a four-line stanza, *quatrain*. See also SCANSION.

STOCK CHARACTER A familiar, conventional character who appears often in certain kinds of literary works. Stock characters include the epic hero, the knight and his lady, the disconsolate lover and his cruel mistress, the villain, the braggart soldier, the clever servant, the cruel stepmother, the clown or fool, the proud tragic hero, the virtuous heroine, the *femme fatale*, et al.

STOCK EPITHET Frequently repeated lines or phrases, such as occurred in the long, orally recited heroic poems. For example, Homer's "rosy-fingered dawn."

STOCK RESPONSE An unsophisticated reader's predictable emotional reaction to certain stimuli, such as the word *mother* in a poem. Stock responses are like sentimentality in that they suspend judgment and prevent a deeper understanding and enjoyment of poetry.

STOCK SITUATION Stock situations are circumstances that appear frequently in literature: mistaken identities, love triangles, separations of twins by shipwreck, etc.

STREAM OF CONSCIOUSNESS A term coined by William James (*Principles of Psychology*, 1890) to refer to the continuous flow of inner experiences. In literature it refers to a technique of presenting the perceptions, thoughts, and feelings of characters in a narrative. The narrative progresses through psychological association rather than linguistic conventions such as sentences. The term is usually applied to prose fiction—e.g., James Joyce's *Ulysses*—but it might also be applied to the floating consciousness of T. S. Eliot's Prufrock and to parts of *The Waste Land* and Pound's *Cantos*.

STRESS Synonym for *accent*, the emphasis given to certain syllables of words. If a word (usually longer than three syllables) has more than one accented syllable, the heavier accent is called the primary stress, the lighter is the secondary stress, and the other syllables are unstressed.

STROPHE See ODE.

STRUCTURALISM, POST-STRUCTURALISM, STRUCTURALIST POETICS

The generic name for several interpretative methodologies based on the idea of a communicative system as a set of signs and the rules by which these signs may be combined. Meaning is not intrinsic to the signs or even to their combinations, but arises from the systematic interplay of their mutual differences. Such differentiation is the basis of the system. The paradigm system is language as defined by structural linguistics. The Swiss linguist Ferdinand de Saussure distinguished language (*langue*), the abstract system, from speech (*parole*), the individual utterances meaningful within the system. He described the "sign" as a duality: one aspect is the sound (or mark) called the "signifier," while the other is the conceptual referent called the "signified." Current usage replaces "system" with "structure." Structuralism aims to reveal the codes, the symbolic logic as it were, of such structures or systems, all of which are studied as analogous to language.

In France, structuralism has been applied to the ethnology of kinship and myth by Levi-Strauss, to psychoanalysis by Lacan, to literature by

Barthes, and to the whole range of socio-cultural phenomena. Pure structuralist criticism tries to describe how literary texts differ from other writings, but because such differences make the literary text seem "strange" they lead to extra-literary studies of how texts become meaningful. Generally, structuralism tries to make explicit the codes which determine both the text and its interpretation as social products. In Barthes's later work on pop-culture and Foucault's historical studies of the power structures of western society, structuralism took on political implications. Where history and/or politics are involved, structuralism, supposedly neutral and abstract, becomes post-structuralism, although it is often hard to distinguish them.

In America, Culler's *Structuralist Poetics* (1973) became probably the major exposition of literary structuralism in English, although it has been criticized as too purist, avoiding the wider scope of French structuralism and homogenizing its radical implications. Culler proposed a poetics (or theory of literature) which would make explicit the conventions that enable a reader to respond to a literary work as such. Despite numerous structuralist studies of individual works, most American literary theoreticians of this persuasion have been post-structuralists. More recently, the major French influence (even on Culler) has been Derrida's DECONSTRUCTION (q.v.)

Robert Losada

STRUCTURE   The underlying logic or arrangement and movement in a literary text; its skeleton or paraphrasable content. The term *structure* usually refers to the organization of elements other than words. For the latter the term *style* is used. See ARGUMENT and TEXTURE.

STYLE   The choice and arrangement of words, sentences, and larger units in a literary text. The term is very broad and includes consideration of the choices a writer must make about diction, figurative and rhetorical devices, tone, and sound patterns of the language (alliteration, rhyme, meter, etc.). Styles may be classified according to authors (Miltonic, Shakespearean), or periods (classical, Renaissance, romantic), or books (Biblical), or subjects (legal, journalistic). Styles may also be classified as high (or grand), middle, and low (or plain).

SUBJECTIVITY   The quality in a literary work which reveals the author's personality, his or her own feelings and attitudes. Wordsworth's *The Prelude* is subjective because it records the growth of the poet's own mind. Shakespeare's plays, in contrast, are impersonal and objective, for they tell us virtually nothing about the poet's personality. The term may be used to refer to the characters in a work, rather than to the author who created them; Browning's dramatic monologues are subjective in that they reveal the personality of the character, or persona, in the poem. In literary criticism, subjectivity means emphasis on the critic's personal taste and response, "impressionistic" criticism.

SUBLIMITY (THE SUBLIME)

Sublimity is a certain distinction and excellence in expression, and . . . it is from no other source than this that the greatest poets and writers have derived their eminence and gained an immortality of renown. The effect of elevated language upon an audience is not persuasion but transport. At every time and in every way imposing speech, with the spell it throws over us, prevails over that which aims at persuasion and gratification. Our persuasions we can usually control, but the influences of the sublime bring power and irresistible might to bear, and reign supreme over every hearer. . . . Sublimity flashing forth at the right moment scatters everything before it like a thunderbolt. . . . For, as if instinctively, our soul is uplifted by the true sublime; it takes a proud flight, and is filled with joy and vaunting, as though it had itself produced what it has heard.

On the Sublime, traditionally ascribed to Longinus

SUBSTITUTION   See INVERSION.

SURREALISM   A literary and artistic movement vigorous in the 1920s and 1930s, and still productive. Surrealists want to go "beyond" realism (normal perception of the outer world) deep into the inner world of the unconscious mind. Their work often resembles the stark, strange imagery and nonsyntactical narrative of dreams. In general, surrealists are hostile to, or "go beyond," rationality, bourgeois morality, and artistic conventions. The French poet Guillaume Appollinaire invented the word surrealism; André Breton led the movement. Poets who use surrealist techniques include Aragon and Eluard in French, Lorca and Neruda in Spanish, and Dylan Thomas in English. Max Ernst and Salvador Dali are surrealist painters. A *surrealist image* is not so much "the thing perceived" as "anything as it might be perceived." In practice, most surrealist images are merely juxtapositions of objects that have no relationship in the normal world. However, the effective surrealist images are more than this; they seem to be formed by a logic of the subconscious, as things are in dreams.

When the sun is only a drop of sweat
the sound of a bell
the red pearl falling down a vertical needle

Michel Leiris, "Marécage de sommeil"

Surrealist techniques have always existed in verse. Breton remarks that the eighteenth-century poetry of Edward Young, in *Night Thoughts*, was surrealist. The deliberate, intense application of these techniques in the twentieth century has created a kind of literature that seems, in spite of absurdities, original and stimulating. The following poem by the Chilean Pablo Neruda, here printed in its entirety in translation by Angel Flores, describes the art of a surrealist and uses surrealistic techniques:

Ars Poetica
Between shadow and space, between garrisons and maidens,
endowed with singular heart and doleful dreams,
precipitately pale, the forehead withered,
and with the mourning of an angry widower for each day of life,
alas, for each invisible drop of water which I drink sleepily
and for each sound which I receive, trembling,
I have the same absent thirst and the same cold fever,
an ear that is born, an indirect anguish,

628

as if thieves or ghosts were approaching,
and in a shell of fixed and deep extent,
like a humilitated waiter, like a bell slightly hoarse,
like an old mirror, like the smell of a lonely house
whose roomers enter by night dead drunk,
and there is a smell of clothing thrown about on the floor, and an
    absence of flowers
possibly in some other way even less melancholy,
but, in truth, suddenly, the wind that strikes my chest
the nights of infinite substance dropped into my bedroom,
the noise of a day that burns with sacrifice,
demand, sadly, whatever there is of prophetic in me,
and there is a knocking of objects which call without being answered,
and a ceaseless movement, and a confused name.

See the discussion of Dada and Surrealism on pages 27–30.

SYLLABIC VERSE (SYLLABICS)   Verse in which the system of measurement is based
    on the number of syllables in the line, rather than on stress or quantity. In
    the first of the following stanzas, the syllable count by lines is 11, 10, 13,
    8, 8, 3. The second stanza is made on the same pattern—with a variation,
    14 syllables in the third line.

Dürer would have seen a reason for living
        in a town like this, with eight stranded whales
to look at; with the sweet sea air coming into your house
on a fine day, from water etched
        with waves as formal as the scales
on a fish.

One by one in two's and three's, the seagulls keep
        flying back and forth over the town clock,
or sailing around the lighthouse without moving their wings
rising steadily with a slight
        quiver of the body—or flock
mewing where

                                    Marianne Moore, "The Steeple-Jack"

See Thomas Campion, "Rose-Cheeked Laura," p. 87.

SYMBOL   A symbol is a thing that stands not only for itself but for something
    else as well. It is the visible expression of a hidden meaning. "The Infi-
    nite," said Thomas Carlyle, "is made to blend with the Finite, to stand
    visible, and as it were, attainable there" (Sartor Resartus).
        Literature is filled with symbolism. The sword, the rose, and the
    cross have come down through the centuries carrying definite associa-
    tions. But in modern literature, symbolism may evoke a complex of
    thought and feeling that can be understood only in the context of the
    work itself, or express "an unconscious content whose nature can only be
    guessed because it is still unknown" (C. J. Jung, "The Collective Uncon-
    scious and Archetypes"). Thus Eliot borrows from Mallarmé to create an
    image with symbolic overtones:

Garlic and sapphires in the mud
Clot the bedded axle-tree.

"Burnt Norton"

"I incline to think," says Bodelsen, "that garlic symbolizes the lower, and sapphires the higher, elements in life." But we cannot know—we can only approximate a meaning from our sense of the work as a whole.

The world is a temple whose walls are covered with emblems, pictures and commandments of the Deity . . . there is no fact in nature which does not carry the whole sense of nature.

Ralph Waldo Emerson, "The Poet," 1844

Nature is a temple where living pillars
From time to time let confused words come forth;
Man passes there through forests of symbols
That observe him with familiar eyes.

Charles Baudelaire, "Correspondences," 1857

See SYMBOLISM (SYMBOLIST MOVEMENT) and the discussion of Yeats's "The Stare's Nest by My Window," pp. 23–25.

SYMBOLISM (SYMBOLIST MOVEMENT)   A literary movement originating in France in the 1880s. The name *symbolist* was chosen by Jean Moreas, rather than "decadent," to define the new poetry, and disseminated in a manifesto and a magazine, *Le Symbolist*.

Baudelaire was a forerunner—"True Symbolism has been shown to us by Baudelaire—the search for a fundamental correspondence, a real and constitutive analogy between our soul and the universe" (Guy Michaud, *Message Poétique du Symbolisme*). Stéphane Mallarmé led the movement. At the moment when Taine and Zola proclaimed that literature must become "scientific," the symbolists made the counter-claim that it must be based in mystery, that beyond the veil of appearances there is an infinite Beauty of which our senses give hints and guesses. "Beauty alone exists," said Mallarmé, "and it has only one perfect expression, poetry."

Mallarmé aimed at "pure poetry," that is, the purely lyric, placing narrative and discursive poetry in an inferior category—an idea that can be traced, by way of Baudelaire, back to Poe's essay of 1848 on "The Poetic Principle." The poet, said Mallarmé, should suggest, never state: "To name a thing is to suppress three quarters of the joy of the poem, which consists in guessing, little by little; suggestion makes the dream."

Symbolist technique has been described as setting images at a certain distance from one another and letting the meaning flower out of the spaces between. Mallarmé called this forming "constellations."

These, also, were important in the movement: René Ghil, Gustave Kahn, Stuart Merrill, Emile Verhaeren, Maurice Maeterlinck, Villiers de l'Isle Adam, Jules Laforgue, Paul Verlaine, and Arthur Symons, who introduced W. B. Yeats to the symbolists. Besides Yeats, among poets writing in English, T. S. Eliot, Wallace Stevens, and Dylan Thomas show the influence of symbolism.

SYNCOPE   Omission of one or more sounds or letters in a word, as in *fo'c'sle* for *forecastle*.

SYNECDOCHE   A figurative use of language in which a part of something is substituted for the whole, or the whole for a part. *Roof* is used to mean *house*, *sail* to mean *ship*, etc. Synedoche is often regarded as a special type of *metonymy* (q.v.).

SYNESTHESIA   Description of one kind of sense perception in words that usually describe another.

> There are perfumes fresh and cool as the bodies of children, mellow as oboes, green as fields; and others that are perverse, rich, and triumphant.
> Charles Baudelaire, "Correspondences" (trans. by Francis Scarfe)

TENOR   See METAPHOR.

TENSION   A technical term in the vocabulary of New Criticism (q.v.). Allen Tate arrived at it by "lopping the prefixes off the logical terms *extension* and *intension*" and combining their meanings, so that the term *tension* refers to the extent to which the abstract and concrete elements in a poem have an integral relationship or are unified with the idea embodied in images. An additional meaning of the term *tension* involves "conflict-structures," listed by Robert Penn Warren as "tension between the rhythm of the poem and the rhythm of speech . . . between the formality of the rhythm and the informality of language; between the particular and the general, the concrete and the abstract; between the elements of even the simplest metaphor; between the beautiful and the ugly; between ideas; between the elements involved in irony; between prosisms and poeticisms."

TERCET   A three-line stanza. If there is a single rhyme for all three lines, the tercet is a triplet. The term *tercet* may also refer to half the sestet in a Petrarchan sonnet, or to the *terza rima* stanza.

TERMINAL RHYME   See RHYME.

TERZA RIMA   An Italian fixed verse form of tercets with rhymes interlocking in the pattern *a b a, b c b, c d c, d e d*, etc. The form was used by Dante in *The Divine Comedy*. See Shelley, "Ode to the West Wind," p. 226.

TETRAMETER   A line of four metrical feet:

> How thĕ | Chímnĕy | -swéepĕr's | crý
> Every black'ning Church appalls;
> And the hapless Soldier's sigh
> Runs in blood down Palace walls.
>   Blake, "London"

TETRASTICH   A four-line stanza; synonym for quatrain.

TEXTURE   The surface detail of a text, especially the phonetic patterns, the sensory quality of the images, and the additional richness of meaning suggested by the connotations of the words. Texture is contrasted with structure, which is the argument or paraphrasable content of the work. With reference to meter, John Crowe Ransom calls the basic meter the structure and the variations on it the texture.

THEMATIC DEVELOPMENT The process by which a theme unfolds to the reader or undergoes changes in a work.

THEME A central idea or major point of a literary work; its thesis, as stated in sentence form. Also, loosely used, *theme* can mean the subject of a work, such as time, love, death, beauty, and so on.

THRENODY See DIRGE.

TONE The attitude of the writer toward his or her audience, as it is implied in the text and inferred by the reader. The tone may be serious or light, formal or intimate, scornful or sympathetic, straightforward or given a double edge by irony.

TRADITION A body of beliefs, laws, and customs handed down from generation to generation. In literature, the totality of conventions—of technique, form, subject matter, and point of view or attitude—characteristic of a group of writers in a period. Thus we may speak of the Puritan tradition, the Cavalier tradition, the metaphysical tradition of the seventeenth century, the neoclassical tradition of the eighteenth century, or the romantic tradition of the nineteenth century. The term may also be used to refer to a complex of conventions and themes common to writers of various periods, such as the classical tradition, the Neoplatonic tradition, and the pastoral tradition.

TRANSFERRED EPITHET See EPITHET.

TRAVESTY See BURLESQUE.

TRIMETER A line of three metrical feet.

My silks | and fine | array,
My smiles | and lan | guish'd air
By Love | are driv'n | away; . . .

Blake, "Song"

TRIOLET a French fixed form used by late nineteenth-century English poets. It has eight lines, but only two rhymes; the first two lines are repeated as the last two, and the fourth is the same as the first. The rhyme scheme is *a b a a a b a b*.

TRIPLE METERS Meters whose feet consist of three syllables. Dactylic ($'\smile\smile$) and anapestic ($\smile\smile'$) are triple meters. See DUPLE METERS.

TRIPLE RHYME See RHYME.

TRIPLET A three-line stanza with a single rhyme.

TRISTICH A three-line stanza; synonym for *tercet*.

TROCHEE, TROCHAIC A metrical foot of two syllables, with a strong stress followed by a weak: $'\smile$. See also METER and FALLING METER.

TROPE Literally, a "turn," or use of a word with a definite change or extension of its meaning, from literal to figurative. See FIGURATIVE LANGUAGE.

TROUBADOUR One of a class of lyric poets who flourished in southern France (and eastern Spain and northern Italy) from the eleventh to the thirteenth centuries. They wrote in the Provençal dialect about courtly love and chivalry. Their interest in metrical technique led to the development of many of the intricate French fixed verse forms. Among the more famous of the troubadours were Bertrans de Born, Arnaut Daniel, and William, Count of Poitiers. See also TROUVÈRE.

TROUVÈRE   One of a class of court poets of northern France who flourished at the same time as the Provençal troubadours and were greatly influenced by them. Trouvères, one of whom was Chrétien de Troyes, wrote chivalric romances, love lyrics, and *chansons de geste*.

TRUE RHYME   See RHYME.

TRUNCATION   See CATALEXIS.

TUMIDITY   Pompous, turgid, bombastic language or literary style.

"UBI SUNT" MOTIF   A common theme in lyric poetry: lamenting the vanished past. The phrase is Latin for "where are," as in Villon's "Where are the snows of yesteryear?"

UNDERSTATEMENT (MEIOSIS)   A figurative use of language in which less is said than is meant. Only a part of the meaning is stated, so that the reader, in order to complete the thought, must enter into the mind and feelings of the author. In doing so, the reader obtains a better understanding than he or she would from explicit statement. Shakespeare's Othello says: "Keep up your bright swords, for the dew will rust them." He is speaking of a quarrel in the street, between men armed with swords, as though it were a promenade. The effect is to draw the reader into the heroic calm of Othello's mind: He is a man of experience, particularly of battle, to whom a streetfight would be insignificant.

But now go the bells, and we are ready;
In one house we are sternly stopped
To say we are vexed at her brown study,
Lying so primly propped.
          John Crowe Ransom, "Bells for John Whiteside's Daughter"

In this stanza about the death of a little girl, the "brown study" is death, and being "vexed" is being grieved. The words seem insufficient; in order to complete the poet's meaning, the reader is compelled to imagine the scene and give of his or her own feelings.

UNITY   The coherent relationship of all the parts of a work to the whole, with nothing essential omitted and nothing irrelevant included. The *three unities* of the drama are those of action, time, and place. During the Renaissance, French and Italian critics who derived the *unities* from Aristotle's *Poetics* insisted that a play should be the imitation of a single action taking place within a single day in a single place. However, the only unit that Aristotle himself had insisted upon was unity of action.

VEHICLE   See METAPHOR.

VERS DE SOCIÉTÉ   French for "society verse," brief epigrammatic or lyrical light verse concerning polite society. It is usually witty and highly polished, using a conversational tone and one of the intricate French fixed verse forms, such as the rondeau or villanelle. It may be gently satiric or elegantly amorous, paying a witty compliment to a lady.

VERS LIBRE   See FREE VERSE.

VERSE   (1) Any individual line of a poem. (2) Strictly metrical language; verse as distinguished from prose. Verse is not necessarily poetry, however; it may be mere doggerel.

> A rhymer, and a *poet*, are two things.
>
> Ben Jonson, *Timber*

VERSE PARAGRAPH   A group of lines, frequently in blank verse, considered as a rhetorical unit similar to a prose paragraph, and indicated as such by the indentation of the first line.

VERSIFICATION   Synonym for *prosody* (q.v.).

VICTORIAN PERIOD   The period dated from either 1832 (the first Reform Bill) or 1837 (the accession of Queen Victoria to the throne) until the Queen's death in 1901. Much of the writing of this period reflected contemporary social, economic, and intellectual problems, such as the Industrial Revolution, pressures for political and economic reforms, and the impact of the Darwinian theory of evolution. Tennyson, Browning, and Arnold were the more prominent poets. Arnold, Carlyle, and Ruskin were influential essayists. Among the novelists were Dickens, Thackeray, George Eliot, Meredith, Trollope, Hardy, and Samuel Butler.

VILLANELLE   A French fixed verse form of six stanzas (five tercets and a quatrain), characterized by the use of only two rhymes and the repetition of lines as refrains. The opening line is repeated at the ends of the second and fourth stanzas, and the third line at the ends of the third and fifth. The two refrain lines conclude the poem. The rhyme scheme is *a b a, a b a, a b a, a b a, a b a, a b a a*. The form was originally used for pastoral subjects (the name derives from *villa*, a farm or country house), and later used for light verse. See Theodore Roethke, "The Waking," p. 416, and Dylan Thomas, "Do Not Go Gentle into That Good Night," p. 444.

VIRELAY   A name applied to two verse forms derived from old French poetry, neither of which is strictly fixed in form or common in English. The short one has only two rhymes and alternates the first and second lines as refrains. The other has an indefinite number of stanzas with one rhyme in long lines and the other rhyme in short lines. The short lines always provide the rhyme for the long lines of the next stanza, and the short lines of the last stanza rhyme with the long lines of the first.

VIRGULE (SLASH)   The short slanting line used to mark the division between one line and another when quoting poetry in a prose paragraph.

> No use of lanthorns; and in one place lay/ Feathers and dust, today and yesterday.
>
> Donne, "The Calm"

VOICE   T. S. Eliot has described "The Three Voices of Poetry":

> The first voice is the voice of the poet talking to himself—or to nobody. The second is the voice of the poet addressing an audience, whether large or small. The third is the voice of the poet when he attempts to create a

dramatic character speaking in verse; when he is saying, not what he would say in his own person, but only what he can say within the limits of one imaginary character addressing another imaginary character.

See PERSONA.

WEAK ENDING   At the end of a line of verse, a syllable which, though it is stressed metrically, would be unstressed in ordinary speech, and leads right on to the following line:

Thy mother was a piece of virtue, and
She said thou wast my daughter.

Shakespeare, The Tempest

WIT   (1) Intelligence or wisdom (Renaissance usage). (2) Fancy or nimbleness of thinking (seventeenth-century usage, often applied in discussion of metaphysical poetry). (3) The ability to see similarities, as opposed to *judgment*, which was considered the ability to see differences (late seventeenth-century usage). (4) In the eighteenth century, according to Pope,

True wit is Nature to advantage dressed,
What oft was thought, but ne'er so well expressed.

(5) In the twentieth century, wit is associated with humor in original, clever remarks.

WORD ACCENT   See ACCENT.

WRENCHED ACCENT   See ACCENT.

ZEUGMA   a Greek word literally meaning "yoking" and applying to the use of a single word standing in the same grammatical relationship to two other words, but with significant differences in meaning:

Or *stain* her honor, or her new brocade.

Pope, The Rape of the Lock

636

637

638

INDEX OF AUTHORS AND TITLES

646